Laurie,

Thank you for being you!!

May God bless you in fact for

all you've given m

Love,

Kathy Dodd

5/2005

Susanna Wesley

Susanna Wesley

The Complete Writings

Edited by

CHARLES WALLACE JR.

2036

New York   Oxford   ❦   Oxford University Press   1997

Oxford University Press

Oxford   New York

Athens   Auckland   Bangkok   Bogota   Bombay   Buenos Aires
Calcutta   Cape Town   Dar es Salaam   Delhi   Florence   Hong Kong
Istanbul   Karachi   Kuala Lumpur   Madras   Madrid   Melbourne
Mexico City   Nairobi   Paris   Singapore   Taipei   Tokyo   Toronto

and associated companies in
Berlin   Ibadan

Copyright © 1997 by Oxford University Press, Inc.

Published by Oxford University Press, Inc.
198 Madison Avenue, New York, New York 10016

Library of Congress Cataloging-in-Publication Data
Wesley, Susanna Annesley, 1670–1742.
[Works. 1996]
Susanna Wesley : the complete writings / edited by Charles Wallace, Jr.
p.   cm.
Includes bibliographical references
ISBN 0-19-507437-8
I. Wallace, Charles.   II. Title.
BX8495.M55A2   1996
287'.092—dc20   95-8821
[B]

1 3 5 7 9 8 6 4 2

Printed in the United States of America
on acid-free paper

To
Miriam Shroyer Wallace
(1921–1985)
and
Charles I. Wallace Sr.,
not Susanna and Samuel (thank goodness!),
but extraordinary parents in the Wesleyan tradition

Preface

Given the keen interest in recovering women's voices in the history of both church and society, the time is ripe for a careful presentation of the work of Susanna Wesley. Though much of her literary output has appeared in print since her death, a good deal of it has suffered at the hands of Victorian editors or has only been published in obscure and now defunct denominational journals. The entire corpus has heretofore never been gathered in one place.

I offer this edition in the hope that her own voice may be heard more fully than before, thus providing material for a careful reassessment of a remarkable woman. She deserves to be regarded not just as the mother of the founders of Methodism but also as a fascinating figure in her own right, a woman enmeshed in and yet pushing against many of the patriarchal constraints of early eighteenth-century church and society. In addition, her story will supplement those of other women and give a more balanced and complete picture of religion, literature, and society in the early eighteenth century.

Thirteen years is a long time to be occupied with an editing project, even if the subject matter is the nearly lifelong output of a prolific individual. Along the way many debts have been accrued and many changes have taken place.

In the first category, I am happy first to name Frank Baker, doyen of Wesley scholars and my graduate school mentor. His presentation on Susanna Wesley at the pioneering Women in New Worlds Conference in 1980 helped focus United Methodist historical work on the recovery of women's experience and, in particular, prodded me to investigate a "complete works" of Susanna. Typically, his support included not only advice and counsel but also access to his collection of rare Methodistica. Other scholars in the field have also aided and abetted me in various ways: John Newton and John Vickers in England; Bob Burtner, Doug Chandler, Dale Johnson, Fred Maser, Russ Richey, and Ken Rowe in the United States; Joanne Brown and the late Elizabeth Hart (whose scholarship and enthusiasm I miss greatly) in Canada.

In addition to those sharing my specialized interests, I am grateful for the support of colleagues at Western Maryland College (Ira Zepp and Bob Hartman), Wesley

Theological Seminary (particularly the late Clarence Goen), and especially at Willamette University (Jim Hand, Dave McCreery, Doug McGaughey, and Lane McGaughy). Peter Williams and Charles Hambrick-Stowe, distinguished scholars in American religious history and good friends, have contributed in both these capacities.

The librarians and staffs of the two major depositories of Susanna Wesley manuscripts deserve special thanks: the Methodist Archives at the John Rylands University Library, Manchester, and the library at Wesley College, Bristol. Thanks also go to Hartley-Victoria College, Manchester, which provided hospitality and accommodations for the week I spent working in the Methodist Archives. I am grateful to the other owners of manuscripts: Wesley's Chapel, London; the Methodist Historical Society, Baltimore; the Melbourne Public Library; and Peter Conlan of Bromley, Kent. Two major research libraries were indispensable in the detective work connected with tracing many of Susanna Wesley's intellectual sources: the British Library and the Henry E. Huntington Library. Willamette University provided funds from the National Endowment for the Humanities to subsidize a trip to the latter. When research forays were not possible, the Mark O. Hatfield Library at Willamette was a ready source of interlibrary loans and computer search expertise. Willamette president Jerry Hudson and three successive deans of the College of Liberal Arts, Jerry Berberet, Julie Ann Carson, and Lawrence Cress, also provided support, both moral and financial, in the course of the project.

I am happy to list the string of conscientious work-study student assistants at Willamette who have entered text, proofread, and helped with the annotation: Rachel Hill, Meg Dupuis, John Watson, and Julie Weddle. Leslie Bandfield, Carolyn Kilday, and Betty Smith lent their word-processing expertise. My administrative assistant, Holli Davenport, kept the Chaplain's Office functioning when I was distracted with Susanna. Ed Arabas provided the two expertly drawn maps.

I note with pleasure that Susanna Wesley is receiving her academic due in this edition, however indirectly, from the university that educated her father, husband, and sons but had no place for her (or any other women) in her own day. Special thanks for their complicity, therefore, go to the helpful and patient editors at Oxford University Press, Cynthia Read, Cynthia Garver, Paula Wald, and Peter Ohlin.

Feminist scholarship has reinforced the historian's proclivity to examine the context of any intellectual work. My greatest debts in this project are to the women in my life, all of whom participate in what a Methodist Jungian might call the Susanna "archetype" (though I hasten to add that that may be more my projection than their objectively viewed character traits). In naming them, I am aware of the mystery of change that is as central to our lives as it is to the history we study. Still alive when I began the project were Edna Laird Wallace and Helen Rex Shroyer, my grandmother and step-grandmother, and Miriam Shroyer Wallace, my mother. They are gone, but they live on as examples of strong women. Four others of a similar persuasion have, wittingly or not, marked this project over its long duration. I gratefully acknowledge Betsy Sargent, quondam uxor and continuing friend; Dee-dee Walters, gifted priest and affectionate companion; and my daughters, Hannah and Molly Wallace, wonderful uppity women of the rising generation.

Norman Maclean concludes his profoundly "male" book, *A River Runs through It*, with the phrase, "I am haunted by waters." Many men in the church and the academy (myself included) would have to admit that we are "haunted by women"—and will continue to be, until we give real women, not idealized or demonized projections, their due. For that reason, as well as for the enrichment of the historical record and for simple justice, I have undertaken this project.

Contents

PART III / EDUCATIONAL, CATECHETICAL,
AND CONTROVERSIAL WRITINGS

A section of maps and illustrations appears after p. 16.

Important Dates in
Susanna Wesley's Life

20 January 1669	Birth, London (probably at Annesley home, Spital Yard, Bishopsgate).[1]
c. 1681	"Conversion" from Nonconformity to the Church of England.
12 November 1688	Marriage to Samuel Wesley, St. Marylebone Parish Church, London.
1688	Samuel curate at St. Botolph, Aldersgate, London (about one year).[2]
1689	Samuel chaplain on a man-o'-war (about 6 months); ended November 1689.
10 February 1690	First child, Samuel Jr., born, in Annesley home, London.[3]
1690	Samuel curate at Newington Butts, Surrey, for nearly a year.
Summer 1691	Samuel rector of South Ormsby, Lincolnshire.
May/June 1697	Samuel resident as rector of Epworth, Lincolnshire.
17 June 1703	Birth of John, later founder of Methodism.
1705	Samuel Wesley jailed in Lincoln Castle, ostensibly for debt, exacerbated by a political grudge.
9 February 1708/9	Fire destroys Epworth rectory; family saved, but all possessions (including Susanna's earlier writings and her father's literary remains) lost.
February 1711/12	Susanna holds controversial Sunday evening services in the rebuilt rectory while Samuel attends convocation in London.
December 1716–January 1717	Poltergeist incident in the Epworth rectory.
c. 1724	Nearby parish of Wroot given to Samuel Sr.; family occasionally lives there.[4]

28 April 1735	Death of Samuel Wesley Sr. forces Susanna to vacate rectory.
By November 1735	Moves to nearby Gainsborough with daughter Emilia.[5]
September 1736	Moves to Tiverton, Devon, with Samuel Jr.[6]
c. July 1737	Moves to Wooton, Wiltshire, near Marlborough, and afterward to Fisherton, near Salisbury, with the Halls (daughter Martha and son-in-law Westley).[7]
April 1739	Moves with Halls to London.[8]
Late 1739	Moves to the Foundery, son John's newly acquired Methodist headquarters.
30 July 1742	Death at the Foundery, London.
1 August 1742	Burial, Bunhill Fields, City Road, London.

Notes

1. Frank Baker, "Investigating Wesley Family Traditions," *Methodist History* 26.3 (April 1988): 162. I have drawn on this authoritative source for all references to Wesley family births, marriages, and deaths.

2. Details on the couple's early married life, until 1698, have been gleaned from the recent investigations of H. A. Beecham, "Samuel Wesley Senior: New Biographical Evidence," in *Renaissance and Modern Studies* 7 (1963): 78–109. See also Frank Baker, "Salute to Susanna," *Methodist History* 7.3 (April 1969): 3–12.

3. The first of 18 or 19, 10 of whom (7 girls and 3 boys) survived infancy. See Baker, "Investigating Traditions," p. 162, for names and dates.

4. Susanna Wesley to John Wesley, 19 August 1724. Samuel Sr. to Lord Chancellor York, 14 January 1733. Adam Clarke, *Memoirs of the Wesley Family; Collected Principally from Original Documents* (New York: N. Bangs and T. Mason for the Methodist Episcopal Church, 1824), 174.

5. Susanna Wesley to John Wesley, 27 November 1735.

6. Samuel Jr. to Charles Wesley, 21 September 1736; Clarke, *Wesley Family*, p. 315.

7. Samuel Jr. to Charles, 21 September 1736; Clarke, *Wesley Family*, p. 316. Susanna Wesley to Mrs. Alice Peard, 5 August 1737. Eliza Clarke, *Susanna Wesley* (London: W. H. Allen, 1886), p. 183, identifies Wooton incorrectly as a parish in Gloucestershire. The move to Fisherton had taken place by early 1738. See W. Reginald Ward and Richard P. Heitzenrater, eds., *The Works of John Wesley*, vol. 19, *Journals and Diaries, II (1738–42)* (Nashville: Abingdon, 1990), p. 227.

8. See letter to Samuel Jr., 8 March 1738/39.

Abbreviations

AM	*Arminian Magazine*, 20 vols. (London: J. Fry, 1778–1797)
AV	The Authorized (King James) Version of the Bible
BCP	The Book of Common Prayer
Clarke	Adam Clarke, *Memoirs of the Wesley Family, Collected Principally from Original Documents* (New York: N. Bangs and T. Mason for the Methodist Episcopal Church, 1824)
DNB	*Dictionary of National Biography*
FB	Frank Baker, ed., *Letters, I: 1721–1739*, in *The Works of John Wesley*, vol. 25 (Oxford: Clarendon Press, 1980)
LB	John Wesley's Letter Book, Methodist Archives, Manchester
MA	Methodist Archives, John Rylands University Library, Manchester
MH	*Methodist History* (Lake Junaluska, N.C.: Commission on Archives and History, The United Methodist Church, 1962–)
MSS A, B, C	The "Headingley" Manuscripts of Susanna Wesley, owned by Wesley College, Bristol
OED	*Oxford English Dictionary*
Priestley	Joseph Priestley, ed., *Original Letters, by the Rev. John Wesley and His Friends* . . . (Birmingham: Thomas Pearson, 1791)
PWHS	*Proceedings of the Wesley Historical Society* ([Burnley, Eng.]: Printed for the Society, 1897–)
Stevenson	George J. Stevenson, *Memorials of the Wesley Family* (London: S. W. Partridge; New York: Nelson and Phillips, 1876)
SWJr Letter Book	Samuel Wesley Jr.'s Letter Book, Methodist Archives, Manchester
Walmsley	Robert Walmsley, "John Wesley's Parents: Quarrel and Reconciliation," in PWHS 29.3 (1953–1954): 50–57
WB	*The Wesley Banner*, 4 vols. (London: Partridge and Oakley, 1849–1852)

Susanna Wesley

Introduction

Who is Susanna Wesley? The quick and obvious response is John Wesley's mother, the woman behind the founder of Methodism in eighteenth-century England. True as far as it goes, this answer nevertheless limits her appeal to a smaller audience than she deserves. Moreover, it perpetuates the assumption of her own day that a woman's identity derives from her relationships with close male relatives. It would be a pity if late-twentieth-century interpretation would follow late-seventeenth- and the early-eighteenth-century commonplace and represent her only as the daughter of a prominent Nonconformist minister, Samuel Annesley; as the wife of an Anglican priest who never quite became prominent, Samuel Wesley; and as the mother of Methodist founders John and Charles Wesley, whose undeniable prominence first brought her widespread recognition. Of course, in her day such relationships were underwritten and carefully constructed by contemporary piety, and how much more so for a woman attached to clergy in all demographic directions. Today piety continues to be part of the reason her identity is still dependent on the men in her life. But another factor in our less religious age is the practice of history, which has made useful beginnings but has still not succeeded in recovering the stories of all the notable women or in fully describing women's experience in the past.

Who is Susanna Wesley? In different communities of interpretation she has been a Methodist saint, an archetype of evangelical womanhood, and even (in a certain psychological reading) an overweening mother who prevented her son from experiencing any marital happiness.[1] Most recently, however, as feminist approaches have claimed scholarly prerogatives in literary and historical, as well as religious, studies, her identity is ripe for reinterpretation. There are stirrings that suggest she is becoming something of a foremother for latter-day Christian feminists and an example of early "writing women" who employed intellect and spirituality to subvert (however gently) some of the very religious-based conventions that ordinarily worked to keep women modest, chaste, and silent. Until now, those who would like to pursue such explorations (and could not make forays to the archival collections) have had

3

to work from secondary sources and scattered, incomplete, and sometimes unreliable transcriptions of her own writing.[2]

In pulling together material for this collection, I am assuming that Susanna Wesley's own writings allow her finally to speak for herself and yield a richer and fuller identity than she has ever been accorded before. Not that any edition, however complete and however judiciously prepared, can ever avoid constructing her or at least shaping her and in some way prejudicing our interpretation of her. Nor for that matter can archives boast a complete lack of bias—the letters and other papers that survive already represent a process of selection, dependent partly on the reflected glory of her famous son and the concerns of his admiring successors. Despite all that, we still have a remarkably rich collection from which to work. There is no reason that Susanna Wesley's own voice should not be heard; assessed; and brought into historical, literary, and theological conversations at the turn of the third millennium.

This new edition will no doubt spark many more readings of her work and life. Some will continue to approach her from within the Wesleyan tradition and find in her writings further corroboration for her status as a sort of Methodist Madonna. Others, prompted (as I have been) by a concern to recover the works of women in various religious traditions, will delve into these pages for clues to women's struggles and triumphs in more restrictive times and places. Still others, with little commitment to faith or particular interest in the study of religious history, will nevertheless read Susanna Wesley's religious writings as discourse that encouraged woman's education and afforded some psychic space, some "room of one's own," for her own self-expression and self-development.[3] With such readers in mind, I have striven to provide as complete and accurate a collection as possible, edited from holographic and manuscript sources whenever available, and furnished with all necessary annotations and contextual information. It is, I believe, a step in the enriching process of reclaiming another woman's voice from the past.

The rest of this general introduction will attempt to sketch and characterize Susanna Wesley's life and suggest how both religious studies and literary historical studies can profit from examining her—and perhaps in the process can contribute to a fuller picture of her. More detailed introductory material, appropriate to the particular writings, will appear in each major part and subsection of the collection.

Biographical Sketch

The epitaph on her original tombstone identified Susanna Wesley as "the youngest and last surviving daughter of Dr. Samuel Annesley."[4] Born on 20 January 1669,[5] she was part of a large family, as an anecdote reported by her eccentric brother-in-law John Dunton amply illustrates. At her baptism (or possibly her younger brother's) when the officiating minister asked Dr. Annesley how many children he had, the answer was a slightly uncertain "two dozen or a quarter of a hundred."[6] Traces of "only" nine of the Annesley children have turned up in recent research, suggesting that less than half survived infancy, seven girls and two boys. Apart from Susanna, we know little about them, though there are intriguing snippets in Dunton's autobiography and in a funeral sermon for her sister Elizabeth, Dunton's wife.[7] There is even less information on Annesley's two wives, Mary Hill (d. 1646) and Susanna's mother, Mary (?)White (d. 1693), though contextual evidence indicates that the latter was, like her youngest daughter, pious, educated, and energetic.[8]

Inevitably, we know quite a bit more about Susanna's father.[9] Graduating from Oxford in 1639, he was ordained in Presbyterian fashion and served as a chaplain in the parliamentary navy before settling down as rector of Cliffe in Kent. Additional service at sea kept him away from his parish temporarily, but he soon lost it completely, probably because of his opposition to the execution of Charles I and the fact that there was no great love lost between him and Cromwell. Annesley then moved to London, briefly taking a small parish before being appointed (by Oliver's son Richard) to the important living of St. Giles, Cripplegate. For nine years he distinguished himself as a preacher and an editor of a sermon series he hosted in the church.

At the Restoration, however, he was ejected from St. Giles in 1662 for conscientiously refusing subscription to the Book of Common Prayer according to Act of Uniformity. Following the practice of many other displaced Puritans, he organized a congregation of like-minded Nonconformists, occasionally running afoul of the laws penalizing such religious Dissenters. His large Presbyterian congregation gathered in Spitalfields, less than a mile east of St. Giles. Though the church no longer survives, Annesley's nearby house still stands; here he lived; here he worked in his well-stocked study; here his last daughter, Susanna, was born and raised; and here he died in 1696.[10] Among his friends and colleagues were numbered all the prominent Nonconformists of the day, including Richard Baxter, and among his parishioners was Daniel Defoe, who published a flattering obituary, extolling him for the "Greatness of his Soul."[11]

This quality served him particularly well when his daughter Susanna precociously decided to forsake Nonconformity and join the Church of England, the ostensible cause of his persecution.[12] As she indicated in a letter to her son Samuel, this leave-taking was rather remarkable—not only for her youth but also for the methodical way in which she researched and decided the issue.[13] Remarkable, too, was the equanimity with which her father responded; as his library shows, he had something of what his most famous grandson would later describe as a "catholic spirit." Whatever Samuel Annesley's inner hurt, Susanna "departed" with his blessing and remained his favorite daughter, receiving all his letters and papers at his death. Lacking further evidence, we can only speculate about her mother's impact on her education and development. However, we can be sure of the powerful gift her father gave her when he affirmed the conscientious choice of an adolescent daughter, even if it registered as a dissent against his cherished Dissenting tradition.

Young Susanna Annesley's ecclesiastical migration from Nonconformity to the Church of England coincided with a similar move made by a young theological student from Dorset, one Samuel Wesley.[14] She met him at the time of her sister Elizabeth's wedding to John Dunton in 1682, possibly at the ceremony itself. Some half-dozen years her senior, he was not only the son but also the grandson of Nonconformist ministers. Like her, and notwithstanding subsidized training in two London Dissenting academies, he also sought membership in the established church.

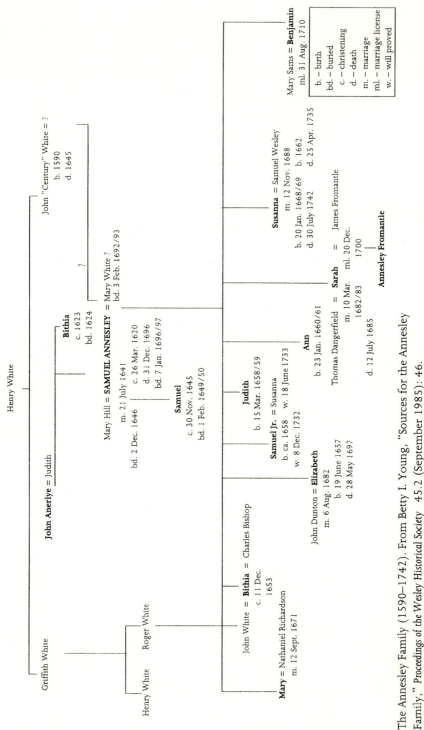

The Annesley Family (1590–1742). From Betty I. Young, "Sources for the Annesley Family," *Proceedings of the Wesley Historical Society* 45.2 (September 1985): 46. Used with permission.

As a man, this afforded him one advantage that Susanna could not have: the opportunity to pursue an ecclesiastical career by matriculating at one of the universities.[15] He did so, entering Exeter College, Oxford, in 1684; graduating with a B. A. in 1688; and receiving deacon's and priest's orders in the Church of England by 1689. Meanwhile, intellectual and theological affinity had grown,[16] as had their love, and the two lapsed Dissenters were married in the parish church of St. Marylebone on 12 November 1688. Thus began a 46 year marriage, ending with Samuel's death in 1735. As many of the collected letters and journals reveal, it was not always a smooth relationship; but on the whole it probably deserves the label Lawrence Stone has attached to the more enlightened, affective liaisons of the day, a "companionate marriage."[17]

A temporary curacy at St. Botolph's, Aldersgate, did not bring much in the way of financial support, so the young couple lived in the Annesley household. This arrangement proved useful when Samuel Wesley signed on for a six-month naval chaplaincy (considerably more lucrative than parish work for a beginning clergyman), leaving Susanna behind in her first of many pregnancies. Following the birth of their first son, Samuel Jr., at the Annesleys', Wesley was invited to fill another curacy, this one south of the Thames at Newington Butts, Surrey. There he served for a year and rented lodgings for himself, Susanna, and young Samuel.[18] Still unable to make ends meet, he picked up some literary work on the side; considered emigrating to Virginia; and finally secured his first living in the summer of 1691, the parish of South Ormsby, Lincolnshire.[19]

Off today's main road between Louth and Skegness, about 25 miles east of the cathedral city of Lincoln and 150 miles from London, South Ormsby is still in the rural heart of the Lincolnshire wolds. For city-born Susanna, this was a radical change of scene. In this setting, financial problems did not abate, and they were exacerbated by other woes, borne more directly, one imagines, by Susanna. As Samuel Wesley wrote to a friend in 1692

> This [i.e., the expense of buying "all sorts of household stuff" together] with first fruits, Taxes, my wives lying in about last Christmass & threatening to do the same the next, & two children & as many servants to provide for (my wife being sickly, having had 3 or 4 touches of her Rheumatism again . . .) yet has and still does . . . Reduce Me to greater Extremitys. . . .[20]

The two children spoken of would have been the young Samuel, whom they brought with them from London, and their first daughter, Susanna, born in South Ormsby but also buried there not long after her first birthday. The "threatened" child turned out to be Emilia, their oldest surviving daughter. And four more followed: twin boys, Annesley and Jedidiah, who lived a month and a year, respectively; and two girls, a second Susanna and Mary, both of whom survived into adulthood.

One other detail from the family's sojourn at South Ormsby merits inclusion to show the young priest's penchant for getting himself into trouble: the scrupulous rector lost his job by directly confronting the mistress of his patron. As John Wesley later recalled the family story, Samuel was incensed by the woman's attempts to pay social calls on Susanna:

	Nickname	Birth	Baptism	Place	Marriage	Spouse	Place	Death	Burial	Place	Age
Samuel W. Sr.		?	*17 Dec. 1662*	Winterb.	*12 Dec. 1688*	Sus. Anny.	Marybone	25 Apr. 1735	*28 Apr. 1735*	Epworth	72
Susanna Annesley		20 Jan. 1669	?	London	*12 Dec. 1688*	Sam. W. Sr.	Marybone	23 July 1742	*1 Aug. 1742*	London	73
Samuel Jr.	Sammy	10 Feb. 1690	?	London	*c. 1724*	Urs. Berry	Westm.?	6 Nov. 1739		Tiverton	49
Susanna		?	*31 Mar. 1692*	S. Ormsby					*17 Apr. 1693*	S. Ormsby	1
Emilia	Emily, Emly, Em	31 Dec. 1692?	*13 Jan. 1693*	S. Ormsby	*c. 1735*	Rob Harper	?	c. 1771	?	London?	79?
Annesley		?	*3 Dec. 1694*	S. Ormsby					*3 Jan. 1695*	S. Ormsby	1 mo.?
Jedidiah		?	*3 Dec. 1694*	S. Ormsby					*31 Jan. 1696*	S. Ormsby	1
Susanna	Suky	c. 1695	?	S. Ormsby	*c. 1719*	Rd. Ellison	?	Dec. 1764			69?
Mary	Molly, Moll	c. 1696	?	Epworth	*21 Dec. 1733*	J. Whitelamb	Epworth		*1 Nov. 1734*	Wroot	38?
Mehetabel	Hetty	c. 1697/98?	?	Epworth?	*13 Oct. 1725*	Wm. Wright	Haxey	21 Mar. 1750		London	53?
[?unknown]		c. 1698?	?	Epworth?				c. 1698?	?	Epworth?	?]
John		16 May 1699	?	Epworth				c. 1700?	?	Epworth	?
Benjamin		16 May 1699	?	Epworth				c. 1700?	?	Epworth?	?
John Benjamin		17 May 1701	*31 May 1701*	Epworth				27 Dec.?	*30 Dec. 1701*	Epworth	6 mo.
Anne	Nancy	17 May 1701	*31 May 1701*	Epworth	*2 Dec. 1725*	Jn. Lambert	Finningley		?		
John	Jacky, Jack	17 June 1703 [28 June (NS)]	*3 July 1703*	Epworth	*18 Feb. 1751*	M. Vazeille	London?	2 Mar. 1791	*9 Mar. 1791*	London	87
[son]		29 May 1705?	?	Epworth				30 May 1705	*31 May 1705*	Epworth	1 day
Martha	Patty	c. 1706	?	Epworth	*13? Sept. 1735*	Westl. Hall	London	12 July 1791	*19 July 1791*	London	85
Charles	[no nickname]	18 Dec. 1707	*29 Dec. 1707*	Epworth	*8 Apr. 1749*	Sa. Gwynne	Garth. Mer.	29 Mar. 1788	*5 Apr. 1788*	London	80
[?unknown]		Mar. 1709?	?	Epworth?				Mar. 1709?	?		]
Kezia	Kezzy	Mar. 1709?	?	Epworth?				9 Mar. 1741	?	London	30?

The Wesley Family of Epworth (1662–1796). Dates in italics are taken from contemporary parish registers or transcripts. From Frank Baker, "Investigating Wesley Family Traditions," Methodist History 26.3 (April 1988): 162. Used with permission.

> Coming in one day, and finding this intrusive visitant sitting with my mother, he went up to her, took her by the hand, and fairly handed her out. The nobleman resented the affront so outrageously as to make it necessary for my father to resign the living.[21]

A principled but perhaps ill-advised response to local custom, such behavior would bring continuing problems to the Wesley family in their new parish.

Epworth was in its own way more isolated than South Ormsby, situated some 30 miles north of Lincoln in the Isle of Axholme, fen country drained earlier in the century by Dutch engineers. The king presented Wesley to the living in 1695, but he and the family did not take up residence until 1697. They remained there with occasional sojourns in the nearby parish of Wroot, later also held by Wesley, until his death in 1735. Here were born the remaining Wesley children, Mehetabel, Anne, John, Martha, Charles and Kezia, all of whom survived, as well as four to six (such is the uncertainty of the details about a couple of these short-lived babies) who did not.[22]

Even given the Wesleys' love for the written word (and subsequent Methodists' attempts to preserve every scrap they produced),[23] the texture of family life during the 39-year Epworth period is not fully recoverable. Nevertheless, certain patterns and certain particular incidents stand out. If they have been staples of Wesleyan legend in the past, they deserve continued attention when viewed from Susanna's perspective; and, in fact, most of these are well represented in her writing, some even finding their original expression there.

The details of daily life occasionally gain expression in Susanna's writing: managing a household, facing illness and other such "afflictions," and raising and educating a large family. The perennial family debts, due in part to Samuel's mismanagement and inattention, weigh heavily on her and sometimes find expression in her letters. It was a major concern, for instance, in the long letter to her brother Samuel Annesley Jr., a merchant in India, from whom the family expected some financial aid. In the process of outlining their needs (and defending Samuel Wesley's ability to manage money wisely), she alludes to the time in 1705 when her husband was detained in debtor's prison in Lincoln. She writes of the "testimony" she had given at the time to the Archbishop of York, whose aid she sought. In answer to his question about whether the family had "ever really wanted bread," she had replied:

> My lord . . . . I will freely own to your grace, that strictly speaking, I never did want bread. But then I have had so much care to get it before 'twas eat, and to pay for it after, as has often made it very unpleasant to me. And I think to have bread on such terms is the next degree of wretchedness to having none at all.[24]

While Archbishop Sharp had been touched and responded with "a handsome present," her brother was unmoved by the implication that he should follow suit and barely mentioned the Wesleys in his will.[25] As other of her letters (and those of her husband) bear witness, their finances were often in this straitened mode.[26]

As the one who ran the household, Susanna felt responsibility for their plight, and thus the topic occasionally intrudes even into her devotional life. Her journal recalls, for example, her bargain with God to worship more sincerely in return for an easing of financial pressures:

You did sometime since make this vow, that if God would in very deed give you food to eat and raiment to put on without exposing you to the temptation of anxious care or reducing you to the necessity of borrowing for the necessaries of life, that then the Lord should be your God.[27]

Next to money problems, ill health seems to have challenged her most on a continuing basis—not surprising given the energy drain of her reproductive life and the "primitive physic" available from eighteenth-century medicine. Already noted above from their time at South Ormsby were the "three or four touches of rheumatism" that afflicted her even as a young woman.[28] In her correspondence, there are at least a dozen mentions of her bouts of illness, though usually without any specific description. In an early letter to her son Samuel, she is "so ill." In another she explains why she and her husband were sleeping in separate rooms the night of the rectory fire: "I having been very ill, we were obliged to lie asunder." In early 1722 she writes her brother, perhaps exaggerating for sympathetic effect, "I am rarely in health." In the autumn of 1724, she escapes the small pox that the rest of the family contracted but is "very ill, confined to my chamber" the following February. In summer 1727 she reports "very ill health," the following year is laid low by fever and sickness, and the summer after that is "ill for want of tea" (and happy therefore to have a present of tea—and chocolate). Letters from the decade of the 1730s (her 60s) almost always assume ill health, only mentioning situations in which she feels somewhat better. Occasionally, as in a letter to her son Charles (well after her husband's death and her departure from Epworth), her difficulties serve as apologies: "I should write oft'ner had I better health."[29] Health was for her, as for most people, a natural concern, heightened in her day no doubt by the relatively primitive state of sanitation, medicine, and birth control. It was also a subject for spiritual reflection, so that its preservation was a blessing to thank God for and its dissolution was an affliction, like poverty, to be improved "to our spiritual advantage."[30] The bottom line, both on fortune and on health, is probably accurately expressed in a letter to Samuel Jr. a few months after the rectory fire in 1709. "Truly my health and fortune is much alike," she writes, "neither very good or extremely bad. I have constantly pain enough to mind me of mortality and trouble enough in my circumstances of fortune to exercise my patience."[31]

By all odds the greatest concern of her day-to-day life was her role as educator of her children. Explicitly present in her famous child-rearing letter of 1732,[32] as well as in her other "catechetical" essays and numerous journal entries, this focus is also implicit in virtually every letter to her children. Heir to the traditional Protestant concern for education as embodied both in her Puritan upbringing and in her adopted Anglicanism,[33] Susanna also absorbed many of the newer intellectual assumptions of her own age, voraciously reading contemporary "practical divinity," with its penchant for the "reasonableness" of "natural and revealed religion," and keeping current with such intellectual pace-setters as John Locke.

Though her initial educational attempts with her first pupil Samuel Jr., must have taken place in South Ormsby—apparently something of a slow start[34]—the process began in earnest in the Epworth rectory. Here, in what John Newton describes as an atmosphere resembling "a small private boarding school,"[35] she wasted no time putting her children into "a regular method of living" from birth and then taking them aside on their fifth birthday to teach them the alphabet and start them off on the first chapter of Genesis. The personal attention continued in necessarily methodical fashion: each pupil had her or his special day of the week for a one-on-one tutorial with the headmistress.[36] As the letters to her grown sons and the essays prepared particularly with her daughters in mind indicate, she never forsook her pedagogical role, even when her children graduated from her classroom.[37]

The results of the Epworth experiment in home schooling were gratifying enough in their own day. Three boys were well prepared for a career track that led to actual boarding schools in the metropolis, to Oxford, and thence to ordination in the Church of England. And the seven sisters received equal preparation, well beyond the normal expectation of their gender and community. Susanna cannot be blamed if that was to their detriment when it came to finding suitable intellectual matches among the young men of the fens, marriage being the primary assumed "career" of a clergyman's daughters.[38] Beyond the immediate pedagogical success, however, many observers have additionally supposed that Susanna's schoolroom and rectory life in general put the initial discipline, the original "method," in John Wesley's Methodism and ensured that a continuing ideal of the movement would be the joining of "knowledge" with "vital piety."[39]

These general elements of family life provide a backdrop for several particular incidents, which leap from Susanna's writing and give vivid testimony not only to "remarkable occurrences" in Wesley family history but also to the extraordinary character of its matriarch. Worth mentioning briefly are the rectory fire of 1709; two signal occasions of Susanna's conscientious insubordination, to husband and governmental authority in one case and to husband and ecclesiastical authority in the other; and the saga of the notorious family poltergeist.

The rectory fire of 1709 is a key reference point in the Methodist story, giving John Wesley himself and thousands of the faithful thereafter an example of providential intervention. Given up for lost, he was snatched from a fiery upstairs room, "a brand plucked from the burning," a person chosen for God's future purposes.[40] The event is also central to Susanna's life and experience.

The fire exemplifies the difficulties that came too regularly to the rectory family to be described as merely bad luck. Rather, like their dismissal from South Ormsby and like the financial problems that plagued the family, the fire was probably attributable to the rector's running afoul of disgruntled parishioners. Not that he should be held responsible for the extremes of rough justice that local men sought to impose on the aloof, scholarly, stubborn outsider. Already, the attempts of local retribution had included threats of harm during the parliamentary election of 1705 and, indirectly, the death of a nameless newborn son; a trip to debtors' jail in Lincoln; and the maiming of some of his animals. From this perspective, the flames that engulfed the rectory on the frosty night of February 9, 1709, were only the latest and most vicious assault on an unpopular parson.

The family, including the nearly lost young "Jacky," survived the fire unscathed, but otherwise the losses were complete and devastating. House, furniture, clothing, money (just received for some crops), a "good quantity" of some additional crops, all their pewter and brass, all but "25 ounces of plate," some hemp and corn, and a few sticks of lumber were gone, the makings of continuing financial disaster. Perhaps even more distressing was the loss of Samuel's books and manuscripts, including one ready for the press (worth £50 to the family fortune), and the destruction of the letters and papers willed to Susanna by her late father. A further casualty was Susanna's own manuscripts; everything we have of hers apart from a few letters preserved by their recipients thus dates after the fire.

Without minimizing the ruinous effects of the fire, Susanna Wesley nevertheless came away from it focused and reinvigorated for the rest of her life. She was on the verge of menopause, her last child, Kezia, being born either in 1709 or 1710. This impending change of life thus coincided with the fire and produced a renewed devotional life, the result of which may be seen in the journals I have collected in part two of this volume. The transition to a motherhood that no longer involved childbearing may have reinforced the conviction born out of her contemplation, and in practical response to the farming out of her children after the fire, that a revitalized sense of educational purpose was called for. In October 1709 she wrote Samuel Jr., still a pupil in Westminster:

> There is nothing I now desire to live for, but to do some small service to my children, that, as I have brought 'em into the world, so that it might please God to make me (though unworthy) an instrument of doing good to their souls. I had been several years collecting from my little reading, but chiefly from my own experience, some things which I hoped would ha' been useful to you all. . . .[42]

Thus began the arduous project of sustained writing that makes up the bulk of part III of this volume: an exposition of the Creed, a partial exposition of the Decalogue, and a dialogue on natural and revealed religion. Here again Susanna "improved" the affliction, in this important instance gaining a second wind and reviving her sense of vocation for the remainder of her life.

We have already noted Susanna's independence of character when, as a well-read, strong-willed preadolescent, she forsook her father's Nonconformity. Now we may follow the same trait as it was played out on two occasions, a decade apart, in her married life. The first instance took place when Susanna refused to add her "Amen" to Samuel's prayer for the king one evening in late 1701 or early 1702. Though both were High Church and Tory, Samuel was favorably disposed toward William and Mary, who had been invited to rule by Parliament in 1688, while Susanna regarded them as usurpers. She believed James II continued to be king by divine right. It is somewhat unclear why she waited so long to register her protest—Mary, with Stuart blood in her veins, had died in 1694, leaving William to reign on his own in the eight intervening years. Perhaps it was the death of the exiled James II in 1701 that brought the whole issue to mind.[43]

In any case, the significant omission at family prayers was noted by the rector, who confronted her and, when she refused to recant, took a solemn oath not to touch her until she begged forgiveness. She remained obstinate, and they broke off marital relations for nearly half a year. John Wesley's version of the story included his father's memorable line, "You and I must part: for if we have two kings, we must have two beds."[44] Susanna's version, much more complete and intriguing, may be read in her first four extant letters, in part I of this volume. She wrote for counsel to natural allies—a local noblewoman who had been a maid of honor in the Stuart court and one of the most prominent Nonjurors, that sect of divine-right Anglicans who conscientiously refused to swear allegiance to William and Mary.[45] The issue for them in the wider political arena and for Susanna in her marriage was liberty of conscience. Ironically, a signal trait that had been instilled in her from the Dissenting side of the English religious spectrum was now employed for the sake of an ultra–High Church cause. With the support of Lady Yarborough and the Rev. George Hickes (he had written her, "stick to God and your conscience which are your best friends"),[46] Susanna stood her ground. Only after some time in London and a fire in the rectory (not as destructive as the later one, though bad enough) had brought Samuel to his senses were the two finally reconciled. The fruit of their reconciliation arrived June 17, 1703, a baby boy, christened John.

The saga of Susanna standing up against Samuel's (and conventional authority's) sway was to recur a few years after the 1709 rectory fire. In the winter of 1711–1712, the offended authority was not so much political as ecclesiastical convention. Samuel, in London as a delegate to the Church of England's convocation, got word from his temporary curate that parishioners were absenting themselves from morning prayer in favor of an irregular Sunday evening service conducted by Mrs. Wesley in the rectory kitchen. Wesley wrote back rebuking his wife, and she replied with a strong letter that answered him point by point, claiming her right to exercise a kind of ministry in his absence. To his objection about a woman presiding at public worship, she replied:

> As I am a woman, so I am also mistress of a large family. And though the superior charge of the souls contained in it lies upon you, as head of the family, and as their minister, yet in your absence I cannot but look upon every soul you leave under my care as a talent committed to me under a trust by the great Lord of all the families of heaven and earth.[47]

She further explained that she had been inspired by an account of Danish missionaries in India "to do somewhat more than I do," beginning with her own children—thus the genesis of her scheme of individual meetings with each of them once a week. The inspiration also increased her zeal in the conduct of Sunday evening family prayers, and when the circle of attenders widened and servants' families and then the general public sought to attend, she felt she could not turn them away. The limit, in fact, got to be the capacity of the rectory ground floor, something on the order of 200. The rector was still not convinced and wrote her again, asking her to stop. In due course she replied with a further account of the good her "society" was doing among the people and concluded with one of her more stunning rhetorical flourishes:

> If you do after all think fit to dissolve this assembly, do not tell me any more that you desire me to do it, for that will not satisfy my conscience; but send me your positive command in such full and express terms as may absolve me from all guilt and punishment for neglecting this opportunity of doing good to souls, when you and I shall appear before the great and awful tribunal of our Lord Jesus Christ.[48]

The rector relented; Susanna's conscience had once more withstood husbandly and churchly attempts at control, though this time her actions more closely paralleled her ancestral tradition of Nonconformity. Not believing she had contravened any law, she nevertheless had created a competing institution (an irregular "conventicle" according to her accusers) when the church could not provide for the needs of the parish as she perceived them. Years later, John Wesley, who had been present at the Sunday evening meetings as a boy of nine, read over the correspondence after his mother's death, and concluded, "I cannot but farther observe that even she (as well as her father and grandfather, her husband, and her three sons) had been, in her measure and degree, a preacher of righteousness."[49] By then, Wesley himself had replicated the same model in his own Methodist societies and was here implicitly acknowledging another debt to his mother.

Any description of the Epworth years is incomplete without a mention of Old Jeffrey, the poltergeist that plagued the rectory during December 1716 and January 1717 and has bedeviled historians ever since. A variety of noises and apparitions immediately attracted the household's attention, first the servants and the children, then Samuel and Susanna. Letters to Samuel Jr., by then teaching at Westminster School, quickly aroused his curiosity and that of his brother John, also in London, a pupil at Charterhouse School. The correspondence from Epworth and the informal depositions that John took in 1720 constitute what one writer on psychic phenomena called the "most fully documented case in the history of the subject."[50] This evidence fascinated others, as well; at the end of the century, it surfaced in the hands of the chemist and Unitarian minister Joseph Priestley, who published it to demonstrate John Wesley's captivity to that bane of eighteenth-century rationalism, "enthusiasm."[51]

John Wesley indeed was predisposed to believe in the existence of an invisible supernatural world and thus was ready to accept his family's evidence at face value, another good argument against atheism, Deism, and materialism. Each member of the family, except daughter Hetty, reported his or her experiences in straightforward fashion, as did a hired man and a neighboring clergyman. There seems to have been no apparent hoax. Indeed, in years of wrestling with it, no obvious and satisfying explanation has emerged in bemused Methodist historiography, either.

More to the point of our discussion is what the poltergeist meant to the family, particularly Susanna, and what that says about the worldview of the Epworth rectory. Because one of the poltergeist's favorite disturbances was to knock during the rector's evening prayer for the king (by then George I), the family concluded that the ghostly being had Jacobite leanings. John went so far as to connect the hauntings to his father's rash oath on the occasion of Susanna's refusal to say amen to his prayers for King William 15 years earlier. He wrote, "I fear his vow was not forgotten before God."[52] The eldest daughter, Emily, suggested that the commotions might have some link to an alleged outbreak of witchcraft in a nearby parish, which had moved Samuel to preach "warmly against consulting those that are called cunning men, which our people are given to." As this occurred just before the onset of Old Jeffrey, she concluded that the supernatural visitant was acting to spite the rector, though it might also suggest another subset of flesh-and-blood parishioners with a motive to disrupt the pretentious inhabitants of the parsonage.[53]

Susanna herself was initially skeptical at the reports of the servants and children. On first hearing noises, she suspected rodents and called in someone to blow a horn to drive them away. But the tactic did not work, and matters deteriorated. Noises (groans and all matter of knockings, stampings, and clatterings) and appearances (Susanna thought she saw a badger-like creature scurrying across the floor) became too outrageous to deny. At length she decided the visitation portended the death of a close relative, either the rector or someone at a distance, such as Samuel Jr., en route to London, or her brother in India. Finally, at about the time the ghost gave up the rectory, she expressed exasperation at her son Samuel's continuing curiosity about "our unwelcome guest." She was "tired with hearing or speaking of it" and invited the young man to come home to Epworth and experience it for himself.[54]

The episode paints in bold relief Susanna's, her family's, and perhaps the age's continuing predisposition toward supernaturalism against the background of reasonableness and science. Priestley and other eighteenth-century commentators might accuse her of enthusiasm and credulity. We might more charitably contend that the irrational and the emotional imply another, not necessarily an inferior, worldview, an alternative discourse in which a woman could express and discover herself quite well—especially when held in tension with rational and experiential considerations. Pascal himself, another anomaly of the era, whom Susanna read and commented on in her journal, expresses an appropriate agnosticism for those rationalists who would too quickly foreclose on the "superstitious" side of eighteenth-century thought: "the heart has its reasons which reason cannot know."[55]

The death of Samuel Wesley Sr. in 1735 signaled the beginning of a new life-phase for Susanna. In addition to the loss of her husband of some 46 years, it also meant her removal from the Epworth rectory (a place that for all the disruptions had been home for nearly as long). Now she would no longer be mistress of a household but would sojourn for a seven-year period as a guest, albeit a welcome one, with various of her children. She first stayed with Emily, now a schoolmistress in nearby Gainsborough. Then she moved southwest to live with Samuel Jr., a headmaster in Tiverton, Devon, leaving him two years before his unexpected death in 1739 to be with her daughter Martha (called Patty) and her clergyman husband, Westley Hall, in three locations (Wooton, Wiltshire, near Malborough; Fisherton near Salisbury; and London). From that last brief arrangement it was an easy step to finally take up residence with her son John at his London headquarters, the Foundery, within hailing distance of her birthplace.

Communication with friends loomed larger in her final years, as several of her letters attest.[56] Staying with her children in various corners of the land allowed her to make new friends, as far as we can tell from letters, all female. One such was Alice Peard, a woman she met while staying with Samuel in Tiverton and wrote to at least once after joining Martha and Westley Hall in Wiltshire. Another was the countess of Huntingdon, an influential player in the evangelical revival, who had sent her a bottle of madeira and, apparently, a generous gift of financial support at the Foundery.[57] If some of her new acquaintances were not up to that standard of affability and/or generosity,[58] that did not cause Susanna to pull back from social contacts in her advanced years.

Although friends could help her deal with the loss of husband and home and all the difficulties that came with widowhood and aging, they were no substitute for family. Thus, she began to rely on her children, not just for room, board, and financial support but also for their visits and, when that was not possible, their correspondence. For instance, the string of letters to Charles in 1738 and 1739 contain frequent references to the help, both temporal and spiritual, that he and John were providing her. She expresses her strong desire to be visited by Charles so they can talk over some of her problems. She would even like more time with John, whom she infrequently saw. She wrote of him:

> My dear Son Wesley hath just been with me and much revived my spirits. Indeed I've often found that he never speaks in my hearing without my receiving some spiritual benefit; but his visits are seldom and short, for which I never blame him, because I know he is well employed, and, blessed be God, hath great success in his ministry.[59]

To this example of family support may be added one other episode, reported in a conversation with John. She spoke to him of the strong sense of forgiveness she felt while receiving the cup from her son-in-law Hall at Communion one Sunday in August 1739. Though John and Charles both made a bit too much of the incident, "assurance of pardon" being an expected mark of Methodist experience, and though she would have been scandalized had she known of Hall's unfaithfulness to her daughter, which came out only later,[60] Susanna was genuinely touched. She, who had spent most of her life serving others, could at this point in her life also gratefully receive service from those close to her.

This is not to say that she had become passive and had relinquished her maternal, intellectual, and theological authority. She still had an active mind and continued to advise and confront when occasion demanded. While fiercely proud of her sons' evangelical work, she was not above puncturing some of their early enthusiastic pretensions, as when she accused Charles of falling into "an odd way of thinking" in saying he had "no spiritual life nor any justifying faith" before his conversion earlier that year.[61] Her misgivings were not to be taken as disavowals of the Methodist movement, as some of John's and Charles's enemies tried to make it seem, but rather attempts to further the important work she saw them doing.[62]

Perhaps the best example of her continuing decisiveness involves her role in convincing John to adopt one of the most important innovations of the movement, the employment of unordained but spiritually gifted people in preaching. One Thomas Maxfield began the practice without permission during one of Wesley's frequent absences. Before returning to take care of the situation, Wesley spoke to his mother, who replied, "My son, I charge you before God, beware what you do; for Thomas Maxfield is as much called to preach the Gospel as ever you were!"[63] Taken aback by her blunt statement and perhaps remembering her own "irregular"preaching in the Epworth rectory years before, he saw her wisdom and adopted the new practice, which developed into a trademark of Methodism and one reason for its early success.

The culmination, in many ways, of her life's work was the final document of this collection, her anonymous pamphlet of 1741 that defends her son John in his quarrel with George Whitefield. *Some Remarks on a Letter from the Reverend Mr. Whitefield to the Reverend Mr. Wesley, in a Letter from a Gentlewoman to Her Friend* brought together in a public

Susanna Wesley's England. Susanna Wesley began and ended her life in London but spent most of it in the remote Lincolnshire parish of Epworth (and its yoked neighbor, Wroot). After leaving London and before moving to Epworth, she lived in South Ormsby, her husband Samuel's first parish, also in Lincolnshire. Following her husband's death, she sojourned briefly with various of her children—in nearby Gainsborough, Tiverton (in the southwest), Wooton, and Salisbury (in south-central England)—before she finally returned to London.

Susanna Wesley's London. Susanna Annesley was born and raised in London, married Samuel Wesley there, and bore her first child there. After many years away, she returned as a widow and died there, under the care of her son John.

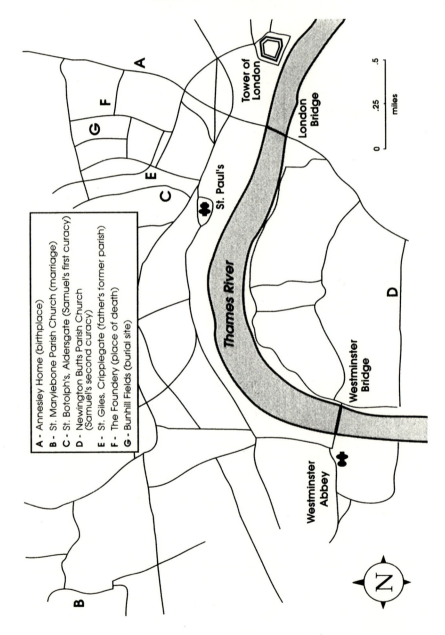

A - Annesley Home (birthplace)
B - St. Marylebone Parish Church (marriage)
C - St. Botolph's, Aldersgate (Samuel's first curacy)
D - Newington Butts Parish Church (Samuel's second curacy)
E - St. Giles, Cripplegate (father's former parish)
F - The Foundery (place of death)
G - Bunhill Fields (burial site)

Thames River

Tower of London

London Bridge

St. Paul's

Westminster Bridge

Westminster Abbey

0   .25   .5
miles

N

S Wesley

Susanna Wesley as a young woman. Late-nineteenth-century engraving, possibly from an authentic early portrait. A copy of the engraving hangs in the Old Rectory in Epworth.

Susanna Wesley at age 68. John Williams, a pupil of Samuel Richardson, painted Susanna's portrait in 1738, several years before her death. This engraving was made from the portrait a year or two after she died. The portrait has survived and is currently owned by Wesley College, Bristol, but it was inaccurately restored with a younger woman's face in 1891. The engraving is therefore probably her most authentic likeness.

Susanna Wesley as an older woman. W. H. Gibbs engraving, following the original John Williams oil painting of 1738. Taken from the frontispiece of John Kirk, *The Mother of the Wesleys*, 6th edition (London: Jarrold and Sons, 1876).

Susanna Wesley's birthplace, Spital Yard, off Bishopsgate, London. Her father, the dissenting minister Samuel Annesley, and his family lived here at some point following his ejection from the living of St. Giles, Cripplegate, in 1662. Susanna probably also stayed here briefly as the young wife of Samuel Wesley during his brief chaplaincy on a man-of-war. During that period, her first son, Samuel Wesley Jr., was born in 1690. The building has survived—though just barely—the 1990s commercial development around Liverpool Street Station.

St. Leonard's Church, South Ormsby, Lincolnshire, Samuel Wesley Sr.'s first ecclesiastical preferment. During the family's time in this rural parish (1691–1697), Susanna Wesley bore six children, three of whom died in infancy.

The Epworth rectory, rebuilt after the devastating fire of 1709. The rectory was the primary Wesley family residence from late 1697 until Samuel Wesley's death in 1735. Restored as a place of pilgrimage by the World Methodist Council in the 1950s, it was the site of Susanna's home school and her Sunday evening public prayer services; it was also the haunt of "Old Jeffrey," the erstwhile family poltergeist.

Blundell's School, Tiverton, Devon, where Samuel Wesley Jr. served as headmaster from 1732 until his death in November 1739. The widowed Susanna Wesley lived here with her eldest son and his family from September 1736 to July 1737, probably in apartments on the left side of the building. Blundell's outgrew the facility in the middle of the nineteenth century and still flourishes in larger premises a mile or two away. The original building has since been renovated as a retirement home.

St. Andrew's Church, Wooten Rivers, Wiltshire. Susanna lived in the rectory of this agricultural parish with her daughter Martha and son-in-law, the Reverend Westley Hall, in 1737–1738, before moving with them to the Salisbury suburb of Fisherton in 1738 and finally to London in 1739.

The Foundery, formerly a royal foundry for cannon, was renovated and used by John Wesley as his London headquarters from 1740 to 1778. In addition to a preaching house, a schoolroom, and his own apartments, the facility afforded space for traveling preachers and their families and for his mother, Susanna Wesley. Here, probably in the gabled section on the right, she lived the final two years of her life. Here she died on 30 July 1742.

Susanna Wesley's grave, Bunhill Fields, London. After Susanna's death in 1742, John Wesley buried his mother in this dissenters' cemetery across City Road from the eventual site of his chapel (built in 1774). The stone, recently cleaned and restored, actually dates from 1828, when Methodist officials replaced the original, less-descriptive one put there by her son. Her neighbors in Bunhill Fields include John Bunyan, Isaac Watts, and William Blake.

way several important strands of her life. First, it called on her adversarial personality, nurtured in Puritanism, further cultivated in her Nonjuring phase, and continually reinforced in the struggles of her personal and devotional life. Second, it allowed her to demonstrate her intellectual acuity, to draw on her wide reading, and to employ the ready style she had developed in all her years as a closeted writer. Finally, public and private concerns coincided when she was able to identify her sons' cause with God's intention for the nation and defend them both. Though it might have been more gratifying to have her name on the pamphlet's title page, her anonymity seems appropriate: she had the quiet satisfaction of seeing her work in print and yet could assure herself that she was not transcending the boundaries of female modesty. And perhaps there was, in addition, the canny realization that the work would be more effective if readers did not perceive it as a mother defending her son.

Mother and son were together at the end, Friday, 30 July 1742, as were most of her surviving daughters. Before she lost her speech, she had addressed them, "Children, as soon as I am released, sing a psalm of praise to God," and they afterward obliged her. "An innumerable company of people" gathered for her funeral, John preached the sermon, and she was buried (appropriately, given both her origins and her own dissenting style, even as an Anglican) in the Dissenters' burial ground in Bunhill Fields just across from the future site of Wesley's City Road Chapel. Commented Wesley in his *Journal*, "It was one of the most solemn assemblies I ever saw, or expect to see on this side eternity." [64]

(Re)assessments

The basic hagiographical, not to say romantic, view of Susanna Wesley is well exemplified in Adam Clarke's early-nineteenth-century assessment. Recounting her roles as wife, mistress of a large family, Christian, mother, and friend and the impact she had, especially on John Wesley, he exclaims, "If it were not unusual to apply such an epithet to a *woman*, I would not hesitate to say she was an able divine!" He confesses not having seen her like among all the pious females he has known, heard of, or read about, and he concludes by inserting her name into the famous description of a good woman in the book of Proverbs: "Many daughters have done virtuously: but SUSANNA WESLEY has excelled them all." [65]

"Able divine" and "good woman" are not bad places to start in any overview of Susanna Wesley. Without capitulating to the hagiographic and romantic readings of the past, we may nevertheless contend that she deserves a place both in theological discussion and in the wider consideration of women's history. Granted, Clarke's first phrase sounds a bit quaint (and a bit obvious, now that women have long since filled ministerial roles); and early Methodists and late-twentieth-century feminists might disagree on the meaning of the second catchall expression, the proverbial good woman. But if "able divine" may be employed to suggest a particular vocational subculture (a language, a set of theological and devotional assumptions, a worldview) and "good women" can hint at the more generic sense of what it has meant for women to excel, these two descriptions may not be far from the mark. If so, Susanna Wesley may prove to be a fit subject for feminists and for those who study women, their history, and their literature, as well as for Christians and for those who study that tradition and its interaction with society and culture. Our age may not regard her as St. Susanna, mother of St. John, any longer, but it might justly discover her to be a competent, practical theologian-educator and a complex and extraordinary woman in her own historical context.

It will not be difficult to convince religionists to take a fresh look at Susanna, particularly those who stand in and/or study any of the same traditions that she inhabited: the Puritan, the Anglican, and the Methodist. For them, Susanna's life and work provide clues to the links between and among these three important strands of English Protestantism. For instance, those searching for the origins of Methodist religious experience and emotionalism might usefully find in Susanna a connection to what Gordon Rupp has called a "devotion of rapture" among English Puritans.[66] Students of John Wesley's sometimes troublesome doctrine of Christian perfection, and for that matter Anglicans interested in the development of the "holy living" strand of their tradition, might notice Susanna's own wrestlings with that subject as guided by the blind Welsh theologian Richard Lucas.[67] In a waning ecumenical age, when communities are urged to celebrate their particularities, constructive attention might be paid to the tension between partisan identity and "catholic spirit" as it plays out in Susanna Wesley's life. How could she read so widely (Puritans, continental Catholics, all stripes of Anglicans) but at times focus so narrowly (e.g., in her Nonjuring phase) and yet over the course of her life find some sort of continuity in three movements in early modern English religion?

An obvious special focus of current religious studies of Susanna Wesley is her femaleness. How did gender affect her participation in religious life? How did the religious traditions that she was part of condition, limit, and possibly liberate her? In two earlier studies I have attempted to discover some of the possibilities. I have argued, for instance, that certain elements of her spirituality (conscience, reason, and religious experience) did in fact act as solvents "against the patriarchal biases then prevailing."[68] I have further explored her intellectual life—her reading and the writing amply displayed in this volume—as a factor in the resistance she mustered against her father, her husband, her sons, and her pamphlet opponent George Whitefield, in effect, against the patriarchal authority of the Establishment.[69] Among other discoveries or confirmations that emerged in her writing, "a conscience void of offense," a God-given reason that is closely related to self-reverence and the "dignity of your nature," and the experience of "loving and being beloved by [God]," all might offer a woman the eighteenth-century equivalent of empowerment.[70] The premium put on education and literacy by Protestantism, particularly in its Enlightenment phase beginning in the late seventeenth century, could be applied with revolutionary effect to women as well as to men. This is not news to students of Western religion, though surprisingly few have paid attention to the period between the Civil War sects and the rise of Methodism.[71] A thorough reconsideration of Susanna Wesley, based on the documents assembled here, should immensely enrich our understanding of that process.[72]

Though some literary historians have neglected women who wrote in a spiritual vein,[73] others have recognized them, deferring to the number of women writers if not to their theological assumptions. As Patricia Crawford has noted, "Religious writing of various kinds was the most important area of publication for seventeenth-century women." And the same would be true, if to a somewhat lesser extent, in the eighteenth century.[74] Women like Susanna who wrote out of a religiously constructed worldview are beginning to gain the recognition of scholars in this field. And the day is not far off when Susanna herself will garner similar notice: she—along with her sometime black sheep daughter Hetty, that is, Mehetable Wright,[75]—has recently been certified as a "woman writer" in the spate of dictionaries and "companions" that are beginning to recover names and sources.[76]

In fact, feminist literary historians have already made helpful approaches. Opening up the literary canon to religious women writers has involved paying positive attention to previously ignored "women's" genres such as the diary, autobiographical writing, the meditation, and the conversion narrative.[77] Each of the three genres that we have identified in her writing and used as organizing principles in this collection—letters,[78] diaries,[79] and published essays[80]—have been illuminated in recent work.

Clearly, whether we read Susanna Wesley as an early "able [female] divine" or simply as a "good woman" who wrote and lived in a religious idiom, like many another in her day, we can no longer regard her only as John Wesley's mother. She most assuredly is that, and that relationship brought her to public view and led to the preservation of the documents we can now proceed to explore. As we delve into these texts, though, her identity may begin to emerge in a richer form than ever before. Who is Susanna Wesley? Mediated by her own writings, a woman of her own time and place, she emerges in these pages as a complex and compelling personality who has much to teach.

I have organized Susanna Wesley's work into three parts, corresponding to three discernible genres that she employed. Part I consists of her letters, which are the best-dated and most complete record of her connection to her family and the world around her. Part II offers her devotional diaries. They are rarely dated, probably from a relatively narrow slice of years early in the century, but they open up her spirituality and, more clearly than the other writings, reveal her deepest self in process. Finally, part III presents her longer theological and educational writings—not that these themes are absent from letter and journal, but they are more sustained here, written with self-consciousness and intended for either real or informal publication. This is Susanna boldly trying her hand at a "male" task, albeit for the best of female motives, the education of her children and the defense of her son.

In general I have sought to present the most accurate transcription of Susanna Wesley's own writing consistent with easy comprehension by the modern reader. I wish to avoid her Victorian editors' attempt to expunge, correct, dress up, and otherwise tamper with her work. At the same time, I have restrained the urge to reproduce a text so exactly that every archaism and quirk of handwriting becomes a stumbling block to the interested general reader.

In pursuit of this goal the following guidelines have been used.

Spelling has been corrected and usually modernized, using the *Oxford English Dictionary* (OED) as standard. For instance, *chuse* becomes *choose*, but *centre* and *Saviour* remain as they are—Susanna should still be allowed to write with a British accent. Commonly occurring colloquial or shorthand spellings such as *bin* and *som* and *coud* are regularized to *been* and *some* and *could*.

Contractions and abbreviations are expanded unless they indicate speech patterns that would otherwise be lost. Thus *'tis* and *I've* and *'em* are maintained, but *wn* is expanded to *when* and *yt* becomes *that*.

Punctuation has been left alone unless alterations are required for sense or to avoid the distraction of excessive use, for example, of commas. Many of her sentences, particularly in letters and journal, tend to run on without adequate punctuation, in which case I have revised them according to modern convention and my own best judgment. Her sometimes excessive use of exclamation points is occasionally left as is to indicate her emotional state; when I have limited them a bit to preserve the flow of her sentences, I have so noted. Though she does occasionally employ quotation marks, I have frequently introduced them as part of my editorial attempt to track down her use of biblical and other material, and I so indicate in the notes.

I have tried to follow manuscript paragraphing, but given the excessive length of some of her paragraphs, I have from time to time introduced my own, and I have so indicated.

Notes, in addition to citing sources of quotations and allusions when available, also provide definitions of technical theological terms and archaic usage and give some more wide-ranging explanations if they have not already been covered in introductory material. Definitions have been taken, usually uncited, from the *Oxford English Dictionary.*

Thankfully, other textual apparatus has not often been necessary, but the following should be kept in mind:

[Brackets] are used for editorial insertions where the text is deficient but a fairly reliable guess may be made. Also, where noted in one or two instances, brackets are employed to indicate manuscript variations.

[?] precedes a probable reading of an illegible word.

Ellipses (. . .) indicate omissions in a manuscript, for example, when the only manuscript of a letter is the excerpted copy in John Wesley's letter book.

A blank (———), occasionally employed by Susanna herself, indicates words, usually names, that she intentionally omitted on her page.

Italics in text indicate Susanna's own underlining, unless otherwise noted. (Note, however, that such emphasis could have been added by any subsequent reader of the manuscript.)

Notes

1. Typical of the hagiographic tradition is John Kirk, *The Mother of the Wesleys: A Biography,* 6th ed.(London: Jarrold, 1876), first published in 1864. That S. W. (I will employ her initials for brevity's sake in the notes) was promoted as a saintly model is clear from the bookplate inside my second-hand copy of Kirk. In 1898 it had been awarded to a young woman, Myrtle Hodge, for winning the Circuit Prize (Middle Division), Examination in History of Meth-

odism, by the Cornish Wesleyan Methodist Church Council. Elsie G. Harrison, *Son to Susanna: The Private Life of John Wesley* (London: Ivor Nicholson and Watson, 1937), argues John's continuing emotional links to his mother. Writing of his most promising relationship with a woman, Harrison observes, "It was clear that neither Grace Murray nor anyone else ever really had a fair chance with John Wesley. S. W. had seen to all that under the old thatched roof of Epworth Rectory . . . ."(p. 323.)

2. All told there are at least a half dozen full-length biographies and a host of articles or parts of larger works that treat S. W.'s life. John Wesley himself began the hagiographical tradition during the eighteenth century in the pages of his *Journal* and his *Arminian Magazine*, (AM) in which anecdotes, references, and some of her writings take their place with notices of other exemplary Christians. The beatification continued in 1823 with the English publication of Adam Clarke's *Memoirs of the Wesley Family; Collected Principally from Original Documents* (New York: N. Bangs and T. Mason for the Methodist Episcopal Church, 1824). As the subtitle suggests, this volume is an anthology, as well as a biographical-hagiographical study. S. W. is the focus of about a fifth of the book, which deals with the entire Wesley family except for John and Charles. See the Bibliography for a more complete listing of relevant works. And see also John Newton, the author of the best biography, *Susanna Wesley and the Puritan Tradition in Methodism* (London: Epworth, 1968), for his analysis of his predecessors in that endeavor, "Susanna Wesley (1669–1742): A Bibliographical Survey," *Proceedings of the Wesley Historical Society* [subsequently, PWHS]37 (1969–1970): 37–40. For an introduction to the subsequent mishandling of much of S. W.'s writing, see Elizabeth Hart, "Susanna and Her Editors" PWHS 48.6 (1992): 202–209; and 49.1 (1993): 1–10.

3. Now that we have a Foucauldian reading of John Wesley, Henry Abelove's *Evangelist of Desire* (Stanford, Ca.: Stanford University Press, 1990), and given the plethora of feminist literary historical work, there are doubtless many critical approaches that might be applied to S. W.'s texts. I have noted in an as yet unpublished paper that, for some, a devotional discipline might provide the private space Virginia Woolf advocated for a woman to write and think: "The Prayer Closet as 'A Room of One's Own': Two Anglican Women Devotional Writers at the turn of the Eighteenth Century"; an earlier version was presented under a slightly different title at the American Society of Church History meetings, Washington, D.C., December 1992. See Virginia Woolf, *A Room of One's Own* (London: Triad Grafton, 1977).

4. W. Reginald Ward and Richard P. Heitzenrater, eds., *The Works of John Wesley*: Vol. 19. *Journals and Diaries, II (1738–42)* (Nashville: Abingdon, 1990), p. 283. For a discussion of this and other details of the Annesley family, see the authoritative study by Betty Young, "Sources for the Annesley Family," PWHS 45.2 (1985): 47–57.

5. Sometimes written 1668/69 to indicate that the Old Style calendar, still in official use until 1752, did not begin the new year until March 25.

6. John Dunton, *The Life and Errors of John Dunton*, 2 vols. (London: J. Nichols, Son, and Bentley, 1818), 1:166.

7. Timothy Rogers, *The Character of a Good Woman. . . Occasion'd by the Decease of Mrs. Elizabeth Dunton. . .*(London: John Harris, 1697). Filtered through the lens of a Nonconformist minister, the sermon shows numerous parallels between Elizabeth and her younger sister Susanna. Like Susanna, she kept a diary, and in it she "made a great many Reflections, both on the State of her own Soul, and on other Things, that as far as could be judged by the Bulk, would have made a very considerable Folio" (sig. e5).

8. Young, "Sources for the Annesley Family," pp. 55–56.

9. See John A. Newton, "Samuel Annesley (1620–1696)," PWHS 45.2 (1985): 29–45.

10. The house, a plain three-story brick structure with an attic garret just off Bishopsgate, is called "Susannah [sic] Wesley House" and most recently served as a solicitor's office. It is dwarfed by the current spate of office-block developments above and around Liverpool Street

Station, but the site is apparently noteworthy enough to have survived destruction and redevelopment. However, it has recently been flanked on the Bishopsgate side by an American-style "Fatboy's Diner." A plaque on the north side commemorates Susanna Annesley's birth. For a sense of Samuel Annesley's extensive library, see the sale catalogue prepared after his death, in Edward Millington, ed., *Bibliotheca Annesleiana:. . . The Library of the Reverend Samuel Annesley,* . . . (London, 1697). An original is in the British Library; Wesley Theological Seminary, Washington, D.C., owns a microfiche copy.

11. *The Character of the Late Dr. Samuel Annesley, by Way of Elegy . . . by One of His Hearers* (London: E. Whitlock, 1697).

12. Newton, "Samuel Annesley," p. 39.

13. See the letter to Samuel Wesley Jr., 11 October 1709.

14. The most authoritative recent account of Samuel Wesley's early years, based on newly discovered materials, is H. A. Beecham, "Samuel Wesley Senior: New Biographical Evidence," *Renaissance and Modern Studies* 7 (1963): 78–109.

15. Ibid., pp. 85–87. See also Newton, *Susanna Wesley,* pp. 65–66.

16. For instance, discussions with her future husband seem to have persuaded her to pull back from a temporary inclination toward Socinianism (Unitarianism). See Newton, *Susanna Wesley,* p. 66.

17. Lawrence Stone, *The Family, Sex and Marriage in England 1500–1800,* abridged ed. (New York: Harper Colophon, 1979), pp. 217–253.

18. At the time a semirural suburb, Newington Butts is now inner city, a stone's throw from Elephant and Castle underground station. The parish church is long since gone, and the only ecclesiastical edifice is Spurgeon's London Tabernacle, relic of a later time, itself seeming out of place in the tangle of council flats, shopping centers, and speeding traffic.

19. See his long letter of 22 August 1692, in Beecham, "Samuel Wesley," pp. 102–108.

20. Ibid., p. 108.

21. Clarke, *Wesley Family,* p. 61.

22. For details on the Wesley offspring, see Frank Baker, "Investigating Wesley Family Traditions," *Methodist History* 26.3 (1988): 159–162.

23. See especially Clarke, *Wesley Family.*

24. Letter to Samuel Annesley Jr., 20 January 1721/22, in part I of this volume.

25. See Young, "Sources for the Annesley Family," p. 52.

26. See, among others, her letter regarding the 1709 fire to Joseph Hoole, 24 August 1709. Even at the end of her life, she was not in good financial shape. See the letter to Charles Wesley, 19 October 1738. For Samuel Wesley's perspective, see Clarke, *Wesley Family,* pp. 76–82, 86–96, and 128–133, and Beecham's publication of a recently discovered letter from the South Ormsby period, in "Samuel Wesley," pp. 102–108. A letter from Emilia to John, 7 April 1725, details the pinch she felt when called home from her boarding school job to keep her mother company (George Stevenson, *Memorials of the Wesley Family . . .* (London: S. W. Partridge; New York: Nelson and Phillips, 1876), pp. 262–64.

27. See journal entry 119, dated 17 October 1715, in part II of this volume.

28. Beecham, "Samuel Wesley," p. 108.

29. See the following letters: 27 November 1707; 14 February 1708/09; 20 January 1721/22; 10 September 1724; 23 February 1724/25; 26 July 1727; 12 August 1728; 11 August 1729; 21 February 1731/32; 5 August 1737; 6 December 1738.

30. See journal entries 105 and 13, respectively. See also entries 25, 160, and 253 and her letter to her son John, 26 July 1727.

31. Letter to Samuel Wesley Jr., 11 October 1709.

32. See "On Educating My Family," the first essay in part III of this volume.

33. See the brief introduction to ibid.

34. The family story told to Adam Clarke by John Wesley was that Samuel Jr. did not speak at all until he was between four and five years old. One day when the family could not find him, S. W. combed the house, frantically calling his name. Suddenly, a small voice was heard speaking a complete sentence from under a table: "Here am I, mother!" Looking down they found "Sammy" and his favorite cat. "From this time," says Wesley, "he spoke regularly, and without any kind of hesitation." Clarke, *Wesley Family*, pp. 213–214.

35. *Susanna Wesley*, pp. 109–110.

36. See journal entry 79 and the letter to her husband, 6 February 1712.

37. Note the insistence of Richard Allestree's influential *The Whole Duty of Man* . . . (Oxford: George Pawlet, 1684), p. 115, that after children are "past the age of education," parents are still to observe them "and accordingly to exhort, incourage, or reprove, as they find occasion."

38. S. W.'s concern for her children's marriages, particularly her daughters', is visible in several letters to John, for example, 12 October 1726 (on Hetty's problematic relationship), 1 January 1733/34 (her reservations on Molly's marriage), and 31 January 1727 (some straight talk on what she regarded as an inappropriate, albeit platonic, relationship of his own). Her dissatisfaction with her daughter Suky's choice is recorded in her letter to her brother Samuel Annesley Jr., 20 January 1721/22. The same letter indicates that at least one of the sisters tried for a while the only other option, that of governess or teacher. The bad luck of the Wesley daughters in later life is the subject of Frederick E. Maser, *The Story of John Wesley's Sisters, or Seven Sisters in Search of Love* (Rutland, Vt.: Academy Books, 1988).

39. The Methodist nickname came later, one of several slung at the devotional group the Wesley brothers led at Oxford, but the way of life, in both its well-ordered and obsessive-compulsive aspects, clearly originated in the Epworth rectory. John Wesley understood the importance of his mother's childrearing and educational methodology and gave wide circulation to her letter describing it. For its continuing influence, see the introduction to "On Educating My Family," in part III of this volume.

40. Family letters started the legend, including S. W.'s own to Samuel Jr., 14 February and 11 October 1709, and one to the Rev. Joseph Hoole, 24 August 1709.

41. See the convenient summary of these sad episodes in Maldwyn Edwards, *Family Circle: A Study of the Epworth Household in Relation to John and Charles Wesley* (London: Epworth, 1949), pp. 18–20. The baby was "overlaid" by the nurse to whom it was entrusted the night before the election. Noisy partisans had kept her awake by discharging pistols and making a general disturbance where she and the Wesleys were lodged for the night in Lincoln; when she finally fell into a deep sleep, she unknowingly rolled over on the infant and smothered him. See the account in Samuel Wesley's letter to the archbishop of York in Clarke, *Wesley Family*, p. 90

42. To Samuel Wesley Jr., 11 October 1709. See also the various journal entries in which she wrestles with this issue, for example, 51, 52, and 56, and the opening lines of her letter to Suky on the Creed, in part III of this volume, as well as the journal entry 2, in part II, which alludes to the "misfortunes that have separated" the family.

43. Gordon Rupp, *Religion in England, 1688–1791* (Oxford: Clarendon Press, 1986), p. 6, explains that there were "recurring problems of conscience" for some half a century for those who refused to swear an oath of allegiance to the new succession. Clearly the abortive attempts to return the Stuarts to power in 1715 and 1745 provoked such soul-searching; but so did the death of a monarch, whether the deposed James II or the actually reigning William, Anne, and George I.

44. This bit of family oral tradition was recorded by Clarke, *Wesley Family*, p. 83.

45. See Rupp's helpful chapter on the phenomenon in *Religion in England*, pp. 5–28.

46. Quoted in Robert Walmsley, "John Wesley's Parents: Quarrel and Reconciliation," PWHS 24.3 (1953): 55. Walmsley first discovered and published S. W.'s letters to Lady Yarborough and Dean Hickes.

47. To Samuel Wesley Sr., 6 February 1711/12.

48. To Samuel Wesley Sr., 25 February 1711/12.

49. Ward and Heitzenrater, *Journals and Diaries* (30 July 1742), p. 284.

50. Harry Price, *Poltergeist over England*, quoted in Edwards, *Family Circle*, p. 95.

51. Joseph Priestley, *Original Letters, by the Rev. John Wesley and his friends* . . . (Birmingham: Thomas Pearson, 1791), p. iv.

52. Clarke, *Wesley Family*, p. 143.

53. Ibid., p. 154. Beliefs and practices of this sort were certainly part of the popular religious mix of the time. James Obelkevich has detailed their existence in nineteenth-century Lincolnsire (though in another part of the county) in *Religion and Rural Society: South Lindsey, 1825–1875* (Oxford: Clarendon Press, 1976): pp. 259–312. He finds belief in ghosts, witches, and wise men—who could in some ways be seen as rivals to the clergy—among village people (pp. 282–291) and accounts for it in part by the weaknesses of official Christianity, "the remoteness of its high God, the social elevation of its clergy," and so on (p. 301). However, "wise men rushed in where Anglicans feared to tread . . ." (p. 304), dealing with everyday problems concerning weather, crops, animals, health, love, and death in immediate ways. In the Epworth case a century before, members of the Wesley family found themselves, against their natural Enlightened inclinations, pulled into the popular worldview. Their fascination is evident, but so is their discomfort; they were very much in Epworth but not of it, and that distinction may at some level help explain the whole episode.

54. See her letters to Samuel Jr.—12 January 1716/17; 25 or 27 January 1716/17; and 27 March 1717—and her "Account to Jack," dated 27 August 1726, which I have included immediately thereafter, in part I. The fullest collection of all the material on Old Jeffrey is in Clarke, *Wesley Family*, pp. 136–167.

55. See entries 84, 131, 133–135, 138–139, and 207. The quotation is from the modern edition, *Pascal's Pensées*, introducton by T. S. Eliot (New York: Dutton, 1958), p. 78.

56. Though we should not conclude that she lacked friends in earlier stages of her life just because few nonfamily letters survive from those periods.

57. To Alice Peard, 5 August 1737; to the countess of Huntingdon, 1 July 1741.

58. An objectionable woman seems to have attempted to cozy up to S. W. at the Foundery, driving off other, more compatible companions. See the letter to Charles, 27 December 1739.

59. To Charles Wesley, 27 December 1739.

60. See Ward and Heitzenrater, *Journals and Diaries*, II, (3 September 1739), pp. 93–94. Hall later turned out to be, in Clarke's words, "a Moravian and Quietist, an Antinomian, a Deist, if not an Atheist, and a Polygamist, which last he defended in his teaching, and illustrated by his practice" (*Wesley Family*, p. 421). Charles celebrated her newfound "assurance" in a poem composed for her tombstone, making it appear as if she had lived in darkness, evangelically speaking, for the previous 70 years. See Ward and Heitzenrater, *Journals and Diaries*, II (1 August 1742), pp. 283–284.

61. To Charles Wesley, 6 December 1738.

62. See Clarke, *Wesley Family*, pp. 275–286, refuting the claim made by Samuel Badcock in 1782 and afterward circulated for purposes of controversy that Mrs. Wesley "lived long enough to deplore the extravagances of her two sons John and Charles. . . ."

63. Ibid., p. 236.

64. Ward and Heitzenrater, *Journals and Diaries*, II, pp. 282–84. The original tombstone was notable for its lack of biographical information and its inclusion of a four-stanza hymn composed by Charles Wesley:

Here lies the body of Mrs. Susanna Wesley, the youngest and last surviving daughter of Dr. Samuel Annesley.

In sure and steadfast hope to rise
And claim her mansion in the skies,
A Christian here her flesh laid down,
The cross exchanging for a crown.

True daughter of affliction she,
Inured to pain and misery,
Mourned a long night of grief and fears,
A legal night of seventy years.

The Father then revealed the Son,
Him in the broken bread made known.
She knew and felt her sins forgiven,
And found the earnest of her heaven.

Meet for the fellowship above,
She heard the call, "Arise, my love."
"I come," her dying looks replied,
And lamb-like, as her Lord, she died.

Having worn badly, this stone was replaced by a more descriptive one in 1828, maintained by Methodist pilgrims ever since. A larger monument was erected on the grounds of Wesley's Chapel in 1870. See Stevenson, *Memorials*, pp. 228–229.

65. Clarke, *Wesley Family*, pp. 291–292; his emphasis. See Proverbs 31:29.

66. Gordon Rupp, "A Devotion of Rapture in English Puritanism," in R. Buick Knox, ed., *Reformation, Conformity and Dissent: Essays in Honour of Geoffrey Nuttall* (London: Epworth, 1977), p. 119. I have enlarged on this in my article "Susanna Wesley's Spirituality: The Freedom of a Christian Women," *Methodist History* 22.3 (1984): 168.

67. See the host of journal entries that quote Lucas and/or discuss Christian perfection: 193–196, 202–203, 205, 208, 212–214, 219, 226, 228, 231–233, 237–238, 240–243, and 252.

68. Wallace, "Susanna Wesley's Spirituality," p. 160.

69. See Charles Wallace Jr., " 'Some Stated Employment of Your Mind': Reading, Writing, and Religion in the Life of Susanna Wesley," *Church History* 58 (1989): pp. 354–366.

70. See her journal entries 181 (following Bishop Beveridge's sermon on conscience), 51, and 191. Patricia Crawford has recently sketched the wider landscape, even including S. W. (and her conscientious refusal to say "amen" to the prayer for King William) as one of the details in the picture: "Public Duty, Conscience, and Women in Early Modern England," in John Morrill, Paul Slack, and Daniel Woolf, eds., *Public Duty and Private Conscience in Seventeenth-Century England: Essays Presented to G. E. Aylmer* (Oxford: Clarendon Press, 1993): pp. 57–76. Her conclusion is that conscience "justified some women's wifely disobedience and their participation in English social and political life" (p.76).

71. Checking some of the important anthologies on women and Christianity, I find significant gaps that further study of S. W. could help fill. There is no chapter on women of her generation or on early female Methodists in Rosemary Ruether and Eleanor McLaughlin, eds., *Women of Spirit: Female Leadership in the Jewish and Christian Traditions* (New York: Simon and Schuster, 1972). Elizabeth Clark and Herbert Richardson's anthology, *Women and Religion: A Feminist Sourcebook of Christian Thought* (New York: Harper and Row, 1977), moves from John Milton to Ann Lee to Schleiermacher with not a look at anything Anglican or Methodist. Dale Johnson's anthology, *Women in English Religion, 1700–1925* (New York and Toronto: Edwin Mellen, 1983)

is better, including in its narrower focus both Anglican and Methodist sources and referring to S. W. as part of an introduction to the evangelical revival; but it includes nothing of her writing. Richard L. Greaves, ed., *Triumph over Silence: Women in Protestant History* (Westport, Conn., and London: Greenwood, 1985), skips directly from a chapter on sectarian women in late-seventeenth-century England to chapters on Puritanism and Methodism, respectively—in America. Barbara J. MacHaffie, *Her Story: Women in Christian Tradition* (Philadelphia: Fortress, 1986), moves directly from the Reformation to religion in the American colonies, giving only the briefest of details about any Englishwomen in the interim. The recent collection, Lynda L. Coon, Katherine J. Haldane, and Elisabeth W. Sommer, eds., *That Gentle Strength: Historical Perspectives on Women in Christianity* (Charlottesville and London: University of Virginia Press, 1990): totally neglects English religion prior to the Victorian era. And W. J. Sheils and Diana Wood, eds., *Women in the Church: Papers Read at the 1989 Summer Meeting and the 1990 Winter Meeting of the Ecclesiastical History Society* (Oxford: Basil Blackwell, 1990), provide no direct treatment of the Church of England between the Reformation and the Victorian era. As one might expect, Methodist denominational history has done better. Witness, for example, and just to mention book-length treatment, Earl Kent Brown, *The Women of Mr. Wesley's Methodism* (New York and Toronto: Edwin Mellen, 1983); Paul W. Chilcote, *John Wesley and the Women Preachers of Early Methodism* (Metuchen, N.J.: Scarecrow, 1991); and of course, John Newton's *Susanna Wesley* and Rebecca Lamar Harmon's *Susanna: Mother of the Wesleys* (Nashville and New York: Abingdon, 1986).

72. The stage has recently been well set by Patricia Crawford's splendid monograph, *Women and Religion in England, 1500–1720* (London and New York: Routledge, 1993). Though she, too, gives only scant coverage to turn-of-the-century issues that deal with women and the established church, her chapter on "Piety and Spirituality" is a treasure trove of helpful background. In fact, she uses Susanna Wesley (misspelling her given name with a final h) as an example of how "godliness and piety could develop a woman's sense of rectitude which would enable her to defy her husband" (pp. 95–96).

73. For instance, Marilyn L. Williamson, *Raising Their Voices: British Women Writers, 1650–1750* (Detroit: Wayne State University Press, 1990), defends her decision to omit any consideration of religious poetry: "I admit that in seventeenth-century England, religious values are social and political, but the issues are so complex that they would have required another framework besides that of gender ideology, which I have used. That would be another study, and one does what one can" (p. 10).

74. Patricia Crawford, "Women's Published Writings 1600–1700," in Mary Prior, ed., *Women in English Society, 1500–1800* (London and New York, Methuen, 1985), p. 221. Other studies that take women's religious writing seriously include Sara Heller Mendelson, "Stuart women's diaries and occasional memoirs," ibid., pp. 181–210; Elaine Hobby, *Virtue of Necessity: English Women's Writing, 1649–88* (Ann Arbor: University of Michigan Press, 1989); Felicity A. Nussbaum, *The Autobiographical Subject: Gender and Ideology in Eighteenth-Century England* (Baltimore and London: Johns Hopkins University Press, 1989); and Margaret J. M. Ezell, *Writing Women's Literary History* (Baltimore and London: Johns Hopkins University Press, 1993).

75. I have recounted in the introduction to chapter 9 of the letters, part I of this volume, the story of Hetty's forced marriage and the disruption it caused the family. For glimpses of the issue in S. W.'s letters, see those to her son John, 23 February 1724/25 and 12 October 1726.

76. For instance, S. W. claims a listing of a column and a half in Janet Todd, ed., *A Dictionary of British and American Women Writers, 1660–1800* (London: Methuen, 1987), p. 319; a one-column entry in Virginia Blain, Patricia Clements, and Isobel Grundy, eds., *The Feminist Companion to Literature in English: Women Writers from the Middle Ages to the Present* (New Haven, Conn., and London: Yale University Press, 1990): p. 1150; and a brief (and somewhat misleading)

paragraph in Maureen Bell, George Parfitt, and Simon Shepherd, eds., *A Biographical Dictionary of English Women Writers, 1580–1720* (Boston: G. K. Hall, 1990), p. 211.

77. See, for example, Mendelson, "Stuart Women's Diaries"; Harriet Blodgett, *Centuries of Female Days: Englishwomen's Private Diaries* (New Brunswick, N.J.: Rutgers University Press, 1988); Felicity A. Nussbaum, "Eighteenth-Century Women's Autobiographical Commonplaces," in Shari Bentock, ed., *The Private Self: Theory and Practice of Women's Autobiographical Writings* (Chapel Hill and London: University of North Carolina Press, 1988): pp. 147–171; Elaine Hobby, Virtue of Necessity, pp. 54–75.

78. For example, Patricia Meyer Spacks, "Female Rhetorics," in Benstock, *Private Self*, p. 178, reads eighteenth-century letters to show how women developed rhetorical strategies allowing them to elucidate themselves without falling prey to the "troubling threat of egotism." The tension between self-deprecation and self-assertion pervades S. W.'s letters and her other writings as well. (See *Introduction to the Letters* in part I of this volume) As Allison Weber has shown, *Teresa of Avila and the Rhetoric of Femininity* (Princeton, N.J.: Princeton University Press, 1990): pp. 11, 48–50, 80–81, such rhetorical strategizing was not limited to eighteenth-century English Protestant women.

79. Felicity A. Nussbuam performs a similar service for various forms of female "self-writing" (diaries, commonplace books, and autobiographies), arguing that such texts both reproduce and challenge the reigning ideology. In the process of representing herself in the relatively safe space of her diary, a woman might in part "confirm the conventions for 'woman,'" but at the same time "alternative configurations of identity" might emerge ("Eighteenth-Century Women," p. 156). She further calls out for "mapping the territory of Restoration and eighteenth-century female autobiographical subjectivity more fully" and specifically incorporates "the spiritual autobiographers, including Quaker, Baptist, and Methodist journalists" into her wish list of future research (p. 151). In my analysis of S. W.'s diaries in part II of this volume, I have relied on Blodgett's book-length treatment of similar issues in *Centuries of Female Days*.

80. Elaine Hobby, examining seventeenth-century women who published religious books, discovered a "repertoire of devices to make their writing a 'modest' act" (*Virtue of Necessity*, p. 9). If women were to write and publish, both regarded as highly inappropriate, "immodest" activities, they could follow no better strategy than to assert divine approval, precisely the claim S. W. made in rationalizing her "publications." See ibid., p. 9 and chaps. 1 and 2, pp. 26–75, also part III of this volume. "Publication" for purposes of this discussion might be broadened to include any piece of writing intended for an audience of more than one, even if not commercially printed and distributed.

PART I

Letters

Introduction to the Letters

Susanna Wesley's letters give us a better view of the whole person than do her larger theological and educational writings and her devotional journal. Theological and spiritual concerns are never far from the surface in her correspondence (indeed, word for word, they predominate) and so are moments of introspection, but family news and relationships also frequently come up in interesting, though not always explicit, ways. The everyday world at least frames the theological and devotional content of the letters and enables the reader to fill in the life details and sketch more fully the worldview of this remarkable woman.

The collection presented in this part consists of 72 letters—74, if we count the second parts of two double letters. Because of their length and intentional composition, three additional letters have been grouped in part III as theological treatises. The first extant letter dates from 1702, when Susanna was a young wife of 33, and the last, from 1741, when she was a 72-year-old widow, a year before her death. Unfortunately, we have no writing of any kind from the period before her marriage. However, each decade of the century, up to and including that of the 1740s, is represented, though some better and more consistently than others.

Most of the letters were written to family members. Not surprisingly, we have 36 letters to John, whose fame would ensure the saving and eventual archiving of a voluminous correspondence. Beginning with his time at Oxford, they focus intensely on issues of "practical divinity," imparting theological advice appropriate for the various early career stages he was going through.

Slightly less than half that amount, 17, are addressed to Susanna's eldest son, Samuel Wesley Jr., owing in part to his keeping a letter book (his mother's idea) full of copied correspondence that has otherwise disappeared. All but two of these were written before the end of 1710, and they mainly consist of moral and spiritual counsel during his years as a scholar at Westminster School. Two letters illustrate her conversation with him as an adult, one during his teaching career at Westminster School and one near the end of his life when he was headmaster of Blundell's School in Tiverton.

Her youngest son, Charles, received at least nine, two of which were included in those double letters just mentioned that were sent as part of letters to John. She was writing Charles during and after his Oxford career, in part arguing against what she perceived to be theological exaggerations of her recently converted son.

Two letters are addressed to her husband, Samuel Wesley Sr., penned to defend her alleged liturgical irregularities while he was in London attending the Church of England convocation in early 1712. And her brother Samuel Annesley Jr., the East India merchant, is represented by a long letter that both justifies her husband's lack of business acumen and pleads on behalf of her family, then as always in dire financial straits. Two of the three "letters" included in part III are addressed to Suky, her next to eldest daughter, and the third relegated to that part of this volume is the well-known letter to John recounting her child-rearing and educational approach.

Surviving letters to people outside the family number only nine. Two each were written to Lady Yarborough and the Rev. George Hickes, the earliest ones in this volume and four of the most interesting in the way they shed light on a political, religious, and marital quarrel between Susanna and her husband. Two were addressed to a neighboring clergyman, the Rev. Joseph Hoole, in 1710 and 1716; and one each was sent near the end of her life to two women friends or acquaintances, Mrs. Alice Peard and the countess of Huntingdon. There is also one letter to an unknown person, a young clergyman seeking advice on how best to obtain ecclesiastical preferment.

We may surmise that this collection represents only a sampling of her letters, those that for one reason or another have survived. It is particularly disappointing that we have so few letters written to women. Correspondence with her grown daughters, her sister Ann Annesley in London, and other women relatives and friends was probably discarded at an early stage. Apart from the two treatises in letter form addressed to her daughter Susanna (in part III of this volume), there are only four in the entire collection, those mentioned above: the two to Lady Yarborough, the one to Alice Peard, and the one to the countess of Huntingdon.

I have been able to work from original manuscripts in most cases. The Methodist Archives (MA) at the John Rylands University Library, Manchester, owns a number of holographs and also both Samuel Jr.'s (SWJr) and John's letter books (LB). An additional holograph each has surfaced at Wesley's Chapel, London; at the Melbourne Public Library in Australia; and in a private collection in London, all of which I have been able to examine in photocopied form. The first four letters in this series (the Yarborough and Hickes correspondence) were carefully edited for publication in 1953; as I judge these to be trustworthy, I have not sought out the originals. For a few, I necessarily depend on John Wesley's editing when he prepared a number of his mother's letters for publication in his *Journal* and in his *Arminian Magazine* (AM) later in the century. For one other, I am at the mercy of George Stevenson, the nineteenth-century Methodist historian whose editorial work on dozens of letters is not always reliable.[1]

The chronological arrangement I follow allows the reader to witness the unfolding of Susanna Wesley's personality throughout a good portion of her life. Coincidentally, this sequence also breaks fairly conveniently into thematic sections, or chapters, to which I have prefixed brief introductions that give a sense of the personal, family, and theological issues in each. Endnotes also help with the identification of unfamiliar names and terms.

We need not be detained here with details on letters and letter writing in the eighteenth century, though such knowledge obviously enriches one's appreciation for Susanna's output.[2] More to the interpretive point and more helpful in the reading of these letters as literary texts is a recent perspective on the "strategies of deflection" used by women correspondents in that era.[3] Patricia Meyer Spacks has argued, "Eighteenth-century letters by women reflect and elucidate the conflict between the desire for self-assertion and the need for self-suppression."[4] A reading of Susanna Wesley's letters reveals a similar conflict and the development of a similar "rhetoric" to help in the process of self-definition. The self-deprecation that Spacks finds in her research[5] echoes again and again in Susanna's letters. However, that lip service to contemporary social convention is undercut by a deeply formed sense of self, a Puritan self-understanding that ultimately values the individual and empowers her when in conflict with "the world," however that might be construed. That sense of self allows her not only to love and support her family but also to advise, teach, argue with, and sometimes stubbornly resist even her husband, brother, and sons.

Notes

1. *Memorials of the Wesley Family* . . . (London: S. W. Patridge; New York: Nelson and Phillips, 1876), passim.

2. See Professor Frank Baker's excellent, concise introduction to his first volume of John Wesley's correspondence: *The Works of John Wesley: Vol. 25. Letters I (1721–1739)* (Oxford: Clarendon Press, 1980), especially pp. 11–28 ("An Age of Correspondence").

3. Patricia Meyer Spacks, "Female Rhetorics," in Shari Benstock, ed., *The Private Self: Theory and Practice of Women's Autobiographical Writings* (Chapel Hill and London: University of North Carolina Press, 1988), pp. 177–191. Her analysis focuses on the letters of Lady Mary Wortley Montagu, Elizabeth Carter, and Mary Granville Delany (coincidentally, a sometime friend and correspondent of John Wesley).

4. Ibid., pp. 177–178.

5. Ibid., p. 188.

ONE

Religious and Sexual Politics

Yarborough and Hickes Correspondence

*T*he earliest extant Susanna Wesley letters stem from 1702, when she was a young wife of some 13 years, mother of six children, and for some five years the mistress of the Epworth rectory. They record the political quarrel that for six months disrupted her marriage. At issue was the legitimacy of William III's claim to the English throne. While most, Samuel Wesley included, supported his reign and the "Glorious Revolution" that brought him to power, a small, conscientious minority refused to take an oath to him and his consort, Mary, on the grounds that the deposed James II remained king by divine right. As these letters show, Susanna Wesley put herself in that camp, writing to two members of the church's Nonjuring party for advice in her domestic dispute.

The incident also involves sexual politics, demonstrating how far a woman might go in resisting the will of her husband and on what grounds. In this case Susanna's Puritan conscience, now serving (and being bolstered by) a sectarian right-wing Anglicanism, enabled the otherwise obedient 32-year-old wife to withstand the bluster of her politically more moderate 39-year-old husband. Having vowed to live apart from her until she apologized, the rector left for London in a huff. Far from accepting the charge of "pride and obstinacy," she felt herself to be "pretty innocent" and stood her ground until circumstances brought him back.

The story was known to John Wesley.[1] Indeed, when the quarrel was resolved (the rectory fire described in the second letter to George Hickes brought Samuel around), John Wesley himself, born the following June, was the most obvious result of the healed rift.

Lady Yarborough was born Henrietta Maria Blagge and had been a maid of honor of the duchess of York at Charles II's court. Thomas Yarborough, later a member of Parliament (MP), married her in 1663 and brought her to Snaith in a corner of Yorkshire just a few miles from Epworth. Susanna made her acquaintance there and trusted her Nonjuring sympathies enough to ask for advice. Lady Yarborough referred her to a much more eminent Nonjuror, the Rev. George Hickes. As a result of his principles, Hickes had been deprived of the deanship of Worcester and was by this time styled Suffragan Bishop of Thetford, one of the highest-ranked clerics in the samll schismatic movement.

The letters were discovered by Robert Walmsley in the early 1950s in a manuscript book, "The Genuine Remains of the Late Pious and Learned George Hickes, D. D., and Suffragan Bishop of Thetford, consisting of Controversial Letters and Other Discourses." Walmsley published them in the *Manchester Guardian*, 3 July 1953, and soon thereafter in the *Proceedings of the Wesley Historical Society*, from which we reprint them here.

❧

To Lady Yarborough
7 March 1702
Reprinted from Robert Walmsley, "John Wesley's Parents: Quarrel and Reconciliation," PWHS 29.3 (1953–1954): 52–53. Paragraphing introduced by Walmsley. Occasional punctuation, indicated in brackets, and notes have been added in this volume.

To the lady Yarborough.
Saturday night March 7, 1701–2.

Madam

I'm infinitely obliged to your Ladyship for your charming civility to a person so utterly unworthy of your favours, but oh Madam! I must tell your Ladyship you have somewhat mistaken my case. You advise me to continue with my husband and God knows how gladly I would do it but there, there is my extreme affliction[:] he will not live with me. 'Tis but a little while since he one evening observed in our Family prayers I did not say Amen to his prayer for K[ing] W[illiam] as I usually do to all others; upon which he retired to his study, and calling me to him asked me the reason of my not saying Amen to the Prayer. I was a little surprised at the question and don't well know what I answered, but too too well I remember what followed: He immediately kneeled down and imprecated the divine Vengeance upon himself and all his posterity if ever he touched me more or came into a bed with me before I had begged God's pardon and his, for not saying Amen to the prayer for the K[in]g.

This Madam is my unhappy case. I've unsuccessfully represented to him the unlawfulness and unreasonableness of his Oath; that the Man in that case has no more power over his own body than the Woman over her's; that since I'm willing to let him quietly enjoy his opinions, he ought not to deprive me of my little liberty of conscience. But he has opened his mouth to the Lord and w[ha]t help? What's past is Fate, nor can God or man recall the time that is actually elapsed, or undo an action once performed. I should be eternally obliged to your Ladyship would you be pleased to consult one of our Divines about it that might be trusted with such an important secret. 'Tis a fearful thing to fall into the hands of the living God,[2] or to trifle with the divine Vengeance which we can never sufficiently deprecate. He is too great to be affronted or mocked, to[o] wise to be deceived, no artifice or evasion could possibly pass upon him were I so impious to attempt it. I have no resentment against my Master, so far from it that the very next day I went with him to the Communion, though he that night forsook my bed to which he has been a stranger ever since.

I'm almost ashamed to own what extreme disturbance this accident has given me, yet I value not the world. I value neither reputation[,] friends or anything in comparison of the single satisfaction, of preserving a conscience void of offence towards God and man;[3] and how I can do that if I mock almighty God, by begging pardon for what I think no sin, is past my discerning. But I am inexpressibly miserable, for I can see no possibility of reconciling these differences, though I would submit to anything or do anything in the world to oblige him to live in the house with me. I appeal to your Ladyship if my circumstances are not strangely unhappy. I believe myself an Original of misery. I don't think there's any precedent of such a case in the whole world; and may I not say as the Prophet, "I am the person that has seen affliction."[4] I'm almost afraid I've already complied with him too far, but most humbly beg your Ladyship's direction.

I am etc.

S. Wesley.

I've a great deal more to say but am afraid of being troublesome, and ask pardon for what I've already given your Ladyship. My Master is for London at Easter, when I hope I shall be able to wait on your Ladyship if I can live so long, and in the meantime earnestly desire your prayers and direction.

To Lady Yarborough
15 March 1702
Reprinted from Robert Walmsley, "John Wesley's Parents: Quarrel and Reconciliation," PWHS 29.3 (1953–1954): 53–54.

March 15 [1701–2]

Madam

The shortness of my time will I hope excuse the brevity of my answer. I'm extremely obliged to your Ladyship for your generous concern and pity of my misfortunes, and return my humblest thanks for your Letters, which have been a great cordial to me and given me unspeakable satisfaction. I find the Gentleman that has seen my Letters is of opinion that I ought not to comply any further, but persevere in following the dictates of my own conscience, which I hope is not erroneous. I thank God I'm much better satisfied in all things than I was, and find God has by these unusual afflictions vouchsafed me many favours; they have greatly inclined my mind to patience and a more entire resignation to the divine Will, I am not so much affected as formerly with these sublunary affairs, which as your Ladyship rightly observes are but for a time, and a very little inconsiderable time indeed. I've represented as long as I could be heard the sin of the Oath and ill consequences of it to my Master, but he cannot be convinced he has done ill, nor does the present change in State[5] make any alteration in his mind; I am persuaded nothing but an omnipotent power can move him and there I leave it. He is for London at Easter where he designs to try if he can get a Chaplain's place in a Man of War.

I'm more easy in the thoughts of parting because I think we are not likely to live happily together. I have six very little children, which though he tells me he will take good care of, yet if anything should befall him at Sea we should be in no very good condition, but still I believe that that charitable Being which feeds the Ravens and cloathes the Lilies[6] will never think me or mine below his care and Providence, though none in the world is more unworthy of either. I've offered since I last writ to your Ladyship to put this business to a reference, provided I might choose one Referee and my Master another, but I fancy he'll never agree to it. He is fearful of my communicating it to any person, which makes me somewhat more confined than usually, but when he is gone I hope I shall be able to wait on your Ladyship to discourse more fully of things, and to return you my repeated thanks as well as to confirm my sincere profession of being, Madam, your Ladyship's   S. W.

I am extremely concerned for Sir Thomas's illness and pray God to mitigate it, and in the meantime to sanctify all his afflictions. I humbly beg the Gentleman would be careful that the world may know nothing which may reflect upon my Master, but that the business may be concealed.

To George Hickes
? April 1702
Reprinted from Robert Walmsley, "John Wesley's Parents: Quarrell and Reconcili-ation," PWHS 29.3 (1953–1954): 54. The address at its close (Snaith) indicates this letter was written from Lady Yarborough's home, some 13 miles northeast of Epworth.

To the Rev Mr Dean Hickes

Reverend Sir, I should not at this time trouble or divert your better thoughts, but you having been already acquainted by the Lady Yarborough with some uneasy circumstances I at present am under, and expressing so generous a pity and compas-sion for an unfortunate stranger, makes me presume to beg your direction in this particular. My Master will not be persuaded he has no power over the conscience of his Wife, and though I believe he's somewhat troubled at his Oath yet cannot be persuaded 'tis not obligatory. He is now for referring the whole to the Archbishop of York and Bishop of Lincoln, and says if I will not be determined by them, he will do anything rather than live with a person that is the declared enemy of his country, which he believes himself obliged to love before all the world.

I very well know before such Judges I'm sure to be condemned without a fair hearing; nor can I see any reason I have to ask either God Almighty's or his pardon for acting according to the best knowledge I have of things of that nature. If I thought or could be persuaded I'm in an error I would freely retract it and ask his pardon before the whole world. He accuses me of pride and obstinacy and insists upon my making him satisfaction for the injury he believes I've done him. I dare not plead not guilty to such an Indictment, but yet I hope however I may in other instances be culpable, in this I'm pretty innocent. I most humbly beg the favour of your direction and prayers, and your acceptance of most humble thanks and service from, Sir, your most humble Servant

(Snaith).   S. Wesley

My Master is at London, and the extreme difficulty of receiving a Letter when he's at home without his knowledge is the reason I would humbly beg the favour of a speedy answer.

To George Hickes
31 July 1702
Reprinted from Robert Walmsley, "John Wesley's Parents: Quarrel and Reconciliation," PWHS, 29.3 (1953–1954): 55–56.

Reverend Sir, 'Twas not want of the most grateful sense of your great charity and goodness made me so long defer writing, but some other reason which I shall acquaint you with when I wait on you. This however comes at last, though 'tis long first, with my humblest thanks for the great favour of yours which found me in circumstances that very much needed advice. My Master was then at London and had given me time to consider what to do, whether I would submit to his judgment and implicitly obey him in matters of conscience. I foresaw a great many evils would inevitably befall me if I refused to satisfy his desires, and had scarce courage enough to support me in the melancholy prospect when your Letter came, which was the noblest cordial, and gave me the greatest satisfaction of any thing in my whole life. When he returned he absolutely refused a reference, and so I thought it unnecessary to write to the Archbishop. He stayed two days and then left me early one morning with a resolution never to see me more, but the infinite Power that disposes and overrules the minds of men as he pleases, and can speak to their wild unreasonable passions as he does to the waves of the sea, hitherto shalt thou go and no farther,[7] so ordered it, that in his way he met a Clergyman to whom he communicated his intentions, and the reason that induced him to leave his Family: He extremely pitied him and condemned me, but however, he prevailed with him to return.

But as it often happens that great mischiefs take their rise from very small beginnings, so his long absenting himself upon that account occasioned abundance of trouble to himself and Family; the particulars of which I shall not, Sir, at present trouble you with, but if I live to see you as I hope I shall, I must beg the liberty of informing you of as strange a complication of misfortunes as perhaps as ever happened to any persons in the world. Yet though I've had so much trouble, since Sir you have fully satisfied me I do my duty in following the dictates of my conscience, I will as you advise persevere, and against hope believe in hope, since I know after all there is an inseparable connection betwixt virtue and happiness; for let it be granted that a vicious person may and often does find a great deal of present satisfaction in the enjoyment of their irregular inclinations and desires, yet we can by no means allow that to be any part of a rational Happiness that is immediately succeeded by ungrateful reflections, and must inevitably end in unspeakable eternal misery: so on the other side though Virtue may be here oppressed and despised, yet as sure as God himself has said it the end of Virtue is peace and endless Felicity.

I'm afraid I'm troublesome already, yet must once more beg direction in some other cases when I know how to write; I'm forced at present to give my Lady Yarborough the trouble of superscribing my Letter. Before I've finished my Letters I'm alarmed by a new misfortune; my house is now fired by one of my servants, I think not carelessly but by so odd an accident as I may say of it, as the Magicians of Moses's fourth Miracle, "This is the finger of God."[8] Two thirds are burnt, and most of our goods though they have escaped the flames are utterly spoiled. May heaven avert all evil from my children and grant that the heavy curse my Master has wished upon himself and Family may terminate in this life. I most earnestly beg the continuance of your prayers, that God may at last have mercy upon us, at least that he would spare the innocent Children however he is pleased to deal with the unhappy parents. I am Sir

Your most obliged humble Servant.

S. Wesley

Epworth, July ult[imo,] 1702.

Notes

1. See Robert Walmsley, "John Wesley's Parents: Quarrel and Reconciliation," PWHS 29.3 (1953–1954): 50, quoting Wesley's own accounat in AM, 1784, p. 606 and the version Adam Clarke recorded in *Memoirs of the Wesley Family; Collected Principally from Original Documents* (New York: N. Bangs and T. Mason for the Methodist Episcopal Church, 1824), p. 83.
2. Hebrews 10:31.
3. Close paraphrase of Acts 24:16.
4. Lamentations 3:1; quotation marks added.
5. The king's death on March 8. This note appears in brackets in the PWHS edition.
6. See Psalm 147:9; Luke 12:24, 27.
7. Job 38:11, closely paraphrased.
8. Exodus 8:19; quotation marks added.

TWO

"Dear Sammy"

Samuel Wesley Jr. School Correspondence

*T*he next grouping of letters was sent to the Wesleys' eldest child, Samuel Jr., between March 1704 and February 1707, his first years away from home. Young Samuel had been born in London in 1690 before the family moved to Lincolnshire, first to South Ormsby and finally to Epworth. Education at his mother's knee did not begin propitiously: the family story had it that he did not speak until the age of four or five, though then, quite suddenly, in a complete sentence.[1] Nevertheless, he became the first object of the home-schooling enterprise, which Susanna Wesley later detailed in a famous letter to her son John, included in part III of this volume. In 1704 Samuel was sent to Westminster School in London to begin the rudiments of a classical education and prepare for university and, ultimately, the priesthood.

These letters to her adolescent son are full of an anxious parent's normal apprehensions when a first child leaves home. In addition, however, they bespeak a teacher's concern that sound moral and religious education continue. This emphasis becomes a hallmark of her calling and reappears later, not only in letters to her sons John and Charles, but also in educational materials prepared for her daughters.

The young Samuel Wesley matriculated at Christ Church College, Oxford, and upon graduation was recalled to teach at Westminster, where he was also ordained. Having hitched his career to the ill-fated Francis Atterbury (banished for his supposed part in a plot to return the Pretender to power), Wesley was passed over for advancement both in school and in church. His only chance for promotion came in 1732, when he accepted the headmastership of Blundell's School in Tiverton, Devon, where he was able to offer brief hospitality to his widowed mother in 1736 and where he died three years later.

In these early letters, his mother discourses on natural and revealed religion and on the moral standards she would have him follow. In addition to long passages of typical "reasonable" religion, occasional glimmers of family life do appear, including her request that he transcribe her letters for future use, her disappointment at an instance of apparently poor school performance, the story of a drunken parishioner's (deserved?) death, and an admission that her abstemiousness (and her own rule as an adolescent to balance time spent in exercise with time spent on her devotions) might not be appropriate for her son.[2] Diffusing this entire section of correspondence is her special concern for "Sammy," her first-born son.

That the letters survived at all is a tribute to the young man's heedful discipline. They are preserved not in original form but in response to his mother's request as part of a letter book, into which he laboriously copied them nearly word for word.

ᴡ

To Samuel Wesley Jr.
11 March 1704
MA; SWJr Letter Book, pp. 9–34

[Greeting and a number of pages missing.]

. . . teaches us to pray that we might conform to the will of God [?]here on earth, as those pure and happy spirits did in heaven.

The eternal law with respect to man is called the law of reason; when 'tis more clearly explained by revelation, divine; when it orders natural agents, which obey it unwittingly yet constantly and regularly, we style it the law of nature and instinct. And you may here take notice that in the observation of his law consists the happiness of all creatures, and 'tis only that which conserves the being and composes the harmony which we observe in the works of the creator. God made a law for the rain and gave his decree to the sea that the waves thereof should not pass his commandment. And should nature swerve ever so little from those rules God has prescribed her; should the principal elements of which all things are composed suspend or lose their native qualities; if the frame of the heavenly arch erected over our heads were loosened or dissolved; if celestial spheres should forget their regular motions and turn away as might happen; if the sun that rejoiceth as a giant to run his race should neglect his wonted course or the moon wander from her beaten way, the various seasons of the year mix and become disordered, the winds cease and the clouds afford no rain—the earth would pine for want of their influence and could produce no fruits, and what would become of man for whose use all these things were created?

And if God has taken such care of natural agents to prepare a law for them and to secure their obedience to it, we may conclude that he would not suffer man to be without law, since, if he were, he must be the most miserable of all beings in the world. It's therefore plain and undeniable that God has also given a law to mankind because their nature requires it. He has a right to do it as creator, wisdom and goodness to direct our actions to what is best, and power to enforce his laws by rewards and punishments of infinite weight and duration.

Now by what has been said, you may learn that a law is the rule of an action. Now where this is taken from the nature of things and respects rational voluntary agents, 'tis called moral, and our agreement or conformity to it, a moral virtue. The law of reason (which is the foundation of morality) is also (and not improperly) called the law of nature, because 'tis not only a rule of action to rational voluntary agents but 'tis a rule we are capable of discerning by our natural light without the assistance of revelation. So you plainly perceive you are obliged as a man to observe all the precepts of morality or natural religion, though you had never heard of Christ or Moses. I cannot here enumerate all the particulars of this great law. I shall therefore only hint at those that are most obvious and easy to be understood. I intend you an entire discourse upon it when I have more time.

The first thing that seems dictated by nature's law is self-preservation. I know that Christians generally hold that the glory of God and increase of his kingdom should be first in our desires and designs. And in order to it we should chiefly aim at being virtuous and religious. But forasmuch as virtuous life presupposes life, I think the first thing nature teaches us is the care of our life and to avoid all penury or want of those things that sustain and preserve it. Hence it was that, as soon as mankind became sensible of want and conscious of their weakness when single and alone, they began to form societies, then communities and regular governments; and from the same desire of self-preservation all human laws which tend to the welfare of mankind take their rise.

I've already told you by what method of thinking you might come to the certain knowledge of a God. Whether or no mankind at first attained the idea of a God by the same way concerns not us to know, since we find in the first ages of the world men's reason did teach them to believe a supreme independent Being. Nor does natural religion only teach us to believe his existence, but it likewise assures us that he is the creator and governor of all things, and that nothing can justly be attributed to him that implies the least imperfection; that he is one we may discern also by the light of nature, because many infinities is a palpable contradiction.

All his fore mentioned attributes we may plainly perceive by the same light. As also the first principles of natural religion, which is founded on the knowledge of God and our selves.

We may distinguish the propositions of natural religion into theoretical and practical. I've already said enough of the first. I proceed to the second and shall divide the propositions of practical natural religion into two parts: first the internal, secondly the external worship of God.

The internal part consists in honouring and loving God. His honour proceeds from a high opinion of his power, wisdom, justice, truth, etc.; hence we learn to fear his power and justice, to adore his wisdom, to acquiesce in his will, and to depend on his veracity. From our belief of his goodness we learn to love him, particularly for the effects of it towards us.

The external worship of God is chiefly shown in these instances: that we pray to him for what we want and give thanks to him for what we receive, and this not only privately, but publicly, to show we are not ashamed of our devotions and to excite others to do the like.

We learn by the law of nature likewise a great part of our duty to ourselves and neighbours. Our duty to ourselves is the practice of all moral virtues in order to perfect our natures, and therefore upon our own account, we are obliged to practice all social virtues, since we cannot be completely virtuous without it.

Moral virtues have been divided into two parts. The principal are reckoned four, viz. prudence, justice, temperance and fortitude. The others are called magnanimity, magnificence, liberality, modesty, gentleness, courtesy, truth, and urbanity. Of your duty to your neighbour I shall speak more particularly when I come to tell you your obligations as a member of a community.

Perhaps you may here ask what need there was of revelation if man were capable of knowing and worshiping God without it. To which I answer that the effects of natural religion considered with regard to the present state of mankind are concluded within the prospect of this life. I say considered with regard to the present state of man, for we are to consider him now not as he was first created, perfect and innocent, but fallen from his primitive purity, and so obnoxious to the justice and wrath of God. Now though all men may clearly perceive their pravity and a strong propension in themselves to moral evil, yet no man's reason, nay not the united reason of all mankind, could ever discover how their natures became defective, nor by what means they must now escape that justice or appease the anger of the Almighty, had not he mercifully revealed it to them.

Again, consider, though the works of nature in every part of them carry sufficient evidence of a deity, and natural reason could discern him and the duties of natural religion, yet in process of time the greatest part of the world made so little use of their reason, that they became ignorant of God and the true way of worshipping him. Sense and passion blinded some; and a careless inadvertency in others and wrong apprehensions in most of them that believed any supreme beings misled mankind into superstition and polytheism, and that occasioned infinite error and mischief in the world. And though the rational and thinking part of mankind, when they sought after him, found the supreme invisible God, yet they acknowledged him and worshipped him in their own minds, they kept the truth locked up as a secret in their own breasts and very rarely suffered it to go any further, and so were not likely to do much good to the bulk of mankind. Nor were those men of thought easily to be found; their number was small, and those few scattered throughout the world. We find but one, Socrates in Athens, who disbelieved polytheism and laughed at their wrong notions of a deity; and you know how they rewarded him for it. And so much had superstition and idolatry prevailed, that whatever Plato and the soberest philosophers thought of the being and nature of a God, they were forced in their outward professions and worship to go along with the herd and keep to the religion established by law. Thus, whatever light there was in the works of the creation and providence to lead men to the knowledge of the true God, yet very few found him; but the generality of the world were so much in the dark that they thought the Godhead like to gold and silver and stone, graven by art and man's device.

The knowledge of God and the law of nature is no way to be attained without the assistance of revelation, but by a train of deductions from self-evident principles, which the greatest part of mankind had neither leisure to weigh nor (for want of using their reason) skill to judge of. But whether this was the chief cause, or any of those already mentioned, 'twas plain in fact men failed in their great and proper business of morality. Nor was the law of nature collected into an entire body or practised to any purpose till the coming of our Saviour.

Thus revelation became very necessary to lead man into the knowledge of God's unity and his other perfections, as well as to instruct men in their duty towards him. Those moral virtues which were necessary to hold societies together and preserve the quiet of governments was indeed taught by the civil laws of communities and some obedience to 'em forced from men by their magistrates; but even in this case their virtue was very defective, and the just measures of right and wrong stood not on their surest basis, I mean a universal belief of a God, superintending the actions of all mankind in order to a future retribution. Their thoughts of another life were at best but very obscure and expectations uncertain. They sometimes talked of manes and shades of departed men, of Styx and Acheron and Elysian fields, which they fancied the seats of the blessed; but they received these notions from their poets and took 'em rather for inventions of wit and ornaments of poetry than for truths that were to influence their practice. The immortality of the soul and a future state was never made an article of faith till men had the light of revelation.

It may be you may ask whether the revelation the Jews received by Moses did not teach men all this and was not sufficient without that by Jesus Christ. I answer, No. It was not sufficient for all men. For though the knowledge of one invisible God and the moral law was revealed to the Jews, yet they were confined to a corner of the world and by the very law they received from Moses, excluded from commerce with the rest of mankind. Therefore the gentile world could have no great benefit by the law of Moses. What attestation they had of the miracles on which the Jews built their faith they received chiefly from the Jews themselves: a people contemned and despised by those nations that knew them, and therefore very unfit to propagate the faith or worship of God in the world.

And it was long enough after the law had been given on Mount Sinai that men were entirely given up to idolatry and immersed in all manner of vice and wickedness; even the Jews, God's peculiar people, forgot and forsook the laws of their fathers and worshipped the gods of those very nations which were delivered into their own hands by God himself for a punishment of their unreasonable idolatry. And though God sent his servants the prophets to admonish 'em, and they frequently warned them of that destruction that would inevitably overtake them if they did not reform and return to their obedience to the law of the true God, yet so miserably were they corrupted and hardened that they would not hearken to the voice of God speaking by his prophets till they were conquered and carried captive into Babylon. Nay, after God pitied their miserable captivity and brought 'em back to their own country and assisted them against their enemies, and they had rebuilt their temple and renewed their covenant with the Almighty, they relapsed into all their former sins (idolatry excepted) and continued impenitent even after the coming of our Saviour till they were at last utterly defeated and ruined by Titus, son to Vespasian, the tenth emperor of Rome.

In this wretched state of darkness and error our Saviour found mankind and brought light and immortality to light by his coming. "For this purpose the Son of God was manifested, that he might destroy the works of the Devil."[3] And this could no way be done but by a complete morality established in all its parts upon its true foundations to which man might have recourse upon all occasions. And upon its true foundations morality could never be fixed without a clear knowledge of the lawmaker and a just acknowledgement of him and belief of the rewards and punishments prepared for those that would or would not obey him.

'Twas also necessary for the common salvation that this law should be promulged[4] with that authority it was, for nothing less than an assurance of Jesus's being the Messiah and a clear evidence of his mission could be able to prevail upon such men to repent and conform to his doctrine. For this reason our blessed Saviour wrought so many miracles in the view of all the world. And as his love and pity to unhappy men was universal, so he broke down the wall of sanction between the Jews and gentiles and did not confine his miracles and doctrine to the worshippers at Jerusalem, but he preached at Samaria and wrought miracles in the borders of Tyre and Sidon, and people followed him from all quarters. And so publicly were his miracles wrought, as well as those of his apostles, that the enemies of Christianity have never dared openly to deny them.

I've already observed that we could neither know how we became depraved, nor by what means we must be reconciled to the offended Deity. 'Tis true by the power of natural reason we might have attained some knowledge of God and our own minds, but I cannot see how we could have had any certain knowledge of the being and orders of the angels or that some of them fell from their primitive purity and became devils, had we been without revelation. Nor could we have discovered by our natural light that through the temptations of those apostate spirits, our first parents (in whom were virtually included the whole species of mankind) lost their innocence. And that by eating of that fatal tree of the knowledge [of good and evil] they forfeited the tree of life and with it bliss and immortality.

Whoever reads and carefully observes the tenor of the New Testament will find the whole doctrine of redemption is founded on the supposition of Adam's fall. Nor can they fail to observe that as our first parents lost paradise, so all their posterity were born out of it in a state of sin and mortality. But as in Adam all died, so in Christ were all made alive,[5] that is were brought into a salvable condition.

You see now plainly the use and necessity of revelation and the reasons why the blessed Jesus condescended to assume humanity: that he might satisfy the justice of God by the sacrifice of himself for us; that he might plant good life among men and give us an example of perfect obedience to the divine will, which, though we are not absolutely capable of following, yet he hath taught us that our sincere endeavours to do our duty shall be accepted, though we fail in the performance. And though we often fall, we may rise again by faith and repentance. For which reason he has vouchsafed us the assistance of his Holy Spirit, and 'tis no small encouragement to a man under the difficulty of his nature, beset with temptations and surrounded with prevailing custom, to practice true religion, to be assured he shall be assisted by an almighty Power that can preserve and support him in a constant and steady course of virtue.

I hope what has been said has convinced you there was great need of revelation. I come now to the second thing I proposed, which was to show you what you are obliged to as a Christian. And here I shall distinguish your duty into two parts of equal consideration, viz. faith and obedience.

First, of faith. You are most firmly to believe that the man Jesus, born of the Virgin Mary, when Herod was tetrarch of Galilee, in the reign of Augustus, second. . . .

[Two sides, one manuscript (MS) sheet, pp. 25–26 of SWJr Letter Book, are missing, breaking the flow of the letter.]

. . . [con]formity as far as possible to all the precepts of the moral law or law of reason which he has confirmed and established, and all moral virtues are now become Christian virtues. Think not (says our Saviour) I am come to destroy the law and the prophets. I am not come to destroy, but to fulfill,[6] the meaning of which is, he came not only to fulfill the predictions of the prophets concerning [him][7] the Messiah, but also to complete, advance and give authority to the moral precepts of Moses his law, which was founded on the eternal law of reason and to free this law from the corrupt glosses the scribes and pharisees had put upon it. And this seems to be the main and proper intention of Christianity.

I proceed to the particulars of your obedience, and what they are you may best learn from our Saviour's own mouth. He began his preaching with a command to repent, St. Matthew 4.17.[8] And this, considering the fallen state of mankind, was most necessary to be first taught. Everyone of common sense knows that Repentance implies forsaking of, as well as sorrow for, sin. And, that unless men are convinced they have done amiss, they are never likely to become better.

Therefore, it was agreeable to the wisdom of our blessed Saviour to inculcate that duty first which must be first practiced in order to a good life. He proceeds in the fifth chapter to command men to be exemplary in good works. "Let your light so shine before men that they may see your good works and glorify your Father which is in heaven."[9] And after he had confirmed the moral law, verse 17, he goes on to explain it and tells them that not only murder, but causeless anger and contemptuous words were forbidden. He forbids not only actual impurity, but irregular and unchaste desires, upon pain of condemnation. All swearing in conversation as well as forswearing in judgement. And so strictly does he forbid all malice and revenge, that he positively commands men to love their enemies, to do good to those that hate them, and to pray for such as despitefully use and persecute them; and closes all his particular injunctions with this general rule: "all things whatsoever you would that men should do to you, do ye even so to them, for this is the law and the prophets."[10]

From what our Saviour has anywhere forbidden we may learn those positive duties he commands, which are always included in his prohibitions. Thus by forbidding murder, causeless anger and words of contempt, he commands that we contribute all we reasonably may towards the preservation of our neighbour's life, goods, and fame. To be compassionate and liberal, patient, meek, courteous and friendly to all mankind. By forbidding impure desires, looks, etc., he commands unspotted chastity in heart and life. By prohibiting customary or unnecessary oaths, he enjoins a useful innocent conversation, free from pride or passion which usually leads men into that unreasonable practice.

But our blessed Saviour goes further and directs 'em to the highest and most noble part of Christian life, which consists in loving God. When the lawyer asked our Lord what he should do to inherit eternal life, he said, "What is written in the law, how readest thou?" He answered, "Thou shalt love the Lord thy God with all thy heart, with all thy soul, with all the mind, and with all thy strength, and thy neighbour as thyself." Jesus said, "This do and thou shalt live,"[11] that is, shalt be eternally happy, for happiness in scripture is usually called life.

By this answer of our Saviour we may learn that to love the eternal ever-blessed God with the full power and energy of the soul is the principal duty of a Christian and the complement of Christian perfection and happiness.

Love is a simple act or motion of the soul whereby it is carried towards and presses to a union with the beloved object, which is always apprehended to be good.[12] Now to make this act or motion of the soul truly rational 'tis necessary, first, that the object be really good as it appears to be. And that the degree of love hold proportion with the degree of goodness in the object beloved.

The first part of this rule we are sure to follow in our loving God, since he is all perfect and amiable. The second can't be strictly observed, because no act of a finite being can bear any proportion to what is infinite. However, we must go as far as we can and love him to the utmost of our capacity. And this love to God must be predominant over all our love to any creature whatever, as our blessed Saviour teaches us in the tenth of St. Matthew. He that loveth father or mother or son or daughter more than me is not worthy of me.[13] Nay, he goes farther in the fourteenth of St. Luke and says, "If any man come to me and hate not his father and mother and wife and children and brethren and sisters" (where they stand in competition with him), "yea, and his own life also, cannot be my disciple."[14]

This is sufficient to show what love our Lord requires.

'Tis an opinion that hath been commonly received that there are two sorts of love: a love of benevolence or good will and a love of complacency or delight.[15] This, I think, is an error that arises from a want of clear ideas of the nature of love, which, as I said before, is a simple act or motion of the soul and determined to its several modes and operations by the nature of the thing beloved. If we have an idea of positive, absolute perfection in the object of our love, as in God, then the acts of our love are adoration, praise, complacency,[16] etc. And we do not wish well to or desire to benefit him, because we are assured his most glorious perfection and infinite essential happiness are incapable of any admission.[17] And since his most blessed nature can receive no advantage from his creatures, we express our love to God by being friendly and beneficent to all that bear his image and are ever ready to do good offices where we perceive the smallest ray of his divinity.

There are two natural effects of love which are inseparable from it, viz. a desire to please and a desire to enjoy. These in divine love are the springs of all those virtuous actions and religious duties we perform. Thus we endeavour to perfect our natures by recovering that image of God we lost in Adam, which alone can render us pleasing to that most holy Being and qualify us for the beatific vision we hope to enjoy when we have put off our mortality and are admitted into the region of happy spirits and "just men made perfect."[18]

God is the true and proper centre[19] of the mind, towards which it had always regularly moved, had not sin interposed and cast a shade between him and its noblest faculties. But however as depraved as it is, it can nowhere find rest or an adequate lasting happiness on this side its ever-blessed and glorious Creator; nor must you ever expect to please or enjoy him unless you obey all his commandments. And this obedience is the only way to evidence the sincerity of your love to him.

That you may more perfectly know and obey the law of God, be sure you constantly pray for the assistance of the Holy Spirit. Observe that assistance implies a joint concurrence of the person assisted; nor can you possible be assisted if you do nothing. Therefore, use your utmost care and diligence to do your duty and rely upon the veracity of God, who will not fail to perform what he has promised.

Besides the promise of his Holy Spirit he has already given us the Holy Scripture, which is a perfect rule of faith and manners. This read and study constantly and, in all cases that occur where you want direction, have recourse to the law and to the testimony. And if there be any thing therein you cannot understand, your father will gladly assist you; or if you have not time to write, your master[20] or any good man you are acquainted with will very willingly instruct you in the way to salvation.

I should proceed to give you some particular directions for your devotions, etc. But I'm afraid I have already tried your patience too far and will therefore omit them till I come to discourse of the last thing I proposed, which was the virtues of a social life or your obligations as a member of a community, which shall be the subject of another letter.

To God's blessed protection I commit you and earnestly beseech him that his Holy Spirit may illuminate and steer your soul through all the changing scenes of life and at the last conduct you to his eternal glory.

Susanna Wesley

Epworth. March 11
An[no]: Dom[ini]: 1704

To Samuel Wesley Jr.
N.d. (possibly late spring or early summer 1704)
MA; SWJr Letter Book, pp. 35–37. The bottom of the last page, where Samuel usually notes the date and address, is cut out. George Stevenson, *Memorials of the Wesley Family* . . . (London: S. W. Partridge; New York: Nelson and Phillips, 1876), 182–183, dates it 4 August 1704. Perhaps he saw the missing piece; more likely he has identified it with the succeeding letter, clearly dated 4 August 1704.

Dear Sammy!

I've been ill a great while, but am now, I thank God, well recovered. I thought to have been with you long ere this, but I doubt I shall hardly see you this summer. Therefore send me word particularly what you want.

I would ere now ha' finished my discourse, begun so long ago, if I had enjoyed more health, but I hope I shall be able to finish it quickly and then would have you transcribe all your letters, for they may be more useful to you afterwards than they are now, because you'll be better able to understand them.

I shall be employing my thoughts on useful subjects for you when I have time, for I desire nothing in this world so much as to have my children well instructed in the principles of religion, that they may walk in the narrow way which alone leads to happiness. Particularly, I am concerned for you, who were even before your birth dedicated to the service of the altar, that you may be an ornament of that

Church of which you are a member and be instrumental (if God shall spare your life) in bringing many souls to heaven. Take heed, therefore, in the first place of your own, lest you yourself should be a castaway.

You have had great advantages of education. God has entrusted you with many many talents, such as health, strength, a comfortable subsistence hitherto, a good understanding, memory, etc. And if any one be misemployed or not improved, they will certainly one day rise up in judgement against you.

If I thought you would not make good use of instruction and be the better for reproof, I would never write or speak a word to you more while I live, because I know whatever I could do would but tend to you[r] greater condemnation. But I earnestly beg of God to give you his grace. And I charge you, as you will answer for it at the last great day, that you carefully "work out your own salvation with fear and trembling,"[21] lest you should finally miscarry.

You say you know not how to keep a secret without sometimes telling a lie. I don't know what secrets you may have. I'm sure nobody with you has authority however to examine you, but if any should be so impertinently curious to do it, put 'em civilly off if you can. But if you can't, resolutely tell 'em you will not satisfy their unreasonable desires and be sure you never, to gain the favour of any, hazard losing the favour of God, which you will do if you speak falsely.

To God's merciful protection I commit you.

Susanna Wesley

[The last quarter of the page is torn off at this point.]

To Samuel Wesley Jr.
N.d. or 4 August 1704
MA; SWJr Letter Book, p. 38 or pp. 38–43. Manuscript pp. 39–40 are missing; thus there may be two letters here.

Dear Sammy!

'Tis a great while since I heard from you, but yet I hope you are in health. Be sure you write to me next post.

I am very sorry that I should have any reason to complain of or find fault with you at this distance, but you have not answered the expectation I had of you at all. I thought you would have been so wise when you so well knew our circumstances and how hard a thing it is for us that have had such uncommon misfortunes and have so many children beside yourself to maintain you at such a place. I say I thought and hoped you would have used your utmost care and diligence to surpass all others in virtue and learning, but instead of that I find you do not so much as keep pace. . . .

[The bottom quarter of the page is missing: perhaps a maternal indictment of Samuel's slow progress at school, later removed by an embarrassed member of the family or Methodist hagiographer; MS pp. 39–40 are also missing.]

. . . er obligation than others that are not so, to "let your light so shine before men that they may see your good works and glorify your Father which in Heaven." [22]

Examine well your heart and observe its inclinations; particularly observe what the general temper of your mind is, for let me tell you 'tis not a fit of devotion now and then speaks a man a Christian but 'tis a mind universally and generally disposed to all the duties of Christianity in their proper times, places, etc. For instance, in the morning and evening or any other time when occasion is offered, a good Christian will be cheerfully disposed to retire from the world that he may offer to his creator his sacrifice of prayer and praise and will account it is happiness, as well as duty, so to do. When he is in the world, if he have business, he will follow it diligently, as knowing that he must account with God at night for what he has done in the day, and that God expects we should be faithful in our calling, as well as devout in our closets. A Christian ought and in the general does converse with the world like a stranger in an inn; he will use what is necessary for him and cheerfully enjoy what he innocently can, but at the same time he knows it is but an inn. And he will be but little concerned at what he meets with there, because he takes it not for his home. The mind of a Christian should be always composed, temperate, free from all extremes of mirth or sadness, and always disposed to hear the still small voice of God's Holy Spirit, which will direct him what and how to act in all the occurrences of life, if in all his ways he acknowledge him and depend on his assistance. I cannot now stay to speak of your particular duties. I hope I shall in a short time send you what I designed.

In the mean time I beg of you as one that has the greatest concern imaginable for your soul, I exhort you as I am your faithful friend, and I command you as I am your parent, to use your utmost "diligence to make your calling and election sure." [23] To be faithful to your God. And after I've said that, I need not bid you be industrious in your calling.

Sammy! Think of what I say, and the blessed God make you truly sensible of your duty to him and also to me. Renew your broken vows; if you have wasted or misemployed your time, take more care of what remains. If in anything you want counsel or advice, speak freely to me and I'll gladly assist you.

I commit you to God's blessed protection.

Susanna Wesley

August. 4. 1704

Notes

1. Adam Clarke, *Memoirs of the Wesley Family; Collected Principally from Original Documents* (New York: N. Bangs and T. Mason for the Methodist Episcopal Church, 1824), pp. 213–214.

2. See, respectively, n.d. (?) Summer 1704; n.d. or 4 August 1704, 22 May 1706, 27 November 1707.

3. 1 John 3:8; quotation marks added.

4. Archaic equivalent of promulgated.

5. Close paraphrase of 1 Corinthians 15:22.

6. Close paraphrase of Matthew 5:17.

7. Brackets in MS.

8. S.W.'s citation in MS. The AV translation reads, "From that time Jesus began to preach, and to say, Repent: for the kingdom of heaven is at hand."

9. Matthew 5:16; quotation marks added.

10. Matthew 7:12; quotation marks added.

11. Luke 10:27–28, slightly altered; quotation marks added.

12. Cf. John Norris, *The Theory and Regulation of Love* . . . , 2nd ed. (London: S. Manship, 1694), p. 25, where Norris characterizes love in general as "a Motion of the Soul towards Good," and the "love of Concupiscence or Desire" as a "simple Tendency of the Soul to Good."

13. Matthew 10:37–38, condensed.

14. Luke 14:26; quotation marks added.

15. Cf. two other related discussions, one in her "Obedience to the Laws of God: A Brief (Unfinished) Exposition on the Ten Commandments," in part III of this volume, written c. 1709–1711; the other a brief reference to the distinction made by the philospher John Norris in a letter to John Wesley, 30 March 1726. The Norris distinction is between "love of benevolence" and "love of desire" in his "A Discourse concerning the Excellency of Praise and Thanksgiving," in *[Practical] Discourses upon Several Divine Subjects*, 3rd ed. (London: Samuel Manship, 1697), 2:92–93. See a related discussion in her spiritual journal in part II of this volume.

16. Disposition to please, oblige, or comply with the wishes of others.

17. In two similar passages, one in another letter to Samuel, the other in her unfinished exposition of the Decalogue in her discussion of the first commandment, S. W. uses "accession" (i.e., addition, augmentation, increase). The OED does not indicate any equivalent meaning of "admission." See To Samuel Wesley Jr., 27 November 1707; and part III, chapter 3, "Obedience to the Laws of God: A Brief (Unfinished) Exposition on the Ten Commandments."

18. Hebrews 12:23; quotation marks added.

19. The SWJr Letter Book spells it *center*, an acceptable alternative at the time. However, "*centre*" won out as the preferred British spelling.

20. That is, schoolmaster.

21. Philippians 2:12; quotation marks added.

22. Matthew 5:16; quotation marks added.

23. 2 Peter 1:10, quotation marks added.

THREE

More Letters to "Dear Sammy"

Susanna Wesley's correspondence with her son continues, but our record of it is incomplete. A gap of nearly two years (between consecutively numbered pages of his Letter Book) probably is explained by Susanna's reference to a theft in her letter of 18 March 1707. Samuel probably had accumulated a large batch of her letters and lost them before he had the opportunity to copy them.

✿

To Samuel Wesley Jr.
22 May 1706
MA, SWJr Letter Book, pp. 44–47.

Dear Sammy!

You cannot imagine how much your letter pleased me, wherein you tell me of your fear lest you should offend God; though if you state the case truly, I hope there is no danger of doing it in the matter you speak of.

Proper drunkenness does, I think, certainly consist in drinking such a quantity of strong liquor as will intoxicate and render the person incapable of using his reason with that strength and freedom as he can do at other times. Now there are those that by habitual drinking a great deal of such liquors can hardly ever be guilty of proper drunkenness, because never intoxicated; but this I look upon as the highest kind of the sin of intemperance.

But this is not, nor I hope ever will be your case. Two glasses cannot possibly hurt you, provided they contain no more than those commonly used. Nor would I have you concerned, though you find yourself warmed and cheerful after drinking 'em, for 'tis a necessary effect of spirituous liquors to refresh and increase the spirits; and certainly the divine Being will never be displeased at the innocent satisfaction of our regular appetites.

But then have a care. Stay at the third glass; consider you have an obligation to strict temperance, which all have not. I mean your designation to holy orders. Remember under the Jewish economy it was ordained by God himself that the snuffers of the temple should be perfect gold;[1] from which we may infer that those that are admitted to serve at the altar, a great part of whose office it is to reprove others, ought themselves to be most pure and free from all scandalous actions; and if others are temperate, they ought to be abstemious.

Here happened last Thursday a very sad accident. You may remember one Robert Darwin of this town. This man was at Bawtry fair, where he got drunk, and, riding homeward down a hill, his horse came down with him, and he, having no sense to guide himself, fell down with his face to the ground and put his neck out of joint. Those with him immediately pulled it in again, and he lived till next day, but never spake more. His face was torn all to pieces, one of his eyes beat out and his under lip cut off, his nose broke down, and in short he was one of the dreadfullest examples of the severe justice of God that I have known.

I have been the more particular in this relation, because the man, as he was one of the richest in this place, so he was one of the most implacable enemies your father had among his parishioners, one that insulted him most basely in his troubles, one that was most ready to do him all the mischief he could, not to mention his affronts to me and the children. And how heartily he wished to see our ruin, which God permitted him not to see. This man and one more has been now cut off in the midst of their sins, since your father's confinement.[2] I pray God amend those that are left.

I am, Dear Sammy!

Your faithfull

Friend and mother

Susanna Wesley

Epworth. May
22. A. D. 1706

To Samuel Wesley Jr.
18 March 1706/07
MA; SWJr Letter Book, pp. 70–74.

Dear Sammy!

I'm sorry you have lost my letters. Not that they contain anything very valuable, but because you have not now so many witnesses of my great love for you and unfeigned desire of your eternal happiness.

What use any person can make of 'em is past my comprehension! Or for what end any should be so impertinently curious to steal letters from a mother to a son that concerns none but himself, I cannot imagine. However, I hope you remember the main things which are therein expressed; but lest you should not, I shall again repeat some things which by the good blessing of God may be useful to you.

Be sure always to retain a firm belief of the being and perfections of the eternal ever-blessed God. Remember he is your Creator, to whom you owe your being; your governor, whose most holy laws you are indispensably obliged to obey.

Endeavour to impress upon your mind the reason for which you were created;

not only to eat, drink, etc. and perform other natural actions relating only to this life, but to know, love and obey God.

This life is nothing in comparison to eternity! So very inconsiderable and withall so wretched that 'tis not worthwhile to be, if we were to die as the beasts! What mortal would sustain the pains, the wants, the disappointments, the cares, and thousands of calamities we must often suffer here? But when we consider this as a probationary state, wherein we are placed by the Supreme Being, and that, if we wisely behave ourselves here, if we purify our souls from all corrupt and inordinate affections, if we can, by the divine assistance, recover the image of God [moral goodness]³ which we lost in Adam and attain to a heavenly temper and disposition of mind, full of the love of God, etc., then we justly think that even this life is an effect of the inconceivable goodness of God towards us, especially since we know that all things shall work together for good to those that love God,⁴ and that these light afflictions, which are but for a moment, shall be recompensed with an exceeding and eternal weight of glory.

I am almost afraid that I should tire you with such frequent repetitions of the same things, but "out of the abundance of the heart the mouth speaketh."⁵ I've such a vast inexpressible desire of your salvation and such dreadful apprehensions of your failing in a work of so great importance, and do moreover know by experience how hard a thing it is to be a Christian, that I cannot forbear, I cannot but most earnestly press you and conjure you over and over again to give the most earnest heed to what you have already learned, lest at any time you let slip the remembrance of your final happiness or forget what you have to do in order to attain it!

Sammy! Believe me! The flesh, the world and the devil,⁶ are very formidable enemies! But above all the flesh (by which, I think, is meant all our corrupt sensual appetites) is the most to be apprehended! That man of sin, the old Adam, still lives in us, and it is by ourselves we are still betrayed. Not all the pomps and vanities of the world, nor all the united powers of hell could prevail so far as to make us swerve in the least from our duty, did not these sordid, impure desires of our own given 'em the advantage they gain over us! This is the enemy that will to the last maintain a conflict! Which will sometimes be very difficult, and 'twill require our utmost skill and strength to come off conquerors, which yet would be impossible without the grace of God! You may perhaps in the course of your duty meet with those trials which our Saviour expresses by pulling out a right eye and cutting off a right hand, and you have great reason to pray daily that God would proportion your strength to your trials and that his grace may be sufficient for you.⁷ I say not these things to discourage you, but to quicken you, to impress on your mind a greater sense of the necessity you lie under to use your utmost endeavour to get a stock of virtue, that you may not have grace to seek, when you have it to use.⁸

Dear child! Remember how short and how uncertain this life is! And what depends upon it! Make a stand! Recollect your thoughts! Think again upon eternity! An endless duration! A perpetual now! That admits of no parts, succession or alteration! Of what vast importance is it, since our souls must, whether we will or no, be immortal! Of what vast importance, I say, is it, that we should be possessed of those divine virtues that will necessarily make them eternally happy!

I have a great and vast desire that all your sisters and your brother[9] should be saved, as well as you, but I must own I think my concern for you is much the greatest. What! You, my son! You! who was once the son of my extremest sorrow in your birth and in your infancy! Who is now the son of my tenderest love! My friend in whom is my inexpressible delight! My future hope of happiness in the world! For whom I weep and pray in my retirements from the world, when no mortal knows the agonies of my soul upon your account! No eye sees my tears which are only beheld by that Father of Spirits, of whom I so importunately beg grace for you that I hope I may at last be heard! Is it possible that you should be damned! Oh! That it were impossible! Indeed, I think I could almost wish my self accursed, so I were sure of your salvation! But still I hope—still I would fain persuade myself that a child for whom so many prayers have been offered to heaven will not at last miscarry!

To the protection of the ever-blessed God I commit you. Humbly beseeching him to conduct you by his grace to his eternal glory.

Epworth March 18   Susanna Wesley
  M1706/7

To Samuel Wesley Jr.
7 May 1707
MA; SWJr Letter Book, pp. 75–76.

Dear Sammy!

Though I writ so lately, yet having received advice that your election is so much sooner than I expected, I take this opportunity to advise you about it.[10]

The eternal ever-blessed God that at first created all things by his almighty power and that does whatever please him, as well among the inhabitants of the earth as in the armies of heaven, you know is the only disposer of all events; and therefore I would by all means persuade you solemnly to set apart some portion of time (in the Sabbath, if you can) to beg his more especial direction and assistance upon a business on which a great part of your future prosperity may depend.

I would have you in the first place humbly to acknowledge and bewail[11] all the errors of your past life, as far as you can remember them; and for those that have escaped your memory, pray as David did that God would cleanse you from your secret faults.[12]

Then proceed to praise him for all the mercies which you can remember you have received from his divine goodness; and then go on to beg his favour in this great affair, and do all this in the name and through the mediation of the blessed Jesus.

Sammy, don't deceive yourself. Man is not to be depended on. God is all in all. Those whom he blesses shall be blest indeed! When you have done this, entirely resign yourself and all your fortunes to the almighty God, nor be too careful about your being elected nor troubled if disappointed.

If you can possibly, set apart the hours of Sunday in the afternoon from four to six for this employment, which time I have also determined to the same work. May that infinite Being, whose we are and whom I hope we endeavour to serve and love, accept and bless us.

Epworth May. 7.
    1707   Susanna Wesley

To Samuel Wesley Jr.
20 August 1707
MA; SWJr Letter Book, p. 77.
Written after Samuel's election to a scholarship. He was still at Westminster, though now with higher status and additional duties. Samuel notes in his letter book, "The following letters were sent to me since my admittance into the Colledge."

Dear Sammy!

Prithee how do you do in the midst of so much company and business to preserve your mind in any temper fit for the service of God? I'm sadly afraid lest you should neglect your duty towards him! Take care of the world, lest it unawares steal away your heart and so make your prove false to those vows and obligations which you have laid upon yourself in the covenant you personally made with the ever-blessed Trinity before your reception of the Holy Communion.

Have you ever received the Sacrament at London? If not, consider what has been the cause of your neglect, and embrace the next opportunity.

    Epworth Aug. 20.
        1707   Susanna Wesley

To Samuel Wesley Jr.
10 October 1707
MA; SWJr Letter Book, pp. 78–79.

Dear Sammy!

Since it has now pleased God to afflict you with bodily pains, 'tis a very proper season to recollect your past life to the end you may discover whether or no there be not some secret cause of his displeasure. "For he does not afflict willingly or grieve the children of men" [13] without reason.

Particularly, consider whether you have been mindful of your sacramental vows and obligations. Assure yourself if you have not, if still the divine Goodness continues his merciful intentions towards you, he will punish you for your neglect.

I know physicians are apt to say that rheumatic distempers carry no danger of death in them, but I'm of opinion that all diseases whatever, if God sees we unworthily abuse his mercies and that we shall continue to trifle away our time here, which is our only opportunity of working out our salvation, and may certainly put a period to our days, as well those called chronical as the most acute.

Nor are you too young to think of dying or to prepare for that eternal duration which succeeds this transitory uncertain life!

May the God of mercies give you grace to remember your Creator in the days of your youth![14] And may his Holy Spirit preserve you from the temptations of the world, the flesh and the devil![15]

Epworth. Oct 10
1707   Susanna Wesley

To Samuel Wesley Jr.
27 November 1707
MA; SWJr Letter Book, pp. 79–96.

Dear Sammy!

We both complain of not having often heard from each other. What foundation there is for complaint on your side I know not, but I'm apt to suspect you've written more letters to me than I've received. For you lately sent one that never came to my hands, though I was advertised of some part of the contents of it, as of your having received the Sacrament, at which I'm greatly pleased; and that you desire some direction how to resist temptations, and some particular advice how to prepare for the reception of the blessed Communion.

You never informed me of any particular temptation to which you are exposed, and 'tis impossible from dark hints and general expressions to collect the true state of your case. Therefore, I can but offer at general things and if I happen to omit *anything that I should* chiefly insist on, I can't help it.

I think all temptations of what kind soever may be comprehended under these two general heads: first, the pleasure which is found in indulging the irregular motions of the mind or the gratification of the sensual appetite; or the pain, difficulty or danger which we do suppose we shall meet with in our entrance upon, or perseverance in, a course of virtue. And both these kinds of temptations are to[16] be conquered by very different ways.

If you have ever made any serious reflections on the state of your own soul, you must know that human nature is fallen from its primitive innocence. The ever-blessed God, which needed not the service or assistance of any creature, his essential perfections being fully sufficient for his own eternal blessedness, did out of a principle of pure goodness create angels and men, that he might communicate that perfection and happiness, which in himself were incapable of any accession.[17] Man, therefore, taking his original from the divine nature, must necessarily in the state of his first creation have been most perfect, since nothing evil could possibly proceed from infinite goodness; nor could evil any way have entered into the world but by man being left to his own liberty. And if he had not been left to his own liberty, but had God made him a necessary and not a free agent, the divine glory had been apparently diminished and the virtue of man's obedience utterly destroyed and had been rendered incapable of any reward. Liberty in man being the foundation of rewards and punishments, as well as of moral virtue.

I need not enlarge upon the present corrupt state of human nature. The Scripture account of Adam's fall is very clear and every way agreeable to the reason and experience of any that will give themselves leave to think. How Adam's sin hath been transmitted to all his posterity we do not well know, but we are sure the fact is true, and therefore I would have you take some pains to get a clear knowledge and deep sense of the corruption of your nature. For the better you are acquainted with your disease, the better you may apply a remedy.

The disease of the understanding is in general that ignorance which proceeds from an indisposition to know the truth. But as the goodness of any object is what we ought principally to regard, so clearly to perceive the truth concerning what is good or evil is the chief business of the understanding. And its averseness from that kind of knowledge and contemplation is the greatest corruption.

Knowledge hath been distinguished into immediate and mediate. The former is when the being, qualities, etc. of anything, or truth of any proposition is known by its own proper evidence, which is called self-evident truth. As that fire is hot, ice cold, etc. or that a part of anything is less than the whole, etc. Mediate knowledge is when the being, qualities, etc. of a thing or truth of a proposition is known by the intervention of some other thing, whose clearer evidence affords us light to discern it; and when we thus proceed from the evidence of one thing to argue and infer another, this is what we call argument or discourse, and this kind of knowledge is properly scientifical.

When the medium of our knowledge is the testimony of any person, 'tis called belief or faith, which Bishop Pearson well defines, "An assent to anything credible as credible,"[18] in which you may observe that credibility is the formal essence of faith, as the supposed ability and integrity of the relator is the formal essence of credibility.[19]

In these cases the fault of the understanding is either a privation of the act or an indisposition to it or else a want of rectitude in the act. When we should know a thing by its proper evidence, the privation of the act is ignorance, and the privation of its rectitude is error, which differ as not judging at all or judging falsely. When it should know by testimony, the privation of the act is unbelief, and the privation of the rectitude is either disbelief, when we without sufficient reason think the reporter erreth or would deceive us, or misbelief, when we believe a testimony which we ought not to believe. So you see, the diseases of the understanding are in general ignorance, error, unbelief, misbelief and disbelief.

The will is supposed to act in subordination to the understanding and to be determined by the judgment, since no man can will anything under the formal notion of evil. But whatever excites its motions, the corruption of it is plainly discovered by its strong tendency to sensual forbidden objects and its unreasonable aversation from God and the position of its act in relation to spiritual things.

The depravity of the memory is discerned in its retentiveness of evil and its neglect in retaining the impressions of spiritual matters.

I think that the sin of imagination or fancy consisteth in a disposition to think of evil or worldly sensual things and an unaptness to think upon what is good, and when we force ourselves to holy thoughts, they are generally disordered, confused, and unskillfully managed.

The corruption of the passions manifestly appears in their being so easily and strongly excited by the sensitive appetite which precipitates them into such violent motions as generally cause them to err in point of excess, where their objects are sensual or evil, and in defect when the object is spiritual and good.

You may perhaps think that this long digression is nothing to the purpose, it seeming at first view very foreign to the business of temptation. But I'm of another mind, since 'tis from these corrupted faculties and appetites that Satan draws all his auxiliary forces and fights us with our own weapons. And if it were not for the impurity and treachery of that strong party within us that adhere to his interest, all the powers of hell could never prevail against us.[20]

You may remember I said that temptations of all kinds might be comprehended under two general heads. Your business is to take notice to what kind of temptation you lie most exposed and what it is that most usually prevails over you.

If your temptations are of a spiritual nature, and you find that the devil takes advantage from your ignorance and natural indisposition to think on spiritual things to tempt you to a great aversion from God, and a total neglect of what you know is your duty towards him, as praise, prayer etc. or else suggests vain, sinful or unnecessary thoughts in the performance, which corrupts the purity of the sacrifices and renders them altogether ineffectual. And you likewise perceive that he takes advantage from the defection of your will, corrupt imagination and irregular passions, etc. to represent religion to your mind as a melancholy thing, and that 'tis a matter of great difficulty to serve God, and next to impossible to reduce a mind so totally depraved to order and a universal obedience to the law of God. And these thoughts dishearten you, either from making any attempt or else so far indispose your mind that you move faintly and unwillingly and so make no progress in the paths of virtue.

If you are assaulted by these or such like temptations, then your case is reducible under the second head and your method of conquering must be: after having humbly acknowledged your own impotence before God and earnestly implored his assistance, to resolve upon a courageous and vigorous encounter of all difficulties, which is the only way to overcome them. For if you give ground, you are lost! Whereas, by repeated acts of piety, you'll gain a facility of acting, and then you'll find that all those difficulties will vanish; and your uneasiness and aversion from duty will decrease as your mind is renewed, till at last you attain such virtuous habits as will make religion the most agreeable and delightful thing in the world.

But Satan does not usually assault the young converts with temptations of this kind, especially those whose complexion is so sanguine as yours. But he commonly makes his attacks upon the sensitive appetites, which he excites by proper objects to such strong commotions as put the whole frame of nature out of order, and drowns the voice of reason, to whose conduct and government God hath committed them. I have not time to discourse at large upon this copious subject. I shall therefore single out two instances that include many particulars. First, impurity; secondly, intemperance in meat, drink or recreation. Both of which are included in the second branch of the first general head, viz. the pleasing the sensual appetites.

And I shall here propose a general direction that I think will be of use in all such kind of temptations. Whenever the matter of any temptation is sensual pleasure, you must immediately fly from it, nor so much as suffer yourself to think upon it, till the first motions of the passions are over and the mind is reduced to such a composure as renders it capable of receiving the influences of the Holy Spirit, which you must earnestly implore, for that pure and Holy Spirit moves not in storms and tempests, nor can his small still voice[21] be heard amidst the uproar of tumultuous passions. Therefore you must take special care to resist the first motions to any impurity with the utmost vigour. If they are indulged, the second will be harder to overcome, and the third more difficult than the second, and so on.

I cannot say that the first motion of the sin of impurity is always (though I believe very often) from Satan. But this I'm sure of, that whether they proceed from him or the natural constitution of the body or any other cause, that he is very careful to observe how these first motions are received and takes vast advantage from the least inclination to indulge them. Therefore, if this be your case, fly all incentives to so base and sordid a sin as you would from present death. Suffer not your eyes to look upon, nor your ears to hear, nor your tongue to speak one word that may have the least tendency towards begetting an impure desire. If you find Satan solicits you very strongly, cry mightily to God for assistance. If you have not opportunity for retired devotions, yet at least you may offer up some private ejaculations, which he will regard (if sincere) and answer as soon as the most enlarged petitions. At such times seriously advert to the omnipresence of God. Think or say to yourself, "I am now in the presence of the holy God who perfectly knows me and particularly regards how I behave myself in this time of trial. This is my probationary state, and the resisting of temptation is the way to Glory. And shall I presume to sin willfully, when the eternal Majesty of heaven and earth is looking upon me?"[22] Then in a full sense of his presence, cry out unto him, "Lord, help me—Save me or I now perish[23]—Suffer not the flesh or the Devil in thy presence to prevail against that soul which thou sentest thine own Son into the world to redeem—I am weak of myself, unable to do anything that is good, but I throw myself upon thy mercy—Lord, save or I perish!"[24] These or such like fervent ejaculations may prove very effectual and discourage Satan from making further attempts.

But you must watch as well as pray.[25] And that you may always be in a capacity so to do, remember the second instance I mentioned: intemperance in meat, drink, etc. Perhaps you'll think that the small provision made for you in the college is a sufficient guard against the first. But may there not be more danger of eating intemperately, if you are accidentally at another table? I don't know, but I think it concerns you to take care.

Nor can I tell what temptations you may meet with to immoderate drinking. But since in this licentious age few are secure, it behoves you to fortify yourself against that brutish destructive sin which generally proves an inlet to all kinds of wickedness, especially to the sin of impurity. For temperance is the peculiar guard of chastity. Nor can I see how 'tis possible for a person to resist any temptations that nature, whose blood is fired and filled with more spirits than they can command and whose reason is so weakened by the pernicious fumes of strong liquors, that it can no longer maintain its own authority. 'Twill be very necessary to think often upon the true end of eating and drinking, which is to repair the decays of nature and thereby to strengthen and refresh the body, that it my be serviceable to the mind, as both must be to God. And whatever other end is proposed, as pleasure, company etc., are directly contrary to the will of God and the great law of nature. And I think all the pretences men make to colour their intemperance are very good arguments against it.

The common plea of pleasure answers itself; for if the devil and corrupt nature have already gained so considerable a point as to make anyone drink for the pleasure of drinking, 'tis high time for such a one to look to himself and carefully avoid all temptations to intemperance, lest he should, ere he is aware, be engaged beyond a possibility of retreat. I would not have you think that I believe it a sin to be pleased with the provision God has made for us, or that I would propose my own way of living (which perhaps is too abstemious) as a rule for you to walk by. No; all I intend is that we should by no means make pleasure our principle end in eating or drinking. But whether we eat or drink or whatsoever we do, let us do all to the glory of God,[26] which I'm sure the intemperate and voluptuous can never do.

The other pretence of drinking for the sake of company is more ridiculous than the former. To drink for our own pleasure carries some show of reason, but to drink to humour or comply with another man's appetite is such an unaccountable piece of nonsense that, did not frequent experience assure us of the fact, no mortal could believe a man would ever do it. Should anyone subject his body to the power of diseases and bring his soul under the wrath of God and forfeit his hopes of heaven in compliance with a foolish custom for a compliment to please those that perhaps don't care a farthing for him! 'Tis too much, God knows, to be so often conquered by our own appetites, but 'tis a thousand times worse more inexcusable to be enslaved by another man's! Nor should it ever be in anyone's power to say they had such an ascendant over me, that they could either flatter or force me to drink one glass beyond what I thought necessary for my health or refreshment!

But there is another thing that often prevails more with young inexperienced persons than either flattery or force. And that is a fear of being thought singular and precise and that they shall be laughed at if they refuse to do like the rest of the company. To this I shall only say, remember what you are, a Christian, the disciple of a crucified Jesus—and he has commanded that all his disciples should take up the cross and follow him. Consider how "he made himself of no reputation," but "was despised and rejected of men,"[27] and therefore how little reason have you to regard the unjust censures of a mistaken world or being made the subject of a little raillery because you will not be ashamed of or deny your Master? And be assured that though they laugh now, you will have infinitely more reason to rejoice, if by the grace of God you can preserve your innocence. Alas, you don't know the world. If you did, you'd plainly see that there's no passing through it without meeting with many reproaches and reflections and often very hard usage from such as will take it very ill if you don't think 'em very good Christians. And then what wonder is it if you are affronted and reviled or laughed at by the licentious part of mankind, who will be sure to be highly displeased if you "run not with them into the same excess of riot"?[28]

But after all, consider what they are which are against you, and who they are that are on your side. All good men will esteem you and have a certain veneration for you when they see your mind superior to those temptations that prevail over others, and that the sincerity of your piety is evidenced by your constant temperance and sobriety. The holy angels that are employed about you will rejoice over you, their charge, and gladly minister to you in your spiritual warfare.[29] You will be an inexpressible comfort to your parents in their declining years, who will think the care, trouble and hardship they have undergone for you well rewarded, if after all they see that you are truly devoted to the service of God. And what is infinitely more than all this, your blessed Saviour will in the end vouchsafe you his plaudit and pronounce that most joyful sentence before all the world, "Well done, good and faithful servant. Thou hast been faithful over a few things, I will make thee ruler over many things. Enter thou into the joy of thy Lord!"[30]

The last instance of temperance in recreation I shall say little to. I don't know what time is assigned you for it, and I think your health and studies require you should use a pretty deal of exercise. You best know whether your heart be too much set upon it. If it be, I'll tell you what rule I observed in the same case, when I was young and too much addicted to childish diversions, which was this: never to spend more time in any matter of mere recreation in one day than I spent in private religious duties. I leave it to your consideration whether this is practicable by you or no. I think it is.

I am so ill and have with so much pain writ this long letter, that I gladly hasten to a conclusion and shall leave *your request* about the Sacrament unanswered till I hear from you, and then, if I am in a condition to write, I'll gladly assist you as well as I can. May God of his infinite mercy direct you in all things.

Epworth. Nov. 27
1707   Susanna Wesley

Notes

1. See 1 Kings 7:50.
2. The elder Wesley was arrested for debt (at the hands of political enemies among his parishioners) and spent several months of 1705 in Lincoln Castle. Apparently, the victim of drink in S. W.'s grisly story was one of his persecutors.
3. Brackets in MS.
4. Close paraphrase of Romans 8:28.
5. Matthew 12:34; quotation marks added.
6. BCP, Litany.
7. See Matthew 5:29–30 and 2 Corinthians 12:9.
8. Possibly a somewhat garbled aphorism.
9. Four-year-old John. The third and last son, Charles, was not born until 29 December 1707, and the last surviving daughter, Kezia, was born in March 1709.
10. Probably his election as a King's Scholar at Westminster School. See Adam Clarke, *Wesley Family; Collected Principally from Original Documents* (New Youk: N. Bangs and T. Mason for the Methodist Episcopal Church, 1824), p. 293; and George Stevenson, *Memorials of the Wesley Family . . .* (London: S. W. Partridge; New York: Nelson and Phillips, 1876), p. 233.
11. BCP, communion service, confession.
12. Paraphrase of Psalm 19:12.
13. Lamentations 3:33; quotation marks added.
14. See Ecclesiastes 12:1.

15. BCP, Litany.

16. "Must" written here above the line.

17. Addition, augmentation, increase.

18. John Pearson, *An Exposition of the Creed*, 6th ed. (London: J. Williams, 1692), p. 2: direct quote; my quotation marks. The MS begins the quotation with a dash. Pearson begins the paragraph, "*Belief* in general I define to be. . . ." Pearson (1613–1686), bishop of Chester from 1673, was a royalist and a scholar.

19. Ibid., p. 5: "Whereas if it be any matter of concernment in which the interest of him that relateth or affirmeth any thing to us is considerable, there it is not the skill or knowledge of the Relater which will satisfie us, except we have as strong an opinion of his fidelity and integrity. . . ." S. W. has here quickly summarized several pages of the bishop's dense prose.

20. Echoes of Matthew 16:18.

21. See 1 Kings 19:12.

22. Quotation marks added.

23. See Matthew 8:25.

24. Quotation marks added.

25. Matthew 26:41: "Watch and pray, that ye enter not into temptation."

26. Paraphrase of 1 Corinthians 10:31.

27. A combination of Philippians 2:7 and Isaiah 53:3; quotation marks added.

28. 1 Peter 4:4; quotation marks added, question mark added.

29. As they ministered to Jesus in his temptation. See Matthew 4:1–11.

30. Nearly exact quotation of Matthew 25:21; quotation marks added.

❦ FOUR ❦

The Rectory Fire

*T*he night of Wednesday, 9 February 1709, looms large in Susanna Wesley's life story, as well as in Methodist legend. Near midnight a fire, probably the latest mischief of the rector's enemies in the parish, engulfed the house. The family all rushed or were carried to safety—miraculous enough, it might have seemed, that night. However, the subsequent career of John Wesley has focused special attention on the rescue of the then six-year-old "Jacky," trapped in an upstairs bedroom by the flames. With the help of neighbors he was lifted down to safety, leading him to regard himself as providentially set apart, a "brand plucked from the burning,"[1] a phrase eagerly repeated by his Methodist followers.

Mythologizing aside, the event had personal consequences deep and far-reaching enough for Susanna Wesley. For a start, their home and all their belongings were destroyed, necessitating the dispersal of the children until money could be scraped up for the construction of a new rectory (the one that still exists as a place of Methodist pilgrimage). Among the losses of the fire were the rector's library and writings; the Epworth parish registers; the manuscripts left to Susanna by her father, Samuel Annesley; and her own manuscripts.

Several letters in the days and months immediately following the fire recount what happened and how Susanna meant to cope. Of particular consequence to her own identity and sense of calling was her redoubled dedication to producing materials useful in the education of her growing children. Evidence that she energetically continued in this calling may be found in later correspondence with her sons, even as they undertook an Oxford education and pursued their own priestly vocations, and in the longer moral and theological treatises she directed to her daughters, who in that era could not even aspire to university training.

All but one of these letters were sent to Samuel Wesley Jr., near the end of his school days in Westminster. We find Susanna by turns eager to fill him in on the family tragedy (14 February 1708/9); recording her emotional response to the fire, urging him to follow a "method" in his living, and detailing "the little manual" she had been writing for her children when the flames struck (11 October 1709);

commending, though with the self-deprecation expected of an "uneducated" woman, her finished work on the Creed (7 April 1710); and answering his call for spiritual direction, though again with considerable disparagement of her talents (28 December 1710).

The one letter from this period not sent to "Sammy" is addressed to the Rev. Joseph Hoole, vicar of the neighboring parish of Haxey. A later letter demonstrates that Susanna was to find in Hoole a conversation partner for exploring one of the intellectual issues of the day (see 12 October 1716). In the present correspondence, however, she recounts the tragic events of the fire to one of her husband's colleagues. Getting the details down on paper for someone only a few miles removed from the event might seem odd, unless, as appears to be the case, it was necessary to inform him so that he could better fill the role of fund-raiser for a new Epworth rectory.

🔥

To Samuel Wesley Jr.
14 February 1708/9
MA; SWJr Letter Book, pp. 103–105.

Dear Sammy!

When I received your letter wherein you complain of want of shirts, I little thought that in so short a space we should all be reduced to the same, and indeed a worse condition. I suppose you have already heard of the firing of our house by what accident we cannot imagine, but the fire broke out about eleven or twelve o'clock at night, we being all in bed; nor did we perceive it till the roof of the corn chamber was burnt through and the fire fell upon your sister Hetty's bed, which stood in the little room joining upon it. She waked and immediately run to call your father, who lay in the red chamber, for I being ill, he was forced to lie from me. He says he heard some crying fire in the street before, but did not apprehend where 'twas till he opened his door. He called at our chamber and bid us all shift for life, for the roof was falling fast and nothing but the thin wall kept the fire from the staircase.

We had no time to take our clothes, but ran all naked. I called to Betty to bring the children out of the nursery. She took up Patty and left Jacky to follow her.[2] But he, going to the door and seeing all on fire, ran back again. We got the street door open, but the wind drove the flame with such violence that none could stand against it. I tried thrice to break through, but was driven back. I made another attempt and waded through the fire, which did me no other hurt than to scorch my legs and face. When I was in the yard, I looked about for your father and the[3] children, but seeing none, concluded 'em all lost. But I thank God, I was mistaken! Your father carried sister Emly, Suky and Patty into the garden; then, missing Jacky, he ran back into the house to see if he could save him. He heard him miserably crying out in the nursery and attempted several times to get upstairs, but was beat back by the flame; then he thought him lost and commended his soul to God and went to look after the rest. The child climbed up to the window and called out to them in the yard; they got up to the casement and pulled him out just as the roof fell into the chamber. Harry broke the glass of the parlour window and threw out your sister Molly and Hetty, and so by God's great mercy we all escaped. Don't be discouraged. God will provide for you.

Epworth. Feb. 14   Susanna Wesley.
        1708/9

To Rev. Mr. [Joseph] Hoole
24 August 1709
MA; the copy is in a florid hand, endorsed later by John Wesley, who later edited it heavily in the first issue of *A M* in 1778: "My mother's account of the fire, August 24th, 1709. Not exactly right with regard to me. J. W." Paragraphing, completely lacking in the MS, has been supplied.

Epworth 24th Augst. 1709

Revd. Sir,

My master is much concerned that he was so unhappy as to miss seeing you at Epworth and is not a little troubled that the great hurry of business he is in about his building will not afford him leisure to write at present. He has therefore commanded me to make a tender of his humblest thanks and service to yourself and his unknown benefactors that by your application were moved to so laudable and generous a charity; and since he is not acquainted here with any good hand that can give you the particulars of our late misfortunes, he has ordered me to satisfy your desire as well as I can, which I shall do by a simple relation of matter of fact; nor can I at this distance of time recollect every calamitous circumstance that attended our strange reverse of fortune.

On Wednesday night February 9th between the hours of eleven and twelve o'clock our dwelling house was fired by what accident God only knows, which was discovered by some sparks falling from the roof upon a bed where one of the children lay that burnt her foot. She immediately ran to our chamber and called us, but I believe none [heard] her, for Mr. Wesley was alarmed by a cry of fire in the street, upon which he arose, not imagining 'twas his own house burning. On opening his door, he found it full of smoke and perceived the roof was already burnt through. He immediately came to my room (for I having been very ill, we were obliged to lie asunder) and bid us rise quickly and shift for our lives, [as] the house was all on fire. Then he ran and broke open the nursery door and called to the maid to bring out the children; she snatch[ed] up the youngest and bid the rest follow, which they did, except Jacky, for he, coming to the entry and seeing the fire, ran back to his bed; nor did we presently miss him. When we were got into the hall and saw ourselves surrounded with flames and that the roof was upon the point of falling, we concluded ourselves inevitably lost, for in the fright we had forgot the keys of the house, which were in my master's chamber; but he ventured upstairs once more and recovered them a minute before the staircase took fire. When we opened the street door, it being a strong northeast wind, the flames poured in with such violence that none could stand against them. Mr. Wesley only had such presence of mind as to think of the garden door, out of which he helped some of our children, and our men broke the bars and glass of the hall and dining room windows, by which the rest escaped. I was not in a condition to stir like the rest, nor could I climb a window or get to the garden door. I endeavored thrice to force a passage through the flames that had seized the street door and was as often beat back by the fury of the fire. In this distress I made my particular application to our blessed Saviour and besought him if it were his will to preserve me from that death, when I made another attempt and waded through the fire (naked as I was) which did me no further harm than a little scorching of my hands and face, which immediately brought into my mind that passage in Isaiah 43:2, "when thou walkest through the fire, thou shalt not be burned; neither shall the flames kindle upon thee." [4]

While my master was carrying the children into the garden, we heard the child in the nursery cry out miserably for help, which extremely moved him, but his affliction was much increased when he had several times attempted the stairs, then on fire, and found it was impossible to get near him. He then gave him for lost and, kneeling down, commended his soul to God and left him, as he thought, burning. But the boy, seeing none came to his assistance and being frighted by the hanging of the chamber and his bed being on fire, climbed up to the casement, where he was presently spied by the men in the yard, who immediately got up and pulled him out just in that article of time that the roof fell and beat the chamber to the earth. So by the infinite mercy of almighty God our lives were well preserved by little less than [a] miracle, for there passed but a few moments between the first discovery of the fire and the falling of the house.

Though Mr. Wesley and I and seven small children were all naked and exposed to the inclemency of the air in a night which was as severely cold as perhaps anyone can remember and though we had before our eyes the melancholy prospect of our house and goods consuming in the flames, nor knew we whither to wander or what to do with our little ones that now cried out as much with the cold and because the frost cut their naked feet as they had just before done for fear of the fire; yet so deeply were our minds affected with the goodness of God in preserving our and our children's lives that for a while we essayed no reflection on the condition to which we were reduced. Nor did the consideration of our having no house, money, food or raiment for the present much affect us.

We had a good quantity of wheat and malt in the house and my master had received a considerable sum of money the day before for flax, but we had no time to save anything, nor could we afterwards recover more than about 25 ounces of plate, though perhaps more might be found. I had the week before (as I used to do when in that condition) brought all my pewter, brass, etc., which was most valuable, into my store chamber and so increased our loss; but the greatest almost irrecoverable loss was that of my master's books and manuscripts, particularly that book which he had just before prepared for the press, upon the delivery of which he should have received £50. We had a little hemp and some corn unthrashed that was preserved, and they got some lumber out of the low rooms, but the worth is very inconsiderable. Thus, sir, it pleased God by a strange turn of his Providence to take from us what before he had most liberally given us, and I can assure you, sir, whatever some men's philosophy may persuade them to the contrary, such involved and mysterious methods of divine Providence are as hard to bear with [?]temper and submission as they are to understand; and the calming our tumultuous passions and suppressing those motions of discontent and murmuring that are wont to take their rise from such occurrences, are some of those difficult acts of mortification which our Saviour aptly expresses by pulling out a right eye and cutting off a right hand.[5] Yet it hath pleased the almighty Being hitherto to support us and to raise some friends whose charity has supplied us with daily bread and something towards the rebuilding our house; and more, I believe, had been done but that there are a sort of people who find a malicious pleasure in inventing and spreading false reports that our losses are abundantly made up by the liberal contributions of our neighbours. I love not to complain, neither with nor without reason, nor would I be unthankful to God or man, and therefore gratefully acknowledge we have received very considerable benefactions from several worthy persons. Yet notwithstanding, we are, I fear, far from having a sufficiency to defray the charge of building, and when that is finished, any man of sense may easily conceive that the furnishing a house for so large a family (to say nothing of necessary clothing for [our]selves and ten children and the books which my master cannot be without) will require full as much, if not more than the house itself. Yet notwithstanding all that the great enemy of mankind can suggest or any person can do against us, if it pleases God to raise us from the dust as he did Job, he can easily do it, for omnipotence knows no difficulty, and the almighty Power from whom we received our being can, if he sees it best for us, quickly restore us to our former condition. But if his infinite wisdom has otherwise determined concerning us, his will be done. All is best that he orders, and his ways are ever equal, and his actions are [in] number, weight and measure most perfect. I humbly beg the continuance of *your* prayers for us that God would assist and direct us. And I am

Sr Yr Obliged hble sert.

S. W.

P. S. I gave my master the eight guineas and fifteen shillings in silver.

To Samuel Wesley Jr.
11 October 1709
MA; Wesley College, Headingley MS C (draft)

Epworth, October 11, 1709

Dear Sammy,

Though nothing in the world could ever make me forget you or prevent my having the tenderest regard for your happiness and concern for your immortal soul, yet my mind has been so terribly shocked by our late misfortunes that, though I cannot say I never had leisure, yet I could not dispose myself to write to ye. A long series of adverse fortunes had before inclined me to a too melancholy temper, but this most strange and surprising accident, attended by so many calamitous circumstances, gave my soul so strong a bent to extreme sadness that I have not been able to recover myself till within a few days, but have been as one dead to the world, uncapable of enjoying any of those comforts which God in his mercy hath yet left me. Now I am, heaven be praised,[6] a little free from that unhappy paroxism, the first thing I shall enquire after is the health of your soul.[7]

I hope you retain the impressions of your education, nor have forgot that the vows of God are upon you. You know that the first fruits are his[8] by an unalterable right, and that as your parents devoted you to the service of the altar, so you yourself made it your choice when your father was offered another way for your subsistence. But have you duly weighed what such a choice and such a dedication imports? Sammy, consider what purity, what devotion, what separation from the world! What exemplary virtues[9] are required in those who are to guide others in their way to glory! Exemplary, I say, for low and common degrees of piety are not sufficient for those of that sacred function. You must not think to live like the rest of the world; but your light in a more special manner must so shine among men that they may see your good works and thereby be led to glorify your Father which is in heaven.[10] For my part I cannot see how any clergyman can reprove sinners or exhort men to lead a good life when they themselves indulge their own corrupt inclinations and by their practice contradict their doctrine. If the holy Jesus be in truth their Master, and they are really his ambassadors, surely it becomes them to live like his disciples; and if they do not, what a sad account they must one day give of their stewardship you would do well to consider. Nor would I have you now give yourself liberty to comply with the vain or sinful customs of the[11] world, foolishly flattering yourself that it will be time enough to begin a strict course of life when you enter into Orders, when the eyes of the world will be more upon you. For let me tell you, now is the time to lay a good foundation, now is the time to wean yourself from vanity and sensual pleasures.[12] If you indulge your unruly passions, if now you suffer yourself to love the world or anything in it more than God, if you now neglect your private duties, your daily sacrifices of prayers and thanksgiving,[13] or grow remiss or cold in their performance. If now you permit impurity, anger, hatred, malice or any kind of danger of intemperance to gain an ascendant over your mind, you are in danger of being eternally lost. Believe me, first motions are most easy to restrain; if they pass unheeded and unchecked, how soon do they prevail upon the inclination, and when that point is gained, how insensibly are we led into act[s], which, being multiplied, naturally beget a habit; and how hard that is to be cured you very well know.

I have already given you so many particular directions, how to perform your duty to God, yourself and your neighbour, that I shall not at present speak much o' those subjects, but shall only mention some few things and beseech the great Father of Spirits to direct and assist your mind to practice what you already know.

First I would advise you as far as 'tis possible in your present circumstances to throw all your business into a certain method, by which means you'll learn to improve every precious moment and find an unspeakable facility in the performance of your respective duties. Begin and end the day with him who is the Alpha and Omega, and though my ignorance of the orders of your school makes it impossible for me to assign what time you should spend in private devotion, yet I'm sure, if you do but really experience what it is to love God, you'll redeem all the time[14] you can for his more immediate service. What is in your own power you may dispose of, nor are your rules so strict as not to admit of some diversions. I'll tell you what method[15] I used to observe when I was in my father's house and perhaps had as little, if not less, liberty than you have now. I used to allow myself as much time for recreation as I spent in private devotion;[16] not that I always spent so much, but so far I gave myself leave to go, but no farther. So likewise in all things else, appoint so much time for sleep, eating, company etc. Remember what the divine Herbert advises on[17] this head:

> "Slight them who say amidst their Sickly Healths,
>   Thou livest by rule. What doth not so but man?"[18]

And 'tis the shame and ignominy of our minds that we who alone were created after the image of the God of order should be the only part of his creation that is irregular and disorderly. But above all things, my dear Sammy, I command you, I beg, I beseech you to be very strict in your observance of the Lord's day. That blessed day of God, that most dear and sacred type of the great sabbath which we hope to enjoy with him in glory. Believe me, dear child, there is more depends on this one duty than the unthinking world is aware of. I am verily persuaded that our most gracious God is more ready to grant our petitions and more pleased with our devotions on that day than any other. Though he is ever present with us and carefully adverts to the particular actions of each individual creature at all times, yet he has promised to be in a more peculiar[19] manner present in the assemblies of his saints; and to be sure he takes particular notice of the behaviour of his servants on his own day. Nor do those blessed guardian spirits that are sent forth to minister for those who are the heirs of salvation behold a devout soul in its seraphic aspirations towards that Being whom we jointly adore without the greatest pleasure and satisfaction imaginable. We then hold communion with all saints, with the celestial hierarchy; with angels and archangels and all the company of the heavenly host we join in admiring and praising our great Creator,[20] our blessed Redeemer, and the Holy Spirit of grace by whom we are sealed unto the day of redemption.[21] Indeed I heartily wish that I could persuade all my children to such a love and honour of the sabbath, that they might by it be known and distinguished from the rest of the world.

In all things endeavour to act upon principles. Do not live like the greater part of mankind, who pass through the world like straws upon a river, which are carried what way soever the stream or the wind drives 'em. Accustom yourself often to put the question: Why do I this or that? Why do I pray, read, study, eat, sleep, use diversions, etc.? And so as much as possible moralize all your thoughts, words and actions, which will bring you[22] to such a steadiness and consistency as becomes a reasonable being and a good Christian.

Be very nice in the choice of your company, and never rely upon your own virtue so far as to associate with the vicious and profane.[23] Our blessed Lord, who knew what was in man, commands us to pray daily, "Lead us not into temptation."[24] And indeed, considering what the world is, 'tis most prudent to avoid a great acquaintance, for let us be we're so careful, much company will strongly divert the mind[25] from serious thoughts; nor can we possibly serve God so well in a crowd as in solitude. In all places and at all times be most[26] careful to avoid that most odious but common vice of intemperate drinking. I have formerly writ largely on that subject. I'll therefore only remind you to observe a constant rule in drinking. Nor can I name a better than that of Mr. Herbert: "Stay at the third glass"[27]—one for thirst and one for refreshment is sufficient, especially for one designed for a clergyman. Nor is temperance always the utmost that is required from them: they must for the most part be abstemious, especially where the tide runs strongly o' the contrary side. For old Seneca's maxim is yet good; "Those are the best instructors who preach by their lives and prove their words by their actions."[28] And that man may with courage boldly reprove another for being drunk who will never himself be guilty of an intemperate glass.[29] Nor do I think it possible for any persons to keep a due guard upon their minds against impurity or any irregular passion if they indulge themselves in[30] immoderate drinking. I do protest, though I love you perhaps as much as ever parent loved a child, I had much rather see you die than have you commit that sin which I abhor above anything whatever.

Sammy, there is nothing I now desire to live for, but to do some small service to my children,[31] that, as I have brought 'em into the world, so that it might please God to make me (though unworthy) an instrument of doing good to their souls. I had been several years collecting from my little reading, but chiefly from my own experience, some things which I hoped would ha' been useful to you all; and had begun to[32] form all into a little manual wherein I had designed you should ha' read what were the particular reasons which prevailed upon me to believe the being of a God and the ground of natural religion, together with the motives that first[33] induced me to embrace the faith of Jesus Christ, under which was comprehended my own private[34] reasons for the truth of revealed religion and upon what convictions I professed myself a Christian. And because I was educated among the Dissenters, and there was somewhat remarkable in my leaving 'em at so early an age, not being full 13, I had drawn up an account of the whole transaction, under which head I had included the main of the controversy between them and the Established Church as far as it had come to my knowledge; and then followed the reasons that determined my judgment to the preference of the Church of England. I had fairly transcribed a great part of it, but you writing to me for some directions about the receiving the sacrament, I begun a short discourse on that subject,[35] intending to send all together; but before I could finish my design the flames consumed this with all the rest of my writings. I would have you[36] do somewhat like this yourself when you've leisure and write down the principles upon which you build your faith, and though I cannot possibly recover all I formerly writ, yet I'll gladly assist you what I can in explaining any difficulty that may occur to your thoughts, that you may be able to give a reason of the faith that is in you.[37]

Since I begun to write this I received a letter from you dated [?][38] wherein you tell me you know not whether you should congratulate my good, or condole my ill, health or fortune. Truly my health and fortune is much alike, neither very good or extremely bad.[39] I have constantly pain enough to mind me of mortality and trouble enough in my circumstances of fortune to exercise my patience. I shall shortly write to your Aunt Annesley a particular account of our late losses (which letter I'll enclose in one to you) which will inform you of those things that you say you are ignorant of. I take it mighty kindly that you offer me part of your small library, but I am not willing to receive anything from one to whom I can give so little. Your sister Emly [*sic*] has wrought you a purse in which I have sent a small present. 'Tis a very pretty one and you ought to thank her. I beseech God to bless you with health of mind and body.

S. Wesley

Let me hear from you when you've leisure.[40]

To Susanna("Suky") Wesley
13 January 1709/10
Wesley College, draft. This "letter" is really an extended treatise on the Apostles' Creed, and thus is included in part III of this volume.

To Samuel Wesley Jr.
7 April 1710
MA; SWJr Letter Book, pp. 106–107. Cover letter sent with copy of exposition of Apostles' Creed, originally addressed to Suky. See part III of this volume.

Dear Sammy!

I thought I should have heard from you e'er now, but I find you do not think of me as I do of you. Indeed, I believe you would be very easy were you never to hear from me more, but I cannot satisfy myself without writing sometimes, though not so often as I would!

I have sent you a letter which I writ to your sister Suky at Gainsbro, which I would have you read and copy if you have time.

When I have any leisure, I think I can't be better employed than in writing something that may be useful to my children; and though I know there are abundance of good books wherein these subjects are more fully and accurately treated of than I can pretend to write, yet I am willing to think that my children will somewhat regard what I can do for 'em, though the performance is mean, since they know it comes from their mother, who is perhaps more concerned for their eternal happiness than anyone in the world. And, as you had my youth and vigour employed in your service, so I hope you will not despise the little I can do in my declining years, but will for my sake at least carefully read these papers over, if it be but to put you upon a more worthy performance of your own.

April 7th 1710   Susanna Wesley

To Samuel Wesley Jr.
28 December [1710]
AM, 1788, pp. 36–38, 83–86 (dated there "about the year 1706"). This is not in the SWJr Letter Book, which concludes with Samuel's transcription of Susanna's

letter to Suky on the Creed. Clarke, pp. 298–301, and Stevenson, pp. 236–238, date the letter 1710. This is corroborated by a December 1710 letter from Samuel Jr., which this one answers, and the fact that December 28 did fall on a Thursday in 1710.

Thursday, Dec. 28 [1710]

Dear Sammy,

I am much better pleased with the beginning of your letter than with what you used to send me, for I do not love distance or ceremony; there is more of love and tenderness in the name of mother than in all the complimental titles in the world.

I intend to write to your father about your coming down, but yet it would not be amiss for you to speak of it too. Perhaps our united desires may sooner prevail upon him to grant our request, though I do not think he will be averse from it at all.[41]

I am heartily glad that you have already received and that you design again to receive the Holy Sacrament; for there is nothing more proper or effectual for the strengthening and refreshing the mind than the frequent partaking of that blessed ordinance.

You complain that you are unstable and inconstant in the way of virtue. Alas! what Christian is not so too? I am sure that I, above all others, am most unfit to advise in such a case; yet, since I cannot but speak something, since I love you as my own soul, I will endeavour to do as well as I can; and perhaps while I write I may learn, and by instructing you I may teach myself.

First, endeavour to get as deep an impression on your mind as is possible of the awful and constant presence of the great and holy God. Consider frequently that wherever you are, or whatever you are about, he always adverts to your thoughts and actions in order to a future retribution. He is about our beds,[42] and about our paths, and spies out all our ways. And whenever you are tempted to the commission of any sin or the omission of any duty, make a pause, and say to yourself, "What am I about to do? God sees me! Is this my avowed faithfulness to my Creator, Redeemer, and Sanctifier? Have I so soon forgot that the vows of God are upon me? Was it easier for the eternal son of God to die for me than it is for me to remember him? For what end came he into the world but to satisfy the justice of God for us and to reconcile us to God and to plant good life among men in order to their eternal salvation? What! cannot I watch one hour with that Jesus[43] who veiled his native glory with our nature, and condescended so low as to make himself of no reputation, by putting on the form of a servant, that he might be capable of conferring the greatest benefit upon us that man could receive, by his suffering such a shameful and cursed death upon the cross for our redemption?"[44] Oh, Sammy, think but often and seriously on Jesus Christ, and you will experience what it is to have the heart purified by faith!

Secondly, consider often of that exceeding and eternal weight of glory that is prepared for those who persevere in the paths of virtue. "Eye hath not seen, nor ear heard, not hath it entered into the heart of man to conceive what God hath prepared for such as love and serve him faithfully."[45] And when you have so long thought on this that you find your mind affected with it, then turn your view upon this present world and see what vain inconsiderable trifles you practically prefer before a solid, rational, permanent state of everlasting tranquility. Could we but once attain to a strong and lively sense of spiritual things, could we often abstract our minds from corporeal objects and fix them on heaven, we should not waver and be so inconstant as we are in matters of the greatest moment, but the soul would[46] as naturally aspire towards a union with God, as the flame ascends; for he alone is the proper centre of the mind, and it is only the weight of our corrupt nature that retards its motions towards him.

Thirdly, meditate often and seriously on the shortness, uncertainty, and vanity of this present state of things. Alas! had we all that the most ambitious, craving souls can desire; were we actually possessed of all the honour, wealth, strength, beauty, etc., that our carnal minds can fancy a[nd][47] delight in; what would it signify, if God should say unto us, "Thou fool, this night shall thy soul be required of thee"?[48] Look back on[49] your past hours and tell me which of them afford you the most pleasing prospect. Whether those spent in play or vanity or those few that were employed in the service of God? Have you not in your short experience often found Solomon's observations on the world very true? Has not a great part of your little life proved in[50] reflection nothing but vanity and vexation of spirit?[51] How many persons on a deathbed have bitterly bewailed the sins of their past life and made large promises of amendment if it would have pleased God to have spared them; but none that ever lived, or died, repented of a course of piety and virtue. Then why should you not improve the experience of those who have gone before you, and your own also, to your advantage? And since it is past dispute that the ways of virtue are infinitely better than the practice of vice, and that life is not only short at best, but likewise uncertain,[52] and that this little portion of time is all we have for working out our salvation, for as the tree falls, so it must lie, as death leaves us, judgment will certainly find us; have a good courage, eternity is at hand. Lay aside every weight, and the sin that doth so easily beset you, and run with patience and vigour the race which is set before you.[53] And if at any time present objects should make so great an impression on your senses as to endanger the alienating your mind from the spiritual life, then look up to Jesus, the author and finisher of our faith,[54] and humbly beseech him, that since he for our sake suffered himself to be under temptation, he would please to succour you when you are tempted, and in his strength you will find yourself enabled to encounter your spiritual enemies;[55] nay, you will be more than a conqueror through him who hath loved us.[56]

I am sorry that you lie under a necessity of conversing with those that are none of the best, but we must take the world as we find it, since it is a happiness permitted to a very few to choose their company. Yet, lest the comparing yourself with others that are worse may be an occasion of your falling into too much vanity, you would do well sometimes to entertain such thoughts as these:

"Though I know my own birth and education and am conscious of having had great advantages and many means of grace,[57] yet how little do I know of the circumstances of others? Perhaps their parents were vicious or did not take early care of their minds to instill the principles of virtue into their tender years, but suffered them to follow their own inclinations till it was too late to reclaim. Am I sure that they have had as many offers of grace, as many strong impulses of the Holy Spirit, as I have had? Do they sin against such[58] clear conviction as I do? Or are the vows of God upon them as upon me? Were they so solemnly devoted to him at their birth as I was?"[59] You have had the example of a father who served God from his youth; and, though I cannot commend my own to you, for it is too bad to be imitated, yet surely earnest prayers for many years, and some little good advice, have not been wanting.[60]

But if after all self-love should incline you to partiality in your own case, seriously consider your own many failings, which the world cannot take notice of because they were so private; and if still, upon comparison, you seem better than others are, then ask yourself who is it that makes you to differ, and let God have all the praise, since of ourselves we can do nothing. It is he that worketh in us both to will and to do of his own good pleasure;[61] and if at any time you have vainly ascribed the glory of any good performance to yourself, humble yourself for it before God, and give him the glory of his grace for the future.

I am straitened for paper and time, therefore must conclude. God Almighty bless you and preserve you from all evil! Adieu.

Notes

1. See Amos 4:11 and Zechariah 3:2.
2. Emphasis in MS, but probably that of some later reader.
3. See previous note.
4. Quotation marks added.
5. See Matthew 5:29–30.
6. MS C substitutes "I thank God."
7. Paragraph break inserted here.
8. MS C substitutes "heaven's."
9. MS C phrases the first part of this sentence as "Sammy, consider well what separation from the world, what purity, what devotion, what exemplary virtues are required. . . ."
10. Paraphrase of Matthew 5:16.
11. In MS C: "this bad."
12. MS C adds, "and to endeavor to get requisite graces, that you may not have them to seek when you should have them to use." Note the similar phrase in her earlier letter to Sammy, 18 March 1706/7: "get a stock of virtue, that you may not have grace to seek, when you have it to use."
13. See BCP, Holy Communion.
14. See Ephesians 5:16 and Colossians 4:5.
15. In MS C: "Rule."
16. S. W. is repeating a point she had already made in her letter of 27 November 1707.
17. In MS C "upon."
18. The poet and priest George Herbert (1593–1633) was successively rector of Leighton Bromswold and Bemerton. These lines are from "The Church-Porch," stanza 23, lines 133–145, from *The Temple*, in F. E. Hutchinson, ed., *The Works of George Herbert* (Oxford: Clarendon Press, 1941), p. 12. The edition S. W. might have read is *The Temple, Sacred Poems and Private Ejaculations*, 12th ed. (London: Jeffery Wale, 1703). The entire stanza in the latter, p. 5, reads:

Slight those who say amidst their sickly healths,
Thou liv'st by rule. What doth not so, but man?
Houses are built by rule, and Common-wealths.

Entice the trusty sun, if that thou can,
>   From his Ecliptick line; becken the sky.
>   Who lives by rule then keeps good company.

19. In MS C: "more especial."
20. Echoes of the Sanctus, Holy Communion, BCP.
21. Paraphrase of Ephesians 4:30.
22. MS C substitutes, "by which means you will come. . . ."
23. MS C substitutes, "so far as to run into temptation."
24. Matthew 6:13; quotation marks added.
25. In MS C: "our minds."
26. MS C substitues "exactly."
27. "The Church-Porch," stanza 7, line 41, in Hutchinson, *George Herbert*, p. 8. The relevant surrounding material, quoted from the 1703 edition, p. 2, puts the line in context:

Shall I, to please anothers wine-sprung mind,
Lose all mine own? God hath giv'n me a measure
Short of his Can and Body; must I find
A pain in that, wherein he finds a pleasure?
>   Stay at the third Glass: if thou lose thy hold,
>   Then thou art modest, and the wine grows bold.
If reason move not Gallants, quit the room,
All in a shipwrack shift their severall way:
Let not a common ruin thee intomb:
Be not a beast in courtesy; but stay,
>   Stay at the third cup, or forgo the place.
>   Wine above all things doth God's stamp deface.

Quotation marks have been substituted for the dashes that surround Herbert's phrase in the MA MS.
28. The Roman writer Lucius Annaeus Seneca (4 B.C.–A.D.65) had considerable attraction for Enlightenment England. His various works, especially his "Moral Epistles," reveal a man who combines reason, morality, and (in his own pagan way) piety in a manner that S. W. must have found congenial. The most likely source of this quotation—R. L'Estrange, ed., *Seneca's Morals by Way of Abstract*, 7th ed. (London: Jacob Tonson, 1699)—does not yield it up, though there are similar phrases, for example, "[Wisdom] teaches us to Do, as well as to Talk; and to make our Words and Actions all of a Colour" (164). S. W. may have possessed it in some other form or read it in another author.
29. The passage beginning "Nor is temperance," which includes the Seneca quotation and concludes with this reference to a temperant person's ability to reprove an immoderate drinker, is not found in the draft version of the letter, MS C.
30. MS C originally inserted, then crossed out here, "that shameful vice of. . . ."
31. MS C here adds, then crosses out, "to be some way instrumental. . . ."
32. MS C adds, "to correct and. . . ."
33. "First" does not appear in the MS C draft.
34. S. W. first wrote "particular" in MS C, then crossed it out and inserted "private."
35. MS C "on that head."
36. MS C inserts "at your leisure" here, replacing the phrase "when you've leisure" further on in the sentence.
37. Paraphrase of 1 Peter 3:15.
38. The date, omitted in MS C, is nearly totally obscured by a worn creasemark in the

holograph. A reasonable guess would be "Sept. 12," but a case could be made for the letter of June 9, printed (and probably excerpted) in Clarke, p. 296, and Stevenson, p. 234, and apparently no longer extant. His frantic questions about what was happening at Epworth following the fire and his offer of two books to his mother seem to fit her reply, the lateness of which is attributable both to its length and to the bout of melancholy mentioned in the first paragraph.

39. MS C substitutes "nor extremely ill."

40. There follows an unsigned postscript of 11 lines answering a moral question posed by Samuel Jr. in a previous letter and quoting the Roman grammarian Aulus Gellius and the apocryphal book of Tobit. Handwriting, content, and tone point to the Rev. Samuel Wesley Sr. as the writer.

41. Paragraph break (not found in AM version) introduced by Clarke, p. 299.

42. In AM: "bed."

43. See Matthew 26:40 and its parallels.

44. See Matthew 2:40 and Philippians 2:7–8; quotation marks added.

45. Paraphrase of 1 Corinthians 2:9; quotation marks added.

46. Clarke, p. 299, reads, "would be naturally aspiring towards. . . ."

47. Ibid., p. 300, reads, "or."

48. Luke 12:20; quotation marks added.

49. In Clarke, p. 300, "upon."

50. Ibid. Reads, "on."

51. See Ecclesiastes 1:14.

52. In Clarke, p. 300, "life is only short at best and uncertain. . . ."

53. Paraphrase of Hebrews 12:1.

54. See Hebrews 12:2.

55. See Hebrews 4:15–16.

56. See Romans 8:37.

57. The phrase "many means of grace" not found in Clarke, p. 301.

58. Ibid., "as" substituted for "such."

59. Quotation marks added.

60. Paragraph break not in AM added by Clarke.

61. See Philippians 2:13.

FIVE

The Evening Prayers Controversy

A dispute in the winter of 1711/1712 over Susanna's conduct of irregular worship services gives another stunning example of how far a woman's conscience might oppose both the prerogatives of her husband and priest and the canons of the established church. The story, well known in Methodist legend because of its presumed impact on the nine-year-old John Wesley, ranks with the earlier theological, marital, and political quarrel over who was rightfully king (see chapter 1, the Yarborough and Hickes correspondence, in part I of this volume).

On several occasions, Samuel Wesley Sr. attended the Church of England's governing convocation in London. Whatever influence he might have had on church law—or might have gained hobnobbing with church power brokers—was bought at a considerable price. The cost of travel, food, lodging, and a curate to substitute for him at Epworth put a considerable dent in the family income. On this occasion, it also put him in conflict with his wife. During his absence she made a special effort in the continuing process of providing spiritual formation for her children. In addition to meeting with each child individually one evening a week, she also began to give special emphasis to family prayers on Sunday evening. Such a practice, which involved reading prayers and a sermon and discussing devotional topics, would not have been exceptional had it remained within the family. However, word got out, and neighbors began attending in considerable numbers. More to the point, they began staying away from morning prayer, as conducted by the lackluster curate the Rev. Mr. Inman. Inman, hurt and scandalized, contacted the rector in London, who in turn wrote his wayward wife implying that she desist from holding her public meetings. The two letters suggest his side of the argument and give full scope to her effective rhetorical strategy, a fascinating balance of deference and defiance.

Her son John, future organizer of the Methodist movement, may not have sensed the controversy, but he was surely present at the Sunday evening services. His own society and class meetings, innovations that he likewise did not intend to rival the official church worship, may have had an unconscious model in his mother's earlier experiment. Summing up her life at the time of her death, he was ready to place her in the same category as her many male clerical relatives and grant her the biblical title a "preacher of righteousness."[1] The effectiveness of his mother presiding at a public religious gathering may also have made him more receptive to the work of women in his own societies.

❧

To Samuel Wesley Sr.
6 February 1711/12
Original missing. John Whitehead, *The Life of the Rev. John Wesley* . . . (New York: Worthington, 1881), 1:40–44, and Clarke, pp. 267–269, present the same full version, differing from one another only in punctuation. Thomas Coke and Henry Moore, *The Life of the Rev. John Wesley, A.M.* (London: Paramore, 1792), pp. 241–244, greatly excerpt and somewhat rearrange it, following John Wesley's own transcription in his *Journal*, 1 August 1742. The *Journal* version does add the address: "To the Rev. Mr. Wesley, In St. Margaret's Church-Yard, Westminster."

Epworth, February 6th, 1712

I heartily thank you for dealing so plainly and faithfully with me in a matter of no common concern. The main of your objections against our Sunday evening meetings are, first, that it will look particular; secondly, my sex; and lastly, your being at present in a public station and character. To all which I shall answer briefly.

As to its looking particular, I grant it does; and so does almost everything that is serious, or that may any way advance the glory of God or the salvation of souls, if it be performed out of a pulpit, or in the way of common conversation; because in our corrupt age the utmost care and diligence have been used to banish all discourse of God or spiritual concerns out of society, as if religion were never to appear out of the closet, and we were to be ashamed of nothing so much as of professing ourselves to be Christians.

To your second, I reply that as I am a woman, so I am also mistress of a large family. And though the superior charge of the souls contained in it lies upon you as head of the family and as their minister, yet in your absence I cannot but look upon every soul you leave under my care as a talent committed to me under a trust by the great Lord of all the families of heaven and earth. And if I am unfaithful to him or to you in neglecting to improve these talents, how shall I answer unto him, when he shall command me to render an account of my stewardship?

As these and other such like thoughts made me at first take a more than ordinary care of the souls of my children and servants; so, knowing that our most holy religion requires a strict observation of the Lord's day, and not thinking that we fully answered the end of the institution by only going to church, but that likewise we are obliged to fill up the intermediate spaces of that sacred time by other acts of piety and devotion, I thought it my duty to spend some part of the day in reading to and instructing my family, especially in your absence, when, having no afternoon service, we have so much leisure for such exercises; and such time I esteemed spent in a way more acceptable to God than if I had retired to my own private devotions.

This was the beginning of my present practice: other people coming in and joining with us was purely accidental. Our lad told his parents—they first desired to be admitted; then others who heard of it begged leave also; so our company increased to about thirty and seldom exceeded forty last winter; and why it increased since, I leave you to judge after you have read what follows.

Soon after you went to London, Emily found in your study the account of the Danish missionaries,[2] which, having never seen, I ordered her to read it to me. I was never, I think, more affected with anything than with the relation of their travels, and was exceeding pleased with the noble design they were engaged in. Their labours refreshed my soul beyond measure; and I could not forbear spending good part of that evening in praising and adoring the Divine goodness for inspiring those good men with such an ardent zeal for his glory, that they were willing to hazard their lives and all that is esteemed dear to men in this world, to advance the honour of their Master Jesus. For several days I could think or speak of little else. At last it came into my mind, though I am not a man nor a minister of the gospel, and so cannot be employed in such a worthy employment as they were; yet if my heart were sincerely devoted to God, and if I were inspired with a true zeal for his glory and did really desire the salvation of souls, I might do somewhat more than I do. I thought I might live in a more exemplary manner in some things; I might pray more for the people and speak with more warmth to those with whom I have an opportunity of conversing. However, I resolved to begin with my own children, and accordingly I proposed and observed the following method: I take such a proportion of time as I can best spare every night to discourse with each child by itself on something that relates to its principal concerns. On Monday I talk with Molly, on Tuesday with Hetty, Wednesday with Nancy, Thursday with Jacky, Friday with Patty, Saturday with Charles, and with Emily and Sukey together on Sunday.

With those few neighbours who then came to me I discoursed more freely and affectionately than before. I chose the best and most awakening sermons we had, and I spent more time with them in such exercises. Since this our company has increased every night, for I dare deny none that asks admittance. Last Sunday I believe we had above two hundred, and yet many went away for want of room.

But I never durst positively presume to hope that God would make use of me as an instrument in doing good; the farthest I ever durst go was, "It may be: who can tell? With God all things are possible."[3] I will resign myself to him; or, as Herbert better expresses it,

Only, since God doth often make
Of lowly matter, for high uses meet,
  I throw me at His feet;
There will I lie until my Maker seek
For some mean stuff whereon to show His skill;
Then is my time.[4]

And thus I rested without passing any reflection on myself or forming any judgment about the success or event of this undertaking.

Your third objection I leave to be answered by your own judgment. We meet not on any worldly design. We banish all temporal concerns from our society; none is suffered to mingle any discourse about them with our reading or singing; we keep close to the business of the day, and as soon as it is over they all go home. And where is the harm of this? If I and my children went a-visiting on Sunday nights, or if we admitted of impertinent visits, as too many do who think themselves good Christians, perhaps it would be thought no scandalous practice, though in truth it would be so. Therefore, why any should reflect upon you, let your station be what it will, because your wife endeavours to draw people to the church and to restrain them by reading and other persuasion from their profanation of God's most holy day, I cannot conceive. But if any should be so mad as to do it, I wish you would not regard it. For my part, I value no censure on this account. I have long since shook hands with the world, and I heartily wish I had never given them more reason to speak against me.

As for your proposal of letting some other person read. Alas! you do not consider what a people these are. I do not think one man among them could read a sermon without spelling a good part of it; and how would that edify the rest? Nor has any of our family a voice strong enough to be heard by such a number of people.

But there is one thing about which I am most dissatisfied; that is, their being present at family prayers. I do not speak of any concern I am under barely because so many are present, for those who have the honour of speaking to the great and holy God need not be ashamed to speak before the whole world, but because of my sex. I doubt if it be proper for me to present the prayers of the people to God.

Last Sunday, I fain would have dismissed them before prayers, but they begged so earnestly to stay that I durst not deny them.

To Samuel Wesley Sr.
25 February 1711/12
MA. John Wesley's endorsement, part missing, "of her reading on Sund. Eveng." Addressed to her husband "at Mr. Farmery's in St. Margarets Churchyard, Westminster" and postmarked; yet there is no signature. The word (?) "copy" is scrawled at the bottom, after what appears to be a postscript, perhaps added by a later collector or compiler.

Dearest!

Some few days since I received a letter from you (I suppose) dated the 16th instant, which I made no great haste to answer, because I judged it necessary for both of us to take some time to consider before you determine in a matter of such great importance.

I shall pass no censure upon the hasty and unexpected change of your judgment, neither shall I inquire how it was possible that you should be prevailed on by the senseless clamours of two or three of the worst of your parish to condemn what you so very lately approved. But I shall in as few words as possible tell you my thoughts, which perhaps you'll regard just as much as you did my last long, though otherwise not impertinent letter.

There is not that I can hear of more than three or four that is against our meeting, of which Inman is the chief, for no other reason, as I suppose, but that he thinks the sermons I read better than his own. He and Whitely, I believe, may call it a conventicle,[5] and the other full as wisely calls it a puppet show. But we hear no outcry here, nor has any one person ever said one word against it to me. And what does their calling it so signify? Does that alter the nature of the thing? Or do you think that what they say is a sufficient reason for the forbearing a thing that hath already done much, and by God's blessing may do more good? If its being called so by those that know in their own conscience they are mistaken did really make it one, what you say would be somewhat to the purpose; but 'tis plain in fact that this one thing has brought more people to church than ever anything did in so short a time. We used not to have above twenty or twenty-five at evening service, whereas now we have between two and three hundred, which is many more than ever came before to hear Inman in the morning.

Besides the constant attendance on the worship of God, it has wonderfully (as you guessed it would) conciliated the minds of this people toward us, insomuch that we now live in the greatest amity imaginable, and what is still better, they are very much reformed in their behaviour on the Lord's Day, and those people which used to be playing in the streets, come now to hear a good sermon read, which surely is more acceptable to almighty God.

Another reason I have for what I do is I have no other way of conversing with this people and therefore cannot possibly do them any good beside, but by this I have an opportunity of exercising the greatest and noblest charity, viz. charity to their souls.

Some families which very seldom came to church now go constantly. One person that has not been there this seven year is now prevailed on to go with the rest.

There are many other good consequences of this meeting which I have not time to mention. Now I beseech you weigh all things in an impartial balance. On the one side the honour of almighty God, the doing much good to many souls, the friendship of the best among whom we live; on the other (if folly, impiety and vanity may abide in the scale against so ponderous a weight) the malicious senseless objections of a few scandalous persons, their laughing at us and censuring us as precise and hypocritical. And when you have duly considered all things, let me know your positive determination.

I need not tell you the consequences if you determine to put an end to our meeting. You may easily foresee what prejudices it may raise in the minds of these people against Inman especially, who has had so little wit as to speak publicly against it. 'Tis true I can now keep them to the church, but if 'tis laid aside, I doubt[6] they'll never go to hear him more, at least those that come from the lower end of the town. Whereas, if this be continued till your return (which now will not be long), it may please God by that time so to change their hearts that they may love and delight in his public worship so as never to neglect it more.

I shall add but a few words more.

If you do after all think fit to dissolve this assembly, do not tell me any more that you desire me to do it, for that will not satisfy my conscience; but send me your positive command in such full and express terms as may absolve me from all guilt and punishment for neglecting this opportunity of doing good to souls, when you and I shall appear before the great and awful tribunal of our Lord Jesus Christ.

I dare not wish this practice of ours had never been begun, but it will be with extreme [?]grief that I shall dismiss them, because I foresee the consequences. I pray God direct and bless you.[7]

Mr. Hall desires to know of you whether Caywoods Instruments for Navigation are approved of at London, because if they be, he would get them.

Notes

1. 2 Peter 2:5. See his *Journal* entry for 1 August 1742. For evidence, he published his mother's letter of 6 February 1711/12 to his father.

2. The king of Denmark, inspired by the Society for the Propagation of the Gospel (SPG), founded by Anglicans in 1701 to evangelize and organize church work in North America, sent Henry Pluetschau and Bartholomew Ziegenbalg to Tranquebar on the southern coast of India. Their letters home were translated into English in 1709 and dedicated by the translator, A. W. Boehm, to the SPG. The society, of which Samuel Wesley was an ardent supporter and for which his son John would later work in Georgia, bought and distributed 500 copies. It was probably one of these that Emily discovered in the rector's study, though a Part II was published in 1710 and might have been in the Wesley home by the time this letter was written. A final volume, Part III, was published in 1718 by the direction of the Society for the Promotion of Christian Knowledge, an organization allied to the SPG., See C. F. Pascoe, *Two Hundred Years of the S. P. G.* . . . , 2 vols. (London: SPG, 1901), 1:471–472.

3. See Mark 10:27.

4. "The Priesthood," lines 34–39, from "The Church" in *The Temple*, in F. E. Hutchinson, ed., *The Works of George Herbert* (Oxford: Clarendon Press, 1941), p. 161. She has extracted verses from two stanzas, here quoted from the 1703 edition, p. 155:

Wherefore I dare not, I, put forth my Hand
To hold the Ark, although it seem to shake
Through th'old Sins and new Doctrines of our Land.
Only, since God doth often Vessels make
Of lowly Matter for high Uses meet,
　　　I throw me at his Feet.

There will I lie, untill my Maker seek
For some mean Stuff whereon to show his Skill:
Then is my Time. The distance of the Meek
Doth flatter Power. Lest good come short of Ill
In praising might, the Poor do by Submission
　　　What pride by opposition.

5. The derogatory term for a Dissenter's place of worship. Prior to the Toleration Act of 1689, conventicles were not only outside the Church of England, but also outside the law.

6. That is, suspect.

7. Several extra lines of space appear here, but the expected signature is missing. The subsequent few lines function as a sort of postscript.

SIX

An Age of Reason—and Credulity

*H*istorians of the early modern and modern periods have for some time noticed the seemingly odd juxtaposition, illustrated frequently in the eighteenth century, of reasonableness and superstition. The Age of Reason, itself a designation that privileges high intellectual history, yields up new insights when the historian of popular culture is permitted to notice elements of the irrational, the emotional, the supernatural, and the magical among the beliefs and behaviors of many (and not just unlettered village and country folk). Such disparate elements are amply represented in the next batch of correspondence.

On the side of the reasonableness so prized by eighteenth-century intellectuals, we offer Susanna Wesley's letter to the neighboring clergyman, Joseph Hoole, vicar of Haxey. She engages him in an interchange on John Locke's *An Essay concerning Human Understanding*, presenting a fairly sophisticated analysis of "power" and "person" in Locke's philosophy. As may be seen throughout her writing, an active intellect wrestled with difficult issues, whether biblical revelation, natural religion, ethics, or current topics in philosophy. Clearly, she and her husband discussed such issues in the rectory, but this letter indicates that she also looked beyond her home for intellectual companionship. As in the disputes with her husband, so in this instance of debate outside her home: though she defers to authority (in this case Locke and Hoole), she does not shy away from arguing with it.

Hoole also figures in one of Epworth's more notorious examples of the less rational side of the eighteenth-century worldview. As "an eminently pious and sensible man,"[1] he was called in to corroborate the family's own experience of a supposed poltergeist in December 1716 and January 1717. The details of the various knockings and other unexplained noises were written down to satisfy the curiosity of the two older sons, Samuel, by then a schoolmaster in Westminster, and John, a scholar at the Charterhouse School in London. Jeffrey, as the Wesley girls dubbed the raucous spirit, was variously interpreted. John supposed, for instance, that it was the rector's vow in the 1702 dispute with Susanna come back, literally, to haunt him.[2]

In any case, by the end of the century the "disturbances" had piqued the interest of the public. John Wesley, unwilling to give up any evidence of the supernatural, published his analysis in the *Arminian Magazine*, and Joseph Priestley, Unitarian minister, chemist and materialist, printed many of the original documents, by way of tainting Methodism's credulity and "enthusiasm."

Susanna, along with other members of the family, played the part of experimentalist and believer. In the 12 January 1716/17 letter, initially skeptical, she quickly jumped to the conclusion that the preternatural noises portended someone's death (her husband, her eldest son, or her brother). In the subsequent one (25 or 27 January), as in the account she dictated to her son John ten years later, she carefully details the facts of the case in good Lockean fashion as she experienced them. The paradox of the age is well represented in her writing on the subject: crediting and arguing from sense experience (her own and that of trustworthy witnesses), while simultaneously accepting a realm of meaning beyond the ken of a crass materialism.

❧

To Rev. Joseph Hoole
12 October 1716
MA, copy, not in Susanna Wesley's hand. Endorsement in another hand: "Sent copy of the above to Mr. Wesley, 5th Octr 79." An additional endorsement reads, "For Sophia."

Fry. Oct 12th 1716

Revd. Sir!

Permit me to interrupt your better thoughts a few minutes while you read this, which I send humbly to entreat you'd be pleased to recollect the argument we were discoursing t'other day concerning Mr. Locke's notion of *personal identity*, since I cannot upon second thoughts entirely agree with you any more than I can with him, your notion seeming to me attended by as ill, if not the same, consequences as his.

Mr. Locke supposes *personal identity* consists in *self-consciousness*.[3] You are pleased to define it rather, a *capacity of self-consciousness*.

Now with great deference and submission to two superior minds, I think neither of these notions comes fully up to the matter under debate.

When we apply the word *capacity* to *immaterial* substances, I humbly conceive it signifies (and indeed it is but another word for) *power*. So the difference between Mr. Locke and you lies only here: you would place identity in the power itself, he in the act or operation of that power. To both [of] which I reply: Power is always a relative term and does necessarily suppose some *being* that hath or sustains or to whom that power belongs or in whom it is placed. For of power abstracted from all relation we can have no idea. Now as vegetables and animals to whom we ascribe such qualities or accidents as extension, form, colour and whom we can know no otherwise than by those qualities or accidents (for their substances come not within the verge of our senses), we do yet notwithstanding all allow that there must be a substratum to support those accidents, since they cannot otherwise subsist. So to spiritual immaterial beings in whom we plainly perceive the capacities or powers of reason, volition, judging, etc. there must likewise be granted some substratum (if I may so express it) to sustain those capacities or powers or properties, call 'em as you please. And this something, whatever it is, must have a real being, for nonentity hath no power, and what hath no power cannot act. Now though we may possibly attain some perception of this *something* by its proper ties and by defining what it is not; yet by what certain marks or signs its *identity* may be known and plainly distinguished from all other beings endued with like powers, I cannot conceive. I grant indeed that I can see no way whereby we can discern our personal identity but [by] self-consciousness, which infers capacity. But may not God or any other superior mind by some marks or signs unknown to us distinguish each individual spirit from its brother spirit and discern their identity as clearly and certainly by such marks or signs, as we know and distinguish the various kinds of plants and animals by their specific forms and qualities though they are all made of the same matter? I see no absurdity in this supposition, but I submit that and all I have said to your better judgement and humbly beg you would favour me with your thoughts on this subject, either by letter or as you think fit.

You may please to observe that I go upon a supposition that Mr. Locke's explanation of the word *person* is good, though at the same time I doubt[4] it is very defective, but since we did not dispute it then, I will not now. 'Tis sufficient for my present purpose to say that, though we should grant that the word *person* signifies no more than *an immaterial thinking being that hath reason, reflection etc.* as Mr. Locke defines it, yet still in this sense of the word I humbly conceive its *identity* cannot consist in *self-consciousness.*[5]

You know Mr. Locke, to be sure, better than I do and can remember the consequences of his hypothesis. Therefore, I shall only desire you would please to compare his notions and yours together and then see whether the same consequences do not belong to both. I hope you'll pardon this trouble, and I take the liberty of professing myself with much sincerity,

Revd Sir,
Yr obliged Frd & mo. obt Servt
Susanna Wesley

I humbly desire you'd please to favor me once more with a sight [of] the last volume of Clarendon's History, if you have it by you.[6]

Our humble service attends Mrs. Smith.

I doubt[7] Mr. Locke leaves out the word *immaterial* in his definition of *person*. But my master has taken him from me.[8] I desire you'd please to see whether he has or not.

To Samuel Wesley Jr.
12 January 1716/17
Priestley, pp. 119–122, working from a MS of Samuel Wesley Jr.'s.

January 12, 1716–7

Dear Sam,

This evening we were agreeably surprised with your pacquet, which brought the welcome news of your being alive, after we had been in the greatest panic imaginable, almost a month, thinking either you was dead, or one of your brothers by some misfortune been killed.

The reason of our fears is as follows. On the first of December our maid heard at the door of the dining room several dismal groans, like a person in extremes at the point of death. We gave little heed to her relation and endeavoured to laugh her out of her fears. Some nights (two or three) after, several of the family heard a strange knocking in divers places, usually three or four knocks at a time, and then stayed a little. This continued every night for a fortnight; sometimes it was in the garret, but most commonly in the nursery or green chamber. We all heard it but your father, and I was not willing he should be informed of it, lest he should fancy it was against his own death, which, indeed, we all apprehended. But when it began to be so troublesome both day and night that few or none of the family durst be alone, I resolved to tell him of it, being minded he should speak to it. At first he would not believe but [said] somebody did it to alarm us; but the night after, as soon as he was in bed, it knocked loudly nine times, just by his bedside. He rose and went to see if he could find out what it was, but could see nothing. Afterwards he heard it as the rest.

One night it made such a noise in the room over our heads as if several people were walking, then run up and down stairs, and was so outrageous that we thought the children would be frighted; so your father and I rose, and went down in the dark to light a candle. Just as we came to the bottom of the broad stairs, having hold of each other, on my side there seemed as if somebody had emptied a bag of money at my feet; and on his, as if all the bottles under the stairs (which were many) had been dashed in a thousand pieces. We passed through the hall into the kitchen, and got a candle, and went to see the children, whom we found asleep.

The next night your father would get Mr. Hoole to lie at our house, and we all sat together till one or two o'clock in the morning and heard the knocking as usual. Sometimes it would make a noise like the winding up of a jack, at other times, as that night Mr. Hoole was with us, like a carpenter plaining deals;[9] but most commonly it knocked thrice and stopped, and then thrice again, and so many hours together. We persuaded your father to speak, and try if any voice would be heard. One night about six o'clock he went into the nursery in the dark and at first heard several deep groans, then knocking. He adjured it to speak if it had power and tell him why it troubled his house, but no voice was heard, but it knocked thrice aloud. Then he questioned it if it were Sammy and bid it, if it were and could not speak, knock again, but it knocked no more that night, which made us hope it was not against your death.

Thus it continued till the 28th of December, when it loudly knocked (as your father used to do at the gate) in the nursery and departed. We have various conjectures what this may mean. For my own part I fear nothing now you are safe at London hitherto, and I hope God will still preserve you. Though some times I am inclined to think my brother is dead. Let me know your thoughts on it.

To Samuel Wesley Jr.
25 or 27 January 1716/17
Priestley, pp. 125–127.

Jan. 25, or 27,[10] 1716–7

Dear Sam,

Though I am not one of those that will believe nothing supernatural, but am rather inclined to think there would be frequent intercourse between good spirits and us, did not our deep lapse into sensuality prevent it; yet I was a great while e'er I could credit anything of what the children and servants reported concerning the noises they heard in several parts of our house. Nay, after I had heard myself, I was willing to persuade myself and them that it was only rats or weasels that disturbed us; and having been formerly troubled with rats, which were frighted away by sounding a horn, I caused a horn to be procured and made them blow it all over the house. But from the night they began to blow, the noises were more loud and distinct both day and night than before, and that night we rose and went down, I was entirely convinced that it was beyond the power of any human creature to make such strange and various noises.

As to your questions, I will answer them particularly, but withal I desire my answers may satisfy none but yourself; for I would not have the matter imparted to any. We had both man and maid new this last Martinmas, yet I do not believe either of them occasioned the disturbance, both for the reason above mentioned and because they were more affrighted than anybody else. Besides, we have often heard the noises when they were in the room by us; and the maid particularly was in such a panic that she was almost incapable of all business, nor durst ever go from one room to another or stay by herself a minute after it began to be dark.

The man, Robert Brown, whom you well know, was most visited by it lying in the garret and has been often frighted down bare foot and almost naked, not daring to stay alone to put on his clothes; nor do I think, if he had power, he would be guilty of such villainy. When the walking was heard in the garret, Robert was in bed in the next room in a sleep so sound that he never heard your father and me walk up and down, though we walked not softly, I am sure. All the family has heard it together in the same room at the same time, particularly at family prayers. It always seemed to all present in the same place at the same time, though often before any could say it is here, it would remove to another place.

All the family, as well as Robin, were asleep when your father and I went down stairs, nor did they wake in the nursery when we held the candle close by them; only we observed that Hetty trembled exceedingly in her sleep, as she always did, before the noise awaked her. It commonly was nearer her than the rest, which she took notice of, and was much frightened because she thought it had a particular spite[11] at her. I could multiply particular instances, but I forbear. I believe your father will write to you about it shortly. Whatever may be the design of providence in permitting these things, I cannot say. *Secret things belong to God;*[12] but I entirely agree with you, that it is our wisdom and duty to prepare seriously for all events.

S. Wesley

To Samuel Wesley Jr.
27 March 1717
Priestley, p. 140 (extract).

March 27, 1717

I cannot imagine how you should be so curious about our unwelcome guest. For my part, I am quite tired with hearing or speaking of it; but if you come among us, you will find enough to satisfy all your scruples and perhaps may hear or see it yourself.

S. Wesley

Addendum: Susanna Wesley's Account of the Rectory Poltergiest
"My Mother's Account to Jack"
27 August 1726
Priestley, pp. 152–155. This narrative eventually found its way into Samuel Wesley Jr.'s collection of papers and thence to Priestley, who published it along with the various other letters on the subject. It is, however, not a letter but the record of a conversation, taken down ten years after the events by John Wesley.[13]

Aug. 27, 1726

About ten days after Nanny Marshall had heard unusual groans at the dining room door, Emily came and told me that the servants and children had been several times frighted with strange groans and knockings about the house. I answered that the rats John Maw had frightened from his house by blowing a horn there were come into ours and ordered that one should be sent for. Molly was much displeased at it and said if it was anything supernatural, it certainly would be very angry and more troublesome. However, the horn was blown in the garrets; and the effect was that whereas before the noises were always in the night, from this time they were heard at all hours, day and night.

Soon after, about seven in the morning, Emily came and desired me to go into the nursery, where I should be convinced they were not startled at nothing. On my coming thither, I heard a knocking at the feet and, quickly after, the head of the bed. I desired if it was a spirit, it would answer me, and knocking several times with my foot on the ground with several pauses, it repeated under the sole of my feet exactly the same number of strokes with the very same intervals. Kezzy, then six or seven years old, said, "Let it answer me too, if it can,"[14] and stamping, the same sounds were returned that she made many times successively.

Upon my looking under the bed, something ran out pretty much like a badger and seemed to run directly under Emily's petticoats, who sat opposite to me on the other side. I went out, and one or two nights after, when we were just got to bed, I heard nine strokes, three by three, on the other side the bed, as if one had struck violently on a chest with a large stick. Mr. Wesley leapt up, called Hetty, who alone was up in the house, and searched every room in the house, but to no purpose. It continued from this time to knock and groan frequently at all hours, day and night; only I earnestly desired it might not disturb me between five and six in the evening, and there never was any noise in my room after during that time.[15]

At other times I have often heard it over my mantle tree, and once, coming up after dinner, a cradle seemed to be strongly rocked in my chamber. When I went in, the sound seemed to be in the nursery. When I was in the nursery, it seemed in my chamber again. One night Mr. Wesley and I were waked by someone running down the garret stairs, then down the broad stairs, then up the narrow ones, then up the garret stairs, then down again, and so the same round. The rooms trembled as it passed along, and the doors shook exceedingly, so that the clattering of the latches was very loud.

Mr. Wesley proposing to rise, I rose with him, and went down the broad stairs, hand in hand, to light a candle. Near the foot of them a large pot of money seemed to be poured out at my waist and to run jingling down my night gown to my feet. Presently after we heard the noise as of a vast stone thrown among several dozen of bottles, which lay under the stairs: but upon our looking no hurt was done. In the hall the mastiff met us, crying and striving to get between us. We returned up into the nursery, where the noise was very great. The children were all asleep, but panting, trembling, and sweating extremely.

Shortly after, on Mr. Wesley's invitation, Mr. Hoole staid a night with us. As we were all sitting round the fire in the matted chamber, he asked whether that gentle knocking was it?[16] I told him yes, and it continued the sound, which was much lower than usual. This was observable, that while we were talking loud in the same room, the noise, seemingly lower than any of our voices, was distinctly heard above them all. These were the most remarkable passages I remember, except such as were common to all the family.

Notes

1. John Wesley's description, reprinted in Clarke, p. 143.

2. See ibid., pp. 136–167, for most of the original documents, and Maldwyn Edwards, *Family Circle: A Study of the Epworth Household in Relation to John and Charles Wesley* (London: Epworth, 1949), pp. 87–99, for a modern analysis. A Jacobite ghost's timing was right: Queen Anne, the last Stuart, had died in 1714, and here was Samuel Wesley praying again for another usurper, this time the Hanoverian George I! In fact Jeffrey often made his presence felt most vociferously during the Prayer for the King's Majesty.

3. Locke develops this idea in *An Essay concerning Human Understanding*, Peter H. Nidditch, ed. (Oxford: Clarendon Press, 1975), 2.27.9 (p. 335): "since consciousness always accompanies

thinking, and 'tis that, that makes every one to be, what he calls *self*; and thereby distinguishes himself from all other thinking things, in this alone consists *personal Identity*."

4. Once again the archaic usage for "suspect."

5. Locke's definition of person (ibid., p. 335) is "a thinking *intelligent* Being, that has reason and reflection, and can consider it self as it self" (my emphasis). As S. W. suspects in her postscript, he does not use the word "immaterial," which she here attributes to him.

6. Edward Hyde Earl of Clarendon, *The History of the Rebellion and Civil Wars in England* . . . , 3 vols.(Oxford: Printed at the Theatre, 1712). If she is reading from this most recent edition of this royalist history, the last volume she requests takes up the narrative in the spring of 1648 and recounts, among other things, the execution of Charles I. The second part of the last volume (actually a sixth volume since each volume in this edition has two separately bound parts) covers the commonwealth period and, as the title page puts it, Charles II's "blessed Restoration and Return . . . in the year 1660." It is probably more than coincidence that a woman of Nonjuring principles would be mulling over these stories from this perspective, given the recent unsuccessful attempt of Bonnie Prince Charlie to reassert his family's claim to the throne in 1715.

7. See note 4.

8. Why? Without knowing the details of the situation, we might be excused for suspecting that Samuel did not fully support his wife's intellectual interests.

9. Planks (archaic usage).

10. The indecisive dating apparently represents Priestley's inability to decipher the original.

11. Priestley reads: "spight."

12. Deuteronomy 9:29, closely paraphrased. Emphasis in Priestley may be in lieu of quotation marks.

13. Frank Baker writes that this is corroborated by Wesley's MS diary entry for that day. Private correspondence, 28 August 1988. Wesley's "Oxford" diaries are being edited as volume 32 of the current ("bicentennial") *Works of John Wesley*.

14. Quotation marks added.

15. The time for her evening devotional reading, meditating, and writing? See part II of this volume.

16. Priestley punctuates these sentences thus: "Mr. Hoole staid a night with us: as we were all sitting round the fire in the matted chamber. He asked whether. . . ."

SEVEN

A Rich Brother in India

*T*he Wesley family was often in financial straits. To begin with, there were many mouths to feed and bodies to clothe, and the Epworth living, even when augmented a few years later with the nearby parish of Wroot, did not always provide enough to meet the family's needs. The rectory fire of 1709 did not help. Samuel Wesley, moreover, was neither a good businessman nor politically astute, thus exacerbating the problem. As efficient a household manager as she was, there were times when Susanna despaired of making ends meet. Some of the more interesting entries in her devotional journal are the record of her vows with God, promising increased piety in return for the necessities of life for herself and her children.[1]

If large families were part of the problem, they might also be seen as part of the solution. Samuel's brother Matthew, a London surgeon and apothecary, for instance, had provided upkeep and/or room and board for three of his nieces at various times: Sukey, Hetty, and Patty.[2] Susanna, herself the youngest sister among 24 or 25 siblings, could look to her side of the family, too. One Annesley who had done well was her brother Samuel Jr. Born about 1658, he left home at age 16 to seek his fortune in India. First in the employ of the East India Company, then as a merchant in his own right at Surat, he flourished. He died there in 1732, never returning to England.[3]

The following long letter, which makes up this entire chapter, reveals both the expectations and the pitfalls of family ties where money is concerned. It highlights, as well, Susanna's assessment of her husband, gives us further glimpses of the Epworth rectory's household economy, and suffuses it all with theological musings on riches and poverty.

Susanna tries to moderate a quarrel between her husband and brother over some botched business the latter entrusted to the former, recommending they put the matter to arbitration. She describes what it's like to be past 50 with a large family and in financial distress. Carefully detailing the "unprosperous events" that have put them there (debts incurred as far back as the rectory fire, bad health, a badly married daughter, and another "in service"), she implies her brother's responsibility for the situation. Answering his charges from previous letters, she admits that her husband is in fact "not fit for worldly business" and that his talents are wasted in an "obscure corner of the country." She also makes an apt observation when she notes who are hurt while the two men wrangle over blame: "The right or wrong belong to you and Mr. Wesley, the suffering part belongs to me and mine."

The effort she put into this production and her rhetorical strategies (not least of which was dating it "January 20th . . . my birthday") all went for nought. When her brother died in 1732, his will barely mentioned Susanna and her family.[4]

To Samuel Annesley Jr.
20 January 1721/22
Wesley College: Concluding fragment in S. W.'s hand with many corrections, possibly a draft of the letter, endorsed by J. W., "To Mr Annesley at Surrat"; MA: entire letter in a fairer hand, not S. W.'s, probably a copy, endorsed by J. W., "My mother to Mr. Annesley, Jan 20, 1721—& his answer," to which latter phrase a subsequent reader has added "(no!)" Various vertical lines and deletions suggest later editorial work, perhaps Stevenson, who edits out the same passages in his edition, pp. 198–200.)

[no heading]

Sir,

The unhappy differences between you and Mr. Wesley have prevented my writing some years, not knowing whether a letter from me would be acceptable and being unwilling to be troublesome. But feeling life ebb apace and having a desire to be at peace with all men, especially you, before my exit, I've ventured to send one letter more, hoping you will give yourself the trouble to read it without prejudice.

You cannot but be sensible that I've a very hard part to act between an only brother and a husband, which are names full of tenderness and ought to be regarded with the utmost kindness and respect; and that 'tis next to impossible to speak a word between ye without offence to one, perhaps to both. To approve all you have done or said, I cannot. To condemn ————[5] or any man without full evidence of matter of fact, I dare not. Yet would I fain offer somewhat by way of accommodation, and I earnestly beseech the God of peace and love to inspire your hearts with a reasonable proportion of brotherly affection and Christian charity and direct ye to use such prudent measures as may beget a good understanding between ye. I am not well apprised of the merits of the cause, but upon the best of my knowledge, I think much may be said on both sides.[6]

On the one side, sir, he is accused of having laid out your money not only without, but expressly against, your order. Of having received several sums for which he never accounted, or, which is still worse, of which he has given a very dishonest account. A heavy charge, indeed! On the other hand he says he has orders to produce for the money he hath laid out. That his personal expences, though great, were no more than were necessary by reason of his living so far from London, and being compelled to hire a curate in his absence. That the involved state of your affairs obliged him to a long and frequent attendance on persons of different characters living at a distance from each other, which, besides the vast fatigue to himself, must needs be very chargeable to you. He positively insists on the justice and honesty of his dealings, [and] challenges the whole world to prove him a knave, though he will not vindicate each particular of his conduct in point of prudence. He denies that ever he received any sum of money but what he has faithfully accounted for, and that ninety pound he had from Chamberlain he told you of, but did not return, waiting to see whether you'd be pleased to recollect what you wrote him August 24, 1715. "I shall send a large consignment, so expect you'll charge nothing for your own coming up, on which account I give not my sister the forty pound[s]. I wrote Mr. Eaton and Dodsworth to give you half commission."[7] The same in that of September 24. In several other letters you say you will allow his expenses when about your business those three years he sat in Convocation, if the public did not allow his expenses.

This promised commission he never received, either in whole or part.

The public did not bear his charges or any part of them while he sat in Convocation.

Ergo—   Good English Logic.

He thinks if these allowances were made and these promises fulfilled, he should not remain your debtor, humbly conceives he has hard measure, particularly in the case of the salary, says by indefatigable industry he brought the matter to bear; he beat the bush, and others went away with the bird. He is informed that if he had money to try the cause in chancery it would certainly be given on his side. But as he is not much inclined to law, so that method I cannot bear against a brother, a benefactor and (I wish I were permitted to add) a friend.

It must be an exact judgement that holds the balance even between ye, and I will not presume to determine on either side. But I cannot help thinking that you might compromise this matter betwixt yourselves without the intervention of any man; and this is what I most earnestly desire. But if my hard fortune permit it not, surely the thing ought in reason to be put to an arbitration. And this is what Mr. Wesley tells me he hath often proposed to your attorneys, but could never prevail with 'em to agree to it, which has a shrewd aspect on their side. For though it is not an infallible argument that he is on the wrong side of the question which declines a reference, yet 'tis an undoubted proof of a man's honest intentions and that at *least*[8] he believes himself to be in the right when he desires to have his cause brought to a fair hearing. This, therefore, sir, is what with submission I propose and most humbly request: that if you do not think fit to recede from some strong demands, impossible to be granted without the total ruin of his family; that if you are pleased to recall your word to forget the several promised commissions etc.; that then you will likewise be pleased to appoint one or more on your part, and he will choose the same number on his, before whom the whole case may be fairly stated, and, when after a calm and dispassionate debate, what is justly due to you is made apparent, we shall both be very willing that you should satisfy yourself by sequestering his living, provided that his other creditors be joined with you in the sequestration, or that you will give security for the payment of their debts, after your own is discharged. And this I humbly conceive is as much as can *reasonably* be desired; and more than *reason*, I presume you are too much a Christian and a gentleman to require.

Mr. Eaton often writes to my master, sometimes saying he has positive orders to see Mr. Chamberlain's heirs (which is in effect to sue Mr. Wesley), at other times that he has order to proceed directly against himself, etc. But, dear brother, what do these threats avail? An honest man will pay his debts (if able) without compulsion, and if he be not able, besides one reason more proper for your penetration to suggest than me to mention, I cannot for my life see what manner of good would accrue to you by throwing an aged minister into prison and starving your sister and her children. Will the misery of his family add any access to your happiness? I once hoped better things from you.[9] I am, I believe, got on the right side of fifty, infirm and weak; yet, old as I am, since I have taken my husband[10] for better or worse, I'll make my residence with him. Where he lives will I live and where he dies will I die and there will I be buried. God do so to me and more also, if ought but death part him and me.[11] Confinement is nothing to one that by sickness is compelled to spend great part of her time in a chamber; and I sometimes think that if it were not on account of Mr. Wesley and the children, t'would be perfectly indifferent to my soul whether she ascended to the supreme Origin of being from a jail or a palace. For God is everywhere! No walls, nor locks or bars, nor deepest shade, nor closest solitude excludes his presence, and in what place soever he vouchsafes to manifest himself that place is heaven![12] And that man whose heart is penetrated with divine love and enjoys the manifestations of God's blissful presence is happy, let his outward condition be what it will, is rich "as having nothing yet possessing all things."[13] This world, this present state of things, is but for a time. What is now future will be present, as what is already past once was, and then, as Mr. Pascal observes, "a little earth thrown on our cold head will forever determine our hopes and our condition,"[14] nor will it signify much who personated the prince, who the beggar, since with respect to the exterior all must stand on the same level after death.

I insensibly lengthen this letter, but I'll make a few short remarks on some of your latest writing and then trespass on your patience no longer.

In one of your letters to me, dated March 17, 1715/6, you say very truly "that a contented mind is the best riches, and without it, what do riches avail—even nothing.["] And upon the best observation I could ever make of such as have them, I am induced to believe that 'tis much easier to be contented without riches than with them. 'Tis so natural for a rich man to make his gold his God. (For whatever a person loves most, that thing, be it what it will, he certainly makes his God.) 'Tis so very difficult not to trust in, not to depend on, them for support and happiness, that I do not know one rich man in the world with whom I would change conditions.

You tell, me "you are perfectly tired, or rather, overpressed, with business."[15] This would excite my greatest compassion, but that I hope 'tis in your power to quit it if you please. In another place you say, "I hope you've recovered your loss by fire long since." No, and 'tis to be doubted never shall. Mr. Wesley rebuilt his house in less than one year, but near thirteen are elapsed since 'twas burnt, and yet 'tis not half furnished, nor his wife and children half clothed to this day. 'Tis true by the benefactions of his friends, together with what he had [himself],[16] he paid the first, but the latter is not paid yet, or, what is much the same, money which was borrowed for clothes and furniture is yet unpaid. You go on, sir,[17] "And then my brother's living of three hundred a year (as they tell me). . .["] They—who? I wish those that say so were compelled to make it so. ". . . so far from London is a plentiful maintenance with ordinary frugality.["] And in another to Mr. Wesley you have these words: "you write things are triple the price at London as at Epworth. I have heard the same and may compute your three hundred pounds a year income worth about a thousand near London." I mention these distant passages together, being willing to reply to them both at once. My master positively denies he ever wrote anything of that nature; and indeed 'tis inconceivable what should move a man to write such a palpable falsehood in his own prejudice. It may full as truly be said that his living is ten thousand a year as three hundred, and if it were three hundred a year, yet there is no such difference in the price of things there and here, as will justify your computation. I have, sir, formerly laid before you the true state of our affairs, have told you that the living was always let for eight score pound[s] a year;[18] that taxes, poor assessments, out-rents, tenths, procurations, synodals, etc.[19] took up near thirty pounds yearly of that moiety,[20] so that there needs no great skill in arithmetic to compute what remains. Some things are cheaper here than at London, and some things are dearer, as all silks, most sorts of stuff, all manner of groceries, candles,[21] soap, etc., chandlers and milleners ware. And if the goodness of commodities in or near London were set against the meanness of such as are lower priced here, the matter, as I told you before, would be brought to a par, or very near it. And this the better sort here are so well apprised of, that they send to London for most of their clothes, groceries, candles, soap, etc. as the more frugal way of having their wants supplied. But to proceed with your letter to me: ". . . so that you'll need no small accession from me hereafter.["] What we shall, or shall not, need hereafter, God only knows; but at present there hardly ever was a greater coincidence of unprosperous events in one family than is now in ours. I am rarely in health; Mr. Wesley declines apace; my dear Emily, who in my present exigencies would exceedingly comfort me, is compelled to [go to] service in Lincoln, where she is a teacher in a boarding school. My second daughter, Suky, a pretty woman and worthy a better fate, when by your last unkind letters she perceived that all her hopes in you were frustrated, rashly threw herself away upon a man (if man he may be called, that is little inferior to the apostate angels in wickedness) that is not only her plague, but a constant affliction to the family.[22] Oh, sir, oh, brother, happy, thrice happy are you, happy is my sister, that buried your children in infancy! Secure from temptation, secure from guilt, secure from want or shame or loss of friends, they are safe! beyond the reach of pain or sense of misery; being gone hence, nothing can touch them further. Believe me, sir, 'tis better to mourn ten children dead than one living, and I have buried many. But here I must pause awhile.

The other children, though wanting neither industry nor capacity for business, we cannot put to any, by reason we have neither money nor friends to assist us in doing it. Nor is there a gentleman's family near us in which we can place them, unless as common servants, and that even you yourself would not think them fit for, if you saw them, so that they must stay at home while they have a home; and how long that will be—[23] Innumerable are other uneasinesses too tedious to mention. Insomuch that what with my own indisposition, my master's infirmities, the absence of my eldest, the ruin of my second daughter, and inconceivable distress of all the rest, and, to make up the complement, your most unfortunate affairs, I have enough to turn a stronger head than mine. And were it not that God supports and by his omnipotent goodness often totally suspends all sense of worldly things, I could not sustain the weight many days, perhaps hours. But even in this low ebb of fortune I am not without some lucid intervals.

Unspeakable are the blessings of privacy and leisure! when the mind emerges from the corrupt animality to which she is united and, by a flight peculiar to her nature, soars beyond the bounds of time and place in contemplation of the invisible Supreme, whom she perceives to be her only happiness, her proper centre, in whom she finds repose inexplicable, yet such as the world can neither give nor take away!

But to return. "I hope Mr. Wesley will take care of coz Charles[24] and advance more than ten pound a year . . ." Sir, I wish that were continued, but we have not heard from him these three years and know not whether he be dead or alive.[25] So that had not our eldest son lent us money to support him (much of which I doubt[26] he borrowed), we must have sent for him home, which would ha' been pity, for he is a brave scholar and is this year chosen into the Kings College at Westminster. You proceed to mention the ingratitude of your nieces, which I shall compare with one passage in a letter to my master, where, after you had been speaking of our supposed thousand a year, you are pleased to add, "I look upon the sixty pound you have paid yourself thrown away, which might have done (otherwise employed) a great deal of good. Which was your fault in deceiving me, and you are to answer for it." Here I cannot forbear to observe that 'tis incident to all men, wise or otherwise, to judge of things by their events, which cannot be right, since they make no alteration in the nature of moral actions, which take their denomination of good or evil from the intention and will and not from the understanding or event. Therefore, certainly we are to do what we think best according to the present sense of our minds upon such views as we have, and leave events to God, to whom alone it belongs to order them. Thus, sir, you are pleased to condemn yourself for what you did for [y]our nephews and nieces and for what you gave me. But you must give me leave to say, sir, that in this you are very wrong. You acted upon good principles, according to the generous sentiments of your own heart; nor was you in the least to blame, since you could not then certainly know that they would prove ungrateful, or that I was so unworthy of your favours, as in truth I am. I speak with respect to the personal merit; for in relation to your business, neither against God or you have I erred a tittle. Alas, in things of that nature, I am a person more sinned against than sinning. The right or wrong belong to you and Mr. Wesley, the suffering part belongs to me and mine. But you now think we did not want that sixty pound. Dear Brother, do you think nobody wants but he that asks an alms at your door? This calls to mind what the late Archbishop of York once said to me when my master was in Lincoln Castle, among other questions. "Tell me," says he, "Mrs. Wesley, whether you ever really wanted bread." "My lord," said I, "I will freely own to your grace, that strictly speaking, I never did want bread. But then I have had so much care to get it before 'twas eat, and to pay for it after, as has often made it very unpleasant to me. And I think to have bread on such terms is the next degree of wretchedness to having none at all." "You are certainly in the right," replied my Lord, and seemed for awhile very thoughtful.[27] Next morning he made me a handsome present, nor did he ever repent having done so. On the contrary I've reason to believe it afforded him some comfortable reflections before his exit. I am not altogether of Seneca's opinion that he which upbraids me with a benefit, cancels the obligation and that he which suspects me, gives me thereby a right to deceive him.[28] For I never will forget the pleasing ease from care you gave me near two years by that sixty pound, with part of which I clothed myself and children, and the residue paid debts as far as 'twould go. For all which I very heartily thanked almighty God and do again and again a hundred times thank you, be you pleased or angry with me for so doing. And though I have the mortification to be esteemed by you as a person of no credit, yet I can cheerfully say that I never endeavored to impose upon you in anything I ever wrote. And if I am not Christian or Stoic enough to read some passages in your letter without emotion, yet your distrust shall never make me deceive you.

You subjoin to Mr. Wesley, ". . . which was your fault in deceiving me, and you are to answer for it." This article is almost above my comprehension. Do you think, sir, he deceived you by a false representation of the circumstances of his family? This could not be, for none can conceive our condition to be what in truth it was and is. Nay, he himself does not know it. I conceal our wants from him as much as possible, lest he should be afflicted above measure and because I know that if he were made acquainted with each particular, he would hazard his health, perhaps his life, in riding to borrow money, rather than I or his children should be so distressed. For to do him justice, he hath often gone beyond his proper ability to supply us with necessaries, and several debts has he contracted to support a worthless life below his care, and that is now become insignificant and useless to the world. Therefore, he hath not deceived you; and to say the truth, among all his wants sincerity is none. I have not reason to complain of his being deceitful, but have often blamed him for speaking his mind too freely, which sometimes exposes people to the malice of ill men. For though he can't be called an honest man that speaks contrary to his thoughts, so neither is he to be called a wise man that always[29] speaks all he thinks. "He must answer for taking what you gave me." And so he may both to God and man with a very good conscience.[30] "These things are unkind, very unkind."[31] Add not misery to affliction; if you will not reach out a friendly hand to support, yet I beseech you forbear to throw water on people[32] already sinking.

But[33] I shall go on with yours[34] to me. You proceed, "When I come home (ah, would to God that might ever be), should any of your daughters want me (as I think they will not), I shall do as God enables me." I must[35] answer this with a sigh from the bottom of my heart. Sir, you know the proverb, "While the grass grows the steed starves."[36] That passage relating to Annesley[37] I've formerly replied to;

therefore shall pass it over together with some [dark] [38] hints I am not willing to understand.

"My brother has one invincible obstacle to my business, his distance from London." Sir, you may please to remember I put you in mind of this long since. "Another hindrance, I think he is too zealous for the party he fancies in the right and has unluckily to do with the opposite faction." [39] Whether those you employ are factious or not, I shall not determine, but very sure I am Mr. Wesley is not so. He is zealous in a *good cause*, [40] as every one ought to be, but the farthest from being a party man of any man in the world. [41] "Another remora [42] is these matters are out of his way." That is a remora, indeed, and ought to have been considered on both sides before he entered on your business. For I am verily persuaded that *that*, and *that* alone, [43] has been the cause of any mistakes or inadvertency he has been guilty of, and the true reason why God hath not blessed him with desired success. [And 'tis on the same account that those things we fondly hoped should have been for our wealth, has proved an occasion of stumbling.] [44] "He is apt to rest on deceitful promises." Would to heaven that neither he, nor I, nor any of our children had ever trusted to deceitful promises. But 'tis a right hand error, and I hope God will forgive us all. "He wants Mr. Eaton's thrift." This I can readily believe. "Is not fit for worldly business." This I likewise assent to. And must own I was mistaken when I did think him fit for it. My experience hath since convinced me that he is one of those whom our Saviour saith is not so wise in their generation as the children of this world. [45] And did I not know that almighty Wisdom hath views and ends in fixing the bounds of our habitation which are out of our ken, I should think it a thousand pities that a man of his brightness and rare endowments of learning and useful knowledge in relation to the church of God should be confined to an obscure corner of the country, where his talents are buried, and he is determined to a way of life for which he is not so well qualified as I could wish. And 'tis with pleasure I behold in my eldest son an aversion from accepting a small country cure; since, blessed be God, he has a fair reputation for [46] learning and piety, preaches well, and is capable of doing more good where he is. You conclude, "My wife will make my coz Emily . . ." Indeed, 'twas a very small and insignificant present to my sister; [47] but, poor girl, 'twas her whole estate, and if it had been received as kindly as 'twas meant, she would ha' been highly pleased.

I shall not detain you any longer, not so much as to apologize for the tedious length of this letter.

I should be glad if my service could be made acceptable to my sister, to whom with yourself the children tender their humblest duty. We all join in wishing ye both a happy new year and very many of them. [48].

    I am

          Sr

               Your Obligd

                  &

Epworth Jan. 20th, 1721/2   Most Obedient Servt

  My Birth Day   & Sister

                  Susanna Wesley

Notes

1. See part II of this volume.

2. See Susanna's letter to John, 12 July 1731, which Clarke excerpts, pp. 47–56.

3. For a helpful look at the basic details of his life and those of other Annesley family members, see Betty I. Young, "Sources for the Annesley Family," PWHS 45.2 (September 1985): 44–57.

4. Ibid., p. 52.

5. Line added, representing the short gap in the MS, possibly indicating the erasure of (?)Samuel's name.

6. This last phrase ("on both sides") is crossed out in the MS, perhaps by a later hand.

7. Quotation marks in MS.

8. Emphasis here and elsewhere in the letter is found in the MS.

9. A vertical line through the text—corresponding to material left out of the letter in Stevenson, beginning with the second paragraph—ends here, augmented by a horizontal line that finishes the deletion of the sentence. The next sentence is the one with which Stevenson resumes his excerpt of the letter.

10. "Him" is crossed out; "my husband" is inserted above the line.

11. Paraphrased from Ruth 1:16–17.

12. Stevenson, p. 198, sets up the preceding passage, beginning "No walls, nor locks," as a quotation of poetry but without attributing it.

13. From 2 Corinthians 6:10; quotation marks added.

14. Close paraphrase of Pascal's *Thoughts on Religion, and Other Subjects* . . . Basil Kennett, trans. (London: A. and J. Churchil, R. Sare, J. Tonson, 1704), p. 312 (chap. 29, par. 44): "The last Act of Life is always Bloody and Tragical; how pleasantly soever the Comedy may have run thro' all the rest. A little Earth, cast upon our Cold Head, for ever determines our Hopes, and our Condition." Quotation marks added.

15. The MS closes this and several other quotations with a dash. I have inserted a quotation mark.

16. Editorial insert in MS, replacing crossed-out "in Mr. Hoar's hands."

17. Preceding word crossed out.

18. Inserted here in (?)Stevenson's hand, "£ 160."

19. That is, the various taxes and fees, civil and ecclesiastical, that Samuel Wesley was required to pay.

20. That is, half.

21. Crossed out.

22. Suky, the second surviving Wesley daughter, was born about 1695 in South Ormsby. She married Richard Ellison about 1719 and bore at least four children before the marriage soured and she and Ellison separated. From this letter, things were not going well at all even early in the marriage. See Clarke, pp. 387–389; and Frank Baker, "Investigating Wesley Family Traditions," MH, 26.3 (April 1988): 162.

23. The dash in the MS would probably be supplied today by ellipses, implying a missing but easily imaginable conclusion such as "no one can tell."

24. This familiar form was often used to designate a niece or a nephew, as well as a cousin.

25. Charles, the youngest of three surviving Wesley sons, was born in 1707. After home schooling with his mother, he was sent in 1716 to Westminster School, where, as indicated here, he was supported by his elder brother Samuel, by then an under master there. The Mr. Wesley referred to in Samuel Annesley's letter may be Matthew, the rector's brother, the surgeon-apothecary. While the family might not have heard from him in three years, it is scarcely credible that they would be out of contact with Charles.

26. Suspect.

27. The incident is from the summer of 1705 when Samuel Wesley Sr. spent several months in debtors' prison. Quotation marks in this reported conversation have been added. A wavy line stretching from the end of the sentence to the right margin and continuing for the space of a word on the following line suggests that material may have been left out in this copy.

28. S. W. is probably referring to Roger L'Estrange's translation, *Seneca's Morals Abstracted: In three parts. I. Of Benefits. II. Of a Happy Life, Anger, and Clemency. III. A Miscellany of Epistles.* (London: Henry Brome, 1679). *Seneca's Morals by Way of Abstract. Of Benefits. Part I . . .* (London: Henry Broome, 1678). Though there are sections dealing with these points (e.g., chap.13, "There Are Many Cases Wherein a Man May Be Minded of a Benefit, but It Is Very Rarely to be Challeng'd, and Never to Be Upbraided," pp. 90–102; chap. 14, "How Far to Oblige, or Requite a Wicked Man," pp. 103–115; chap. 15, "A General View of the Parts, and Duties of the Benefactor," pp. 116–124; and chap. 16, "How the Receiver Ought to Behave Himself," pp. 125–137), I do not think Seneca makes them quite so baldly as S. W. indicates in her rhetorical defense of her family to her brother.

29. The Wesley College draft MS of the letter begins at this point.

30. Followed in the Wesley College draft by these crossed-out words: "But tis time to return to [above the line: "go on with"] ?[garbled word] letter to me."

31. Quotation marks in the Wesley College draft.

32. Followed in the Wesley College draft by the crossed-out "sinking apace."

33. Followed in the Wesley College draft by the crossed-out "'tis time to return to."

34. The Wesley College draft has crossed out "letter" and apparently added an "s" to "your."

35. In the Wesley College draft: "shall."

36. Quotation marks added.

37. Possibly Annesley Fromantle, son of their sister Sarah and her husband James Fromantle. Young, "Sources for the Annesley Family," p. 53, identifies him as figuring in Samuel Annesley's will.

38. Crossed out in the Wesley College draft.

39. The Wesley College MS originally had "and my business etc." inserted before "has," but S. W. crossed it out.

40. Underlined in the Wesley College MS; enlarged letters in the MA MS.

41. The Wesley College MS adds here, crossed out, "In all eager disputes he is rather like Ishmael, his hand is against every man, and every man's hand against him," a close paraphrase of Genesis 16:12.

42. Obstruction, impediment.

43. Emphasis in the Wesley College MS.

44. An asterisk ("*") in the Wesley College MS probably refers to this phrase, not otherwise visible there but included in the MA MS.

45. Paraphrased from Luke 16:8. The sentence is preceded by the crossed-out "Worldly business, for." Likewise, in the biblical paraphrase she has crossed out "his," replacing it with "their" immediately preceding "generation," and crossed out "life" at the end of the sentence, replacing it with "world."

46. The Wesley College MS adds "for" in place of the crossed-out "of."

47. That is, her sister-in-law, Samuel's wife, also named Susanna. See Young, "Sources for the Annesley Family," p. 52. S. W. had originally written "her" but crossed it out and replaced it with "my sister." "Coz." in this instance can also mean "niece."

48. In the Wesley College MS, the sentence originally began with the words "if my," which were subsequently crossed out.

EIGHT

Advice to an Oxford Man

Not surprisingly, more letters survive addressed to S.W.'s son John than to any other correspondent. His success as evangelist and organizer of "the people called Methodists" ensured that his literary remains would be privileged, closely followed by those of his family. Beyond this obvious observation, however, lie several other explanations for the large quantity of Susanna's correspondence with John. First, like his brother Samuel, he adopted the habit of transcribing incoming letters into a notebook, giving us access to many that have otherwise disappeared.[1] Second was his editorial ability, coupled with the insight that the preparation and distribution of appropriate literature would enhance Methodism's success. In his published *Journal* and in his *Arminian Magazine* he was as likely to include letters from his mother as extracts from the lives of saints or any other improving literature. Third, though the point is debatable, there is some indication that Susanna meant to pay special attention to the education of this son. Without denying the pedagogical energy she invested in her other children, her keen attention to John's formation does seem borne out in the correspondence that follows.[2]

The first batch of letters to John focuses on the end of his undergraduate career and his determination to pursue ordination. As in most of her correspondence, two types of discourse vie for attention here. Given pride of place—usually in beginning and concluding paragraphs—are family matters, including but not limited to the news from Epworth and Susanna's concerns for John. In terms of quantity, though, the prime topic is theology or "practical divinity," as Susanna would prefer it to be known and taught.

Money or the lack thereof is a continuing theme of family conversation. The issue of an overdue "college loan" is raised in the letter of 19 August 1724; further hopeful talk of financial salvation through Samuel Annesley Jr., the India merchant, crops up there and in the succeeding letter, that of 10 September. She keeps track of family travel: her own rare trip to Oxford and London (in the letter of 24 November) and young Charles's difficult journey to Epworth with his brother and bossy sister-in-law (described in the 23 February 1724/25, letter). She worries over various personal tensions, among them her distrust of a suitor for her daughter Emily (in that same letter and those on 8 and 21 June 1725) and the barest hint of the melodramatic problem that was about to develop in the love life of Hetty, found in the cryptic postscript to the 23 February letter. Her own health occasionally intrudes (10 September, 23 February, and 21 June) but only briefly.

Her theological concerns begin very practically with her urging of John to seek ordination (10 September, reinforced 23 February) and continue with her helping him to work through various scruples as he prepares for that step. As she states in an oft-quoted passage from the 23 February letter, her concern (and she hopes it is her son's, as well) is with "practical divinity" rather than with the "critical studies" that her husband, the rector, favored. In that vein she knowledgeably discusses Thomas à Kempis (8 June), Jeremy Taylor (21 June and 18 August), and the Anglican church's Article on Predestination (18 August). In each case she is not afraid to take issue with theological authority; nor does she flinch from contradicting her pupil, as her straightforward judgment in the 18 August letter ("you are somewhat mistaken in your notion of faith") amply illustrates.

In one sense, the family talk includes the theologizing: her love for Jacky (as previously for Sammy and in other instances for Suky, Emily, Charles, and the rest) drives her to participate in his spiritual formation, even as he studies at Christ Church College. However, her theological pedagogy is qualitatively, as well as quantitatively, deserving of regard in its own right. The dialogues she pursues with her son, the about-to-be ordained Oxford graduate, push the boundaries of epistolary convention and point to the treatises she was fully capable of (see part III of this volume).

Readers interested in seeing her son's side of the correspondence may turn to Frank Baker's edition of John Wesley's letters, vol. I,[3] which also includes most (but not all) of the Susanna Wesley material brought together here. For convenience, citations from Baker's edition (FB) are included at the heading of each letter to John.

᭡

To John Wesley
19 August 1724
LB, pp. 24–25; FB, 1:148.

Wroot, August 19, 1724

Dear Jacky

I am somewhat uneasy, because I've not heard from you so long and think you don't do well to stand upon points and write only letter for letter, since I decline apace, and 'tis more trouble for me to write one than for you to write ten times. Therefore let me hear from you oftener, and inform me of the state of your health, how you go on, and whether you are easier than formerly, and have any reasonable hopes of being out of debt.

We have dismal weather, and can neither get hay, corn, nor firing,[4] which makes us apprehensive of great want. I am most concerned for that good, generous man that lent you £10 and am ashamed to beg a month or two longer, since he was so kind to grant us so much time already. Give my service to him and thanks, however.

We were strangely amused with your uncle's coming from India, but I suppose those fancies are laid aside. I wish there had been anything in it; then perhaps it had been in my power to have provided for you. For if all these things fail, I hope God will not forsake us: we have still his good providence to depend on, which has a thousand expedients to relieve us beyond our view . . .

Dear Jacky, be not discouraged; do your duty, keep close to your studies, and hope for better days; perhaps, notwithstanding all, we shall pick up a few crumbs for you before the end of the year.

Dear son, I beseech Almighty God to bless thee!

Susanna Wesley

To John Wesley
10 September 1724
LB, pp. 25–26; FB, 1:149.

Wroot, September 10 [1724]

Dear Jacky,

'Tis above a week since I received your kind letter, which has greatly revived my spirits; and though I should not have an ill opinion of you though there had really been some neglect on your side, yet I find I am much better pleased to think you do not grudge the pains of writing.

I'm nothing glad that Mr. ———— has paid himself out of your exhibition . . . Though I cannot hope, I do not despair of my brother's coming, or at least remembering me where he is; for I am persuaded God will yet order things so that either I or mine shall sometime be the better for that man; though most of my family are of another opinion . . .

The smallpox has been very mortal at Epworth most of this summer. Our family have all had it besides me, and I hope God will preserve me from it, because your father can't yet well [spare money to bury me] . . .[5]

I heartily wish you were in Orders and could come and serve one of his cures. Then I should see you often and could be more helpful to you than 'tis possible to be at this distance . . .

Dear Jacky, I beseech Almighty God to bless thee!

To John Wesley
24 November 1724
LB, pp. 26–27; FB, 1:152–153.

Wroot, November 24 [1724]

Dear Jacky,

I have now three of your letters before me unanswered and take it very kindly that you would write so often though you heard not from me. Indeed I'm afraid of being chargeable, or I should miss few posts, it being exceeding pleasant to me in this solitude to read your letters, but I believe they would be pleasing anywhere.

Your disappointment in not seeing us at Oxford[6] was not of such ill consequence as mine in not meeting my brother at London. Naught[7] but your wonderful curiosities might excite a person of greater faith than mine to travel to your museum on purpose to visit them. 'Tis almost pity that somebody does not cut the weson[8] of that keeper with Adam's sword, to cure his lying so enormously . . .

I wish you would save all the money you can conveniently spare, not to spend on a visit, but for a wiser and better purpose: to pay debts and make yourself easy. I am not without hope of meeting you next summer, if it please God to prolong my worthless life. If then you will be willing and have time allowed you to accompany me to Wroot, I'll bear your charges, and do other ways for you, as God shall enable me . . .

The story of Mr. B[arnesley] has afforded me many curious speculations.[9] I do not doubt the fact, but cannot conceive for what reason those apparitions should come unto us. If they were permitted to speak to us, and we had strength to bear such conversation; if they had commission to inform us of anything relating to their invisible world that would be of any use to us in this; if they could instruct us how to avoid any danger or put us in a way of being wiser and better, there would be sense in it. But to appear for no end that we know of unless to fright people almost out of their wits, seems altogether unaccountable.

. . . I hope at your leisure you will oblige me with some more verses, on any, but rather on a religious subject . . .

Dear Jacky, I beseech almighty God to bless thee!

To John Wesley
5 January 1725
LB, p. 27; FB, 1:157.

Jan. 5, [17]25

Dear Jacky,

(About sending money)[10]

Your brother talks of coming hither at Whitsuntide; perhaps between this and that something may occur, or it may happen that you may come with him . . .
God bless thee!
I wish you a happy new year.

To John Wesley
23 February 1724/25
Wesley's Chapel, London (holograph);
LB, pp. 23–24; FB, 1:159–160.

Wroot Feb: 23, 1724[/5]

Dear Jacky,

I have received two letters from you, neither of which I've answered. Your father kept the first, it being included in one to him, and since the receipt of the last I have been very ill and confined to my chamber, but I thank God I'm much better.

Your last brings surprising news indeed about the pope, whom I doubt[11] the conclave will not permit long to live. His justice to the young gentleman in restoring him the estate his bigoted father gave from him to the monks is really very commendable, but his allowing the scriptures to the laity and declaring against his own infallibility are actions truly Christian. In the latter he has given a mortal wound to the infallibility of that see, and whether he were in the right or whether he was in the wrong, the matter is the same, for both horns of the dilemma strikes them. They must resign their more profitable than honest pretence to infallibility. The king of Prussia talks often, but is not to be depended on for action. Emly has answered for herself. 'Tis strange Mr. Leybourne[12] should send any service to me, but I accept the compliment, and without one, wish him health and happiness.[13]

The alteration of your temper has occasioned me much speculation. I, who am apt to be sanguine, hope it may proceed from the operations of God's Holy Spirit, that by taking off your relish of sensual enjoyments, would prepare and dispose your mind for a more serious and close application to things of a more sublime and spiritual nature. If it be so, happy are you if you cherish those dispositions and now in good earnest resolve to make religion the business of your life. For, after all, that is the one thing that strictly speaking is necessary; all things beside are comparatively little to the purposes of life. Dear Jacky, I heartily wish you would now enter upon a serious examination of yourself, that you may know whether you have a reasonable hope of salvation by Jesus Christ, that is, whether you are in a state of faith and repentance or not, which you know are the conditions of the gospel covenant on our part. If you are, the satisfaction of knowing it will abundantly reward your pains; if not, you'll find a more reasonable occasion for tears than can be met with in a tragedy. This matter deserves great consideration in all, but especially those designed for the clergy ought above all things make their calling and election sure, lest after they have preached to others, they themselves should be cast away.

Now I mention this, it calls to mind your letter to your father about taking orders. I was much pleased with it and liked the proposal well, but 'tis an unhappiness almost peculiar to our family that your father and I seldom think alike. I approve the disposition of your mind. I think this season of Lent the most proper for your preparation for orders, and I think the sooner you are a deacon the better, because it may be an inducement to greater application in the study of practical divinity, which of all other I humbly conceive is the best study for candidates for orders. Mr. Wesley differs from me, would engage you, I believe, in critical learning (though I'm not sure) which, though of use accidentally and by way of concomitance, yet is in no wise preferable to the other. Therefore I earnestly pray God to avert that great evil from you of engaging in trifling studies to the neglect of such as are absolutely necessary. I dare advise nothing. God Almighty direct and bless you.

Adieu,

I have much to say but cannot write more at present. I even long to see you.

We hear nothing of H., which gives us some uneasiness. We have all writ, but can get no answer. I wish all be well.[14]

To John Wesley
8 June 1725
LB, pp. 28–32; collated with AM 1:33–36 (1778), following FB, 1:164–167. The first and last paragraphs, containing family references, appear only in LB. The intervening paragraphs, more theological in nature, were edited by Wesley for AM in a slightly expanded manner. Frank Baker believes that he was working from the now missing holograph and that the expansions sometimes represent Susanna's original words (not fully transcribed in LB) and sometimes John's own editorial changes. See FB, 1:166–167.

Wroot, June 8, 1725

Dear Jacky,

Whatever satisfaction you may think your brother Charles would find in his journey, I believe it did in no wise answer his expectation. They were at Mr. Berry's before they came hither, where he was much mortified with your sister Wesley's ungenteel[15] usage of him, and for want of liberty [for eating and drinking].[16] The case was somewhat mended here, for I would so far overrule in my own house as to let him [fill his belly],[17] but we were none of us very easy. She resented my taking notice of him, and I her behaviour on the other side. To say truth, I never heard her once speak well of him all the time they were here; nor have I used the meanest servant I ever had in my life with less civility than she observed towards him. Not to mention the rest of the children, who were very unnecessarily provoked, in doing which she was very wrong.[18]

I've Kempis[19] by me, but have not read him lately, and therefore cannot recollect the passages you mention. But believing you do him justice, I do very positively aver that he is extremely in the wrong in that impious, I was about to say blasphemous, suggestion, that God by an irreversible decree hath determined any man to be miserable in this world. His intentions, as himself, are holy, just, and good, and all the miseries incident to men here or hereafter proceed from themselves. The case stands thus. This life is a state of probation, wherein eternal happiness or misery are proposed to our choice, the one as the reward of a virtuous, the other as a consequence of a vicious life. Man is a compound being, a strange mixture of spirit and matter; or rather, a creature wherein those opposite principles are united without mixture, yet each principle after an incomprehensible manner subject to the influences of the other. The true happiness of man under this consideration consists in a due subordination of the inferior to the superior powers, of the animal to the rational nature, and of both to God. This was his original righteousness and happiness that was lost in Adam; and to restore man to this happiness by the recovery of his original righteousness was certainly God's design in admitting him to his state of trial in the world and of our redemption by Jesus Christ! And surely this was a design truly worthy of God! And the greatest instance of mercy that even Omnipotent Goodness could exhibit to us!

As the happiness of man consists in a due subordination of the inferior to the superior powers, so the inversion of this order is the true source of human misery. There is in us all a natural propension towards the body and the world: the beauty, ease, and pleasures of the world strongly charm us; the wealth and honours of the world allure us; and all, under the manage of a subtle, malicious adversary, give a prodigious force to present things. And if the animal life once get the ascendant of our reason, it utterly deprives us of our moral liberty and by consequence makes us wretched.

Therefore for any man to endeavour after happiness in gratifying all his bodily appetites in opposition to his reason is the greatest folly imaginable, because he seeks it where God has not designed he shall ever find [it].[20] Yet this is the case of most men. They live as mere animals, wholly given up to the interests and pleasures of the body; and all the use of their understanding is to 'make provision for their flesh, to fulfil the lusts thereof',[21] without the least regard to future happiness or misery. 'Tis true our eternal state lies under a vast disadvantage, in that it is future and invisible. And it requires great attention and application of mind, frequent retirement, and intense thinking to excite our affections and beget such an habitual sense of it as is requisite to enable [us][22] to walk steadily in the paths of virtue, in opposition to our own corrupt nature and the vicious customs and maxims of the world. Our blessed Lord, who came from heaven to save us from our sins, as well as the punishment of them, as knowing we could not be happy in either world without holiness, did not intend by commanding us to "take up the cross"[23] that we should bid adieu to all joy and satisfaction [indefinitely],[24] but he opens and extends our views beyond time to eternity. He directs us where to place our joy, that it may be durable as our being;[25] not in gratifying but retrenching our sensual appetites; not in obeying but correcting our irregular passions,[26] bringing every appetite of the body and power of the soul under subjection to his laws, [if we would follow him to heaven].[27] And because he knew we could not do this without great contradiction to our corrupt animality, therefore he enjoins us to take up this cross [and to fight under his banner against the flesh, the world, and the devil].[28] And when by the divine grace[29] we are so far conquerors as that we never willingly offend, but still press after greater degrees of Christian perfection [sincerely endeavouring to plant each virtue in our minds that may through Christ render us pleasing to God];[30] we shall then experience the truth of Solomon's assertion, "The ways of virtue are ways of pleasantness, and all her paths are peace."[31]

I take Kempis to have been an honest, weak man, that had more zeal than knowledge, by his condemning all mirth or pleasure as sinful [or useless, in opposition to so many direct and plain texts of Scripture].[32] Would you judge of the lawfulness of unlawfulness of pleasure, [of the innocence of malignity of actions? Take this rule.][33] Whatever weakens your reason, impairs the tenderness of your conscience, obscures your sense of God, or takes off your relish of spiritual things; in short, whatever increases the strength and authority of your body over your mind; that thing is sin to you, however innocent it may be in itself. And so on the contrary.

'Tis stupid to say nothing is an affliction to a good man. "That's an affliction that God makes an affliction,"[34] either to good or bad. Nor do I understand how any man can thank God for present misery. Yet do I very well know what it is to rejoice in the midst of deep affliction: not in the affliction itself, for then it must necessarily cease to be one. But in this [we may rejoice],[35] that we are in the hand of a God who never did, nor ever can exert his power in an act of oppression, injustice, or cruelty! In the power of that superior wisdom which disposes all events and has promised that all things shall work together for good (for the spiritual and eternal good) of those that love him![36] We may rejoice in hope that Almighty Goodness "will not suffer us to be tempted above what we are able, but will with the temptation make a way to escape, [that we may be able to bear it]."[37] In a word, we may and ought to rejoice that God has assured us he will never leave or forsake us; but if we continue faithful to him, he[38] will take care to conduct us safely through all the changes and chances of this mortal life[39] to those blessed regions of joy and immortality where sorrow and sin can never enter!

Your brother has brought us a heavy reckoning for you and Charles. God be merciful to us all. Prithee, Jacky, what reception did Mr. Leybourne[40] give your sister Wesley? Or did you ever affront her? I have somewhat against that same man, but I hope he is good in the main, and I think humanity and good breeding are not among his wants.

Dear Jacky, I earnestly beseech Almighty God to bless you. Adieu.

To John Wesley
21 July 1725
MA; LB, pp. 32–34; FB, 1:172–173.

Wroot, July 21, [1725]

Dear Jacky

Whether Charles have given occasion for her contemptuous usage or no I can't determine; but his time of bondage is now near expired, and if it be n't his own fault, his future life may be easier . . . 'Tis well your sister has ever been civil to you, and would have you also so to her. But never put it in the power of that woman to hurt you; stand upon your guard and converse with caution; and I wish Mr. L[eybourne] would take the same advice. He has in my opinion done much to oblige those that have not the most grateful sense of his kindness.

Though I have a great deal of unpleasant business, am infirm and but slow of understanding, yet 'tis a pleasure to me to correspond with you upon religious subjects; and if it may be of the least advantage to you, I shall greatly rejoice. May what is sown in weakness be raised in power![41]

I know little or nothing of Dr. Taylor's Holy Living and Dying,[42] having not seen it above twenty years; but I think 'tis generally well esteemed, therefore can't judge of the rules you suppose impracticable. Of humility I'll tell you my thoughts as briefly as I can.

What he calls humility is not the virtue itself, but the accidental effects of it, which may in some instances, and must in others, be separated from it.

Humility is the mean between pride or an overvaluing ourselves on one side and a base abject temper on the other. It consists in an habitual disposition to think meanly of ourselves, which disposition is wrought in us by a true knowledge of God, his supreme, essential glory, his absolute, immense perfection of being! A just sense of our dependence on and past offences against him, together with a consciousness of our present infirmities and frailty.

In proportion to the sense we have of God's infinite majesty and glory, and our own vileness and unworthiness, this disposition will be stronger or weaker. And those who are arrived to a great degree of Christian perfection, that know and are assured by reason and experience[43] that there is none good but God, will be sure to hold him in the highest estimation, and are generally observed to be the most humble and mortified of men. Such persons as these make the glory of God the principal aim in all their actions; and to please him is to them more eligible[44] than to enjoy the esteem of the whole universe.

They will be very well content "to be slighted or undervalued,"[45] provided their conscience do not reproach them, and the honour of God be unconcerned in the case. But where it is concerned, none are more wary in their outward deportment, lest they give occasion of scandal to the profane, or of stumbling to the weak. None are more careful to observe, "Whatsoever things are lovely, whatsoever things are of good report,"[46] and if through surprise or inadvertency they have said or done amiss, such slips commonly make them more watchful and humble ever after.

As we should not covet to be little esteemed, because a fair reputation is of excellent service in promoting the glory of God, so neither should we desire the praise of our good actions to terminate in ourselves; for of a right it belongs to him of whose grace it is that we either will or do according to his good pleasure.[47]

If we are in disgrace,[48] either we deserve it or we do not. If we do, his caution is good; if not, he is wrong; for we certainly may, and I believe should be pleased with consciousness of our innocence.

I will not say we must judge of ourselves as he directs, but believe there are some who are much inclined to think themselves not only the worst in a particular company, but worse than any in the world. For being strongly pressed on by thirst after universal righteousness, they behold their own deficiencies with great severity: every mote in their own eye appears a beam, while every beam in their brother's eye seems to them as a mote.[49]

"Weakness, deformity, and imperfection"[50] of body are not moral evils, and may accidentally become good to us.[51] Yet surely they are not to be desired, for strength and comeliness are valuable blessings, may be of great use, and ought to be enjoyed with thankfulness. If they prove incentives to pride, 'tis our own fault: a humble man will improve all those advantages for God's service, and a . . .[52]

To John Wesley
18 August 1725
LB, pp. 39–43. The beginning of the letter is in four pages of LB, missing by the time Wesley edited it for AM, pp. 36–38, concluding portions only; misdated as 18 July 1725; FB 1:178–180.

(. . .)but still insist on that single point in Dr. Taylor, of "thinking ourselves the worst in every company";[53] though the necessity of thinking so is not inferred by my definition. But this I perceive much affects you, and you can't well digest it. Therefore you employ your wit in making distinctions and formal arguments; which arguments I shall reply to after I've observed that we differ in our notions of the virtue itself.[54] You will have it consist in thinking meanly of ourselves, I in an habitual disposition to think meanly of ourselves; which I take to be more comprehensive, because it extends to all the cases when that virtue can be exercised, either in relation to God, ourselves, or our neighbour, and renders the distinction of absolute and comparative perfectly needless.[55]

We may in many instances think very meanly of ourselves without being humble. Nay, sometimes our very pride will lead us to condemn ourselves, as when we have said or done anything which lessens that esteem of men we earnestly covet. As to what you call absolute humility with respect to God, what greater matter is there in that. . . . Had we no more than a mere speculative knowledge of that Awful Being and only considered him as the Creator and Sovereign Lord of the universe, yet since that first notion of him implies that he is a God of absolute and infinite perfection and glory, we can't contemplate that glory or conceive him present without the most exquisite diminution of ourselves before him!

The other part of your definition I can't approve, because I think all those comparisons are rather the effects of pride than humility.

The truth is the proper object of the understanding, and all truths, as such, agree in one common excellence; yet there are some truths which are comparatively of so small value, because of little or no use, that 'tis no matter whether ever we know them or not. Nay, in some instances 'tis better never to know them. Among those I rank the right answer to that question, whether our neighbour or we be worse. Of what importance can this enquiry be to us? Comparisons in this case are very odious or do most certainly proceed from some bad principle in those that make them. So far should we be from reasoning upon the case, that we must not permit ourselves to entertain such thoughts, but if they ever intrude, should reject them with abhorrence.

Suppose then in some cases the truth of that proposition "my neighbour is worse than me"[56] . . . be ever so evident, yet what does it avail? Since two persons in different respects may be both better and worse than each other. As in your own instance. One who in company with a free-thinker or other person signally debauched in faith and practice (we must suppose he is debauched in neither) can't avoid knowing himself to be the better of the two. He may be so in appearance; but if he trust in his own righteousness, and value himself upon it, he may appear more vile and contemptible in the sight of God than the other, merely on account of his self-idolizing pride. Though the Pharisee might speak very truly with respect to many of his neighbours when he said, "I am not as other men are," [57] and probably his outward behaviour was more regular and decent than the poor publican's had been, whom perhaps he despised because he knew he had been a scandalous offender; yet we find the humility of the publican . . . rendered him acceptable to his Maker, while the Pharisee returned unjustified.

If we are not strictly obliged to think ourselves the worst in every company, I am perfectly sure that a man sincerely humble will be afraid of thinking himself the best in any, though it should be his lot (for it can never be his choice) to fall into the company of notorious sinners. "Who makes them to differ?" or "What hast thou that thou hast not received?" [58] is sufficient, if well adverted to, to humble us, and silence all aspiring thoughts and self-applauses; and may instruct us to ascribe our preservation from enormous offences to the sovereign grace of God and not to our own natural purity or strength.

There's nothing plainer than that a free-thinker as a free-thinker, an atheist as an atheist, is worse in that respect than a believer as a believer. But if that believer's practice does not correspond with his faith . . . he is worse than an infidel . . .

You are somewhat mistaken in your notion of faith. All faith is an assent, but all assent is not faith. Some truths are self-evident, and we assent to them because they are so. Others, after a regular and formal process of reason, by way of deduction from some self-evident principle, gain our assent; and this is not properly faith but science. Some again we assent to, not because they are self-evident, or because we have attained the knowledge of them in a regular method by a train of arguments, but because they have been revealed to us, either by God or man, and these are the proper objects of faith.

The true measure of faith is the authority of the revealer, the weight of which always holds proportion with our conviction of his ability and integrity. Divine faith is an assent to whatever God has revealed to us, because he has revealed it. And this is that virtue of faith which is one of the two conditions of our salvation by Jesus Christ . . . But this matter is so fully and accurately explained by Bishop Pearson (under "I believe") that I shall say no more of it . . . . [59]

I have often wondered that men should be so vain, to amuse themselves with searching into the decrees of God, which no human wit can fathom; and do not rather employ their time and powers in working out their salvation, [60] and making their own calling and election sure. [61] Such studies tend more to confound than inform the understanding, and young people had better let them alone. But since I find you've some scruples concerning our Articles of Predestination, [62] I'll tell you my thoughts of the matter, and if they satisfy not, you may desire your father's direction, who is surely better qualified for a casuist than me.

The doctrine of predestination, as maintained by the rigid Calvinists, is very shocking and ought utterly to be abhorred, because it directly charges the most holy God with being the author of sin. And I think you reason very well and justly against it. For 'tis certainly inconsistent with the justice and goodness of God to lay any man under either a physical or moral necessity of committing sin and then punish him for doing it. "Far be this from thee, O Lord . . . Shall not the Judge of all the earth do right?" [63]

I do firmly believe that God from eternity hath elected some to everlasting life. But then I humbly conceive that this election is founded on his foreknowledge, according to that in the 8th of Romans: "Whom he did foreknow, he also did predestinate, to be conformed to the image of his Son . . . Moreover, whom he did predestinate, them he also called . . . [64] and whom he called, them he also justified, and whom he justified, them he also glorified." [65]

Whom in his eternal prescience God saw would make a right use of their powers and accept of offered mercy, . . . he did predestinate, adopt for his children, his peculiar treasure. And that they might be conformed to the image of his Son, he called them to himself, by his external Word, the preaching of the gospel, and internally by his Holy Spirit. Which call they obeying by faith and repentance, he justifies them, absolves them from the guilt of all their sins, and acknowledges them as just persons, through the merits and mediation of Jesus Christ. And having thus justified, he receives them to glory—to heaven.

This is the sum of what I believe concerning predestination, which I think is agreeable to the analogy of faith, since it neither [66] derogates from God's free grace nor impairs the liberty of man. Nor can it with more reason be supposed that the prescience of God is the cause that so many finally perish, than that our knowing the sun will rise tomorrow is the cause of its rise.

I am greatly troubled at your increasing debts. [67] Your brother writes for your father to get you sixty pounds before you stand for the fellowship . . . Alas!

I shall not cease to pray for you, that God would sanctify all conditions and deliver you out of present distress.

Jacky, may God Almighty bless thee!

Notes

1. John Wesley kept his letter book by using abbreviations and a sort of primitive shorthand, which have been expanded without further notice. For example, from comparisons of the letter book and existing holographs, we know that "D. J." at the beginning of a letter should be read "Dear Jacky." Similarly (and obviously), "S. W." at the end may be expanded to "Susanna Wesley" and "W" just before the date indicates that the letter was written at Wroot, the small neighboring parish that Samuel Wesley had recently acquired and where the family occasionally lived. Wesley seems to use dashes to indicate material in the original that he has not felt necessary to copy. To indicate these occasions in this volume, I have used ellipses (. . .).

2. See the entry in her Devotional Journal, dated 17 May 1711, in part II of this volume, in which she vows to "be more particularly careful of the soul of this child that thou hast so mercifully provided for, than ever I have been, that I may do my endeavours to instil into his mind the disciplines of thy true religion and virtue." See Henry D. Rack, *Reasonable Enthusiast: John Wesley and the Rise of Methodism* (Philadelphia: Trinity Press International, 1989), p. 57, for a discussion of the issue.

3. *Letters I: 1721–1739* in Frank Baker, ed., *The Works of John Wesley*, vol. 25 (Oxford: Clarendon Press, 1980); hereafter FB.

4. That is, fuel for a fire.

5. Bracketed material in cipher, decoded from Wesley's private shorthand by Prof. Richard Heitzenrater, in FB 1:149.

6. In LB: "Oxon."

7. The MS reads "not."

8. Throat.

9. John Wesley's letter of November 1 had described Barnsley, an Oxford undergraduate, who saw a frightening apparition at the exact time, he later found out, that his mother had died in Dublin. The Wesley household's own experience of a poltergeist in 1716/17 was obviously still in the minds of the two correspondents.

10. Occasionally, Wesley uses a phrase in parentheses to indicate a section of a letter he has not transcribed.

11. Suspect.

12. Robert Leybourne (c. 1694–1759), friend of Samuel Wesley Jr. and at the time fellow of Brasenose College, Oxford, had been mentioned as a match for Emily Wesley. Susanna and Samuel Jr. prevented it from happening. See FB 1:159, n. 4, and subsequent appearances of his name in later Susanna letters. Here she spells the name without the final "e".

13. John Wesley summarizes this paragraph in his letter book: "Of news, the pope, the King of Prussia, and of Mr. L."

14. These last lines (from "We hear nothing of H") are not found in the body of the Wesley Chapel holograph but unaccountably appear in LB. The reference is probably to Hetty, who was then in service and involved in a relationship that would lead to much anguish in the family. Susanna expressed her concerns more clearly as the story developed. See her letter to John, October 12, 1726.

15. In LB: "ungentile," that is, uncourteous, impolite, unobliging.

16. These words in cipher, translated in FB, 1:164.

17. Again in cipher.

18. Charles Wesley had been traveling with his elder brother Samuel and Samuel's wife, Ursula. It was natural for Charles to be journeying with them, as he was then attending the Westminster School in London, where Samuel taught. Before visiting Wroot, they had stayed briefly with Ursula's father, the Rev. John Berry, vicar of Watton, Norfolk.

19. Thomas à Kempis, *The Christian's Pattern; or a Divine Treatise of the Imitation of Christ* (London: John Williams, 1677). In contrast to the implication in FB, 1:162, n. 7, it was this edition, rather than the later translation of George Stanhope, *The Christian's Pattern: Or, a Treatise of the Imitation of Jesus Christ. . . . To Which Are Added, Meditations and Prayers, for Sick Persons* (London: Gillyflower et al., 1698), that John Wesley later excerpted for his *Christian Library* in 1735. The material he was describing to his mother in his letter of 28 May 1725, is possibly bk. 1, chap. 22, titled in the Stanhope translation "The Miserable Condition of Man Considered," p. 52. One of Stanhope's phrases may have stuck in Wesley's craw: "Since therefore so ordained it is, that all must suffer and be miserable. . . ." Significantly, the earlier anonymous translation Wesley followed in his abridgement skips over this pessimistic material, relieving him of the necessity of deleting it in his 1735 publication. See *The Christians Pattern . . .* " (London: John Clark, 1659), p. 59, another edition of the translation (1677) Wesley refers to in the Preface of his 1735 edition, p. iii, n., and p. xxiv. Thomas à Kempis (1380–1471), a member of the Canons Regular near Zwolle in Holland, wrote with a devotional spirit that has attracted readers on both sides of the Reformation divide ever since his lifetime.

20. Not in LB, but supplied in AM.

21. Romans 13:14, paraphrased. LB has a beginning, but not a concluding quotation mark.

22. Supplied in AM.

23. Mark 10:21 and so on. Again, LB supplies a beginning but not a concluding quotation mark.

24. In AM only.

25. AM substitutes for this clause "how to seek satisfaction durable as our being."

26. In AM: "which is not to be found in gratifying, but retrenching our sensual appetites; not in obeying the dictates of our irregular passions, but in correcting their exorbitancy."

27. In AM only. LB does not indicate any omitted material.

28. In AM only; no ellipses in LB. For "the flesh, the world and the devil," see BCP, Litany.

29. In AM: "by the Grace of God's Holy Spirit."

30. In AM only; LB does not indicate an omission.

31. Proverbs 3:17, paraphrased in both LB and AM. The AV reads, "*Her* ways are ways of pleasantness" (my emphasis). It is Wisdom, not Virtue, that the writer of Proverbs is personifying.

32. In AM only; LB does in this case show a dash, indicating missing material.

33. In AM only; LB indicates material missing.

34. Aphorism attributed to Samuel Annesley in S.W.'s later letter to Charles Wesley, 29 November 1739, on the occasion of Samuel Jr.'s death. Quotation marks added.

35. In AM only; no ellipses in LB.

36. Loose paraphrase of Romans 8:28.

37. Close paraphrase of 1 Corinthians 10:13; my quotation marks. The last phrase is missing in LB but indicated by a dash; AM includes it.

38. Supplied in AM.

39. In AM; LB reads, "In a word, we may and ought to rejoice that we are assured he will never forsake us, but if we continue faithful to him will conduct us safely through this mortal life." FB, 1:166, n. 5, believes Wesley is reproducing the holograph in the longer AM version and that LB represents a summary.

40. See S. W. to John, 23 February 1724/25. Susanna was interested in Samuel and Ursula's visit at Oxford with Leybourne, a possible match for her daughter Emily. John reported details in his letter of 18 June 1725. See FB, 1:167–168.

41. Paraphrasing 1 Corinthians 15:43.

42. Jeremy Taylor (1613–1667), bishop of Down and Connor. John Wesley was reading the two books—first published in 1650 and 1651, respectively, but by the late seventeenth century often bound together—*The Rule and Exercises of Holy Living* . . . and *The Rule and Exercises of Holy Dying* . . . , 15th ed. (London: Luke Meredith, 1690). Wesley's letter to his mother, 18 June 1725 (FB, 1:168–169), raises the issue of whether Taylor's rules are not too legalistic and impractical, quoting several passages. Among these are the ones on humility (*Rules*, chap. 2, sect. 4) that S. W. comments on in the rest of this letter, as well as in her letter of 18 August.

43. Note the juxtaposition within two short clauses of several themes that were later to become prominent in Wesleyan theology: perfection, assurance, reason, and experience.

44. That is, desirable, suitable.

45. My quotation marks; this is Wesley's paraphrase (FB, 1:168) of Taylor's rule (*Rules*, p. 85) which begins, "Love to be concealed, and little esteemed: be content to want praise, never being troubled when thou art slighted or undervalued."

46. Philippians 4:8; beginning quotation mark in LB.

47. Paraphrase of Philippians 2:13.

48. Responding to Wesley's paraphrase: "Please not thyself when disgraced by supposing thou didst deserve praise, though they understood thee not, or enviously detracted from thee" (FB, 1:169). Cf. Taylor, *Rules*, pp. 86–87: "Make no suppletories to thy self, when thou art disgraced or slighted, by pleasing thy self with supposing thou didst deserve praise, though they understood thee not, or enviously detracted from thee."

49. See Matthew 7:4–5 and Luke 6:41–42.

50. Quoting Wesley's close paraphrase of Taylor; quotation marks added (FB, 1:169):

"Give God thanks for every weakness, deformity, or imperfection, and accept it as a favour and grace, an instrument to resist pride." Wesley has shortened the end of the original, which reads, "as a favour and grace of God, and an instrument to resist pride and nurse humility" (Taylor, *Rules*, p. 88).

51. In editing Wesley's letter to his mother on 18 June 1725, Baker (FB 1:169, m. 3) found S. W.'s written annotation added to the original: "Weakness, deformity, or imperfection of body are not evil in themselves, but accidentally become good or evil according as they affect us and make us good or bad."

52. The remainder of the letter, part of four pages torn from LB, is missing. See FB, 1:173, note on source. It probably dealt with the remainder of Wesley's other questions on Taylor, namely, the issue of repentance, raised in *Rules*, pp. 269–280.

53. *Rule of Holy Living*, p. 87; my quotation marks. Taylor's exact wording: "Never compare thy self with others, unless it be to advance them and to depress thy self. To which purpose we must be sure in some sense or other to think our selves the worst in every company where we come."

54. That is, humility; see the discussion in her previous letter to John, 21 July 1725.

55. In LB: "pfectl Us needl," possibly construed as "perfectly useless and needless."

56. Quotation marks added.

57. Luke 18:10. Beginning quotation mark in LB.

58. Quotation marks added.

59. John Pearson, *An Exposition of the Creed*, 6th ed., rev. (London: J. Williams, 1692). S. W. is referring to the opening section ("Article I. I believe in God the Father Almighty, Maker of Heaven and Earth"), pp. 1–15. See especially p. 12: "To *believe* therefore as the word stands in the Front of the CREED . . . is to assent to the whole and every part of it, as to a certain and infallible truth revealed by God, (who by reason of his infinite knowledge cannot be deceived, and by reason of his transcendent holiness cannot deceive) and delivered unto us in the Writings of the blessed Apostles and Prophets immediately inspired, moved and acted by God." S. W. knew the work from a much earlier reading. See her letter to Samuel Jr., 27 November 1707, where she quotes directly from this section, and note her use of it in "The Apostles Creed explicated in a letter to her daughter Susanna," in Part III of this volume.

60. Philippians 2:12, paraphrased.

61. 2 Peter 1:10, paraphrased.

62. BCP, Articles of Religion, XVII, Of *Predestination and Election*. The article does not explicitly insist on predestination to damnation, and it acknowledges the harmful potential of the doctrine to "curious and carnal persons," but it is at bottom a Calvinist, not an Arminian, statement: "Predestination to Life is the everlasting purpose of God, whereby (before the foundations of the world were laid) he hath constantly decreed by his counsel secret to us, to deliver from curse and damnation those whom he hath chosen in Christ out of mankind, and to bring them by Christ to everlasting salvation."

63. Genesis 18:25; first clause paraphrased, second phrase quoted exactly. Initial quotation mark in LB.

64. Dash in LB indicates omitted material, even though the verse in Romans continues directly at this point.

65. Verses 29–30, quotation marks in LB.

66. In LB: "nr"; FB has "never," probably following the force of Wesley's editorial change in AM, p. 38: "it in no wise derogates."

67. These two words are in cipher.

NINE

Distinction at Oxford,
Scandal at Home

Young John Wesley soon crossed clerical and academic thresholds. On 19 September 1725, Dr. John Potter, bishop of Oxford, ordained him deacon, and the following spring, 17 March 1725/26, he was elected fellow of Lincoln College, to the great delight and relief of the family. Susanna, for one, was ready with advice in her letter of 30 March 1726, about how her son should deal with his newfound "riches." Nevertheless, despite these new attainments and responsibilities, he remained "Dear Jacky" to her, as she continued to fill her letters with theological counsel. Though the young don did not always put the details into his letter book, he did transcribe the authors she discussed for his benefit: Berkeley, Pearson, and Fiddes in the 10 November 1725, letter (in addition to an intriguing, but long, discourse on religious zeal) and Norris on love in the 30 March 1726 letter.

Occasionally, even in the Wesley family, life prevailed over theology. The news from Epworth (actually, from Wroot, Samuel Wesley's other parish, where the family now resided) was dominated in these letters by an ill-fated love affair followed by an ill-arranged marriage involving daughter Mehetabel, known to the family as Hetty. Finding suitable suitors for the bright and lively Wesley daughters from among the residents of the fen country was not easy. Hetty became infatuated with a lawyer (she had met him in the household where she was in service) and was in the process of eloping when she discovered that he was not really interested in a wedding. Her behavior (and the resulting pregnancy) scandalized the family, especially the rector, who set up a quick, unsuitable match with a local plumber. Only her sister Molly and her brother John sympathized in the least with the unfortunate young woman. The sad story cast a gloom over these letters that even for a time put the perennial concern about indebtedness in the shade.

One letter in particular rewards close study, that of 12 October 1726. Here Susanna recounts a visit with Hetty and her attempt to work out some reconciliation with her estranged daughter. It sheds considerable light on the mother-daughter relationship, on the Wesley marriage, and on that battle in Susanna's own mind between her sense of justice and mercy in the middle of a family crisis.

❦

To John Wesley
10 November 1725
MA; addressed "For the Revd. Mr John Wesley, Commoner of Christ Church . . .
Oxon"; LB, pp. 44–45; FB, 1:183–185, but with considerable material missing.

Wroot, Nov. 10th, 1725

Dear Jacky,

I believe I've received three letters from you since I wrote to you; but the dismal situation of our affairs, which has found me full employment at home, and my unwillingness to burden you, prevented my writing hitherto. But I will now look over your letters, and reply to each if there be occasion.

Your first of August 4th requires no answer, only there's one passage in it which I don't well understand. You say Berkeley has convinced you "that there is no such thing as matter in the world, if by the real existence of matter is meant a subsistence exterior to the mind, and distinct from its being perceived." What does he mean by imperceptible matter?[1]

Your second bears date August 24th, wherein you are satisfied about humility, and I wish you had also a better notion of that faith which is proposed to us as a condition of salvation. I think Pearson's definition of divine or saving faith is good and no way defective.[2] For though the same thing may be an object of faith as revealed and an object of reason as deducible from rational principles, yet I insist upon it that the virtue of faith, by which through the merits of our Redeemer we must be saved, is an assent to the truth of whatever God hath been pleased to reveal, because he hath revealed it, and not because we understand it. Thus St. Paul, "By faith we understand that the world was made"[3]—q.d.,[4] rejecting the various conjectures of the heathen and not resting upon the testimony of natural reason but relying on the authority of God, we give a full assent to what he hath been pleased to reveal unto us concerning the creation of the world. Now the reason why this faith is required is plain, because otherwise we do not give God the glory of his truth, but prefer our weak and fallible understanding before his eternal word, in that we will believe the one rather than the other. If you will but read Bishop Beveridge on faith, and repentance, Vol. 7th,[5] you'll find him a better divine than Fiddes.[6]

I can't recollect what book I recommended to you, but I highly approve your care to search into the grounds and reasons of our most holy religion, which you may do if your intention be pure, and yet retain the integrity of faith. Nay, the more you study on that subject, the more reason you will find to depend on the veracity of God; inasmuch as your perceptions of that awful Being will be clearer, and you will more plainly discern the congruity that there is between the ordinances and precepts of the gospel and right reason; nor is it a hard matter to prove that the whole system of Christianity is grounded thereon.

If it be a weak virtue that can't bear being laughed at, I am very sure 'tis a strong and well confirmed virtue that can stand the test of a brisk buffoonery. I doubt there are too many instances of people that, being well inclined, have yet made shipwreck of faith and a good conscience, merely through a false modesty, and because they could not bear the raillery of their companions. Some young persons have a natural excess of bashfulness, others are so tender of what they call honour that they can't endure to be made a jest of. Nay, I've often observed that those very people which will on all occasions take the liberty to play upon their neighbours are of all living the worst able to bear being so used themselves. I would therefore advise young persons in their beginning of a Christian course to shun the company of profane wits as they would the plague or poverty; and let 'em never contract an intimacy with any but such as have a good sense of religion. And if 'tis their hap to live where few of that character can be found, let them learn the art of living alone; and when once they are masters of that rare secret, and know how to converse with God and themselves, they'll want no other company. For properly speaking no man wants what he can be happy without.

I now proceed to answer your last, of October 14th. And in this you desire me to speak on a subject above my comprehension. I do not mean as to the nature of zeal, for that is easily defined; but to assign precisely every instance wherein it is allowable or we are required to show that zeal to the world, needs a better head and pen than mine. However, I'll offer some hints, which you may correct or improve by your own meditation.[7]

Zeal or jealousy is an effect of love; and the more intense the love is, the greater is our desire of the good and possession of what we love, and the more vigorously shall we strive to repel and exclude everything that is repugnant to the belov'd object or may prevent our attainment or quiet enjoyment of what we so love. As we observe in friendship, whoever really loves his friend always desires the good of that friend, and if his love be strong, it moves him against everything that is contrary to it; and accordingly he is said to be zealous for his friend and for his reputation when he endeavors all he can to repel everything that is said or done against him. Thus on account of the great love he bears to us, Almighty God is frequently in holy writ represented as zealous or jealous over us, lest we bestow that honour and love which is due to him on anything else—particularly in the Second Command where he says that as he will show mercy unto thousands of those that love him, so he will punish to the third and fourth generation those that hate him,[8] i.e., transfer their love from him to a creature. And the reason is because he is a jealous God.

Zeal with respect to God consists in an awful regard and tender concern for his glory and will, and it ever holds proportion with the degree of our love towards him. If our love be cold, so will our zeal be, too; if fervent, we shall endeavor what is in our power to advance his honour and service in the world, and shall feel much displicency[9] and grief when either we ourselves or any other is guilty of dishonouring or offending him and shall strive what we can to prevent or repel whatever is done against his honour and will. So Elijah says of himself, "I have been very jealous, or zealous, for the Lord God of Hosts, for the children of Israel had forsaken his covenant and thrown down his altars."[10]

The habit of this zeal is always necessary, being indeed inseparable from our love to God; but the visible expressions of it must be ever under due restriction, always according to knowledge, and strictly guarded by prudence and Christian charity; for without restriction and such a guard 'tis the most pernicious thing in nature and has done more mischief in the world than even licentiousness or infidelity. These have slain their thousands, but zeal its ten thousands,[11] as might be shown in many instances. This sacred fire must be kindled at the altar; nor should the perturbation arising from malice, revenge or any private interest or selfish regard presume to mingle with it. Otherwise we may fitly apply to zeal what St. James says of an unbridled tongue: " 'Tis a fire, a world of iniquity, it setteth on fire the course of nature; and it is set on fire of hell."[12]

Now that the outward expressions of our zeal may be acceptable to God and useful to men, 'tis necessary in the first place that our intention be good, that the glory of God and good of others be really our aim without any private views or worldly consideration. Let nothing be done through strife or vainglory. And herein prudence is of great use in choosing such means and using them in such a manner as is most proper and worthy the ends we propose. For prudence ever has respect to time, place, persons and manner of speech or action. As to time it directs us to observe and improve that special season for speaking or acting which we call opportunity, when we are likely to do most service to God, i.e., to make him better known and loved in the world, as for instance if we have an opportunity of instructing the ignorant, to confirm the weak or reprehend[13] the [?]sinner. Or if we would administer relief to our neighbor, it must be done when he stands most in need of it and when we can best spare it without injuring our dependents or creditors; the former must first be provided for, nor will God accept robbery for sacrifice.

Prudence also considers place, and in all these instances the most private is the best, unless in some exempt cases which I can't stay to mention particularly.

Persons also it regards, and here I must advise that if we sincerely desire to promote the glory of God or would successfully attempt anything for his service or the good of mankind, that we do first turn the point of our zeal against ourselves. Let us be careful to sanctify the Lord God in our own hearts by holding him in the highest estimation, by bearing equal respect to all his commands, by purifying our minds from whatever is contrary to his will, and planting each virtue there that may through Christ render us acceptable to God. For [it is] in vain that we appear zealous for that glorious Being, if we do not inwardly esteem and revere him ourselves. In vain shall we attempt to serve him while we indulge ourselves in any known sin and do not vigorously proceed in our own reformation. For otherwise, instead of a plaudit we must expect to meet with that sad expostulation from God: "who hath required this at YOUR hand? Bring no more vain oblations; the incense of your service is an abomination unto me."[14] Nor can we expect better success in instructing or reproving our neighbor who fail to observe the disproportion between our lives and professions; and instead of taking our good offices kindly they will, and may justly, retort upon us, "physician, heal thyself."[15]

Again, prudence requires all persons with or without distinction to keep with their own sphere of action. The inferior magistrate must not intrench[16] upon the prerogative of his prince, nor any private person assume the office of the magistrate. Neither should any secular person of what degree soever invade the province of a priest. But princes, magistrates, husbands, wives, parents, children, masters, servants must all observe their several stations; nor will any pretense of zeal justify a man's acting out[17] of his own proper character. For our God is a God of order and not of confusion.[18] Nor does he require ought of us but what is consistent with a due performance of relative duties. And indeed there's work enough for our zeal in accurately discharging the duties of each relation.

But in the last place prudence is more especially concerned in the manner of our speaking or acting either for God or our neighbor. For be our intention never so good, our zeal ever so fervent, unless we perform all after a due manner, we shall not compass our design. If we would serve Almighty God, we must do it with that vigor, that cheerful gravity and becoming reverence as [the] importance of the work requires. If we are about to instruct the ignor[ant let] us proceed with so much seriousness that they may see we are well appriz[ed of the] truths we teach, and are ourselves under the same impressions we endea[vour to] make on their minds. If we would confirm the weak, it should be done witho[ut any] reproach and with that tenderness and arguments so well adapted to their cas[e,] as may serve to convince them that we are really concerned in their safety and happiness. If we reprove the sinner, let us avoid pride and vainglory and be careful lest we fall into indecent passion or be guilty of unchristian revilings and contemptuous language, which would probably prove a greater sin in us than that we are about to reprehend in another. As we should never undertake a matter of this nature without desiring to do good, so we ought by all proper methods to make the person spoken to sensible of that desire; for we gain a great point if we can persuade them that we really bear them good will and have no design to upbraid, much less expose them, but merely to do 'em good.

The second thing mentioned as a guard of our zeal was charity, which I shall briefly speak of and so conclude.

Love to God and love to our neighbour, which often in scripture is called charity, is, or ought to be, the principle and rule of all our thoughts, words and actions with respect to either. And whatever we do for God or man that flows not from this principle and is not squared by this rule is wrong, as wanting a good foundation and a right conduct. Thus St. Paul: "Though I give my body to be burned and all my goods to feed the poor and have not charity, it profiteth me nothing."[19]

I have not time to discourse on divine charity, but shall only mention a few instances wherein charity must correct our zeal in thought, word, and deed in relation to our neighbour.

And first we must never conclude any man so bad as 'tis possible for him to be; nor think because he is guilty of many sins, that therefore he must be guilty of all; nay, we should not judge that the most profligate sinner cannot possibly amend. For what are we that we should presume to limit the omnipotent mercy of God or consign any to eternal misery whom that almighty Goodness for ought we know may intend to save at last.

Secondly, our charity should strictly confine our zeal within the bounds of truth and soberness. We must not lie for God nor falsely accuse our brethren; nor in a pretended zeal run into censoriousness and evil-speaking, crimes utterly to be abhored of all good men.

Thirdly, no pretence of zeal should make us lay aside our humanity or exercize any act of injustice or cruelty towards our neighbour. Nor must we suffer a bad man to perish for want of our relief. For we have no commission to slay the wicked or right to invade any man's property because he is a sinner. But we must be careful to do our duty to all men, let 'em be what they will.

Yet after all that can be said, though prudence and charity should correct the irregular motions of our zeal, they must by no means extinguish it. But we must keep that sacred fire alive in our breasts and carefully lay hold of all opportunities of serving God, nor should we tamely endure to hear his glorious name blasphemed in execrable oaths or impious discourses without expressing a just indignation against such offences. And if we happen to be in presence of those that either are so superlatively wicked or too much superior to admit of reproof, we may find some way to testify our dislike of such conversation and leave their company.[20]

I've room to add no more but that I send you my love and blessing.

S. W.

Your sisters send their love.
I've just received a letter from you, which I'll answer if I've leisure.
Your brother Wright fetches your sister Hetty from hence the end of this week.[21]

To John Wesley
7 December 1725
LB, pp. 45–46; FB, 1:189–190.

Wroot, December 7th [1725]

Dear Jacky,

(Of Mr. Norris's Sermon on Divine Love)[22]

Who but an atheist will deny that God, and God alone, is the supreme efficient cause of all things, the only uncreated good! But can it be inferred from hence that he hath imparted no degree of goodness to his creatures? . . . We may full as well argue that because they are not self-existent, therefore they have no being at all . . .

Your sister Wright went with her husband about three weeks since to their house in Louth, with Molly to keep her company this winter.[23] Your sister Anne was married last Thursday at Finningley to John Lambert and goes this day home with him. He has hired the red house as we go to church, which they have made very pretty and comfortable, and we hope they will do well.[24]

Emly sends her love to you, as do all the rest. She goes not hence this winter, and greatly desires to hear from you.

I suppose the election at Lincoln College draws near, and your father gives me small encouragement to hope for your success[25] . . . Our crop at Wroot was almost destroyed by floods; and of the small remains your sister Nancy has the best part in dowry, besides near if not quite £30 for hers and Hetty's clothing, which I've yet to pay. What then can I do for you? Nothing but pray for you; nothing but lift my helpless eyes and hands to heaven and beseech Almighty God, to whom all power belongs, to do that for you which I cannot: to appoint some expedient for your relief and raise you some friend in this time of distress. And who can tell? Perhaps he may condescend to hear the unworthiest of his creatures . . . I will not despair, but against hope, believe in hope: for I know that often man's extremity is God's opportunity, wherein he delights to manifest his mercy to such as call upon him.

Dear Jacky, I send you my love and blessing. Adieu!

To John Wesley
30 March 1726
LB, pp. 46–47; FB, 1:193–194.

Wroot, March 30, 1726

Dear Jacky,

I think myself obliged to return great thanks to Almighty God for giving you good success at Lincoln.[26] Let whoever he pleased be the instrument, to him, and him alone, the glory appertains. For as the best concerted measures often prove ineffectual, so sometimes things that carry little probability in them shall succeed beyond expectation. And why is this? But because God prospers the one, and (as his Spirit expresses it) blows upon the "labour of the other."[27]

I am much more pleased and thankful because I have observed sometime that the Holy Jesus (to whom the whole manage of our salvation is committed) seems to have taken the conduct of your soul into his own hand, in that he has given you a true notion of saving faith and, I hope, an experimental knowledge of repentance. Therefore I trust that he will be pleased to direct your intentions, and assist you in the exercise of your[28] ministerial office, that he will incline your heart to the love of justice, so that you will not look on the small addition to your fortunes as given you to make provision for the flesh, but as a talent committed to your charge: to pay your debts in the first place, and the residue to be employed as religion and prudence direct.[29]

(Of Norris's distinction between compla[cenc]e and goodwill.)[30]

Many and great are the trials it has pleased God to exercise us with; and though that is not the reason of my not writing so long, yet I must say they have found me sufficient employment to keep my mind from utter[31] fainting. And your father being displeased at my writing so often, because of the expense it was to you, our pressures disposed me to a more implicit obedience than perhaps I should otherwise have paid him.[32] I would not inform you of anything that might grieve, but Dr. Morley advising your coming into the country, 'tis not probable any unhappy circumstances or practices of some of our family should remain concealed from you.[33] Dear Jacky, I hope you are a good Christian, and as such do firmly believe that no events happen but by the commission, or rather at least permission of divine Providence. Therefore do not much afflict yourself, let what will befall. God hath promised, "All things shall work together for good to those that love him."[34]

(Of my father's getting money for me.)

How or when do you intend to come hither? It will be necessary to let us have timely notice of your intentions. Dear Jacky, all send their love, I my love and blessing.

To *John Wesley*
9 April 1726
LB, p. 47; FB, 1:198.

Apr. 9 [1726]

Dear Jacky,

. . . I thought to send a servant the 25th of this month with two horses . . .
Send now a speedy answer, that we may give them a little food extraordinary.[35] Dear
Jacky, I beseech Almighty God to bless Thee!

To *John Wesley*
16 April 1726
LB, pp. 47–48; FB, 1:198.

Apr. 16 [1726]

Dear Jacky,

. . . Your father has ordered his servant, Alexander Clark, to set out hence on
the 18th instant . . . One thing I suppose needful to admonish you of, that you do
not propose to yourself too much satisfaction in coming hither; for what the world
calls joy lives not within these walls. But if your heart be right and you can rejoice
in God whether you have or have not anything else to rejoice in; if he be the
pleasure of your mind, so that you can feel delight in each perception of his presence, though encompassed with [poverty, reproach] and shame,[36] then you may
spend a few months in Wroot as happily as in any place of the world . . .
    Dear Jacky, God bless thee!

To *John Wesley*
27 August 1726
Priestley, pp. 152–155.
This is not a letter but John Wesley's written account of Susanna's "testimony"
concerning the rectory hauntings in 1716/17. See chapter 5 in part I of this
volume, where it is printed as an addendum to her more timely record of Old
Jeffrey.

To *John Wesley*
28 September 1726
LB, p. 48 (one-line summary); FB, 1:199.

Sept. 28 [1726]

Dear Jacky,

    (Of my father's mare, left ill at Banbury, and my plaid[37] nightgown)

To *John Wesley*
12 October 1726
LB, pp. 48–49; FB, 1:199–200.

Oct. 12 [1726]

[Dear Jacky,]

(Of my father's mare, and my nightgown)

I greatly rejoice that your lot is cast among such agreeable companions, nor am I a little pleased with the hopes of your being [out of debt].[38] Would Almighty God now permit me the satisfaction of being so myself and seeing my children [clear][39] in the world, with what pleasure could I leave it!. . .

Your brother and sister Wright are now in Wroot at John Lambert's.[40] By your father's permission I went to see her and was surprised to find that she met me without the least emotion of joy or grief. I desired a private conference, which she could not deny, though I found she was not pleased with it. I spoke what I thought proper for the occasion, but observed she was on the reserve, nor could I prevail with her to speak freely on anything. To induce her to it I used as much mildness as I am mistress of, told her I freely forgave all her offences against me, and spake more than perhaps was required on my part. She heard me with great indifference, made no acknowledgment of my proffered kindness, but seemed rather not pleased that I supposed she stood in need of my pardon. I then proposed a reconciliation between her and Mr. Wesley and asked her if she would not see him if he were willing to see her. She told me she had no desire to see him, because she knew he would reproach her with what was past, and that she could not bear. I replied, he would certainly put her in mind of her faults, which I thought he was obliged to do, as a father and as a clergyman; and that she was not to call the just rebukes of a parent reproaches, but submit herself to him, which she would certainly do if she were truly penitent. She repeated her not desiring to see him and added she wished for no reconciliation with him till one of 'em came to die. What effect my discourse had on her I know not, but I'm sure I returned home strangely mortified, neither pleased with her nor myself. I hoped from Molly's representation of matters to have found her in a different temper from what I did. Therefore I did not say enough to convince her of her duty and was troubled to find her averse from her father, whom I take to be as well disposed to be reconciled to her as man can be. For he seemed pleased that I went to her and never restrains any of the children from being with her as much as they will. I verily believe that I could by a few words speaking reconcile him to her, but God forbid those few words should be spoken by me till she is better disposed. What her inward frame of mind is, is best known to the Searcher of hearts, to whose mercy I leave her, beseeching him to give her true repentance, without which I desire to see her face no more.

Charles is greatly to blame in not writing to Sam . . .

Dear Jacky, I pray God to bless thee!

I desire what I've spoken of Hetty may be concealed. I have not spoken so freely of her to our folks, nor is it necessary they should know my thoughts. Let all think as they please.

To John Wesley
29 November 1726
LB, p. 50; FB, 1:200.

Nov. 29. Tues. 1726

Dear Jacky,

. . . The mare cost £4.10s.9d before we got her home. (Of the money I left at Wroot.) Dear Jacky, I must say unto thee as Naomi to her daughters, "It grieveth me much for your sake that the hand of the Lord is gone out against me."[41]

This has withheld me from writing, though I had a great desire to hear from you and poor starving Charles. For it seemed a palpable piece of cruelty to make you pay for a letter unless I could send money too. But [as] I can't fix a time of payment, I now think it better to write, lest you should impute my silence to a worse cause.

. . . Let us know how you like your plaid . . .

I heartily wish your converse with your friend[42] may prove innocent and useful; but old folks are scrupulous and much given to fear consequences. May God preserve you from sin and danger.

Dear Jacky, I pray God bless thee.

Mr. Wesley is this day gone to Mr. Farmery's (late Minister of Blighton's) funeral.

Notes

1. John Wesley summarizes this and the following paragraph with a brief phrase in LB, p. 44: "Of Hylas and Philonous and the nature of faith." His letter of 4 August no longer seems to be extant. This early work of Berkeley is titled *Three Dialogues between Hylas and Philonous. The Design of Which Is Plainly to Demonstrate the Reality and Perfection of Humane Knowlege, the Incorporeal Nature of the Soul, and the Immediate Providence of a Deity: In Opposition to Sceptics and Atheists. Also, to Open a Method for Rendering the Sciences More Easy, Useful, and Compendious* (London: Henry Clements, 1713). Wesley was reading the second edition, 1725. See FB, 1:186, n. 1. George Berkeley (1685–1753) was a fellow of Trinity College, Dublin, when he published this work. He later became dean of Derry and, in 1734, bishop of Cloyne. In 1752 he retired to Oxford. Though she responds intelligently to some of the issues raised, S. W. appears not to have read the book.

2. For Pearson's view of faith, see chapter 8, note 59, on S. W.'s letter of 18 August 1725.

3. Paraphrase of Hebrews 11:3. In the AM MS the passage begins with a quotation mark and ends with a dash. I have added the final quotation mark.

4. *Quasi dicat:* "as if he were to say."

5. Probably his two sermons, "Repentance and Faith, the Two Great Branches of the Evangelical Covenant" (nos. 88 and 89), *Theological Works* (1844), 4:185–224. The texts for both discourses is Mark 1:15, "Repent ye, and believe the Gospel"; the first sermon emphasizes repentance, the second faith. Beveridge's handling of these two imperatives interestingly anticipates Wesley's later insistence on both faith and works: "as they err on the one hand, who are altogether for faith without repentance, and good works; so they err too on the other hand, who are altogether for repentance and good works, without faith. And therefore, if we desire to go to Heaven, we must be sure to keep the middle betwixt these two extremes: and what Christ hath joined together in His preaching, we must not put asunder in our practice" (pp. 210–211). The definition of faith that S. W. is recommending includes both assent to

certain propositions, a familiar element in the rational theology of the day, as well as a deeper element of trust in Christ: "Faith, therefore, or belief in general, is nothing else but the assent of the mind to what is attested by another, grounded upon the authority of him that doth attest it" (p. 215). "In matters Divine," this means assenting "to any truth only upon the testimony of God Himself; which is most certainly the highest kind of faith which we can possibly exert, because it hath an infallible testimony for the ground and foundation of it" (pp. 216–217). But this assent leads to something more: "For he that firmly and steadfastly assenteth unto this proposition, that God upon our repentance will pardon, accept, and save us, in and through Jesus Christ; cannot but trust and confide in the same Jesus Christ. . . . And in this, doubtless, consisteth the very essence of saving or justifying faith; even in trusting and relying upon Christ alone for pardon and Salvation, so as to expect it from Him, and from none but Him . . . the faith which our Saviour requires, is not such a light assent which swims only in the brain, but such a firm and solid assent as sinks into the heart, and there moves and inclines the will to Christ, and resting upon Him for pardon and acceptance with the Most High God" (p. 218).

6. Wesley had been reading Richard Fiddes (167–1725) and was mulling over his definition of faith, in Wesley's paraphrase, "an assent to any truth upon rational grounds." See his letter to S. W., 29 July 1725; FB, 1:175, n. 3. V. H. H. Green, *The Young Mr. Wesley* . . . (New York: St. Martin's, 1961), pp. 70, 305, believes he was reading Fiddes' *A General Treatise of Morality* (London: S. Billingsley, 1724).

7. This paragraph and the following 14 are omitted in LB and summarized with the phrase "Of the nature, properties and expressions of zeal." FB, 1:184–185, includes only a few excerpts of this long section.

8. Paraphrase of Exodus 20:5–6. Quotation marks erroneously placed in the MS between "says" and "that" have been omitted.

9. Dissatisfaction.

10. Close paraphrase of 1 Kings 19:14. The MS has quotation marks at the beginning of the verse and a dash after "Hosts" and "altars." Susanna added the words "or zealous" in the middle of her quotation. I have set the whole verse apart with quotation marks.

11. She is playing off 1 Samuel 18:7.

12. Close paraphrase, though with several phrases omitted, of James 3:6; S. W.'s quotation marks.

13. Reprove.

14. Paraphrased from Isaiah 1:12–13; quotation marks added. "Your" is emphasized in the MS with large lowercase letters.

15. Luke 4:23; my quotation marks.

16. Encroach.

17. Outside.

18. Echoes of 1 Corinthians 14:33, 40.

19. 1 Corinthians 13:3, paraphrased; quotation marks added.

20. Note S. W.'s interest in the subject in her letter to John, 14 March 1726/27. There she recommends a sermon on the subject by Bishop Sprat of Rochester. Her thoughts here, though similarly concerned with guarding against excesses, do not seem to be dependent on that discourse.

21. Hetty Wesley was married to William Wright, a plumber, on 13 October 1725 in the parish church of nearby Haxey. By the time of this letter he would have been ready to take her to his home in Louth, a town some 40 miles to the southeast. Baker has determined from baptismal records in the Louth parish registers that she was by then likely to be five months pregnant, probably by the lawyer that she had gone away with (against her father's wishes) on a mistaken promise of marriage. The match with the rather coarse Wright was promoted

by her mortified father. For brief details, see Frank Baker, "Investigating Family Traditions," in MH 26.3 (April 1988): 157–158. For a retelling of the entire episode, see Frederick Maser, *The Story of John Wesley's Sisters, or Seven Sisters in Search of Love* (Rutland, Vt.: Academy Books, 1988), pp. 51–71. The Cambridge don Arthur Quiller-Couch was so taken by the story that he converted it into a novel, *Hetty Wesley* (London and New York: Macmillan, 1903).

22. Susanna Wesley has probably been commenting on "A Discourse concerning the Measure of Divine Love, with the Natural and Moral Grounds Upon Which It Stands." in John Norris, [Practical] *Discourses upon Several Divine Subjects*, 2nd ed., 4 vols. (London: S. Manship, 1701), 3:1–68. The sermon, based on Matthew 22:37—"Thou shalt love the Lord thy God with all thy heart, and with all thy soul, and with all thy mind"—seeks to demonstrate "that God is the only Author or Cause of our Love" and "that he is also the only proper Object of it" (p. 10). Note S. W.'s continuing interest in Norris, expressed in another reference in the letter of 30 March 1726. For details on Norris (rector of Bemerton and sometime collaborator with Samuel Wesley on the *Athenian Mercury*), see Richard Acworth, *The Philosophy of John Norris of Bemerton (1657–1712)* (Hildesheim, Ger., and New York: Georg Olms, 1979), especially chap. 7, "The Theory of Love," pp. 154–183.

As in other letters for which our only source is LB, the ellipses and the summaries in parentheses represent material that Wesley himself has omitted.

23. See note 21.

24. Anne Wesley ("Nancy") married John Lambert, a fairly well-off land surveyor, on 2 December 1725. As indicated here, they set up houskeeping in Wroot, though later they moved to the London area, where Anne met with Charles and John and was present at her mother's death. Apart from her husband's slight drinking problem and some financial ups and downs, Anne appears to have had one of the happier marriages of any of the Wesley children. For additional details, see Maser, *John Wesley's Sisters*, pp. 72–78.

25. A fellowship had become open, it was restricted to a native of the diocese of Lincoln, and Samuel Wesley Sr. pulled out all the ecclesiastical political stops to ensure his son's selection. See Green, *Young Mr. Wesley*, pp. 76–80.

26. Wesley had been elected a fellow on 17 March 1725/26.

27. Quotation marks in LB, probably misplaced; I have been unable to find a direct scriptural reference, although there are resonances of Psalm 90:17 (BCP)—"prosper thou the work of our hands"—and Isaiah 40:24 (AV)—"he shall blow upon them, and they shall whither."

28. FB has "the."

29. His income as a fellow would vary but run somewhere in the neighborhood of £30 per annum. See Green, *Young Mr. Wesley*, pp. 320–321. S. W. here reinforces a lesson in personal stewardship that would stick with her son throughout his life.

30. The one-line parenthetical summary of this paragraph in LB (or Susanna in the first place) may not have it right. "Complae-GWill" in the MS probably does stand for "complacence and goodwill." But if Susanna is referring to *The Theory and Regulation of Love, A Moral Essay in Two Parts. To Which Are Added Some Letters Philosophical and Moral, between the Author and Dr. Henry More*, 2nd ed. (London: S. Manship, 1694), the primary distinction there is between "concupiscence and benevolence." Samuel Wesley (or one of his literary friends) favorably reviewed the book in *The Compleat Library* (London: John Dunton, 1694), 3:92–97, calling attention to these two main branches in Norris's taxonomy of love. Concupiscence is "a Simple tendency of the Soul to Good," that is, good in general (p. 93), and benevolence is "a willing of Good to some Being or another" (p. 94). In a later work Norris distinguished between the "love of benevolence" (appropriate toward our neighbor, whose good we can selflessly will) and the "love of desire" (appropriate toward God, whom we cannot hope to wish any good, from whom we can only seek the fulfillment of our want). Desire, even when used in this theological sense, seems better represented by "concupiscence" than "complacence." See his "Dis-

course concerning the Excellence of Praise and Thanksgiving," in [*Practical*] *Discourses*, 2:92–94. It is possible that the mislabeling of the distinction is attributable to Susanna—she certainly used the same terms when writing to Samuel Jr. on 11 March 1704. If she were remembering it without the book in hand, "good will" would be a plain English equivalent of the Latinate "benevolence," and "complacence" (OED, def. 3, "disposition to please") is a word that a rusty memory might substitute for the slightly racier "concupiscence." Compare the related discussion in her "Obedience to the Laws of God: A Brief (Unfinished) Exposition on the Ten Commandments," in part III of this volume. The related Platonic distinction between the "concupiscible" and the "irascible" affections is also alluded to in S. W.'s devotional journal, entry 73.

31. FB omits.

32. For her role vis-à-vis Samuel, see my article, " 'Some State Employment of Your Mind'. . ." *Church History*, 58.3 (September 1989): 354–366.

33. John Morley was rector of Lincoln College, 1719–1731, and also resided occasionally in Scotten, his parish, near Gainsborough, not far from Epworth. The family difficulties S. W. refers to probably centered on Hetty's forced marriage. The whole process had estranged her from the family in general and her father in particular. John, home during the summer vacation, was later to take Hetty's part in a sermon he preached at Wroot in August. See his letter to his brother Samuel, defending his stand, in FB, 1:201–205. Susanna, on having the MS read to her, noted, "You writ this sermon for Hetty; the rest was brought in for the sake of the last paragraph" (p. 205).

34. Nearly exact quotation of Romans 8:28; quotation marks in LB.

35. That is, over and above what is usual.

36. "Poverty" and "reproach" in cipher. S. W. is taking pains to warn her son what he is coming back to. On leave from Lincoln College, he in fact walked home, arriving 23 April and remaining until 19 September.

37. In LB: "plad"; in FB: "plain."

38. In cipher.

39. In cipher.

40. Not particularly welcome at the rectory while visiting from her new home in Louth, the disgraced Hetty found sanctuary of a sort with her sister Anne and her husband. See preceding letters of 10 November and 7 December 1725 (and notes). The visit set the stage for the rather remarkable mother-daughter interview described in this letter.

41. Ruth 1:13; quotation marks in LB.

42. Most likely Sarah (Sally) Kirkham, daughter of a Cotswold rector, to whom Wesley had been attracted. Despite the fact that she had by now married a local schoolmaster, John continued a slightly more than platonic correspondence with her. She was probably the friend who had recommended both Thomas à Kempis and Jeremy Taylor to his attention. See Green, *Young Mr. Wesley*, pp. 205–211. There is explicit mention of her in the letter of 31 January 1726/ 27. Susanna's scruples doubtless reflect the family's recent experience vis-à-vis Hetty.

TEN

A Continuing Cure of Souls

Susanna maintained her regular correspondence with her son John, whose career was continuing apace. A year later (14 February 1727) he took his master of arts degree, and in August of the same year a leave of absence—to become his father's curate with a special charge for the parish of Wroot. Apart from the brief visit for his ordination as priest (22 September 1728), he did not return to Oxford for good until the fall of 1729.

These letters, primarily from late January until late July 1727, were written to John at Oxford before his return to the family. The last three in the set frame his time at Epworth and Wroot: two from the time of his ordination and a final one after leaving for Oxford for good in late summer of 1729.

Not surprisingly, there is a continuing focus on John's ecclesiastical career; Susanna still writes to him as his tutor in "practical divinity" and is keenly interested in his prospects, including, she hopes, a stint at home helping his father. However, more than in the previous correspondence with her son, these letters reveal a wider care for, as she says in the letter of 9 January 1727, "the state of my family." John would have his ecclesiastically sanctioned curacy over the parishioners of Wroot; Susanna's cure of souls continued to be her family, the young women and men who had been committed to her care through birth.

The children were coming of age, and their mother shouldered multiple burdens: helping them through the life crises of vocation and marriage; facing her (and her husband's) advancing age; experiencing the loneliness of a rapidly emptying nest—all in the context of the family's perennial debts. The sons needed to be worried through university, ordination, search for preferment, and marriage. Her daughters, especially, required a good match or, failing that, an appropriate placement "in service."

Thus we find Susanna the practical theologian writing about Sherlock on Providence or Sprat on zeal (in the 14 March 1727 letter) and about zeal and love (and preaching) in the letter of 14 May. But pastoral and parental issues predominate: John's platonic relationship with a married woman (9 January and 14 March), his health (14 May), the hope that he lead a "regular course of life" (22 April), and the possibility of his coming home as curate (22 April, 14 May, 26 July); Charles, as well as John, not getting enough to eat (22 April); the children all leaving home (22 April); an allusion to Hetty's problems; a desire to see the Lamberts' fortunes improve (11 August 1729); Emily's moving to Lincoln as a schoolteacher (9 January 1727).

It is not unusual for women in patriarchal situations to use indirect, manipulative approaches to gain desired ends. Such a premise might help us understand the guilt she seems to be putting on her son for not rushing to Epworth immediately (14 May) as well as at least part of her speculation about her own death and whether her children would grieve and whether it could be useful for them (26 July).

〜

To John Wesley
31 January 1726/27
LB, pp. 51–53; collated with AM, 1778, pp. 38–39; FB, 1:209–211. Ellipses indicate missing material in LB. Bracketed material comes from the fuller AM version.

Jan. 31, 1727

Dear Jacky,

. . . Emly can have no time to work the chairs, having given her promise to Mrs. T. to go with her at Lincoln at May Day. The small interval between this and that is hardly sufficient to prepare for her removal. I would gladly have kept her here, but it cannot be: our seas run high, and each succeeding wave impairs her health, so that I plainly perceive she has not strength to ride out the storm; but must either make some other port, or shortly leave the world. For which reason I am content to part with her, however pleasing or useful she might otherwise be to me.[1]

. . . I often revolve the state of my family and the wants of my children over in my mind. And though one short reflection on the sins of my youth and the great imperfection of my present state solves all the difficulty of Providence relating to myself, yet when I behold them struggling with misfortunes of various kinds, some without sufficiency of bread, in the most literal sense, all destitute of the conveniences or comforts of life, it puts me upon the expostulation of David, "Lo, I have sinned, and I have done wickedly, but these sheep, what have they done?"[2] Though thus the tenderness of a mother pleads their cause, yet I dare not dispute God's justice, wisdom, or goodness. I know that to allot all men such a sphere of action as all things considered is best for them is the proper exercise of his providence, as it is what none but he can do. We yesterlings[3] do not know whether prosperity or adversity, health or sickness, honour or disgrace, would most conduce to our good . . . What then to desire for myself or children I wot not. One thing I know, that the unsearchable wisdom of God is a good reason why we should not censure those mysterious methods of Providence which we cannot comprehend, but rather vigorously apply ourselves to do our duty in our several stations, leaving all things else to be disposed of by that almighty Goodness which was exhibited to us in the redemption of the world by Jesus Christ. Only let us join in this petition to our Incarnate God, that as our day is, so our strength may be![4] Amen!

(Of my father's borrowing money for brother Charles, detained by brother Sam.)

I have many thoughts of the friendship between Varanese[5] and thee, and the more I think of it, the less I approve it. The tree is known by its fruits,[6] but not always by its blossoms; what blooms beautifully sometimes bears bitter fruit . . .

(Against the continuing the acquaintance with Varanese.)

I often muse on the prodigious force of present things and am grieved to observe with what a strong impetus passion and appetite bear us in pursuit of sensitive[7] enjoyments, contrary to our best informed understandings.

. . . We would freely serve God with what costs us naught, but if he require a costly sacrifice, a right eye, or a right hand, we are ready to say, "These are hard saying, Who can bear them?"[8] We are apt to think heaven too dear a purchase if our favourite must be given for it . . .

. . . [I am verily persuaded that][9] the reason why so many "seek to enter into the kingdom of heaven, but are not able,"[10] is because there is some [Delilah, some one][11] beloved vice, they will not part with; hoping that by a strict observance of other duties that one fault will be dispensed with. But [alas!][12] they miserably deceive themselves. The way to heaven is so narrow, the gate we must enter in so strait,[13] that it will not permit a man to pass with one known unmortified sin about him. Therefore let everyone in the beginning of a Christian course seriously weigh what it will cost to finish it.[14] "For whosoever having put his hand to the plough, looketh back, is not fit for the kingdom of God!"[15]

[I am nothing pleased we advised you to have your plaid; though I am, that you think it too dear, because I take it to be an indication that you are disposed to thrift, which is a rare qualification in a young man who has his fortune to make. Indeed, such an one can hardly be too wary, or too careful.][16] Not that he should take thought for the morrow,[17] any farther than is needful for his improvement of today, in a prudent manage of the talents God has committed to his trust. So far I think 'tis his duty;[18] I heartily wish you may be well apprised of this, while life is young.

Believe me, youth, for I am read in cares,
And bend beneath the weight of more than fifty years.[19]

Believe me, dear son, old age is the worst time we can choose to mend either our lives or our fortunes. If the foundations of solid piety are not laid betimes in sound principles and virtuous dispositions and if we neglect, while strength and vigour last, to lay up something ere the infirmities of age overtake us, 'tis a hundred to one odds but we shall die both poor and wicked.

Ah! My dear Jacky,[20] did you with me stand on the verge of life and see before your eyes a vast expanse, an unlimited duration of being, which you were obliged shortly to enter upon, you can't conceive how all the inadvertencies, mistakes, and sins of youth would rise to your view. And how different [the][21] sentiments [of sensitive pleasures, the desire of sexes, and pernicious friendships of the world] would be then . . . from what they are now, while health is entire, and seems to promise many years of life! . . .

My love and blessing attends you and your brother. Dear Jacky, adieu!

To John Wesley
14 March 1726/27
LB, pp. 53–54; FB, 1:211–212.

March 14 [1726/27]

Dear Jacky,

. . . I congratulate your good success in taking your Master's degree . . .[22]

I'm greatly pleased with your reflections on the methods of divine providence relating to our family and am entirely of your mind, that less violent motives would not have prevailed (on me at least) to make us seriously apply ourselves to the study and practice of the virtues you mention.

(Commendation of Sherlock on Providence.)[23]

The relation I have to your friend Theod[osius][24] made me think it my duty to speak freely on his friendship to V[aranese]; which having done, I have no more to say or do, but only earnestly to pray for him; and to commit the conduct of his soul to that superior Wisdom which alone can guide it into the ways of truth and peace. I have a good opinion of the honesty of his intention and believe he proposes to himself no happiness at present but what appears to him solid, rational, and Christian. But age has less fire and more caution than youth and may perhaps sometimes be afraid where no fear is. But I hope it is excusable, and that no offence will be taken, where none was intended.

(Of Bishop Sprat's Sermon on Zeal.)[25]

. . . I wish I had that funeral sermon you preached; but if that can't be, prithee send me the text, and bring the sermon, if you should come again ere I die.

Dear Jacky, I beseech Almighty God to bless you!

To John Wesley
22 April 1727
LB, pp. 54–56; FB, 1:215–216.

April 22 [1727]

Dear Jacky,

I have so much to say that I verily believe I shall forget at least one half of it . . . Therefore 'tis the best way to begin with that which seems of most importance.

(Of my cutting off my hair; reasons for it.)

Your drawing up for yourself a scheme of studies highly pleases me, for there is nothing like a clear method to save both time and labour in anything. 'Tis a pretty observation of Seneca's, "Most people pass through the world like straws upon a river, which are carried on by the wind or stream without having any proper action of their own."[26] Whether it proceed from mere impotence of mind, intemperate love of pleasure, want of[27] courage, or indolence, 'tis certain there are very few that will persevere in a regular course of life, and 'tis as certain that without such a course a man must necessarily spend most of his days in doing nothing, or nothing to the purpose . . . I know very well that if a man . . . will resolutely break through the foolish customs and maxims of that world . . . he must submit to be often the sport, perhaps the scorn, of the profane and the witty; but

Slight those that say, amidst their sickly healths,
Thou liv'st by rule. What does not so, but man?[28]

A little well-timed neglect or a prudent withdrawing from such company is the best answer in those cases; and the inward peace that results from a well-ordered life is an ample recompense for all its difficulties.

There is another thing in your last letter that almost equally pleases me, and that is your wise and honest resolution of not being trusted again by anyone. I heartily wish, Dear Jacky, that God may enable you to keep it . . ., and that his merciful providence will ever grant you all things that are necessary for life and godliness without your being compelled to live the life that I have done; and that you may have such power over yourself as to be able to live cheerfully without such things as his wisdom thinks fit to withhold from you . . .

How you account for your being weak and little I know not; but I believe the true cause of your being so is want of sufficiency of food for ten or twelve years when you were growing and required more nourishment. If your contracting any ill habit was a means of your acquiring or confirming any good ones, the reason of God's permitting you to contract it is very clear. He often demonstrates the power of his mercy toward us by bringing good out of sin, the greatest evil; and his not hearing our prayers proves sometimes, in the event, the greatest instance of his favour.[29]

I am not sorry that you missed the school.[30] That way of life would not agree with your constitution, and I hope God has better work for you to do . . . I would not have you leave making verses . . . Rather make poetry sometimes your diversion, though never your business.

I must own I vehemently suspect your doctrine and practice did not well agree. I know Mr. Griffiths was a favourite on more accounts than one or two. Be that as it will, I am glad you are better; though I verily believe you will never have any good state of health while you keep your hair.[31]

My L[ord] Nottingham has given Mr. Pennington a small living, about £74 a year, paid in money, to which he goes the tenth of May[32] . . . 'Tis your father's intention to serve both his cures for a year, which (beside that I think it too much for him) I know would satisfy neither parish. Now I think if it will be no great prejudice to your affairs, and you can submit to live as we must do in his absence, it will be a charitable thing to come hither and supply his place during that time. I am persuaded that if it be in your power to help us, you will do it . . .

Thus far I had written when Mr. William Hume, who succeeds his father in Laughton living, sent a servant to tell Mr. Wesley that his third brother, Daniel, enters into Holy Orders on Trinity Sunday; and that he desires, since Mr. Pennington is preferred,[33] he would accept of him for a curate. On Thursday next the two young gentlemen are to meet here about it. I shall not fail to inform you of what they resolve, as soon as it comes to my knowledge.

Your sister Emly is upon the point of leaving us, and we intend, if God permit, to put Molly to trade at midsummer. So we shall have only Patty and Kezzy at home.[34]

Dear Jacky, I beg of you to leave drinking green tea. It ill agrees with a weak constitution. If you drink sage, be sure you make it of sage well dried . . .

I beg Almighty God to bless and guide you in your ways.

Dear Jacky, adieu.

I have abundance more to say, had I time.

Jacky, do you really think Charles has [victuals][35] enough? He writ me a mighty kind letter, with an air of great sincerity; but yet I am sometimes afraid he represented his case rather too well, out of mere goodness, to make me easy.

To John Wesley
14 May 1727
LB, pp. 56–59; collated following FB, 1:217–218, with AM, 1778, pp. 78–79 (which leaves much out and adds several sentences).

Wroot May 14 [1727]

Dear Jacky,

I wrote some [time] since to your brother Charles and you, but have not yet heard whether either of you received my letter. Yours, dated the 7th of April, found me engaged in much business, and if I had not I should have made no great haste to answer it, because you told K[ezzy] you were to be absent from College for some time . . . And now I am about to answer it, I don't know how to do it to your satisfaction; for I've very little to say on zeal more than I've said already. Yet I can deny you nothing that is in my power to grant, though I write to no purpose. (Of zeal.)[36]

The difficulty of separating the ideas of things that nearly resemble each other, and whose properties and effects are much the same, has made some think that we have[37] no passion but love and that what we call hope, joy, fear, etc.,[38] are no more than various modes of it.[39] This notion carries some show of reason, though I can't acquiesce in it. I must confess I never yet met such a definition of love[40] as fully satisfied me. 'Tis indeed commonly defined, "a desire of union with a known or apprehended good."[41] But this directly makes love and desire the same thing, which[42] I conceive they are not, for this reason: desire is strongest and acts most vigorously when the beloved object is distant, absent, or apprehended unkind or displeased; whereas when the union is attained,[43] delight and joy fills [sic] the[44] lover, while desire lies quiescent; which plainly shows[45] that desire of union is an effect of love, not love itself.

What then is love? How shall we define its strange, mysterious essence? It is—I don't know what: a powerful something; source of our joy and grief! Felt by every-one, yet unknown to all! Nor shall we ever comprehend what it is till we are united to our First Principle and there read its wondrous nature in the clear mirror of Uncreated Love! [Till which time it is best to rest satisfied with such apprehensions of its essence as we can collect from our observation of its effects and properties; for other knowledge of it in our present state is too high and wonderful for us, neither can we attain unto it.][46]

Dear Jacky,[47] suffer now a word of advice. However curious you may be in searching into the natures or distinguishing the properties of the passions or virtues [of humankind] for your own private satisfaction, be very cautious of giving nice definitions in public assemblies, for it does not answer the true end of preaching, which is to mend men's lives, not to fill their heads with unprofitable speculations . . .[48] [And after all that can be said, every affection of the soul is better known by experience than any description that can be given of it. An honest man will more easily apprehend what is meant by being zealous for God and against sin when he hears what are the properties and effects of zeal, than by the most accurate defini-tions of its essence.][49] And it is of incomparably greater concern to every individual soul of your auditory to be well instructed how to temper zeal than to have the most accurate definition of its essence . . .

I've now received yours dated May 8th and find by it you have my last. If you are so averse from parting with your hair . . . I've no more to say . . . I wish you health, and, if it please God, a long life . . .

Your being subject to frequent bleedings at the nose is no sign of the fluids being too thick, but . . . of the contrary . . . The cramp is a nervous distemper and proceeds from some obstruction that prevents the regular circulation of the spirits. 'Tis no wonder you should be afflicted with it, when your father has had it so violently, especially when he was young. One of the best remedies in this case is eight or nine hours of sleep and moderate exercise, avoiding as much as possible the being abroad after sunset . . . Water does certainly increase the fluids, but whether it corrects their viscidity[50] or no I cannot tell . . .

(A r[ecipe] for viscidity or sharpness in the blood.)

What curate your father will hire I don't know. I think Mr. Hume will be the man. Till Martinmas he designs to serve both cures himself . . . I did once with some degree of earnestness wish you here, but I don't now; rather I am glad that there is no occasion for your coming at all. For 'tis best for me to have as few attachments to the world as possible.

Dear Jacky,[51] the conclusion of your letter is very kind. That you were ever dutiful I very well know, but I know myself enough to rest satisfied with a moderate share[52] of your affection. Indeed it would be unjust of me to desire the love of anyone.

Your prayers I want and wish; nor shall I cease while I live to beseech Almighty God to bless you! Adieu![53]

I congratulate your composure of mind; for sure 'tis a happy temper and can never make you unfit for good conversation. 'Tis my simple opinion that no man is so well qualified for converse in the world as he that most despises it.

Charles has writ a letter to your father which much pleases him.

Em is gone to Lincoln.

To John Wesley
5 July 1727
MA and LB, p. 59; FB, 1:226–227. This is part of a double letter from Samuel and Susanna.

[Wroot], Jul. 5, [1727]

Dear Jacky,

I had answered your letter but was prevented by an unusual illness, which I thank God is pretty well over. When I wrote last I thought your father had laid aside his design of sending for you hither, but perceive now he has altered his purpose and has desired you to come. He does certainly want an assistant, though I believe if you stay a little longer ere you come hither he will want none. How Charles can get to Wroot I can't tell. 'Tis impossible for us to send horses farther than Nottingham, and I suppose he may scruple coming so far with the carrier.[54]

In great haste I send ye both my love and blessing.

S. W.

To John Wesley
26 July 1727
LB, pp. 59–61; collated with AM, 1778, pp. 79–80; following FB, 1:228–229.

July 26, [1727][55]

Dear Jacky,

The very ill health I have had this two or three last months makes me much indisposed to write, or I should have answered yours of the 15th instant sooner.

'Tis certainly true that I have had large experience of what the world calls ill[56] fortune; but as I have not made those improvements I ought to have made under the discipline of Providence, I humbly [conceive][57] myself to be unfit for an assistant to another in affliction.[58] But blessed be God you are at present in pretty easy circumstances, . . . [59] [which I thankfully acknowledge is a great mercy to me, as well as you.][60] Yet if hereafter you should meet with troubles of various sorts, as 'tis very probable you will in the course of life, the best preparative I know of for suffering is a [regular and exact][61] performance of present duty. For this will surely make[62] a man pleasing to God and put him directly under his protection, so that no evil shall befall him but what he will certainly be the better for.

'Tis incident to all men to regard the past and the future, while the present moments pass unheeded; whereas in truth neither [the][63] one nor the other is of use to us any farther than they put us upon improving the present time . . .

You did well to correct that fond desire of dying before me, since you do not know what work God may have for you to do ere you leave the world. And besides, as you observed, I ought surely to have the pre-eminence in point of time, and go to rest before you. Whether you could see me die without any motion of grief I know not; perhaps you could. 'Tis what I've often desired of the children, that they would not weep at our parting, and so make death more uncomfortable than it would otherwise be to me. If you, or any other of my children, were like to reap any spiritual advantage by being with me at my exit, [I][64] should be glad to have you with me. But as I have been an unprofitable servant[65] during the course of a long life, I have no reason to hope for [so great an honour,][66] so high a favour, as to be employed in doing our Lord any service in the article of death. It were well if you spoke prophetically, and that joy and hope might have the ascendant over my other passions at that important hour. But I dare not presume, nor do I despair, but leave it to our Almighty Saviour to do with me both in life and death just what he pleases; for I have no choice . . .[67]

The family you mention under some affliction I suppose to be that of Varanese. I hope no branch of it has proved so bad as Hetty. If it has, I pray God to comfort the rest of them, for they have trouble enough . . .

I have writ so often to my sister Annesley and have received no answer, that I believe she either never got my letters, or has forgotten me.[68] I wish you would see her . . . and enquire whether my sister Richardson[69] be alive and how she lives.

Your father, I suppose, is for your coming hither presently. But what becomes of poor Charles? I'm ill, and can't write to him.

I shall be glad if your coming to Wroot may be to your satisfaction. We are under some pressures, but will endeavour to make things as easy to you as possible. 'Tis well you've left [drinking tea];[70] for 'tis doubtful whether I shall be able to get you any.

Dear J[acky], God bless thee!

Your sisters Patty and Kezzy, who are both recovering from a fever that has brought them very low, send their love to you; and do humbly petition that if you have any [old shirts],[71] you would give 'em to them.

Once more, Adieu!

This[72] letter was not sent till the 15th of August. We have been sick, and I could not finish it.

To John Wesley
12 August 1728
LB, pp. 61–62; FB, 1:232. The gap between this and the last letter represents the initial period of John's service as his father's curate. With her son living at home, she had no need to write to him.

Epworth, August 12, 1728

Dear Jacky,

I had not failed to give you advice of your box sending, but that I have been ill ever since you went hence. Within these few days the fever left me, and now, I thank God, I'm pretty well . . . My sickness, and somewhat worse, has made our work here go on very slowly; and when you return you'll not find the house much better than you left it.

I am glad you met with so good a reception at London and that the place of your residence is so pleasing to you. Whatever my circumstances are, or wherever it seems good to Infinite Wisdom to cast my lot, I am greatly delighted to hear that others are more easy in their fortunes, company, or habitation; and have as true a taste of what they enjoy as they have themselves. Were it in my power to make all men happy I should not fail of being so too. Though, blessed be God, as it is I am far from miserable.

You did well to visit poor Tim; 'tis a little hearty mortal, and I dare say was very glad to see you. If you happen to see him again, pray return his services . . .

(R[ecipe]s for Syrup of Mulberries, Mulberry Wine, or Wine and Shrub).

If there be anything else in which I can serve you, let me know. I beseech Almighty God to bless thee!

To John Wesley
September 1728
LB, p. 62 (two-line summary); FB, 1:233.

September [17]28

Dear Jacky,

(Of my brother's coming to Epworth)

If he come, he must not think of returning till after winter.

To John Wesley
11 August 1729
LB, p. 62; FB, 1:239–240. Again, the long gap between letters represents a long period of residence with his family, as his father's curate.

August 11, [17]29

Dear Jacky,

I need not tell you I should be glad to see you, because you know it already; and so I should to see poor Charles too; but what to say to his coming I know not. J[ohn] L[ambert], his w[ife] and ch[ild],[73] we are still like to keep, for we hear no news of a place for him; though I would fain hope it would please God to provide for him some way ere winter and take off their w[eigh]t, which really grows very heavy.

I wrote with some earnestness to your brother Sam Wesley to persuade him to come to Epworth; but I find I can't prevail . . . He will be here toward the end of the month . . . He sent me a pound of Bohea tea[74] and two pounds of chocolate, which were very acceptable; for none could I buy, and I was somewhat ill for want of tea . . .

I think you had better contrive to meet your brother at Lincoln and then come all together . . . I have a bad arm and write in much pain, or I have a deal to say else . . . Perhaps I may live to see you.

May Almighty God bless and preserve you!

Notes

1. Emilia, the eldest Wesley daughter, had already had her relationship with a young man broken up by the family. That same winter she found herself in near total charge of the family during the indisposition of Susanna. Finally, she left home for a teaching position in a Lincoln boarding school for five years. After another brief stint at home (this time, Wroot), she again became a teacher in Lincoln, this time in the school of Mrs. Taylor (the Mrs. T. mentioned in this letter). Though Susanna would have preferred to keep her daughter with her, she seems to have acquiesced to her leaving. See the letter of 20 January 1722, in this volume, chapter 7, and two of Emily's in Stevenson, pp. 263–267.

2. Nearly exact quotation of 2 Samuel 24:17; quotation marks in LB.

3. Not in OED; perhaps colloquial or dialect.

4. Deuteronomy 33:25, paraphrased.

5. The name John used in correspondence with his friend Sally Kirkham, now Mrs. Chapone. See S. W.'s letter of 29 November 1726.

6. Cf. Matthew 7:20.

7. That is, sensuous.

8. John 6:60 reads, "This is an hard saying; who can hear it?" Quotation marks are in LB.

9. This is the beginning of the extract Wesley published in the AM.

10. A summary, not a direct quotation, of Matthew 7:21–23; quotation marks are in LB but not AM.

11. In AM only. A pointed personification of vice, given her disapproval of Wesley's relationship with "Varanese" only a few lines above! If this is John's interpolation, it is no less interesting. See Judges 16:4–21.

12. In AM only.

13. Paraphrase of Matthew 7:14.

14. AM substitutes, ". . . weigh what our Lord says in St. Luke xiv. ver. 27, 28, 29, 30, 31."

15. Nearly exact quotation of Luke 9:62; quotation marks in LB.

16. LB begins the paragraph. "One who has his fortunes to make, can hardly be too careful." The reference to a seemingly insignificant detail (the plaid nightgown) strengthens the argument that Wesley left material out of LB and in 1778 was editing from the holograph, which he occasionally transcribes in his AM edition.

17. See Matthew 6:34.

18. In AM: "I would not recommend taking Thought for the Morrow any further than is needful, for our improvement of present opportunities, in a prudent manage of those talents God has committed to our trust. And so far I think it is the Duty of all, to take Thought for the Morrow. And. . . ."

19. I have not been able to trace the source of this couplet.

20. In AM: "my dear Son."

21. In LB: "your."

22. Conferred February 14.

23. S. W. is not referring to Thomas Sherlock (1678–1761), at this time not yet embarked on his episcopal career (bishop of Bangor, 1728; Salisbury, 1734; and London, 1748), but to his father, William Sherlock (1641?-1707). The elder Sherlock, a Cambridge graduate whose clerical career culminated in the deanship of St. Paul's in 1691, was a noted controversialist. He wrote against Dissenters, Catholics, and Socinians and for the divine right of kings. Like S. W. he was initially a Nonjuror but soon backed off from that position, recognizing William and Mary as governing de facto—thereby avoiding deprivation and assuring further preferment. His *a Discourse Concerning the Divine Providence* (London: William Rogers, 1694) is dedicated to the Queen, invoking the "same Good Providence, which has advanced Your Majesties to the Throne." Among other things that would interest S. W., Sherlock argues that God's "Praescience does not destroy [human] Liberty" (p. 181); that people should "take care of the Religious and Vertuous Education of their Children" (p. 337); and that we ought "humbly to acquiesce in what God does, and faithfully to discharge the duties which belong to that state, and condition, and circumstances of life, which the Providence of God has placed us in" (p. 354). Samuel Wesley (or one of his close literary associates) gave the book a long favorable review in *The Compleat Library* (London: John Dunton, 1694), 3:3–14.

24. The name given to another of the Cotswold circle in which the the young Wesley moved. His own appellation in the group was Cyrus.

25. "A Sermon Preached before the King at White-Hall, December 22, 1678," in *Sermons Preached on Several Occasions* (London: R. Bonwicke et al., 1722), pp. 143–190. Sprat (1635–1713) was dean of Westminster and then bishop of Rochester, in which latter capacity he ordained Samuel Wesley Sr. a deacon in 1688. Preaching on Galatians 4:18 ("It is good to be zealously affected always in a good thing"), he both commends "true religious zeal" and shows the "due limitations of such zeal" (pp. 144–145) Note S. W.'s disquisition on this subject in her letter to John, 10 November 1725 (chapter 9, this volume). A test of true zeal is "First, That which is guided by a good Light in the Head. Secondly, That which consists of good and innocent Affections in the Heart. Thirdly, That which employs the Head and the Heart about good Things, and those only" (p. 157). Sprat's desire is to show the Stuart king that true religious zeal does not mean violence, resistance, or open rebellion against those in authority (pp. 188–189); with this political point S. W. is in accord, but she may be commending the sermon to John in hopes that he will be careful to temper in this instance his "natural passions," that is, with respect to Varanese (p. 153).

26. Quotation marks in LB. I have been unable to locate the passage in Roger L'Estrange, ed., Seneca's Morals by Way of Abstract, 7th ed. (London: Jacob Tonson, 1699).

27. In LB: "or."

28. George Herbert, "The Church-Porch," stanza 23, lines 133–135, from *The Temple*, in F. E. Hutchinson, ed., *The Works of George Herbert* (Oxford: Clarendon Press, 1991), p. 12. See note to S. W.'s letter to Samuel Jr., 11 October 1709, where it is also quoted.

29. S. W. is answering a query John made in his letter to her, 19 March 1727. FB, 1:212–213.

30. John had indicated that he was in the running for the headmastership of a school in Skipton, in the West Riding of Yorkshire, not too far from Epworth (FB, 1:213–214). By the time of her writing, S. W. had heard it had not come through, probably from another letter from her son that does not survive. See FB, 1:714.

31. An answer to details in a letter that seems not to have survived. The reference may be to John (Robin) Griffiths, an undergraduate friend of Wesley, who died suddenly during the previous Christmas vacation.

32. With his curate's departure, Samuel Wesley was left to minister alone in both Epworth and Wroot. See his letter to John, 6 June, 1727, in Luke Tyerman, *The Life and Times of the Rev. Samuel Wesley* . . . (London: Simpkin, Marshall, 1866), p. 400.

33. That is, elevated to a parish of his own.

34. Emily was going to her teaching post at Lincoln. Charles had come up to Christ Church College in 1726. Suky had made a bad match, c. 1719, with Richard Ellison, a rich but boorish and irreligious landowner. Hetty and Anne, as we've seen, were married; Samuel Jr. was teaching school; and John, for a few more months at least, was at Oxford.

35. In cipher.

36. This paragraph is found only in LB.

37. In AM: "the human soul has. . . ."

38. In AM: "and that all those Passions or Affections, which we distinguish by the names of hope. . . ."

39. In AM: "of Love."

40. In AM: "such an accurate definition of the passion Love. . . ."

41. Quotation marks in LB; I have not uncovered this reference.

42. AM adds, "upon a close inspection. . . ."

43. AM adds, "and Fruition perfect, Complacency. . . ."

44. AM adds, "soul of the. . . ."

45. AM adds, "at least to me. . . ."

46. Added from AM, following FB; the last clause is a paraphrase of the AV version of Psalm 139:6.

47. Omitted in AM.

48. Dash in LB indicating omitted material; material that follows from AM, added here in brackets, seems to fill that gap.

49. The following material, down through "as few attachments to the world as possible," appears only in LB.

50. Stickiness, glutinousness.

51. "Dear Son" in AM.

52. In AM: "degree."

53. AM version ends here.

54. In LB: "I can't tell . . . perhaps he may scruple coming by the carrier."

55. AM.

56. In AM: "adverse."

57. Missing in LB; supplied in AM.

58. AM substitutes, "but I have not made those improvements in piety and virtue, under the discipline of Providence, that I ought to have done; therefore I humbly conceive myself to be unfit for an assistant to another in affliction, since I have so ill performed my own duty."

59. LB indicates material missing, probably that supplied by AM.

60. AM.

61. AM. In LB: "an exact. . . ."

62. In AM: "render." LB mistakenly reads, "will surely will make a man. . . ."

63. AM.

64. Left out in LB; supplied by AM.

65. See Matthew 25:30.

66. Added in AM.

67. AM version ends here.

68. Probably either her unmarried sister Ann, born 1661, or her younger brother Benjamin's wife, Mary. See Betty Young, "Sources for the Annesley Family," PWHS, 45.2 (September 1985): 46–57. None of these letters seems to have survived, though on the evidence of the following letter, MA, dated 12 August, 1731, S. W. seems finally to have gotten through to her sister via her sons:

Dear Sister

I am sorry the providence of God has placed us at such a distance that we can't hope to meet in this world or have one hour's chat to talk over our past lives before we die. But be that as it will, we must submit to what we can't help, for though I have neither money nor friends, yet I live as happy as anyone in my circumstances can do, for I never grieve at [?]inevitable things. I hope to hear better news when my nephews return to London, for they told me you had a very ill state of health, but the sight of them, I believe, will so revive you that they will do you more good than a doctor. Pray give my love to my brother and all my nieces, and be assured I am,

Dear Sister, your affectionate Sister
and Servant
Anne Annesley

69. Mary Annesley, one of Susanna's older sisters, married Nathaniel Richardson in 1671. No record of her death has been found; if she was alive at the time she would have been near 80. See Young, "Sources for the Annesley Family," p. 51.

70. In cipher.

71. In cipher.

72. Baker misreads as "your."

73. Susanna's son-in-law, the surveyor, and her daughter Anne and child had not yet moved to London.

74. Black tea from China.

ELEVEN

Advisor to the Holy Club

*T*he "method" instilled by Susanna Wesley, both in her rectory home-school and in correspondence, became an early form of "Methodism" in the autumn of 1729. It was then that her son John returned to Oxford to take up his duties as a tutor and was pulled into a small circle of undergraduates (his brother Charles and a couple of his friends) who met from time to time to read devotional works together. Under his leadership the group grew into a "shifting network"[1] of Oxonians who engaged in various pious and charitable activities and earned for themselves such nicknames as Supererogation Men, the Holy Club, and Methodists. More serious notoriety came in August 1732 with the death of William Morgan, one of the original members; his demise, as well as the mental and physical symptoms attending his illness, was attributed to the ascetic excesses of Oxford Methodist discipline.[2]

Susanna's response to all this is predictably supportive of her sons. In correspondence with John and (beginning here in two double letters) also with Charles, she offers advice and sympathy in the early stages of the Morgan case (see 12 July 1731 and both parts of the double letter of 21 February 1732). Further, in the 25 October 1732 letter there is warm agreement with the aims of their "small society" and "all its pious and charitable actions"; continuing helpful discussion about the most useful devotional books; and interest expressed in other members of her sons' circle, two of whom (John Whitelamb and Westley Hall) would soon become her sons-in-law.

However, she also shows a more critical side, most clearly visible in the accusation that John might "rigorously impose any observances on others" (fragments of a letter written before 16 August 1733). And there are several maternal jibes at her sons' lack of concern for their health and at their habit, as "two scruffy travelers," of saving money by walking home from Oxford (see again the letter of 25 October 1733).

As in other sets of correspondence, family news provides the other main interest in these letters. Two extended narratives—one on Samuel Wesley's near-disastrous fall from a wagon, the other detailing Uncle Matthew Wesley's "surprise" visit to Epworth and his offer to "adopt" Patty—and an additional shorter one on the intricacies of renting (or working) the glebe (see in the following letter) furnish further evidence of the precarious financial situation at home. The girls have not all been provided for, and the Rev. Mr. Wesley is failing—no wonder the plaintive note at the end of the 25 October letter, where she begins expressing concern over what happens when he dies.

Κ

To John Wesley
12 July 1731
MA: addressed to "John Wesley Fellow of Lincoln . . . Oxon." Note added to Charles Wesley. John Wesley's endorsement: "m[y] F[athe]r's Fall." FB, 1:291–292, with two omissions.

July 12, [1]731

Dear Jacky,

I am sorry to put you to the expense of another letter so soon, but I'm so uneasy about poor John Whitelamb[3] that I hope you will excuse it. I presently desired your father to give him one of those guineas you mentioned in yours by Mr. Horbery,[4] and he very readily consented to it, being I believe much pleased with Whitelamb's letter to him. This I hope will be some small relief, though it can bear no proportion to his great necessities. I am glad you have chosen Mr. Isham[5] your rector, for I think he is friendly to you, as the late rector was, and perhaps you may have power to get something for poor starving Johnny, whose deplorable case I have much at heart and do daily most earnestly recommend to divine providence, for I know what a great temptation it is to want food convenient.

The particulars of your father's fall are as follows. On Friday before Whit Sunday (the 4th of June) he and I, Molly, and young Nanny Brown were going in our waggon to see the ground we hire of Mrs. Knight at Low Melwood. He sat in a chair at one end of the waggon, I in another at 'tother end, Molly between us, and Nanny behind me. Just before we reached the Close, going down a small hill, the horses took into a gallop. Out flew your father and his chair. Nanny, seeing the horses run, hung all her weight on my chair, and kept me from keeping him company. She cried out to William to stop the horses and that her master was killed. The fellow leapt out of the seat and stayed the horses, then ran to Mr. Wesley. But ere he got to him Harry Dixon, who was coming from Ferry, Mrs. Knight's man, and Jack Glew, were providentially met together, and raised his head, upon which he had pitched, and held him backward, by which means he began to respire, for 'tis certain by the blackness in his face that he had never drawn breath from the time of his fall till they helped him up. By this time I was got to him, asked him how he did, and persuaded him to drink a little ale, for we had brought a bottle with us. He looked prodigiously wild, but began to speak, and told me he ailed nothing. I informed him of his fall. He said he knew nothing of any fall, he was as well as ever he was in his life. We bound up his head, which was very much bruised, and helped him into the waggon again, and set him at the bottom of it while I supported his head between my hands, and Will led the horses softly home. I sent presently for Mr. Harper, who took a good quantity of blood from him, and then he began to feel pain in several parts, particularly in his side and shoulder. He had a very ill night, but on Saturday morning Mr. Harper came again to him, dressed his head, and gave him something which much abated the pain in his side. We repeated the dose at bedtime, and on Whit Sunday he preached twice, and gave the Sacrament, which was too much for him to do, but nobody could dissuade him from it. On Monday he was ill, slept almost all day. On Tuesday the gout came, but with two or three nights taking Bateman it went off again, and he has since been better than could be expected. We thought at first the waggon had gone over him, but it only went over his gown sleeve, and the nails took a little skin off of his knuckles, but did him no further hurt.

My brother Wesley[6] had designed to have surprized us and had traveled under a feigned name from London to Gainsbro. But there sending his man out to see for a guide into the Isle[7] next day which was Thursday, the man told one that keeps our market his master's name and that he was going to see his brother, which was minister of Epworth. The man thus informed met with Molly in the market about an hour before my brother got thither; she, full of the news, hastened home and told us her uncle Wesley was coming to see us, but we could hardly believe her. 'Twas odd to observe how all the town took the alarm and were upon the gaze as if some great prince had been about to make his entry. He rode directly to John Dawson's, but we had soon notice of his arrival and sent John Brown with an invitation to our house. He expressed some displeasure at his servant for letting us know of his coming, for he intended to have sent for Mr. Wesley to dine with him at Dawson's and then come to visit us in the afternoon; however, he soon followed John home, where we were all ready to receive him with great satisfaction. His behaviour among us was perfectly civil and obliging. He spoke little to the children the first day, being employed (as he afterwards told them) in observing their carriage and seeing how he liked them. But afterwards he was very free and expressed great kindness to them all. He was strangely scandalized at the poverty of our furniture and much more at the meanness of the children's habit. He always talked more freely with your sisters of our circumstances than to me and told them he wondered what his brother had done with his income, for 'twas visible he had not spent it in furnishing his house or clothing his family. We had a little talk together sometimes, but it was not often we could hold a private conference, and he was very shy of speaking anything relative to the children before your father, or indeed of any other matter. I informed him as far as I handsomely[8] could of our losses etc., for I was afraid lest he should think I was about to beg of him, but the girls (with whom he had many private discourses) I believe told him everything they could think on. He was particularly pleased with Patty, and one morning before Mr. Wesley came down, he asked me if I was willing to let Patty go and stay a year or two with him at London. "Sister," says he, "I have endeavoured already to make one of your children easy while she lives,[9] and if you please to trust Patty with me, I will endeavour to make her so, too." Whatever others may think, I thought this a generous offer, and the moreso because he had done so much for Suky and Hetty. I expressed my gratitude as well as I could and would have had him speak to your father, but he would not himself; he left that to me. Nor did he ever mention it to Mr. Wesley till the evening before he left us.

He always behaved himself very decently at family prayers and in your fathers absence said grace for us before and after meat. Nor did he ever interrupt our privacy, but went into his own chamber when we went into ours. He staid from Thursday till the Wednesday after, then left us to go to Scarborough. From whence he returned the Saturday sennight[10] after, intending to stay with us a few days. But finding your sisters gone the day before to Lincoln, he would leave us on Sunday morning, for he said he might see the girls before they set forward for London. He overtook them at Lincoln and had Mrs. Taylor, Em., [and] Kez. with the rest to supper with him at the Angel.[11] On Monday they breakfasted with him; then they parted, expecting to see him no more till they came to London, but on Wednesday he sent his man to invite them to supper at night. On Thursday he invited them to dinner, at night to supper, and on Friday morning to Breakfast, when he took his leave of them and rode for London. They got into town on Saturday about noon, and that evening Patty writ me an account of her journey.

Before Mr. Wesley went to Scarbro' I informed him of what I knew of Mr. Morgan's case.[12] When he came back he told me that he had tried the spa[13] at Scarbro', and could assure me that it far excelled all the spas in Europe, for he had been at them all, both in Germany and elsewhere. That at Scarbro' there were two springs, as he was informed, close together, which flowed into one basin, the one a chalybeate[14] the other a purging water, and that he did not believe there was the like in any part of the world. Says he, "If that gentleman you told me of could by any means be gotten thither, though his age is the most dangerous time in life for his distemper, yet I am of opinion those waters would cure him." I thought good to tell you this, that you might, if you please, inform Mr. Morgan of it, if 'tis proper.

The matter of the tithe stands thus.[15] You know Charles Tate died about Easter. His sons after his death desired Mr. Wesley to continue them in partnership this year, which he granted. But afterwards, when the great drought had consumed most of the flax, they sued for a release, of which I was glad, though he was nothing pleased; yet however he released them, and now we have it all in our own hands. This has thrown us into more debt for two horses and another waggon, but still I hope we shall do pretty well, for though line[16] fails, we are likely to have a large crop of barley, which they say will bear a good price.

This new turn in our affairs will make it very expedient for Emly to come home, for I cannot manage both house and tithe, and though Molly be a good girl, she is unequal to the work. If Mr. Wesley will but agree with her I shall be very glad; if not, I doubt[17] he must let his tithe. I am old and infirm and can't do as I have done, therefore must have help, or drop the business.

Your father has let Wroot tithe to Will Atkinson this year, and a brave year he is like to have. But he would not take Canby ground off our hands, so we have burned near twenty acre of it, which if it please God to bless and to send us a good crop of rapes,[18] we may come to get something by that unfortunate bargain at last.

Dear Jacky, I can't stay now to talk about Hetty and Patty; only this, I hope better of both than some others do.

I pray God to bless you. Adieu.

Dear Charles,

Though I have spent my time and almost filled up my paper, yet I must thank you for yours by Mr. Horbery. That same gentleman came to Epworth last Thursday about noon and told us the pleasing news of your and your brother's health. I suppose ere this ye have received mine of the 5th instant; you would do well to burn yours, for I wrote perhaps too warmly about the Christ Church gentlemen, though I was strangely provoked at them.[19]

Dear Charles, my love and blessing attends ye both.

Adieu.

Remember my love to poor starving Johnny.[20] Service to Mr. Kirkham.[21]

To John Wesley
21 February 1731/32
MA (a double letter, including one to Charles Wesley also). FB 1:326–327, omits sections of the second and third paragraphs.

Monday, February 21, [1]731–2

Dear Jacky,

I thank God I am much better than I have been, though far from being in health; yet a little respite from much pain I esteem a great mercy. If you had any design to visit our family this spring (which for your own sake I could wish you had not) my health or sickness will be of little consequence; your entertainment would be the same, and I am no company.

I have time enough now, more than I can make a good use of, but yet for many reasons I care not to write to anyone. I never did much good in my life when in the best health and vigour, and therefore I think it would be presumption in me to hope to be useful now; 'tis more than I can well do to bear my own infirmities and other sufferings as I ought and would do. All inordinate affection to present things may, by the grace of God and a close application of our own spirits to the work, be so far conquered as to give us very little or no trouble. But when affliction comes once to touch our purely natural appetites, which we can never put off but with the body itself, when every member of the body is the seat of pain and our strong and, I think, innocent propension to ease and rest, is crossed in every article, then comes on the severity of our trial. Then it is not an ordinary measure of divine succour and support that will enable us to continue steadfast in the spirit and disposition of Jesus Christ. This was the very case of our dear Lord! He had no irregular passions or sinful appetites ever to combat with, but he had what was infinitely harder to be sustained, the greatest contradiction of sinners against the purity of his nature, to undergo, and all his innocent natural appetites voluntarily to sacrifice in a death exquisitely painful! and attended with circumstance very grievous to be borne by human nature, though in its utmost perfection!

I am heartily sorry for Mr. Morgan. 'Tis no wonder that his illness should at last affect his mind; 'tis rather to be admired that it has not done it long ago. It's a common case, and what all who are afflicted with any indisposition a great while together experience as well as he. Such is our make, such the condition of embodied spirits, that they cannot act with freedom or exert their native powers when the bodily organs are out of tune. This shows how necessary it is for people (especially the young) to improve the present blessing of health and strength by laying a strong foundation of piety towards God, of submission, patience and all other Christian virtues before the decline of life, before the shadows of the even lengthens [sic] upon them and those years draw nigh in which without solid piety they can find no pleasure.

The young gentleman you mention seems to me to be in the right concerning the real presence of Christ in the sacrament. I own I never understood by the real presence more than what he has elegantly expressed, "that the divine nature of Christ is then eminently present to impart (by the operation of his Holy Spirit) the benefits of his death to worthy receivers." [22] And surely the divine presence of our Lord, thus applying the virtue and merits of the great atonement to each true believer, makes the consecrated bread more than a bare sign of Christ's body, since by his so doing we receive not only the sign but with it the thing signified, all the benefits of his incarnation and passion! But still, however this divine institution may seem to others, to me 'tis full of mystery. Who can account for the operations of God's Holy Spirit? Or define the manner of his working upon the spirit in man, either when he enlightens the understanding or excites and confirms the will, and regulates and calms the passions without impairing man's liberty? Indeed the whole scheme of our redemption by Jesus Christ is beyond all things mysterious. That God! the Mighty God! the God of the spirits of all flesh! The possessor of heaven and earth! Who is being itself! And comprehends in his most pure nature absolute perfection and blessedness! That must necessarily be infinitely happy in and of himself! That such a being should in the least degree regard the salvation of sinners! That he himself! the offended, the injured, should propose terms of reconciliation and admit them into covenant upon any conditions! is truly wonderful and astonishing! As God did not make the world because he needed it, so neither could that be any reason for his redeeming it. He loved us, because he loved us! And would have mercy, because he would have mercy! [23] Then the manner of man's redemption, the way by which he condescends to save us, is altogether incomprehensible! Who can unfold the mystery of the hypostatic union! Or forbear acknowledging with the Apostle, that "without controversy, great is the mystery of godliness, God manifested in the flesh!" [24] That the divine person of the Son of God should (if it may be permitted so to speak) seem so far to forget his dignity and essential glory! as to submit to a life of poverty, contempt, and innumerable other sufferings for above thirty years and conclude that life in inexpressible torments! And all this to heal and save a creature that was at enmity against God and desired not to be otherwise. Here is public and benevolent affection in its utmost exaltation and perfection! And this is "the love of Christ," which, as the Apostle justly observes, "passeth knowledge!"[25]

I have been led away so far by this vast subject! that I have hardly left myself time or room to add more. The writing anything about my way of education I am much averse from.[26] It can't (I think) be of service to anyone to know how I, that have lived such a retired life for so many years (ever since I was with child of you), used to employ my time and care in bringing up my children. No one can, without renouncing the world in the most literal sense, observe my method, and there's few (if any) that would entirely devote above twenty years of the prime of life in hope to save the souls of their children (which they think may be saved without so much ado); for that was my principal intention, however unskillfully or unsuccessfully managed.

Dear Jacky, my love and blessing is ever with you. Adieu.

To Charles Wesley
21 February 1731–1732
MA. Part of a double letter immediately following the preceding one to John.

[No heading, see previous half of the same double letter.]

Dear Charles,

Though you have not had time to tell me so since we parted, yet I hope you are in health, and when you are more at leisure, I shall be glad to hear you are so from yourself. I should be pleased enough to see ye here this spring, if it was not upon the hard condition of your walking hither. But that always terrifies me, and I am commonly so uneasy for fear ye should kill yourselves with coming so far on foot, that it destroys much of the pleasure I should otherwise have in conversing with ye.

I fear poor Patty has several enemies at London and that they have put it in her head to visit us this summer. I am apt to believe that, if they get her once out of my brother's house, they will take care to keep her thence for ever. 'Tis pity that honest, generous girl has not a little of the subtlety of the serpent with the innocence of the dove.[27] She is no match for those which malign her, for she scorns to do an unworthy action and therefore believes everybody else does so, too. Alas, 'tis great pity that all the human species are not so good as they ought to be.

Prithee what is become of J[ohn] Whitelamb: is he yet alive? Where is Mr. Morgan? If with you, pray give my service to him. I am sorry the wood drink did him no service. I never knew it fail before, if drank regularly; but perhaps he was too far gone before he used it. I doubt[28] he eats too little or sleeps cold, which last poisons the blood above all things.

Dear Charles, I send you my love and blessing.

Em, Molly, Kez send their love to ye both.

To John Wesley
24 July 1732
AM, 1784, pp. 462–464 ("On Obedience to Parents"); collated with *Journal*, 3 (1 August, 1742): 34–39 FB, 1:330–331. This famous long letter on the education of her children appears in part III of this volume.

To John Wesley
25 October 1732
State Library of Victoria, Melbourne; copy in MA;
FB, 1:344–346

October 25, [1]732

Dear Jacky,

I was very glad to hear ye got safe to Oxford and should have told you so sooner had I been at liberty from pain of body and other severer trials not convenient to mention. Let everyone enjoy the present hour. Age and successive troubles are sufficient to convince any reasonable man that 'tis a much wiser and safer way to deprecate great afflictions than to pray for them; and that our Lord well knew what was in man when he directed us to pray, "Lead us not into temptation."[29]

I think heretic Clark[e], in his exposition on the Lord's Prayer, is more in the right than Castaniza concerning temptations.[30] His words are as follow: "We are encouraged to glory in tribulation, and to count it all joy when we fall into divers temptations, etc. Nevertheless 'tis carefully to be observed that when the scripture speaks on this manner concerning rejoicing in temptations, it always considers them under this view, as being experienced, and already in great measure overcome. For otherwise, as to temptations in general, temptations unexperienced, of which we know the danger but not the success, our Saviour teaches us to pray, Lead us not into temptation. And again, Watch and pray, lest ye enter into temptation. Our nature is frail, our passions strong, our wills biased; and our security, generally speaking, consists much more certainly in avoiding great temptations than in conquering them. Wherefore we ought continually to pray that God would pleased so to order and direct things in this probation state as not to suffer us to be tempted above what we are able, but that he would with the temptation also make a way to escape, that we may be able to bear it. Our Lord directed his disciples, when they were persecuted in one city, to flee into another. And they who refuse to do it when it is in their power lead themselves into temptation, and tempt God."[31]

I can't tell how you represented your case to Dr. Huntington.[32] I have had occasion to make some observation in consumption and am pretty certain that several symptoms of that distemper are beginning upon you and that unless you take more care than you do, you'll put the matter past dispute in a little time. But take your own way. I have already given you up, as I have some before which once were very dear to me. Charles, though I believe not in a consumption, is in a fine state of health for a man of two or three and twenty that can't eat a full meal but he must presently throw it up again. 'Tis great pity that folks should be no wiser and that

Oct. 25th 732

Dear Jacky.

I was very glad to hear ye got safe to Oxford, and shou'd have told you so sooner had I been at
liberty from Pain of Body, and other severer trials not convenient to mention. Let every one enjoy the present Hour,
the, and successive troubles are sufficient to convince any reasonable man that 'tis a much wiser, and safer way to Deprecate great Afflictions, than to pray for them; and that,
our Lord well knew what was in man, when He directed
us to Pray "Lead us not into Temptation —
I think Herric Clark, is more in the right than (as time a
concerning Temptations, his Words are as follow—"We are
encourag'd to glory in Tribulation and to count it all joy
when we fall into divers Temptations &c— nevertheless 'tis
carefully to be observ'd, that when the Scripture speaks on this
manner concerning rejoicing in Temptations, it always
considers them under this View, as being experienc'd, and already in great measure overcome. for otherwise, as to Temptations
in general, Temptations unexperienc'd, of wch we know the Danger,
but not the Success. Our Saviour teaches us to pray, Lead us not into
Temptation— And again, Watch & Pray, let ye enter into Temptation
Our nature is frail, our passions strong, our Wills biass'd; and our Security generally speaking, consists much more certainly in avoiding great
Temptations, than in conquering them. Wherefore we ought continually
to Pray, That God wd be pleas'd to to order and direct things in this Probate
on State, as not to suffer us to be tempted above what we are able,
but that He wd with the Temptation also make a way to Escape, that we may
be able to bear it. Our Lord directed His Disciples, when they were persecuted in one City, to flee into another. And they who refuse to do it when
it is in their power, Lead themselves into Temptation & Tempt God."

I can't tell how you represented yr Case to Dr Huntington, I have
had occasion to make som observation in Consumptions, and am
pretty certain, that several Symtoms of that Distemper are beginning
upon you, and that unless you take more care than you do, you'll

First page of a typical letter by Susanna Wesley, this one written on 25 October 1732 to her son, John. It is now owned by the State Library of Victoria in Melbourne. Note her use of his family nickname, Jacky, despite his age (29) and station (fellow of Lincoln College, Oxford).

they can't hit the mean in a case where it is so obvious to view that none can mistake it, which do not do it on purpose.

I heartily join with your small society in all their pious and charitable actions, which are intended for God's glory; and am glad to hear Mr. Clayton and Mr. Hall[33] has met with desired success. May ye still in such good works go on and prosper.[34] Though absent in body, I am present with ye in spirit and daily recommend and commit ye all to divine providence. You do well to wait on the bishop, because 'tis a point of prudence and civility, though (if he be a good man) I can't think it in the power of anyone to prejudice him against you.[35]

Your arguments against horse races do certainly conclude against masquerades, balls, plays, operas, and all such light and vain diversions, which, whether the gay people of the world will own it or no, does strongly confirm and strengthen "the lust of the flesh, the lust of the eye, and the pride of life";[36] all which we must renounce, or renounce our God and hope of eternal salvation. I will not say 'tis impossible for a person to have any sense of religion which frequents those vile assemblies, but I never throughout the course of my long life knew so much as one serious Christian that did. Nor can I see how a lover of God can have any relish for such vain amusements.

The Life of God in the Soul of Man[37] is an excellent good book and was an acquaintance of mine many years ago; but I have unfortunately lost it. There's many good things in Castaniza, more in Baxter,[38] yet are neither without faults, which I overlook for the sake of their virtues; nor can I say of all the books of divinity I have read which is the best; one is best at one time, one at another, according to the temper and disposition of the mind.

Mr. Horbery is for Oxford soon, by whom if I can I will write Mr. Whitelamb, to whom pray give my love and service and tell him though I can't show my esteem for him all the ways I would, yet I daily remember him.

I must tell ye, Mr. John Wesley, Fellow of Lincoln, and Mr. Charles Wesley, Student of Christ Church, that ye are two scrubby travellers and sink your characters strangely by eating nothing on the road [. . .][39] to save charges. I wonder ye are not ashamed of yourselves. Surely if ye will but give yourselves leave to think a little, ye will return to a better mind.

Your sisters send their love to you and Charles, and I my love and blessing to ye both.[40]

Adieu

Your father is in a very bad state of health; he sleeps little and eats less. He seems not to have any apprehension of his approaching exit, but I fear he has but a short time to live. 'Tis with much pain and difficulty that he performs divine service on the Lord's day, which sometimes he is forced to contract very much. Everybody observes his decay but himself, and people really seem much concerned both for him and his family.

The two girls, being uneasy in the present situation, do not apprehend the sad consequences which (in all appearance) must attend his death so much as I think they ought to do; for as bad as they think their condition now, I doubt[41] it will be far worse when his head is laid.

To John Wesley

Before 16 August 1733

John Whitehead, *The Life of the Rev. John Wesley* . . . (Dublin: John Jones, 1805), 1:443–445; FB, 1:354–355. Fragments of an "angry letter from my mother" are quoted in John's reply, 17 August 1733. S. W. was apparently criticizing the (overly strict?) discipline of the Holy Club.

. . . the devil hates offensive war most, and . . . whoever tries to rescue more than his own soul from his hands will have more enemies and meet with greater opposition than if he was content with "having his own life for a prey." [42]

. . . [you] rigorously impose any observances on others . . .

Notes

1. The phrase is Henry D. Rack's, *Reasonable Enthusiast: John Wesley and the Rise of Methodism* (Philadelphia: Trinity Press International, 1989), p. 87.

2. For a summary and useful primary sources on this phase of Wesley's life see Richard P. Heitzenrater, *The Elusive Mr. Wesley: Vol. One. John Wesley His Own Biographer* (Nashville: Abingdon, 1984), pp. 63–74.

3. A native of Wroot, Whitelamb was taken under the wing of Samuel Wesley, who helped send him to Oxford, where John Wesley gave him free tuition. Upon graduation and ordination, the elder Wesley arranged for Whitelamb to succeed him as rector of Wroot and authorized his marriage to his daughter Mary in December 1733.

4. Matthew Horbery had been an undergraduate at Lincoln and in 1733 would be elected a fellow of Magdalen. His father had been vicar of Haxey, a parish adjoining Epworth, which he still occasionally visited.

5. Eusby Isham had been a fellow of Lincoln since 1718 and was elected rector on 9 July 1731, with John Wesley's support, following the death of the incumbent, John Morley. See V. H. H. Green, *The Young Mr. Wesley* . . . (New York: St. Martin's, 1961), pp. 127–29.

6. Samuel's brother Matthew, the physician who had taken care of Suky and Hetty after the rectory fire until a new rectory could be built. Following this visit he would also take his niece Patty (Martha) to spend time with his family in London. His will provided considerable sums for Martha, Hetty, Anne, and two of their children. See Stevenson, pp. 52–53.

7. The Isle of Axholme, local designation for the fen-surrounded area where Epworth was situated.

8. Appropriately.

9. Probably a reference to Hetty, to whom he gave £500 at her marriage. See Frederick Maser, *The Story of John Wesley's Sisters, or Seven Sisters in Search of Love* (Rutland, Vt.: Academy Books, 1988), p. 59.

10. "Seven night," that is, a week.

11. Emily and Kezzy were both employed in Mrs. Taylor's school in Lincoln. Their presence there was good reason for the other sisters to stop en route from Epworth to London.

12. William Morgan, an undergraduate of Christ Church College, was a "charter member" of the Holy Club, the small group of pious students that John Wesley led after his return to Oxford in 1729. It was largely Morgan who moved the club to begin a ministry to prisoners and their families. His increasing ill health, madness, and subsequent death in August 1732 were attributed by his father, a government official in Dublin, to the excessive religious zeal of the Holy Club. See Green, *Young Mr. Wesely*, pp. 168–71. Further references crop up in ensuing letters.

13. S. W. uses the archaic spelling "spaw."

14. A mineral spring.

15. This paragraph gives insight into the business problems surrounding a rectory family. Part of the priest's maintenance was whatever profit he could make from the glebe land, which could either be managed himself or rented out. In the Wesley family it is apparent that much of this burden fell to the rector's wife.

16. Flax.

17. Suspect.

18. Turnips.

19. Charles had earlier described his college as "the worst place in the world to begin a reformation in," a place where religion was ridiculed. Green, *Young Mr. Wesley*, p. 152.

20. John Whitelamb. See note 3.

21. Robert Kirkham, undergraduate of Merton College, friend of the Wesley brothers, and member of the Holy Club.

22. John Wesley's letter of 26 January to his mother has not survived, but his answering letter of 28 February 1731/32 indicates that he was probably quoting William Morgan. See FB, p. 328.

23. Echoes of Exodus 33:19 and Romans 9:15.

24. Nearly exact quotation of 1 Timothy 3:16; quotation marks in holograph.

25. Ephesians 3:19; my quotation marks.

26. Susanna finally relented, supplying her son with a summary of her child-rearing practices in the famous long letter of 24 July 1732, reprinted in part III of this volume.

27. See Matthew 10:16.

28. Suspect.

29. Matthew 6:13; Luke 11:4.

30. A reference to Lorenzo Scupoli, *The Spiritual Combat*, Richard Lucas, Trans. (London: Samuel Keble, 1698), then falsely attributed to Juan de Castaniza; the Wesleys probably read from the 1698 translation of Richard Lucas, whose own work on religious perfection S. W. commented on at some length in her journal, q.v. in part II of this volume. Lucas was at the time rector of St. Katherine, Coleman Street. S. W. probably has several of the book's chapters in mind: chap. 7, "Of the Manner of Fighting Against Sensual Motions, and of the Acts That the Will Must Produce to Acquire a Habit of Vertue"; chap. 10, "Of the Manner of Fighting or Subduing the Lusts of the Flesh or Concupisence"; chap. 17, "How the Devil, by the Means of General Good Purposes, Endeavours to Hinder Our Progress in Virtue"; chap. 18, "How the Devil Strives to Draw Us from the Way of Virtue." Samuel Clarke (1675–1729), a friend of William Whiston, flirted with Arianism and Unitarianism but successfully avoided official censure, retaining the living of St. James's, Westminster, until his death.

31. S. W. is excerpting material from Samuel Clarke's *An Exposition of the Church-Catechism* (London: James and John Knapton, 1729), published posthumously. In discussing the sixth petition of the Lord's Prayer, he says: "Nay, on the contrary, we are incouraged even to glory in Tribulations [Rom.v.3]; and to count it all joy, when we fall into divers Temptations [Jam.i.2]: Considering that the Tryal of our Faith, is much more pretious than of Gold that perisheth [I Pet.i.7]; and that Blessed is the man that endureth temptation; for when he is tried, he shall receive the Crown of Life [Jam.i.12].

"Nevertheless 'tis carefully to be observed, that when the Scripture speaks in this manner concerning Rejoicing in Temptations, it always considers them under This view, as being experienced, and already in great measure overcome. For otherwise, as to Temptations in general, Temptations unexperienced, and of which we know the Danger, but not the Success; our Saviour teaches us to pray, 'Lead us not into temptation:' And again, Watch and pray, least ye enter into Temptation [Mar.xiv.38]. Our Nature is frail, our Passions strong, our Wills biassed; And our security, generally speaking, consists much more certainly in avoiding great Temptations, than in conquering them. Wherefore we ought continually to pray, that God would be pleased so to order and direct things in This Probation-state, as not to suffer us to be tempted above what we are able [1 Cor.x.13]; but that he would with the Temptation also make a way to escape, that we may be able to bear it. Our Lord directed his Disciples, when they were persecuted in One City, to flee into another [Matt.x.23]. And they who refuse to do so, when it is in their Power; lead Themselves into Temptation, and tempt God" (Pages 267–269, with marginal biblical citations inserted).

32. Apparently a physician he was consulting; I can find no other references to him.

33. John Clayton, a fellow of Brasenose College, and Westley Hall, an undergraduate of Lincoln, one of Wesley's pupils and later his brother-in-law (in a disastrous marriage to his sister Martha in 1735), were both members of the Holy Club. As the singular verb might indicate, S. W. has included Hall as an afterthought: "& Mr. Hall" is inserted above the line after the sentence was finished.

34. Resonances of 1 Kings 22:15 and 2 Chronicles 18:14.

35. Earlier in the month, Wesley and Clayton had visited John Potter, then bishop of Oxford and later archbishop of Canterbury, to discuss the confirmation of a prisoner they had been working with under Holy Club auspices. See Green, *Young Mr. Wesley*, p. 182.

36. Nearly exact quotation of 1 John 2:16; my quotation marks.

37. This work, published anonymously, has since been attributed to the Scottish Episcopalian Henry Scougal. Its subtitle reads, "*Or, the Nature and Excellency of the Christian Religion: With the Methods of Attaining the Happiness It Proposes; Also an Account of the Beginnings and Advances of a Spiritual Life*, 2nd ed.(London: T. Dring and J. Weld, 1691). The MS has the title in quotation marks.

38. S. W. could be referring to any of dozens of the practical works of Richard Baxter (1615–1691), the best known of which are *The Christian Directory* and *The Saints Everlasting Rest*. John Wesley later abridged the latter in his *Christian Library*. Baxter had been an old friend of Susanna's father, Samuel Annesley. See John Newton, *Susanna Wesley and the Puritan Tradition in Methodism* (London: Epworth, 1968), pp. 29, 138ff. For details on Baxter's approach and a complete checklist of his publications, see N. H. Keeble, *Richard Baxter: Puritan Man of Letters* (Oxford: Clarendon Press, 1982), particularly, chap. 4 ("The Pastor and Practical Divine"), pp. 69–93, and the "Baxter Bibliography," pp. 156–84.

39. Several words are clipped out of the letter.

40. There follows here an endorsement in John Wesley's hand, employing the same abbreviate script used in LB: "Eating on Road: J. Whitelamb: my father: Society."

41. Suspect.

42. See Jeremiah 38:2; quotation marks in MS.

TWELVE

More Advice, More Concern

*I*n this set of letters for 1734 and early 1735, the aging Susanna Wesley continues to provide counsel to her correspondents (including, in the first one, a person not of her family) and to discuss important events within the family circle. Perhaps reflecting on her husband's deteriorating condition and intimations of her own mortality, she also falls into paragraphs of devotional rapture, reminiscent of pages in her journal.[1]

The initial letter, difficult to place concerning both date and recipient, shows her at her practical best, trying to help a young clergyman think through the ecclesiastical, political, and legal issues involved in getting his first parish. As in other instances in which she has something important to say, her tactic is modestly to deny her own abilities and then boldly to proceed to impart her well-considered advice. She writes in this letter as one who understands "the system" but who also knows the spiritual and theological bases that the system ought to serve.

In three substantial letters to her son John at Oxford in early 1734, Susanna combines a number of her typical themes. The marriage of her crippled daughter, Molly, to John Whitelamb, Samuel Wesley's protégé and John's pupil at Oxford, exercises her in the 1 January letter. She is against the match, lets John know in no uncertain terms, and closes by asking him to "burn this letter." He did not, probably in part because she also provided perspective on William Law, whose mysticism John was struggling to comprehend at the time. Of additional interest to us is a reference to the "despised Methodists" at Oxford (she was already taking her sons' controversial part) and her almost existential confession of faith: "I cannot know him. I dare not say I love him—only this, I have chose him. . . ."

The letter of 14 February reveals her as a sort of pastor's pastor, helping John figure out how to be the spiritual director of his student Richard Morgan, brother of William (whose death had caused such controversy for the Oxford Methodists). In the process she criticizes the "heathen philosophers" and recommends the ethics of the New Testament by reporting a remark of John Locke.

The Morgan case and the Holy Club are still on her mind in her letter of 30

March, in which she also reports taking issue (on paper) with a preacher she has been hearing (perhaps her husband, perhaps young John Whitelamb). She passes on some free advice to Westley Hall, another of John's Oxford contacts and the soon-to-be husband of her daughter Patty, recognizing that it is "none of my business." Then, in a section recommending more time for meditation, she waxes eloquent on the glory of God, nevertheless observing that lack of fervor should not be interpreted as lack of faith. She has gotten carried away: "I am got to the end of my paper before I am aware."

For the early part of 1735, just prior to Samuel Wesley Sr.'s death, we have no full letters, only notes for a letter to John and part of one to Charles. In the former, Susanna responds to John's query about Christian liberty by reaffirming her belief in the hierarchical order of things and subservience to authority. Practically liberated she may be, but theoretically she still sees social and political distinctions as part of the divinely ordained scheme. In the fragment of the letter to Charles she again is commending meditation as a spiritual discipline to one of her children, concluding with what is by now her old refrain from George Herbert's poetry.

❧

To Unknown
N.d. (possibly 1734)
MA. This is possibly a draft, given its many deletions and insertions. Internal clues suggest that it is intended for a young, local clergyman trying to find a decent living during Samuel Wesley Sr.'s lifetime. Perhaps the man is John Whitelamb, before he succeeded to the living of Wroot in 1734; surely, however, Whitelamb would not have to be urged to "advise with Mr. Wesley," having been his protégé and a member of the household for some time before he went to Oxford and (see following letter) became his son-in-law. Concern for a daughter's prospect would certainly account for Susanna's interest in such a case, though her practical advice might well have been sought in any case.

[No heading or greeting]

I was greatly surprised when Mrs. Piggot[2] told me that your friend is like to be engaged in a suit of law about the living he pretends to, and though I do not care to meddle or interfere in other people's business, especially where my advice is not desired and perhaps will not be well taken, yet I think myself obliged in charity to speak my mind freely, since none of your brethren,[3] Mr. [?]Lug etc., would be so kind to deal faithfully with you; but 'tis no new thing for a man to have a great acquaintance and yet want a friend.

You know when you were first pleased to tell me the reason of your journey, that I spake very cautiously of it, yet I could not forbear saying that I did not like your miscalled friend's proceedings, and I must tell you plainly, sir, that I like him now worse than ever. He has not dealt fairly with you in representing his case; for he told you that he was sure of the place and wanted nothing but your name in the presentation and that you immediately be inducted, whereas now it appears that there must be a reference, if not a suit, before he can enter upon it, which may take up a great deal of time. And, though I am but a novice in these matters, yet I think you would do well to inquire whether your having your name put into his presentation by which you are entitled to the living will not prove a bar to your own preferment till the matter is decided. I am afraid you'll find yourself incapable of any other cure without a dispensation. And are you sure, sir, your friend will be at the trouble and charge of procuring you one if you should want it? Or that he will support you in the meantime without one? If not, to what purpose should you make such a costly compliment to any man? You stand as fair and are as well qualified for preferment as another, and why should you involve yourself in such a dishonourable and troublesome business to oblige anyone?[4] Indeed, I'm much afraid that you'll gain a great deal of disreputation by [?]engaging in this affair, and you know we are not only obliged to whatever things are honest, but to whatever is of good report.[5] 'Tis in my opinion this affair is of the same complexion with Occasional Conformity;[6] for as that is a wicked evasion of one law, so is this of another. 'Tis well if that friend of yours be not a little heterodox in his principles and, if there be not too much love of this world in the bottom of it.

I should not take upon me to advise those that are wiser than myself, nor to teach where I ought to learn, but I think I may without offence to any say that the clergy would do well to consider with what temper and sincerity of mind they reply when they are questioned before they enter into the sacred priesthood, whether they think they are moved by the Holy Ghost to take upon themselves that holy order.[7] Though it is permitted to those who serve the altar to be partakers with the altar, yet that does by no means justify the entering upon the ministry only for interest without principally regarding the glory of God and the salvation of the souls committed to their cure. And you very well know, sir, that those that followed our Saviour only for the loaves were upon that account severely reprehended by him.[8] Whether this be the case of your friend, I am not able to determine. God and his own conscience are the most proper judges, and there I leave it.

To be short, though you have gone so far, yet be advised and go no farther. You do not know your man, nor can you possibly foresee the event of a law suit. But grant you were sure he would get the better; yet are you also sure it will be the better for you if he does? What terms are agreed upon between you? Or what advantage can he propose that will be equivalent to the tarnishing of your reputation upon your first appearing in the world? But above all other things, this consideration ought to weigh most with you, whether or no you can answer before God your being accessory to his plain neglect of his duty, to say no worse of it. And if you cannot, I need not tell you what you are to do. What, though this small thing you have at [sic][9] now be precarious and you have at present no prospect of another cure, yet never be discouraged that God that has been with you, that has fed and clothed you hitherto ever since you came into the world, and that has preserved you, will never forsake you, if you do but heartily rely upon his Providence, and he has a thousands expedients to relieve and provide for us that we cannot possibly foresee. Nay, though your friend should entirely cast you off and should refuse to bear the charges of the journey (which, by the way, would prove him a great————),[10] yet if you have but the testimony of a good conscience and can but say to yourself, "this loss and damage I sustain because I would be guilty of an ill action,"[11] I am very confident that God will abundantly make it up to you, even in this life, though if he should not, heaven would make large amends for all.

Pardon me, sir, that I have spoke my thoughts so freely, but I have a true concern for you, and would not have you under the management of a designing man that perhaps may lead you into a great deal of mischief and then drop you. I wish you would advise with Mr. Wesley. Depend upon it, he is a just, honest man, and I am sure will be very faithful, if you please make a friend of him.

I am, sir, your friend and servant
[no signature]

To John Wesley
1 January 1733/34
MA; FB, 1:362–364.

Tuesday, Jan. 1st [1]733/4

Dear son,

I was highly pleased with receiving a letter from you last Sunday,[12] for I have long wanted to write to you, but knew not whether you were at London or Oxford. My principal business with you was about Whitelamb, to reprehend your too great caution in not informing me what his moral character is, and about his intrigue at Medley. Had you let me know of the looseness of his principles and his disreputable practices, I should never have forwarded his going into orders, neither would I have suffered him to renew his addresses to Molly, after such a notorious violation of his promises to her. Indeed when he came hither first he was so full of his new doxy that he could not forbear telling Molly and Kezzy of his amour, which the former informed me of, and I discoursed him about it and would have convinced him that it was sinful and dishonourable for him to court another woman when he was pre-engaged, [but] he was not much moved with what I could say. So I told him plainly he should presently renounce one or the other, and that if he did not presently write to Robinson[13] (who is his pimp) and tell him that he would never more have any conversation with his doll at Medley, I would immediately send Molly away, where he should never see her more; though withal I advised him rather to take his Betty than your sister, for I thought her a much fitter wife for him. Besides, I was extremely unwilling Molly should ever marry at all. But Molly, who was fond of him to the last degree, was of another mind, and persuaded him to write to Robinson, and show[14] me the letter. I did not much approve it, because he seemed to justify those vile practices, which I thought he ought to have condemned; yet to satisfy her importunity I permitted them to go on. Whitelamb wrote to ask your father's leave to marry his daughter, which Mr. Wesley gave him, and on St. Thomas's Day[15] married they were at Epworth by Mr. Horbery; full sore against my will, but my consent was never asked, and your father, brother Wesley,[16] etc., being for the match, I said nothing against it to them, only laboured what I could to dissuade Molly from it. But the flesh and the devil were too hard for me. I could not prevail. Yet with God nothing is impossible,[17] and though this unequal marriage has to me a terrible aspect, 'tis possible for God to bring good out of this great evil; or otherwise he can take me away from the evil to come. Still, Jacky, I have somewhat more to tell you, but dare not write it, only this. Pray let Robinson (your pupil) know that Whitelamb is married; let him know I was against the match; give my service to him; and tell him from me, I am as good as my word, I daily pray for him, and beg of him, if he have the least regard for his soul or have yet any remaining sense of religion in his mind, to shake off all acquaintance with the profane and irregular; for it is the free thinker and sensualist, not the despised Methodists,[18] which will be ashamed and confounded when summoned to appear before the face of that Almighty Judge whose Godhead they have blasphemed and whose offered mercy they have despised and ludicrously rejected. The pleasures of sin are but for a short, uncertain time, but eternity hath no end. Therefore one would think that few arguments might serve to convince a man which has not lost his senses that 'tis of the last importance for us to be very serious in improving the present time and acquainting ourselves with God while it is called **Today,**[19] lest being disqualified for his blissful presence, our future existence be inexpressibly miserable.

You are entirely in the right in what you say in the second paragraph of your letter. The different degrees of virtue and piety are different states of soul, which must be passed through gradually; and he that cavils at a practical advice plainly shows that he has not gone through those states which were to have been passed before he could apprehend the goodness of the given direction. For in all matters of religion, if there be not an internal sense in the hearer corresponding to that sense in the mind of the speaker, what is said will have no effect. This I have often experienced. Yet sometimes it falls out that while a zealous Christian is discoursing on spiritual subjects the Blessed Spirit of God Incarnate will give such light to the minds of those that hear him as shall dispel their native darkness and enable them to apprehend those spiritual things of which before they had no discernment. As in the case of St. Peter, who preaching the gospel to Cornelius and his friends, it is said, "While Peter yet spake these words the Holy Ghost fell on all them which heard the word."[20]

Mr. Law is a good and a valuable man; yet he is but a man; and therefore no marvel that he could not be so explicit as you could have wished in speaking of the presence of God.[21] Perhaps his mind was too full of the sense of that Blessed Being readily to hit upon words to express a thing so far above their nature. Who can think, much less speak, on that vast subject—his greatness, his dignity, astonishes us! The purity of his goodness, his redeeming love, confounds and overwhelms us! At the perception of his glory our feeble powers are suspended, and nature faints before the God of nature.

For my part, after many years' search and inquiry I still continue to pay my devotions to an unknown God. I cannot know him. I dare not say I love him—only this, I have chose him for my only happiness, my all, my only God, in a word, for my God. And when I sound my will, I feel it adheres to its choice, though not so faithfully as it ought. Therefore I desire your prayers, which I need much more than you do mine.

That God is everywhere present, and we always present to him, is certain; but that he should be always present to us is scarce consistent with our mortal state.

Some choice souls, 'tis true, have attained such a habitual sense of his presence as admits of few interruptions. But what, my dear—Consider, he is so infinitely blessed! So altogether lovely![22] That every perception of him, every approach (in contemplation) to his supreme glory and blessedness imparts such a vital joy and gladness to the heart as banishes all pain and sense of misery—And were eternity added to this happiness it would be heaven.

I have much to say, but time is expired.

Pray burn this letter, for I would not that any know my thoughts of W[hitelamb] and M[olly], since they are married. She thinks she can reform what is amiss in him. I think myself he grows more serious and regular. My love and blessing to ye both. Wishing ye a Happy New Year. My service to Mr. Hall.[23]

To John Wesley
14 February 1734
AM, 1778, pp. 81–84; FB, pp. 377–378. When Wesley edited this letter for *AM*, he misdated it as 14 February 1735. In fact, it answers John's letter to S. W. of 28 January 1734 (FB, 1:71–373).

Feb. 14 [1734]

Dear son,

I cannot well say whether it will answer any good end to let the young gentleman[24] know that you have heard of what he has said against you. I doubt it will make him desperate. I remember a piece of advise which my brother Matthew[25] gave in a parallel case: "Never let any man know that you have heard what he has said against you. It may be he spake upon some misinformation, or was in a passion or did it in a weak compliance with the company; perhaps he has changed his mind, and is sorry for having done it and may continue friendly to you. But if he finds you are acquainted with what he said, he will conclude you cannot forgive him and upon that supposition will become your enemy."

Your other question is indeed of great weight, and the resolving it requires a better judgment than mine. But since you desire my opinion, I shall propose what I have to say.[26]

Since God is altogether inaccessible to us but by Jesus Christ, and since none ever was or ever will be saved but by him, is it not absolutely necessary for all people, young and old, to be well grounded in the knowledge and faith of Jesus Christ? By faith I do not mean an assent only to the truths of the gospel concerning him, but such as assent as influences our practice, as makes us heartily and thankfully accept him for our God and Saviour upon his own conditions. No faith below this can be saving. And since this faith is necessary to salvation, can it be too frequently or too explicitly discoursed on to young people? I think not.

But since the natural pride of man is wont to suggest to him that he is self-sufficient and has not need of a Saviour, may it not be proper to show (the young especially) that without the great atonement there could be no remission of sin; and that in the present state of human nature no man can qualify himself for heaven without that Holy Spirit which is given by God Incarnate? To convince them of this truth, might it not be needful to inform them that since God is infinitely just, or rather that he is justice itself, it necessarily follows that vindictive justice is an essential property in the divine nature? And if so, one of these two things seems to have been absolutely necessary, either that there must be an adequate satisfaction made to the divine justice for the violation of God's law by mankind; or else that the whole human species should have perished in Adam (which would have afforded too great matter of triumph to the apostate angels)—otherwise how could God have been just to himself? Would not some mention of the necessity of revealed religion be proper here? Since without it all the wit of man could never have found out how human nature was corrupted in its fountain, neither had it been possible for us to have discovered any way or means whereby it might be restored to its primitive purity. Nay, had it been possible for the brightest angels in heaven to have found out such a way to redeem and restore mankind as God hath appointed, yet durst any of them have proposed it to the uncreated Godhead?—No. Surely the offended must appoint a way to save the offender, or man must be lost for ever. "O the depth of the riches of the wisdom, and knowledge, and goodness of God! How unsearchable are his judgments, and his ways past finding out!"[27] "As the heavens are higher than the earth, so are his thoughts higher than our thoughts, and his ways than our ways!"[28] Here surely you may give free scope to your spirits, here you may freely use your Christian liberty and discourse without reserve of the excellency of the knowledge and love of Christ, as his Spirit gives you utterance.—What, my son, did the pure and holy person of the son of God pass by the fallen angels, who were far superior, of greater dignity, and of an higher order in the scale of existence, and choose to unite himself to the human nature? And shall we soften (as you call it) these glorious truths? Rather let us speak boldly without fear; these truths ought to be frequently inculcated and pressed home upon the consciences of men. And when once men are affected with a sense of redeeming love, that sense will powerfully convince them of the vanity of the world and make them esteem the honour, wealth, and pleasures of it as dross or dung, so that they may win Christ.[29]

As for moral subjects,[30] they are necessary to be discoursed on; but then, I humbly conceive, we are to speak of moral virtues as Christians and not like heathens. And if we could indeed do honour to our Saviour, we should take all fitting occasions to make men observe the excellence and perfection of the moral virtues taught by Christ and his apostles, far surpassing all that was pretended to by the very best of the heathen philosophers. All their morality was defective in principle and direction, was intended only to regulate the outward actions, but never reached the heart, or at the highest it looked no farther than the temporal happiness of mankind. "But moral virtues evangelized, or improved into Christian duties, have partly a view to promote the good of human society here, but chiefly to qualify the observers of them for a much more blessed and more enduring society hereafter."[31] I cannot stay to enlarge on this vast subject, nor indeed (considering whom I write to) is it needful. Yet one thing I cannot forbear adding, which may carry some weight with his admirers, and that is, the very wise and just reply which Mr. Locke made to one that desired him to draw up a system of morals. "Did the world," says he, "want a rule, I confess there could be no work so necessary, nor so commendable. But the gospel contains so perfect a body of ethics that reason may be excused from that enquiry, since she may find man's duty clearer and easier in Revelation than in herself." [32]

That you may continue steadfast in the faith and increase more and more in the knowledge and love of God, and of his Son, Jesus Christ! That holiness, simplicity, and purity (which are different words signifying the same thing), may recommend you to the favour of God Incarnate! That his Spirit may dwell in you, and keep you still (as now) under a sense of God's blissful presence, is the hearty prayer of, dear son,

    Your affectionate mother,
     And most faithful friend,
      S[usanna] W[esley]

To John Wesley
30 March 1734
MA; FB, 1:382–385.

             Sat: March 30th [1]734

Dear son,

The young gentleman's father,[33] for ought I can perceive, has a better notion of religion than many people have, though not the best; for few insist upon the necessity of private prayer, but if they go to church sometimes and abstain from the grossest acts of mortal sin, though they are ignorant of the spirit and power of godliness and have no sense of the love of God and universal benevolence, yet they rest well satisfied of their salvation and are pleased to think they may enjoy the world as much as they can while they live and have heaven in reserve when they die. I have met with abundance of these people in my time, and I think it one of the most difficult things imaginable to bring them off from their carnal security and to convince them that heaven is a state, as well as a place; a state of holiness, begun in this life, though not perfected till we enter upon life eternal;[34] that all sins are so many spiritual diseases, which must be cured by the power of Christ before we can be capable of being happy, even though it were possible for us to be admitted into the kingdom of heaven hereafter. If the young man's father was well apprized of this, he would not venture to pronounce his son a good Christian upon such weak grounds as he seems to do. Yet notwithstanding the father's indifference, I can't but conceive good hopes of the son, because he chooses to spend so much of his time with you (for I presume he is not forced to it), and if we may not from thence conclude he is good, I think we may believe he desires to be so. And if that be the case, give him time. We know that the great work of regeneration is not performed at once, but proceeds by slow and often imperceptible degrees, by reason of the strong opposition which corrupt nature makes against it; yet if one grain of divine grace be sown in the heart, though (to use our blessed Lord's simile) it be but as a single grain of mustard seed, it will take root, and bring forth fruit with patience.[35]

Mr. Clayton and Mr. Hall[36] are much wiser than I am, yet with submission to their better judgments I think that though some marks of a visible superiority on your part is convenient to maintain the order of the world, yet severity is not; since experience may convince us that such kind of behaviour towards a man (children are out of the question) may make him a hypocrite, but will never make him a convert. Never trouble yourself to inquire whether he loves you or not: if you can persuade him to love God, he will love you as much as is necessary; if he love not God his love is of no value. But be that as it will, we must refer all things to God, and be as indifferent as we possibly can be in all matters wherein the great enemy, self, is concerned.

If you and your few pious companions have devoted two hours in the evening to religious reading or conference, there can be no dispute but that you ought to spend the whole time in such exercises which it was set apart for; but if your evenings be not strictly devoted, I see no harm in talking sometimes of your secular affairs. But if (as you say) it does your novice no good and does yourselves harm, the case is plain—you must not prejudice your own souls to do another good; much less ought you to do so when you can do no good at all. Of this ye are better judges than I can be.

'Twas well you paid not for a double letter. I am always afraid of putting you to charge, and that fear prevented me sending you a long scribble indeed a while ago. For a certain person[37] and I had a warm debate on some important points in religion wherein we could not agree. Afterwards he wrote some propositions, which I endeavoured to answer, and this controversy I was minded to have sent you, and to have desired your judgment upon it. But the unreasonable cost of such a letter then hindered me from sending it, since I have heard him in two sermons contradict every article he before defended, which makes me hope that upon second thoughts his mind is changed; and if so, what was said in private conference ought not to be remembered, and therefore I would not send you the papers at all.

I can't think Mr. Hall does well in refusing an opportunity of doing so much service to religion as he certainly might do if he accepted the living he is about to refuse. Surely never was more need of orthodox, sober divines in our Lord's vineyard than there is now; and why a man of his extraordinary piety and love to souls should decline the service in this critical juncture I can't conceive. But this is none of my business.

You want no direction from me how to employ your time. I thank God for his inspiring you with a resolution of being faithful in improving that important talent committed to your trust. It would be of no service to you to know in any particular what I do, or what method in examination, or anything else, I observe. I am superannuated, and don't now live as I would, but as I can. I can't observe order, or think consistently, as formerly. When I have lucid interval I aim at improving it, but alas! it is but aiming.

I see nothing in the disposition of your time but what I approve, unless it be that you do not assign enough of it to meditation, which is (I conceive) incomparably the best means to spiritualize our affections, confirm our judgments, and add strength to our pious resolutions of any exercise whatever. If contrition be as 'tis commonly defined, that sorrow for and hatred of sin which proceeds from our love to God, surely the best way to excite this contrition is to meditate frequently on such subjects as may excite, cherish, and increase our love to that blest Being! And what is so proper for this end as deep and serious consideration of that pure, unaccountable love which is demonstrated to us in our redemption by God Incarnate! Verily, the simplicity of divine love is wonderful! It transcends all thought, it passeth our sublimest apprehensions! Perfect love indeed! No mixture of interest! No by-ends[38] or selfish regards. If we be righteous, what give we him? "In him we live, and move, and have our being,"[39] both in a physical and moral sense; but he can gain nothing by us, nor can we offer him anything that is not already his own. He can lose nothing by losing us, but in our loss of him we lose all good, all happiness, all peace, all pleasure, health, and joy; all that is either good in itself, or can be good for us. And yet this great, this incomprehensible, ineffable, all-glorious God deigns to regard us! Declares he loves us! Expresses the tenderest concern for our happiness! Is unwilling to give us up to the grand enemy of souls, or to leave us to ourselves, but hath commissioned his ambassadors to offer us pardon and salvation upon the most equitable terms imaginable! How long doth he wait to be gracious! How oft doth he call upon us to return and live! By his ministers, his providences; by the still, small voice[40] of his Holy Spirit! By conscience, his vicegerent within us and by his merciful corrections and the innumerable blessings we daily enjoy! To contemplate God as he is in himself we cannot; if we aim at doing it we feel nature faints under the least perception of his greatness, and we are presently swallowed up and lost in the immensity of his glory! For finite in presence of Infinite vanishes straight into nothing. But when we consider him under the character of a Saviour we revive, and the greatness of that majesty which before astonished and confounded our weak faculties now enhances the value of his condescension towards us and melts our tempers into tenderness and love.

But I am got to the end of my paper before I am aware. One word more and I am done. As your course of life is austere, and your diet low, so the passions, as far as they depend on the body, will be low, too. Therefore you must not judge of your interior state by your not feeling great fervours of spirit and extraordinary agitations, as plentiful weeping, etc., but rather by the firm adherence of your will to God. If upon examination you perceive that you still choose him for your only good, that your spirit (to use a Scripture phrase) cleaveth steadfastly to him,[41] follow Mr. Baxter's advice, and you will be easy:

> Put your souls, with all their sins and dangers, and all their interests, into the hand of Jesus Christ your Saviour; and trust them wholly with him by a resolved faith. It is he that hath purchased them, and therefore loveth them. It is he that is the owner of them by right of redemption. And it is now become his own interest, even for the success and honour of his redemption, to save them.[42]

When I begin to write to you I think I don't know how to make an end. I fully purposed when I began to write to be very brief, but I will conclude, though I find I shall be forced to make up such a clumsy letter as I did last time.

Today J[ohn] Brown, Sr.[43] sets forward for London in order to attend your father home.

Pray give my love and blessing to Charles. I hope he is well, though I have never heard from him since he left Epworth.

Dear Jacky, God Almighty bless thee!

To John Wesley
Notes for an answer written on the back of his letter to S. W., 14 February 1735; MA; FB, 1:418–419. John's letter continues a discussion they have been having on Christian liberty.

The visible order of Providence is to be observed by all, whether strong or weak in the faith, and this can't be done, nor civil government be established and the due subservience of one man to another preserved, without ensigns of authority, and difference in houses, furniture, and apparel, all which are marks of distinction, and as such in obedience to the will of God, and not for vainglory, they ought to be used, and he that breaks his rank and goes out of character, so far as he does so, so far he breaks the external order of the universe and abuses his Christian liberty.

To Charles Wesley
1735 (no month or date)
MA. Fragments, mainly advising a daily devotional routine; heading missing; brief postscript from Samuel Wesley Sr.: "Since you desire me to write, I will, though with great pain and to little purpose. I pity and love you, but that's all I can do unless praying to God to help you. Yr Aff: Fa: Sam Wesley." Endorsed by Charles Wesley: "My father and mother 1735." The letter would have to have been written before Samuel Wesley's death on 25 April 1735 and before Charles and John walked home from Oxford, arriving to be with their dying father on 4 April (FB, 1:422, n. 1).

. . . that as pleases God, but if while I have life and any remains of health, it may be useful or pleasing to you, that we hold a correspondence together by letters, I shall gladly do it. But then, dear Charles, let us not spend our time in trifling, in talking of impertinent matters that will turn to no account. Rather, let us converse as beings whose existence on earth is of short continuance, and yet have a work of great, I should say, of the greatest, importance, to finish in this uncertain duration, or we are lost forever.

This consideration will readily suggest to your good sense that we ought carefully to improve our time.[44] And in order to do it effectually, I must earnestly conjure[45] you to set apart two hours every day for private devotion; one in the morning, the other in the evening, which will answer to the morning and evening sacrifices that you know were appointed by God himself![46] It is not for me to fix the particular hours; those must be determined by yourself, who best know the method of your studies and what time you are least engaged. But then having once made your choice, you must peremptorily adhere to it, nor suffer company, pleasure, or any business that is not truly unavoidable to break in upon you, and cause you to neglect your retirement. For what is once devoted to God, ought never to be alienated from him. 'Tis probable you will find some difficulty in this practice at first, and when it is observed, perhaps you may sometimes lie under the imputation of singularity, moroseness, or ill breeding—but let not such things trouble you, for they are not worth regarding. What wise man would not be singular among such as have no [?]taste of sincere piety? Or would not rather be thought defective in complaisance [47] and good breeding by men of license, than neglect such an excellent means of advancing spiritual life?

> Slight those that say amidst their sickly health,
> Thou livest by rule. What doth not so but man? . . . [48]

[Page cut; material missing.]

. . . knew of my [?]worry.
Dear Charles, my love and blessing attend thee.

S. Wesley

Notes

1. See part II of this volume.
2. Wife of the vicar of Doncaster, c. 1732/33(?) See Stevenson, p. 135.
3. "Brethren" replaces the crossed-out "acquaintance."
4. "One" replaces the crossed-out "man."
5. Echoes from Philippians 4:8. This last clause, beginning "and you know" is written lengthwise in the right-hand margin; an asterisk after the word "affair" in the text calls it to the reader's attention.
6. The practice of a Dissenter's receiving communion in the Anglican church on only one or two occasions to qualify for government office. An attempt to close this loophole was on the books from 1711 until 1719, when it was repealed to relieve George I's Nonconformist subjects. In the present instance S. W. is complaining that the spirit of the canons relating to a priest's induction into a parish was being similarly violated.
7. She actually has in mind the first question asked candidates for the *diaconate* in the BCP: "Do you trust that you are inwardly *moved by the Holy Ghost to take upon you this Office and Ministra-*tion, to serve God for the promoting of his glory, and the edifying of his people?" (My emphasis.) The equivalent question in the ordination of priests is "Do you think in your heart, that you be truly called, according to the will of our Lord Jesus Christ, and the order of this Church of England, to the Order and Ministry of Priesthood?"
8. See John 6:26–27.
9. She originally wrote "at present," then substituted "now" without striking out both words of the first phrase.
10. Dash in MS, indicating that S. W. has omitted the word, possibly to be inserted in a subsequent draft.
11. My quotation marks.
12. Wesley's letter of 19 December 1733 has not been found.
13. Probably Wesley's pupil at Lincoln, Matthew Robinson, who later became a fellow of Brasenose.
14. In MS: "shew."
15. 21 December; see BCP.
16. That is, Samuel Jr.

17. Luke 1:37.

18. By now the standard nickname for the Wesleys' circle at Oxford.

19. My boldfacing; S. W. emphasized the word in the MS by writing it in larger letters.

20. Acts 10:44; S. W.'s quotation marks.

21. William Law (1686–1761), unwilling to take an oath of allegiance at George I's accession, forswore a career in the church and university. He wrote his two most famous works, *A Practical Treatise upon Christian Perfection* (London: William and John Innys, 1726) and *A Serious Call to a Devout and Holy Life . . .* (London: William Innys, 1729) while serving as tutor for the Gibbon family in Putney. John Wesley, much influenced by the ideal of a "new life perfectly devoted to God" (*Christian Perfection*, p. 41), visited Law in July of 1732 and again, just before writing the letter that Susanna Wesley is here answering, on 28 November 1733. In his diary for that day John Wesley notes, "with Mr. Law, not understood all he said." V. H. H. Green, *The Young Mr. Wesley . . .* (New York: St. Martin's, 1961), p. 277, n. 4. Though no copy of his letter exists, his mother's reply indicates that he was asking her to help him understand the interview. Despite her interest in the meditational life and her political affinity for him, there is no evidence that she had ever read Law. John Wesley later broke with Law, the former pulling away from mysticism after his sojourn in Georgia, the latter delving deeper into it with his increasing appreciation of the work of Jacob Boehme.

22. Song of Solomon 5:16.

23. The last sentence is written sideways along the top left-hand margin of the page.

24. Richard Morgan Jr. was the brother of William, whose death had been attributed by some to the zeal and discipline of the Holy Club. A new undergraduate, he was chafing under the close scrutiny of John Wesley, under whose tutelage his father had placed him—notwithstanding the elder brother's unfortunate experience. See Green, *Young Mr. Wesley*, pp. 194–200.

25. That is, brother-in-law Matthew Wesley.

26. Still speaking of Richard Morgan, John had asked, "Should we converse then in the simplicity of the gospel; and speak as we are enabled, with zeal, of the nothingness of things present, the greatness of things future, and the excellency of the love of Christ? Or should we rather soften these glorious truths, and talk morally? 'Tis an important question, and of constant use" (FB, 1:372).

27. Romans 11:33; first sentence slightly misremembered. The original: "O the depth of the riches both of the wisdom and knowledge of God!" AM encloses both biblical verses in the same set of quotation marks.

28. Isaiah 55:9, slightly condensed and with changed pronouns.

29. See Philippians 3:8.

30. Paragraph break not found in AM but introduced here to divide up an extraordinarily long block of discourse.

31. Quotation marks in AM. I have been unable to trace this reference.

32. I cannot find a direct quotation, although S. W. writes as if she is looking at Locke's exact words (thus my quotation marks). However, the substance of the story was available in a letter of 25 August 1703 to the Rev. Richard King, in which he recommends the New Testament as a special source of religious knowledge and moral guidance. See *The Works of John Locke*, 12th ed. (London: C. and J. Rivington, 1824), 9:305–306. Cf. Thomas Jefferson's similarly "enlightened" view in his *Life and Morals of Jesus* (Washington: Government Printing Office, 1904).

33. Richard Morgan Sr.; see note 24.

34. Cf. the doctrine of perfection as developed by John Wesley a few years later.

35. See Matthew 13:31–32 and parallels.

36. Members of the Holy Club.

37. FB, 1:383, n. 1, suggests that this may be her husband, Samuel, or perhaps her son-in-law John Whitelamb, soon to be incumbent of Wroot.

38. That is, subordinate ends or aims.

39. Acts 17:28.

40. See 1 Kings 19:12.

41. Psalm 78:9, BCP (AV 78:8): "a generation . . . whose spirit cleaveth not stedfastly unto God."

42. I have not been able to find the exact passage amid Baxter's voluminous works. It may be that it is tucked in among similar directions for the faithful in his *A Christian Directory*, 2nd ed. (London: Nervil Simmons, 1678), for example, Grand Direction XII, in bk. 1 ("Christian Ethicks"), chap. 3, p. 131: "Trust God with that soul and body which thou hast delivered up and dedicated to him; and quiet thy mind in his Love and faithfulness, whatever shall appear unto thee, or befall thee in the world." Like material is found also in *The Life of Faith* (London: Nevil Simmons, 1670), for example, p. 175: "By faith deliver up yourselves to God, as your Creator and your Owner, and live to him as those that perceive they are absolutely his own . . . . By faith deliver up yourselves to God, as your Sovereign Ruler, with an absolute Resolution to learn, and love, and obey his Laws." Another treatise dealing with these issues is *The Right Method for a Settled Peace of Conscience and Spiritual Comfort* in *The Practical Works of the Rev. Richard Baxter*, 23 vols., ed. William Orme (London: J. Duncan, 1830), vol. 9. For easier reading I have chosen to indent this passage from Baxter, removing the quotation marks in the MS.

43. In MS: "Senr."

44. See Colossians 4:5.

45. Appeal solemnly to.

46. See Exodus 29:38–42 and Numbers 28:3–8.

47. That is, willingness to please others.

48. George Herbert, "The Church-Porch," stanza 23, lines 133–34, from *The Temple*, in F. E. Hutchinson, ed., *The Works of George Herbert* (Oxford: Clarendon Press, 1941), p. 12. S. W. is fond of these lines and recommended them to each of her three sons. See her letter to Samuel Jr., 11 October 1709 (and note), chapter 4, and her letter to John, 22 April 1727, chapter 10.

❧ THIRTEEN ❧

A Widow and a Supportive Critic
of Revival

Society (Susanna would have said Providence) appointed a further set of roles for her in her old age. Her husband, Samuel, died on 25 April 1735, necessitating her departure from the Epworth rectory and a kind of itinerancy among her children: Emily in Gainsborough, Lincolnshire; Samuel Jr. in Tiverton, Devon (he was to die prematurely less than five years after his father); Patty and her husband, Westley Hall, in Wooten Rivers, Wiltshire, and Fisherton near Salisbury, before moving to London; and finally John at his newly renovated headquarters, the Foundery, a stone's throw from her birthplace. Widowhood forced this further dependence on her, but it also opened up new vistas—new locations; new people; new challenges; and a new religious perspective to wrestle with, one sponsored by her two increasingly famous younger sons.

The passage to a new stage of life was not without its difficulties, both temporal and spiritual. Not dwelling on her financial arrangements, she nevertheless acknowledges them, thanking her sons for what they have been able to contribute to her upkeep (19 October 1738, 6 December 1738, 29 November 1739, 27 December 1739). And she takes time to reassure a new friend, Mrs. Peard in Tiverton, that she's being well treated by the Halls in Wiltshire (8 April 1737). Her main concerns, however, are not worldly. In seeking their counsel, she admits to both John (27 November 1735) and Charles (19 October 1738 and 27 December 1739) various instances of what she considers her own "want of faith." In that last letter she even observes, "I am become a little child."

Nevertheless, she has not completely relinquished the teacher's role. She energetically confronts what she regards as the excesses of his language in Charles's early evangelical effusions (19 October 1738) and cautions him against his "odd way of thinking," putting too much stock in feeling as a measure of his assurance of salvation (6 December 1738). Partly, she is feeding on Samuel Jr.'s suspicions about the early revival, as is revealed in her letter to him of 8 March 1739. However, in the same letter she reports rather positively on a visit from George Whitefield, whose ecclesiastical irregularities would in some ways outstrip her sons' (and whose subsequent theological break with them would prompt her only published work).[1]

By the end of 1739 she was, literally and figuratively, at home with her son John, living at the Foundery and supporting his and Charles's cause. If her companions there weren't always conducive to Christian conversation, if her sons were out and about more than she might have liked, she nevertheless heartily prayed that God might prosper their work (27 December 1739).

To John Wesley
27 November 1735
AM, 1778, pp. 84–85; FB, 1:445–446

Gainsborough,[2] Nov. 27, 1735

[Dear son,]

. . . God is being itself! The I AM![3] And therefore must necessarily be the supreme good! He is so infinitely blessed that every perception of his blissful presence imparts a vital gladness to the heart. Every degree of approach toward him is in the same proportion a degree of happiness. And I often think that were he always present to our minds as we are present to him, there could be no pain or sense of misery. I have long since chose him for my only good! My all! My pleasure, my happiness in this world, as well as in the world to come! And although I have not been so faithful to his grace as I ought to have been, yet I feel my spirit adheres to its choice and aims daily at cleaving steadfastly unto God. Yet one thing often troubles me, that notwithstanding I know "while we are present with the body, we are absent from the Lord,"[4] notwithstanding I have no taste, no relish left for anything the world calls pleasure, yet I do not long to go home as in reason I ought to do. This often shocks me; and as I constantly pray (almost without ceasing)[5] for thee, my son, so I beg you likewise to pray for me, that God would make me better and take me at the best.

> Your loving mother,
> Susanna Wesley

To Mrs. Alice Peard, Tiverton
5 August 1737
Clarke, 2nd ed., (New York: Lane and Scott, 1851), pp. 397–399; Stevenson, pp. 213–214. Written from Wooton, Wiltshire, where she was living with her daughter and son-in-law, Martha and Westley Hall. Mrs. Peard was a woman she had apparently met through her son Samuel.

Wootton, Aug. 5, 1737[6]

Dear Madam,

To your goodness I am obliged for the kind present sent by Charles and return many thanks, particularly to good Mrs. Norman. I heartily sympathize with the young lady in her affliction and wish it was in my power to speak a word in season that might alleviate the trouble of her mind, which has such an influence on the weakness of her body. I am not apprised of her particular complaints but am apt to believe that want of faith and a firm dependence on the merits of Christ is the cause of most if not all her sufferings. I am very well satisfied she doth not allow herself in willful sin, and surely to afflict herself for mere infirmities argues weakness of faith in the merits of our Redeemer. We can never be totally freed from infirmity till we put off mortality, and to be grieved at this is just as if a man should afflict himself that he is a man and not an angel. It is with relation to our manifold wants and weaknesses, and the discouragements and despondencies consequent thereupon, that the blessed Jesus hath undertaken to be our great High-priest, Physician, Advocate, and Saviour. His satisfaction related to the forfeiture of all the good we had in possession, and his intercession is with respect to our great distance from God and unworthiness to approach him. His deep compassion supposes our misery; and his assistance and the supplies of his grace imply our wants and the disadvantages we labour under. We are to be instructed, because we are ignorant; and healed, because we are sick; and disciplined, because so apt to wander and go astray; and succoured and supported, because we are so often tempted. We know there is but one living and true God, though revealed to us under three characters—that of Father, Son, and Holy Spirit. In God the Father we live, move, and have our natural being;[7] in God the Son, as Redeemer of mankind, we have our spiritual being since the fall; and by the operation of his Holy Spirit the work of grace is begun and carried on in the soul; and there is no other name given under heaven by which men can be saved, but that of the Lord Jesus.[8]

And here, madam, let me beseech you to join with me in admiring and adoring the infinite and incomprehensible love of God to fallen man, which he hath been pleased to manifest to us in the redemption of the world by our Lord Jesus Christ. He is the great God, "the God of the spirits of all flesh,"[9] "the high and lofty One that inhabiteth eternity,"[10] and created not angels and men because he wanted them, for he is being itself, and as such must necessarily be infinitely happy in the glorious perfections of his nature from everlasting to everlasting; and as he did not create, so neither did he redeem because he needed us; but he loved us because he loved us, he would have mercy because he would have mercy, he would show compassion because he would show compassion.[11] There was nothing in man that could merit anything but wrath from the Almighty. We are infinitely below his least regards; therefore this astonishing condescension can be resolved into nothing but his own essential goodness. And shall we, after all, undervalue or neglect this great salvation? Who should be so much concerned for our eternal happiness as ourselves? And shall we exclude ourselves from an interest in the merits of the blessed Jesus by our unbelief? God forbid. But you will say, "We are great sinners." Very true, but Christ came into the world to save sinners;[12] he had never died if man had never sinned. If we were not sinners we should have had no need for a Saviour, "but God commended His love towards us, in that while we were yet sinners Christ died for us."[13] The greatest saints in heaven were once sinners upon earth, and the same redeeming love and free grace that brought them to glory are sufficient to bring us also thither. I verily think one great reason why Christians are so often subject to despond is that they look more to themselves than to their Saviour; they would establish a righteousness of their own to rest on, without adverting enough to the sacrifice of Christ, by which alone we are justified before God. But I need not say more, considering to whom I am writing; only give me leave to add one request, which is that you would commit your soul in trust to Jesus Christ as God incarnate, in a full belief that he is able and willing to save you. Do this constantly, and I am sure he will never suffer you to perish.

I shall be very glad to hear often from you. I thank God I am somewhat better in health than when I wrote last; and I tell you, because I know you will be pleased with it, that Mr. Hall and his wife are very good to me; he behaves like a gentleman and a Christian, and my daughter with as much duty and tenderness as can be expressed, so that on this account I am very easy. My humble service waits on your sister and Mr. and Mrs. Norman. I heartily wish you all happiness, temporal, spiritual, and eternal. I earnestly recommend myself to all your prayers, who am, dear madam, your obliged and most obedient servant,

Susanna Wesley

To Charles Wesley
19 October 1738
MA. In Charles Wesley's hand: "My mother of faith in Xt." Part of MS missing.

Thurs: 19th. Oct: [1]738.

My Dear Charles,

I received yours of the eleventh instant on Monday night and am somewhat surprised at its being so long in coming.

'Tis with much pleasure I find your mind is somewhat easier than formerly, and heartily thank God for it. "The spirit of man may sustain his infirmity, but a wounded spirit who can bear?"[14] If this hath been your case, it has been sad indeed. But blessed be God which gave you those convictions of the evil of sin as contrary to the purity of the divine nature and the most perfect goodness of His laws. Blessed be God! that showed you the necessity you were in of a saviour to deliver you from the power of sin and Satan (for Christ will be no saviour to such as see not their need of one) and directed you by faith to lay hold on that stupendous mercy offered us by redeeming love! Jesus is the only physician of souls, his blood the only salve which can heal a wounded conscience. 'Tis not in wealth or honour or sensual pleasure to relieve a spirit heavy laden and weary of the burden of sin; these things have power to increase our guilt by alienating our hearts from God, but none to make our peace with him, to reconcile God to man, and man to God, and to renew the union between the divine and human nature which was broken by the disobedience of our first parents. No, there is none but Christ, none but Christ is sufficient for these things. But blessed be God he is an all-sufficient Saviour! And blessed be his holy name that thou hast found him a Saviour to thee, my son. Oh, let us love him much, for we have much to be forgiven.

I would gladly know what your notion is of justifying faith, because you speak of it as a thing you have but lately obtained.

I never thought it in your power to remove my troubles nor ever had a hard thought of you on that account. I've been much obliged by what you have already done, and if God be pleased to give power, I doubt not your will to help me. I have indeed been under a state of what the world calls deep affliction, but alas, pain, poverty, want of friends are the least part of my sufferings. Nor have they been so grievous to me as some imagine. Temporal things are of short continuance and will soon be over; therefore they do not much affect me. I have not time, therefore shall say no more at present, only this—*God hath not forsaken* me,[15] nor hath his consolations (at times) been small unto me. And I hope that all the dispensations of his providence towards me will prove at last to have worked together for my spiritual and eternal good. I believe that God the Father, as Parent of the universe, doth by his general providence sustain, provide for, and govern all the works of his creation. And that God the Son, as saviour of mankind, doth by his Holy Spirit overrule and dispose the events of God's general providence so as to make them work together for the spiritual good of those which by faith are united to him. And this government of Christ I take to be signified by Ezekiel's vision of a wheel within a wheel[16] and of what our Lord said to his disciples, "My Father worketh hitherto, and I work."[17]

I thank you for minding me of the promises. I often think of them and have been often comforted by them. But I have had great conflicts with the powers of darkness who have laboured hard to persuade me that these promises belong not to me. Yet in this God hath not forsaken me, nor hath he suffered the gates of hell to prevail against me;[18] but I yet hope that in the end I shall be more than conqueror through him that loveth us.[19] But I must hasten to a conclusion.

[Subsequent page with concluding paragraph(s) and signature is missing.]

To Charles Wesley
6 December 1738
MA. Charles Wesley's endorsement: "My mother (not clear) of faith Dec. 6. 1738." Addressed to "The Revd Mr Charles Wesley at Mr Bray's in Little Brittain, London." Several key phrases in the holograph are underlined. However, we must be cautious in attributing them to S. W., who rarely uses this form of emphasis; they are more likely Charles's or the work of some later reader-editor. Consequently they are indicated here only in the notes.

Dec: 6th 1738

Dear Charles,

I should write much oft'ner had I better health and should be very glad if you received as much benefit from my letters as I do comfort from yours.

My notion of justifying faith is the same with yours, for that trusting in Jesus Christ or the promises made in him is that special act of faith to which our justification or acceptance is so frequently ascribed in the gospel. This faith is certainly the gift of God wrought in the mind of man by his Holy Spirit. But then, as the Gospel promises are conditional, I can't believe that the Spirit of Holiness will give that faith to any but such as sincerely desire and endeavor to perform the conditions of the gospel covenant required on their part. Sincerely, I say, for perfection no man ever did, or ever will, attain to in this life. Now because "the commandments of God are exceeding broad"[20] and by reason of our manifold imperfection and infirmities we are so frequently subject to deviate from the perfect law of God, 'tis incident to many (I hope) good Christians often to doubt the sincerity of their faith. They make not the least question of the power or will of God incarnate to save them, but they keep a jealous eye upon themselves and are sometimes afraid that they do not all which is required of them; therefore they do in the most literal sense "work out their salvation with fear and trembling."[21] And truly I am inclined to think that such humble, fearing Christians are in a safer, thought not so comfortable a state, than those which think themselves sure of salvation.

I do not judge it necessary for us to know the precise time of our conversion. 'Tis sufficient if we have a reasonable hope that we are passed from death to life by the fruits of the Holy Spirit wrought in our hearts. Such are repentance, faith, hope, love, etc. Our Lord acts in various ways and by various means on different tempers, nor is the work of regeneration begun and perfected at once. Some (though rarely) are converted by irresistible grace. Others (rarely too) have been sanctified from the womb, and like Obadiah, have served the Lord from their youth.[22] But from these exempt cases we can draw no general rules, nor ought we too curiously to search after the knowledge of the operations of God's Holy Spirit. His ways are past finding out![23] 'Tis observed by du Moulin[24] that

> many devout souls yield a wrong obedience to this precept of St. Paul, "Examine your own selves, whether you be in the faith."[25] For instead of examining themselves, they examine God, seeking with an over busy care what degree of comfort and assurance of salvation they feel in their hearts, which is the work of God, not of men.[. . .] Wherefore, when we examine whether we are in the faith, it is not the work of God we must examine, but our own. We must call ourselves to account whether we love God and our neighbour, and what care we take to serve him, to keep his commandments, and receive his promises with obedience of faith. In these things, where the work of God's grace is joined with ours, we have but our performance to examine, looking upon God's work with reverence and ascribing to him all the good that is in us. Which reverence must be redoubled when we consider in us that work of Grace wherein man hath no share, and such are heavenly comforts, and spiritual joys. Of these we must not curiously examine the manner or measure as though the seal of our adoption consisted in them. For it is not in feeling comfort, but in departing from iniquity that this seal consisteth.[26]

Thus far this excellent divine, and I think he is in the right.

I think you are fallen into an odd way of thinking.[27] You say that till within a few months you had no spiritual life nor any justifying faith. Now this is as if a man should affirm he was not alive in his infancy, because, when an infant he did not know he was alive. A strange way of arguing, this! Do you not consider that[28] there's some analogy in spiritual to natural life?[29] A man must first be born and then pass through the several stages of infancy, childhood, and youth, before he attain to maturity. So Christians are first born of water and the spirit and then go through many degrees of grace, be first infants, or babes in Christ, as St. Paul calls them,[30] before they become strong Christians. For spiritual strength is the work of time, as well as of God's Holy Spirit. All then that I can gather from your letter is that till a little while ago you were not so well satisfied of your being a Christian as you are now.[31] I heartily rejoice that you have now attained to a strong and lively hope in God's mercy through Christ. Not that I can think you were totally without saving faith[32] before, but then 'tis one thing to have faith and another thing to be sensible we have it. Faith is the fruit of the Spirit and is the gift of God, but to feel or be inwardly sensible that we have true faith requires a further operation of God's Holy Spirit. You say you have peace but not joy in believing. Blessed be God for peace. May his peace rest within you. Joy will follow, perhaps not very close, but it will follow faith and love. God's promises are sealed to us but not dated. Therefore, patiently attend his pleasure. He will give you joy in believing. Amen.

The other part of your letter gave me pain and pleasure. I was glad to find you still retain so much tender affection for me, but sorry you should be grieved because you can do no more when you have already done far more than you were well able. It was nothing but necessity (having more to pay than your brothers' money came to) made me take the last you sent, for which, as for all other kindnesses, I much thank you.[33]

This is my only paper or I should write more, for I have much to say.

My tender love and blessing ever attends thee. Continue to pray for me, as I do for you.

S. W.

I wish you a cheerful Christmas and happy New Year, and many of them.

Your brother sent me word the 25th of November that he had that post writ to Mr. Bentham to receive some money for me the beginning of December. I hope he has got it, for having paid that money sent before, I was compelled to give Mr. Randall Hall a note upon him for 5lb.[34] to be paid ten days after date thereof. So it will be payable the [?]14th instant. Dear Charles, inquire after it.

To Samuel Wesley Jr.
8 March 1738/39
Priestley, pp. 91–94. See also Clarke, pp. 276–278, quoting from John Whitehead, *The Life of the Rev. John Wesley . . .* (Dublin: John Jones, 1805). Priestley records an address ("For the Rev. Mr. Wesley, Tiverton, Devon") but cannot be reading from the holograph when adding a "return address": "From Mrs. Wesley, of Epworth." This editorial insertion would identify S. W. to his readers, but it gives the erroneous impression that she was still residing in her deceased husband's Lincolnshire parish rather than with her daughter in Wiltshire. Priestley records no concluding salutation or signature.

Thursday, 8th March, 1738–9

[Dear Son,]

Your two double letters came safe to me last Friday. I thank you for them and have received much satisfaction in reading them; they are written with good spirit and judgment, sufficient, I should think, to satisfy any unprejudiced mind that the reviving these pretensions to dreams, visions, etc. is not only vain and frivolous as to the matter of them but also of dangerous consequence to the weaker sort of Christians. You have well observed, "That it is not the method of providence to use extraordinary means to bring about that for which ordinary ones are sufficient." Therefore the very end for which they pretend that these new revelations are sent seems to me one of the best arguments against the truth of them. As far as I can see, they plead that these visions, etc. are given to assure some particular persons of their adoption and salvation. But this end is abundantly provided for in the holy scriptures, wherein all may find the rules by which we must live here and be judged hereafter are so plainly laid down, "That he who runs may read;"[35] and it is by these laws we should examine ourselves, which is a way of God's appointment, and therefore we may hope for his direction and assistance in such examination. And if upon a serious review of our state we find that in the tenure of our lives we have, or do now sincerely desire and endeavour to perform the conditions of the gospel covenant required on our parts, then we may discern that the Holy Spirit hath laid in our minds a good foundation of a strong, reasonable, and lively hope of God's mercy through Christ.[36]

This is the assurance we ought to aim at, which the apostle calls the *full assurance of hope,* which he admonish us to *hold fast unto the end.*[37] And the consequence of encouraging fanciful people in this new way of seeking assurance (as all do that hear them tell their silly stories without rebuke) I think must be the turning them out of God's way, into one of their own devising. You have plainly proved that the scripture examples and that text in Joel which they urge in their defence[38] will not answer their purpose, so that they are unsupported by any authority, either human or divine (which you have very well observed), and the credit of their relations must therefore depend on their own single affirmation, which surely will not weigh much with the sober judicious part of mankind.

I began to write to Charles before I last wrote to you, but could not proceed: for my chimney smoked so exceedingly that I almost lost my sight and remained well nigh blind a considerable time. God's blessing on eye-water I make[39] cured me of the soreness, but the weakness long remained. Since I have been informed that Mr. Hall intends to remove his family to London, hath taken a house, and I must (if it please God I live) go with them,[40] where I hope to see Charles, and then I can fully speak my sentiments of their new notions, more than I can do by writing; therefore I shall not finish my letter to him.

You have heard, I suppose, that Mr. Whitefield[41] is taking a progress through these parts to make a collection for a house in Georgia for orphans and such of the natives' children as they will part with to learn our language and religion. He came hither to see me, and we talked about your brothers. I told him I did not like their way of living, wished them in some places of their own, wherein they might regularly preach, etc. He replied, I could not conceive the good they did in London, that the greatest part of our clergy were asleep, and there never was greater need of itinerant preachers than now. Upon which a gentleman that came with him said that my son Charles had converted him and that both my sons spent all their time in doing good. I then asked Mr. Whitefield if my sons were not for making some innovations in the church, which I much feared. He assured me they were so far from it, that they endeavoured all they could to reconcile dissenters to our communion; that my son John baptized five adult Presbyterians in our way on St. Paul's day, and he believed would bring over many to our communion. His stay was short, so I could not talk with him so much as I desired. He seems to be a very good man and one who truly desires the salvation of mankind. God grant that the wisdom of the serpent may be joined to the innocence of the dove.[42]

My paper and sight are almost at an end; therefore I shall only add that I send you and yours my hearty love and blessing.

Service to Mrs. Berry.[43]

I had not an opportunity to send this till Saturday the 17th ult.[44]

Love and blessing to Jacky Ellison.[45]

Pray let me hear from you soon. We go in April.

To Charles Wesley
29 November 1739
MA. Endorsement: "Nov. 29, 1739. My Mother on my Br.'s Death."

Nov: 29, [1]739

Dear Charles,

Upon the first hearing of your brother's death,[46] I did immediately acquiesce in the will of God without the least reluctance. Only I somewhat marveled that Jacky did not inform me of it before he left me, since he knew thereof. But he was unacquainted with the manner of God's dealing with me in extraordinary cases, which indeed is no wonder, for though I have so often experienced his infinite power and mercy in my support and inward calmness of spirit when the trial would otherwise have been too strong for me, yet his ways of working are to myself incomprehensible and ineffable!

Your brother was exceeding dear to me in his life, and perhaps I've erred in loving him too well. I once thought it impossible for me to bear his loss, but none knows what they can bear till they are tried. As your good old grandfather often used to say, "That's an affliction, that God makes an affliction."[47] For surely the manifestation of his presence and favour is more than an adequate support under any suffering whatever. But if he withhold his consolations and hide his face from us, the least suffering is intolerable. But blessed and adored be his holy name, it hath not been so with me, though I am infinitely unworthy of the least of all his mercies! I rejoice in having a comfortable hope of my dear son's salvation. He is now at rest and would not return to earth to gain the world. Why then should I mourn?[48] He hath reached the haven before me, but I shall soon follow him; he must not return to me, but I shall go to him, never to part more.

I thank you for your care of my temporal affairs. 'Twas natural to think that I should be troubled for my dear sons's death on that account, because such a considerable part of my support was cut off. But to say the truth, I've never had one anxious thought of such matters. For it came immediately into my mind, that God by my child's loss had called me to a firmer dependence on himself. That, though my son was good, he was not my God—and that now our heavenly father seemed to have taken my cause more immediately into his own hand; and therefore, even against hope, I believed in hope[49] that I should never suffer more.[50]

I can't write much, being but weak. I've not been down stairs above ten weeks, though better than I was lately. Pray give my kind love and blessing to my daughter and Philly.[51] I pray God to support and provide for her.

[. . .][52]I doubt my dear you have been unmindful in this thing.[53]

To Charles Wesley
27 December 1739
MA. Written from her lodgings in the Foundery, though the place is not mentioned in her own letter. Addressed to "The Revd. Mr Wesley at Mrs Grevill's Grocer in Bristol." Endorsement: "Dec. 27, 1739 My Mother—wanting Faith." Italics may be S. W.'s, Charles's, or the work of some subsequent reader of the MS.

Thurs: Dec: 27, [1]739

My dear Charles,

You cannot more desire to see me than I do to see you. Indeed, your brother (whom henceforward I shall call Son Wesley, since my dear Sam is gone home)[54] hath done more, I think, than could be expected to supply temporal wants; but though they were not small, and relief was welcome, yet that was not the principal thing which I desired. I am in a state of great temptation and want to talk with you about many things. I need your direction and instruction how to act in the present situation, particularly in relation to my very disagreeable companion,[55] who does not scruple to declare that she hates spiritual people and looks upon them as the worst people in the world. If she hath talked at Mr. [?]Priest's and among other true Christians as to me, no wonder that they showed a dislike of her company. Those with whom I lodge are an excellent people and would be glad to converse with me on spiritual subjects, but they are discouraged from coming to me (and to them I cannot go) by her either leaving the room as soon as they enter, or by something she says that discovers her aversion from them. Other matters I would speak with you about concerning my worldly affairs, but these are comparatively of little moment; yet still they are by no means to be neglected.[56] My dear Son Wesley hath just been with me and much revived my spirits. Indeed, I've often found that he never speaks in my hearing without my receiving some spiritual benefit; but his visits are seldom and short, for which I never blame him, because I know he is well employed, and, blessed be God, hath great success in his ministry.

But, my dear Charles, still I want either him or you, for indeed in the most literal sense I am become a little child and want continual succour. "As Iron sharpeneth iron, so doth the countenance of a man his friend."[57] I feel much comfort and support from religious conference when I can obtain it. Formerly, I rejoiced in the absence of company and found the less I enjoyed of creature comforts (be not offended at the expression) the more I had from God. But, alas, I am fallen from that spiritual converse I once enjoyed, and why is it so? Because I wanted faith. God is an omnipresent, unchangeable Good, "in whom is no variableness, neither shadow of turning."[58] The fault is in myself, and I attribute all mistakes in judgement, all errors in practice to want of faith in the blessed Jesus. Oh, my dear, when I consider the dignity of his person! The perfection of his purity! The greatness of his sufferings! But above all his boundless love! I am astonished and utterly confounded. I am lost in thoughts. I fall into nothing before him. Oh, how inexcusable is that person which hath knowledge of these things, and yet remains poor and low in faith and love. I speak as one guilty in this matter.

You desired me to write to you, and I've a great desire to do it. But from the date hereof I have been prevented finishing my letter. I complained I had none to converse with me of spiritual things, but for these several days I've had the conversation of many good Christians that have refreshed in some measure my fainting spirits. And though they hindered my writing, yet 'twas pleasing and, I hope, not an unprofitable interruption that they gave me. I hope we shall shortly speak face to face, and I shall then, if God permit, impart my thoughts more fully. But then, alas, when you come, your brother leaves me. Yet that is the will of God, in whose blessed service ye are engaged, who hath hitherto blessed your labours and preserved your persons. That he may continue so to prosper your work and protect ye both from evil—and give ye strength and courage to preach the true gospel in opposition to the united powers of evil men and evil angels, is the hearty prayer of,

my dear Charles,

thy loving mother, SW.

I wish you a happy year—and many, very many such.

Notes

1. Her anonymous pamphlet of 1741, *Some Remarks on a Letter from the Reverend Mr. Whitefield.* . . . See part III of this volume.

2. After her husband's death and the induction of a new rector at Epworth, Susanna's first move was to Gainsborough, a dozen miles away, where Emily had established a small school of her own. See Stevenson, p. 268.

3. See Charles J. McCracken, *Malebranche and British Philosophy* (Oxford: Clarendon Press, 1983), p. 166, n. 32. The phraseology is similar to Nicolas Malebranche, *Malebranche's Search after Truth* . . . 2 vols., trans. Richard Sault (London: J. Dunton, 1694), bk. 3, part. 2, chap. 5. Or it might be derived from his English disciple, John Norris, *Reason and Religion* . . . (London: Samuel Manship, 1689), part 1, contemplation 15, pp. 22–23: "We must attend in the first place to the true sense and signification of this Name of God, *I am that am,* or *I am.* Now this can signifie no other but *Being it self,* or *Universal Being,* or *Being in General, Being in the Abstract,* without any restriction or limitation. As if God had said, You enquire who I am, and by what Name I would be distinguish'd. Know then, that, *I am he that am, I am Being itself.*" S. W. uses the same phrase in her "Religious Conference" in discussing the attributes of God. See part III of this volume.

4. 2 Corinthians 5:6, slightly paraphrased; my quotation marks. AV says, "whilst we are at home in the body."

5. See 1 Thessalonians 5:17.

6. Clarke's reading of the MS, now lost. Stevenson reads "April 8," but he is not as trustworthy an editor as his predecessor.

7. See Acts 17:28.

8. Acts 4:12, paraphrased.

9. Numbers 16:22; my quotation marks.

10. Isaiah 57:15; my quotation marks.

11. See Romans 9:15 and Exodus 33:19; a similar expression is found in S. W. to John Wesley, 21 February 1731/32.

12. 1 Timothy 1:15 and BCP, Holy Communion, "Comfortable Words," following the absolution.

13. Romans 5:8; quotation marks in Stevenson.

14. Nearly exact quotation of Proverbs 18:14; initial quotation mark is S. W.'s; I have supplied the closing one.

15. Underlined in MS, though possibly by a later hand.

16. See Ezekiel 1:16ff.

17. John 5:17; S. W.'s initial quotation marks, my concluding quotation marks.

18. See Matthew 16:18.

19. Paraphrase of Romans 8:37.

20. Psalm 119:96, paraphrased; S. W.'s quotation marks.

21. Philippians 2:12, paraphrased; my quotation marks.

22. Neither the prophet Obadiah nor the pious official in the court of Ahab (1 Kings 18) seems to fit this description. A more apt example is Samuel (1 Samuel, chaps. 1–3).

23. Paraphrase of Job 9:10.

24. Pierre du Moulin (1601–1684), French-born Anglican priest. His father, of the same name (1568–1658), was a Reformed theologian who settled in England. Several books appear under this name (father and/or son) in the catalogue of Samuel Annesley's library sale.

25. 2 Corinthians 13:5; my quotation marks.

26. Nearly exact quotation of Peter [Pierre] du Moulin, *A Treatise of Peace and Contentment of Mind*, 3rd ed. (London: John Sims, 1678), bk. iv, pp. 464–465; S. W. set it off with a concluding quotation mark; for ease of reading I have put it into an indented block. I have inserted bracketed elipses to represent material she skips in du Moulin: "And, as in the searches of jealousie, when a man seeks for that which he fears to find, they draw upon them that which they fear by seeking with too much curiosity, and frame doubts to themselves, by examining of their confidence.

"To heal themselves of that timorous curiosity, they should not take for Gospel whatsoever godly men have written of the manner how the Holy Ghost is working in the conscience; for it is certain, that he worketh diversely according to the diversity of natures, and doth vary the dispensation of his graces according to his good pleasure."

27. Phrase "*an odd way of thinking*" underlined in MS; see note 15.

28. S. W. originally followed with "Christians are," but crossed out the two words.

29. Original punctuation a semicolon.

30. 1 Corinthians 3:1.

31. Phrase *a Christian as you are now* underlined in MS; see note 15.

32. Phrase "*without saving faith*" underlined in MS; see note 15.

33. Phrase "*kindnesses, I much thank you*" underlined in MS; see note 15.

34. Likely reading. "Lb.," an abbreviation of Latin "libra," was then used to stand for pounds sterling as well as for the measure of weight.

35. Paraphrase of Habakkuk 2:2; quotation marks in Priestley.

36. See 1 Peter 1:3.

37. Hebrews 6:11, slightly enhanced; emphasis in Priestley.

38. Probably Joel 2:28–29; cf. Acts 2:17–18.

39. A lotion for the eye, such as the one John Wesley later would recommend in his *Primitive Physick*, (London: Strahan, 1747).

40. Indication that this letter was written from the home of her daughter and son-in-law near Salisbury.

41. The Rev. George Whitefield (1714–1770), one-time member of the Holy Club at Oxford, gained fame in both Britain and North America as an evangelist. His theological break with John led to Susanna's anonymous pamphlet against him. See *Some Remarks* . . . in part III of this volume.

42. See Matthew 10:16.

43. That is, Samuel's mother-in-law.

44. "Ultimo," that is, "in the last [month]." She may have meant to put "inst." (i.e., of the present month). Priestley provides no information on postmark.

45. John Ellison, eldest son of daughter Susanna (Suky) and her husband Richard Ellison.

46. Samuel Jr. died on 6 November 1739 at the age of 49.

47. S. W. also used this saying without attributing it to Samuel Annesley in her letter to John Wesley, 8 June 1725. Beginning quotation marks in MS; I have substituted concluding quotation marks for the dash S. W. uses to set off the end of her father's saying.

48. Question mark inserted in place of S. W.'s comma.

49. See Romans 4:18.

50. One and a half lines follow but were crossed out; the words are now indecipherable.

51. That is, to her widowed daughter-in-law, Ursula, and her granddaughter. On hearing of their brother's death, Charles and John had gone to Tiverton to comfort their sister-in-law and niece.

52. Three lines beginning a new paragraph follow, but are crossed out. The first two words are "Yr Sister"; the second is probably "Emly," but the rest is indecipherable.

53. End of letter; closing courtesies and signature may have been on another page, now missing.

54. Samuel Jr. had died November 6, leaving John the elder surviving son. See previous letter.

55. These two words are underlined in MS; see note above.

56. Phrase *to be neglected* underlined in MS; see note 15.

57. Paraphrased from Proverbs 27:17; S. W.'s quotation marks.

58. James 1:17; S. W.'s quotation marks.

FOURTEEN

Last Letters

*B*y the end of 1739 Susanna Wesley had moved into what was to be her final home, her son John's newly acquired and renovated Methodist headquarters, the Foundery. There her last four extant letters (and doubtless a number of others that haven't survived) were written. Not always in the best of health, Susanna nevertheless continued to be a lively correspondent. To the familiar themes of her sons' work and her own spiritual and temporal condition are added here a hint of her role in the community at the Foundery and a unique perspective on her personality in a letter to the countess of Huntingdon.

The first letter (to Charles, 2 October 1740) continues in the mode of previous ones she has wrtten to him: a sparring but loving spiritual conference. To his "accusations" she pleads guilty, assuring him that she knows he is writing with her eternal well-being in mind. But the deference is only temporary; she comes back at what appears to be his own self-effacement. "I cannot conceive why you affirm yourself to be not Christian," she replies, and she expresses her offense at people who go on and on about their sins with very little to say thankfully about God's grace.

The 13 December 1740 letter to John, then on one of his trips to Bristol, illustrates her pastoral concern for a Methodist who has been committed to a madhouse in Chelsea. Susanna is convinced the crisis is more spiritual than medical and begs the prayers of both her sons for the unfortunate man.

The recently recovered letter to Charles (28 April 1741) begins with a point of practical theology that he has raised and turns it into another opportunity to retell the story of Christ's passion and death—in this case as a way of fully convicting an individual of sin. The second part, however, delves into the theological politics of the young revival movement and speaks as an insider about the twin dangers that Satan has used to oppose the awakening her sons have helped sponsor: the Moravians and the Calvinists. The "practical atheism" of the one and the "pernicious controversy" of the other must be fought; John has already valiantly entered the fray, and Charles is urged to do his part as well. Though she does not mention it, her similarly incisive critique of Whitefield and the Calvinists would soon be (perhaps already was) in print, albeit anonymously. *Some Remarks on a Letter from the Reverend Mr. Whitefield* . . . appeared in the same year and is reprinted in its entirety in part III of this volume.

In early adulthood Susanna had written a noblewoman on a point of conscience; the letter to Lady Yarborough is the first of her letters we still have. At 72 she wrote another member of the nobility, though for different purposes, in what we now may regard as her last letter. Selina, countess of Huntingdon, an early patron of the revival, followed Whitefield in his Calvinism and eventually founded her own "connexion." At this point, though, she was on friendly terms with John Wesley and, it appears from this letter, with Susanna.

Susanna writes to thank the countess for "her generous benefaction." A bottle of Madeira is specifically mentioned, but much more (perhaps a financial contribution toward her expenses) is broadly hinted at. Again, the twofold strategy. While she clearly writes to indicate she knows her place, both vis-à-vis nobility (she praises the countess's "condescension" and employs all appropriate courtesies) and the divine-human hierarchy ("I am the greatest of sinners"), she proudly basks in the work of her sons, who compare favorably, in her humble opinion, to two lords spiritual, the archbishops of Canterbury and York. Moreover, she plunges forward with candid revelations of her "own little affairs." Her Ladyship is the first person she has ever asked anything of; she hides her wants from John and Charles, who are already doing what they can for her. Boldness in the context of careful respect typifies this last letter, as it does so much of the rest of her writing.

❦

To Charles Wesley
2 October 1740
No MS seems to exist. Stevenson, pp. 220–221 closing sentence lost.

Foundry, London, October 2nd, 1740

Dear Charles,

I do heartily join with you in giving God thanks for your recovery. He hath many wise reasons for every event of providence, far above our apprehension, and I doubt not but his having restored you to some measure of health again will answer many ends which as yet you are ignorant of.

I thank you for your kind letter. I call it so, because I verily believe it was dictated by a sincere desire of my spiritual and eternal good. There is too much truth in many of your accusations; nor do I intend to say one word in my own defence, but rather choose to refer all things to him that knoweth all things. This I must tell you: you are somewhat mistaken in my case. Alas, it is far worse than you apprehend it to be! I am not one of those who have never been enlightened or made partaker of the heavenly gift or of the Holy Ghost, but have many years since been fully awakened, and am deeply sensible of sin, both original and actual. My case is rather like that of the church of Ephesus: I have not been faithful to the talents committed to my trust, and have lost my first love.[1] "Yet is there any hope in Israel concerning this thing?"[2] I do not, and by the grace of God I will not, despair; for ever since my sad defection, when I was almost without hope, when I had forgotten God, yet I then found he had not forgotten me. Even then he did by his Spirit apply the merits of the great atonement to my soul, by telling me that Christ died for me. Shall the God of truth, the Almighty Saviour, tell me that I am interested in his blood and righteousness, and shall I not believe him? God forbid. I do, I will believe; and though I am the greatest of sinners, that does not discourage me: for all my transgressions are the sins of a finite person, but the merits of our Lord's sufferings and righteousness are infinite! If I do want anything without which I cannot be saved (of which I am not at present sensible), then I believe I shall not die before that want is supplied.

You ask many questions which I care not to answer; but I refer you to our dear Lord, who will satisfy you in all things necessary for you to know. I cannot conceive why you affirm yourself to be not Christian; which is, in effect, to tell Christ to his face that you have nothing to thank him for, since you are not the better for anything he hath yet done or suffered for you. Oh, what great dishonour, what wondrous ingratitude, is this to the ever-blessed Jesus! I think myself far from being so good a Christian as you are, or as I ought to be; but God forbid that I should renounce the little Christianity I have: nay, rather let me grow in grace and in the knowledge of our Lord and Saviour Jesus Christ. Amen.[3]

I know not what other opinion people may have of human nature, but for my part I think that without the grace of God we are utterly incapable of thinking, speaking, or doing anything good: therefore, if in any part of our life we have been enabled to perform anything good, we should give God the glory. If we have not improved the talents given us, the fault is our own. I find this is a way of talking much used among this people, which has much offended me, and I have often wished they would talk less of themselves, and more of God. I often hear loud complaints of sin, etc., but rarely, very rarely, any word of praise and thanksgiving to our dear Lord, or acknowledgment of his infinite. . . .

To John Wesley
13 December 1740
MA; FB, 2:629, notes the letter but does not transcribe it. Nehemiah Curnock, *The Journal of the Rev. John Wesley, A.M.* . . . 8 vols. (London: Epworth, 1912-1916 [Reprint, 1938]), 8:273, includes a facsimile. Address torn: "To . . . The Rev. Mr . . . at the school . . . Horse-fair Br[istol]. Endorsed in Wesely's hand: "m[y] mr Dec. 13. 1740/ ad to b Humph!/& Mrs Maccune."

Sa[turday]: Dec: 13 1740

Dear Son,

I hope this will find you safe at Bristol, and if you would be so kind as to write as soon as conveniently may be, I should rejoice.

The reason of my writing so soon is I'm somewhat troubled at the case of poor

Mr. MacCune. I think his wife was ill-advised to send for that[4] wretched fellow Monroe, for by what I hear, the man is not lunatic, but rather under strong convictions of sin; and hath much more need of a spiritual, than bodily physician.[5] However be it as 'twill, Monroe last night sent him to a mad-house at Chelsea, where he is to undergo their usual methods of cure in case of real madness; notwithstanding in their treatment of him he behaved with great calmness and meekness, nor ever but once swore at them, for which he presently condemned himself and said, "Lord, what a sin have I been guilty of,"[6] and cried to God for mercy and pardon. This probably may confirm the doctor in the opinion of his madness, but to me 'tis a proof of his being in a right mind.

I am sure that our blessed Lord is superior to all the powers of evil angels and men and that, if he hath begun to awaken and call this poor sinner to himself, neither men nor devils can be able to stand before him!

Dear son, I desire you and your brother would pray for this poor afflicted man.[7] My love and blessing to ye both.

[signature missing]

To Charles Wesley
28 April 1741 (with an earlier section possibly written on 7 September 1739)
Private collection of Mr. Peter Conlan, Bromley, Kent.
Copy in United Church Archives, Toronto. Address in John Wesley's hand: "To The Revd. Mr. Wesley in Bristol." Endorsement in Charles Wesley's hand: "April 1741/ My Mother on/ Xt Crucified/ the [indecipherable word or words]." See *MH*, 28.3 (April 1990); 202–209, for more detailed introduction and notes.

Dear Son,

Your brother[8] hath more than once desired me to write to you, but as I knew there was a constant correspondence between ye, I thought he would inform of anything relating to me which was necessary for you to know.

I rejoice in your being so much employed in the service of our Lord and that he is pleased to set his seal to your ministry. May you ever retain the same humble thoughts of yourself and continue to ascribe all the glory of your usefulness to him to whom it properly belongs.

I don't well understand what you mean by the baptism which remains for us to be baptized with,[9] but suppose by what follows you think we are not yet fully convinced of sin. I hope we are in good measure convinced already that we do feelingly[10] know we are poor sinners—but to be fully apprized of the evil of sin in its nature and consequences it is, I humbly conceive, necessary that we have a more full and perfect knowledge of God. The sight of our sins may humble us indeed, but when by the eye of a strong faith we behold him that is invisible to the eye of sense; when we clearly apprehend that he is almighty power, justice and purity and yet almighty love (demonstrated by sending his only son to die for us), then we may say as Job, "We have heard of thee by the hearing of the ear, but now our eye seeth thee, wherefore we abhor ourselves and repent in dust and ashes."[11] Then we feelingly believe the exceeding sinfulness of sin, then true contrition springs up in the soul and the utmost self abhorrence—we stand amazed and confounded at the view of our own vileness and base ingratitude against God! That God which gave us being, that hath upheld us and fed and clothed us and by his blessed providence hath preserved us from innumerable evils all our life long, notwithstanding we have in no wise answered the end of our creation. But if reflection on our ingratitude for these temporal blessings (though exceeding valuable) renders us vile in our own eyes, how much viler do we appear when we consider we have all this while been sinning against redeeming love. If anyone would be deeply convinced of the evil of sin, if we would be more strongly affected with a sense of our own guilt, let us behold ourselves in the sufferings of the Son of God for the sins of mankind, more particularly for our own. Let us, my son, attend our Lord from the Passover to the Garden in which his soul was made an offering for sin. That as in a Garden the first Adam by his disobedience lost himself and all his posterity (which were then virtually included in him), so a principal part of the sufferings of the second Adam for sin were undergone in a Garden. It seems as if there was a gradual withdrawing of the light of God's countenance from the time of eating the Passover—he "began to be sorrowful and very heavy," saith St. Matthew, "sore amazed and very heavy," saith St. Mark.[12] Again that strange request to his three disciples, "Tarry ye here and watch with me,"[13] argued an astonishing weight of horror and grief in his soul! But how can we behold him in the Garden, prostrate on the earth agonizing to that strange height as far surpassed the power of human nature to sustain, insomuch that an angel was sent from heaven to strengthen him, after which we find that he prayed more earnestly till his sweat was in great drops of blood falling to the ground![14] I do humbly conceive that our dear Lord at that time did sustain the whole weight of the grief, anguish and sorrow which is due to divine justice for the sins of all mankind;[15] and then was his spotless soul made an offering for sin indeed! He knew God, the infinite purity of the divine nature! He perfectly knew the nature and felt the full weight and guilt of sin, as far as was possibly consistent with his unity with the Godhead!

'Tis certain our blessed Lord had a perfect foreknowledge of every article of his suffering long before and at that time had them all in view. But what does the Apostle mean by these words: "In the days of his flesh, when he had offered up prayers and supplications with strong crying and tears unto him that was able to save him from death; and *was heard* in that he feared."[16] If this is a right translation, what was it our Lord feared? It was not contempt and shame or pain or death; all this he patiently suffered—and therefore if it had been these things he deprecated, how was he heard? I humbly conceive then that what our Saviour deprecated was the terrible insupportable hiding of the Father's face: at the zenith of his passion, having probably some diffidence of his own human ability to finish the great work of man's redemption if the Godhead remained quiescent.[17] Set me right in this.

To your prayer that we may never rest till we rest in God, I say a hearty Amen.

Sept[ember] 7.[17]39[18]

The present state of the Christian Church affords but a melancholy prospect. Great numbers of the clergy as well as laity have either never known the gospel of

Jesus Christ or else hath forgot it. There hath of late been such a strange awakening throughout the Kingdom as has not been in my time before, as if our Saviour now made his last effort to bring people out of their carnal security before he comes to judgment; for in my apprehension that awful time draws very near. Satan has taken the alarm too, and perceiving that many are become obedient to the faith by which means he feels his kingdom strongly shaken, he hath exerted all his power in making opposition to the success of the gospel; he soon found the wicked too weak to serve his interest and therefore hath transformed himself into an angel of light[19] (under which disguise he is ever most formidable) and has prevailed with many that had been led into the way of truth to turn out of it. And now again our dearest Lord is wounded in the house of his friends.[20] First the little Moravian foxes attempted to spoil our vines and destroy the tender grapes.[21] These endeavoured to lead people into practical atheism by teaching them (out of a pretence of greater purity) that when they were regenerated and born again, they were at liberty to lay the ordinances[22] aside as useless: not considering that thereby they denied their Lord in setting aside his authority which appointed [them and refusing][23] to do him that public honour which he requires and has told us beforehand that such as will not confess him before men, the same will he deny before his father at the last judgment.[24] Further, they have taught that we are not to obey God's commands because he hath commanded us so to do, but because the doing, or forbearing such or such a thing, is agreeable and pleasing to spiritual self (a shameful contempt of divine authority again), whereas in truth, if when after we have been enlightened, have tasted the heavenly gift and been made partakers of the Holy Ghost, we decline from a pure intention of glorifying God by an entire sacrifice of self, and make either peace of conscience or the pleasure we find in any religious actions, the principal end of those actions; we exalt self into the place of God and are guilty of idolatry (more refined and spiritual, indeed) but as [?]flat idolatry as if we fell down and worshiped a graven image. This practical atheism their principles naturally lead men into.

April 28, 1741[25]

Thus these little foxes have endeavoured to destroy our Lord's vineyard and throw it open to common; but now, "the wild boar out of the wood" is labouring "to root it up: and the wild beasts of the field to devour it."[26] 'Tis an old maxim of Satan's, "Divide that you may destroy."[27] In order to practice his own rule, he hath thrown a bone of contention among the brethren about a point which hath been formerly much controverted in the Christian world, but of late years hath been very wisely laid aside.[28] The bait has taken among the weaker sort of people and numbers are greatly shaken, and no doubt but the Grand Adversary triumphs in his success and exults to see that he hath prevailed so far over our men as to engage them in a pernicious controversy which will effectually divert them from working out their own salvation with fear and trembling.[29] I am fully persuaded that if Whit[efield] could live more years than he will live, he will never do so much good as he has done harm since his return to England. God forgive him.[30]

Your brother hath made a noble defence against the enemies; has given them no quarter indeed! But continues daily to serve the Predestinarians as Samuel did Agag—he hews them in pieces before the Lord.[31] I admire his zeal and so much more as it is tempered with great meekness and patience and longsuffering—and though he strenuously opposes their doctrine, he does it always in the true spirit of Christian charity! Before they beset and [?]assaulted him so furiously on every side, he was very weak, and having no assistant, was often ready to faint under his labours. But our dear Lord hath had compassion on him and hath renewed his strength to such a degree as is truly astonishing! Asher's blessing is fallen on him: as is his day, so is his strength.[32] Glory be to God!

I have had many thoughts about you, because I knew the weakness of your body, I was under some apprehension of its being cast down by incessant labours;[33] but now I see the power of our Lord so plainly manifested in your brother and consider that his God and Saviour is yours also, my fears are at an end, and I need not desire you to join hand and heart with your brother in vindicating the glory and honour of our ever blessed Redeemer! Proclaim his universal love and free grace to all men. And that ye may go on in [the power of the Lord and in][34] the strength of his might and be preserved from yielding place to those bold blasphemers so much as for an hour is the hearty prayer of your loving mother. I send thee my love and blessing.

To the Countess of Huntingdon[35]
1 July 1741
MA. Addressed "To/ The Right Honble./ The Countess of Huntington." No postmark visible; possibly hand-delivered or never delivered.

Madam,

Your ladyship's great condescension in writing so kindly to such a one as I am had been sooner acknowledged, but I have not had opportunity, neither knew how to direct till last Sunday night. And now I have leisure, I really do not know what to say. Your goodness utterly confounds me, but the infinite goodness of God much more! Your ladyship doth not know me; you write as to one that is an heir of eternal glory (I am not without hope), but our Lord knoweth I am the greatest of sinners.[36] Yet, Christ came into the world to save sinners![37] Therefore, I have no fear.

I do indeed rejoice in my sons and am much pleased that they have in any measure been serviceable to your ladyship. You'll pardon the fondness of a mother, if I exceed in commending them, but I've known few (if any) that have laboured more diligently and unweariedly in the service of our dear Lord. And, blessed be his great name, he hath set his seal to their ministry and hath made them instrumental in bringing many souls to God. And though in the eye of the world they appear despicable, men of no estate or figure, and daily suffer contempt, reproach and shame among men, yet to me they appear more honourable than they would do if the one were Archbishop of Canterbury and the other of York; for I esteem the reproach of Christ greater riches than all the treasures in England.

Give me leave, my lady, to speak freely now of my own little affairs. I had it once in my mind to have given your ladyship some account of many incidents in my life, to which you are a stranger; but upon second thoughts it appeared presumption to trouble you too much. It may, therefore, be sufficient to say that your ladyship is the first person that ever I asked anything of in my life. For I rarely, if ever, complain, nor ask anything but of God. Some weeks before I heard from your ladyship, I had been in somewhat more than usual distress and had earnestly begged of God to open some door of hope, to send some relief by the hand of some person whom he would send. A few days after, Mrs. [?]Mott came hither and told me she came by your ladyship's order, who was so good as to order me some madeira, a welcome present, indeed, for which I return humble thanks. It came into my mind to speak freely to her, which accordingly I did, and find by what followed that I was not mistaken when I thought that you was the person, Madam, by whom God would answer my prayer, and I can never be too thankful to him and your ladyship; for never was a more seasonable charity. If the giving only a cup of cold water [38] entitles to a reward, how ample will be their recompense, Madam, that give such generous benefactions as yours!

I am far advanced in the decline of life and can't live now as I could have done forty or fifty year ago. I cannot dig; to beg I am ashamed. My sons, indeed, are very good to me, even beyond their proper power. Therefore I am careful to hide all wants from them. God in his good time will either call me home or appoint me sufficiency of food convenient, which is all I desire.

Though what your ladyship hath done for me may seem now like casting your bread upon the waters, yet be assured, Madam, you will find it again, though perhaps it may be after many days. [39]

I am,

Madam,

From the Foundry
July. First. 1.7.4.1.

Your Honour's
MostOblig'd
&
Most Obedient Servt:
Susanna Wesley

Notes

1. See Revelation 2:4.
2. Ezra 10:2, rearranged as a question; quotation marks in Stevenson.
3. Paraphrase of 2 Peter 3:18, the letter's final verse.
4. Crossed out: "perni," perhaps meaning pernicious.
5. I find no reference to this particular case in John Wesley's *Journal*, but the confusion of madness with conviction of sin was not uncommon in early Methodism. See, for example, his entry for 21 September 1739. Dr. Monroe, who figures there and also in the entry for 17 September 1740, seems to have been the eighteenth-century equivalent of a psychiatrist, making decisions on who needs institutionalization.
6. My quotation marks.
7. Her letter had an additional effect: according to his diary, John acted on the notes made when endorsing the letter and "writ to . . . Mrs. MacCune . . . Humphreys." See

W. Reginald Ward and Richard P. Heitzenrater, eds., *The Works of John Wesley*: Vol. 19. *Journals and Diaries*, II (*1738–42*) (Nashville: Abingdon, 1990), p. 444. Joseph Humphreys was one of Wesley's first "assistants," working with him in the early days at the Foundery but eventually leaving to follow Whitefield in 1741.

8. That is, John.

9. See such passages as Matthew 20:22–23, Luke 3:16, and Acts 1:5.

10. That is, consciously.

11. Job 42:5–6, substituting the second person plural. S. W.'s quotation marks.

12. Matthew 26:37 and Mark 14:33; my quotation marks. Note the same citations in her long letter to her daughter Susanna, 13 January 1709/10, expounding the Apostles' Creed, in part III of this volume.

13. Matthew 26:38; my quotation marks.

14. See Luke 22:43–44.

15. Phrasing close to another sentence in the same 1709/10 letter. See note 12.

16. Hebrews 5:7; my quotation marks. Underlined in MS.

17. In the letter to young Susanna on the Creed, cited in note 12, see a similar reference under the word "crucified": "There was, but after what manner we cannot conceive . . . a sensible withdrawing of the comfortable presence of the Deity, which caused that loud and passionate exclamation, 'My God, my God, why hast thou forsaken me.' "

18. This date is a bit mysterious. It may indicate that the first part of the letter was indeed written at this earlier time, then laid aside unfinished until April 1741.

19. Paraphrase of 2 Corinthians 11:14.

20. Paraphrase of Zechariah 13:6.

21. Song of Solomon 2:15. While John had come to a new assurance of salvation through the agency of the Moravians he had met during his mission to Georgia, he broke away from their influence when he discovered their quietist and antinomian tendencies. As he notes in his *Journal*, 18 July 1740, Susanna had some part in the proceeding: "A few of us joined with my mother in the great sacrifice of thanksgiving; and then consulted how to proceed with regard to our poor brethren of Fetter-Lane. . . ."

22. That is, the sacraments.

23. Bracketed words are reasonable guesses. Only the tops of several words are visible at the bottom of the MS page.

24. See Matthew 10:32–33.

25. This date runs top to bottom in the left-hand margin near the end of the preceding paragraph at the top of the letter's third page.

26. Nearly exact quotation from Psalm 80:13, BCP; my quotation marks.

27. S. W.'s quotation marks.

28. That is, predestination, the source of the Wesleys' dispute with Whitefield.

29. See Philippians 2:12.

30. George Whitefield departed for his second trip to North America in August 1739 and returned March 1741, at which point he joined the controversy by publishing *A Letter to the Rev. Mr. John Wesley . . .*, the reply to Wesley's sermon, *Free Grace*. See Iain Murray, ed., *George Whitefield's Journal* (London: Banner of Truth Trust, 1960), pp. 564–568. Cf. Susanna's rather positive assessment of Whitefield in the letter of 8 March 1739.

31. See 1 Samuel 15:33.

32. Paraphrase of Deuteronomy 33:25.

33. Or "labour."

34. Bracketed words added in left margin; probable reading.

35. Selina Hastings, countess of Huntingdon (1707–1791), was an early supporter of John Wesley and the evangelical revival. During the dispute over Calvinism, however, she sided

with George Whitefield and eventually created her own Nonconformist denomination, "The Countess of Huntingdon's Connexion."

36. This last declaration is written in slightly larger script.

37. 1 Timothy 1:15 and BCP, "Comfortable Words" following the absolution in Holy Communion.

38. See Matthew 10:42.

39. A paraphrase of Ecclesiastes 11:1.

PART II

Journals

Introduction to the Journals

*I*n an early entry (17 according to the system used in this edition) Susanna Wesley gives her rationale for keeping a diary and hints at her method.

> Keep the mind in a temper for recollection, and often in the day call it in from outward objects, lest it wander into forbidden paths. Make an examination of your conscience at least three times a day and omit no opportunity of retirement from the world.

Setting aside three periods of meditation at the beginning, middle, and end of a busy day was a typically Puritan approach. So, too, was the recording of spiritual questions and insights in a devotional diary, a custom followed by various members of the Annesley and Wesley families, both Anglican and Nonconformist. Her emphasis on the sabbath (see entries 165–168) also exemplified her Puritan background.[1] However, her spirituality was eclectic enough (paralleling English spirituality in general at the time) to draw also on method and content from other strands of Christianity. The devotional journal may have been a Puritan substitute for the confessional, but Anglicans also kept them.[2] There was a rigorous devotional tradition among the Nonjurors she so admired, as well as among the Caroline divines, whose spirituality has been described as the "disciplined response to the leading of the Spirit."[3] In places her diary becomes a virtual commonplace book of excerpts from and/or responses to such diverse non-Puritan sources as the French historian Lewis Maimbourg and his compatriot the philospher Nicolas Malebranch; Anglican divines William Beveridge, Richard Lucas, Gilbert Burnet, and possibly George Rust; not to mention figures with a more enduring reputation, Blaise Pascal, John Locke, and George Herbert. The Book of Common Prayer claims her attention in two instances, there are hints of Platonic language in at least one place, and the whole is suffused with biblical quotations and allusions.

Whatever the genre's origin, the diary functions for Susanna Wesley as a "means of grace," as well as a spiritual account book. It is first and foremost an explicit and important part of her spiritual life.

However, there is more to Susanna Wesley's journal than personal piety (and the fleeting revelations it gives about her family and home life). After all, diaries were, in addition to letters, the main mode of written self-expression open to early eighteenth-century women. As recent examinations of this genre have shown,[4] women's diaries in the early modern period not only provide a previously over-looked women's-eye view of their lives but also give us evidence, in the very act of writing to, for, and about themselves, that women could wrest a sense of self apart from the male-dominated assumptions of church and society.[5]

Religious diaries predominated in the seventeenth and eighteenth centuries: three-quarters of the Stuart women's diaries that Sara Heller Mendelson studied had substantial sections devoted to piety, and more than half were initiated, like Susanna Wesley's, for religious reasons.[6] The devotional journal (in Harriet Blodgett's terms, "the formulaic diary of conscience") did emerge under Puritan auspices as a way of searching the individual soul, recounting the ups and downs of the spiritual life, and thus supporting the "lifelong struggle with the enemy."[7]

One notable characterstic that Susanna Wesley's devotional journal shares with other women's diaries is a certain reticence, a discomfort about writing with complete openness and spontaneity. Women's diaries were often inhibited—whether by the fear of a husband or other family member finding and reading the diary or by the power of one's own internalized censor, for instance, the feeling that self-expression, even in a private diary, might contravene the ideal of female modesty. For such reasons Blodgett finds many diaries to be "neither self-reflective nor self-revealing, except minimally and inadvertently," and the epigraph on the flyleaf of Susanna Wesley's first journal notebook could have been taken directly from one of the popular conduct books that inculcated modest expression among women: "Think much and speak little."[8]

Susanna Wesley's older sister, Elizabeth, was avoiding the appearance of prideful and inappropriate self-expression when she tried to prevent others from reading the diary she kept over a period of some 20 years. According to the preface to her funeral sermon,

> she was so far from Vain-Glory, or Affectation of being talkt of after Death, that she desired that all those large Papers might be burnt, though even much of what she writ was in a Short-hand of her own Invention.[9]

The literal coding of thoughts in private shorthand (and there are several brief and indecipherable instances of this in Susanna Wesley's journal), suggests that a more figurative "encoding" may have taken place, as well.[10] Thus, while most Englishwomen diarists have accepted their male-dominated lot without complaint, there have always been some who "show conscious and unconscious defiance of that arrangement of power and its ramifications."[11] Paradoxically, the acceptance and the defiance seem not to be mutually exclusive.

All of this is to say that Susanna Wesley's private devotional diaries may be read on at least two levels. There is, first, a more conventional reading, which emphasizes her traditional spirituality, her submission to God and to the divinely ordered scheme of things. Then there is a second, less obvious approach, which requires a certain amount of decoding and reading between the lines but ultimately reveals a woman attempting to define herself over against the established powers. This second reading will help us make sense of the questioning, the bold resolutions, the exploration, and the wrestling with contemporary ideas that are woven into the fabric of Susanna Wesley's diaries.

Part II of this volume is based on some 255 entries or meditations that survive in three notebooks and two fragments in her handwriting and in two nineteenth-century printed sources. Only a handful of the entries are dated, but they do give us some sense of the historical context in which Susanna Wesley was writing. The earliest journal entries are from 1709 and the latest date is 1727, with the bulk of the work probably belonging to the first half of that period.[12]

Thus we are granted a fairly close look at the inner life of Susanna Wesley beginning at age 40, with all of her childbearing done but a good deal of her child rearing still before her. Though according to an early source she started keeping her diary nearly a decade earlier,[13] the 1709 date at least represents a new beginning, all of the family's books and papers having been destroyed by the rectory fire early that year.

Extracts of the journals have appeared from the time of Whitehead's biography up to the present day. In good Victorian fashion, they have often been excerpted and/or heavily edited for reasons of theology or taste; a twentieth-century English edition has even turned some of them into prayers for the Methodist faithful. Though scholars have had access to many of the entries at various points in the past, this volume is the first time they have been assembled, annotated, and introduced in one place.[14]

To facilitate reference and ease of reading, I have prefixed my own bracketed number and title to each of the journal entries. The consecutive numbers are a fairly reliable guide to chronological order within each manuscript but do not necessarily indicate priority among entries in different manuscripts.

Notes

1. See John Newton, *Susanna Wesley and the Puritan Tradition in Methodism* (London: Epworth, 1968), pp. 136 and 140, especially his entire chapter, "Serious Godliness," pp. 131–158, in which he connects S. W. with her birthright tradition through her father, Samuel Annesley, as well as through other prominent Puritans like Richard Baxter. On the sabbath, see Gordon S. Wakefield, "The Puritans," in Cheslyn Jones, Geoffrey Wainwright, and Edward Yarnold, S.J., eds., *The Study of Spirituality* (New York and Oxford: Oxford University Press, 1986), p. 442. S. W.'s sister Elizabeth Dunton kept a diary, as did at least one of her daughters, Martha Hall. On the former, see the preface to her funeral sermon by Timothy Rogers, *The Character of a Good Woman* . . . (London: John Harris, 1697), and John Dunton's *The Life and Errors* . . . , 2 vols. (London: J. Nichols, Son, and Bentley, 1818), 1:277–278; original ed. (London: S. Malthus, 1705). For the latter, see Adam Clarke, *Memoirs of the Wesley Family; Collected Principally from Original Documents*, 2nd ed. (London: Thomas Tegg, 1843–1844), 2:361–369. Her two most famous sons also kept diaries and/or journals, though of considerably wider scope than their mother's. John Wesley's journal, currently being edited in seven volumes by W. Reginald Ward and Richard Heitzenrater as part of the bicentennial edition of Wesley's works, continues to be one of the classics of the genre.

2. The provocative insight is William Haller's in *The Rise of Puritanism* (New York: Columbia University Press, 1938), pp. 38, 96–97; reprint ed. (Philadelphia: University of Pennsylvania

Press, 1984); it is taken up approvingly in Newton, *Susanna Wesley*, p. 140, and Owen C. Watkins, *The Puritan Experience: Studies in Spiritual Autobiography* (New York: Schocken, 1972), p. 18. However, Wakefield, in Jones et al, *Study of Spirituality* p. 439, claims that Haller is "not wholly justified" in making that assertion. Haller himself notes, pp. 229–230, that Archbishop Laud, archfoe of the Puritans, kept a diary.

3. Martin Thornton, "The Caroline Divines and the Cambridge Platonists," in Jones et al., *Study of Spriituality*, p. 436.

4. Sara Heller Mendelson, "Stuart Women's Diaries and Occasional Memoirs," in Mary Prior, ed., *Women in English Society 1500–1800* (London and New York: Methuen, 1985), pp. 181–210, nicely sets the stage for Susanna Wesley's earliest diaries. Harriet Blodgett, *Centuries of Female Days: Englishwomen's Private Diaries* (New Brunswick, N.J.: Rutgers University Press, 1988), puts the genre into a wider historical perspective. Both provide helpful suggestions for further reading on diaries in general and Englishwomen's diaries in particular.

5. Mendelson looks to diaries for "women's own sensibilities or the *minutiae* of their daily lives" ("Diaries," p. 181, elaborated on at some length, pp. 189–200) and hints only occasionally at their role in developing a new sense of female identity (e.g., pp. 194, 201). Blodgett, using her larger canvas, can paint a more detailed picture of how the genre functioned in changing women's lives, though she, too, is interested in what diaries can tell us about their lives. Not only are diaries "confidants" and "consciences," they also "support and reinforce the female sense of self." (*Female Days*, pp. 63ff., her second chapter, "Personal Time: Motivations and Justifications for Diary Keeping.") The theme recurs throughout the book.

6. Mendelson, "Diaries," p. 185.

7. Blodgett, *Female Days*, is quoting Watkins, *Puritan Experience*, p. 18, on her p. 265, n. 16. She regards the religious diary as one of the ancestors of the modern diary (p. 23), but she tries (not always successfully, given the pervasiveness of religiosity in the early modern worldview) to exlude it from her study (p. 12). Even so, her analysis is often provocatively helpful in reading Susanna Wesley's unapologetically devotional outpourings.

8. Blodgett, *Female Days*, p. 41; see also pp. 41–62 for her extended discussion on the various reasons for such reticence. Angeline Goreau makes a good case for the importance of a broadly defined modesty, a metaphorical extension of the virtue of chastity, in silencing women. As inculcated by seventeenth-century moralists in "conduct books," modesty was not just a matter of avoiding ostentatious dress and flirtatious behavior but could extend to any perceived boldness of expression. As the anonymous author of *The Whole Duty of a Woman* puts it: "Your looks, your speech, and the course of your whole behaviour, should own an humble distrust of your selves; rather being willing to learn and observe, than to dictate and prescribe. . . . There is scarce any thing to be found that appears more indecent, than to be proud, or too forward in overmuch talk, or indecent behaviour." Angeline Goreau, *The Whole Duty of a Woman: Female Writers in Seventeenth-Century England* (New York: Dial, 1985), pp. 52–53. See also her introduction, pp. 1–20, and extended excerpts from other conduct books in the chapter "Education: 'Modesty,' " pp. 35–64. S. W.'s epigraph is remarkably close to the complaint of a protofeminist tract, *The Female Advocate*: ". . . one great commendation of our sex is to know much and speak little . . ." (quoted in Goreau, p. 13). Of course, an even more egregious breach of modesty than keeping a diary would be writing for publication, an issue S. W. faced only once (see part III of this volume).

9. Timothy Rogers, *The Character of a Good Woman . . . in a Funeral Discourse . . . of Mrs. Elizabeth Dunton . . .* (London: John Harris, 1697), quoted in Mendelson, "Diaries," p. 184. Rogers was able, however, to coax some of her writings from her during her last illness and made excerpts of pious passages, which he included in the sermon

10. Blodgett, *Female Days*, p. 59.

11. Ibid., p. 135. She further suggests the techniques employed in expressing such defi-

ance: "grumbling, outright complaining, undercutting and manipulating of men, and even . . . outright insubordination."

12. Headingley MS A ranges from 1709–1718 (seven dates, including one on the flyleaf and the others scattered among 165 entries); a second set, beginning at the back of the same notebook, dates from 1709 to 1727 (six dates in 19 entries). Headingley MS B contains no dates in 15 entries, as does Headingley MS C in 17 entries, though the latter is part of a notebook with draft letters from 1709, 1710, and possibly 1711. The fragments from archives in Baltimore and Manchester contain no dates in six entries; nor do any of the 26 additional entries in the *Wesley Banner* and the six entries in Clarke's *Wesley Family*.

13. John Whitehead, *The Life of the Rev. John Wesley* . . . (New York: R. Worthington, 1881, p. 34; original ed. London, 1793 and 1796.

14. All subsequent publication until now seems to have come from one or more of the following three collections. (a) Ibid., pp. 34–36, selects those we have designated entries 191 (from Headingley MS B) and 250–255 (missing material). (b) *Wesley Banner*, 1852, includes the following: on pp. 201–205, 245–248 entries 219 (from the Baltimore fragment), missing material 220–228, 229–230 (Baltimore fragment), missing material 231–247; and on pp. 282–287, 323–326, 365–366, 404–406, 443–445 entries 4–21, 162, 22–27, 29–36, 164, 37–43 (somewhat oddly ordered) from MS A. (c) Clarke includes on pp. 257–263 entries 185–199 (from MS B) and on pp. 263–265 missing material entries 250–255. The remaining entries in MS A (1–3, 28, 44–161, 163, 165–184) have, as far as I can tell, never been published. In the twentieth century, W. L. Doughty, *The Prayers of Susanna Wesley* (London: Epworth, 1956), and following him, Donald L. Kline, *Susanna Wesley: God's Catalyst for Revival* (Lima, Ohio: C. S. S, 1980), have heavily edited various entries for modern devotional purposes.

FIFTEEN

"Think Much and Speak Little"

First Surviving Entries

*O*n the initial title page of her most substantial journal notebook (a page now nearly obscured by notes in a later hand), Susanna Wesley has written hurriedly and upside down: "S. W. 1709"; and at the top, right side up, an epigraph: "Think much and speak little." More than a maxim with a general appeal to the meditative sensibility (and in accord with reigning views of female modesty), this sentence also catches something of the special predicament a thoughtful woman like Susanna Wesley found herself in—and something of the promise that a devotional journal might provide to such a woman.

In this earliest surviving portion of her private writing (any previous notebooks would have been lost in the flames in the rectory fire early in 1709), we begin to glimpse the interplay of her devotional musings and her life. The preponderance of her writing is theological, but it is almost always practical: either stemming from her own experience (as interpreted in the light of Christian revelation and the "reasonableness" of the age) or having profound implications for the way she and her family should order their lives.

Thus the calls for humility (1, 14) and submission to Providence (9), the tension between a life of quiet devotion and service to her large family, and concerns for improving the time and finding an "exact and regular course of life" (11) are scattered throughout these pages. Of particular note is the early reference in entry 11 to the importance of educating her children, a vocation she methodically and successfully pursued and would later reflect on at length at the request of her son John.[1]

In addition there is even a rare political entry here. Her Nonjuring sympathies were still well enough intact in 1709 for her to question English military aggression toward France (4). The importance to her of "a Conscience void of offense," already visible in her letters, will appear again and again in the private confessional of her devotional journals.

The 14 entries transcribed here begin the most substantial of Susanna Wesley's journal notebooks still extant. Designated "Headingley MS A" in the collection of Wesley College, Bristol, it contains meditations from the period 1709–1727 on 192 pages (numbered by a subsequent hand), beginning at one end of the notebook, and 35 pages (unnumbered) beginning at the other.

🖋

[1. Humility.]

"Lord, I am not high-minded, etc."² David gives that as an instance of his not being high minded (that he does not exercise himself in things too high for him, nor had he any proud looks—³

[2. The point of parables: the Prodigal Son.]

In all the parables and metaphors our Lord makes use of in the Gospel there seems to be one principal design, and the parts of which they are composed are only to illustrate and plainly set forth that design so that we are chiefly to observe what that is and not to raise any point of faith or doctrine or weight upon the rest of the story. Thus in the parable of the prodigal⁴ we may observe that the intention of the parable is to show us the exceeding infinite goodness and mercy toward one repenting sinner and the readiness and willingness of God to accept of such.⁵

[3. Reflections on atonement.]

Pardon of Sin, What?⁶

All sin deserves eternal punishment or death, and therefore every sinner is under an obligation to suffer death for his sins—sins are said to be pardoned when that obligation to death or punishment is taken off. And they are said to be pardoned by or through or for the sake of Christ, because that death which we should have suffered for sin, he was pleased to suffer in our stead, and thereby he hath discharged the sinner. Did Christ then suffer eternal death? No—but he suffered death here upon the cross for us, and he, being the eternal son of God, his once dying for our sins is more than equivalent for the eternal sufferings of all mankind.⁷

[. . .] protect them. And as our principles, so our practice is greatly corrupted, and unless the almighty Goodness should almost miraculously interpose in our favour,⁸

[4. Conscientious objection to war with France and to public prayers for its success.]

For these reasons I think fasting and prayer was never more necessary than now, and we ought with great humility to bewail the sins⁹ of guilty England and to cry mightily to God for mercy on this nation which seems so ripe for vengeance. But still I cannot join with the public assemblies for these reasons. First, the end for which this fast is assigned. I am not satisfied in the lawfulness of the war on our part, because 'tis offensive.¹⁰ The common reasons which were given for it do by no means satisfy me, such as the checking the power of France, securing our religion, etc. Though it must be owned that the F[rench] K[ing] did extend his dominions beyond the just limits and might be guilty of an exorbitant ambition, yet he did not actually invade us, nor should we upon a supposition of a probable danger have made use of indirect means for our preservation, but ought rather to have resigned the care of our safety to that providence which presides over all the kingdoms of this world and disposes of them to whom he pleases.

As for the security of our religion, I take that to be still a more unjustifiable pretense for war than the other. For whatever some men of a sanguine complexion may persuade themselves, I am of opinion that as our Saviour's kingdom is not of this world,[11] so 'tis never lawful to take up arms merely in defense of religion. 'Tis like the presumption of Uzzah, that audaciously stretched out his hand to support the tottering ark,[12] which brings to mind those verses of no ill poet:

> In such a cause, 'tis fatal to embark,
> Like the bold Jew, that prop'd the falling ark,
> With unlicens'd hand, he durst approach;
> And though to save, yet it was death to touch.[13]

And truly the success of our arms hitherto has no way justified our attempt, but though God has not much seemed to favour our enemies, yet neither has he altogether blessed our forces.

But though there is often many reasons given for an action, yet there is commonly but one true reason that determines our practice. And that in this case I take to be the securing those that were the instruments of the revolution from the resentments of their angry master and the preventing his return and settling the succession in a line they resolved. . . .[14]

Whether they did well in driving a prince from his hereditary throne, I leave to their own consciences to determine—though I cannot tell how to think that a king of England can ever be accountable to his subjects for any maladministrations or abuse of power, but, as he derives his power from God, so to him only he must answer for his using it. But still I make a great difference between those who entered into a confederacy with————[15] against their prince and those who, knowing nothing of the contrivance, and so consequently not consenting to it, only submitted to the present government, which seems to me to be the law of the English nation and the duty of private Christians and the case of the generality of this people. But whether the praying for a usurper and vindicating his usurpations after he has the throne be not a partaking in his sins is easy to determine.[16]

Second, since I am not satisfied of the lawfulness of the war, I cannot beg a blessing on our arms till I can have the opinion of one wiser and a more competent judge than myself in this point, viz., whether a private person that had no hand in the beginning of a war, but did always disapprove of it, may, notwithstanding, implore God's blessing on it and pray for the good success of those arms which were taken up, I think, unlawfully?

In the mean time I think it my duty, since I cannot join in public worship, to spend that time others take in that in humbling my soul before God for my own and the nation's sins and in beseeching him to spare this guilty land, wherein are many thousands that are, notwithstanding, comparatively innocent, and not to slay the righteous with the wicked, but to put a stop to the effusion of Christian blood, and in his own good time to restore us to the blessing of public peace.

Since then I do not absent from church out of any contempt of authority or out of any vain presumption of my own goodness, as though I needed no solemn humiliation, and since I endeavour according to my poor ability to humble myself before God and do earnestly desire that he may give this war such an issue as may most effectually conduce to his glory, I hope it will not be charged upon me as a sin, but that it will please almighty God by some way or other to satisfy my scruples and to accept of my honest intentions and to pardon my manifold infirmities.

[5. Vows and prayers as means of grace against temptation.]

Even[ing] M.[editation?]

How evidently does the Holy Spirit concur with the means of grace; and how certainly does he assist and strengthen the soul, if it be but sincere and hearty in its endeavours to avoid any evil or perform any good! If once the mind be but brought to an inclination toward any virtue, it hath gained a considerable point; nay, 'tis one step to goodness to have but a good desire; a fervent aspiration towards God shall not pass unregarded. I have found by experience that 'tis of great use to accustom oneself to solemn vows against any particular sin, but then I would have them never made for longer time than from morning till night and from night till morning, that so the impressions they make on the mind may be always fresh and lively; this many years tried with good success in the case of———.[17] Glory be to thee, O Lord.

One step made towards virtue, in that I find that whenever there is any fervent prayer against any particular imminent, dangerous temptation, the remembrance of that prayer is a check upon the mind, nor dares it indulge a thought, a wish or an inclination so prayed against, which is a great and strong proof of an invisible power that does advert to our actions and hear our prayers and that is ever ready to assist and help such as sincerely, though weakly, devote themselves to him.

Glory be to the sacred and ever blessed God! Father, Son, and Holy Ghost!

[6. Finding a means of grace in the ordinary course of life.]

Even[ing] M[editation]

What shall I call it, providence or chance, that first directed my eye to the first verse of the thirteenth chapter of Zechary[18] when for several nights the bible always opened in that place when I took it to read in the evening? Whatever it was, I have found a good effect of it, for by that means I have for so long a time had an opportunity of praising the eternal infinite love of God for sending his Son into the world to die for sinners, nor can I see that verse without "Glory be to thee, O Lord."[19]

From which I cannot but observe that, if the temper and disposition of the mind be good, there is very few things that occur in the ordinary course of life, however trivial or inconsiderable they may seem in their own nature, but what may prove a mean[s] of conveying grace into the soul, and 'tis only want of advertence and a due care to implore the divine blessing and direction in all our ways that makes us so little the better for those little accidents we meet with in our daily converse in the world.[20]

[7. Christ's passion can save as many worlds as God's omnipotence can create.]

As the infinite power of almighty God was not exhausted in the creation of the universe, nor could possibly be so, though he should create more, but though he should still continue to create *ad infinitum*,[21] his essential goodness is the same. So neither is the merits of our Saviour's passion exhausted by those that are actually redeemed. But were there as many worlds to save as omnipotence could create, his one sacrifice of himself would be sufficient to save them all.

[8. God's governance of, and our disengagement from, the world; a "conscience void of offence."]

Even[ing] M[editation]

Considering the present state of mankind, the corruption of their natures, variety of dispositions and circumstances, their different and often contrary designs and interests, which almost all pursue with as much passion and eagerness as if they were to live here forever; considering, I say, these things, there is no such relief and satisfaction to the mind as a firm belief of God's governing the world, nor does anything afford such practical arguments for patience and resignation to divine providence as the often reflecting that the tumultuous and irregular actions of sinful men are nevertheless under the direction of that wise, good and omnipotent Being that hath promised to make all things work together for good to those that love him.[22]

And since we must expect to meet with many difficulties, much opposition, many disappointments and daily trials of faith and patience in our passage through this world, 'tis our highest wisdom to disengage our affections, as much as we lawfully may, from all these transitory temporal enjoyments and to fix 'em on those more solid, more rational and spiritual pleasures we are to enjoy when we enter upon our state of immortality. To endeavour to secure our eternal happiness by using our utmost endeavours to gain a treasure that lies beyond the reach of all the storms and tempests of this world, a kingdom that cannot be shaken by faction, cannot be disturbed by ill men or ill angels, where there are no parties or separate interests to engage or divide men's affections, but all shall most perfectly agree to make up a divine harmony praise and adoration.[23]

In the mean time 'tis best to resolve to keep a "conscience void of offense towards God and man."[24] Does many nowadays seek to advance their worldly interest, endeavour to raise their families by fraud, oppression, by making shipwreck of faith and a good conscience?[25] Let it then be my great care to have a special regard to justice and charity, to preserve the principles of faith inviolate, and in all cases to perform present duties with the greatest exactness and integrity. And then whatever crosses or troubles are met withal, all will be well within, and the consciousness of one's own innocence will be an admirable preservative against all exterior calamities.

Nor shall it be in the power of any to rob me of that peace which results from a firm faith in God through the merits of our blessed Saviour, to whom with the Father and the sacred Spirit all glory!

[9. Focus away from worldy disappointments, "the incommodities of a little house and a great family," and toward eternity.]

E[vening] M[editation]

'Twas well resolved not to be much concerned at what is met with in this world, however contrary to our present inclination. Whatever were the accidents that disappointed ——— in the pursuit of R———,[26] the event was ordered by that unerring Wisdom that disposes all things and fixes the bounds, determines the place of our habitation.[27]

Now all things are sufficiently uneasy, and the incommodities of a little house and great family are great impediments to ———[28] when the body is weak and the mind not strong, but all things must be endured with patience, seeing the end of all troubles is at hand, for life wears apace, and in a few years (perhaps days) we shall pass into another state very different from this, wherein we shall always enjoy that tranquility that is in vain sought for in any temporal enjoyment. Nor shall we sin or sorrow more. Courage then—think on eternity.

[10. Integrity establishes a better reputation than vanity.]

E[vening] M[editation]

'Tis a weakness very incident to persons that live a retired life, when they accidentally come abroad into the world, to be talking of themselves, of their own affairs or employments, of their families or business, their relations, their acquaintance[s], servants, etc. This vanity generally proceeds from a desire of being taken notice of, or else from a partial fond opinion men are apt to conceive of themselves, which makes them think all things that relate to them or any way concern them must needs be very considerable and well worthy the notice or imitation of the rest of the world.

Now what needs all this ado? To what purpose should we desire to be observed or esteemed of by those whose good or ill opinion is of so little consequence, since it possibly may no way conduce to our eternal happiness, nor will it add any weight to our future glory?

I have often observed that a simple, plain, unaffected honesty that has had little or no advantages from great sense or human prudence has established a better reputation than the most refined arts and best laid designs of worldly wisdom hath ever been able to reach without integrity. Nay, often times it happens that, though a man hath some weak degrees of virtue and is, as we used to say, honest in the main, yet if he has too great a desire to be known and esteemed by men, he hath for that very reason never been able to acquire any considerable reputation in the world. Perhaps because his too eager desire to please may put him upon mean and unworthy compliances,[29] may make him neglect his guard and often speak or act inconsistently, or may possibly render him an easy prey to crafty and designing men, and by that means engage him in factions or interests that in the end may ruin the fame he designed to build by such practices.

After all, "he that walketh uprightly, walketh most securely." [30] He may in some rare and exempt cases, 'tis true, incur the displeasure of men, but he is always assured of the favour and protection of God, which can, if he see it best for him, even in this world make his righteousness shine as the sun and his just dealing appear clear as the noon day. [31] However it be, this world is but for a short time, and those that have their treasure and heart in heaven need not, nor will they be very solicitous about, these temporal concerns. Honours, riches, sensual pleasures appears to such a person truly as they are, vain, unsatisfactory, perishing trifles, not worth much care to get or keep, nor will they barter heaven and eternal happiness for things which, in themselves considered, have no real value, nay, that are rather a clog and burden than anything else to a soul truly devoted to God and that had rather enjoy the blessed opportunities of frequent retirement from the world than have all those things in possession which foolish mistaken men account the chief ingredients of happiness.

Indeed, 'tis a thing much to be admired [32] that men which know they were born to die, that know and are morally assured that this life is only a prelude to eternity and that this short uncertain space of time is all that is allowed for the working out their salvation, that still notwithstanding they should with so much eagerness and concern pursue wealth and honour, fame etc., which, if attained, could neither satisfy in the enjoyment nor be kept one moment after death, while in the mean time they take no thought of what shall be their state in their future existence. [33]

[11. Contemplation in the context of "a numerous family and a narrow fortune." Redeeming the time through education of children.]

N. M-R. [34]

'Tis perhaps one of the most difficult things in the world to preserve a devout and serious temper of mind in the midst of much worldly business, and therefore I would advise that no person voluntarily involve themselves in or take upon them the management of more business than they can throw into such a method as may not distract their thoughts or take up too much their time which was given us to work out our salvation. But where a numerous family and a narrow fortune oblige to it, it is not to be declined, lest we break the order of providence, and therefore in such a case we must do as a wise workman that takes a piece of work by the great upon hard terms; we must work so much harder, we must be careful to redeem time from sleep, eating, dressing, unnecessary visits, and trifling conversation, that we be not forced to contract our private devotions into such a little space as may deprive us of the benefit and comforts of them.

Were I permitted to choose a state of life or positively to ask of God anything in this world, I would humbly choose and beg that I might be placed in such a station wherein I might have daily bread with moderate care without so much hurry and distraction; and that I might have more leisure to retire from the world without injuring my ———— [35] or children. Nor should any consideration of interest, of riches, honour, pleasure prevail upon me to encumber myself with such a multiplicity of business as I now submit to only in obedience to the order of divine providence.

This is my present thoughts, but yet I do not know whether such a state of life would really be best for me. Nor am I assured that, if I had more leisure, I should be more zealously devoted to God and serve him better than now. Perhaps there might be as many temptations in a quiet and private life as there is in this, or suppose there should not, yet how can I tell but that a constant state of suffering may be necessary to purify the mind and to keep a check upon it, lest it run into vanity, worldly regards, etc., which ought carefully to be avoided, and possibly such a proportion of punishment for some sins is necessary in this life, or otherwise we should not escape punishment hereafter.

After all, 'tis undoubtedly best to keep the mind in a habitual submission and resignation to that Being which is infinitely incomprehensibly wise and good, which cannot possibly err, but must certainly know what is best for everyone in the world. He that made us best knoweth how and where to fix the bounds of our habitation,[36] what relations, what circumstances, what business, what diversions, what company, what trials are best for every individual person in the world; and he hath given us his word that all things shall work together for good to those that love him,[37] which is enough to support and calm the mind in all the adverse or uneasy circumstances of life.

The main thing to be done, then, is to endeavour all we can to be assured that we love God, which assurance can no way be attained but by the evidence of a good life.[38] If the mind does habitually press after a conformity to the divine will and doth in all its actions chiefly desire to please and approve itself to God, and this without regarding the world or the favour or displeasure of man any further than his honour and glory is concerned, if it have an habitual tendency and desire of union and enjoyment of him and does in all circumstances, places, and times preserve a habit of submission and entire resignation to the order of his providence, as well when it crosses our worldly interest and prevents our best laid design and contrivances for the advancement of his glory as when it favours them, if it be content to be laid aside,[39] as an unprofitable useless thing of no value or esteem and can rejoice in the disposal of his wisdom though in all things it seems to contradict our judgments and cross our inclinations.[40] And though order and an exact regular course of life be desired above all things in the world and to have certain set times for retirement and leisure to worship and adore the supreme fountain of being be an unspeakable happiness, yet "obedience is better than sacrifice,"[41] and, if the order of his providence doth sometimes plainly interrupt or prevent such retirement, etc., the same love of God that inspires the soul with the desire of such a state will calm and quiet it, though disappointed, and cause it humbly to acquiesce in and submit to whatever he seeth best for us to do or suffer.

Take courage, then, and suffer not thy mind to faint or grow weary. God is no hard master, and, though it seemeth best to his infinite wisdom to determine us to such a station as will necessarily involve us in much business and does daily exercise our faith and patience, yet rest assured that all things shall at last have a happy issue, if the heart be but sincerely devoted to him. Nor shall his Spirit be wanting to guide and support those that principally intend his honour and glory in all their actions.

Though the education of so many children must create abundance of trouble and will perpetually keep the mind employed, as well as the body, yet consider 'tis no small honour to be entrusted with the care of so many souls, and if that trust be but managed with prudence and integrity, the harvest will abundantly recompense the toil of the seed time, and it will be certainly no little accession to the future glory to stand forth at the last day and say, "Lord, here are the children which thou hast given me, of whom I have lost none by my ill example, nor by neglecting to instill into their minds in their early years the principles of thy true religion and virtue."[42]

[12. Using one's talents. Aristotle's error corrected by Trinitarian revelation.]

Morn[ing]

That God that made us and fixed each individual creature within such a certain sphere of activity beyond which he knows it cannot act, will never require more of any man than he has power to do. The unprofitable servant was not condemned for having only one talent, but for letting that talent lie useless.[43] The case is the same with us. No man shall be finally condemned for the smallness of his understanding or the natural and involuntary weakness of his judgment, but for neglecting to improve and make good use of the powers God has given him.

Aristotle supposes the world to have been eternal, that is, streamed by connatural[44] result and emanation from God, as the light from the sun, and that there was no instant of duration assignable of God's existence in which the world didn't also actually coexist.[45]

This error seems grounded on a true notion of the eternal infinite goodness of God, which he truly supposes must eternally be communicating good to something or other, and it was his want of the knowledge of revealed religion that probably led him into it. For had he ever heard of that great article of our Christian faith concerning the Holy Trinity, he had then perceived the almighty Goodness eternally communicating being and all the fullness of the Godhead to the divine Logos, his uncreated Word, between whose existence and that of the Father there is not one moment assignable. As likewise the eternal Spirit, streaming from the Father and Son by connatural result and emanation as light from the sun, though that simile does not[46] . . . of the three divine persons.

[13. Making true use of dissappointments: separation from worldly things; pursuit of everlasting happiness.]

March 1st, 1710/11

R—[47] Nothing comes to pass but by the appointment of God, and he hath a sovereign right of disposing all persons and things according as his infinite wisdom shall determine. Nor is it for a creature to dispute the will of his creator. In all disappointments whatever, in all the crosses and troubles we meet with in this life, we must therefore submit with cheerfulness, and when our expectation and comforts of this world run lowest, the expectations and comforts relating to another life must in proportion rise higher, and the nearer we must approach towards heaven, or the heart is not right with God. If faith cannot conquer and triumph over riches, honour, and sensual pleasures, 'tis undoubtedly very weak and can never save us. Resolve, therefore, to make the true use of all disappointments and calamities in this life and let them more closely unite the heart to God; let them separate the affections from worldly things and inspire the soul with more vigour in the pursuit of everlasting happiness. For, till this temper of mind be attained, till we can thus improve affliction to our spiritual advantage, the mind can never enjoy any settled peace, much less perfect serenity. Nothing but God can satisfy an immortal soul, nor are any but spiritual treasures proper for its nature, and till we are well apprised of this, till we can have a firm and deep impression of this upon our minds, we can never be happy, for we shall still be pursuing after happiness in the enjoyment of something or other below, where it can never be found. I have often experienced that the less there is of worldly comforts the more there is of God, and the sweeter and stronger are the consolations of God to the mind, when there is not any one creature it can fly to for help or comfort. Till the soul can stay and centre itself in God, till it can confine its desires, hopes and expectations of happiness to him alone and calmly attend to the dispensations of his providence, till it have a firm habitual resignation to his will, it is not truly devoted to God, however specious[48] the profession of religion may be to the world. And, as "obedience is better than sacrifice,"[49] so all external performances without sacrificing our whole selves to him, without being ready to part with whatever we enjoy, if he think fit to require it, signifies nothing.

There is a great deal of difference between taking off the affections from the world and fixing them on heaven, and 'tis much easier to do the one than the other. 'Tis very natural upon a present disappointment of a pleasing expectation or a bodily indisposition, which takes off the relish of our enjoyments, to reflect on the vanity of the world and of the folly of placing our happiness in and of expecting any solid permanent satisfaction from the present state of things; and we are very ready to say in such cases as Solomon did, "All is vanity and vexation of spirit."[50]

But this is not sufficient for our happiness. What if the unclean spirit of ambition, sensuality, immoderate love of the world be gone out of the man, if love to God, pure desires, holy affections, and a fixing of the heart on heaven do not succeed this separation from the world?[51] 'Tis great odds but Satan, when he finds the soul thus empty of grace, will quickly return and bring with him seven other spirits worse than the other, and the last state of that man shall be worse than the first.[52]

We must love the Lord our God with all the heart, with all the mind, with all the soul, and with all the strength.[53] We must love him so as to desire him, desire him so as to be uneasy without him, without his favour, without some resemblance (such as our nature in this imperfect state can bear) of him. We must . . .[54]

[14. Mean estate ordered by God; no cause for shame.]

He that is ashamed of a poor or mean estate would certainly be proud of a great one. For the man is not well informed, has not a true sense and therefore does not make a due estimate of things. He wants a strong and clear sense of God upon his mind and does not advert sufficiently to his government of the world. He wants the principles of true humility, which would teach him to think so worthily of God and so meanly of himself, that he would easily perceive that whatever that blessed Being is pleased to order, whatever part he hath assigned him to act upon the stage of the world, be it that of a prince or a beggar, 'tis certainly best, and that he himself can never have less than he deserves, and therefore he is so far from being ashamed of his poverty or want of many things others enjoy, that he stands amazed at the divine goodness for giving him anything, that deserves nothing.

Notes

1. See her famous letter to John Wesley on child rearing, 24 July 1732, the first document in part III of this volume.

2. Psalm 131:1; Coverdale's sixteenth-century translation in BCP; my quotation marks.

3. Paraphrase of Psalm 131:1b–2. There follows a break of a line or two and then a new thought, written, it appears, with a new pen.

4. Luke 15:11–32.

5. An inch or so is torn from the bottom of the page, but her meditation has already ended, and there is an inch of blank space between her last line and the tear.

6. One of S. W.'s own subtitles, a rare instance.

7. Two pages torn out at this point, before they were numbered. Scraps of the pages remaining next to the binding indicate that there was writing on them. Consequently, we have missed two sides' worth of an entry and join the next meditation, already in progress (in fact nearly finished), at the top of the following page. Nevertheless, there seems to be continuity in the discussion.

8. Meditation breaks off in mid-sentence. Two lines are left blank before she continues with a new but related turn of thought. This new paragraph begins material published in the *Wesley Banner*, 1852, pp. 282–287.

9. Paraphrase from General Confession, Holy Communion, BCP.

10. As the note in the *Banner* indicates, this was probably written in 1709, shortly before Marlborough defeated Marshal Villars at Malplaquet. Though the French were defeated, the battle was a costly one for the British and their German allies. It took place on 11 September.

11. John 18:36.

12. 2 Samuel 6:6–7.

13. I have been unable to determine who this "no ill poet" is. It appears not to be the work of her husband, Samuel (who might deserve such faint praise), nor is it that of the better poets of the age, such as Milton, Dryden, or Pope.

14. Her apparent reference is to the Glorious Revolution of 1688, which effectively deposed James II in favor of his son-in-law (and nephew), William of Orange. William reigned jointly with James's daughter Mary until her death in 1694 and alone until his death in 1702. James fled to France, where he died in 1701. The Act of Settlement of that same year stipulated that the throne must pass only to a Protestant heir; thus in 1702 Mary's sister Anne became queen. War with France, punctuated with Marlborough's victories at Blenheim and at Malplaquet, could at least in part be attributed to an attempt to weaken the power of the Old Pretender, James's son, who would in fact attempt an invasion not long after Anne died without an heir in 1714.

15. William of Orange is the likely reference. See note 16.

16. Cf. Susanna's quarrel with her husband over King William's legitimacy, outlined in

her letters to Lady Yarborough (7 and 15 March 1701/02) and George Hickes (? April and 31 July 1702). Did she mean to leave a negative out of the last clause: "is [not] easy to determine"? Or is she still continuing in her Nonjuring ways, contrasting a Christian's duty to obey the new sovereign with the danger of praying for him or her and thus in some sense participating in what seemed to her a travesty against rule by divine right?

17. A strong internal censor and/or the fear that someone might read her journal has kept her from describing the subject of her vow on paper.

18. Zechariah 13:1: "In that day there shall be a fountain opened to the house of David and to the inhabitants of Jerusalem for sin and for uncleanness."

19. My quotation marks; S. W. uses dashes before and after the phrase.

20. This reflection ends, and several lines are left blank at the bottom of the page. A new thought begins at the top of the facing page, though without a new heading.

21. This clause originally (and more clearly) read: "nay though he should still continue eternally to create *ad infinitim*." She has crossed out "nay," substituting "but," and has crossed out "eternally." I have added the emphasis due the Latin phrase.

22. Paraphrase of Romans 8:28.

23. Cf. the growing antipathy toward "party" in eighteenth-century English politics and society.

24. Nearly exact quotation of Acts 24:16, a verse she also employed in her letter to Lady Yarborough, 7 March 1701/02, in discussing the same broad issue. Quotation marks added.

25. Loose paraphrase of 1 Timothy 1:19.

26. Again, S. W. does not go so far as to name names and sins, though the following paragraph might indicate that she is thinking along domestic lines. The initial may also be interpreted as a "P" with the dash tailing off so that it resembles a capital "R." A possible reading: "Whatever the accidents that disappointed *Samuel* in the pursuit of *preferment* [i.e., another parish with better economic prospects]. . . ."

27. Echoes here of Acts 17:26.

28. Perhaps she has in mind her difficulty in focusing away from worldly concerns, or perhaps she means her spiritual life in general.

29. Unworthy accommodation or submission.

30. Proverbs 10:9, slightly paraphrased. The original ends, "walketh surely." Quotation marks added.

31. Apparently a half-remembered combination of Job 11:17 and Matthew 13:43.

32. Viewed with wonder.

33. One and a half pages left blank.

34. This abbreviation, underlined in the MS, is difficult to interpret; perhaps "Noon Meditation-Reading"?

35. (?)Husband.

36. Cf. Acts 17:26.

37. Romans 8:28, paraphrased.

38. Cf. the Puritan preoccupation "to make one's call and election sure." See Gordon Wakefield, "The Puritans," in Cheslyn Jones et al., eds. *The Study of Spirituality* (New York and Oxford: Oxford University Press, 1986), pp. 437–445.

39. There are hints of John Wesley's "Covenant Service" here, particularly the phrase of the Covenant Prayer, in which the worshipper in a similar act of submission pledges to be "raised up for thee or laid aside for thee." See Frank Whaling, ed., *John and Charles Wesley* . . . (New York: Paulist Press, 1981), p. 140. Did John hear this phrase at his mother's knee? Was she drawing on the same Puritan sources, the work of Joseph and Richard Alleine, that he was later to discover and edit for his societies?

40. This sentence is getting the better of Susanna. Though she is still piling on conditional clauses and is not finished yet, I follow her own punctuation and add the period here.

41. 1 Samuel 15:22, paraphrased; my quotation marks.

42. My quotation marks.

43. Matthew 25:14–30.

44. Inherent.

45. A sentence fragment follows but was crossed out: "What this philosopher held concerning the world (though an error), yet. . . ." This issue was a common point of discussion in the late-seventeenth-century literature seeking to prove theism on a rational basis. Note the extended discussion of this same topic following "Emily's" fifth response in "A Religious Conference," chapter 27 in part III of this volume.

46. This phrase (from "though that") is crossed out, as are the following several unintelligible words, indicated here by ellipses; the final phrase stands without having been crossed out at the top of the next MS page.

47. I have not been able to trace this reference; the "R" probably stands for an author she was reading. The line following it may be read as a dash, a short blank, or possibly as an indication of a quotation.

48. Outwardly respectable.

49. 1 Samuel 15:22, paraphrased; my quotation marks.

50. Ecclesiastes 1:14; my quotation marks.

51. Question mark added here; no punctuation appears in the MS.

52. Cf. Matthew 12:45; Luke 11:26.

53. Mark 12:30, paraphrased.

54. Meditation breaks off; final one-third of MS page is blank.

"Keep a Due Guard over Your Words"

Subsequent entries in the Headingley MS A notebook continue in much the same vein. This second grouping, like the first, leans heavily toward internal spiritual debate. Vague but vociferous charges of irregularities (sensuality, 17; immoderate mirth and anger, 15; evil speaking, 20; inadvertence and temptations, 16) stand in tension with professions of sincerity, praise, thankfulness, and faith in a God who is both powerful and loving (e.g., in 35, 38, 42, and 43).

Woven into these devotional strivings are entries that offer several more specific insights into Susanna Wesley's life. One is her entry on drinking ale (29); another, her extended reflection on the catechism's requirements for Communion (35); and still another, an outline of what her ideal morning routine might look like (41). Her intent in all this is to take note of "common mercies" and to maintain a "constant sense of God upon the soul," nicely caught in a stanza from George Herbert in yet another meditation (40).

ॐ

[15. Speaking truth.]

R. upon Reflection of Errors in practice[1]

April 21, 1711

Endeavour to keep a due guard over your words, that you may habitually speak nothing but what is true on all occasions. Consider what a high offence it is against the God of truth to speak falsely, either through design or inadvertence. In telling any story or relating past actions be careful to speak deliberately and calmly, avoiding immoderate mirth or laughter on the one hand and uncharitableness and excessive anger on the other, lest your invention supply the defect of your memory, ever remembering you are in the presence of the great and holy God. Every sin is a contradiction and offence to some divine attribute. Lying is opposite and offensive to the truth of God.

[16. The danger of feeling "holier than thou" in contrast to neighbors and of forgetting God's grace.]

Even[ing]

Whenever you find any extraordinary assistance from the Spirit of God, either by illuminating the mind whereby you have a more clear perception of God or spiritual things or when he strengthens the soul or raises the affections, etc., then be sure for some time after to keep a stronger guard upon yourself lest by your unfaithfulness to that good Spirit you provoke him to withdraw his influences and so leave you in a state of uncomfortable darkness.

I am verily persuaded that the inequalities in a Christian's temper is [sic] chiefly owing to their own inadvertence. To a remissness after secret duties and a presumption on their own strength, which makes them careless of improving their graces and unmindful of those many temptations that they are hourly exposed to, which by reason of their smallness (never considering their number) we are apt to despise, when in truth those lesser but numerous temptations are the greatest trials of our virtue.

I have often observed that after the greatest enlargements[2] in prayer and the greatest professions of devotedness to God, we are permitted to fall into great temptations, which I humbly conceive to be commonly for one of these reasons: to try the sincerity of the mind, to show us whether or no we are in our outward conversation the same we profess to be in our retirements. Or else to humble the mind which upon such occasions is too apt to be elated, it being very natural upon reflection on any extraordinary performances to entertain too high a conceit of ourselves, especially if we live among people that are licentious in their lives and that observe no rule in their actions.[3] Then we are presently ready to say, "Stand by thyself, I am holier than thou."[4] So apt is vain, foolish man to turn the grace of God into wantonness and to forget that God that makes them to differ from the rest of the world. To whom be glory!

[17. Working with God's grace through a thrice daily examination of conscience, a performance of duty even in the absence of "full assurance."]

Morn[ing]

What an exceeding condescension is it for the Holy Spirit at any time to vouchsafe his assistance to such sinful worthless creatures as we are![5] And how careful ought we to be lest at any time we should grieve him and provoke him to depart from us. God hath said, "My Spirit shall not always strive with man,"[6] and how know we when we wilfully reject his motions and that by our strong adherence to sensuality, which he would persuade us to forsake, we shall not cause him to leave us, never to return more, the consequence of which can be nothing less than final apostasy.[7] By grace we stand, but if we despise or neglect this grace, what remains but a certain fearful looking-for of judgment and fiery indignation![8]

Be then extremely careful to purify your mind from all that may offend him.

Keep it calm and composed and, as much as possible, separate from the world. That still small voice is not heard amidst the thunder and noise of tumultuous passions.[9]

Keep the mind in a temper for recollection, and often in the day call it in from outward objects, lest it wander into forbidden paths. Make an examination of your conscience at least three times a day and omit no opportunity of retirement from the world.[10]

"My grace is sufficient for thee," was the most that an apostle could obtain upon very earnest prayer.[11] Not *shall be*, but *is*,[12] signifying that his utmost endeavours might be used for obtaining that grace. And if an apostle had not a full assurance given him that it should be actually sufficient for his support, what can such a one as thou art expect?

However, do thy duty, make use of all the means for obtaining that grace which God afford thee,[13] throw thyself upon the divine goodness for success, and firmly rely on the merits of Christ Jesus to supply the deficiencies of thy performances— and if I perish, I perish. . . .[14]

[18. Due regard for the "temper of the soul" in times of prayer and devotion.]

Even[ing]

Beware of immoderate mirth, anger, or any other passion, especially for some time before the family or private devotions. Take care to guard the mind against them. Take at least a quarter of an hour to recollect and compose the thoughts before your immediate approaches to the great God. If but an earthly prince or some person of eminent quality were certainly to visit you, or you were to visit him, would you not be careful to have your apparel and all about you decent before you were to come into their presence? How much more should you take care to have your mind in order, when you take upon yourself the honour to speak to the sovereign Lord of the universe? Upon the temper of the soul in your addresses to him depends your success in a very great measure. He is infinitely too great to be trifled with, too wise to be imposed on by a mock devotion, and he abhors a sacrifice without a heart. An habitual sense of his perfections is an admirable help against cold and formal performances, but the lamp of devotion is always burning. Yet a wise virgin will arise and trim it before they [sic] presume to go forth to meet the bridegroom.[15] Rash and precipitate prayers and abrupt breaking off from them to follow business or pleasure is such an affront to the holy God as he will not endure and will be sure to punish.

[19. Inadvertence to the self-evident principles of religion versus a "constant habitual sense of God."]

Noon

I am inclined to think that all people, even those who have not the light of the Gospel as well as Christians, do know more than they advert to or practice.[16] The common principles of morality are so self-evident, though perhaps not innate,[17] that 'tis hardly to be supposed any person in the world can be really ignorant of them, and the reason why the generality of mankind does so often act contrary to them is rather for want of advertence than for want of knowledge. What creature under heaven that has the use of reason can be ignorant of the being of God and that they ought to live in subjection to him from whom they receive their own being and all things necessary for the support of that being? And yet how few do in reality practice an unfeigned subjection of themselves towards him! And what can be the reason of this, but the want of consideration and advertence to these first principles of Religion.

Be careful to avoid this inadvertence and to maintain a constant habitual sense of God in your mind. Live and act as in his presence. Think often of his omnipresence and omniscience, of his power, wisdom, goodness, justice, truth, etc., and above all of his infinite purity, which will be a check upon the mind and be the best preservative against all temptations.

[20. Avoid speaking evil of the innocent, the dead, and the absent.]

Even[ing]

Innocence is sacred and ought to be reverenced by all, and therefore the honour of persons that are so happy as to preserve it ought always to be held inviolable.

Those that are dead have no longer a part in the land of the living—they are passed into the region of either pure or unhappy spirits and therefore we should not remember their vices, at least not speak of them to others, since they are no longer subject to any earthly power, and we know not what sentence is passed upon them at that tribunal before which we must all appear.

The absent hear not what we say, and, if we speak against them, whether true or false, not hearing, they are not capable of making us an answer. And it seems very unjust and uncharitable to bring an accusation against such as cannot plead in their own defence. And though they should afterwards hear of it and should justify themselves, yet 'tis odds but some that might hear of the crime may not hear the vindication, and so their reputation may be blasted, and their interest weakened past recovery.

This is like wounding a man in the dark, whereas a generous person should rather choose to confront his enemy and allow him fair play for his life. It always argues a base and cowardly temper to whisper secretly what we dare not speak to a man's face. Therefore, be careful to avoid all evil speaking and be ever sure to obey that command of our Saviour, in this case as well as others.[18] "Whatsoever you would that men should do unto you, do you even so unto them."[19] Therefore, be very cautious in speaking of these three sorts of persons, viz., the innocent, the dead, and the absent.

[21. Acquiesce to God's uniting of minds with bodies, but pray for strength to govern and regulate the affections.]

Noon

'Tis in vain to contend with divine Providence or to think of changing the course of nature. And since it hath pleased the infinitely wise God in this state of probation to unite our minds to these gross bodies, we must acquiesce in his appointment and not pretend to separate them wholly from all the inconveniences that are incident to this union. We cannot receive the knowledge of things without us but by our senses, and we cannot altogether prevent the strong impressions that sensual objects are wont to make upon the mind.[20] We must in this case endeavour what we can to maintain the superiority of mind over matter, lest it be corrupted by a too close adherence to sensible objects. We must preserve the government of reason and not suffer our passions to get the ascendant over us. "He that is washed," says our Saviour, "needs not save to wash his feet, and is clean every whit."[21] If our affections are but purified, the work is done. Sensual objects works [sic] immediately upon them, and by means of our passions they prevail over the soul and insensibly influence the last practical dictate of the understanding.

Therefore, be sure to be very hearty and earnest in praying to God for strength to govern and regulate your affections. "It is not in man that walketh to direct his steps."[22] Therefore, humbly implore the divine majesty to steer your soul by his Holy Spirit through all the intricate scenes of human life. Depend not on your own strength or reason, but rely only on his infinite wisdom, and he will guide you by his counsel and at last conduct you to his glory through Jesus Christ our Lord.

[22. Daily problems: opportunities to exercise virtue and receive the benefit of divine strength. Always beg God's direction and assistance.]

Even[ing]

There is hardly one day that does not verify the truth of our Saviour's words, St. Matthew,[23] "Sufficient to the day is the evil thereof." What through the weakness and corruption of our natures, the unavoidable business of our station, many unforeseen accidents, unexpected company, cross occurrences, with abundance of other [. . .],[24] incident to human life, we have occasion given us daily to exercise our virtues of one kind or other. Yesterday you had an extraordinary occasion to use your justice and patience, today your prudence, temperance and charity in forgiving injuries.[25] You did well in applying yourself to the supreme Fountain of virtue for grace in this perplexed affair, and you accordingly succeeded well and found that his "strength is made perfect in weakness"[26] and that he is Truth itself and "all his promises are yea and amen"[27] through Jesus the mediator. Did you ever once in your life in a full sense of your own impotence of mind with humility and sincerity implore the divine assistance without being heard in what you feared? Then may you "set to your seal that God is true,"[28] since you have always found him so. And as you have this day had a fresh instance of his hearing your prayers, so be very careful never to venture upon any business without first begging the direction and assistance of God, which will be a check upon your mind when you would do any thing you know to be unlawful or dubious and will encourage you with hopes of success in your lawful undertakings.

[23. Opportunities for both "retirement" and a particular piece of business; but submit to Providence if illness or family business does intervene.]

Morn[ing]

God gives you many opportunities of retirement for his service. Adore the divine goodness, therefore, and be careful not to neglect improving them. Endeavour somewhat in your business relating to ———. If you can possibly do somewhat in it every day, yet do not lay too much stress upon such performances as to be uneasy if you cannot. If bodily infirmities or extraordinary business in the family, etc., should prevent you, submit to the order of providence, for "obedience is better than sacrifice."[29]

[24. Religion defended against charges of melancholy: allowing for the inevitable imperfections of this life, the only truly happy people are good ones.]

Even[ing]

How unjustly does the profane part of the world charge religion with melancholy and moroseness, as if it tended only to destroy the comforts of our enjoyments and rendered the professors of it fit only to converse with themselves. Whereas, on the contrary, all things in the world where that is wanting cannot possibly make us happy or easy to ourselves or others. Whatever we enjoy of the good things of this life are attended with so much "vanity and vexation of spirit"[30] that any considering person may easily perceive that our happiness even in this world does entirely depend on the favour of God, which we cannot hope to enjoy without the constant practice of piety and virtue.

I will not say but it may sometimes happen that religious persons may now and then be peevish and morose, but I dare say 'tis not religion, but their want of it that makes them so. The best men in the world are here in a state of imperfection, and corrupt nature will not be wholly conquered in this state of mortality.[31] There will be deficiencies in their virtues and oftentimes great imperfections mixed with them.[32] Yet, notwithstanding all the inconveniences or faults which attend good men, they are the only persons that can in any tolerable sense be called happy and well-tempered.

Be not you discouraged with your own failings, nor do not [sic] spend so much time in thinking on them. Consider that perfection is thy Saviour's endowment, sincerity is thine. His merits (if relied on by a firm faith joined with your sincere endeavour to obey the whole will of God) will supply thy deficiencies. That incense which is offered up by the angel of the covenant with the prayers of saints[33] will prevail for the acceptance of thine, if they have but that one ingredient of sincerity, though they too often have a sad mixture of vanity and inadvertence.[34] Therefore, go on, confess, and bewail;[35] who can tell how soon God may be merciful to thee and give thee grace to amend? Amen! Amen!

[25. Patience and submission in bodily infirmities; puzzlement at an acquaintance's lack of faith under her afflictions.]

Even[ing]

Often interrupted by bodily infirmities, indeed. Yet such is the will of God; therefore, in this case your duty is patience and submission. Still remember, "obedience is better than sacrifice."[36]

I cannot conceive how any person that truly fears God can speak such words as M. H.[37] is said to speak, now she is under such afflictions. Those of ——— are great trials, indeed, but still one would think that nothing a person can suffer in the world could be sufficient to provoke them [sic] to say, "I don't know whether there is a God, but if there is, I have but little to thank him for, for he sends me nothing but plagues." [38] Good God! That any person out of hell and that has received being and preservation, food, raiment, etc. from thee near sixty year should think or say that they have nothing to praise thee for! But what is still infinitely more than all we can receive of temporal blessings, thou has sent thy only Son into the world to save sinners, and though thou should deal never so severely with us in relation to the world, that one infinite, inestimable mercy is sufficient to excite us to praise and adore thee to all eternity! [39] How different is this from the temper of J. H. who says, when in contemplation of the love of God in giving us a Saviour, "I can live on and rejoice in the faith of Jesus Christ though I were ready to starve." [40]

Her condition is indeed very pitiable, but the temper of her mind under her affliction is much more deplorable than her circumstances. Remember, therefore, always to pray for her particularly. Who can tell whether God will be merciful to that wretched soul or not?

[26. Practice your own written rules; perform your thrice daily examination better; do good, on pain of damnation, especially to souls committed to your care.]

Morn[ing]

"A little leaven leaveneth the whole lump." [41] A little irregularity in any passion puts the whole mind into disorder. And those persons that are uneasy to themselves can never be easy to those about them. Why do you not take more care to practice your own rules? What reason or for what end do you write them down, if not that you may remember to practice them in your conversation in the world? If it be necessary to keep the affections under due government and to be careful not to offend in speaking of people that are absent, and you are convinced that it is your duty so to do, [42] be more careful for the future not to be guilty in this matter, lest by sinning against the checks of conscience, you provoke the Holy Spirit to forsake you.

Perform your daily examin[ation] three times a day more accurately; let no trifling matter divert you. It requires not much time. Opportunities once lost can never be recovered.

"Whatever your hand findeth to do, do it with all your might," saith Solomon. [43] Doing nothing or nothing to the purpose is in effect the same. This trifling temper in matters of eternal moment is above all things to be avoided. When you have an opportunity, therefore, thankfully and vigorously make use of it. And remember that for all these things God will bring you to judgment. Sins of omission are most dangerous, and our Saviour's charge at the last day will be chiefly made up of such. He when on earth "went about doing good." [44] And you must also do what good you can, especially to the souls God hath committed to your care. If any one soul among your children or servants should perish for want of your example or instruction, your own would be in danger of eternal damnation. Let the thoughts of this be a spur to your undertaking in ———, [45] and do not be discouraged by infirmities or labour. . . . [46]

[27. Thanks to God for peaceful conscience and no violent passions.]

Noon

There is no joy like peace of conscience, nor any pleasure comparable to the satisfaction of the soul when it feels itself strengthened by the grace of God to perform the several duties of one's station.

It would be well if in extraordinary occurrences we could keep the mind from being too warm and speaking too eagerly; yet however, praise God for preventing your falling into violent passion and for any power of recollection. Trust him with all events and beg his blessing on your honest endeavours. May he guard your mind in the afternoon and inspire you with devotion in singing his praise.

[28. Desire for closer union with God; glory to God despite apprehensions of divine displeasure.]

Even[ing] [47]

Give God the praise for any well-spent day—But you are yet unsatisfied because you do not enjoy enough of God, you apprehend yourself at too great a distance from him, you would have your soul united more closely to him by faith and love—You cannot say with the Apostle, "Lord, thou that knowest all things, knowest that I love thee." [48] But you can appeal to his omniscience, that he knows you would love him above all things. He that made you knows your desires, your expectations, your joys all centre in him and that 'tis he himself you desire, his favour, his acceptance, the communications of his grace that you earnestly wish for, more than anything in the world, and that you have no relish nor delight in anything when under apprehensions of his displeasure. You rejoice in his essential glory and blessedness, you rejoice in your relation to him, that he is your Father, you Lord, Your God. . . . [49]

You rejoice that he has power over you and desire to live in subjection to him, and yet he condescends to punish you when you transgress his laws, as a father chastiseth the son whom he loveth [50]—Thank him that has brought you so far, and beware of despairing of mercy, but give God the glory of his free grace.

[29. Strong drink, a vow, and a "nice constitution."]

Morn[ing] [51]

I do not approve of your drinking twice of ale in so short a time. Not that I think it unlawful for another to do so, or that it is a direct breach of your vow, but it is injurious to your health and so does not fall under your own rule, viz., never to drink anything strong but merely for refreshment. You have great reason to adore the great and good God! that hath given you so nice [52] a constitution as will not bear the least degree of intemperance. He might have made you strong to endure the excesses others run into, and so you might often have been exposed to temptations to offend, whereas now you are doubly guarded both by his wise and holy laws and an infirm body. Glory be to thee, O Lord!

[30. A sincere heart can make up for inattentive worship—and various other impediments.]

Noon

"The spirit indeed is willing but the flesh is weak"[53] was the kind excuse that a merciful Saviour pleaded in behalf of his disciples when through infirmity they could not watch one hour with Jesus. And it is said by an apostle that . . .[54]

Therefore, though by reason of infirmities you can rarely exert the powers of the soul and vigorously attend on God's service, yet if the heart be sincere, you may hope for acceptance. A little time, a great deal of weakness, and much business are impediments that much of love will overcome. Purify the mind, then, from all worldly regards, cease from desiring any applause "from man whose breath is in his nostrils, for wherein is he to be accounted of?"[55] And apply yourself vigorously to ———[56]

[31. God is powerful—but willing? Grace is worth waiting for.]

Even[ing]

"God spake once, and twice have I heard the same, that power belongeth unto God," saith David.[57]

The mind of man is naturally so corrupted, and all the powers thereof so weakened by the first man's transgression, that we cannot possibly aspire vigorously towards God or have any clear perception of spiritual things without his assistance.

Nothing less than the same almighty power that raised Jesus Christ from the dead can raise our souls from the death of sin to a life of holiness.

You do not question his power, but you apprehend[58] his will, and indeed that is an obstacle (if it be against you) that cannot be removed. But how do you know that he is unwilling? Whence proceeds these desires if not from him? Perhaps he still defers his assistance to make further trial of your faith and patience. His grace is worth waiting for; therefore, be not discouraged, but remember the words of our Saviour, "that men ought always to pray and not to faint."[59]

[32. A brief essay on government: the human right to govern oneself (albeit in the context of civil and ecclesiastical hierarchy).]

Morn[ing]

Piety, power, prudence and courage seem to be of the essence of government.[60] Piety secures the end, prudence directs to the choice of means, power is requisite to the act and is the nerves and sinews thereof, and courage is needful for the exerting power and encountering the difficulties and obstacles we may meet with.

Piety is the most solid basis of government and doth most effectually secure the end of it, viz., the glory of God and the good of mankind.

Though these qualifications are requisite in the constitution of civil powers, yet, it not being my present design to speak of them, I proceed to say something briefly of that government which every person in the world hath a right to, viz., the government of himself.

The right that a man hath to govern himself is unquestionable, and though almighty God, the supreme Lord and Governor of the universe hath distinguished his creatures into various ranks and orders and amongst men hath established governments ecclesiastical and civil which include[61] all men in one case or other, in one respect or other to be in a state of subjection, yet, as he hath not by any law of his own, so neither has any human law a right to invade or deprive a man of that power which God has given him to govern himself. As he received this right from the author of his being, so in his using it according to the will of his creator consists his glory, perfection and happiness.

[33. Further musings on self-government.]

Even[ing]

By "himself" I mean his better part, his mind or soul, taking the word "mind" in the largest sense,[62] comprehending all his spiritual powers, understanding, will, passions, or affections. Nor do I[63] confine here the term "understanding"[64] only to the simple power or, to speak more properly, act of perception, though the first in order, but include judgment and reason within the verge of that power.[65]

[34. Reason's government of the passions by God's (and Nature's) laws.]

Noon

Whether what we call the several faculties or powers of the mind are really distinct in their own nature or only distinguished by us because of their various operations, concerns us not to inquire at this time;[66] 'tis sufficient that what we call understanding, judgment, and reason ought to have the government of the passions or affections, and this is the province wherein every man ought to rule, this the kingdom wherein a man ought absolutely to govern, and the laws by which he ought to govern are those of God and, what is in effect the same, the laws of pure uncorrupted nature.[67]

[35. The catechism's requirements for communion prompt an extended believing-doubting reflection on repentence, confession, assurance, and prevenient grace.]

Morn[ing]

The Church replies to that question, "What is required of those that come to the Lord's Supper?": "To examine themselves whether they repent them truly of their former sins, stedfastly purposing to lead a new life, have a lively faith in God's mercy through Christ, with a thankful remembrance of his death, and be in charity with all men."[68]

"Whether they repent them truly of their former sins . . ." This you have done, but you still fear that your repentance is partial and that you have not remembered the thousandth part of your transgressions; and indeed who can tell how oft he offendeth![69] But you have taken the commands of God for your rule and have confessed the several kinds of your sins, though not every particular act of each kind. And this you have done, not that you think repentance or confession hath any proper merit in themselves, but you perform as a condition to which the promise of pardon and grace is annexed, and you rely only on the merits of Christ for pardon and acceptance and do humbly hope that the redundance of his merits will supply the deficiencies of your repentance.[70]

You renounce your own righteousness, your own performances in point of merit and rely only on "Jesus the mediator of the new covenant."[71]

You are at a stand about the second general head: "purposing to lead a new life." What is the import of this purposing? If it be you desire to lead a new life, this you fully assent to; 'tis the grief and exceeding trouble of your soul that you have not, nor cannot (as you apprehend) serve God any better. But if it implies a resolution of a more exact obedience, you cannot resolve because, discouraged by the experience of daily renewed failings, you say, "Oh, that it might be so, that you might be entirely devoted to God."[72] But "who is sufficient for these things?"[73] "Better not to vow than not to perform."[74] You cannot, dare not, undertake for your bad self, but you humbly throw yourself upon the mercy of God and beg that his grace may be actually sufficient for you.[75]

"Have a lively faith in God's mercy through Christ." You seem to stagger at the promise of God through unbelief—what is it that you stick at? You do believe that God hath a desire to the work of his omnipotence and that from eternity as he foresaw the fall of man, so he provided a remedy that his creatures, whom he purposed to create in his own image, should not perish.

Consider the infinite boundless goodness of the ever blessed Trinity, adore the stupendous mystery of divine love! That God the Father, Son and Holy Ghost should all concur in the work of man's redemption! What but pure goodness could move or excite God, who is perfect essential blessedness! That cannot possibly receive any accession of perfection or happiness from his creatures. What, I say, but love, but goodness, but infinite incomprehensible love and goodness could move him to provide such a remedy for the fatal lapse of his sinful unworthy creatures? If he had been willing you should perish, he might ha' let you ha' perished without the expense of so many miracles to save you. Why did he give you birth in a Christian country of religious parents by whom you were early instructed in the principles of religion? Why hath he waited so long to be gracious? Why hath his providence so often prevented[76] you? And why hath the same good providence so often reclaimed you by punishments and mercies? Why hath his Spirit so long striven with you, cooperating with the means of grace, illuminating your mind, purifying your affections, in some measure awakening your conscience, not suffering you to enjoy any rest or quiet in a course of sin? And though sometimes you have been impatient under the checks of conscience in lesser miscarriages, yet he hath not given you over till he hath brought you to repentance. You may remember the time when you were strongly inclined to ———,[77] and you cannot forget your state of temptation that you were in two whole years, and what a doubtful conflict you then sustained—but yet the good Spirit of God never totally left you, but the better principle at last prevailed to the eternal glory of free grace. And may you not argue as Ma-noah's wife, "If the Lord were pleased to destroy me, were willing that I should perish, would he have at all regarded my prayers, would he have enabled me through the assistance of his Holy Spirit to conquer this temptation and to break such an inveterate habit of evil thinking?"[78]

'Tis the frequent relapses into the power of the world, etc., that is certainly the occasion of these strange perplexities and so often shocks your faith and trust in God's mercies through Christ. "If any man sin, we have an advocate with the Father, Jesus Christ . . . and he is the propitiation for our sins."[79] "If any man sin . . ."[80] The apostle here does not say such a one should be discouraged or despair of mercy, but directs to look up to Jesus Christ and tells us in such a case that we should remember "he is the propitiation for our sins." That he is "an advocate with the father," pleading his own meritorious sufferings on the behalf of sinners. "If this thy creature hath wronged thee or oweth thee ought, place that to my account."[81]

[36. Reflection on a mind-body problem: intense preparation for the sacrament can lead to temporary spiritual indisposition.]

Noon[82]

You have of late often experienced that the more accurate you have been in the work of preparation for the sacrament, the more indisposed you have been to spiritual things (especially for meditation and reflection) for sometimes one, sometimes two or three days after. And this hath been a great discouragement to you, and you have thought that your soul has received no benefit from that sacred ordinance.

Now the reason of it I apprehend to be this—long intense thinking, keeping the mind for a considerable time to hard exercise, does necessarily impair the bodily strength where persons are of a weak constitution, and then the mind, being under the influences of the body in this imperfect state, it cannot exert itself till that hath again recovered its vigour, which requires some time, and you may observe that as the body is refreshed the soul is strengthened. Therefore, be not discouraged, but endeavour to keep your mind as composed as possible, and pray to God to preserve you from temptation during this bodily indisposition and that, "as your day is, so your strength may be."[83] Amen, Lord Jesus![84]

[37. The sinful self humbled before the great and holy God.]

Morn[ing]

You above all others have most need of humbling yourself before the great and holy God for the very great and very many sins you daily are guilty of in "thought, word, and deed, against his divine majesty"![85] What a habitual levity is there in your thoughts, how broken and inconsistent are they, how many vain impure thoughts pass through the mind in one hour, and though they do not take up their abode for any long continuance, yet their passing through often leaves a tincture of impurity. How many worldly regards, even in sacred actions, what habitual inadvertence,[86] seldom any seriousness or composure of spirit, the passions rude and tumultuous, very susceptible of violent impressions from light and inconsiderable accidents, unworthy a reasonable being, but more unworthy a Christian. "Keep thy heart with all diligence (thy thoughts, thy affections), for out of them are the issues of life."[87]

Who can tell how oft he offendeth in this kind. "O cleanse thou me from my secret faults."[88]

"Out of the abundance of the heart the mouth speaketh."[89] How many vain unnecessary words are you guilty of daily, how many opportunities of speaking for the good of the souls committed to your care are neglected, how seldom do you speak of God with that reverence, that humility, that gravity, that you ought?[90] Your words as well as your thoughts are deficient—you do not conceive or speak of God aright. You do not speak magnificently nor worthily of him who is "the high and lofty one that inhabiteth eternity"![91] The creator of the universe, an immense infinitely perfect mind. Holiness is his essence. 'Tis the eternal infinite rectitude of his nature,[92] causing him to act always suitably to the transcendent excellence and dignity of his own perfections! He is absolutely separated from all moral imperfection. There is no contrariety or contradiction in him, "no variableness, neither shadow of turning!"[93] He is Power! Wisdom! Justice! Goodness! Truth! He is perfection of being which comprehends all and infinitely more than we can possibly conceive!

He is essential glory, nor can his glory admit of access or diminution by any act of his creatures. 'Tis an impropriety of speech to say we glorify his name, for 'tis the exercise of his mercy, goodness, etc., upon man that reflects this glory on those perfections.

[38. Consideration of hell and redemption: abundant reason for praising God.]

Morn[ing]

If a little pain or an uneasy bed be so tiresome for one night, what will you do if God in his infinite wisdom should think fit to afflict you with a long or very painful sickness before he takes you out of the world? Or what will a painful lingering disease be to a state of everlasting torments? Let the torments we suffer in this life be never so severe, yet death will sooner or later infallibly put an end to them, but from hell there is no deliverance, no flying from the power and justice of the Almighty, no alleviation of torment for one single moment, no refreshment, no diversion, nothing but solid substantial misery to all eternity!

O what abundant reason have you to adore, to praise, to magnify the goodness and love of God for sending his Son into the world to die for sinners! What reason have you to praise and adore and love your Saviour that suffered so much to redeem you from that place of torment! What sentiments of gratitude should [you] conceive for such boundless charity to souls! And how gladly and cheerfully should you take up your cross for him that suffered death upon the cross for thee? How ought you to praise and adore the blessed Spirit that sanctifies and illuminates the mind, that cooperates with the means of grace! That condescends to visit and assist and refresh your soul by his powerful influences! Glory be to the Father! Son! and Holy Ghost! Joint authors of man's salvation!

[39. The difficulty of an even temper in devotion.]

Noon

"The heart is deceitful above all things and desperately wicked; who can know it?"[94] How difficult a thing is it to maintain an even temper, one minute praising God, the next averse from that most blessed employment, stupid, dull, and heavy, immersed in matter. Lord, pity and forgive.

[40. Be thankful for common mercies; aim for a "constant sense of God upon the soul."]

Even[ing]

How uneasy is the mind when either company, business or anything else diverts it from its usual course. What reason you have to praise God for suffering you to meet with no more interruptions. Not thankful enough for daily opportunities, common mercies are often unregarded, but this is a great fault, for the more common the mercy, the more valuable. Surely repeated acts of goodness require repeated acknowledgments and praise. When you have been for some time interrupted in your great work, and the thoughts of God have been diverted, how pleasing is it to the mind to feel the motions of his Spirit quickening you and exciting you to return, but how much more delightful is it to find a constant sense of God upon the soul, as Mr. Herbert excellently expresseth it,

> Not thankful, when it pleaseth me;
> As if thy blessings had spare days:
> But such a heart, whose pulse may be
>   Thy praise![95]

This, this is the temper of a good Christian, this is what you should chiefly endeavour to get and keep. Do not despair: "With God all things are possible."[96] To whom be glory!

[41. Clues to her morning routine: a "due method" and even temper help redeem the time.]

Morn[ing]

'Tis only want of temper and recollection that disorders your affairs. If you go not into the family till 8:00, then you have till 9:00 to give orders and oversee, which time is sufficient to manage much business of that kind, if a due method be observed. Beware of vain mirth, immoderate anger, any diversion till family duties are performed, however, and walk not into the air till after ———,[97] for you find that it discomposes your head, and, if possible, redeem some time for preparation for family prayer. . . .[98]

[42. "Mean and contemptible" performances, yet grace and mercy continue.]

Even[ing]

Praise God for any ability to serve him and for enabling you to perform relative duties which are a great part of natural and revealed religion. The constant sense of your infirmities I know discourages you. But God will not "despise the day of small things." [99] 'Tis his grace that makes you what you are, that keeps you to stated times of devotion, and that in any measure preserves you from total apostasy. I grant your performances are mean and contemptible and unworthy the acceptance of God. Yet still, if he utterly rejected them, he would not so often give you grace to repent and mourn over them and enable [you] to rejoice in any little victory you get over your daily infirmities. I know you would not willingly offend; therefore rely upon the merits of your Saviour and never despair of mercy.

[43. The affections (and faith) must keep pace with knowledge: "You must know, that you may adore and love."]

Morn[ing]

Praise God for illuminating your mind and for enabling you to prove demonstratively that his wisdom is as infinite as his power.

The use you are to make of these discoveries is to praise and love and obey; therefore be exceeding careful that your affections keep pace with your knowledge, for if you study the divine perfections as matter of mere speculation, your acquests [100] of knowledge will but enhance your guilt and increase your future torment. You must know, that you may adore and love! And if you are now more rationally persuaded that God is infinitely wise, then learn by this knowledge to practice a more hearty and universal subjection to him, more cheerfully submit to the order of his providence. Submit your reason so far to your faith as not to doubt or scruple those points of faith which are mysterious to us through the weakness of our understanding, and adore the mystery you cannot comprehend. Be not too curious in prying into those secret things that are known only to God, nor too rash in censuring what you do not understand. Those methods of providence that seem to you involved and intricate perplex not yourself about, but resolve them into the infinite wisdom of God, who knoweth "the spirits of all flesh" [101] and best understandeth how to govern those souls he hath created. "We are of yesterday and know nothing," [102] but his boundless mind comprehends at one view all things, past, present and future, and as he sees all things, so he best understandeth what is good and proper for each individual with relation to both worlds. [103]

Notes

1. The allusion here is probably to an author. Though I have not been able to ferret out the reference, one possibility would be the Cambridge Platonist and bishop of Dromore, George Rust, to whom she refers elsewhere. See journal entry 155 and the "Religious Conference," in part III of this volume.

2. Absence of constraint; conscious liberty.

3. She has in mind the sometimes rough country folk, the nonmethodical people living in and around Epworth.

4. My quotation marks; direct quotation of parts of Isaiah 65:5.

5. The exclamation point seems to be inserted in the middle of the sentence after the original draft.

6. Genesis 6:3; quotation marks added.

7. She may be offering her own definition of the variously interpreted, unforgivable "sin against the Holy Ghost" (Matthew 12:31, Mark 3:29, and Luke 12:10).

8. She is outlining a doctrine of synergism, the divine-human cooperation necessary for salvation.

9. Cf. 1 Kings 19:12.

10. S. W. is reinforcing the importance of her own routine of meditation and journal keeping.

11. 2 Corinthians 12:9; my quotation marks.

12. In her notebook S. W. spaced these words out for emphasis; my italics.

13. Her son John was later to emphasize the "means of grace" in early Methodism, similarly interpreting them as extending beyond the church's sacraments.

14. My ellipses replace S. W.'s dash at the end of the entry.

15. S. W. started with a singular subject but switched the reference in the second clause to the more familiar plural of the account in Matthew 25:1–13.

16. There is a hint here of Platonic epistemology. In our own century the scientist-philosopher Michael Polanyi has argued a theory of "tacit knowledge": we know more than we can say.

17. Her Platonism is tempered by her reading of Locke, who contended that there are no innate ideas, only those developed by sensation and reflection.

18. Cf. Matthew 12:34–37.

19. Close paraphrase of Matthew 7:12; my quotation marks.

20. Another reference to Lockean epistemology.

21. John 13:10; direct quote except "needeth" in AV; my quotation marks.

22. Jeremiah 10:23; my quotation marks.

23. Matthew 6:34; S. W. left space for the chapter and verse citation but did not fill it in. I have added quotation marks.

24. Space left blank.

25. Compare the "cardinal virtues" (prudence, temperence, fortitude, and justice) taken over from Greek philosophy by the church fathers and often combined with St. Paul's "theological virtues" (faith, hope, and charity) in subsequent Christian moralizing.

26. 2 Corinthians 12:9; quotation marks added.

27. 2 Corinthians 1:20, paraphrased; my quotation marks.

28. That is, vouch for the conviction that God is true. John 3:33, paraphrased; my quotation marks.

29. 1 Samuel 15:22, paraphrased; my quotation marks.

30. Ecclesiastes 1:14; my quotation marks.

31. Cf. her son John's later doctrine of "Christian Perfection." This sentence, embarrassing to mid-nineteenth-century Methodist editors (who would have assumed that the "best men" could indeed through grace be made perfect in this life), was omitted from The *Wesley Banner* (1852), p. 366.

32. After "imperfections," S. W. originally wrote, then crossed out, "in their graces" before completing the sentence as it stands.

33. Cf. Revelation 8:3.

34. Last phrase omitted in *Wesley Banner*, p. 366.

35. Cf. BCP, General Confession.

36. 1 Samuel 15:22, paraphrased; my quotation marks. Note previous uses of this phrase above, entries 11 and 23.

37. These initials and the blank in the next sentence indicate Susanna's usual reluctance to name persons in her journal, especially those, like her current subject, whom she describes in less than glowing terms. See her motto, above: "be very cautious in speaking of . . . the innocent, the dead, and the absent."

38. My quotation marks in place of dashes in MS.

39. Cf. BCP, Morning Prayer, General Thanksgiving.

40. Possibly John Hacket (1592–1670), bishop of Lichfield and Coventry, reputed author of *Christian Consolations* (1671), a work later attributed to Jeremy Taylor.

41. 1 Corinthians 5:6; my quotation marks.

42. See her entry 20 on this subject.

43. Ecclesiastes 9:10, paraphrased; my quotation marks.

44. Acts 10:38; my quotation marks.

45. The context suggests that the blank might stand for the theological treatises she was composing for her adolescent children or for her overall educational scheme.

46. I have substituted ellipses for the dash with which Susanna punctuates this final sentence.

47. This meditation, which paradoxically echoes both mysticism and Calvinism, appears to have offended the editors of the *Wesley Banner*, who completely omitted it. See ibid., p. 404.

48. Close paraphrase of John 21:17; my quotation marks.

49. My punctuation; MS has a dash.

50. A loose paraphrase of Hebrews 12:6–7 and/or Deuteronomy 8:5, substituting "chastiseth" for the biblical "chasteneth."

51. *Wesley Banner*, p. 404, rejoins the MS here.

52. Fastidious, dainty.

53. Matthew 26:41; my quotation marks.

54. Line skipped. S. W. evidently intended to insert a proof text after finishing her train of thought but never did. Ellipses added.

55. Isaiah 2:22; my quotation marks.

56. Meditation ends. Once again Susanna has failed to spell out what is obviously an important personal project.

57. Psalm 62:11, BCP; my quotation marks.

58. Are anxious, apprehensive about; dread.

59. Luke 18:1; my quotation marks.

60. Possibly a reference to a contemporary political theorist. I have not been able to trace a source.

61. Word unclear in MS; the *Wesley Banner* reads "impel."

62. My quotation marks.

63. MS: "Nor I do not."

64. My quotation marks.

65. As the meditation moves from civil and ecclesiastical government to the governing of oneself, S. W. may be echoing Locke, *An Essay concerning Human Understanding*, ed. Peter H. Nidditch (Oxford: Clarendon Press, 1975), 2.11.1–2 (pp. 155–157), 2.21.5–6 (pp. 236–237).

66. Locke, 2.21.6 (pp. 236–237), wants to discriminate in this matter.

67. Four lines to the bottom of the page are left blank.

68. BCP, catechism, final question and answer; question mark, colon, and quotation marks not in MS. Quotation marks have also been added when S.W. repeats phrases of this passage below.

69. Such scrupulosity was not uncommon among pious people; a good example nearly two centuries before was Luther's anxiety over complete repentance before his "discovery" of grace.

70. Last clause, "and do humbly hope," missing from *Wesley Banner*, p. 405. The editor may have felt that this did not reflect well on Wesley's mother or, more likely, that it did not sound sufficiently perfectionist.

71. Hebrews 12:24; Quotation marks added.

72. My quotation marks.

73. 2 Corinthians 2:16; my quotation marks.

74. Ecclesiastes 5:5, paraphrased; my quotation marks.

75. See 2 Corinthians 12:9.

76. That is, gone before.

77. Probably some former sin, now overcome, yet still not entrusted to paper.

78. An expansion of the idea in Judges 13:23: "If the Lord were pleased to kill us, he would not have received a burnt offering . . . at our hands." Quotation marks and question mark added.

79. 1 John 2:1–2 and BCP, The Communion, the "comfortable words"; quotation marks and ellipses added here and in the phrases from the same passage quoted again below.

80. Quotation marks and ellipses added.

81. S. W. paraphrases Philemon 18 and puts the Apostle's words in Jesus' mouth; my quotation marks.

82. This entry begins a quarter of the way down the page, which has been uncharacteristically left blank to that point.

83. Deuteronomy 33:25, paraphrased; my quotation marks.

84. *Wesley Banner* transcription inserts here a brief meditation from MS p. 190, out of order.

85. BCP, Communion, General Confession; my quotation marks.

86. Inadvertence is a continuing theme. See, for example, entries 15, 16, 19, 24, and 38.

87. Close paraphrase of Proverbs 4:23, adding the parenthetical explanatory words and substituting "them" for "it"; my quotation marks.

88. Psalm 19:12, BCP; my quotation marks.

89. Matthew 12:34; cf. Luke 6:45; my quotation marks.

90. Question mark added.

91. Isaiah 57:15; my quotation marks.

92. I have substituted a comma for the mid-sentence exclamation point that appears here in the MS.

93. James 1:17; my quotation marks; S. W.'s exclamation point.

94. Jeremiah 17:9; quotation marks added.

95. "Gratefulness," lines 29–32 (the concluding stanza), from *The Temple*, in F. E. Hutchinson, ed., *The Works of George Herbert* (Oxford: Clarendon Press, 1941), p. 124; original punctuation, from *The Temple. Sacred Poems . . .* 12th ed. (London: Jeffery Wale), 1703, p. 117, inserted (though the exclamation at the end is S. W.'s).

96. Matthew 19:26 and parallels; my quotation marks.

97. Possibly indicates her morning devotional time.

98. My ellipses replace MS's dash.

99. Zechariah 4:10, paraphrased; my quotation marks.

100. Acquisitions.

101. Numbers 16:22 and 27:16; quotation marks added.

102. Close paraphrase of Job 8:9; my quotation marks.

103. *Wesley Banner* concludes its transcription of MS A here.

SEVENTEEN

"You Write What Is Familiar
to You by Practice"

At the center of this chapter is Susanna Wesley's longish reflection (56) on the writing she had planned as part of her children's education. Here she lays out both the discouraging factors weighing against the project and the more compelling reasons why she must carry on with it. By the meditation's end, her sense of duty and her faith, "familiar to [her] by practice," have convinced her of the plan's importance.

Another entry (47, dated 17 May 1711) serves as a concrete example of her teacher's calling and has provided grist for the mythologizing of John Wesley's early life. Her intention to "be more particularly careful of the soul of this child" may or may not set apart "S[on]. J[ohn]." for special care; it certainly illustrates the devotional seriousness with which she undertook child rearing as a path of service, a vocational identity.

In addition to others in this same vein (51, 52, and 55), there are in this chapter noteworthy examples of her response to contemporary thought. She addresses Locke's *An Essay concerning Human Understanding* explicitly for its theological utility (49); and Locke, together with unnamed Platonists, has her struggling with "constant perverseness in the affections" (in 67–74, among other places). In the process one may also see interesting anticipations of her son John's later approaches: a disagreement with quietist doctrine (64) that he might well own and a somewhat less "Wesleyan" version of sanctification (68).

Two further phrases deserve highlighting. The first (45) might be the basis for a theological epistemology (or at least a spirituality of knowledge): "we must know, that we may love." The second (51) reminds us of how her own spirituality, while it often humbled, also built up: "Preserve the dignity of your nature. Reverence yourself, and do nothing unworthy the reason God has given you."

[44. Fallen sense, perception, and reason useless unless restored by grace.]

Noon

You can no more do anything in your own strength than you can remove mountains or shape the solid foundations of the earth. 'Tis true God did at first bestow on reasonable beings sense, perception, and reason, but sin hath so weakened these powers that, unless divine grace restore them and renew the mind, they are in a manner perfectly useless, or at least will not serve to the end for which they were given.[1]

[45. Knowledge as speculation, knowledge as wisdom: an ethics of knowing.]

Even[ing]

To pursue after knowledge only for its own sake, is a vain and unprofitable curiosity. To labour for it only to furnish matter of discourse that you may be applauded by others is still worse and argues a vain-glorious, weak, and childish temper. Such knowledge puffeth up and is directly opposite to divine charity (the love of God) which alone edifieth,[2] buildeth up, or establisheth the soul in all Christian virtues. 'Tis the end sanctifieth and crowns the work. We must know, that we may love; we must love, that we may cheerfully obey; and we must obey, that we may please God.

Knowledge[3] that goes no further than speculation is like an excellent instrument in the hand of an unskillful person that knows not how to make use of it. Knowledge is indeed an admirable thing, as it is the foundation or basis of wisdom, and the understanding of general rules is much to be desired, but 'tis wisdom that from thence draws conclusions in order to practice them in particular cases. This wisdom you must earnestly pray for, and this is the [?]good[4] use you must make of your knowledge, viz:[5]

[46. Speaking ill of superiors in the presence of inferiors as complicity in the sin of rebellion.]

Noon

Be very cautious in speaking of a parent before a child, of a husband before a wife, and of a master before a servant. Ever since the first man's rebellion against his Maker, man hath been naturally impatient of having any superior, and we have all the same principles and seed of rebellion that Adam had and are apt to think ourselves much fitter to command than to obey. And if we speak ill of any of these superior relations in the presence of those inferior and thereby they should be encouraged to despise their authority, contemn[6] their persons, or neglect their relative duties, we are in a very great measure guilty of the sin they commit in so doing, and if we share in the guilt, 'tis but just we should partake of the punishment.

[47. Intends particular care for "the soul of this child."]

Even[ing] May 17, 1711 S. J.[7]

What shall I render to the Lord for all his mercies? The little unworthy praise that I can offer is so mean and contemptible an offering that I am even ashamed to tender it. But Lord accept it for the sake of Christ and pardon the deficiencies of the sacrifice.

I would (if I durst) humbly offer thee myself and all that thou hast given me, and I would resolve (Oh, give me grace to do it) that the residue of my life shall be all devoted to thy service. And I do intend to be more particularly careful of the soul of this child that thou has so mercifully provided for than ever I have been, that I may do my endeavour to instill into his mind the principles of thy true religion and virtue. Lord, give me grace to do it sincerely and prudently, and bless my attempts with good success.

[48. Prays a Pentecostal blessing so she may believe, obey, and partake of heavenly gifts.]

Morn[ing]

The first thing you have to do this morning is with great humility to implore the divine Majesty that, since he was pleased as at this time to send his Holy Spirit in an extraordinary manner upon the apostles to enable them to propagate the Christian faith, to preach the gospel of Jesus Christ, those glad tidings of salvation, to the sons of men, so he would vouchsafe for the sake of this same Jesus whom they preached, to grant you his Holy Spirit in such a measure as is necessary for your believing and obeying that blessed gospel, that you may be a partaker of those heavenly gifts which, through Christ, are bestowed on true believers.

[49. The usefulness of Locke's theory of knowledge: if we know how ideas enter the mind, we can better guard against sinful ones.]

Noon

"The Original, Certainty, and Extent of Human Knowledge, together with the Grounds and Degrees of Belief, Opinion, and Assent"[8]—*en fin*, L[ocke] of Human U[nderstanding]. Of what use? Of what use is it for persons besieged to know which way and by what method the enemy will approach? If they are certainly informed of the way and means in this case, they may particularly guard and defend that pass.

So if we know by what way we receive our ideas,[9] though it may not always be in our power to prevent their entrance, especially in the case of simple ideas,[10] yet we may be able to observe and distinguish them and to apply them to their proper use. Besides, we may hereby observe what ideas most affect and are longest retained in memory. V.g.,[11] those ideas that are usually attended with pleasure or pain[12] always make the deepest impression, nor is the memory of them easily defaced. Now if any of these ideas are sinful, and we would prevent the mischief they would do, we must particularly guard those senses of the body by which they enter or passions in the mind that they are wont to affect.

[50. The law of reason and the Great Commandment.]

Morn[ing]

Glory be to thee, O Lord, for thy infinite wisdom in giving to rational free agents[13] a law suitable to their natures and tending to their happiness! The whole substance matter of the law of reason is briefly summed up in those two comprehensive duties, the love of God and the love of man, "and upon these two, hang all the law and the prophets."[14]

[51. Practice what you preach when instructing children in the truths of natural and revealed religion; "reverence yourself" as a reasonable creature.]

Noon

"While I teach, I learn," says Seneca. "And while I preach to others, I instruct myself." And again, "Those are the best instructors that teach by their lives and prove their words by their actions."[15] So do, and God will give a blessing to your endeavours. While you instruct your children in the first principles of religion, be careful to impress a sense of them on your own mind, and ever take care of your affections, that they may keep pace with and be agreeable to your convictions of the great truths of natural and revealed religion. Though you have all knowledge, yet if you want divine charity, it profiteth you nothing.[16]

Preserve the dignity of your nature. Reverence yourself, and do nothing unworthy the reason God has given you.

[52. Notes on instructional writings for her children.]

Even[ing] M[ay] 24, 1711

'Tis necessary to observe some method in instructing and writing for your ch[ildren]. Go through your brief exposition on the Ten Commandments, which are a summary of the moral law. Then briefly explain the principles of revealed religion, which will make up the second letter. Subjoin by way of essay a short discourse on the being and attributes of God.[17]

[53. Submission to God's will brings happiness, satisfaction.]

Morn[ing]

When you feel yourself afflicted by pain, sickness, or any other uneasiness, the first thing you do, make an act of submission to the will of God. Then is the time to reflect on that glorious attribute of divine wisdom and to resign yourself in a full sense thereof to the conduct of Providence. Believe it, there is no happiness in this world to be enjoyed without this resignation to the divine will, and as that is more or less perfect, the satisfaction of the mind is more or less sincere and permanent. 'Tis impossible but offences must come, considering the present state of things; 'tis impossible but sometimes we shall meet with things distasteful and uneasy to us. But then we must "look unto Jesus the author and finisher of our faith" [18] and imitate his perfect resignation to our heavenly Father.

[54. Reflection on three sermons: the apostles' eyewitness testimony and the truth of the Gospel.]

Even[ing]

You have this day heard a discourse on those words, Hebrews 2:4, "God also bearing them witness, both with signs and wonders, and with divers miracles and gifts of the Holy Ghost." [19] Proving from thence the truth of our Saviour's mission and, by consequence, of revealed religion. The two former sermons were to show that the miracles our Lord wrought were such as plainly proved the truth of those predictions concerning him, as that he should open the eyes of the blind, should restore feet to the lame, etc., and that those were miracles that surpassed the power of angels or men and therefore clearly proved that it was no less than divine power that wrought them.

The third thing that remained to be proved was that the apostles could have no motive to preach the Gospel unless they themselves were fully persuaded of the truths they taught. Proved by their doing it in direct opposition to the whole Jewish nation, the then only visible church of God on earth. In opposition to the heathen world. And that therefore they were to expect very powerful and numerous enemies, against which they had nothing but simple truth, plain matter of fact, to oppose; that they had no advantage, no prospect of temporal interest, but on the contrary they knew that they should meet with violent persecution, that all the powers of men and hell would engage against them, that they must "suffer the loss of all things," [20] even of life itself, and yet notwithstanding all these discouragements, they boldly preached the Gospel before all their enemies and sealed the truths they declared with their blood.

That which [21] they preached concerning Jesus Christ, his life, death and resurrection were matters of fact such as they were eyewitnesses of. "That which we have seen and heard declare we unto you," says St. John. [22]

The strongest proof that matter of fact can have is the attestation of eyewitnesses that see the things done. And this we have concerning our Saviour. The apostles conversed daily with him, heard his doctrine, saw his miracles, his death and himself after his resurrection. [23]

[55. "Train up a child": an epitome of her child-rearing practice.]

Noon [24]

Never correct your children to satisfy your passions but out of a sense of your duty to reclaim them from their errors and to preserve your authority. And then be exceeding careful to let the measure of correction be proportionable to the fault. Make great allowances for the weakness of their reason and immaturity of their judgments, but never spare them through foolish fondness when they sin against God. Instruct them in their duty and reason with them upon the several branches

of it. Cherish the first dawnings of sense and reason and endeavour to tincture their minds in their early years with a sense of religion. "Train up a child in the way he should go, and when he is old he will not depart from it."[25]

[56. An internal debate on whether to continue writing theological treatises, "the work you designed for your children."]

Morn[ing]

You have long intermitted the work you designed for your children and meet with many discouragements in it. The weakness of your mind and body, it seeming unnecessary because there are already so many excellent discourses written on those subjects,[26] your little time and abundance of other business, your apprehension of censure and contempt, etc. Yet notwithstanding, you do earnestly desire to do somewhat for their souls and are not easy when interrupted in these designs; besides you are willing to have some stated employment of your mind, that you may fill up all the vacant moments of life, that your candle may not burn in vain, and that none of your precious time may pass unprofitably.

Now weigh these things one against another.

Your mind indeed is impotent and corrupt in the highest degree, your understanding is weak and your affections averse from goodness, you have few helps comparatively to what others have and few books, and little assistance from ————.[27] But hath not the inspired apostle said, "If any lack wisdom let him ask it of God who giveth liberally to all and upbraideth no man"[28] that is truly desirous of wisdom, though he have formerly misemployed or neglected to improve his talent; and God can abundantly make up the want of other helps by the illuminations of his Spirit. Your affections are corrupt and averse, but there is "a fountain opened for sin and for uncleanness";[29] therefore there is hope concerning this also, if you have but faith to apply the remedy. As for your bodily infirmities, submit to the will of God, do what you can, and trouble not yourself when interrupted by the order of Providence. The books that have been writ on those subjects affect not you or yours; you have them not, and perhaps your children may never see them. However, if they should, it will be some time first, and what you write will not hinder them from reaping advantage by reading them, but rather prepare their minds (by accustoming them to think and learn) for further instruction. Nor do you envy or repine at the sense of learning of others, but rather adore the divine Goodness for providing such excellent and abundant means of grace for the children of men.

Those that have but little time have still more reason to improve that little. The unprofitable servant was not condemned because he had but one talent, but for not improving it.[30] A little time well spent is more valuable than many years or days or hours spent in vanity. 'Tis not the time spent in God's service, but the sincerity of the heart that he regards. The most wise and holy God requires not more of any than they have ability to perform. He indeed justly demands the heart and a service in some measure proportionable to our receipts,[31] but when he gives but little, much shall not be required.[32]

Business is indeed a great impediment when it necessarily involves the mind in a great deal of care, as well as keeps the body in action, because in the intervals of time which may be redeemed[33] there is a weariness and failure of spirits which greatly indisposes the person for study, but still this does not wholly excuse. If no more time be spent in refreshment than is strictly necessary, some will remain, and if the heart be but sincerely devoted to God, that little will be improved. Besides much study or intense thinking is not always necessary; you write what is familiar to you by practice, and a little recollection will serve the turn,[34] in most cases, and in those which are out of the common way in more perplexed and intricate cases you need not doubt but God will guide you by his Holy Spirit, if you do with great humility and earnestness desire his assistance.

As for censure, contempt, etc., you need not trouble yourself about such things. If any will censure you for doing your duty, what is that to you? And if anyone will contemn you as unlearned and of little sense, why should that affect you when you do not pretend to learning and you think as meanly of your own performances as any other can do?[35] Let those that set up for persons of learning and extraordinary sense mind such things. You do not (or at least ought not to) pretend to what you have not, and let those that desire a reputation in the world seek ways to obtain it. You have long professed to renounce the world, nor do you pretend to seek great things for yourself in relation either to riches or reputation with men. The less esteem you have in the world the better, for you'll have so much less of temptation to pride or vainglory. If you are not in the power of the world, you will not think the esteem of men any part of your happiness and consequently will feel no want of it, nor be uneasy without it.

[57. Not in the world's power.]

Even[ing]

If you "love not the world,"[36] you are not in its power. Whatever we love we take pleasure and delight in, and whatever pleases and delights us has thereby an ascendant over us. And from our misplaced or excess of love arises most of the uneasinesses we suffer in this life. What is beauty, riches, honour, sensual pleasure to them that love none of those things? Or what great uneasiness can they give that mind that hath power over itself and permits not its affections to fix on anything but God?

[58. Amazement at God's mercy to an undeserving humanity.]

Morn[ing][37]

I stand amazed at the boundless and inexhaustible goodness and mercy of God! That he should give to those that are so undeserving, so unmindful of him, and so regardless of and unthankful for his mercies. This is not "after the manner of men,"[38] O Lord! "As the heavens are higher than the earth, so are thy thoughts higher than our thoughts and thy ways than our ways."[39] If we thy sinful creatures do a small inconsiderable kindness for anyone, we expect that it should never be forgotten and greatly resent the least shadow of ingratitude, but how easily do we forget to praise thee for thy daily mercies, and though the want of any one convenience or comfort (though we have innumerable blessings of which we are unworthy) is sufficient (we think) to justify our complaints and murmurings at the order of thy providence, yet when we do not feel the want of them, we find it very hard to preserve a habitual sense of thy goodness and a grateful temper of mind. And yet thy providence maintains its constant course, and thou goest on after a manner worthy of God to shower down blessings on a[n] unthankful world! Thou wilt have mercy because thou wilt have mercy.[40] "Even so, Father, for so it seemeth good in thy sight!"[41] Glory be to the Father! Son! and Holy Ghost!

[59. Spiritual inconsistency.]

Noon

How inconsistent is your practice with your profession! It was but yesterday that you received the pledges of the greatest love that God could show towards the children of men! And you were then inquiring what you should do, what returns you should make your Saviour for all that he did and suffered for sinful man, for his infinite compassion and charity to souls! And yet today you make a difficulty to resist a vain thought or forbear speaking an unprofitable word, though 'tis that Jesus that died for you which requires you so to do.

[60. God's goodness and patience in the face of human sin.]

Morn[ing]

How inconceivable! How incomprehensibly great is the goodness and patience of the divine Mind towards sinful man! How many sins does one sinner commit in the short compass of one day against his most glorious majesty, either in thought, word or deed?[42] Then how innumerable are the sins of the whole world! And yet he does not take vengeance, though he could in a moment consume them. God is strong and patient (or therefore patient), and he is provoked every day. The works of his creation and the redemption of the world by Jesus Christ demonstrate his omnipotence, yet his power over himself, which appears by his sustaining the affronts, contempt and insults of his rebellious creatures, appears to me as . . .[43]

[61. Divine life in a regenerate mind; each unregenerate person's "peculiar temptation."]

Morn[ing]

"We walk by faith, not by light."[44]

Here faith is opposed to sense, and the life of faith to the life of sense, for as a carnal unregenerate man is actuated and influenced by sensitive objects, and the perception and resentment[45] that he hath of them is the great principle of all his motions and is that which determines him in all his actions, so the firm persuasion of spiritual and invisible things is the principle of divine life in a regenerate mind.[46]

The soul by being daily exercised in the study and contemplation of God and spiritual things will acquire such a faculty of discerning, such a clear perception of good and evil, that spiritual things are as plainly seen by the intellectual eye as any material object is by the bodily. But this sense or perception of spiritual things is not natural to man in his lapsed state, nor ever to be attained without much labour and industry.

One man thinks it easy to resist the temptations of women, another those of ill company and intemperance, a third that 'tis the easiest thing in the world to conquer all temptations to covetousness and immoderate love of riches, and all may in some sense be in the right, yet all egregiously mistaken. They are all thus far in the right: if a man hath by the assistance of the Holy Spirit attained to a command of his passions and is actually recovered out of the power of the world and the flesh and consequently the devil,[47] then all external temptations are easily overcome. But if the power of[48] the world and the animal life remains unbroken and he hath not recovered his lapse into corrupt animality, though every man is not equally open to all temptations, yet some one will certainly conquer him. And herein we are apt to put a fallacy upon ourselves, and this is the reason why all things are not equal temptations to all men. Whatever a man's nature most inclines him to love, that is his peculiar temptation, and for want of observing the bent of our particular inclinations, education or customs of living and those of other [?]men, we judge of others by our selves, and what we find has little or no influence upon us we are inclined to think may very . . .[49]

[62. Extraordinary sense of divine mercy apt to degenerate; criteria for a real "sense of God's goodness."]

Noon

You have often experienced that upon any extraordinary sense of mercy in any kind the mind is apt to be too much elated, and if great care and frequent recollection do not prevent it, it is apt to degenerate into light and trivial mirth. What is this but to do as the apostle says, begin in the spirit and end in the flesh?[50] Our sense of God's goodness and of his particular mercies to us is never as it should be, unless it united the soul more closely to him, unless it makes us more vigourous in his service, more serious in our devotions, if it does not separate our affections from this present world and make us more thoughtful of a future state. We must not rest in our present enjoyments as if it were best to be here, but we must "press forward toward the prize, for the mark of the high calling of God in Christ Jesus."[51] Ever remembering that this is only a state of probation, and though our heavenly father is mercifully pleased sometimes to refresh our minds by a pleasing sense of his goodness and doth sometimes indulge us some intervals of rest from care and business, yet all we enjoy here is precarious, and we do not know how soon he may withdraw the beams of his glory and leave us in a state of uncomfortable darkness, if we grow secure or unmindful of our duty, if we turn his grace into wantonness and venture too near the . . . [52]

[63. Human dissatsifaction in this life argues for immortality of the soul and a future state.]

Even[ing]

It seems to me an undeniable argument for the immortality of the soul and the reality of a future state that our duration here is so very uncertain and withal attended with so much "vanity and vexation of spirit."[53] Nor can I conceive so wise and good a being as God is would create man (the noblest of his visible creatures) only to abide a few weary years in a place where he can meet with little, or to say better, nothing of solid happiness but what he draws from the faith and expectation of a future state. We may observe among the variety of creatures that there is none but what enjoys a happiness suitable to its capacity, and as their being seems only designed for the service of man in this life, so they attain in little time to a certain point of perfection, and when they answered the end of their creation, they disappear without any apprehension or fear of an after reckoning. But with man it is quite otherwise; he enjoys the present with dissatisfaction, is anxious for the future, hath boundless capacities and an unsatiable appetite to knowledge which renders him uneasy, and, though he increases in knowledge, yet his sorrows increase likewise, because the further he carries his acquests,[54] the more clearly he perceives his ignorance; the more degrees of light he enjoys, the more plainly he discerns his misery. He sees himself surrounded with a vast expansion of being which he can neither know nor yet be quietly ignorant of.

[64. An activist, rather than a quietist, way of combatting spiritual indisposition.]

Morn[ing]

Some advise that when persons find themselves unapt or indisposed for prayer, meditation or any other part of religious duty, they should not trouble themselves about it or endeavour to perform them at that time, but wait till they have a greater disposition to those duties, wait till they feel themselves moved by the Holy Spirit.[55]

I do not take this counsel to be always good, though too easy to be followed, for unless this indisposition proceeds from bodily distempers which cannot be prevented or striven against, 'tis plain that such a course would give great strength and encouragement to our spiritual enemy.

In this case, then, I humbly conceive the best way is first to consider from whence this hardness of heart or this indisposition to spiritual things proceeds. If from the body, then make an act of resignation to the will of God, and wait a more favourable opportunity, but if the body be in health and this backwardness and averseness proceeds merely from the remains of original corruption or from any late willful omission of known duty or commission of known sin, we must not yield, but strive against it, we must humble ourselves before God for the sin of our nature and those particular sins that we apprehend may be the cause of this defection. And if we cannot readily pray, we may meditate; if by reason of the confusion of our thoughts we cannot do that, we may read to compose the mind; but if still neither prayer, meditation or reading is delighted in, but the soul still remains averse and uneasy, yet however do not quit the field, but retire the appointed time, though you should reap no advantage by it, but only that of crossing and contradicting your own corrupt and carnal inclinations.

[65. Continued reflection: "vigourous resistance" to spiritual lethargy by "crossing your corrupt inclinations."]

Even[ing]

And you will find that by crossing those corrupt inclinations your averseness to spiritual exercise will decrease, and when God's Holy Spirit finds you striving against yourself, against the stream of carnal affections, he will assist you, and I do not know but in this case you may please God better by making a vigourous resistance than you do sometimes when you perform select duties with greater warmth of affection, for this shows that the will and understanding, which are the superior powers of the soul, are conformed to the will of God, and though with the flesh you serve the law of sin, yet with the mind you serve the law of God.

[66. God's glory rather than worldly reputation; an "equal temper of mind" rather than a "dangerous levity."]

Noon

Make not your own esteem or reputation the end of your thoughts, words or actions. If you do, either you will gain your end or not; if you do not, you lose your time [and] labour to no purpose; if you do, then our Saviour says you have your reward already[56] and must expect none from him at the last great day of account. Whereas those that propose in their actions etc. the glory of God principally and the doing good in the station he hath placed them in, though they should not be esteemed or regarded by man, shall not fail of a future recompense infinitely more desirable than anything in this world.

Indulge not yourself therefore in any worldly regards, nor suffer a warm imagination to raise your passions and elevate your fancy by framing discourse of any subject in your mind, as if you were in company with any person, for such things are apt to cherish an overweening conceit of your own parts and naturally lead you into self applauses, which leaves a dangerous levity in the mind, above all things to be avoided.

A grave composure and equal temper of mind is absolutely necessary for such as desire to "live a godly, righteous and sober life."[57]

[67. "Constant perverseness in the affections" as a factor in moral and religious life.]

Even[ing]

'Tis the most stupendous, the most incongruous thing in nature for the mind to be so rationally convinced of and strongly moved with the sense of any evil thought or action and yet in a few minutes be guilty of the same error again. How is it that convictions have so little effect? Whence proceeds this constant perverseness in the affections that they do not immediately follow the dictates of the understanding and judgment? In the order of nature the understanding should direct the judgment, that the will, and that should excite the affections, and in indifferent things it usually is so; but in things of a moral nature 'tis often quite otherwise, and by a stronger corrupt reverse of the actions of the soul the order of nature is inverted and the passions gain the ascendant over the superior powers.

The understanding hath often a clear perception of the truth and reality of spiritual things, yet the judgment stands suspended or weakly and coldly determines. Sometimes the mind both understands and approves, but the will is averse and refuses to submit to their determinations. Other whiles they all concur, and yet the affections yield no obedience but strongly adhere to sensitive objects, and, maugre[58] all the resistance of the superior powers, pursue the worse and refuse the better and by this means raise strong conflicts in the soul, which is too weak to compose these discordant principles. Therefore you must address yourself for cure of these spiritual maladies to that almighty Power that raised this beauteous fabric of the world from a rude chaos of contrary and contending principles,[59] since no less power is required for the one than was for the other.

Think of Jesus Christ, think of Christ crucified! The consideration of Christ crucified as it affords matter of the deepest, most piercing grief, so likewise doth it give occasion for the most sublime and perfect joy, even to exultation and ecstasy![60]

[68. Sanctification: gradual and incomplete, even among the best.]

Noon

Your own corruptions and daily infirmities are no lawful or reasonable plea against your endeavouring to do all the good you can to the souls of others.[61] Nor has any person any more reason to refuse your charitable offers upon that account than they have to refuse advice or physic under any bodily distemper because the physician that prescribes it is mortal himself and therefore incident to the same diseases he attempts to cure in others.

Alas, we are all by nature corrupt and impure, and the best are sanctified but in part and often by slow and almost imperceptible degrees;[62] the work of regeneration is a stupendous work, which is not perfected at once, and though some have wildly imagined and talked of such things as infused habits,[63] yet those that are wiser know of no such things, but say an infused habit is nonsense in terms, for habits are begot by repeated acts and cannot otherwise be acquired. Dispositions indeed may be induced and are by the good Spirit of God, but who does not know that good dispositions may be altered or lost by want of care to improve them, and though they should produce some good actions, yet, unless those acts are frequently repeated, even they will not be effectual for the producing such habits which are absolutely necessary for the perfecting the divine life. 'Tis not grace begun, but carried on and improved that will bring us to heaven. Perseverance crowns the work, nor shall any but those that endure to the end be saved.[64]

But though "all have sinned and come short of the glory of God," though all are by nature "children of wrath,"[65] and even among those who are sanctified there is not one that lives without sin, yet is there a vast difference between those that sin through infirmity of nature and such as offend of malicious wickedness; the one hates, repents of, and strives against their infirmities, the other loves and indulges themselves in their most enormous sins, being altogether alienated from the life of God.

[69. Example more important than precept in the "reforming" of children, each one of which is a talent committed to your trust.]

Morn[ing]

"Cleanse thou me, O Lord, from my secret faults, and keep back thy servant from presumptuous sins, lest they get the dominion over me."[66]

Whosoever would successfully attempt the conversion of others must be careful in the first place to reform themselves. He that does not abstain himself from gross and scandalous vices is of all others the most unfit for a reformer. A drunkard, an unclean person, etc., would meet with nothing but scoffs and derision if they should go about preaching temperance or chastity, and everyone would be ready to say in such a case, "physician, heal thyself."[67]

Precept should weigh more than example, as being grounded generally on the eternal law of reason; but in fact 'tis quite otherwise.[68] Especially young or weak minds will be more apt to observe what you do, than what you say, and such commonly lie upon the catch[69] and are glad when they find you deviating in practice from your own rules, that they may have somewhat to retort upon you when you reprove them, vainly supposing that in your failings they find a just excuse for their own guilt.

'Tis therefore absolutely necessary that you endeavour to prevent all objections of evil persons against your designs of this nature by purifying yourself from all uncleanness of flesh and spirit, carefully avoiding all occasions of scandal and reproach and striving against the infirmities of your nature; but after all, this life is a store of temptation, and if you should fail in your duty in lesser instances, yet you ought not to be discouraged from your endeavouring what you can to instruct your children and to instill into their minds the principles of true religion.

God the great Lord of heaven and earth, the almighty Father of spirits[70] hath placed all mankind in this world in a state of probation and hath committed to each individual a stock of talents, to some more, to some less, commanding us to improve them for his glory.[71] You ought therefore to look upon every child as a talent committed to your trust, and be assured you must give an account at the last great day how you have discharged this trust, and if through your default any soul miscarry, how will you hold up your face in the last judgment?

[70. A forgiving temper is better than anger.]

Noon

There is no age or condition of life but what hath temptations peculiar to itself. Young[72] persons are commonly inclined to anger, impurity, pride and inconstancy.

Though there has [sic] been so many excellent rules given for the government of the passions and of this in particular, for want of actual advertence or through presumption of our own strength and neglect of constant and earnest prayer to God for the guidance and direction of his Holy Spirit, the generality of mankind are little amended by them. It must therefore be your care to preserve a temper of mind disposed to advertence and to rely only on the mercy and grace of God for strength and ability to practice what you know.

A serious and frequent reflection on your own failings, especially in relation to your known duty towards God, may make you more calm and easy when men fail in their duty towards you. Those that have much to be forgiven should surely forgive much, and for one that is daily guilty of repeated offences against his maker and supreme Benefactor, to be of an unforgiving temper to others is the most ridiculous absurd folly imaginable, nor can such a one ask pardon of God without the most consummate assurance. Like the servant in the parable that, when on his desire he had been forgiven so many talents, yet refused to forgive his fellow servant and exacted the most rigorous payment of a few pence.[73]

Nor is anger less unreasonable in respect of yourself. Suppose you are injured, yet what[74] good will it do you to be angry? Why should you revenge another man's fault upon yourself? Perturbation injures the body, it injures the mind, breaks and discomposes the thoughts, betrays the succours of reason, and lays a man open by discovering his impotency of mind to the by-standers, which are too apt to assault a man upon his weak side. It renders a person unfit for business by blinding the judgment and discomposing the body and transports a man into a thousand inconsiderate follies, both in word and action.

And after all, perhaps the supposed injury was no injury at all. Perhaps the person suffers by a misreport, or you yourself have unwittingly given the occasion. It may be he labours under a misapprehension of you, or perhaps there may be some mistake on your side, or suppose the offending party is of so weak parts that what they do amiss may proceed from mere impotence of mind, and then must you be mad because another is a fool? How silly a thing is it to be angry with a child that is not yet arrived to any degree of understanding or with such as, though they are past childhood, yet by reason of the slowness of their parts never can attain to any maturity of judgment, but are children in understanding, thought by their years they are men?

But suppose the injury should be done by a person of competent sense and there[75] should be a degree of malice in it, yet how know you but they have repented of it, and nothing but shame prevents their asking you forgiveness? Yet suppose they should not, still you have the less reason to gratify their malice by letting them know they have a power to make you angry; whoever is your enemy will gladly see you miserable, and there is hardly any misery so great during the time it last as a strong perturbation of mind, and as there is nothing more pleasing to an adversary than to see you uneasy, so on the other side nothing more enrages them or so effectually disappoints their malice as your cheerful calmness and serenity of mind under the injuries you suffer. Nor could a more exquisite and withal a more noble and innocent revenge be contrived than to return mild and gentle words to ill language and good offices for injuries.

[71. Further thoughts on subduing the passion of anger.]

Even[ing][76]

The first motions of anger, as they are commonly involuntary, so they are usually violent, and for the most part a man is transported ere he is aware into some indecent words or gestures, which upon reflection very much grieve and disquiet his mind.

'Tis advisable, therefore, when occasion is offered peremptorily to resolve, "I will not be angry at this time,"[77] and if by this means you can but check the first motion, your passion will cool and not rise so high as a perturbation.

But if upon surprise the passion give a strong shock to your heart and give no leisure for your grace or reason to come in to your assistance, resolve presently not to speak one word, good or bad, till the first tide of passion begins to abate, and then resolve not to be angry till you have duly examined what the provocation is in itself without the false colours of prejudice or passion, view it in all its circumstances, for till you know the true nature of the injury, you cannot tell what proportion of anger is lawful or convenient.

The truth is this passion can no way be subdued without a habitual advertence and presence of mind together with a holy indifference to the things of this world. If we would be free from the perturbation that usually accompanies this and indeed all other passions where they are ill-placed, or err in the excess, we must endeavour by all means to keep out of the power of the world. We must not love wealth, pleasure or honour intemperately, for whether those philosophers were in the right or no, that though[78] the human soul had no passion but love and that all other affections of the will which we call passions, as hope, fear, desire, etc., are only several modes or acts of that passion under the various apprehensions of the beloved object as it is amiable, absent, injured, displeased, kind or averse, etc. . . .[79]

[72. Love, the strongest passion.]

Morn[ing]

This we may be assured of, that love is the strongest passion, the affection that excites and leads the rest to action.

[73. Love, the origin of virtue and vice, happiness and misery.]

Even[ing]

This is the passion that raises and inflames our desire in proportion to its own degree. Our hopes and fears, joys or griefs, all the train of our concupiscible and irascible affections,[80] take their rise from and derive all their vigour and energy from love. All our virtues and vices, happiness and misery have the same origin, and 'tis this passion, well or ill placed, denominates a man either virtuous or wicked.

[74. Love, the "first instance of our duty toward" God.]

Morn[ing]

Therefore, almighty God, the great Father of spirits, who, having made us himself, must to be sure perfectly know the works of his own omnipotence, all the powers of our minds, their various motions and all the springs of action, what it is that moves, excites, impels and determines it in all its operations, hath required it as the first instance of our duty toward him that we "love the Lord our God with all the heart, with all the mind, with all the soul, and with all the strength."[81]

Notes

1. Several lines skipped between the end of this brief meditation and the beginning of the next.

2. Cf. 1 Corinthians 8:1.

3. Preceded by the crossed-out, "Speculative."

4. Indecipherable. "Good" is a reasonable guess for what she intended here.

5. Meditation breaks off with a half page left blank. The implied example was never supplied.

6. Slight, scorn, disdain, despise.

7. "S. J." has been interpreted to mean "son John," and the date of the entry fell on Thursday, the weekday Susanna reserved for him. (see entry 78). His biographers have taken this entry as evidence of an early and special maternal focus.

8. Locke *An Essay concerning Human Understanding*, Peter H. Nidditch, ed. (Oxford: Clarendon Press, 1975), 1.1.2 (p. 43): "This, therefore, being my *Purpose* to enquire into the Original, Certainty . . ." and so on. Early in his book Locke describes what he will (and will not) be discussing. S. W. copies it out as a fair summary of the work.

9. Ibid., 2.1.1 (p. 104): "Whence has it [the mind] all the materials of Reason and Knowledge? To this I answer, in one word, From *Experience*: In that, all our Knowledge is founded; and from that it ultimately derives it self. Our Observation employ'd either about *external, sensible Objects; or about the internal Operations of our Minds, perceived and reflected on by our selves, is that, which supplies our Understandings with all the materials of thinking*. These two are the Fountains of Knowledge, from whence all the *Ideas* we have, or can naturally have, do spring." (Emphasis in the original.)

10. That is, ideas that "enter by the Senses simple and unmixed." Ibid. 2.2.1 (p. 119). In the previous section (2:1:25, p. 118) Locke said, "the Objects of our Senses, do, many of them, obtrude their particular *Ideas* upon our minds, whether we will or no."

11. *Verbi gratia*, for instance.

12. See Locke, *Essay*, 2.7.2 (p. 128). Locke here begins several paragraphs on pleasure and pain with the observation, "*Delight*, or *Uneasiness*, one or other of them join themselves to almost all our *Ideas*."

13. A Lockean concept. See Locke, *Essay* 2.21.16–19 (pp. 241–243).

14. Matthew 22:40, paraphrased; my quotation marks.

15. S. W. has employed one of these quotations, probably from Seneca's *Epistles*—*Seneca Ad Lucilium Epistulae Morales*, ed. and trans. Richard M. Gummere (London: Heinemann; New York: Putnam's, 1935), 1:133—in her letter to Samuel Jr., 11 October 1709; my quotation marks. For Seneca's appeal to S. W. see note 28 on the 1709 letter.

16. Paraphrase of 1 Corinthians 13:2.

17. Second half of page left blank. This meditation helps us date the draft of her commentary on the Decalogue, that is, after the Creed commentary, January 1709/10, and before the present date, 24 May 1711. For the results of this resolution, see the instructional writings in part III of this volume. The designation "being and attributes of God" was a staple of theological discourse at the time. Note, for example, Samuel Clarke's first set of Boyle Lectures, published as *A Demonstration of the Being and Attributes of God: More Particularly in Answer to Mr. Hobbs, Spinoza, And their Followers* . . . (London: James Knapton, 1705).

18. Close paraphrase of Hebrews 12:2; my quotation marks.

19. My quotation marks.

20. Slight recasting of Philippians 3:8; my quotation marks.

21. The MS reads "wt," her usual abbreviation for "what."

22. 1 John 1:3; my quotation marks.

23. Bottom one-third of the page left blank.

24. Begins after a blank top one-third of a page. This entry represents an early expression of her child-rearing practices, later revealed in more detail in the 24 July, 1732 letter to her son John, the first document in part III of this volume. In part this reflection may stem from a reading of John Locke's *Some Thoughts concerning Education*, John W. and Jean S. Yolton, eds. (Oxford: Clarendon Press, 1989), first published in 1693.

25. Proverbs 22:6; my quotation marks.

26. Among the great body of published "practical divinity" dealing with these issues, Susanna would have known about (and is perhaps here referring to) various commentaries and sermons on the Church's catechism. See introduction to part III of this volume.

27. Probably her husband, Samuel.

28. Paraphrase of James 1:5; my quotation marks.

29. Excerpts from Zechariah 13:1; quotation marks added.

30. Parable of the talents, Matthew 25:14–30.

31. That is, mental capacities, powers of apprehension. S. W. spells it "receits."

32. Cf. Luke 12:48.

33. Cf. Ephesians 5:15–16.

34. That is, answer one's purpose or requirement.

35. The two preceding question marks are added in place of a comma and a period as more appropriate punctuation for the MS's long single sentence, beginning "If any will censure you."

36. 1 John 2:15; my quotation marks.

37. Begins after a blank top one-third of a page.

38. A Pauline phrase; quotation marks added. See Romans 6:19, 1 Corinthians 15:32, and Galatians 3:15.

39. Paraphrased from Isaiah 55:9; my quotation marks.

40. Cf. Exodus 33:19.

41. Close paraphrase of Luke 10:21; my quotation marks.

42. Cf. General Confession, Holy Communion, BCP.

43. Discourse breaks off here with the bottom one-third of the page left blank; ellipses added.

44. 2 Corinthians 5:7; my quotation marks.

45. That is, feeling or emotion.

46. Cf. [Henry Scougal], *The Life of God in the Soul of Man* . . ., 2nd ed. (London: T. Dring and J. Weld, 1691).

47. Cf. BCP, Litany.

48. The bottom half of the page is torn out at this point, but the meditation continues overleaf without apparent interruption.

49. The meditation stops in mid-sentence (ellipses have been added), and the bottom half of the page is torn out. However, the thought carries on 26 MS pages later as a Noon meditation, entry 81.

50. Loose paraphrase of Galatians 3:3.

51. Paraphrase of Philippians 3:14, a bit jumbled; my quotation marks.

52. Meditation breaks off in mid-sentence; ellipses added.

53. Ecclesiastes 1:14; 2:11, 17; quotation marks added.

54. Things acquired, acquisitions.

55. This "quietistic" approach ("waiting on the Lord" rather than doing one's duty without a clear sense of spiritual motivation) is one that later caused her son John to break with his Moravian friends.

56. Cf. Luke 6:23–24.

57. General Confession, Order for Morning Prayer, BCP; my quotation marks.

58. Despite.

59. This phrase has the sound of a poetic quotation, but I have not been able to trace it.

60. The bottom five or six lines of the page are left blank.

61. There immediately follows a crossed-out passage: "any more than it is a good reason against taking advice or physic under any bodily distemper."

62. Cf. John Wesley's, and occasionally the Wesleyan tradition's, insistence on "entire sanctification."

63. Imparted by divine influence or by nature.

64. Paraphrase of Matthew 10:22, 24:13; Mark 13:13.

65. Romans 3:23 and Ephesians 2:3; my quotation marks.

66. Psalm 19:12–13, conflated from BCP and AV; S.W. adds "O Lord"; my quotation marks.

67. Luke 4:23; my quotation marks.

68. Proverbial wisdom had already figured this out. One seventeenth-century version is "Example prevails more than precept." Francis Osborne, *Advice to a Son* (Oxford: Thomas Robinson, 1656).

69. Lie in wait, for example, to find fault.

70. Cf. Hebrews 12:9.

71. Matthew 25:14–30.

72. Susanna crossed out her original beginning of this sentence ("Often times middle aged"), replacing it with "Young."

73. Matthew 18:23–35.

74. The MS reads "wd," a slip for "wt."

75. The MS: "their."

76. Heading preceded by what looks like two capital letters: CL.

77. My quotation marks.

78. The MS reads "thought."

79. Ellipses added in lieu of a final expected clause that does not appear; S. W. apparently got lost in her syntax and thought she had completed her sentence.

80. In Platonic thought, the two parts of our irrational nature: concupiscible—characterized by desire or longing; irascible—characterized by, arising from, or exhibiting anger but also having to do with courage, spirit, and passion.

81. Mark 12:30 and parallels, slightly altered; my quotation marks.

EIGHTEEN

"I Cannot Altogether Acquiesce"

A single meditation near the beginning of this chapter and an unusual series of ten meditations at the end claim special attention. At the outset, entry 79 provides one of the rare glimpses into the particulars of personal and family life. In this morning meditation, spanning the best part of two notebook pages, Susanna Wesley details her new resolution to meet each child individually for special conference ("one for every day of the week and two for Sunday") and recalls two previous vows: her own meditational discipline, of which her diaries are a manifestation, taken on nine years previously, and her seven-year-old determination never to "drink above two glasses of strong liquor at one time."

The other rarity is the close attention to a particular line of thought, which she sustains throughout ten meditations (91–100). For half of that space her journal becomes a sort of commonplace book with extended quotations from Bishop William Beveridge's treatise "Holiness the Great Design of the Gospel Dispensation." However, once she has copied, paraphrased, and understood his argument, she pauses and asks herself, "What are your thoughts upon the whole?" In answer she pens six pages of closely considered disagreement and improvement on the bishop's ideas, though with the usual ritual "deference to the judgment of this great and good man." If she "cannot altogether acquiesce" in this theological authority's view of godliness, she will take the trouble to amend it.

Among the other entries in this rich assortment there are typical meditations on creation (86) and redemption (89), another taking off from Locke's thoughts on happiness (75), one quoting Pascal on revelation (84), and a long disquisition on unanswered prayer (77).

🌿

[75. Locke on happiness and misery.]

Noon

Happiness, as Mr. Locke well observes, always moves desire, and though "happiness and misery are the names of two extremes, the utmost bounds whereof we know not, 'tis what 'eye hath not seen, nor ear heard, nor hath it entered into the heart of man to conceive,' yet of some degrees of both we have very lively impressions . . ."[1] Love is the parent of happiness when 'tis centered in God, and of misery when it [is] placed on the creature. For though the intemperate hath pleasure in his excess and the unchaste in his forbidden embraces, cure the diseases of their minds, restore the one to his sobriety and the other to his chastity, and they will reflect on those enjoyments with contempt and abhorrence in which before they placed their supreme felicity.

[76. Let our good works be seen to God's glory.]

Morn[ing]

Let the light of your wisdom and grace so shine among men "that they may see your good works." For what reason? Not that you may receive praise or be esteemed, but that they may "glorify your father which is in heaven."[2]

That this is the plain meaning of our Saviour's words we may learn from those other texts wherein he forbids his disciples to pray or give alms that they may be seen of men,[3] by which prohibition he command[s] us to avoid all vain-glory, all worldly regards, and seeking to advance our own esteem or reputation among men. We must let our good works be seen to the praise and glory of that God which gives us grace to perform those good works, but never that we may be seen or taken notice of or esteemed of men. We must never presume the endeavouring that the praise or glory of them may devolve on ourselves, but if through divine assistance we do any good action let us immediately say, "not unto us, O Lord, not unto us, but to thy name be ascribed all praise and glory!"[4]

[77. Unanswered prayer: "because you ask amiss."]

Even[ing]

God is truth, and 'tis absolutely impossible his word should ever fail. He never said to any of his creatures, "Seek ye my face" (favour) in vain.[5] And again he said, "Ask, and ye shall receive. Seek, and ye shall find. Knock, and it shall be opened unto you."[6]

Whence is it then that your prayers are not answered? It cannot be that God is unmindful or unwilling or unable to grant your petitions.

Why, whence should it be, but from yourself?

You ask and receive not, because you ask amiss.

You either ask irreverently, which is rather a demanding than a begging grace, which argues want of reverence and humility, or you ask coldly without being apprised of the value of that grace you pray for, and so you do not in good earnest desire it, and then 'tis no wonder you speed[7] no better, or you probably pray for some particular virtue, for an ill, or at least not the best end. Perhaps your desires spring not from a principle of love to God and a high estimation of holiness, not from a zeal for his glory and a hearty desire to be conformed to his image and will, but it may be you ask grace that you may be secured of God's protection in this world that you may enjoy a greater affluence of temporal blessings, or may be applauded and esteemed by men. And can you think that God will prostitute his noblest gifts to such unworthy ends? God is a great and a jealous God, nor will he admit a rival in your love; nor impart grace and virtue[8] to such as would divide their affections between him and the world; you must give him all your heart, or he'll accept of none of it. Our Lord requires that such as take upon themselves the honour of speaking to him should approach him with the most profound humility, with the highest reverence and devotion, with a heart (affections) separated from the world, devoted to his glory, and that we most highly esteem, value and prize the grace which we petition for. For what greater affront can we offer to the divine Majesty than to ask with seeming devotion any virtue or grace when we do not in the least regard whether we have it or no? But suppose you offer your petitions to the divine Majesty with the most profound reverence, with humility, with an earnest desire of those things you pray for, and with an ardent zeal for the manifestations of his glory, yet perhaps you ask[9] impatiently; you would indeed have grace, but you would have it just then, you are not willing to tarry the Lord's leisure, you are not willing to be at the pains of repeating your petitions, and therefore, if you are delayed, though not denied, your mind, instead of being more humbled, of being more strongly united to God by faith and love, grows displeased and angry, you say, "What a weariness is it to serve the Lord"[10] or "What profit is it that we serve the Almighty?"[11] Whether these or any other reason prevents the answering of prayers, this you may be assured of, that God is infinite truth, and since he hath graciously promised to hear the prayers that are made to him in the name of Christ, he will certainly do it.

[78. Unconscious inclinations to vices.]

Noon

But I believe upon an impartial examen[12] it may appear that your desires of virtue are not so sincere as you suppose them to be. There may probably be some dispositions or inclinations to the contrary vices, which in absence of temptation or occasion do not exert themselves, by which means they are invisible to you, though apparent to God.

[79. Three personal milestones: individual time with each child; daily devotional routine; temperate drinking.]

Morn[ing]

You have at last begun what you designed[13] and may that infinite Goodness that put into your heart the design give a blessing to it. Amen.

Molly on Monday; Hetty on Tuesday; Nancy on Wednesday; Jacky, Thursday; Patty, Friday; Charles, Saturday. Blessed be God! One for every day of the week and two for Sunday.[14]

Do not by unbelief provoke almighty God to withdraw his Spirit, which will otherwise assist and direct you in this great work. Call to remembrance his past mercy in reclaiming you from a vain and sinful conversation, and do not think so unworthily of him, as that his power or goodness is now less than it was.

'Tis now about nine years since you more solemnly devoted yourself to his service[15] and since you resolved to spend at least one hour morning and evening in private duties, which resolution you have peremptorily adhered to, and though by sickness and sometimes unavoidable business you have contracted your devotions, yet your cons[cience] does not, and I think cannot, accuse you of having once willingly omitted or shortened your private duties, but you have, and still do usually much exceed the allotted time. Glory be to thee, O Lord!

'Tis about seven years since you were in great danger of falling into intemperate drinking,[16] by the persuasion[17] and example of some among whom you lived, and you then made a solemn vow that you never would drink above two glasses of any strong liquor at one time, and though your husband absolved you from the vow as soon as he heard of it, yet you have never broke it, but have peremptorily kept it maugre[18] all the temptations you have met with,[19] and lest you should at any time, through persuasion of company which has pressed you to drink healths, exceed your measure, you have[20] declined drinking any health and have let your resolution to drink none be known to the company to prevent temptation. Glory be to thee, O Lord!

Always give God the glory of his grace. Be assured you are nothing but corruption and misery, and if ever you are restrained from any sin, or inclined to, or enabled to do anything that is good, give him the praise, for 'tis allowing to his undeserved grace, if you either will or do according to his good pleasure.

[80. Principled action, even in common business, conversation, and government of family.]

Even[ing]

Propose some good end to yourself in all your actions. Act always upon principles, even in your common business and conversation in the world. The apostle gives an excellent rule, and much to be observed by all: "Whether you eat or drink or whatsoever you do, do all to or for the glory of God."[21] Be diligent, industrious, and prudent in the government of your family—[22]

[81. The continuation of an earlier entry: differing constitutions incline people to different besetting sins.]

Noon[23]

. . . may very easily be avoided by others. Thus he whose constitution inclines him to sensual pleasures contemns the meanness of his soul that for a little sordid gain will macerate his body, consume his time, and scruple nothing that can any way advance his interest; on the other hand the covetous miser derides the voluptuous epicure that so loosely sacrifices his interest and health to the idol of pleasure.[24]

[82. Avoiding temptation by guarding the affections.]

Even[ing]

Sin is the source and origin of human misery. Our deep lapse into the power of the flesh and the world gives occasion to the devil to strike us with those powers and ensnare our virtue.[25] If you would preserve your liberty, if you would preserve your innocence, guard the affections of your will. 'Tis our concupiscence that continually betrays us. Could we fortify ourselves against the impressions of present things, Satan or the world could never hurt us.[26]

[83. Use divine aid not to change your situation, but to manage it "as well as you can."]

Even[ing]

As God hath not put it in your power, so it is not your business to alter your fortunes or constitution. But 'tis always your duty to manage both as well as you can, as may be most for the glory of God, and this you cannot do without divine succours. "Without me," says our Lord, "you can do nothing."[27] Know yourself.[28]

[84. Believe revealed truth, but prove it by sense and/or reason; a supporting quotation from Pascal's *Pensées*.]

Noon[29]

The evidence of sense and the evidence of reason seem clearer and stronger than that of faith—because that thing we make use of to explain or clear another by, must be clearer and more easy to understand than the thing by which it is explained, cleared or proved.[30] There is nothing more true than that we ought to believe whatever truth God hath revealed upon his authority, but then[31] the truth of the revelation must be proved either by sense or reason or both. 'Tis a just thought of Mr. Pascal that God, "intending no less to reveal himself to those that sincerely sought him than to hide himself from those who were industrious to fly and avoid him, has so tempered the knowledge of himself as to exhibit bright and visible indications to those who seek him and to seem the pillar of a cloud towards those who seek him not."[32]

[85. God's dominion asserted biblically and argued philosophically.]

Morn[ing]

Thy dominion, O Lord, is a universal dominion and thy kingdom ruleth over all.[33] Thy authority is indisputable and hath been acknowledged by all that have acknowledged thy existence. As by thy physical power thou hast an ability to act what thou pleasest, so by thy moral power thou hast an undoubted right to do whatsoever pleaseth thee. Is it not lawful for thee to do what thou wilt with thy own?[34] Glory be to thee, O Lord!

This dominion of God is founded on the superlative excellence of his nature. As none but God could possibly create this universal system of beings, so none but he could have minted[35] and deservedly challenged[36] the government of it, he being the supreme and most excellent of beings. Nor hath anything such a perfection of nature to capacitate it, to enter into a contest with him for a sufficiency to govern. And though among men an extraordinary perfection of nature does not confer a right to govern, though it speaks a great fitness and capacity for government (the right of government being derived from God alone),[37] yet infinite perfection (infinite power, wisdom, goodness, etc.)[38] doth unquestionably give a right and title to the government of the universe. And we find God himself asserting his own authority upon this very account in Isaiah 46:9: "I am God and there is none like me, I will do all my pleasure."[39] And Jeremiah acknowledgeth it for the same reason, Jeremiah 10:6–7: "Forasmuch as there is none like unto thee, O Lord; thou art great, and thy name is great in might. Who would not fear thee, O king of nations? For to thee doth it appertain: forasmuch as there is none like unto thee."[40] And this I take to be the most noble title of dominion, it being essential and such a right as he cannot divest himself of nor communicate to any creature.

[86. Creation as the foundation of God's dominion and humanity's subjection.]

Morn[ing]

As almighty God is the creator of all things and by his sole power he commanded the whole universe to spring from nothing into being, he must necessarily be the absolute sovereign and proprietor of whatever he hath created. His dominion, his jurisdiction, is founded on the act of creation, and he hath an authority over us as creatures before he hath dominion over us as converts. And as this is a strong foundation[41] for a claim of authority over man, so it lays the strong obligation on man to be in entire subjection to God. Shall not all creatures, O God, that received their very being from thee and that entirely depend on thee be subject unto thee? Thou art, O Lord, the only end for which all things were created.[42] The supreme Good must necessarily act for the best and noblest end. Nor can we conceive any end in working worthy of thee but thy own glory,[43] which we see displayed in all thy works of creation and providence. And therefore, since thou hast made all things for thyself, and since thou only preservest that thou hast made and each individual of the creation entirely depends on thee for all they do or can enjoy, it is but just and reasonable that they acknowledge their dependence and that thou hast created them, and that they receive all their blessings from thy bounty and goodness, which is glorifying thee!

[87. Question: what is the glory of God?]

Morn[ing]

I have not methinks a very clear notion of the glory of God. What it is, or in what sense almighty God made all things for himself or, which is all one, for his own glory. Tell me therefore, I desire you, what is meant or what you understand by the glory of God?[44]

[88. God's essential perfection and its manifestation to creatures.]

Even[ing]

A[nswer]. First, I understand by the glory of God his essential perfection. His independence, which infers self-existence. Wisdom, justice, goodness, truth, power, immensity, immutability, holiness or purity, which is the infinite rectitude of his nature, etc., this I call his essential perfection, and this is that glory which is incapable of access or diminution and consequently was and would be ever the same, though he had never created anything. And therefore it could not be of any advantage to him to create, in respect of his essential Glory. It must be, therefore,

Secondly, for the manifestation of his essential glory that he created all things.

Q[uestion]. But does not this seem to reflect some dishonour upon God that he, being so transcendently perfect, should condescend to manifest his glory to things so infinitely below him as the most exalted created being must necessarily be?

An[swer]. This question seems to imply a supposition that God manifested his glory to his creatures for no other end but purely to be admired by them, which is a low and unworthy thought of God. God is no[t] otherwise pleased with the praise and gratitude and admiration of men or angels than as those acts of praise, thanksgiving and admiration are regular acts of the understanding and will.[45]

[89. The prophetic office of Christ and our repentance.]

Noon

Jesus Christ, the eternal son of God, who was by the almighty Father promised in paradise upon the first man's defection and was constituted the second general head of mankind and in the fullness of time was sent into the world to complete the great work of man's redemption, upon the receipt[46] of his mission, entered upon three special offices, viz, prophet, priest and king.[47]

As he was our prophet, he declared to us the whole will of God for man's salvation.[48] And the sum and substance of what he told us we must do, that we may be saved, is comprised in few words, namely, "Repent and believe the Gospel."[49]

Repentance, in short, is "a change of the mind, a change or renovation of all the powers and affections of the soul."[50]

As the whole soul was corrupted and depraved by the fall, so 'tis renewed and restored again to its original purity by the grace of repentance. And this was one great end of our Saviour's coming into the world, "that repentance and remission of sins should be preached in his name unto all nations." St. Luke 24:47.[51]

[90. The understanding—and all other human faculties—are corrupted by the fall.]

Even[ing]

The understanding, which is the eye of the mind, the perceptive faculty by which we discern intellectual and spiritual objects, as we do sensible and material things by our bodily eyes,[52] is naturally eclipsed, for which reason we want a clear perception of immaterial substances and so become guilty of ignorance and an indisposition to contemplate and know truth, which is the proper object of the understanding.

God is truth! And he is the native centre of uncorrupted spirits: And had not sin entered the world, the mind had as naturally and constantly aspired towards him as flames ascend or as heavy bodies press towards their centre.[53] But now as a thick mist or a dark cloud often intercepts the beams of the sun and prevents our seeing it, though it shines with equal glory, so notwithstanding that "God is light, and in him is no darkness at all,"[54] yet by reason of the great depravity of human nature, we are as it were enveloped in a dark cloud of ignorance, [so] that we cannot discern the truth of his essential, infinite perfections.

From dark, confused, imperfect perceptions[55] of the divine Nature, arises the erroneous and mistaken judgments and false determinations that we form concerning him and all things of a spiritual nature.

Our thoughts for the most part are roving and desultory, we can rarely fix them on invisible objects, and, though we essay never so often to raise them to spiritual things, yet they naturally scatter and divide, and if we do by chance fix them a while, 'tis odds but we think amiss, for error is more agreeable to vitiated nature than truth.

And from hence it is that the will is so obstinately averse from goodness and takes so strong a bent towards evil. That we mistake in our notions of good and take evil for good and good for evil. That we prefer natural before moral good, the good of the body before the good of the soul, and what's still worse, the present satisfactions of the sensual appetites before the real good of either soul or body. The enjoying sensual pleasure for a short and uncertain time, before . . .[56]

And as all the superior powers were shaken and the noble faculties corrupted, so likewise are all the inferiour powers, all the passions of the soul, become irregular and disorderly. We love what we should hate, hate what we should love, we desire what we should fly from, and fly from what we should pursue, etc. We delight in what we should be displeased with and find a displicency[57] in those things with which we should be most delighted. In fine, the whole order of nature is inverted by the fall; and man, which was created after the image of God, that had a perfection of intellectual and moral goodness and was constituted by God, himself Lord of all the inanimate and brute creation, is now become a slave to his vassals and is truly more contemptible and vile by reason of his defection and departure from God than anything in nature.

Indeed there is nothing in all the works of God that is vile or contemptible, for all the creation except sinful man do constantly and regularly, though unwittingly, obey the laws of their great and wise Creator and answer the ends for which he made them.

But vain foolish man, as soon as he had received his being and began to be something, rebelled against the power and goodness by which he existed, and by an ingratitude not to be paralleled but by that of the fallen angels, disowned the sovereignty of his Creator, contemned the rule he had given him to walk by, and set up himself, opposed his weak and impotent reason against the dictates of almighty Wisdom. But "whoever hardened himself against God and prospered?"[58] As the presumptuous affecting sovereign Power threw angels from heaven, so the proud aspiring of the first man excluded him and all his posterity from the terrestrial paradise.[59]

[91. Bishop Beveridge's rules for holy living: duty to oneself.]

Noon

Titus 2:11–14. "For the grace of God that bringeth salvation hath appeared to all men;

Teaching us that, denying all ungodliness and worldly lusts, we should live soberly, righteously and godly in this present world."[60]

This place excellently commented on by Bishop Beveridge:[61]

He explains the grace of God to be "God's infinite love and mercy to mankind in sending his Son into the world to die for them."[62] Shows that the whole of man's redemption was owing to God's free and undeserved goodness and not to any merit or worthiness in man. That it is merely through God's favour that we are called, chosen, that our sins are pardoned, our minds renewed, our persons justified, and our souls saved. So that the whole matter of man's salvation must be ultimately resolved into God's infinite grace to mankind in Jesus Christ.[63] Glory be to thee, O Lord.

He explains what it is to live soberly.[64]

"When the grace of God teaches [us] to live soberly, it enjoyns that we avoid whatsoever may disturb or discompose our senses, reason and judgment, so as always to preserve the mind in an equal temper. And for that end it teaches us to avoid,

"1. All excess in meat or drink[. . .].

"2. [. . .] All inordinate love to or desires of the things of this world, which begets immoderate care, for such love hath in it a kind of inebriating quality, making men always looking downward like brutes, minding nothing but dirt. This our Saviour forewarneth us of in St. Luke 21:34. 'Take heed to yourselves lest at any time your hearts be overcharged with surfeiting, and drunkenness, and cares of this life, and so that day come upon you unawares.'[. . .]"[65]

[92. Beveridge on holy living: duty to oneself—and to others.]

Even[ing]

3. All immoderate anger etc. The mind is intoxicated by irregular passions as well as wine.[66]

4. As sobriety teaches us to regulate our passions, so also our thoughts, "especially of ourselves. It doth not suffer a man to be drunk [. . .] with self-admiration and esteem, as too many are, [. . .] insomuch that they cannot forbear venting it at their mouths by self-applause.[. . .]"[67]

5.[68] [. . .] Another "act of sobriety is seldom thought of and that is sobriety in matters of religion. For there is a new kind of riot and drunkenness, which hath intoxicated the age we live in. Men being now grown so unstable and giddy in religion itself, that they reel to and fro and stagger from one opinion to another and are not able to walk steadily in the narrow path that leads to heaven . . ."[69]

As sobriety teaches a man his duty to himself, so righteousness shows him what is his duty to others.

1. To love his neighbour as himself[70]

2. Justice in all our dealings[71]

3. To model all our actions by our Saviour's rule, St. Matthew 7:12, that "whatsoever you would that others should do to you, do you even so to them."[72]

[93. Beveridge on holy living: duty to God.]

(Morn)[ing][73]

Godliness teaches our duty towards God.[74]

The original word which we translate godliness,[75] "according to its true notation or etymology, properly signifies true worship or the worshipping of God or, if you will, right worshiping of the true God.[. . .] Hence it follows that when we speak of godliness, we must not restrain it to some few particular acts, but look upon it as comprehending the whole system of all those duties which we as creatures owe to him that made us; and in the due performance whereof our worship and adoration of him consisteth; so that he that worships God aright, may be justly termed a godly man, and no man else can be properly called by that name."[76] Therefore to understand the nature of true godliness, we must understand "the true nature of divine worship and consider what it is in the scripture sense to worship God."[77]

[94. Beveridge on holy living: duty to God—bodily worship.]

Even[ing]

". . . If we consult the scripture to know wherein the worship of God consists, we shall easily find that God, as he is Creator of soul and body, so he expects we should worship him with both according to their several capacities. And consequently that there are two sorts of acts wherein godliness in general consisteth: the one external, performed by the body with the soul, the other internal, performed by the soul without the body."[78]

The necessity of external worship [is] well proved by the words the Holy Ghost always uses in scripture to express God's worship by. The words are three,[79] the one signifying the bending of the knees, the other bowing the head, and the last the prostration of ourselves on the ground with our hands spread out before him. From whence he[80] argues very well that "it would be very strange if God should use no other words to express his worship by than what denotes the reverential postures of our bodies," if he did not require any bodily worship of us. And he further affirms that those that have entertained such a "blind and groundless conceit[81] never understood the [. . .] meaning [. . .] of the Second Commandment, wherein God expressly enjoins us not to bow or fall down before any image or idol, which certainly he would never have done had not that been an essential part of his own worship."[82] External worship, though necessary, yet [is] not sufficient without the internal worship or acts of the mind from whence these outward performances of the body do, or ought to, proceed.[83] What these are we come now to consider.

[95. Beveridge on holy living: duty to God—internal worship (a "due sense of God upon the heart.")]

(Noon)

"First, to our being or living godly it is indispensably necessary that the mind be possessed with a due sense of God, with right and, if possible, clear conceptions of him; so as not to be only able to discourse of his being the Creator, Governor, Preserver, Possessor and Disposer of all things in heaven and earth," for talking of him is easy, although we have not a due sense of him in the heart. "And though it be necessary that we have such a knowledge of him, [. . .] yet the bare theory or speculation of what he is, and what he hath, and still doth in the world cannot be reckoned among the acts of true godliness, because not only ungodly men, but even the devils themselves, go so far, and yet remain ungodly and devils still. But that knowledge of God which is the first act of godliness and that whereupon all the rest are grounded, although it presupposeth right notions and conceptions of the divine perfections, yet it consisteth principally in a due sense of God upon the heart; what that is I must confess myself unable to express so as that anyone should apprehend it, but they that have it. But only in general we may call it an experimental knowledge whereby a man hath the sense or experience of those perfections upon his own heart, which he knows and believes to be in God, whereby his thoughts and conceptions are so strangely enlarged,[84] that he seems to apprehend him that is altogether incomprehensible, so that he is no longer able to endure himself, but is forced to cry out with Job in the same case, 'By reason of God's highness I cannot endure.' Job 31:23.[85] This is that knowledge of God which the scripture so often enjoins whereby a man sensibly apprehends and contemplates the great God as the first of all beings, the cause of all causes, the chiefest of all goods, the source of all happiness, and the centre of all perfections, as one whose nature is so pure, whose glory is so transcendent, whose wisdom is so incomprehensible, whose power is boundless, and all whose perfections are so high, so glorious, so infinite and eternal that our highest apprehensions of him are still infinitely below him."[86]

[96. Beveridge on holy living: other acts of godliness. Susanna's "thoughts upon the whole."]

Noon

2. Another act of godliness[87] is "to love the Lord our God with all our hearts, souls, etc."[88]

3. To desire him.

4. To rejoice in him. To make him the only object of our joy and felicity.

5. To fear him. To fear "nothing [. . .] so much as his anger and displeasure." "Sanctify the Lord of hosts," saith the prophet Isaiah, "and let him be your dread."[89]

6. To do all that he commands, because he hath commanded it.

7. Believing and trusting in him.[90]

Thus far this reverend prelate. What are your thoughts upon the whole?

A[nswer] 1. I am entirely of his opinion that a bare speculative knowledge of God is not sufficient to make a man godly. No doubt but the fallen angels that were upon creation placed so near the Almighty's throne have a more exact and accurate knowledge of the divine perfections than the most sublime wit of man in this state can possibly attain, and yet, as he observes, are ungodly and devils still. But I cannot altogether acquiesce in his definition of godliness neither,[91] for I take it to be something more than what he calls an experimental knowledge of God.[92]

[97. Continued critique of Beveridge: even devils and ungodly people have "experimental knowledge" of God.]

Even[ing]

For the same reason that he brings against a speculative knowledge, viz., because not only ungodly men, but even the very devils have an experimental knowledge of God's infinite perfections, though it is true the former very rarely adverts to it. This experimental knowledge is indeed common to all men, be they godly or ungodly. We all experience the power, wisdom, and goodness, etc. of God daily, his power in our existence, his wisdom in his providence, his goodness in all the blessings we enjoy, his justice and veracity in the punishment of our sins, etc., and though, as I said before, wicked men seldom think of these things, yet sometimes they can't avoid such thoughts, insomuch that when they hear one of God's ministers discourse upon righteousness, temperance, etc., duties which their own conscience tells them they live in the neglect of, they, as Felix, tremble at the thoughts of a judgment to come; nay perhaps they go further and, like Agrippa, are almost persuaded to become really Christians.[93]

No doubt but[94] godliness principally springs from a "due sense of God in the mind,"[95] but he does not so clearly explain what it is to have this sense of God, for he seems to make it terminate in sublime apprehensions of his perfections, in contemplating God as the First of beings, the Cause of all causes, the Center of all perfections, etc.,[96] whereas, with deference to the judgment of this great and good man, I do humbly conceive that any man who believes there is a God and that hath an ordinary share of common sense must necessarily so apprehend and think of him, whether he be godly or no.

[98. Continued critique of Beveridge: true godliness consists in "being like God."]

Morn[ing]

2.[97] Since you believe that neither experimental knowledge of God nor raised and sublime apprehensions of his perfections can be called true godliness, pray tell me what you think is true godliness and what is the meaning of having a due sense of God upon the mind?

A[nswer]: True godliness I think chiefly consisteth in being like God, in being renewed after the image of God in righteousness and true holiness, etc.[98] When the great work of regeneration is effectually begun in the soul and carried on by the

Holy Spirit, till the mind is restored to that image of God, that moral goodness in which it was first created, then may such a person be said to be truly godly: And in proportion to this divine resemblance, a man is more or less godly. 'Tis true there is a vast dissimilitude in the greatest likeness, even as great as there is between infinite and finite, all created good being not so much when in [the] presence of God, as one spark to the whole element of fire; but still the least[99] degree of good is as truly good as the greatest, as one drop of water is as truly and essentially water as the main ocean.

A soul thus renewed and sanctified loves as God loves, though not in the same measure, for indeed his love has no measure, but is immense and boundless as his essence; yet it loves for the same reason, it loves good as good, and knowing that God is supreme absolute Goodness, it loves God above all created good, and all other good as it bears a resemblance and relation to his eternal goodness, being indeed an emanation from the deity.[100] It rejoiceth with a "joy unspeakable and full of glory"[101] in the infinite perfection of his essential blessedness and glory; and though it feels itself awed and sometimes almost overwhelmed with a sense of the perfect rectitude and majesty of the divine nature, yet 'tis exceedingly delighted with the thoughts of God's being what he is! That he is perfection of being in the abstract and that it is impossible he should suffer any diminution in his essential glory!

[99. Further responses to Beveridge: the godly mind rejoices in God and in God's creation.]

Noon

And as a mind thus truly godly rejoiceth in the contemplation of God, so conse-quently it adores and praiseth him for his essential perfections. It desires above all things to be more perfectly conformed to his will; indeed it has no will but that of God, nor does it ever know any great grief or sensible affliction but when, through weakness, surprise or inadvertence, it deviates from the rule of God's commands and thereby stains that obedience which it would fain offer up to God, an uncor-rupted sacrifice without spot or blemish.

It rejoiceth over all the works of creation and adores in each individual part the infinite power, wisdom, goodness, etc. of the great Creator. Nor can it look upon the meanest herb or most inconsiderable insect without a secret veneration for the power and wisdom that formed it.

[100. Further reflections on Beveridge: extensive description of a godly soul.]

Even[ing]

And it often admires how any reasonable being can content itself with a transient view of the works of God and does not rather penetrate the superficies[102] of things, and adore the divine perfections which are impressed on all the works of creation in such plain and indelible characters that 'tis matter of astonishment that any man can avoid adverting to them, if he would. But though others can slight or disregard these visible effects of omnipotent Wisdom and Goodness, a godly soul cannot so pass them over, but finds and adores God in all the parts of his creation. It casts its eye upon nothing but what affords matter of praise. It sees him in the vast expanse of the heavens, in the beauty, usefulness and harmony of the heavenly bodies. It reads his wisdom and goodness in their position, motions and benign influences on the earth and the children of men. It finds him in all the powers and faculties wherewith it is endowed: in the structure and harmony and usefulness of each part of the body and in the strange mysterious union of itself (which it knows to be a spiritual substance) with a material organized body.

It esteems things truly as they are, makes a right estimation of the worth and value of all things. It regards the body as it is the work of God, and since it hath pleased almighty Wisdom to determine its abode in it during his pleasure, it thinks itself obliged in duty to do its best to keep it in tenantable repair, but it makes no "provision for the flesh to fulfill the lusts thereof." [103] It is neither fond or weary of residing in it, nor does it make any account of its extraction, whether it is noble or base, be that as pleases God. It knows 'tis originally dust and must in a little time be resolved into dust again. [104] But it values itself greatly upon its divine original and upon account of the invaluable price that was paid for its redemption, and rejoiceth more that it can call God Father by creation and adoption, than if its other part were allied to the greatest monarch upon earth.

Such a soul contemns all the pomp and grandeur of the world as sordid and unsatisfactory trifles, below the dignity of its nature and therefore unworthy its pursuit or enjoyment. It is full of humility and hath a very tender sense of its own imperfections and unworthiness and yet at the same time hath the most unbounded ambition, insomuch that nothing less can satisfy its large and comprehensive faculties than the favour of that God that made it, and accordingly it makes it its chief business to obtain his favour by all acts of faith and obedience. It presses after the nearest union and communion with God that it is capable of and vigorously aspires to a divine resemblance, to be like him in all his communicable attributes, his truth, his goodness, mercy, justice, universal charity, etc. and even longs to partake somewhat of his immutability. It is weary of changing, would be always the same, would act consistently, religiously, rationally at all times under all circumstances and therefore endeavours to keep its eye constantly upon the revealed will of God, making that the rule of all its actions. [105]

Notes

1. *An Essay concerning Human Understanding*, ed. Peter H. Nidditch (Oxford: Clarendon Press, 1975), 2.21.41 (p. 258); nearly exact quotation; my quotation marks. Locke's initial sentence, which S. W. paraphrases, is "If it be farther asked, what 'tis moves desire? I answer happiness and that alone." The scriptural quotation is 1 Corinthians 2:9, slightly altered; my quotation marks. The remaining thoughts are not from this section of Locke and are probably her own theological gloss on his passage.

2. Paraphrase of Matthew 5:16.

3. Matthew 6:1–6.

4. Psalm 115:1; close paraphrase and/or conflation of AV and BCP version; my quotation marks.

5. Psalm 27:8; my quotation marks.

6. Close paraphrase of Matthew 7:7 and Luke 11:9; my quotation marks.

7. Succeed, prosper.

8. Replaces the crossed-out "favour."

9. New page beings here with two lines of unconnected copy, crossed out: " 'Tis wonderful to observe the stupidity and blindness of an unregenerate mind".

10. My quotation marks; cf. Malachi 1:13.

11. My quotation marks; paraphrased from Job 21:15.

12. Rare form of "examination."

13. This will have been between 24 May 1711 (the last dated entry, which coincidentally also deals with her educational project, entry 52) and "Jacky's" departure for Charterhouse School in 1714. The next dated entry is 17 October 1715.

14. The "two for Sunday" are the older daughters, Emily (Emilia) and Suky (Susanna), born 1693 and 1695, respectively. The names are supplied in the equivalent passage in a letter to her husband, Samuel, February 6, 1712, a good clue to the dating of this entry. The Wesleys' first child, Samuel, was well out of the nest by this time, and their final child, Kezia, born (?)1709, would have been too young for this scheme.

15. If Clarke is right in saying she began this practice in 1700 (p. 257), this entry might still be dated 1709.

16. See her vow on strong drink, entry 29, some time in April or May 1711.

17. End of page. The next page is cut out of the book, but the meditation continues without a break on the following MS page.

18. Despite.

19. Crossed out here: "from him and from others."

20. Crossed out here: "prudently."

21. Close paraphrase of 1 Corinthians 10:31; my quotation marks.

22. Several lines are left blank before the beginning of the next meditation; a horizontal line separates the following entry. The dash is in the MS.

23. Curiously, this meditation seems to take up where a previous one (61) broke off nearly 30 MS pages earlier, though the last two words of 61 are repeated here. Ellipses added.

24. A line under the final three words may emphasize their content; more likely it simply separates this continuation of an earlier entry (see note 22) from the regular series it has interrupted. The fact that this meditation is framed by a line at the top, separating it from the previous one, also supports this suspicion.

25. Resonances of the Collect for the eighteenth Sunday after Trinity and the renunciation of the devil by godparents in the baptism, BCP.

26. End of page; the following page is torn out, perhaps with some meditations missing. The next page begins with a new entry at the top.

27. John 15:5; my quotation marks.

28. "Know Thyself," inscribed at the Delphic Oracle and popularized in Plutarch's *Morals*.

29. Horizontal line drawn between heading and meditation.

30. Does she mean "than the thing *which is to be* explained"?

31. The MS says "than."

32. *Pascal's Pensées*, Basil Kennett, trans. (London: A. and J. Churchil, R. Snare, J. Tonson, 1704), chap. 18, par. 1, pp. 150–151; my quotation marks. The original reads: "So that intending no less to reveal Himself to those who sought him with their whole Heart, than to hide Himself from those who were alike industrious to fly and avoid Him, He has so temper'd the Knowledge of Himself, as to exhibit Bright and Visible Indications to those who seek Him, and to turn the Pillar of a Cloud towards those who seek Him not."

33. Not a direct quote but perhaps a half-remembered amalgam of Psalm 103:19, 145:13; Daniel 4:34, 7:14.

34. Question mark added.

35. Created, fashioned.

36. Asserted title to.

37. In passing, an assertion of the divine right of kings.

38. Closing parenthesis supplied.

39. In MS: "Esay 46:9." The quotation is actually extracted from verses 9 and 10. My quotation marks.

40. Slightly excerpted; my quotation marks.

41. The orignal phrase, which she subsequently crossed out, is "an unalienable foundation."

42. A possible resonance from the Westminster catechism.

43. Originally, "essential glory," but the adjective has been crossed out.

44. S. W.'s question mark.

45. Three or four lines at the bottom of the page are left blank.

46. In MS: "receit."

47. S. W. seems to be following the Westminster Assembly's Shorter Catechism, Q. 23–24, and the Larger Catechism, Q.42–43.

48. Cf. *The Westminster Shorter Catechism, 1648* in Thomas F. Torrence, ed., *The School of Faith* . . . (London: J. Clarke, 1959), answer to Q. 24: "Christ executes the office of a Prophet, in revealing to us, by His Word and Spirit, the will of God for our Salvation."

49. Mark 1:15; my quotation marks.

50. S. W. sets this definition as if it were a quotation; thus I have added quotation marks. However, it does not seem to match either the *Shorter Catechism*, Q. 87, nor *The Westminster Larger Catechism*, Q. 76.

51. Close paraphrase; my quotation marks, her citation.

52. A Lockean idea, but I do not find the metaphor in the *Essay.*

53. The Newtonian analogy illustrates the attempt of rationalist theology to incorporate current scientific theories.

54. 1 John 1:5; my quotation marks.

55. Followed by the crossed-out "and ideas."

56. Immediately before this sentence is the crossed-out "And as we thus esteem." The entry breaks off here; a new paragraph, albeit following the same line of thought, begins after two or three blank lines. Ellipses added.

57. Condition of being dissatisfied or displeased.

58. Paraphrase of Job 9:4; my quotation marks.

59. The last one-third of this page and the next entire page, overleaf, are left blank.

60. The MS citation: "Tit. 2.11.12..13.4." Actually quoted are only verses 11–12; my quotation marks. Verse 12 comes more quickly to an Anglican mind because of its inclusion in the General Confession, morning and evening prayer, BCP: "that we may hereafter live a godly, righteous and sober life, To the glory of thy holy Name."

61. William Beveridge (1637–1708) had High Church, Nonjuring sympathies but was Calvinist in theology; he held the see of St. Asaph and St. David from 1704 until his death. Susanna is reading and responding to two sermons with the same title and text, "Holiness the Great Design of the Gospel Dispensation" (Sermons 90 and 91), *The Theological Works of William Beveridge* . . . , 12 vols. (Oxford: John Henry Parker, 1844), 4:225–263. A third and a fourth sermon with identical titles, but with texts from verses 13 and 14, respectively, of Titus 2 follow.

62. Close paraphrase, changing the final pronoun from "us" (ibid., p. 228); my quotation marks.

63. Summarizing ibid., p. 233. But note that Beveridge balances this point with the re-

minder, ". . . our Salvation here is wholly attributed to the grace of God, yet so as not to exclude either Christ's satisfaction for us, or our duty and obedience to God" (p. 229).

64. Here S. W. begins quoting and/or closely paraphrasing Beveridge's points, starting on p. 246 (ibid.). Quotation marks have been added whenever she uses Beveridge's words, and bracketed ellipses indicate where she has omitted them.

65. I have inserted the quotation marks indicating Beveridge's (ibid.) exact use of the Luke passage.

66. A brief summary, rather than a quotation. Beveridge (ibid., p. 248) urges his hearers "to keep all our passions within their proper bounds . . . for excessive love or hatred, joy or grief, or any other passion whatsoever, if it be once excessive, will as certainly disturb our reason and pervert our judgment, as excessive drinking can ever do."

67. Ibid., p. 249; close quotation except where syntax is modified to excerpt wordy phrases.

68. The MS mistakenly repeats "4."

69. Close quotation. Beveridge, *Theological Works*, may have in mind, literally and figuratively, the "French Prophets" who came to London at the turn of the eighteenth century, but he might also intend the excesses of commonwealth religion, still fresh in collective memory.

70. Ibid., p. 251.

71. Ibid., p. 252.

72. Ibid., pp. 252–253, substituting "you" for "ye," as does Beveridge; my quotation marks.

73. S. W.'s parentheses.

74. S. W.'s heading for the final point Beveridge, *Theological Works*, makes.

75. Beveridge (ibid.) inserts the Greek: *eusebeia* or *theosebeia*.

76. Though Beveridge is defining worship in broad terms, Anglican preoccupation with liturgy is also visible here.

77. Nearly exact quotation (ibid., pp. 254–255); my quotation marks.

78. Fairly close quotation (ibid., p. 255); my quotation marks.

79. Beveridge (ibid.) inserts Hebrew here.

80. Ibid. S. W. is summarizing at this point before lapsing back into direct quotation.

81. Puritans of various sorts who suspected bodily gestures (such as genuflection and the sign of the cross) as Romish and idolatrous.

82. Exact quotation interspersed amid the summary. Beveridge, *Theological Works*, p. 255, seems to be saying that it is the object of worship that makes it idolatrous, not the fact that it is done "bodily."

83. Ibid., p. 257.

84. Cf. John Wesley's account of his conversion nearly 30 years later. Describing his own religious experience, he wrote, "my heart was strangely warmed," words that became the touchstone of denominational identity but which may have had (in some indirect sense) their origin in his mother's appreciation of Bishop Beveridge. At least it is a reminder that "strangely warmed" (or "enlarged") hearts were possible in the Church of England before the evangelical revival. See Wesley's *Journal*, 24 May 1738.

85. Close paraphrase of Beveridge, *Theological Works*; quotation marks added.

86. Nearly exact quotation (ibid., p. 258).

87. The first act of godliness is the true knowledge of God, the "due sense of God upon the heart," described in the previous entry.

88. Matthew 22:37; my quotation marks. Beveridge, *Theological Works*, p. 259.

89. Isaiah (MS: "Esay") 8:13, slightly excerpted; my quotation marks. The previous sentence echoes Deuteronomy 9:19.

90. S. W.'s quick summary of Beveridge, *Theological Works*, pp. 259–261.

91. Older usage, strengthening the preceding negative "cannot."

92. Line blotted out here, indecipherable apart from the barely legible repetition "there is something more."

93. Paraphrased from Acts 24:25 and 26:28. Cf. John Wesley's sermon "The Almost Christian," preached on the latter verse at Oxford in 1741.

94. The first phrase was originally "He says well that," but S. W. crossed it out and began again.

95. Beveridge's (*Theological Works*) phrase, though S. W. has substituted "mind" for the original's "heart"; see entry 96. My quotation marks.

96. See entry 95.

97. That is, a second point to be made regarding Beveridge's ideas (*Theological Works*). The first is at the final paragraph of entry 96.

98. Cf. Colossians 3:10 and Ephesians 4:24, which seem to be conflated here.

99. In MS: "lest."

100. Platonic rhetoric.

101. 1 Peter 1:8; quotation marks added.

102. The outward appearance.

103. Romans 13:14; quotation marks added.

104. Paraphrase of Genesis 3:19.

105. Ten pages are torn from the notebook at this point; there is evidence of entries on the stubs of paper remaining in the binding.

NINETEEN

"But What Do You Think?"

Susanna Wesley organized much of this chapter in question-and-answer format, not uncommon among authors of her day and certainly a convenient way to arrange an internal conversation. However, as in the first two of three entries on fasting (127 and 128), the device also pushes her to explore her own mind and to justify her position in debate with competing ones. "What do you think of fasting?" and "Why do you think it is not a moral virtue?" are questions that, whatever answers they produce, affirm her thought process and its results.

Another notable series of meditations are those (106–111) that deal with the family's very real financial problems and the attendant spiritual anguish. What do you do when you have entrusted yourself to Providence and still the money (to be spent on "necessaries," not superfluities) fails to appear? Her subsequent reflections on idolatry, covetousness, and "want of subjection" to God's will may impress us as a bit harsh on herself, but they show her working out her "practical divinity" just at that point where experience calls theory into question.

A similar case might be made for her entries on the vow she has taken in imitation of the patriarch Jacob (119–122). We might consider her response to the "perplexity of adverse fortune" naive (saying, in effect, 'I'll give you worship, if you give my family food and clothing without anxiety or the necessity of borrowing'); her critique of idolatrous Christians who have broken their baptismal vows may be overdrawn; but these, too, are the ponderings of a woman who takes life and faith seriously.

Quite a few brief entries crowd this section, and the topics she chooses reflect the usual random pattern, although several deserve attention. The intense concern expressed previously for the inviolability of her own devotional practice also applies in entry 103 to the routine she has established for her children. Bishop Beveridge is again engaged, this time on the conditional nature of God's promises to humanity (114). She affirms the Anglican definition of the church as contained in the Nineteenth Article of Religion (118). And she again displays the concern of a reasonable Christian when she enjoins herself in meditation 117 to "order your passions well."

Apart from the references to the children's education and the family's pinched circumstances, already mentioned, the meditations reveal very little about the home context in which she is writing. The only dated entry in this section is 119 (17 October 1715)—only 67 entries on from the last recorded date, 24 May 1711 (52).

[101. The "why" and "how" of private and family devotions more important than the "what."]

Even[ing]

Judge not of your spiritual state by the multitude of external performances. Neither conclude because you are constant in private and family devotions that therefore you do certainly love God above all things and are in a state of grace.

'Tis the manner more than the matter of such performances that is chiefly to be regarded, and the principles they flow from is more to be observed than the manner of doing them. If you pray often because you love much and delight in discoursing of God and singing his praises with your family because you would fain engage their hearts in his service and, being sensible of your own insufficiency and defects in praising God, are desirous to endeavour to make up in number what is wanting in weight, and since you cannot "praise him according to his excellent greatness," [1] you desire . . . [2]

[102. Three rules for spiritual examination: giving due credit to the triune God.]

(Noon) [3]

Be careful in examination to avoid three things. First, do not arrogate to yourself the praise of any good thought, word, or action, as if they proceeded from or were the effects of your own strength or power, but give God the glory of his grace.

Secondly,[4] neglect not to praise him for any, though the least, influences of his Holy Spirit.

Thirdly,[5] be sure you never forget Jesus Christ, but always acknowledge that you receive any influences of the Spirit or any other blessing, either spiritual or temporal, only for his sake and upon his account.

[103. Family order and devotion: keep the children reading, working, singing psalms.]

Even[ing]

It was your peremptory[6] resolution to observe the rules prescribed to you;[7] that by God's blessing was the cause of your family and children's being first reduced into order. It must be your peremptory adherence to the aforesaid rules which must maintain the order established in your family, and if you will suffer company or any business or little accident to put by or divert the reading of your children, their working, or singing psalms at appointed times, you will find such impediments multiplied upon you, till at last all order and devotion will be lost.

[104. The divine presence—everywhere or in particular locations?]

Morn[ing]

God cannot be properly said to be present more in one place than another. He fills heaven and earth and all the imaginary spaces beyond this universal system of beings.

Q[uery:] Why then is it so often said that God dwelleth in the heavens, that he sitteth in heaven, etc.?

A[nswer:] This is not to be understood of his essential presence, which cannot possibly be circumscribed or determined to one place more than another, but all such expressions I humbly conceive signify the manifestations that he is pleased to make of his glory to those blessed spirits that inhabit those happy regions of light and love. Besides, we must consider that the human nature of the Son of God must be in some place, as all other bodies are, and in that human nature dwells the fulness of the Godhead therefore.

[105. The importance of thanking God for daily mercies: divine assistance in devotions; ability to teach children and perform domestic duties; family's health.]

Noon

"Praise God, my Soul, and all that is within me bless his holy Name!"[8]

Thankfully recognize the mercies of this day hitherto. The assistance of his Holy Spirit in family devotions, the disposition and ability to speak of him, to instruct the children, to perform all domestic duties, the health and preservation of yourself and family from all ill accidents, terrors and dangers. Surely the tribute of our praise is an indispensable and pleasing duty. Heartily thank the omnipotent Goodness that he hath preserved you from all presumptuous sins and trust in and rely on Jesus Christ for the supply of your deficiencies and firmly believe that, as almighty God imputed Adam's sin to all his posterity, so he will, upon account of the perfect obedience his only Son paid to the divine laws in our nature, accept of our sincere, though otherwise imperfect, obedience. Glory be to thee, O Lord!

[106. Managing shaky family finances; finding "mercy in disappointment."]

Even[ing]

You had long hoped and expected by your care, frugality and industry to have provided amply for the ensuing summer;[9] and thought that such a sum which you believed you should receive upon account[10] would infallibly prevent the pressures you lay under last year. Upon review of incomes and exits you find yourself greatly disappointed and that all your prospect of ease and plenty was but a dream, and after all you are like to be involved in greater difficulties than your boasted prudence could foresee. This hath somewhat discomposed your mind and hath disposed it to that anxiety about the things of this world that in obedience to the command of Jesus Christ you have resolvedly avoided for some time. What are your thoughts upon this occasion?

I think myself highly obliged to adore and praise the unsearchable wisdom and boundless goodness of almighty God for this dispensation of his providence towards me. For I clearly discern there is more of mercy in this disappointment of my hopes than there would have been in permitting me to enjoy all that I had desired, because it hath given me a sight and sense of some sins which before I could not have imagined I was in the least inclined to, viz., of idolatry and covetousness and want of practical subjection to the will of God.

Q[uery:] How were you guilty of idolatry in these expectations?

[107. One lesson of diminished expectations: recognition of her idolatry.]

Morn[ing]

A[nswer:] Whatever we trust in or rely upon for our happiness, ease or safety, that thing we make our god. I greatly apprehended want and uneasiness of mind and was exceedingly averse from being reduced to the necessities I had been under the preceding year and thought by my own care and industry to have prevented the like this summer and, having saved what I could, thought I was secure from future want and therefore depended on, and put my trust in, what was so deposited in the hands of ————,[11] which was an act of direct idolatry, for, as was said before, to make any person or thing in the world the object of our trust or dependence to deliver us from any incumbent or impending trouble[12] or danger is to make that thing or person our god.

Q[uery:][13] There was indeed some degree of idolatry in trusting and depending on the creature, and it was a very great sin so to do. Nothing is more incident to corrupted nature than when we either actually enjoy or have, as we imagine, a certain prospect of possessing the riches of this world, for the mind in such a case to rest itself upon the creature and to depend on such riches for preservation from want, contempt, etc., which all men naturally would avoid. And perhaps that is the reason why our blessed Lord said it was so hard for a rich man to enter into the kingdom of God.[14] So hard for him either to comply with or obey the precepts of the gospel or for him to disengage his affections from all sensuality, covetousness and vainglory without which he can never enter in the kingdom of heaven.

[108. A second lesson: recognition of her covetousness, broadly defined.]

Noon

But since you seem to me to have desired no more than a competency of the things of this world, no more but only what was sufficient to preserve you from want and debt, which surely all may lawfully desire (nay, we ought to pray for such a sufficiency),[15] how were you guilty of covetousness in those desires?

A[nswer:] Though we usually restrain covetousness to either unlawfully desiring to intrench[16] upon the property of our neighbour or to a desire of possessing more of wealth than is needful or useful for us, yet I think we may be in some degree guilty of that sin when our desires of necessaries or conveniences are attended with anxiety and uneasiness of mind.

[109. A third lesson: "want of subjection to the will of God."]

Even[ing]

When the thoughts are too much upon the things of this world, and we are too inquisitive after "what we shall eat and what we shall drink and wherewithal we shall be clothed . . . for, since our heavenly Father knoweth that we have need of these things,"[17] and his omnipotent mercy can never want expedients to relieve our wants and supply all our necessities, we ought to acquiesce in all the dispositions of his providence, to do our duty and leave all events and successes to God, who will never forsake us while we continue in his faith and fear, and desire no more of the things of this life than he sees necessary for our spiritual and eternal good.

Q[uery:] Though from what hath been said 'tis easy to collect[18] that you were guilty of some degree of covetousness and idolatry, yet it still remains that you explain how you were deficient in practical subjection to the will of God.

A[nswer:] 'Tis a certain truth that wherever there is anxiety and misgivings or unquietness of mind about the things of this world there is not that practical subjection to the will of God nor that firm trust and dependence upon him that there ought to be. Perfect submission and trust casts out fear and anxiety as well as perfect love.[19]

[110. The poor in spirit are indifferent to the "good things of this life."]

Morn[ing]

Such as are of a humble and lowly mind or, as our Saviour expresses it, are "poor in spirit"[20] can never either passionately desire the riches and honours of this world, nor can they ever value themselves upon them if enjoyed or be much troubled if they are without them. They know that their spiritual and eternal good does not depend on or consist in a multitude of riches, and, as their treasure is not in this world,[21] so they set not their hearts upon it, they alone have learnt the art of being without the good things of this life, as they are called, without wanting them, or if they have them, they always use them with great indifference, as if they used them not.

[111. Continued reflection on poverty of spirit and the things of this world.]

Noon

Poverty of spirit being the first of the beatitudes[22] and the ground and basis of all solid virtue, it highly concerns you to use your utmost endeavours to acquire this blessed temper of mind without which you are uncapable of either the kingdom of grace or glory. Poverty of spirit does undoubtedly exclude all immoderate affection towards the things of this world, so you must in the first place examine yourself whether you love riches or honour, etc. so much as to be the least uneasy without them. Whether you desire them so much as to use any unlawful means to procure them or to be anxious or disquiet if God blesses not your lawful endeavours to obtain them. This is the lowest degree of poverty of spirit, but the more sublime (and yet not impracticable) height of that virtue teaches you utterly to contemn all riches, honours, etc., insomuch that you had rather be without than have them.

[112. A fragment on temptation.]

Even[ing]

Temptation exercises the man and tries the Christian. 'Tis impossible (I think) to know the heart perfectly; we make but weak judgments often of the present and can determine nothing of the future. If upon . . .[23]

[113. Faith, purity, obedience.]

Faith is said to purify the heart[24]—such a faith as makes us obey the precepts of the Gospel must of consequence purify the heart from all filthiness of flesh and spirit— Obedience is purity. 1 St. Peter 1:22.[25]

[114. Comment on Beveridge and God's conditional promises.]

Noon

Bishop Beveridge says we must be very careful to distinguish between the promises of G[od] that are made of godliness and those to godliness. The first, he says, are absolute, the other all conditional.

Q[uery:] What does he mean by absolute promises?

[Answer:] The promises of godliness are the promises of the New Covenant, as that he will put his law in our hearts and write it in our inward parts.[26] That he will give us a new heart and put a new spirit within us.[27] That he will pour out his own Spirit upon us[28] and cause us to walk in his statutes and to keep his judgments,[29] in short, that he will give us grace to repent and turn to him. These he calls absolute promises. But with submission to the judgment of this good man, I think that faith (as he himself otherwhere acknowledges)[30] being indispensably required for the performance of these as well as those he calls the promises to the Gospel, shows that these also are conditional.[31]

[115. Critique of two conversations with parishioners; resolution never to "enter into friendship with the ungodly."]

Even[ing]

A little too warm in the vindication of H,[32] though 'tis a right hand error to incline too much to favour the poor; yet we should always be careful to speak the words of truth and sobriety. It was not so prudent to speak so freely of B[33] to a person that is likely to report the matter to him, since you have been obliged to the family; but however, you did well in pleading the cause of God and arguing against holding any familiarity with such as give evident proof in the course of their conversation that they are altogether strangers to the life of faith. Be faithful to God's grace, never enter into friendship with the ungodly. "Do not I hate," says David, "them that hate

God? Yea, I hate them right sore, as if they were my enemies."[34] Remember what the prophet said to Jehoshophat: "Shouldst thou indeed help the ungodly or love them that hate the Lord? Therefore is wrath upon thee from the Lord."[35]

[116. Moral liberty—by the grace of God.]

Morn[ing]

Q[uery:] Whether or no the perfection of man's nature does not in a great measure depend on his moral liberty?

—What is moral liberty?

—Rectitude of mind. When the mind is as it should be, as God created it, free from all error and sin. Habits of sin are the chains or fetters of the soul which deprive it of its native liberty and reduce it to a true state of captivity, which, while it is under it, hath no more power to act as it ought to do than a body bound with chains of iron can follow its usual labour. The Holy Spirit, which by the grace (or favour)[36] of God is given unto us, is the principal agent in breaking these chains and restoring the soul to liberty. And this he commonly does by illuminating the mind by means of which light it begins first to discern spiritual things, attains to some clearer perceptions of God, the excellence and purity of his nature, the evil of sin and the necessity of forsaking it in order to[37] its freedom and happiness.[38]

[117. Order your passions: love, hate, fear, hope, desire appropriate objects.]

Morn[ing]

Order your passions well. Love nothing but what is truly good. That is truly good, that is perfect in its own nature or kind. And that makes for the real good of yourself or neighbour. Hate nothing but what is truly evil and hurtful; nothing is in its own nature truly evil or mischievous but sin. Fear nothing but what is really evil, hope for nothing but what is truly desirable, and desire nothing but what is justly and fairly to be obtained; rejoice in nothing but what will some way or other make you better or your neighbour.

[118. S. W.'s (and the Church of England's) definition of church.]

Morn[ing]

What is your notion of a Christian church?

A[nswer:] The same with the Nineteenth Article of the Church of England.

"The visible Church of Christ is a congregation of faithful men, in the which the pure Word of God is preached, and the sacraments be duly ministered according to Christ's ordinance in all those things that of necessity are requisite to the same."[39]

[119. A vow: the necessaries of life in return for worship.]

Morn[ing], October 17, 1715, made for life

You did sometime since make this vow, that if God would in very deed give you food to eat and raiment to put on without exposing you to the temptation of anxious care or reducing you to the necessity of borrowing for the necessaries of life, that then the Lord should be your God. What did you mean or intend by this vow?

[120. A patriarchal model for her vow; idolatry in a Christian country.]

Noon

I had been many years under very heavy pressures, which by their continuance and increase grew almost intolerable, nor could I enjoy any ease or composure of mind till God's good Spirit put it into my heart peremptorily to resolve that, in obedience to Jesus Christ, I would never give way to any anxiety of mind about the things of this world, let what would happen. This resolution by God's assistance I kept for some time, nor have I since I made it ever been guilty of murmuring or repining at the good providence of God, but have still acknowledged his justice and mercy in afflictions. But still the perplexity of adverse fortunes lay often like a dead weight on the soul and often disposed to too much sadness. I read the stories of the patriarch Jacob, and, upon reflecting on the mean condition in which he was when he left his father's house, of which he afterward speaks when recognizing God's mercies ("For with my staff," says he, "I passed [over] this Jordan and now I am become two bands."),[40] I imputed his increase to the blessing of God to whom he had offered this vow when he went towards Haran: "If God will be with me, and will keep me in this way that I go, and will give me bread to eat, and raiment to put on, so that I come again to my father's house in peace; then shall the Lord be my God," etc.[41]

A thought then came into my mind: "What if I should imitate this patriarch and make a vow to God, that if God would in very deed, etc.?"[42]

But the case between him and you is vastly different. He went into a country where the people were all idolaters, and 'tis very probable that he would be strongly solicited and under great temptation to worship some of the idols of those people among whom he sojourned; but you live in a country of Christians that profess to acknowledge and worship none but the true God. Therefore there seems to be no liberty for your choice, but you must either worship the true God or none at all. What, therefore, did you intend by your choosing the Lord for your god, when the laws of your country, the custom of the place in which you live, and your own parents by educating you in the Christian religion have already determined your choice?

A[nswer:] The cases may not be so different as at first sight they appear to be. As once the great apostle truly said, "All are not Israel that are of Israel";[43] so all are not Christians or worshippers of the true God that profess themselves to be so. Whatever a man love most and acknowledges his supreme good and places his chief happiness in, that he makes his god. And therefore does our blessed Saviour explain the first command in the Decalogue. "Thou shalt have no other gods but me"[44]— "Thou shalt love the Lord thy God with all thy Heart, with all thy mind, etc."[45] And the apostle therefore calls the covetous man an idolater,[46] because he loves his money above all things else whatever. 'Tis true the blessed laws of the country in which I live do restrain the people from the external worshipping of idols, yet nevertheless I fear if we look abroad into what we call the Christian world we shall find a multitude of people that, notwithstanding all laws of God and man and the custom of the country and their education, are no better than mere idolaters in the sight of God. How many people idolize themselves, their wit, their learning, their strength, or beauty—the sensual and voluptuous man idolizes his carnal pleasures, the covetous his gold and the vainglorious his honour and reputation.

[121. Baptized Christians don't always keep their vows.]

Noon

Query:[47] But all who are baptized into the Christian church have renounced "the world, the flesh and the devil" in their baptismal covenant,[48] have promised to believe all the articles of the Christian faith and to "keep God's holy will and commandments all the days of their life."[49]

A[nswer:] True, all those who have been regularly initiated into the Christian church have either personally, or by their proxies, engaged themselves in the covenant you speak of. But it is not true that all who stand so engaged faithfully and conscientiously endeavour to acquit themselves of the obligations they lie under. As we may easily see, if we take a general view of Christians.[50] How many may we observe that, notwithstanding they have formally "renounced the devil and all his works,"[51] do yet indulge themselves in lying, deceit, fraud, malice, envy, revenge, murder, etc., all which are properly the works of the devil. How many do we see passionately enamoured of the pomps and vanities of this wicked world, and how great a majority are actually under the power of their sensual appetites.[52]

[122. More on Christians who publicly break their baptismal vows.]

Even[ing]

Nor do they content themselves with a private enjoyment of their unworthy desires, but, as if there was something brave and glorious in it, they openly enter the lists against omnipotence and publicly avow and defend their intemperance, unchaste desires, immoderate love of the world, etc., as if they bore the name of Christians for no other end but that they might be thereby enabled to dishonour their maker more effectually.[53]

[123. Don't dispute indifferent matters; keep your temper when debating important issues, especially "matters of religion."]

Morn[ing]

Be calm in arguing, for passion makes error a fault and truth discourtesy.[54]

Why should I feel another man's mistakes more than his sicknesses or poverty?

Decline all disputes as much as possible in all indifferent things; 'tis your wisdom to submit rather than violate your quiet, and in doubtful cases or truths of small importance, better keep silence than violate the bonds of peace and charity. But when the matter is of the highest importance, you must be careful not to lose your temper—especially in matters of religion. He that pleads for God, that will assume to himself the honour of speaking for Jesus Christ, must always do it in the spirit of Jesus Christ, with meekness and sweetness, lest by his intemperate zeal he reflect a dishonour upon his master Jesus and blemish that holy religion in the eyes of men which he labours to defend.

[124. Definition of saving faith.]

Even[ing]

What is saving Faith? Or how is a man saved by Faith?

A[nswer:] He that believes Jesus Christ is the Son of God[55] and that he hath actually by suffering death on the cross made a full compensation to the divine justice, etc. for the sins of mankind, so that now upon condition he repents, i.e., forsakes all his sins, he shall receive a full pardon, or, which is all one, have the punishment of his sins remitted unto him, and accordingly doth repent sincerely of all sin and relies on God's promise of forgiveness for Christ's sake, and that doth also depend on the merits and intercession of the Son of God for sufficient assistances from the Holy Spirit to perform sincere obedience to the laws of God; such a person's faith shall certainly save him.[56]

[125. Human praise and perturbation.]

Noon

'Tis a sign that we make no proficiency[57] in virtue if we are more desirous of the praise or esteem of man than of God.

We are still in the power of the world when anything in it can work us up to a perturbation.

[126. Righteous judgment a demanding exercise.]

Even[ing]

"Judge not according to appearance, but judge righteously," saith our Saviour.[58] 'Tis perhaps one of the nicest[59] things in the world to observe this precept in its true latitude. We hear the words or see the actions of men, but we are not always assured we understand the true sense of the speaker, nor do the springs or principles of action always appear. Some through design, some through inadvertence, others misled by a false modesty, and others by mere impotence of mind depart from or conceal their own judgment and in many instances act quite contrary to them.

[127. Performance of duty leads to happiness; case in point: fasting.]

Morn[ing]

There is nothing can be plainer than that all the duties God requires of man, as they tend directly to the glory of God, so[60] strict performance of them by natural consequence tends to the happiness of man. For moral evil is the proper disease and misery of the mind, and therefore whatever God hath enjoined us in order to purify the mind from sin, if it be conscientiously performed, must necessarily restore the soul to its proper happiness.

This is certainly true. But what do you think of fasting, which by the example of our Saviour and his apostles, the primitive Christians and custom of the church in all ages seems to be enjoined as a duty incumbent on all Christians?

A[nswer:] I think fasting a duty to many and of excellent use to all that can use it. But forasmuch as it is no moral virtue[61] and is as hurtful to some and unnecessary to others as it is profitable for the most, I think we must be determined in our practice in this case by the ends for which it was designed.

Q[uery:] What do you suppose is the true end of fasting?

A[nswer:] To keep under the body, to bring all the sensual appetites into a due subjection to the superior powers of the mind, is, I think, the principal end of fasting. There may be other excellent ends in this custom, such as the gaining time for spiritual exercises, prayer, humiliation for sin, deprecation of judgment, intercession for others, acts of faith, love charity, etc., and doing penance for former excesses, which last I look upon (if there were no other) as a good reason for frequent, total abstinence from whatever may gratify our sensual appetites.

[128. More on fasting: not a "virtue" but a (somewhat less binding) "command."]

Even[ing]

Q[uery:] Since these are all very good reasons for fasting, and such as seem (at least some or other of them) very useful, if not absolutely necessary for all men, why do you think it is not a moral virtue? Or to whom is it hurtful and in what cases unnecessary?

An[swer]:[62] I am so far from thinking it a moral virtue that, strictly speaking, I think it no virtue at all, but rather a way or means to acquire the virtues requisite for the perfection of Christian life.[63] All moral virtues which under the gospel[64] economy are Christian duties have an antecedent foundation in nature and equally respect and oblige all persons of all degrees at all times in all circumstances. But these are very few.

Positive commands[65] have a greater latitude, and among these I reckon fasting.

[129. More on fasting: those who are excused from this command.]

Even[ing]

These do not, I conceive, oblige those who cannot fast without injuring, i.e., all the sick, the weak and infirm, nurses or women with child, the aged, or those who through extreme penury are compelled to a constant abstinence, that seldom or never taste delicious food or rarely have the pleasure of a full meal of the coarsest fare.[66]

Notes

1. Psalm 150:2, both AV and BCP; my quotation marks.

2. The entry, already syntactically tangled, breaks off here, leaving the bottom quarter of the page blank; ellipses added.

3. S. W.'s parentheses.

4. In MS: "2condly."

5. In MS: "3ly."

6. Positively fixed, absolutely determined.

7. Semicolon inserted; no punctuation in MS. Her reference to rules might be Locke's (1693) *Some Thoughts concerning Education,* ed. John W. and Jean S. Yolton (Oxford: Clarendon Press, 1989). See her letter to John, 24 July 1732, in part III of this volume.

8. Psalm 103:1; close paraphrase of AV; my quotation marks.

9. According to the infrequent dating of entries, this one (MS p. 136) is somewhere between 24 May 1711 (MS p. 69), and 17 October 1715 (MS p. 147), though probably much closer to the latter.

10. Probably money owed the Wesleys from renting out parish land.

11. Name omitted; probably someone who owed the family rent but possibly her husband, Samuel, not known for his business acumen.

12. One notebook page is torn out between MS pp. 137 and 138, but the meditation is not interrupted.

13. The actual question is a bit long in coming. Along with its answer, it appears in entry 108.

14. Matthew 19:24 and parallels.

15. My parentheses.

16. To encroach, infringe, or trespass.

17. Paraphrased from Matthew 6:31–32; my quotation marks and ellipses.

18. Gather, deduce, conclude; rare usage.

19. Cf. 1 John 4:18. Knowledge of the verse from John helps restore the sense that her word order clouds. Her meaning would be clear had she written instead, "Perfect submission and trust—as well as perfect love—cast out fear and anxiety." Four lines worth of space at the bottom of the page are left blank after the entry's conclusion.

20. Matthew 5:3; quotation marks added.

21. Matthew 6:19–20.

22. Matthew 5:3.

23. The meditation breaks off at the bottom of the page; three to four lines of space are left at the top of the next page (the other side of the same sheet), followed by an unrelated entry. Ellipses added.

24. See Acts 15:9.

25. "Seeing ye have purified your souls in obeying the truth through the Spirit. . . ."

26. Jeremiah 31:33.

27. Ezekiel 18:31, 36:26,27. Cf. Psalm 51:10.

28. Acts 2:17–18; Joel 2:28.

29. Cf. Ezekiel 33:15.

30. Closing parenthesis added.

31. See William Beveridge, *The Theological Works of William Beveridge* . . . , 12 vols. (Oxford: John Henry Parker, 1844), Sermon 44 ("Christ the Foundation of All the Promises"), 2:326–341. The text is 2 Corinthians 1:20: "For all the promises of God in Him are Yea, and in Him Amen, unto the glory of God by us." If this is the sermon S. W. is reading (Beveridge does not use the terms "of godliness" and "to godliness" here, although he does make the distinction between absolute and conditional promises), she has not given it its due: "although this first grand promise (i.e. the promise of a Saviour) was absolutely made to all mankind, and was accordingly fulfilled, without any conditions required on their part; yet all the other promises grafted upon it, are made only to those who believe this" (pp. 332–333). He further speaks of "one general condition required in all [promises] . . . that whatsoever blessing He

hath promised, we must pray unto Him for it, otherwise we shall not have it" (pp. 338–339). In effect, S. W. is not contradicting Beveridge in her last sentence but agreeing with him.

32. Possibly a destitute parishioner.

33. Another parishioner?

34. Psalm 139:21–22, paraphrased, BCP; my quotation marks.

35. Nearly exact quotation of 2 Chronicles 19:2; my quotation marks. The occasion was Jehoshophat's alliance with Ahab, king of Israel.

36. Closing parenthesis added.

37. That is, for the purpose of.

38. Bottom two lines at the bottom of the page are left blank.

39. BCP, Articles of Religion, XIX; my quotation marks.

40. Genesis 32:10; my quotation marks and parentheses.

41. Genesis 28:20–22; my quotation marks.

42. Quotation marks and question mark added. See her vow in 119.

43. Romans 9:6; quotation marks added.

44. Exodus 20:3, Holy Communion, BCP; my quotation marks. Between this quotation and the succeeding one is the crossed-out "by telling them that the First Commandment is. . . ."

45. Matthew 22:37 and parallels, paraphrased; my quotation marks.

46. Colossians 3:5.

47. In MS: "B)." I believe S. W. intended a "Q" for Query (as in 114 and 116), but wrote "B," her mind already thinking ahead to the "But" that would begin her entry.

48. Publick Baptism of Infants, BCP, contains this idea, slightly expanded, but the actual phrase is from the Litany; my quotation marks.

49. Excerpted from the baptism, BCP; my quotation marks.

50. She originally wrote: "a general view of what we call the Christian," then crossed out "what we call the" and added an "s" to "Christian" before continuing.

51. Baptism, BCP; my quotation marks.

52. A final sentence is crossed out, perhaps sounding a bit harsh as she contemplated it: "And yet all these are called Christians by covenant."

53. The bottom two-thirds of the page is left blank at the end of this entry.

54. This has the sound of a proverb, but I have been unable to trace it.

55. See 1 John 5:5.

56. Meditation ends, leaving one-half page blank.

57. Immediately preceding and crossed out is "great (if any)."

58. Close paraphrase of John 7:24; my quotation marks.

59. Demanding utmost consideration and thought.

60. Immediately following are the crossed-out words, "they by natural."

61. Replaces the original, now crossed-out word, "duty."

62. S. W. began one reply, which she then crossed out: "All moral virtues must, I think, necessarily have an antecedent foundation in nature, and equally respect all persons of all degrees in all times, in all circumstances whatever."

63. That is, a "means of grace" rather than a result of grace.

64. Replaces the crossed-out "Christian."

65. Replaces the crossed-out "duties."

66. The entry ends at the bottom of the page. The following page (same sheet, overleaf) is totally blank.

❦ TWENTY ❦

"Bend the Whole Force of the Mind in a Serious Use of the Ways and Means of Religion"

*T*wo approaches dominate this chapter, the last set of entries in the first half of Susanna Wesley's earliest journal. One might be styled theoretical (though the term is relative since the practical is never far, even from her speculative theology) and involves her engagement with current religious thought, primarily that of Blaise Pascal. The other, clearly practical, emerges in ruminations on her struggles with temptation.

Susanna Wesley's fascination with Pascal was one she shared with numerous other Englishmen and Englishwomen. As is evident from meditations 131–135 and 138–139, she had access to Basil Kennett's 1704 translation of the *Pensées*, which she pondered and plundered for her journal.[1] See Blaise Pascal, *Thoughts on Religion, and Other Subjects* . . . (London: A. & J. Churchil, R. Sare, J. Tonson, 1704). In general she seems to have keyed into Pascal's sense of paradox, typified in his analysis of humanity as both most excellent and most miserable (see 131) and as midway between infinity and nothing (135). Other Pascalian ideas claim her attention, as well—for instance, the insufficiency of metaphysical proofs of God's existence for ordinary people (133); the usefulness of "the habit of believing" (134); the regulation of passions and amusements (139).

No other thinker receives such close and sustained attention in this section, but Locke is brought in (in support of Pascal, meditation 132), and another Frenchman, Malebranche (possibly read through the filter of John Norris), triggers some thoughts on "animal spirits," life after death (142–144), and God's infinite wisdom (147–150). An improving excerpt from Lewis Maimbourg, *The History of the Crusade* . . . , trans. John Nalson (London: Thomas Drink, 1685) (140) and a possible reference to theologian George Rust (155) round out Susanna's clearly detectable connections with current theological discussion.

Her own trials and temptations figure significantly alongside her appropriations of contemporary thinkers and fill most of the section from entry 151 to the end. These entries reveal little of the nature of her sins; even her own diary is not trusted with such specifics—thus the blanks that are not easy to fill in and the initials that are difficult to decipher. Nevertheless, she is speaking the language of personal experience (as filtered through her brand of Enlightenment–evangelical Christianity) when she analyzes the way temptations come through the senses (151), the psychology of gradually yielding to them (153–154), the means of turning away from them (156), and the mystery of God's affliction as a check against them (160 and 164).

Several other issues surface briefly here. The sacraments appear in the first entry (130). In the midst of "bodily pain" and "distress of fortune," not knowing which way to turn, she offers her whole being to Christ (145). Toward the end she advocates a balanced disposition, which would be distracted neither by intemperate joys nor griefs (162). In a similar entry, she recommends balanced thinking, avoiding the impairment brought on by both too much and too little study (163).

Only one of the entries in this chapter (158) carries a date, that of 28 November 1718. Near the end of the entries in MS A, it indicates a nine-year chronological run of meditations in this notebook.

❧

[130. Sacraments duly administered.]

Morn[ing][2]

What is meant by the sacraments being duly administered?[3] Does the word duly relate to time, matter, form or administration or persons to whom they are administered?

Answer: It relates to and may be applied to 'em all. I shall begin with the last. As the sacraments are two, so are the persons capable of receiving them, viz. infants and adult persons.[4]

[131. Thoughts from Pascal.]

Pas[cal]: *Thoughts* with O R U. Morn[ing][5]

"He who passeth days and nights in chagrin or despair for the loss of an employment or some imaginary blemish in his honour is the very same mortal who knows he must lose all by death and yet remains without resentment, disquiet or emotion."[6]

O: 'Tis absolutely necessary in order to know [or] understand our true happiness that we know what is our true nature—[7]

P: Religion teaches "to discern the greatness and meanness of [the] human condition with the cause and reason of both."[8]

O: Love of God and love of man, the foundation of all true religion—[9]

P: That religion that consists only in external appearances (heathen) is popular, but unfit for moving men of parts[10] and genius. "Should religion altogether reside in the spirit, it might be fit to work on men [of] parts, but could have no influence on the gross of mankind. Christianity, alone [is] proportioned to all capacities, being duly composed and tempered of the internal and external way. It raises the ignorant to spiritual acts and abases the intelligent by pressing the obligation to outward performances."—[11]

P: "No religion but the Christian has known man to be the most excellent of visible creatures and the same time most miserable."—[12]

P: "That religion which teaches us to believe the fall of man from a state of glory and communication with God to a state of sorrow, humiliation and estrangement from God, together with his restoration by a Messiah, hath always been in the world."—[13]

O: The gospel was first preached in paradise—[14] As in that blessed place human nature received its fatal wound and was thereby plunged into an abyss of misery, so in the same place was God first manifested to man under the character of a saviour, a healer and repairer of that misery.

Pas[cal:] "The belief of the Messiah has been derived by a constant series and uninterrupted course. The tradition from Adam was fresh and lively in Noah and even in Moses. After them the prophets bore testimony to him."—[15]

Pas[cal:] "Shall it be the religion of those philosophers who proposed no other good but what they would have us find in our own persons? Is this the true and sovereign good? Or have these men discovered the remedy of our evils? Was it a proper cure for man's presumption thus to equal him with God? On the other hand, have they succeeded better in restraining our concupiscence who would level us with beasts and propose the gratification of our sensual appetites for our real and universal happiness?"[16]

The Christian religion alone teaches us to correct our pride and our concupiscence.[17]

[132. Locke's observation supports Pascal on human inattention to an "eternal state of happiness."]

Even[ing]

'Tis incredible how much the things of this world retard our aspiring towards heaven. And did not daily experience prove the truth in fact, 'twould be impossible to conceive our lapse into the powers of externals so easy as we find it, since we all acknowledge and profess to believe that there is an eternal state of happiness or misery attends the issue of this short uncertain life. Nor does the sense of perfect endless blessedness affect us in any proportion to its greatness.[18]

Mr. Locke well observes that there are not many whose happiness reaches so far as to afford them a constant train of moderate mean pleasures without any mixture of uneasiness; and yet they could be content to stay here for ever, though they cannot deny but that it is possible there may be a state of eternal durable joys after this life, far surpassing all the good [that] is to be found here. Nay, they cannot but see that it is more possible than the attainment and continuation of that pittance of honour, riches or pleasure which they pursue and for which they neglect that eternal state. But yet in full view of this difference, satisfied of the possibility of a perfect, secure and lasting happiness in a future state and under a clear conviction that it is not to be had here whilst they bound their happiness within some little enjoyment or aim of this life and exclude the joys of heaven from making any necessary part of it, their desires are not moved by this greater apparent good, nor their wills determined to any action or endeavour for its attainment.[19]

[133. Human self-centeredness adversely affects even the wisest heathen philosophers in their advocacy of virtue.]

Noon

Pas[cal:] "The metaphysical proofs of God are so intricate and so far removed from the common reasonings of men that they strike with little force, or at best their impressions continue but little time."—[20]

O: 'Tis incident to all men, being indeed the original sin of human nature, to desire to be independent on[21] God, thereby making ourselves the centre of our own happiness, which makes us regardless of the divine succours, as if we needed them not. This was the error of the wisest among the heathen philosophers, and those of them that spake the most eloquently in behalf of virtue and argued most strenuously against sensual pleasures did, in effect, only endeavour to raise men from the condition of brutes to place them in that of the apostate angels—[22]

[134. Pride and concupiscence implied by Christ's call to self-denial; the usefulness of custom, "the habit of believing."]

Even[ing]

O: Our blessed Lord frequently declared when on earth that, unless we deny ourselves and take up the cross,[23] we cannot be his disciples. This injunction evidently proves that there is somewhat in us that contradicts the purity of his most holy religion and renders us uncapable of any union or communion with God. What this is a very little reflection on the natural state and temper of our minds will show us. That it is in truth our pride and concupiscence[24] that impedes our salvation and makes us at once contemptible and miserable.

Pas[cal:] "I confess we ought not to begin with this in the search of truth: yet we ought to have recourse to it (custom) when we have once discovered the truth to refresh and invigorate our belief, which decays every moment, for that the regular method and train of arguments should be always present to our minds the business of life will not permit. We ought to acquire a more easy principle, such as is the habit of believing."—[25]

[135. Pride and concupiscence; the Stoics and the inappropriateness of success as an action's justification; humanity's middling place in the universe.]

Even[ing]

Pride alienates us from God: concupiscence fastens us down to the earth—[26]

Pas[cal:] The Stoics "conclude that what has been done once may be done always, and because the desire of glory hath sometimes spurred on its votaries to great and worthy actions, all others may use it with like success. But these are the motions of fever and frenzy, which sound health and judgment can never imitate."—[27]

O: There are many projects so wild and some actions so incongruous to all the reasonable and sober part of mankind that no success can justify 'em. 'Tis sufficient for us if our intentions are good, our end such as is agreeable to our profession of Christianity, and the means we make use of the best that our scantling[28] of reason and prudence can suggest, and, if after all success crowns not our actions, we ought to rest satisfied as knowing that events belong to God, who disposes 'em as he pleaseth. Nor ought we rashly to censure or condemn our own or others' conduct or any particular action for want of that success which none but God can assure.

Pas[cal:] "The whole extent of visible things is but one line or stroke in the ample bosom of nature."—[29]

Pas[cal:] "What is man amongst the natures that encompass him?" (Meaning the heavenly bodies and that vast circle described by the sun o' the one hand and a mite in which he pretends to discover another world.) "In the one view he appears as unity to infinity, in another as all to nothing and must therefore be the medium between these extremes."—[30]

Pas[cal:] "His understanding holds the same rank in the order of beings as his body in the material system, and all the knowledge he can reach is only to discern somewhat of the middle of things, under an eternal despair of comprehending either the beginning or end."[31]

[136. Peace and unity more important than the triumph of your opinion.]

Noon

Be very cautious in giving your judgment on kingdoms or states, neither charge the failings of particular persons on communities or parties. If we have the good fortune to find and embrace truth and do by the good providence of God avoid those errors which others fall into and preserve the principles of religion and loyalty untainted in a general defection, give God the glory, and be not solicitous that others should be of your opinion. But above all things be sure to preserve charity inviolable. These are some truths which, though as truths they partake of one common excellence, yet notwithstanding are of so little importance to the salvation of mankind and our own in particular, that they ought not to be contended for, nor ever asserted at the expense of peace and charity. Let, therefore, the general bent of your mind and conversation tend to peace and unity, and let not the passion, prejudice, or peevishness of any make you ever forget the blessing pronounced by the Saviour of the world on peace-makers.[32]

[137. Causing another to sin.]

Even[ing]

"'Tis impossible," saith our Lord, "but offenses will come, but woe to that man by whom the offence cometh." Woe unto that man that doth by persuasion or example cause his brother to sin against God.[33]

[138. The misfortune stemming from the "roving and restless disposition" of people without faith.]

Morn[ing]

Pas[cal:] "I have often said that the universal cause of men's misfortunes abroad[34] was their not being able to live quietly in a chamber. A person who has enough for the uses of this world, did he know the art of dwelling with himself, would never quit that repose and security for a voyage or a siege; nor would take so much pains to hazard his life, had he no other aim than barely to live.

"But upon stricter examination I found this aversion from[35] home, this roving and restless disposition proceeded from a cause no less powerful than universal, from the native unhappiness of our frail and mortal state, which is uncapable of comfort, if we have nothing to divert our thoughts and to call us out of ourselves.

"I speak only of those who survey their own nature without the views of faith and religion. 'Tis indeed one of the miracles of Christianity that,[36] reconciling man to God, it restores him to his own good opinion, and[37] makes him able to bear the sight of himself; and in some cases renders solitude and silence more agreeable than all the intercourse and action of mankind. Nor is it by fixing man in his own person that it produceth these wonderful effects; 'tis by carrying him to God and by supporting him under the sense of his miseries with the hopes of an assured and complete deliverance in a better life."[38]

[139. Attaining faith by regulating passions and banishing amusements that possess you.]

Noon

Pas[cal:] "You say you are incapable of believing. Endeavour to understand your incapacity, and find out what it is that hinders your faith when reason invites you to it. Labour in your own conviction, not by increasing the proofs of a deity, but by regulating your passions. [. . .] Banish those amusements that have hitherto possessed you."—[39]

"I should soon bid adieu to these pleasures, say you, were I master of faith— And I say, on the other hand, that you would soon be master of faith had you once bidden adieu to pleasure."—[40]

[140. A story of faith from the Crusades.]

Even[ing]

A very memorable passage in Maimbourg's *History of the Crusades*. In the crusade under St. Louis[41] King of France, after the Saracens had entirely defeated the king's army and had killed the greater part and taken the rest prisoners, "an old Saracen, that by his habit and the great number of his attendants seemed to be one of prime quality among them, came into a pavilion where many of the Christian lords were kept and demanded of them by an interpreter whether they really believed that their God was made man and that he had suffered death for them upon the cross and that he was raised from the dead after three days. All the lords, who believed they should instantly be made martyrs upon their frank confession of Jesus Christ, answered with one voice without the least hesitation that this was their firm belief. 'If it be so, messieurs,' replied the wise Saracen, 'comfort yourselves in your affliction; you have not yet suffered death for your God as he hath done for you; and since he had the power to raise himself again, you ought also to believe that, having had so much kindness for you and having so much power, he will very speedily deliver you out of your captivity and misfortunes.' And thereupon, without saying any more, he instantly withdrew." [42]

[141. "I am nothing": A confession of sin and misery.]

Noon

Lord, I am nothing! I have nothing! I can do nothing!

I am nothing in a moral sense, having no power to walk conformably to your laws by reason of my pride and concupiscence.

I have nothing that I can properly call my own but sin and misery. No moral or intellectual goodness but what is given from above.

[142. Speculation on the soul separated from the body after death.]

Morn[ing]

'Tis a pleasing and, I hope, not sinful speculation to consider what shall be the state of souls separate from their bodies in the region of spirits, and, though the most we can apprehend in this case is but guess and conjecture, yet while we reject all thoughts contrary to the analogy of faith, [43] it may not be amiss sometimes for the soul to retire into itself and abstract its thoughts and affections from all material objects to contemplate its own nature and consider its existence in a state of separation from the body.

There are but two ways whereby the soul hath any ideas in this world, viz. sensation [44] and reflection. What sensation (if any) she will carry with her into separate[d] state 'tis impossible to determine. It should seem as if all sense should be destroyed when the organs of sense are by death resolved into their first principles; yet I cannot but believe that the soul will after death be determined to some vehicle, it seeming to me peculiar to the Deity to be perfectly undetermined by all corporeity. [45]

[143. "Animal spirits" as the continuing "vehicle of the soul."]

Noon

It seems probable that the vehicle of the soul in its state of separation from the body will either be formed of purest ether, or the animal spirits, [46] which were in its body in this life, will sustain the form of the body the soul informed here, and to that form the soul will be determined in the region of spirits as it was to the grosser body here.

[144. The spirit's recognizability after death.]

Even[ing]

And perhaps by that form each individual spirit will be distinguished and known to others as men are here by their colour, features, size, etc.

[145. Response to personal distress: offer "your whole being" to God.]

Morn[ing]

In great bodily pain, in much distress of fortune, under many contradictions in almost everything.

I know that God is power, wisdom and mercy, too! From which knowledge I infer that, if I were duly qualified for it, he would soon appoint some expedient for my relief, did he not foresee that 'tis better for the present I should be in the state I am.

What say I then, shall I pray for the continuance of these trials? Considering my impotence, that would be presumption. Shall I absolutely desire deliverance? By no means; the above mentioned reasons shows that unfit. What then? Renounce all choice and again offer up your whole being to him that is your way, your truth, your life.[47]

Saviour God, accept and bless—[48]

[146. Temptation: blame our own "irregular appetite," not Providence.]

Even[ing]

"Let no man say when he is tempted he is tempted of God"[49]—Let no man, when he is under the power of any mortal sin, endeavour to lay the blame on the providence of God, that may seem to lead him into temptation, or on our holy religion, as if it afforded not sufficient light or strength to preserve from or deliver out of a sinful state, for he does certainly deceive himself in so doing and does at once reflect dishonourably on God and himself when he strives to transfer his guilt upon him and would make the violence of his lusts pass for the unkindness of providence or the impotence of religion. Whereas the powers of hell and men could not hurt us, if we did not tamely[50] subject ourselves to them. 'Tis our own concupiscence betrays us, robs us of our liberty, and by giving way to the first motions thereof, we sink by insensible degrees into the powers of the "flesh, the world and the devil"[51] till we lose the very will to resist them; and then what wonder is it, if the divine succours are withdrawn and we are left to feel the weight of our natures, since we have unworthily preferred the satisfaction of an irregular appetite before the favour of God, [and] chose the paths of vice before those of virtue, and a present pleasure rather than eternal happiness in reversion.[52]

[147. God's infinite wisdom, a reflection in response to Malebranche.]

Morn[ing]

Male[branche,] Ques[tion:] [53]

Pray tell me if God's wisdom be infinite?

Answer: To question whether God's wisdom be infinite is in effect to question the infinity of his essence. For his wisdom is not a habit attained or superadded to his essence, but 'tis his very essence itself, as indeed are all his perfections. For God is one. And all those perfections that we attribute to him under various appellations is one and the same perfection in God, distinguished only by several operations on different subjects, all perfections being exerted in every act of the almighty mind. What is that we call wisdom in God but a power of directing, disposing and governing those creatures that he hath created or can create; for wisdom is a branch of intellectual power. And though we usually restrain our notion or sense of God's power to that part or act of it that is manifested in the creation of a thing, yet is the appointing, directing, ordering or fitting that thing to some end as properly an act of power as its simple production.

If it be permitted to distinguish or define the perfections of God, in whom all perfection is one pure simple act, I would choose to say that the power of God exerted in creation is the power of his will; and the wisdom by which he ordered and guided the operations of his will, directing it to work for the most worthy end by the best and most proper means, is the power of his understanding.

[148. More on infinite wisdom: creation *ex nihilo* implies omnipotence.]

Even[ing]

Before I give a direct answer to your question, I would have you weigh the following particulars.

1. To produce anything out of nothing is such an act as necessarily infers omnipotence in the agent. For entity and nonentity are extremes so widely distant that they can never pass into each other without the efficiency of some almighty Power. But God hath actually created all things of nothing; therefore we acknowledge his power infinite or, to speak more properly, inexhaustible.

[149. More on infinite wisdom: displayed in both material and spiritual creation.]

Morn[ing]

2. That the divine Wisdom is manifestly displayed in the works of creation needs no proof. All the inanimate and brute creation, in working for ends unknown to themselves, clearly demonstrate that there is a superior power or wisdom which directs their operations. For when things act regularly by a rule they know not to an end they do not understand, and yet work together in the greatest harmony for that end, we cannot but acknowledge a wisdom in the supreme cause that ranges all these inferior causes in the order we see them and gives law to their several motions, according to their respective natures.

3. As God is the author of the material system, so likewise is he the origin of all

spiritual beings, such as angels and souls of men, and consequently is the fountain of all the powers they have: understanding, will, etc. And he could not have imparted those powers to spiritual substances if he had not had them himself.

[150. More on infinite wisdom: God's power inexhaustible, not limited to this world.]

Even[ing]

4.[54] If the power of God be inexhaustible, as is evident by any single act of creation, then, if he pleaseth he can will the existence of another world, a third, a fourth, and so on *ad infinitum*, for his power can never be exhausted.

I proceed now to give a direct answer to your question, which I shall do in few words.

My first argument is this—

Either God hath power to create more worlds, more spiritual beings endued with wisdom or understanding and to order, dispose and govern them as those already created, or he hath not.

If he hath power to create more worlds, more spiritual beings endued with wisdom or understanding and to order, dispose and govern them as those already created, then is his wisdom or the power of his understanding equal to the power of his will, that is, infinite or inexhaustible.

If he hath not power to create more worlds, more spiritual beings endued with wisdom or understanding and to order, dispose and govern them as those already created, then his power is not infinite, seeing it is actually exhausted and can go no further. The consequence here is very plain: to limit any perfection in God is in effect to deny his being, for, if he be not infinite, he cannot be God—[55]

[151. The senses, "deceitful mediums" of temptation.]

Even[ing]

'Tis the misery of the soul to be determined to the body, that it lives in the senses and is consequently under a necessity of receiving all its ideas of external thing[s] through those deceitful mediums. Yet, considering the lapse of the human soul, it seems necessary it should be so, for otherwise we could be subject to no temptations from the world without us, and if no trial, no virtue; no virtue, no reward.

[152. Her foolish thoughts and amusements: a potentially dangerous precipice.]

Morn[ing]

You are strangely discouraged and complain because you find still an inclination and complacency in those foolish thoughts and amusements of *.[56] Consider the dangerous lapse of the superior powers your voluntary indulging first motions upon a vain presumption of having it in your power at any time to suspend or lay aside such ———— at pleasure.[57] In all irregular appetites or motions of the mind, every repeated act gives an accession of strength to the appetite till by insensible degrees we slide into a habit, which in a little time will be so confirmed that we shall not have it in our power to resist, much less to conquer it.

There is not a more groundless unreasonable presumption incident to man than that of venturing upon the utmost bounds of what is lawful. 'Tis like a person's venturing to walk or look down from the extreme of a precipice. Is such a one sure that the prospect shall not prove fatal? Is he secure that his head shall not turn and put it out of his power to restrain himself from falling?

[153. Her own case of innocent amusement that leads astray.]

Noon

If I mistake not, this is your case. At first you entertained these thoughts only as an amusement to be used or laid aside at pleasure. The matter appeared innocent, attended by no ill consequences to yourself or neighbour. You had some check from the remembrance of former experience, but you wisely resolved that they should never grow to a habit, and therefore could not be prejudicial. At first the delight was faint and transient, often strongly counter-poised by pain and want. But as the one decreased and the other was supplied, the pleasure increased till it gained an ascendant over your inclinations. By this means your soul, which in its pre-existent state was above all spirits most deeply lapsed into the powers of the flesh and the world and had by great conflicts and much difficulty in a good measure conquered both, by swift degrees declined in strength, grew less pleased with its former ac-quests,[58] entertained kinder thoughts of present things. Ideas which seemed totally lost revived and were received with the same satisfaction which usually attends the meeting of friends that have been long separated from each other.

[154. More on her own experience of temptation: enjoyment induces habit.]

Even[ing]

Enjoyment begot sensual pleasure, that mortal enemy to the purity and tranquility of the soul. Pleasure excited to frequent enjoyment till repeated acts induced a habit which is now infinitely more uneasy[59] than any instance of self-denial or penance could ha' been in the beginning of the temptation.

[155. Self-evident truths and an enigmatic reflection on the mind and will.]

Morn[ing]

Self-evident truths can admit of no proof, because their evidence is included in themselves, and there is no medium that can make them appear clearer or more plain than they do at first sight.

He that hath the eternal laws of goodness and rectitude impressed upon his mind cannot set up an arbitrarious[60] will for his rule and guide without doing violence to himself; liberty in the power or principle is nowhere a perfection where there is not an indifferency[61] in the things or actions about which it is conversant.[62]

[156. Further reflection on the cause and cure of her temptation.]

Noon

Two thoughts occurred or possibly suggested by some good spirit. The first, that, instead of spending so much time in complaining of, or only opposing, this single temptation, the best way to conquer it is to bend the whole force of the mind in a serious use of the ways and means of religion. In prayer, reading, meditation, frequenting public worship, the sacrament, fasting, or at least abstinence, self-denial in other instances, etc., which will revive the spirit of piety, the sense of God, of good and evil, strengthen faith, encourage hope and perfect obedience.

[The second,] that whenever the evil spirit suggests any of those vain thoughts, take no further notice of them than immediately to turn the thoughts upon some useful subject and, by a vigorous application to what is good, you will effectually defeat his malice, turn his artillery upon himself, so what he designed for your destruction may be a means of preserving and increasing piety and virtue.

Quere:[63] Is there not some more than ordinary defects in other instances of duty, some other mortal sin indulged that offends God and provokes him to leave you to the insults of evil spirits?

[157. The difficulty—and seriousness—of vices renewed after a long time.]

Even[ing]

The conquest of these foolish T————[64] was the intention of so many years V————[65] and innumerable prayers have [?]ar[isen] on the same occasion.

A habit of thinking, speaking or action once broke and after a long course of time renewed again is seldom with, but never without, almost infinite pains conquered a second time. The same vice or irregular motion is not the same at thirty that it was at twenty, nor at forty[66] that it was at thirty, though it agree in all other circumstances but that of time. That single article greatly changes[67] the guilt, speaks the offender unprofitable in the highest degree and that he well deserves that most terrible sentence should pass upon him. "Let him that is filthy be filthy still."[68] "Cut it down, why cumbereth it the ground?"[69]

[158. Welcome "the severest methods of providence" as means of "breaking an habitual vanity."]

Morn[ing], Nov[ember] 28, [1]718
S. L D—[70]

Still, any suffering rather than sin—Trials of various kinds and degrees—Yet great reason to adore and praise—perhaps nothing less could have been so proper a mean[s] of breaking an habitual vanity, formed and strengthened by so many concurring circumstances. If by the severest methods of Providence the understanding is cleared, the will with its affection purified,[71] strengthened and confirmed in the paths of virtue, complain not of the suffering, but adore the mercy, welcome want, sickness, reproach, loss of friends, welcome any penal evil how painful and uneasy soever it be to flesh and blood if it reclaim the wanderer and bring him back again to God—

[159. On mental and physical extremes.]

Even[ing]

Our make is such we cannot bear extremes in any case, in mind or body. Though we in this life know not the utmost bounds of happiness or misery, yet those lengths we are sometimes permitted to go in either path are equally destructive of our natures, nor could we suffer long what the mind or body is capable of feeling, either of pleasure or pain, in this world. Too much joy dissipates the spirits, too much grief consumes them, both enfeeble the body in a short space and render it altogether unfit for the use it was designed. Therefore the wise God of nature does usually by his providence so order and dispose events that we rarely suffer extremes, but through our own default.

[160. Affliction a "check to the first motions of evil."]

Morn[ing]

You may observe of late that if but one of those vain thoughts come into the mind, though not consented to, but immediately rejected, there is some cross event or uneasy ———[72] presently follows, which I take to be a signal instance of the goodness of God in that he vouchsafes by this method to check the first motions of evil, to give warning of the approach of the Tempter and to call upon you to stand upon your guard. There is strong encouragement to faith and hope while God condescends to afflict and at the same time gives light into the cause of the affliction and excites by his Holy Spirit to repentance.

[161. Don't be elated (or rattled) by the praise (or reproach) of men.]

Even[ing]

You are certainly too much in the power of man, when any man hath power to elate your mind or bias any passion by flattery or to rattle[73] your temper and violate your peace by reproach or calumny. What, are you the better for the praise of men? Or wherein are you the worse, though all men should despise you, if men and devils should all conspire against you, if God be your friend and all be clear between you and heaven?

[162. Avoid "immoderate cares"; "preserve an equal temper."]

Morn[ing]

You sinned last night in giving way to those unquiet thoughts about S. Drs[74] and other seemingly severe dispensations of Providence. Would you be free from presumptuous sins, undefiled and innocent from the great offence, keep a strict guard against all immoderate cares, all anxious thought about anything of this world. If you desire to live under the continual government and direction of the Holy Spirit, preserve an equal temper. That small voice is never heard in storms and tempests,[75] be they raised either by intemperate joys or griefs.

[163. Mental impairment by too much or too little study.]

Noon

Thought is the proper action of the soul as local motion is of the body. And as the body is tired, the spirits exhausted and the whole fabric weakened by too long walking, etc., so is the strength of the mind impaired by too much and intense thinking; indeed too much or too little study renders it extravagant and unruly, the one by over straining its powers, the other too much relaxes them and thereby makes the mind impotent and good for nothing.

[164. Puzzlement at afflictions and trials not caused by intemperance or inadvertence.]

Even[ing]

"Happy is the man that endureth temptation," saith St. James.[76] With submission I would say, "blessed is the person whom God by his providence preserves from too great or constant trials of ———."[77] Though that merciful being never exposes men to, or leads them into, temptation with a design to ensnare or betray their virtue, yet oftentimes for reasons not always obvious he does permit ill men and evil angels to afflict his servants very severely. Sometimes [he] himself, as in the case of acute pains or more lingering distempers, which are not always the effects of intemperance or inadvertence[. . .][78]

Notes

1. On the general popularity of Pascal in England during S. W.'s lifetime, see John Barker, *Strange Contrarieties: Pascal in England during the Age of Reason* (Montreal and London: McGill–Queen's University Press, 1975). On the Wesley family's interest, see pp. 181–195; for women's attraction to Pascal, see pp. 220–221.

2. This meditation is separated from the previous one by an entire blank page. It is further distinguished by an asterisk placed at the top left-hand corner of the page on the same line as the heading, "Morn."

3. See Article XIX, Articles of Religion, BCP.

4. The meditation stops, leaving the remaining two-thirds of the page blank.

5. The initials are somewhat enigmatic: "O" and "R," letters that precede various paragraphs in the text of the meditation, might stand for "Objection" and "Response," but I have been unable plausibly to identify "U," which does not serve as a paragraph tag. Further confusion: the "R" could also be interpreted as a "P" (for Pascal) in front of several of the paragraphs, though later S. W. seems to indicate quotations by the clearer abbreviation: "Pas." Her interest in Pascal has been discussed by Barker, *Strange Contrarieties*, pp. 182–187, 220ff., though he is not aware of these diary entries. Frequently in this entry S. W. ends lines with a dash, possibly an indication of a quotation.

6. Pascal, *Thoughts on Religion*, chap. 1 ("Against an Atheistical Indifference"), par. 1, p. 12; my quotation marks. The original is discussing the manner in which even the enemies of religion illustrate one of its two primary truths, namely, the corruption of nature. It is unnatural that "we find Persons indifferent to the Loss of their Being, and to the Danger of endless Misery" (p. 11). "They are quite other Men in all other Regards: they fear the smallest Inconveniences; they see them as they approach, and feel them if they arrive: and he who passeth Days and Nights in Chagrin or Despair, for the Loss of an Imployment, or for some imaginary Blemish in his Honour, is the very same Mortal who knows that he must lose all by Death, and yet remains without Disquiet, Resentment or Emotion." S. W. separates the quotation from her next paragraph with a short horizontal line.

7. Paraphrase of ibid., chap. 2 ("Marks of the True Religion"), par. 2, pp. 20–21: "To make out the Truth and Certainty of a Religion, 'tis necessary that it should have obtain'd the Knowledge of Human Nature. For our true Nature and true Happiness, true Virtue and true Religion, are things the knowledge of which is reciprocal and inseparable."

8. Ibid., p. 21; my quotation marks continuing from above: "It should also be able to discern the Greatness and the Meanness of the Human Condition; together with the cause and reason of both."

9. Ibid., p. 20. Pascal does not mention love of neighbor in the sentence that begins this chapter ("The True Religion ought chiefly to distinguish itself, by obliging Men to the Love of God"), but S. W. supplies that need in her biblically sound paraphrase. Cf. chap. 28, par. 11, p. 259: "Two Plain Laws might be more effectual in regulating the whole Christian Community, than all Political Institutions; the Love of God, and of our Neighbour."

10. That is, abilities, capacities, talents.

11. Pascal, *Thoughts on Religion*, chap. 2, par. 3, p. 21; my quotation marks. S. W.'s first sentence is a loose paraphrase. The original reads: "Other Religions, as those of the Heathens, are more Popular; as consisting only in External Appearance: But then they are unqualified for moving the Judicious and Prudent. Again, should any Religion reside altogether in the inward Spirit, it might be fitter to work on Parts and Genius, but could hold no influence over the Gross of Mankind. Christianity alone is proportion'd to all Capacities; being duly composed and temper'd of the Internal and the External way. It raises the most Ignorant to inward and spiritual Acts, and at the same time abases the most Intelligent, by pressing the Obligation to outward Performances; and is never compleat, but when it joyns one of these Effects to the other."

12. Ibid., par. 5, p. 22; my quotation marks. The original reads: "No Religion, except the Christian has known Man to be the most excellent of Visible Creatures, and at the same time the most Miserable."

13. Ibid., par. 8, p. 23; my quotation marks: "That Religion which consists in believing the Fall of Man from a state of Glory and Communication with God, to a state of Sorrow, Humiliation, and Estrangement from God; together with his Restoration by a Messiah; has always been in the World."

14. A summary of Pascal's more descriptive words (ibid., p. 24): "For immediately after the first Creation, Adam was the Witness and Depositary of the Promise concerning a Saviour, to be Born of the seed of the Woman."

15. Ibid., par. 10, p. 25. Kennett's sentence begins with "Thus"; otherwise this is an exact quotation.

16. Ibid., chap. 3 ("The true Religion proved by the Contrarieties which are discoverable in Man, and by the Doctrine of Original Sin"), par. 1, p. 34; my quotation marks, although some phrases are rather loosely paraphrased. Exact quotation until "Was it a proper Method for the Cure of Man's Presumption thus to equal him with God? On the other hand, have those succeeded better in restraining our Earthly Desires, who would bring us down to the

level of Beasts, and present us with sensual Gratifications for our real and universal Happiness?"

17. S. W. answers one in a series of Pascal's rhetorical questions: "What Religion shall instruct us to correct at once our Pride and our Concupiscence?" Ibid., p. 35.

18. Probably S. W.'s reflection on the theme of Pascal's chapter; see ibid., pp. 37–38.

19. See *An Essay concerning Human Understanding*, ed. Peter H. Nidditch (Oxford: Clarendon Press, 1975), 2.21.38–42, 58–60 (pp. 255–259, 272–274).

20. Pascal, *Thoughts on Religion*, chap. 20 ("That God Is Not Known to Advantage, but thro' JESUS CHRIST"), par. 2, p. 167; my quotation marks. Exact quotation until "the impression continues but a short Space. . . ."

21. Replaces the crossed-out original, "from."

22. Pascal, *Thoughts on Religion*, chap. 3, par. 1, pp. 36–37. Pascal puts this passage in the mouth of "the Wisdom of God, speaking to us in the Christian Religion." Much of S. W.'s entry is summary, but there is a close paraphrase: "He [man] was dispos'd to make himself the Centre of his own Happiness, and altogether independent from the Divine Succours" (p. 37). Reference to the apostate angels is S. W.'s own (perhaps Miltonic) gloss on Pascal's passage.

23. For example, Luke 9:23.

24. A recurring theme in Pascal's passage. See *Thoughts on Religion*, p. 35.

25. Ibid., chap. 7, par. 3, p. 66. An exact quotation with the exception of Kennett's "when we have once discover'd where Truth is . . ." in place of S. W.'s more succinct "when we have once discovered the truth. . . ." The parenthetical insertion "(custom)" is hers.

26. I have been unable to find this quotation in Pascal. It may be from another source or S. W.'s own observation.

27. Pascal, *Thoughts on Religion*, chap. 21 ("The Strange Contrarieties Discoverable in Human Nature, with Regard to Truth, and Happiness, and Many Other Things"), par. 1, p. 182; nearly exact quotation; my quotation marks.

28. That is, small portion.

29. Pascal, *Thoughts on Religion*, chap. 22 ("The General Knowledge of Man"), par. 1, p. 187; exact quote; my quotation marks.

30. Ibid., par. 1, p. 190. Virtually exact quotation, which continues: "alike distant from that Nothing whence he was taken, and from that Infinity in which he is swallow'd up." The parenthetical explanation is S. W.'s.

31. Ibid., p. 190, exact quotation; my quotation marks.

32. Matthew 5:9. This entry is particularly interesting given S. W.'s own earlier stand as a Nonjuror. A blank space of three or four lines is left at the bottom of the page.

33. Luke 17:1, slightly paraphrased; the second sentence is a much looser expansion on Luke 17:2.

34. This word is S. W.'s insertion.

35. Pascal, *Thoughts on Religion*: "to."

36. S. W. removes "by" (ibid.).

37. S. W. substitutes "and" for "that it" (ibid.).

38. Ibid., chap. 26 ("The Misery of Man"), par. 1, pp. 219–220; exact quotation except where noted in text.

39. Ibid., chap. 7 ("That There Is More Advantage in Believing Than in Disbelieving the Doctrines of Christianity"), par. 2, pp. 64–65; accurate, though somewhat digested paraphrase; my quotation marks. This is from Pascal's famous extended passage on "the wager." The original: "But you say, you are so made as to be incapable of believing. At least therefore, endeavour to understand this your incapacity; and to find what it is that debars you of Faith,

when Reason so manifestly invites you to it. Labour, then, in your own Conviction: not by increasing the proofs of a deity, but by diminishing the power of your Passions . . . banish those Amusements which have hitherto entirely possess'd you."

40. Ibid., p. 65; my quotation marks. "O! I should soon bid adieu to these Pleasures, say you, where [sic] I once but master of Faith. And I say, on the other hand, you would soon be master of Faith, had you once bidden adieu to these Pleasures."

41. In MS: "Lewis."

42. Maimbourg, *History of the Crusade* . . . part iv, bk. ii, p. 371; a nearly exact quotation; my quotation marks.

43. Possibly an allusion to the contemporary theological discussion of analogy, for example, the work of William King (1650–1729), archbishop of Dublin, *Divine Predestination . . . Sermon preach'd at Christ-Church, Dublin, May 15* (Dublin and London: for A. Bell . . . and J. Baker, 1710). *(1709)*. S. W. does not subscribe to King's agnosticism ("If we know anything about Him at all, it must be by analogy and comparison, by resembling Him to something we do know and are acquainted with"), but she apparently does accept a more orthodox use of the term. See James Hastings, ed., *Encyclopedia of Religion and Ethics* (New York: C. Scribner's Sons; Edinburgh: T. and T. Clark, 1908–1926), 1:417, s.v. "Analogy."

44. The meditation continues to the next page, though one notebook leaf has been torn out in between.

45. On "sensation and reflection" see Locke, *Essay* 2.1.2–4, pp. 104–106. S. W. is struggling with the disjuncture between Lockean psychology and Christian belief in disembodied spirits. She might be reflecting on John Norris, *Philosophical Discourse Concerning the Natural Immortality of the Soul* (London: S. Manship, 1708).

46. See Nicolas Malebranche, *Search after Truth. Or a Treatise of the Nature of the Humane Mind. And of Its Management for avoiding Error in the Sciences*, 2 vols., trans. Richard Sault (London: J. Dunton, 1694–1695). Note the connections between this work and S. W.: it is dedicated to the Marquess of Normanby, Samuel Wesley's sometime patron; J. Dunton was Susanna Wesley's brother-in-law and Samuel's literary associate in publishing the *Athenian Mercury*, which sometimes discussed the views of Malebranche (and Locke and Descartes) during its lifetime, 1690–1697; the translator, Sault, and the Platonist divine John Norris were also part of this circle. In fact, it is likely that S. W. got her Malebranchean ideas through Norris, who was the French philosopher's chief English disciple. See Charles J. McCracken, *Malebranche and British Philosophy* (Oxford: Clarendon Press, 1983), pp. 156–179.

Malebranche (1638–1715) synthesized Cartesian philosophy and Platonic-Augustinian theology. The theory of animal spirits, "the most subtle and active parts of the blood" (bk. 2, chap. 2, par. 1, 1:122), which activate the imagination without any necessary external stimulus, is found in bk. 2, chaps. 1–2, 1:118–125. See also Henry More's use of the term in *The Immortality of the Soul*, in *A Collection of Several Philosophical Writings of Dr. Henry More* . . . , 2nd ed. (London: William Morden in Cambridge, 1662), bk. 2, chap. 17, par. 3; Flora Isabel MacKinnon, *Philosophical Writings of Henry More* (New York: Oxford University Press, 1925), p. 158: "the *immediate Instrument* of the Soul are those tenuous and Aereal particles which they ordinarily call the *Spirits* . . . these are they by which the Soul hears, sees, feels, imagines, remembers, reasons, and by moving which, or at least directing their motion, she moves likewise the Body; and by using them, or some subtile Matter like them, she either compleats, or at least contributes to the Bodie's Organization."

47. See John 14:6.

48. Three lines left blank at bottom of page.

49. James 2:13; exact, except for the subject and verb of the final clause, which S. W. makes into an indirect quotation; my quotation marks.

50. That is, without resistance.

51. Litany, BCP, slightly rearranged; my quotation marks.

52. Legal term: the right of succeeding to the possession of something or obtaining it at some future time.

53. Malebranche's *Recherche de la verité* was published in 1674–1675 and translated into English, as in note 46, by Samuel Wesley's associate Richard Sault in 1694. In 1695 Locke wrote a critical analysis, *An Examination of Malebranche's Opinion of Seeing All Things in God*, in *Posthumous Works of Mr. John Locke* (London: for A. and J. Churchill, 1706). John Norris accepted Malebranche's approach in *An Essay towards the Theory of the Ideal or Intelligible World*, 1701–1704. See Frederick Copleston, *A History of Philosophy*, 6 vols. (Garden City, N.Y.: Doubleday, Image Books, 1963), 4:210.

54. In MS: "4thly."

55. Two lines at the bottom of the page left blank.

56. S. W.'s asterisk, in lieu of a name.

57. S. W.'s line, again indicating her unwillingness to be more specific, even in her diary.

58. Acquisitions.

59. Troublesome.

60. Arbitrary, capricious, or (possibly) tyrannical.

61. Freedom of choice.

62. This last half of the sentence (beginning, "liberty in the power or principle . . .") is preceded by the crossed-out phrase "for as Dr. Rust well observes." George Rust (d. 1670), Cambridge Platonist and friend of Jeremy Taylor, whom he succeeded as bishop of Dromore, published, among other items, *A Discourse of the Use of Reason in Matters of Religion, Showing That Christianity Contains Nothing Repugnant to Right Reason, Against Enthusiasts and Deists* (London: for Walter Kettilby, 1683). S. W. also refers to Rust (along with fellow Platonists Henry More and John Norris) in her "Religious Conference." See part III of this volume.

63. Archaic form of "query."

64. Probably an abbreviation: "thoughts" or possibly "temptations."

65. Possibly "vows."

66. Two pages torn from book at this point; meditation continues without interruption on the facing page.

67. In MS: "chanses."

68. Close paraphrase of Revelation 22:11; my quotation marks substituted for S. W.'s dashes before and behind the quotation.

69. Luke 13:7, parable of the fig tree that would not bare fruit; my quotation marks substituted for S. W.'s dashes.

70. I have not been able to determine any special significance of the date and initials in the heading. November 28 was a Friday in 1718.

71. The meditation breaks off at the bottom of the page; an asterisk below the last line corresponds to another asterisk marking a continuation of the thought on MS p. 192 (six pages further on) following the last entry (164) in this section of her journal. That fragment has been added here.

72. Word omitted. I have inserted a line to indicate the blank space left by S. W.

73. Assail.

74. Unclear reference; one possibility: "Samuel's doctors," implying a medical problem.

75. See 1 Kings 19:12.

76. James 1:12, though S. W. has substituted "happy" for "blessed"; my quotation marks.

77. S. W. inserts a line rather than commit her specific "trial" to paper. I have added quotation marks.

78. Meditation breaks off; bottom two-thirds of the page left blank. On the facing page a fragment of a meditation takes up the top one-third of the page; an asterisk and the flow of the thought indicate the continuation of entry 158, and it has been added there. This is the final entry in the notebook from this direction; 18 spreads remain in the book, blank from this side. Upside down and reversed, however—that is, beginning from the "back"—there are more journal entries, which appear in the next chapter.

❧ TWENTY-ONE ❧

"The Most Blest and Happy Day"

*T*his score of uncharacteristic entries occupies some 36 pages, beginning at the back of the same notebook[1] that contains all the diary reprinted to this point. They are uncharacteristic in that they break the normal routine of morning, noon, and evening meditations by including special sabbath reflections and others with a more occasional focus, such as a solemn vow, a sermon she has read, and a series of scripture citations that have for one reason or another intrigued her. In addition, quite a few dates are scattered throughout the pages (nearly as many in 36 pages as in the previous 192), beginning with a flyleaf notation ("*S.W. 1709*") and continuing through 27 November 1727 (entry 172), covering the time period of the previous entries and apparently extending well past them. Though there are a number of more representative meditations in this chapter, it seems likely that Susanna Wesley used the back end of the notebook primarily for special times and needs.

Four "sabbath entries" (165–168) catch the reader's attention at the outset. Dating from 1709 and 1710, they demonstrate her attachment to Sunday, as she gives thanks for it and strives for a "conscientious performance of the several duties of the day" (166). Of course, such contemplation leads her to many of the same themes that also occupy her in her weekday reflections: not forgetting her "true end" (166); preserving a "devout and equal temper" in the midst of her life's difficulties; decrying the "too great a regard for the ease and pleasures of this wretched body" that gets in the way of her intellectual service of God. Students of her son John may also detect early hints of what will not long after form part of the early Methodist ethos: perfection; the quest for assurance and an Arminian view of the atonement; even (in the same entry) an experiential argument for the existence of spirits, so compelling as to be labeled a mathematically clear demonstration (all in 167). The final sabbath entry, that for Palm Sunday (April 2) 1710, demonstrates her attentiveness to the flow of the liturgical year. She has heard the readings for the day and tuned her reflections to the same theme, the "sufferings of the holy and blessed Jesus." Though entrusted to her diary, her writing here is not far from sermonic discourse.

Three entries (170–172) show Susanna Wesley making a resolution in January

1723 and a solemn vow in November 1727 to help extricate her from various anxieties and distresses. The resolution came to her in the midst of a sleepless night, suggested, she writes, "by God's good Spirit"—a resignation of self, relations, and secular concerns "to the entire manage of God's good providence." The vow, the very next entry, though separated by some four years, is a much more specific quid pro quo in which she will offer herself "absolutely" to Christ if he will deliver her from past debts and future necessities "without this extreme distress."

Nowhere else in her extant writings is there anything like the list of scripture citations found in the entry designated 176. Thirty-five passages are listed on four and one-half pages, several with the verses actually copied out, most with the citation alone—and some blank space, suggesting that further comment might be added. Though the section might be a list of sermon texts, it might just as well be a compilation of verses that Susanna Wesley found particularly helpful. Extensive analysis is not possible here, but it is interesting to note that of 18 New Testament passages only two are from the synoptic Gospels, the vast majority coming from John, Acts, and various Epistles. Further, of 17 Old Testament references, 11 are from the prophets (primarily Isaiah), with the remainder divided between the Psalms, Job, and the Pentateuch. Themes of blessing, promise, "glad tidings," and prophecy abound.

Finally, this section once again reveals Susanna Wesley's involvement with current theological and philosophical debate. In entries 169, 177–179, and 182 she pursues the implications of John Locke's *An Essay concerning Humane Understanding*: debates about innate ideas of God in the soul, simple ideas, and abstract substance; reflections on understanding, knowledge, truth, and especially happiness. In 181 she drinks deeply of Bishop William Beveridge's work, proving that high Anglicans of the time could be just as conscientious as Puritans. It is probably also Beveridge that helped her develop (in 183 and 184) a scriptural argument for the Trinity in opposition to Unitarian and Arian ideas that were then contesting with orthodox Christianity.

❧

[165. Praise to God for the sabbath.]

M[orning?] First Sunday, May 22, 170[9] [2]

"This is the day that the Lord hath made;
I will rejoice and be glad therein." [3]

Glory be to thee, eternal Father of spirits, for so kindly and mercifully indulging one day in seven to the souls thou has made, wherein 'tis their duty as well as happiness to retire from the business and hurry of a tumultuous and vexatious world and are permitted to enjoy a more immediate and uninterrupted attendance on the divine Majesty. Oh blessed indulgence! Oh most happy day. Lord, I can never sufficiently adore they infinite love and goodness in appropriating this seventh part of my time to thyself. May these sacred moments ever be employed in thy service; may no vain unnecessary or unprofitable thoughts or discourse ever rob God of his due honour and praise on this day or deprive my soul of the peculiar advantages and blessings which are to be gained by the conscientious performance of the several duties of the day.

"Remember the sabbath day to keep it holy," or "remember that thou keep holy the sabbath day." [4]

Blessed God! That we should need thy memento to put us in mind of such inestimable blessing! To labour six days indeed is very hard, and we may stand in need of a command to make us cheerfully undergo so difficult a task. But one would think that our natural desire of rest after labour after having spent six days in the business of this life, which we know must shortly be determined by death, should be the most pleasing and desirable thing that can be, and indeed if we had no positive command, yet the thing itself is so grateful that we cannot sufficiently bless and praise our God for giving us leave to enjoy a sabbath, for permitting us to refresh our souls by a view of that rest and glory which he hath prepared for those that love him. [5]

I will not take upon me to censure the conduct of those that say, "The sabbath is made for diversion as well as devotion." [6] Nor will I trouble myself to enquire whether or no the severity of the Jewish sabbath is remitted under the Christian economy; 'tis sufficient for my purpose that all agree we may devote the day to God if we will, and therefore let it be in obedience to God's command or under the notion of a free-will offering, if God will be pleased with my strict observation of this day. 'Tis sufficient, 'tis all I ask, and whatever others may think or do, I account this the most blest and happy day of the week. And with all my heart and soul and mind and strength [7] I adore and praise thee, O eternal and ever-blessed God for giving me a dispensation from all worldly business for this day, and, since the weakness and corruption of human nature requires it, for commanding us to keep holy the sabbath day—

Therefore with angels and archangels we praise and magnify thee, O God, the Father, Son and Holy Ghost, to whom be glory and praise for ever and ever. Amen. [8]

[166. More sabbath praise: for our creation, despite its sorrows, and for the eternal sabbath soon to come.]

October 9, Sunday 2nd A. L. T. [9]

Blessed be God for bringing me to another of his own most happy days. The great business of the day is praise and thanksgiving, and to the end that this may be devoutly performed, spend some time in contemplating the essential perfections of the divine nature, and when the soul is duly elevated with those sublime and spiritual thoughts, then praise and adore—

Then consider what that blessed Being is to us—A creator, he made us of nothing; we are the effect of infinite power, wisdom and goodness! He had no need of us being perfectly happy in the contemplation of his own perfections; therefore not to increase but communicate his happiness and glory did he give us being. He is the Father of spirits, and, as such, we owe him the honour and homage due from children. Then give him thanks for our creation—But by reason of the many troubles and calamities of this mortal life it may sometimes be difficult to render that tribute of thanksgiving that we ought for our creation, and possibly Satan or corrupt nature may suggest that, since this life is attended by so[10] many calamitous circumstances, why are we obliged to give thanks for that which is rather a burden than a pleasure to us? 'Tis true, if we had never had being, we had never been capable of happiness, but as we had known no joy, so neither had we felt any pain, no disease, no cold, hunger, thirst, weariness, poverty, losses, contempt, shame, disappointment, ingratitude, no false friends or true enemies, etc.

Indeed, if we consider man with relation to this world only, if all the noble and most excellent powers of his mind were calculated only for the meridian[11] of this life, and were of no use but to contrive and make "provision for the flesh, to fulfill the lusts thereof,"[12] I'd see no great reason to thank God for our creation.

But while we talk thus, we forget the true end of our being here, nor do we consider that this life is only a prelude to eternity. This is our state of probation, to fit us for an eternal state of solid joy and unspeakable tranquility, to prepare us for that happiness which God has designed us and for which he made us, in his heavenly kingdom. He is our Father and, as experience tells what the love of that relation is, so we cannot doubt the love of that blessed Father to his Children. Alas, here we are not in our Father's house,[13] nor are to expect the accommodations we shall meet with there, but this life is but for a little space, a few revolutions of the heavenly bodies shall put a period to this mortal state and resolve these bodies into their first principles.[14] Then shall the body rest in the dust and the souls shall return to God that made it. The principles of that spiritual life we receive here, and the means of grace are appointed to nourish and increase them, by which they proceed from small and imperceptible beginnings "to the measure of the stature of the fulness of Christ,"[15] but here all their perfection is but a perfection of degrees; their proper perfection is reserved till the end and consummation of all these terrestrial beings, till time shall be no more,[16] but shall be utterly lost and swallowed up in the vast unfathomable ocean of eternity.[17] Courage then, my soul. Eternity is at hand; thou shalt not always suffer; these pains and wants and uneasinesses shall all shortly vanish into nothing. You shall not always have these dark and imperfect apprehensions of God, nor shall you always complain of being such a stranger to the spiritual life, nor be always so disquieted by the interpositions of worldly affairs that now so much perplex thy mind and so often retard and divert it from aspiring towards heaven. But a little while and this world shall trouble thee no longer, no more shalt thou suffer such tormenting conflicts with thy spiritual enemies, nor shall Satan have any power to approach the mansions of the blessed. You shall not always labour under the weight of a weak uneasy body nor the heavier burden of an infirm diseased mind; these daily infirmities, these tumultuous passions, these constant temptations shall all be ended "when this mortal shall put on immortality"[18] and thou art once admitted into the region of happy spirits, into "the general assembly and church of the firstborn,"[19] when thou art once a member of that blest society. Then shalt thou enjoy an eternal sabbath, all pain, all sorrow shall forever be done away, and then shalt thou without weariness or disturbance be most delightfully employed[20] in adoring, in loving, in praising the ever blessed God, the Father, Son, and Holy Ghost, to whom be glory!

[167. Further sabbath reflection: the difficulties of preserving a "devout and even temper"; the importance of sincerity.]

Sunday, Third[21]

Another blessed day! Lord, how could we support the cares and pains of life, were it not for the refreshments of the dear and holy day! Glory be to thee, oh eternal ever-blessed Goodness, that has in this probationary state afforded us such a vast invaluable blessing as a sabbath is! But ah, how difficult a thing is it to preserve that devout and equal temper, that separation from the world and freedom from all worldly regards on this blessed day, which we so much desire and so often pray for! How often does unforeseen accidents, indispositions, company, etc. divert the thoughts, alienate the affections, and strongly turn aside the mind from intending and pursuing its eternal happiness! Lord, might thy creature expostulate with thy infinite majesty, I would humbly beseech thee to discover unto me the cause, why I so long labour under such and so many difficulties in my way to heaven as makes me often upon the point of despairing ever to arrive there. I cannot without renouncing my reason as well as faith question or doubt of thy being willing all men should be saved,[22] not only because God that cannot lie hath said it, but also because thou hast sent thy only Son into the world to purchase man's redemption and salvation by suffering not only a weary uneasy life, but a most painful and ignominious death for us. Besides thy Son thou has given the promise of thy Spirit that he may strengthen our decays, purify and exult the soul by renewing and sanctifying our natures, by illuminating our minds and helping us when we labour under infirmities, etc. But still, "straight is the gate, and narrow is the way, that leadeth unto life,"[23] and, what is yet worse, few, comparatively very few, there is that find it—

This thought often damps my devotion and retards the soul when it would aspire towards heaven. How know I whether or no I shall persevere? How shall I be assured that "the world, the flesh nor the devil" shall never be too hard for me?[24] 'Tis true I know that all things in this world are vain, perishing, unsatisfactory enjoyments, that "all is vanity and vexation of spirit,"[25] but still I do not find that the mind has such a strong sense of these things, but that unforeseen accidents, hopes, company, etc. does [sic] often strongly allure it to a liking and complacence for sensual delights, and I am often apt to say, "'Tis good to be here."[26]

I know that, as the mind is infinitely superior to the body,[27] so all its proper satisfaction[s] and enjoyments are more pure, more sublime and more eligible[28] in their own natures than any gratification of the flesh or sensual appetites. But yet I find in fact that the senses are too strong in many instances for the reason, and though with the mind, with the judgment and intellectual powers I serve the law of God and do truly in my sober reflections always prefer him and his service before all sensual enjoyments whatever, yet I often perceive that I have too great a regard for the ease and pleasures of this wretched body, am too careful to provide it necessaries, too much afraid of injuring it, too indulgent to its appetites, and in all things too solicitous for its welfare and continuance in this life. And though no regard for it is of force[29] to cause neglect of fixed stated times of retirement and devotion, yet how often does its weakness and infirmities afflict and divert the thoughts in solitude from intending their proper business, and though there is no reasonable cause of sadness from within, yet how often does only corporal pain (when not violent) create such uneasiness of mind as renders it almost utterly uncapable of rendering to the supreme Fountain of life his just tribute of praise and thanksgiving, without which all other services are maimed and imperfect.

Though I know that the devil, that grand enemy to our salvation, "goeth about as a roaring lion, seeking whom he may devour,"[30] though I know the vigilance, have felt the malice, and often experienced the wiles and stratagems of that accursed spirit, perhaps after such a way and in so strange a manner for so long a time as can hardly be paralleled among a thousand, which hath convinced me beyond all other evidence, hath assured me by a demonstration as clear to me as any in the mathematics, of the being of spirits, and has evinced their power over matter to be much greater than is generally thought on or believed; and though I can often perceive that he takes occasion from bodily infirmities and external occurrences to suggest vain, light and unprofitable thoughts that directly tend to divert and alienate the mind from spiritual employments, yet how hard do I find it to be upon the guard, to maintain a constant watch and a regular habitual advertence to my thoughts, words and actions. And 'tis that irregularity of temper and life that interrupts the comforts which might be found in religion and renders my perseverance suspicious. But this is my infirmity. I ought to consider that God is always the same, fixed, immutable, ever ready to succor and strengthen them that truly and sincerely devote themselves to his service. The whole tenor of the gospel insists upon sincerity as the main condition of salvation. A sincere faith and obedience, though the one may be weak and the other imperfect, yet if they do but determine a person to a habitual temper of obedience, if they do but in the main prove a person devoted to God and that, though they cannot with St. Peter appeal to that omniscient Being that they do love him,[31] yet if they can but heartily say, "Lord, thou that knowest all things, knowest that I desire nothing more than to love thee,"[32] surely God will make great allowances for infirmities, temptations, sudden and unforeseen accidents, etc. Nor ought I so frequently to admit of nice scruples and perplexing thoughts, but rather employ my thought[s] and time in a strict, conscientious performance of present duty, and so entirely depend on the infinite goodness of God to secure me from future temptations. Glory be to thee, O Lord—[33]

[168. Reflections on the readings for Palm Sunday: "the sufferings of the holy and blessed Jesus."]

Palm Sunday, 1710[34]

"Praise the Lord, O my soul, and all that is within me bless his holy Name!"[35]

Forever adored and magnified be the eternal God by all angels and men for his inconceivable purity! and boundless, incomprehensible love to mankind!

Whoever carefully reads and considers the history of the adorable blessed Jesus must, I think, necessarily make these very natural reflections—

First, if we consider what he suffered throughout the whole course of his life and the dignity of the person that suffered such things, it will of consequence follow that we have a very high and sublime idea of the infinite purity of the eternal God and a very great idea of the divine justice that could not be satisfied for the violation of God's most wise and holy laws by a less sacrifice than the blood of Jesus, and this will very naturally lead us to reflect on the evil of sin. When we consider that it is directly opposite to the nature of God, which is inconceivably perfect and holy, 'tis a transgression of those laws which are agreeable to the nature and perfections of this most perfect Being and very adequate to and proper for the nature of man as he was created. And whatever is so diametrically opposite to absolute perfection, to what is infinitely good and holy and so directly contrary to the genuine temper of man, must necessarily be the greatest of evils. And as it is the highest contradiction to his infinite purity, so it must of consequence be most hateful to him. What fellowship hath light with darkness?[36] Nor can anything more clearly and fully show us the averseness of the divine nature from all moral evil than that satisfaction which was required and actually paid to the justice of God for the sins of mankind. Which naturally leads us to reflect on the sufferings of the holy and blessed Jesus.

Jesus Christ the eternal son of God by an ineffable and incomprehensible generation, who is one with the Father and Sacred Spirit, equal to the Father as touching his Godhead, and who therefore "thought it no robbery to take upon himself the title of God,"[37] this Christ, this Jesus, the Son of the Blessed, assumed our nature, "took upon himself the form of a servant,"[38] was made of no reputation only that he might become the Saviour of the world. And had he never gone farther, could the uniting the divine with the human nature have satisfied the justice of God and have given a purity and perfection to that nature without any personal suffering, even this first step of condescension, the veiling his native glory and splendour with our humanity would ha' been so stupendous, so amazing as might justly have exacted a tribute of adoration and praise from the whole human nature for that exceeding abundant honour, for that vast accession of glory which it [?]realized by that mysterious hypostatic union.[39]

But oh when the thoughts proceed further on this vast subject and takes [sic] in the end for which the Son of God took upon him this nature, when we consider 'twas to suffer a lurid, painful, shameful death that he might satisfy the justice of God that loudly called for vengeance on all the race of mankind, that he might purify and reinstate us in the favour of God and purchase eternal salvation for those that believe. But why should the Son of God thus suffer for the sins of men? Why indeed, but because "God so loved the World!"[40] He would have mercy because he would have mercy![41] "As the heavens are higher than the earth, so are his thoughts higher than our thoughts and his ways than our ways."[42] We can resolve the whole of man's redemption by Jesus Christ into nothing but the mysterious, infinite goodness, the boundless and incomprehensible compassion of the blessed God! "Even so, Father, for so it seemeth good in thy sight!"[43]

And, as the love and goodness of God is altogether incomprehensible, so is it wonderful[44] to observe the little effect it hath upon the children of men, how small impression doth the sufferings and death of Christ make upon the minds of the generality of the world.[45]

[169. An innate idea of God not religion's foundation; the usefulness and limitations of natural reason.]

Even[ing] [46]

I cannot but think it a great error in our divines to lay so much stress upon innate principles, making them the foundation of all religion. [47] Whether the idea of a God be connatural with the soul, I know not, nor do I think it of any great consequence to be determined in the point, since God hath given to the whole human species sense, perception and reason. And the being and perfections of God are so clearly manifested in all the visible creation that a small advertence will easily induce any creature so qualified to believe there is a God.

But though the light of nature or natural reason may be sufficient to lead a man to the acknowledgment of a God and point out some of the principal duties consequent to such a belief, yet perhaps it will be difficult to prove there was ever any age of the world wherein God left men only to the conduct of this weak guide. [48]

[170. A revelation on coping with distress and a prayer for strength to obey it.]

January, 1723

After much thought and several projects concerning means to extricate us out of present distress, in the evening—unwise. In the night no care or trouble at all, but quiet rest—mercy! Towards morning several times suggested by God's good Spirit (I believe), " 'Tis better to resign and leave the whole manage of all secular affairs to God! And apply yourself vigorously in good earnest to the duties of Religion, to secure their most important stake, 'the one thing needful.' [49] And if God do not in this world grant deliverance, he will certainly succour and support, and perhaps in a little time take you to eternal rest." [50] Glory be to thee, oh Lord!

But, oh God, that knowest that light without strength is not sufficient for me, since it will only put me in the number of those unprofitable servants that knew their master's will and did it not, [51] vouchsafe for the sake of the Lord Jesus to give me strength and a disposition of heart, to obey the dictates of thy good Spirit. Amen.

[171. A new resolution: resign all secular concerns and anxieties to God's providence.]

Morn[ing], January 29, 1723 [52]

Resolved by the grace of God! which I humbly beg in the name and for the sake of the Lord Jesus! That from this day forward I will resign myself and all relations and secular concerns to the entire manage of God's good providence. Nor will I be anxious or solicitous about events for the future in things relating only to this life.

Glory be to thee, oh Lord!

[172. Another vow: absolute offering of self to God in return for deliverance from debt and distress.]

November 27, 1727

Strongly pressed to make a vow to God under many distresses, as I find was customary among the people of God in all ages; after many thoughts and great perplexity concerning the matter of this vow, not having for several years indulged myself in any particular sinful habit or willful actual transgressions. Began to reflect on numberless infirmities and great deficiencies in all Christian virtues, upon which view it was thought expedient that the subject of the vow should be a universal reformation, a greater accuracy in performance of all duties to God, my neighbour and myself.

Greatly discouraged by remembrance of many attempts o' this nature,[53] which had not such lasting effects as was expected. But more so, or rather altogether confounded with a deep sense of present inability both in mind and body to keep such a vow, looking upon myself not as weak, but as impotence itself. Here stood suspended and astonished for a considerable time.[54]

After this, suggested by some superior power: "If you would resolve on a general reformation in order to greater perfection, do not perplex your mind with such a multitude of confuse[d] ideas, nor dwell so long upon enquiring what you shall do in such a case or under such circumstances, but take the most compendious way to amendment[55] and let your v[ow] run thus—

"If it will please God indeed to bless me and deliver me from these d———[56] to An, Jn, Lr, etc., if he will vouchsafe to give me food to eat and raiment to put on without debt without this extreme distress—Then will I offer up myself absolutely, entirely to Jesus Christ, the incarnate God, only Saviour of the world! To be instructed by his Spirit, strengthened and directed by him to amend in each particular failing, since 'there is no name under heaven given unto men whereby they may be saved' but that of the Lord Jesus![57] And 'no man can come unto the Father but by him! He is our way, our truth, our life.' "[58]

[173. In defense of infant baptism, based on the parallels between Law and Gospel.][59]

Faith was required under the law as well as gospel. The covenant was the same only under different seals. Children were circumcised; children therefore may be baptized.

All nations to be discipled by baptism under the gospel dispensation. Discipled, i.e., brought into the church, which is the school of Christ, there to be instructed by his ministers in the way of salvation. Now though faith is indispensably necessary in adult persons, yet it is not necessary in children under the gospel any more than under the law, and in adult persons faith was as much required of Jewish proselytes as 'tis now of Christian converts. And so was repentance, too. Christ was always the Saviour of the world, and the gospel now preached is the same that was preached to the Jews, only with this distinction: in point of faith they were to believe in a Saviour that was to come, we in one that is come.

Hebrews 4:2. "For unto us was the gospel preached, as well as unto them, but the word preached did not profit them, not being mixed with faith in those that heard it."[60]

1 Peter 4:6 "For this cause was the gospel preached to them that are dead, that they might be judged according to men in the flesh, but live according to God in the spirit."[61]

[174. A description of the basics of our duty and a cure for overly scrupulous consciences.]

Our knowledge is progressive; we cannot possibly attain to a clear and comprehensive view of our duty in all its parts all at once. 'Tis sufficient, I think, if we do as well as we can study to know our duty, and if when we discover anything to be a sin the mind presently feels an averseness from it because 'tis sin and therefore avoids it, I think 'tis what God requires. "Love God and love your neighbour"[62] is known to be a duty at all times—

I would by no means have any person, young people especially, perplex their minds with fears and scruples lest they should come short of their duty when their conscience[63] upon examination does not accuse them of willful sin. 'Tis possible that the best of us may indulge ourselves for a time some evil way, but I am verily persuaded if we are but careful to avoid known sins and to do present duty to the best of our knowledge, God in his good time will reveal even this unto us—[64]

[175. A fragment.]

Morn[ing]
We are apt to think if we find in ourselves[65]

[176. Scripture citations with some commentary.][66]

Galatians 1:8–9
Acts 26:26

13 Acts 32–33 "And we declare unto you glad tidings, how that the promise which was made unto the fathers, God hath fulfilled the same unto us their children, in that he hath raised up Jesus again, as it is also written in the second Psalm, Thou art my son, this day have I begotten thee."[67]

St. John 5:40
St. Luke 24:44–47
Jeremiah 31:33–34
Acts 10:43
Isaiah 59:21[68]
Ezekiel 11:19
[Ezekiel] 36:26–27
Zechariah 12:10
Jeremiah 2:37

Genesis 12:3 [and] 22:18 "And I will bless them that bless thee; and curse him that curseth thee: and in thee shall all families of the earth be blessed." How? By being the Father of the Messiah according to the flesh and in him the Father of the faithful. The same promise repeated 22nd chapter, 18th verse.[69]

Acts 3:25–26 "Ye are the children of the prophets, and of the covenant God made with our fathers, saying unto Abraham, And in thy seed shall all the kindreds of the earth be blessed."[70]

Galatians 3:8, 16–17. "And the scripture, foreseeing that God would justify the heathen through faith, preached before the gospel unto Abraham saying, In thee shall all nations be blessed. [. . .] Now to Abraham and his seed were the promises made. He saith not and to seeds as of many [. . . .]"[71]

2 Corinthians 10:2[72]
Psalm 40:9
Isaiah 40:9, 41:27, 61:1
Isaiah 52:7
Romans 10:15
Isaiah[73]
St. Matthew 13:17
Hebrews 11:13
St. John 12:41
Isaiah 6:1
St. John 8:46
Job 19:25
Hebrews 11:26
John 5:46
Acts 3:24
St. John 12:47–48
All the saints did actually believe in Christ.[74]
Exodus 15:2
Psalm 100 and [?]18:14
Isaiah 12:2
Psalm 6

[177. The understanding, knowledge, and truth.]

Morn[ing]

The regularity of the will and passions seems in great measure to depend on the understanding, for which reason the understanding is generally thought the superior power of the soul.[75] Knowledge is necessary in order to the proper act of that power; indeed it seems the very act or habit of that faculty. Truth is the object of knowledge, or rather the very knowledge itself. All truths agree in one common excellence as truth; but as some truths are of greater use and importance, so consequently the knowledge of the more excellent and important truths is preferable to those of an inferior nature.

[178. Discerning true happiness—with a little help from John Locke.]

Noon

The desire of happiness is connatural with the soul, and 'tis impossible it should be otherwise. We can as easily [?]cease to be, as choose misery, as misery. Nor is the "constant unalterable desire of happiness and the constraint it puts upon us to act for it" any "abridgment of our liberty," as Mr. Locke well observes, "or at least 'tis not an abridgement to be complained of." "God [. . .] himself is under a necessity of being happy, and the more any intelligent being is so, the nearer is its approach to infinite perfection and happiness."[76]

In this state we are placed, the first step to happiness is to discern clearly in what our true happiness consists and, that we may not be mistaken in this important inquiry, God hath endowed us with power to suspend any particular desire and keep it from determining the will and engaging us in action till we have examined whether the satisfaction of such a desire doth interfere with our true happiness and divert us from pursuing it.[77]

[179. Clear perception through the Spirit's illumination.]

Even[ing]

As 'tis absolutely necessary in order to prevent our mistaking imaginary for real happiness that we have a clear perception of true happiness: so we may generally discern that the first operation of God's spirit in the mind is illumination. Darting a new light into the soul, by means of which we look on all things under different views from what we beheld them in the mere state of nature.

[180. Humanity's natural inclination toward "provision for the flesh."]

Even[ing]

Men in their natural state think the body the principal part of the man and that their greatest happiness consists in its preservation and the gratifying its appetites, and accordingly their greatest care is to make "provision for the flesh to fulfill the lusts thereof."[78]

[181. Bishop Beveridge on conscience.]

Conscience—What. Bishop Beveridge in a Sermon, title, "Conscience Void of Offence."[79]

There is in every man naturally a sense of things which we call conscience, whereby he perceives the difference betwixt good and evil. "If a man do but look into his own breast, he may there perceive something putting him in mind of what he should or should not do; and afterwards excusing or else accusing him for doing, or not doing it; which is nothing else, but his own mind or heart as sensible of the difference between good and evil and then reflecting accordingly upon what he doth to see whether it agree with that sense he had of it or no. And if he hath done that which he is sensible is good, then his mind is quiet and at rest. But if he have done that which he is sensible is evil and ought not to have been done, then is his mind offended and disturbed."[80]

This general sense of good and evil is implanted by God in the nature of all men, proved by that famous text in the 2nd [chapter] of Romans, verses 14–15.[81]

"Where we may observe the reason why it is called conscience and not simply science—because it is the same science, or sense of things in a lower degree, with that which God himself hath in a higher; and therefore it doth not simply bear witness, but, as the original word signifies, it bears witness with another, even with God, whether the thing be good or evil."[82]

[182. "Mr. Locke is in the right" on "abstract substance."]

Even[ing]

What idea any man can have of abstract substance I cannot conceive. I think Mr. Locke is right, that our specific ideas of substances are nothing else but a collection of a certain number of simple ideas, considered as united in one thing. Notwithstanding the objections of the Bishop of Worcester,[83] as if Mr. Locke would exclude all substances out of the world because, he says, "whatever be the secret and abstract nature of substance in general, all the ideas we have of particular distinct substances are nothing but several combinations of simple ideas, co-existing in such, though unknown, cause of their union, as makes the whole subsist of itself."[84] And that, "if a man examine his notion of pure substance in general, he will find he has no idea of it, but only a supposition of he knows not what support of such qualities (which are capable of producing simple ideas in us) as are commonly called accidents."[85] Because we cannot conceive "how those simple ideas can subsist by themselves, we accustom ourselves to suppose some substratum, wherein they do subsist, and from which they do result, which, therefore, we call substance."[86] But what this substratum, this support of accidents is, is undetermined, because I think 'tis inconceivable.

[183. Christ's divinity over and against Socinian and Arian views.]

Morn[ing]

Query: What reason have you to believe the divinity of Jesus Christ? What would you answer to the Socinians who deny him to be God or to the Arians who say he is a made or created God?

[184. The Trinity, argued from Hebrew philology, with Bishop Beveridge's help, and from Scripture.]

Noon

Answer: Although if it is to be supposed that God at first when he made man impressed as strong and clear a sense of himself in his mind as he was capable of receiving, yet it is so obscured by the fall of man from his original purity that we can now discern very little of him but what we collect from the revelation he hath been pleased to make of himself in his holy word, wherein he hath by using certain names, titles and expressions (adapted to our capacities), directed us what and how to think and believe concerning him.

There are two names by which he calleth himself in the Old Testament, which very plainly discover him unto us. Jehovah and Elohim. The first, as those that are skilled in the Hebrew inform us, signifies essence or being in general, which can be but one and therefore is always of the singular number; the other is Elohim, which is of the plural number and yet is all along joined with verbs and adjectives of the singular number, as if itself were so, which Bishop Beveridge observes and thence reasonably concludes that it is so used on purpose to show us that, though this universal essence or being be but one, yet there are several persons or subsistences so existing in it that they are all and everyone that essence or being. And accordingly we find frequent mention in scripture as of God himself, so of his Word or Son and also of his Spirit, which three we believe to be all that one Jehovah.[87]

Query: By what you say you seem to infer that the doctrine of the Trinity is only to be found in the scriptures and is not discoverable by the light of nature without assistance of divine revelation.

Answer: I do plainly assert that we could not be certain of the Trinity in the Godhead without God had revealed it unto us. And I think 'tis sufficient to all who believe the scriptures to be given us by the inspiration of the Holy Spirit, if we can clearly prove it by those scriptures that there are three persons or subsistencies (call them as you please) existing in the divine Being after such a manner that each and every person so existing is truly and properly that one Jehovah or essence or being, and this is not hard to do.[88]

Notes

1. MS A.

2. 22 May 1709, was a Sunday; the date matches the title page.

3. Psalm 118:24, slightly paraphrased; my quotation marks.

4. S. W. quotes the Fourth Commandment, first from AV, Exodus 20:8, then from the translation in the catechism, BCP; my quotation marks.

5. Cf. John 14:2–3.

6. My quotation marks.

7. See Matthew. 22:37; Mark 12:30, 33; Luke 10:27.

8. Echoes of the Sanctus, Holy Communion, BCP.

9. I have been unable to decipher these initials. The "A" may also be read as an "H," and the "T" could possibly be an "F." 9 October did fall on a Sunday in 1709.

10. Underlined in MS.

11. Special and distinct sphere.

12. Romans 13:14; my quotation marks.

13. There may be some biographical resonance here, an unconscious longing for her early years in her father's house in London, where cares and responsibilities were fewer.

14. Note that this phrase occurs also in entry 142 in Chapter 20.

15. Ephesians 4:13; my quotation marks.

16. Revelation 10:6.

17. This reflection is further evidence that "going on to perfection," one of John Wesley's later doctrinal emphases, was part of his mother's thought during his childhood.

18. I Corinthians 15:53, paraphrased; my quotation marks.

19. Hebrews 12:23; my quotation marks.

20. Cf. Charles Wesley's hymn "Forth in Thy Name" (1749), which includes the line "For thee delightfully employ / whate'er thy bounteous grace hath given."

21. Undated; this seems to be the third in a series of widely scattered sabbath meditations.

22. This Arminian doctrine, opposed to the Calvinistic idea of limited atonement, would later be another of her son John's theological emphases.

23. Matthew 7:14; my quotation marks.

24. The question of "assurance" is another mainspring of John Wesley's evangelical theology; here is evidence that it also preoccupied S. W. The quoted phrase is from the Litany, BCP; my quotation marks.

25. Ecclesiastes 1:14; my quotation marks.

26. Paraphrasing Peter's remark at Christ's transfiguration: Matthew 17:4, Mark 9:5, and Luke 9:33; my quotation marks.

27. An explicit example of the Platonic dualism that underlies much of S. W.'s (and her era's) thought.

28. Fit or deserving.

29. That is, of binding power; cf. Hebrews 9:17.

30. Close paraphrase of 1 Peter 5:8; my quotation marks.

31. John 21:15–17.

32. My quotation marks.

33. The meditation stops, leaving four or five lines of space at the bottom of the page.

34. 2 April, 1710. Note the lessons for "Sunday next before Easter" in BCP: Philippians 2:5–11 and Matthew 27:1–54. The latter tells the passion story, and the former is a Pauline reflection on it; S. W. seems to be responding to themes presented in both.

35. Psalm 103:1. Conflation of BCP translation, which uses "praise" in both clauses, and AV, which uses "bless." My quotation marks.

36. A conflation of the two parallel phrases in 2 Corinthians 6:14: "for what fellowship hath righteousness with unrighteousness? and what communion hath light with darkness?"

37. Philippians 2:6, paraphrased; my quotation marks.

38. Philippians 2:7; my quotation marks.

39. That is, of the human and divine natures in Christ.

40. John 3:16; my quotation marks.

41. Cf. Exodus 33:19.

42. Isaiah 55:9, paraphrased; my quotation marks.

43. Luke 10:21; my quotation marks. Crossed out at this point: "Adam was the first general head and root of mankind, and in him was virtually included the whole species of human nature."

44. That is, it makes one wonder.

45. Five lines left blank at the bottom of the page; the following page also blank.

46. First meditation not dated on a Sunday, reading from this end of the notebook.

47. S. W. seems here to be siding with John Locke and against the traditional Platonic view of innate ideas as espoused by writers like John Edwards, Joseph Glanvill, William Sherlock, and Edward Stillingfleet. See Richard Ashcraft, "Faith and Knowledge in Locke's Philosophy," in John W. Yolton, ed., *John Locke: Problems and Perspectives* . . . (Cambridge: Cambridge University Press, 1969), pp. 199–202. S. W. also addresses this point in an earlier entry (19) in chapter 16 of this volume, as well as later (182) in this chapter. See also the discussion in her "Religious Conference," in part III of this volume.

48. Entry ends with one-quarter page left blank at the bottom.

49. Luke 10:42; my quotation marks.

50. I have enclosed the entire divine "suggestion" in quotation marks.

51. A conflated reference to two Gospel stories surrounding Matthew 25:30 and Luke 17:10.

52. Under calendar conventions of the time this is probably 29 January 1722/23, a Tuesday (and not 29 January 1723/24, a Thursday).

53. For example, the previous resolution (entry 171), some four years before. The crossed-out "abundance" precedes "many attempts."

54. Followed by the crossed-out "in this view."

55. Replaces the crossed-out "perfection."

56. Probably stands for "debts," though, if so, it is unclear who her creditors are: "An" is perhaps her daughter Anne, who had married John Lambert, a local land surveyor, in late 1725; and "Jn" may be her son John, now on his own as a fellow of Lincoln College and at the time of this journal entry on leave as his father's curate at Epworth and Wroote. In support of John as one of these figures, note S. W.'s concern "to make things as easy . . . as possible" to him in her letter of 26 July 1727. The third potential creditor, "Lr," is more of a mystery.

57. Close paraphrase of Acts 4:12; my quotation marks.

58. Loose paraphrase of John 14:6; my quotation marks there, as well as setting off the entire "suggestion by some superior power" and the vow, itself. Two lines are left blank at the bottom of the page.

59. This entry and the following one, each of which take up a single MS page, lack the usual heading, either a date or the much more common identification of morning, noon, or evening.

60. My quotation marks.

61. My quotation marks.

62. Matthew 22:37–39, summarized; my quotation marks.

63. In MS: "Cs."

64. Three or four lines left blank at the bottom of the page, concluding this entry.

65. Breaks off in mid-sentence. A horizontal line drawn underneath divides this false start from the unique section that follows.

66. Four and one-half MS pages are here uncharacteristically given over to the listing of Scripture verses, spaced out as if for commentary. In only a few instances, however, are the spaces filled, usually with a quotation of or some reflection on the verses cited.

67. My quotation marks; Luke's quotation is from Psalm 2:7.

68. In MS (here and at other Isaiah references): "Esay."

69. My quotation marks.

70. My quotation marks.

71. My quotation marks and ellipses. Half of verse 16 and all of verse 17 are not quoted.

72. In MS: "1.02."

73. No chapter and verse listed.

74. The Scriptures cited seem to be dealing with Old Testament "saints" and the gospel being received by them in some sense.

75. Cf. John Locke, *An Essay concerning Humane Understanding*, ed. Peter H. Nidditch (Oxford: Clarendon Press, 1975), 2.21.5–6 (pp. 236–237).

76. Ibid., 2.21.50 (p. 265); my quotation marks. Her quotation is faithful, though somewhat rearranged. "Unalterable" does not appear in Locke's text.

77. Probably paraphrased from ibid., 2.21.52 (p. 267): "Whatever necessity determines to the pursuit of real bliss, the same necessity, with the same force establishes suspence, deliberation, and scrutiny of each successive desire, whether the satisfaction of it, does not interfere with our true happiness, and mislead us from it."

78. Romans 13:14, a Pauline phrase S. W. also uses in entry 166. Half of the page is left blank at the bottom.

79. William Beveridge (1637–1708), High Church bishop of St. Asaph from 1704. This sermon, based on Acts 24:16, is numbered XVII in *The Theological Works of William Beveridge* . . . , 12 vols. (Oxford: John Henry Parker, 1844), 1:300–319. My quotation marks.

80. Close paraphase, ibid., 1:302–303; my quotation marks.

81. Ibid.: " 'they which have not the Law, do by nature the things contained in the Law; these having not the Law, are a Law unto themselves:' i.e. though they have not God's revealed will or law written among them, yet they . . . have it notwithstanding in their hearts, their own minds telling them what they should or should not do" (p. 303).

82. Close paraphrase, ibid.: "Where we may likewise observe the reason why it is not called simply eidesis, or 'science,' but suneidesis, or 'conscience.' " S. W. has ignored the Greek words, which in Beveridge's original were also printed in Greek characters.

83. Edward Stillingfleet (1635–1699; bishop from 1689) engaged in a prolix published controversy with Locke; they traded three volleys each on their differing understandings of the Christian revelation. See John W. Yolton, *Locke: An Introduction* (Oxford and New York: Basil Blackwell, 1985), pp. 92–103. S. W. is aware of the controversy (see also her journal entries 19 and 169), but it is unclear which of the replies she has read, if any. Her citation is taken directly from Locke's original *Essay*. Stillingfleet's first objections, including the issue of "substance," appeared in the final chapter of *A Discourse in Vindication of the Doctrine of the Trinity* . . . (London: Henry Mortlock, 1697), entitled "The Objections Against the Trinity in Point of Reason Answer'd" (under which heading Locke was surprised to find himself treated). At any rate, she is here taking the more progressive side in an argument that Stillingfleet believed pitched orthodoxy against Unitarian heresy. S. W. implicitly agrees with Locke's protestations that his *Essay* does not call Christian truth into question, though she does seem a bit puzzled by the question at hand.

84. Locke, *Essay*, 2.23.6 (p. 298), lines 11–15; my quotation marks.

85. Close paraphrase of ibid., 2.23.2 (p. 295), lines 17–21; my quotation marks.

86. Ibid., 2.23.1 (p. 295); my quotation marks. Also quoted in Stillingfleet, *Vindication*, p. 236.

87. Beveridge, "The Being and Attributes of God," sermon 13, *Theological Works*, 1:238–247: "And nothing is more usual than for these two names of God, Jehovah and Elohim, to be put together . . . the first denoting the Unity of the Trinity, the second the Trinity in the Unity. . . . For though other adjectives and verbs too of the singular number are all along in Scripture joined with Elohim . . . yet [Hebrew] 'one,' is never joined with it. . . . God is pleased to say of Himself, that He is one Jehovah [Greek: mia ousia], 'one Essence.' In which although there be "Elohim," three distinct Persons . . ." (pp. 238–239). Cf. also "God our Sovereign Good," sermon 46, 2:363: "and it may not be unworthy of our observation, that whensoever God promiseth to be our God, He always doth it by a word [Hebrew] elohim of the plural number, denoting the three Persons subsisting in the Divine Essence."

88. Last entry in the notebook; only three lines at the top of the final page are used.

❦ TWENTY-TWO ❧

"These Blessed Lucid Intervals"

Unlike the previous seven chapters, which contain entries from a single note-book, this one draws on Susanna Wesley's entire journal output in two small notebooks.[1] However, this final batch of journal entries returns to her traditional practice of thrice-daily meditations and continues to deal with the same range of subjects and authors we have come to expect. For instance, there are references to, and wholesale copyings from, such important mentors as John Locke (209–211), George Herbert (205, 216), Pascal (207), Seneca (186), and the relatively unknown theologian Richard Lucas (202–203, 205, 208, 212–214). Even Gilbert Burnet, bishop of Salisbury (an early partisan of the prince of Orange and thus politically distant from the semi-Nonjuring Susanna Wesley) figures in two entries (199 and 215).

Among issues that engage her in these meditations, two stand out. One, a matter of belief, addresses the question "How can we know God?" In a string of entries (187–191) she walks a theological tightrope, acknowledging the positive role of reason and nature but balancing on the other side the necessity of the "experimental" knowledge that claims heart, will, and affections, as well as understanding.

The other issue, a matter of practice, is that of Christian perfection, a much-debated emphasis of her son John in later years. Meditations 193–199 address it in a preliminary way, including the recognition that "corrupt nature" (the same corruption that annuls the sufficiency of natural reason in matters of faith) also invalidates "all our fine speculations" in the pursuit of virtue (193) and, in an oblique reference to Thomas à Kempis's classic, that Christ is a moral pattern, as well as a Savior (194). She finds John Locke of some use here—his argument that "uneasiness" motivates the will helps her understand the human condition after the fall. Her real teacher in this school, however, is Richard Lucas, the blind Welsh priest and author of *Religious Perfection*. She does not buy all of his views, but she is obviously taken with many of them and copies them into her journal for further pondering.

The disciplined faithful life leads her once again to affirm her devotional routine and the vision that underlies her practice. In the final entry (217), as she describes God in classic terms, awe-inspiring yet attractive, she affirms "these blessed lucid intervals when the soul by contemplation holds [God] in view." The phrase is a useful reminder of the journal's importance to her at the deepest level of her life.

Entries from Headingley MS B

Entries 185–199 are taken from Headingley MS B, Wesley College, Bristol: a small notebook also containing poems of the Rev. Samuel Wesley and one bit of doggerel by one of the Wesley daughters, young Hetty. None of the entries are dated or contain internal evidence that gives any sense of when they were written.

ꙮ

[185. Take care not to be diverted from "accustomed exercises."]

Morn[ing]

Such a time devoted [. . .]² Whenever company or business inclines you to quit your retirement and either to omit or cursorily perform accustomed exercises and you instead of resisting comply with such inclinations, you may observe that you are always guilty of some sin or error, that upon reflection gives you more pain than the profit or pleasure gave you satisfaction. Therefore, make it your care to conquer your inclination to any company at such times, nor let any trivial business divert you; for no business, unless it cannot be laid aside or suspended without sin, can be of equal, much less of greater importance than caring for the soul—³

[186. Seneca's standard for friendship better than that of most Christians.]

Even[ing]

That man which will readily believe an ill report of you never was, or at least is not now, your friend. Seneca, a heathen, could say, "In some cases I'll not believe a man against himself. I'll give him however time to recollect himself; nay sometimes I will allow him council, too."⁴ But Christians, bad Christians, are rarely so candid. He is a friend indeed that is proof against calumny. But he is a rare Christian that will not believe a man against himself.

[187. "What is it to know God?"]

Morn[ing]

"This is eternal life: to know thee, the true God, and Jesus Christ, whom thou has sent." ⁵—But what is it to know God? Or what is that knowledge of God on which eternal life depends?

[188. Human reason and nature can teach us of "one supreme, eternal . . . self-existent Being."]

Noon

What can human reason do or how far can the light of nature direct us to find out the knowledge of the most high? From the primordials of the universe⁶ we collect that there is one supreme, eternal, consequently self-existent Being that gave being to all things, since to act presupposeth existence, for nothing can act before it be. That this Being must possess by way of eminence all the perfections we discern in the creatures reason tells us, for nothing can impart that to another which it hath not to impart.

[189. Other divine perfections discoverable by the light of nature.]

Even[ing]

And, as creation demonstrates omnipotence, so that infers wisdom, justice, truth, purity,[7] goodness, etc. for all these perfections are intellectual powers, and were God deficient in any one, he could not be omnipotent. That he is a Spirit, unbodied, undetermined, immense, filling heaven and earth and all imaginary spaces beyond them, most simple (pure), uncompounded, and absolutely separated and free from whatever pollution a spirit is capable of being defiled with, immutable, uncapable of change or alteration for the better or worse, perfectly free,[8] having no superior, no equal that my impel, allure or persuade him, but acting always spontaneously according to the counsel of his own will, we may discover by the light of nature.[9]

[190. Another kind of knowledge: "God known to the heart, the will and its affections."]

Morn[ing]

This is to know God as a man, as a reasonable creature, but this is not that knowledge that leadeth us to eternal life. That is a knowledge of another kind. The one we attain in a scientifical method by a long train of arguments for which the bulk of mankind want either capacity or leisure, the other by frequent and fervent application to God in prayer. The one is an effect of reason assisted by humane learning,[10] peculiar to a few of more noble and refined sense—God perceived, known to the understanding as the creator, preserver and governor of the universe. The other[11] is reason acting by the influence and direction of the Holy Spirit—God known to the heart, the will and its affections, not merely as the author of our being, but as he is exhibited to us under the character of a healer, a repairer of the lapse and misery of human[12] nature, a Saviour, him whom our soul loveth.[13]

[191. "Experimental" more important than speculative knowledge of God.]

Noon

To know God only as a philosopher, to have the most sublime and curious speculations concerning his essence, his attributes, his providence, to be able to demonstrate his being from all or any of the works of nature, and to discourse with the greatest elegancy and propriety of words of his existence or operations, will avail us nothing, unless at the same time we know him experimentally, unless the heart perceive and know him to be her supreme good, her only happiness, unless the soul feel and acknowledge that she can find no repose, no peace, no joy but in loving and being beloved by him, and does accordingly rest in him as the centre of her being, the fountain of her pleasures, the origin of all virtue and goodness, her light, her life, her strength, her all, everything she wants or wisheth in this world and for ever. In a word, her Lord, her God![14]

Thus let me ever know you, oh God! I do not despise or neglect the light of reason, nor that knowledge of you which by her conduct may be collected from this goodly system of created beings, but this speculative knowledge is not the knowledge I want and wish for.[15]

[192. Overcoming an inclination not to obey; exercise virtues of meekness and humility.]

Morn[ing]

'Tis very probable that your hu[mour] last night was rather the effect of fancy and passion[16] than of a clear sound judgment. If otherwise, why did you feel uneasiness at another person's being out of humour? Was it not pride made you resent contradiction? Or from what other principle could that reluctance flow which you felt in[17] obeying a trivial command which perhaps might proceed from narrowness, yet, the matter being indifferent, obedience was unquestionably your duty. A wise person[18] ought seldom, or indeed never when authority is not disputed or contemned, do acts of power, because[19] they are shocking to human nature, which, if not fortified and strengthened by religion, is apt in such cases to throw off a subjection and rebel even against lawful government. But though you should meet with such instances which the pride of man will throw in your way, yet take care not to swerve from your duty. Look upon every such act as a call of divine Providence to exercise the virtues of meekness and humility. When you can bear severe reflections, unjust censure, contemptuous words and unreasonable actions without perturbation, without rendering evil for evil, but with an equal temper can clearly discern and cheerfully do your duty, you may hope that God hath given some degree of humility and resignation.

[193. Enlightenment by "some higher principle," not philosophical speculation, can conquer "corrupt nature."]

Even[ing]

The philosophy of the whole world hath not sufficient force to conquer[20] the propensions of corrupt nature. Appetites and passions will bear sway maugre[21] all our fine speculations, till our minds are enlightened by some higher principle by virtue of which light it discerns the moral turpitude of those things in which before it placed its supreme happiness, and the beauty of that virtue and holiness that it was accustomed to despise.[22]

[194. Imitating Christ and following his precepts.]

Morn[ing]

You commit your soul morning and evening to Jesus Christ, as he is the Saviour of the world—Then observe what he saith unto you, resolutely obey his precepts and endeavor to follow his example in those things wherein he is exhibited to us as a pattern for our imitation.[23] No circumstances or time of life can occur but you may find something either spoken by our Lord himself or by his Spirit in the prophets or Apostles that will direct your conduct if you are but faithful to God and your own soul.

[195. An obstacle to Christian perfection: loving the world.]

Even[ing]

Two great obstacles in the way of Christian perfection, the first [. . .][24] What says our Lord by his apostle St. John? "Love not the world nor the things that are in the world. If any man love the world, the love of the Father is not in him."[25] That man will as certainly be damned whose affections are fixed on sensual pleasures, riches or honours, though he never enjoy any or a very inconsiderable proportion of them, as he that, having them all in his power, indulges himself the satisfaction of his most criminal desires. For 'tis the heart God requires, and he that suffers his heart (his affection) to centre on any thing but God, be the object of his passion innocent or otherwise, does actually make that thing his God and in so doing forfeits his title and pretensions to eternal happiness.[26]

[196. Another impediment to Christian perfection: "deep adversity" or "immoderate anxious care."]

Morn[ing]

Another great impediment is deep adversity, which[27] often affects the mind too much and disposes to anxious doubtful and unbelieving thoughts. Though there be no direct murmurings, no repining at prosperity of others, no harsh reflections on providence, but a constant acknowledgment of the justice and goodness of God, that he punishes less than iniquities deserve and does always in the midst of judgment remember mercy, yet, if you think too severely or unjustly of men, if you are too much dejected or disposed to peevishness, covetousness, or negligence[28] in affairs, if you work too much or too little, are presumptuous or desponding,[29] wholly omit to implore divine blessing and assistance on honest prospects and endeavours, or are too solicitous and earnest in prayer for external blessings, if the thoughts of your circumstances invade your privacies or disturb your rest, if any little access of trouble have power to ruffle your temper and indispose or distract your mind in your addresses to heaven, in reading, meditation or any other spiritual exercise; you are certainly in the power of the world, guilty of immoderate, anxious care. Then observe what your Lord saith by his apostle, "Be careful (anxiously careful) for nothing";[30] what he says himself, "Therefore I say unto you, take no thought [. . .]";[31] and remember that he ranks "cares of this life" with "surfeiting and drunkenness," which are mortal, damning sins.[32]

[197. Lawful enjoyments can become occasions of sin.]

Morn[ing]

The great difficulty we find in restraining our appetites and passions from excess often arises from the liberties we take in indulging them in all those instances wherein there does not at first sight appear some moral evil. Occasions of sin frequently take their rise from lawful enjoyments, and he that will always venture to go the utmost bounds of what he may, will not fail to step beyond them sometimes, and then he uses his liberty for a cloak of his licentiousness. He that habitually knows and abhors the sins of intemperance and will yet stay too long in company of such as are intemperate, and, because God is pleased to indulge us a glass for refreshment, will therefore take it when he really needs none, 'tis odds but this man will transgress, and though he should keep on his feet and in his senses, yet he perhaps will raise more spirits than his reason can command, will injure his health, his reputation or estate, discompose his temper, violate his own peace or that of his family, all which are evils [that] ought carefully to be avoided. It holds the same in all other irregular appetites or passions, and there may be the same temptations in other instances from whence occasions of sin may arise. Therefore be sure to keep a strict guard and observe well lest you use lawful pleasures unlawfully. Fly from occasions of evil.[33]

[198. Christian discipline; practicing any virtue reinforces all others in the "golden chain."]

Noon

The Christian religion is of so complicated a nature, that unless we give up ourselves entirely to its discipline, we cannot steadfastly adhere to any of its precepts. All virtues are closely joined[34] together, and break but one link of this golden chain, you spoil the whole contexture. As vices are often made necessary supports to each other, so virtues do mutually strengthen and assist virtues.[35] Thus temperance and chastity, fortitude and truth, humility and patience, divine charity and charity towards man, all virtues of what denomination soever, reciprocally cherish and invigorate one another.[36]

[199. Readings (unacknowledged) from Bishop Burnet: the "power of religion" alone can effect "inward and universal purity."]

Morn[ing]

Philosophy and morality are not sufficient to restrain us from those sins that our constitution of body, circumstances of life or evil custom strongly dispose us to. Nature and appetite will be too hard for their precepts unless a man be determined by a law within himself. They may teach him caution and give check to his vicious inclinations in public but will never carry him to an inward and universal purity. This is only to be effected by the power of religion, which will direct us to a serious application to God in fervent prayer,[37] upon which we shall feel a disengagement from the impressions sensual objects were wont to make on our minds,[38] and an inward strength and disposition to resist them.[39]

"Good men who felt upon their frequent applications to God in prayer a freedom from those ill impressions that formerly subdued them, an inward love to virtue and true goodness, an easiness and delight in all the parts of holiness, which was fed and cherished in them by a seriousness in prayer, and did languish as that went off, had as real a perception of an inward strength in their minds that did rise and fall with true devotion, as they perceived the strength of their bodies increased or abated, according as how they had or wanted good nourishment."[40]

This replied to Lord R[ochester's] objection against answers of prayer, which he supposes "fancy" and an "effect of a heat in nature"—that it had effect only by diverting the thoughts.[41]

Entries from Headingley MS C

These entries are from Headingley MS C, Wesley College, Bristol. A small (3 ½-by-3-inch) notebook, it is similar to MS A and B, except that its binding is along the short end. In addition to the undated meditations, it also contains, beginning at the other end of the notebook, a draft letter to S. W.'s son Samuel Jr. (11 October 1709) and two draft letters to her daughter Suky (14 January 1709/10, on the Creed, and an undated one on the Decalogue). A number of pages (about ten) seem to be torn from the beginning of the meditation section of the notebook.

[200. Self-criticism for taking up worldly affairs in her meditation time.]

Even[ing]

You did ill in admitting of any discourse about the things of this world in the morn[ing] before the reading the psalms and chapter. It argued, if not a profane, yet a very careless indevout temper, a great deficiency of reverence and love. Do you not yet know that God is a holy and a jealous God! That he abhors all profane mixtures and worldly regards in his service? How long will it be ere you consider and attain to that purity, that perfect abstraction from all earthly things that is required[42] in such as take upon themselves the honour of approaching the divine majesty?

[201. Resolution.]

Morn[ing]

Resolved to be more careful in this matter for the future.[43]

[202. Reaction to Richard Lucas's objections to "solitude and retirement."]

Even[ing]

What Dr. Lucas [on] Christian Perfection[44] observes, that "the practice of wisdom and virtue is the best way to improve both,"[45] is undoubtedly true; but that therefore we ought not to seek solitude and retirement upon a pretense that it cuts off the opportunities of many virtues that may be practised in a public life, I utterly deny, unless our circumstances are such that we cannot without a direct opposition to the order of providence retire from the world, and then are we to exert ourselves and practise those virtues that are more peculiarly proper for persons of a distinguished character. I would fain know what that state of life is wherein the virtues of meekness, patience, charity, zeal, etc. are not necessary, or what place too remote from commerce with mankind as to exclude all occasions of practising these virtues.

I am of opinion that abundance of the temptations we meet with and many of our sins are owing to our too great desire of being known to, and unnecessary converse in, the world. There are but few, ah very, very, few, in whom the prince of this world[46] finds little to work upon. None but he that was God as well as man, in whom he hath nothing;[47] and 'tis great presumption for us to pray daily "lead us not into temptation"[48] and yet expose ourselves unnecessarily to those trials that we are sure to meet with in the common conversations of the world; and he that in confidence of his strength will go abroad to exercise his virtues will, 'tis to be feared, in a little time have no virtue to exercise. For your part neither seek nor shun temptations if providence cast them in your way. Remember this rule which I think will always hold good: fly all temptations to unlawful pleasures, for he that in that case parleys[49] will yield. Encounter trials that carry difficulty and pain with courage and resolution, for he that turns his back is sure to be overcome.

[203. On Lucas: trials and temptations may strengthen some, but most should try to keep out of their way.]

Morn[ing]

He [Lucas] says, "the world is an excellent school to a good Christian; the follies and miseries, the trials and temptations of it, do not only exercise and employ our virtue, but cultivate and improve it [. . .]," etc.[50] This is also truth in some cases, but I doubt[51] where one cultivates and improves his virtue by converse in the world, ten thousand lose their virtue and their souls by willfully plunging themselves into it, that otherwise might have been saved, had they been careful to keep out of the way of temptation. We do not know ourselves, every man is not qualified to enter the lists or take up the gauntlet against pleasure, riches, or honour. No man is always wise, but some are never so, nor have skill or address to combat with such formidable enemies, and therefore 'tis the safest course to keep out of the way as much as we lawfully can. But if providence leads us into danger to exercise our virtue, God's grace is sufficient for us and will certainly preserve us from evil, if we sincerely desire it.

[204. Resolved never to speak against any person, unless God's honor or human good requires it.]

Even[ing]

"Speak evil of no man"[52] is a positive command founded on the eternal law of charity. As all positive commands are to give place to moral duties which, having an antecedent foundation in nature, are of perpetual obligation, so this among the rest, when the glory of God and the good of mankind require it. But when neither the glory of God nor your own nor neighbour's good obliges you to speak ill of any, you ought never to make mention of any person's faults in their absence. Resolved never to speak against any person upon any occasion unless it evidently appear necessary to vindicate the honour of God, the reputation of myself or neighbour, or by way of advice or caution to those spoken to, or for some other good end then[53] in view.

[205. Necessity of spiritual exercises; Lucas (and George Herbert) on appropriate virtues to emphasize in various circumstances.]

Morn[ing]

Experience teaches you that 'tis absolutely necessary to spend a considerable time in spiritual exercises, and therefore be careful to get and improve all opportunities of retirement and recollection. Your mind is weak, consequently inconstant, your thoughts desultory, hard to fix on useful subjects, which is another evident mark of impotence. As in bodily so in spiritual distempers a considerable part of the cure is owing to a knowledge of the disease, and therefore you[54] must carefully observe what state of health your mind is in, what power is defective, what passion irregular and most predominant; for different defects and imperfections, as well as temptations, times, circumstances and opportunities, often makes [sic] the exercise of one virtue more necessary than another. Lu[cas]: three things to be aimed at in all instrumental duties such as prayer, meditation, etc.: "1.[. . .] enlivening the conscience; 2. confirming and strengthening resolutions of obedience; and 3. raising and keeping up holy and devout affections.[. . .] Tenderness of conscience will preserve from all appearance of evil. Spiritual strength renders us steadfast and immovable in good works; holy passion will make us abound in them. To spiritual passion we owe the zeal and pleasure, to spiritual strength [or liberty], the constancy and uniformity of holy life, and both strength and passion are generally owing to an enlightened conscience."[55] Which of these do you most want? I fear all in a great measure. "If," says L[ucas] "a man's temper be such that his passions do soon kindle and soon die again, that he is apt to form wise and great projects and [as] unapt to accomplish anything; in this case it will be his duty to aim especially at the increase of spiritual strength."[56]

And here Herbert's advice is excellent,

> If thou dost purpose ought within thy power
> Be sure to do it though it be but small,
> Constancy knits the bones and makes us stower . . .[57]

"But if on the other hand a man's temper be cold and [phlegmatick, slow and] heavy, it is [but] fit that he should particularly apply himself to the [awakening and] exciting devout affections [in his soul]. For as excellent purposes do often miscarry for want of constancy and firmness of mind, so constancy[58] and firmness of mind doth seldom effect any great matter when it wants life and passion to put it into motion. Again, if [one's] past life have[59] been very sinful or the present unfruitful,[60] it will behove such a one to increase the tenderness of conscience, to add more light and life to its conviction[s], that by a daily repetition of contrition and compunction he may wash off the stain or by the fruitfulness of his following life repair the barrenness of the past." [61]

[206. The capability of receiving divine blessings and human kindnesses.]

Morn[ing]

If you would receive any particular blessing from God or any kind offices from man in any case, you must endeavor to render yourself capable of receiving it. Those that are duly qualified and sincerely apply themselves to obtain, never are denied any instance of his favour they really want. You cannot ask so much as God can give, nor is he ever unwilling to give to such as will worthily receive. Goodness is his essence, bounty, or beneficence, the essence of goodness.

[207. Human ignorance and error prevent the communication of divine goodness and favor; Pascal's thought on human disregard for ultimate concerns.]

Noon

As light and heat are inseparable from the sun, which would always appear with equal lustre, did not clouds interpose and solid bodies obstruct the penetration of his beams; so that immense Fountain of pure goodness would overflow and fill each creature according to the measure of its capacity, did not the clouds of ignorance and error and the more solid bodies of unmortified sins prevent the communications of his favour. Blessed God! that ever you should be willing to impart and condescend to offer that grace which man so much wants, yet is unwilling to receive! Did not constant experience put it out of our power to doubt the truth of it, we should think it impossible for human nature to be so much corrupted as to despise or undervalue that grace which was so dearly purchased and upon which present and eternal happiness depends. But so it is in fact our hopes, our fears, our desires and expectations are commonly concluded within the prospect of this life. Every man living knows he must die; very few but also know that an eternal state of happiness or misery attends the issue of this life, yet with what indifference and ease can we hear or think of these things. As M. Pas[cal] justly observes, "They are quite other men in all other regards: they fear the smallest inconveniences; they see them as they approach and feel them if they arrive; and he who passeth days and nights in chagrin or despair for the loss of an employment or [for] some imaginary blemish in his honour is the very same mortal who knows that he must lose all by death, and yet remains without disquiet, resentment, or emotion. This wonderful insensibility with respect to things of the most fatal consequence in a heart so nicely sensible of the meanest trifles is an astonishing prodigy. . . ." [62]

[208. Spiritual strength through prayer, meditation, and a little help from Dr. Lucas.]

Morn[ing]

Strength and power are equivocal terms; weakness and impotence are so also. The one, if acquired by labour and industry, is a virtue; the other, as far as 'tis voluntary, that is, if it be an effect of sloth, aversion from labour through love of ease or pleasure, unnecessary cares and regards for the things of this life, is a sin. Where either are purely natural, it is not morally good or evil. If you would judge of the strength of your own mind, observe what power you have over your passions and actions, what impressions you receive from the things you are conversant about. If you find your passions quickly raised, your mind soon elated or depressed, your will easily determining to act contrary to your better judgment, your mind is certainly weak, and you must vigorously apply yourself to the gaining of more strength by fervent prayer and frequent meditation.

Dr. Lu[cas] observes that spiritual strength "stands upon two bases, the reduction of sin and the growth of virtue. Whatever does weaken and reduce our propension[s] to evil,[63] whatever promotes the subjection of the body adds power and authority to the mind and renders virtue more easy and pleasant."[64] Whatever strengthens one virtue, strengthens all, because of their mutual connexion and dependence.[65] "Especially, whatever strengthens our hope, quickens our fear, [or] enlarges our knowledge, and increases our faith [, this] does confirm and establish our resolution more than anything else. Faith is the roof, fear the guard, and hope the spur of all our virtues."[66]

[209. The Holy Spirit's role in strengthening the (Lockean) will.]

Noon

The inclining or disposing to, strengthening, and confirming the will in the paths of virtue seems to me the principal design of the Holy Spirit in all his operations. For this end I humbly conceive he enlightens and enlarges the understanding and purifies the affections, and the reason appears obvious, because the will is that "power of the mind that directs the operative faculties of man to motion or rest, as far as they depend on such direction,"[67] which is very far. But I do not [. . .][68]

[210. Understanding does not determine the will; rather, as Locke says, "uneasiness" in the want of some good.]

Even[ing]

[. . .] think it reasonable to suppose that the will always follows the last practical dictate of the understanding, as some have vainly imagined, especially in case of future happiness or misery. "For all absent good," as Mr. Locke says, "by which alone barely proposed and coming in view, the will is thought to be determined and so to set us on action, being only possible but not infallibly certain, 'tis unavoidable that the infinitely greater [possible] good should regularly and constantly determine the will in all the successive actions it directs; and then we should keep constantly and steadily in our course toward heaven without ever standing still or directing our actions to any other end."[69] 'Tis uneasiness that seems immediately to move the will. The understanding has a perception of absent or present good, that perception causes love, love raises desire, which is the most restless passion we have, that desire begets uneasiness, that uneasiness put us upon action, as Mr. Locke has excellently proved, and in proportion to the uneasiness is the vigour of the act.[70]

For let a man's perception of any good be never so clear and evident, it will not "determine his will unless his desire, raised proportionably to it, make him uneasy in the want of it."[71]

[211. More on uneasiness as determiner of the will: an objection to Locke and S. W.'s response in support.]

Even[ing]

It is objected[72] that Mr. Locke is mistaken, that uneasiness can never be the object of desire, therefore cannot determine the will.[73] Good, as good, he thinks, can only move the will—good as good is certainly the proper object of the will, and were not it for the depravity of man's nature, simple good, whether absent or present, and the greatest good would constantly determine all the operations of the will. Nor could there ha' been any uneasiness in the mind, because there would have been no want; but according to the present state of things, though good is still the object of the will and must have power to move it, yet let the good be never so great, and let it appear in the clearest light to the understanding, still, if it be future, and a man can amuse himself with any trifling matters that lie directly in his way and so does not apprehend that absent good as necessary to his present happiness, it will move his will so faintly (if at all) that he shall feel no uneasiness in the want of it, nor will he be at any labour to attain it, so that it appears plainly (I think) that Locke is in the right, that uneasiness is the immediate cause of the operations of the will. 'Tis certain uneasiness can never be the object of desire, for all men naturally desire happiness, and every uneasiness is a degree of misery; were it possible for man to find pleasure in it, he would have no desire to get rid of it, nor does Mr. Locke suppose uneasiness the object of desire, but says that the desire to get rid of uneasiness[74]

[212. Reflection on Lucas: Christian perfection in this life, a "perfection of degrees" only.]

Even[ing]

L[ucas] [on] C[hristian] per[fection]: "Religion is nothing else but the purifying and refining nature by grace, raising and exulting our faculties and capacities by wisdom and virtue. Religious perfection,[. . .] such a maturity of virtue as man is capable of in this life.[. . .] A ripe and settled habit of [true] holiness."[75] "He is a perfect man" (in his sense) "whose mind is pure and vigorous, his body [tame and] obsequious, [. . .] faith firm and steady, [. . .] love ardent and exalted, [. . .] hope full of assurance, whose religion has in it that ardour and constancy and his soul that tranquility and pleasure as speaks him a child of light [. . . .]"[76]

Perfection in the strict notion (notwithstanding all he says of it)[77] in this life amounts to no more than a perfection of degrees. There are many degrees of comparison and a vast difference even in virtuous men. Some, by a singular felicity of temper, a peculiar happiness in the make and constitution of their bodies, seem formed for piety and virtue; others, by education and freedom from great temptations, are all their lives preserved from flagrant scandalous offenses, and such as these may and often do attain to a great degree of perfection unknown to the generality of the world; yet the sublimest pitch of virtue that ever any reached is unworthy the name of true perfection.

[213. Lucas on judging one's spiritual state.]

Morn[ing]

L[ucas on] C[hristian] p[erfection]: His notion of perfection[.] [78] Some rules whereby a man may judge of his spiritual state. [79]

1. "[. . .] If a man's life be very uneven, inconstant [80] and contradictory [to it-self]—if he be today a saint and tomorrow a sinner, if he yield today to the motions of the gospel and impulses of the spirit and tomorrow to solicitations of the flesh and the temptations of the world, he is far from being perfect; so far that there is not ground enough to conclude him a sincere [or real], though imperfect convert. The only certain proof of regeneration is victory; [81] faith [. . .] is not [. . .] saving [and justifying] till it have subdued the will[. . .]." [82] "We may have sudden heats and passions for virtue, but if they are too short lived to implant it in us, this is not that charity or love which impregnates and animates the new creature mentioned in Galatians 5:6, 'faith working by love.' [83] [Lastly,] We may have good purposes [, intentions, nay] and resolutions, but if these prove too weak to obtain a conquest over our corruptions, [. . .] too weak to resist the temptations we are wont to fall by, 'tis plain they are not such as can demonstrate [84] us righteous or entitle us to a crown which is promised to him that overcometh." [85] We are not to conclude anything concerning our progress or perfection too hastily; we are not to determine of the final issue of a war by the success of one or two engagements, but our hopes and assurances are to advance gradually in proportion to the abatement of the enemy's forces and increase of our own. [86]

"A [sincere] Christian [but especially one] of a mature virtue may easily discern his spiritual state." [87] If divine truths make deep impressions, if conviction be clear, faith strong, standing "firm against the shock of carnal objections," if "he earnestly desire to please God" and "thirst more after the consolations and joys of the spirit than that of sensible things," if he laments his heaviness or aridity and frequently aspires toward heaven on the wings of faith and love, if he maintains a constant familiarity and converse with heaven and desires to be "delivered from this body of death" [88] to enter into the peaceful regions of life and immortality, he must be sensible of these things upon reflection. [89]

The animal life, "the reluctancies [90] of the body, the allurements of the world cannot be disarmed and conquered," [91] nor "the hunger and thirst after righteousness [. . .] eager and the relish of spiritual pleasure" so strong and lively [92] as to beget a settled "contempt of worldly things" and the man remain ignorant of his state. [93]

[214. Lucas's checklist for determining "the goodness of our state."]

Even[ing]

L[ucas on] C[hristian] per[fection]: "If [then] we are [94] frequent and fervent in our devotions; [. . .], modest and grateful in successes, patient [and], resigned, calm and serene under the crosses and troubles of life; if we be not only punctual but honourable in our dealings;[. . .] vigorous and generous in the exercise of charity; if [. . .] not only just and true, but meek, gentle and obliging in our words, if we retrench not only the sinful, but something of[95] the innocent freedoms of life[96] and gratifications of sense, to give up ourselves more entirely to the duties and pleasures of faith; if, finally, we are never[97]ashamed of virtue, nor flatter, or wink at vice; if we be ready to meet death with comfort and retain life with some degree of indifferency;[98] if, I say, these things[99] be in us, we have little reason to doubt of the goodness of our state. . .."[100]

[215. "Never despair of pardon"; the necessity of both reason and experience.]

Noon

Despair naturally hardens the heart; this the devil knows by experience as well as observation, and therefore 'tis one of his common artifices, when he sees a person's life hath been very wicked or unfruitful, to suggest they can never be better; and if he can prevail with them to believe their case desperate, he knows they are in the readiest way to make it so. Mark this well, and whatever sins or difficiencies you have been guilty of, never despair of pardon for what is past or of God's grace to prevent the like for the future. Preserve your faith in the Lord Jesus inviolable. All power in heaven and earth is committed to him for this end, that he may be the Saviour of the world. "As the father worketh hitherto," says he, "so do I work."[101] As the eternal Father by the operation of his providence preserveth, governs, and directs each individual creature[102] after such a manner as is best for the good of the whole system of created beings, so Jesus Christ the incarnate Word always presides over the human nature, ordering and disposing all events of God's general providence in such a way as is best for the good of his church and for the spiritual and eternal good of every particular member thereof. So that if you have but a firm faith and dependence on the power of our blessed Lord, you will be able to say, as St. Paul, "I can do all things through Christ strengthening me."[103]

"Reason and experience determine our persuasion. Experience without reason may seem the delusion of fancy. Reason without experience proves oftentimes ineffectual. But when they meet together, they give a man all the satisfaction he can desire."[104]

[216. Submission to God's will; poetic support from George Herbert.]

Noon

Submission and resignation is your present duty. God often times obscures the light of his favour to shine afterwards on the mind with greater splendour. None but he is always the same. 'Tis the peculiar of the deity to be immutable. Be not discouraged, though your good intentions have no effect. Purity of intention is your duty and happiness, but events belong to God.

> Besides things sort not to my will,
> Even when my will doth study thy renown,

Thou hon'st the edge of all things on me still
Taking me up to throw me down.[105]

was Mr. H[erbert's] complaint long ago. Throw yourself on divine mercy, and rest there.

[217. Holding God in view by contemplation.]

Morn[ing]

Pursue the thought you had lost of the purity of God which is very awful[106] and indeed exceeding terrible to the willfully unclean. Purity is his essence. His power, wisdom, justice, goodness, truth, etc. are perfectly simple. No mixture of weakness or injustice pollutes his power; his wisdom is infinitely holy, admits not the least shadow of ignorance, error, folly or inadvertence. His justice, impartial, severe, equal and immutable. His goodness, sincere, absolutely separated from whatever implies impotence or instability. His truth is holy! Rectitude itself! Eternal, invariable, uncapable of fraud, deceit, etc.[107]

"But who can by searching find out God, who can find out the Almighty to perfection?"[108] To know you, Oh God, is impossible; not to know you, intolerable. Our understanding is too weak, is dazzled, confounded and overpowered, and faints at the perception of your glory. We cannot bear the smallest ray thereof, but nature sinks under the weight of an incumbent[109] deity. Yet is the thoughts of you sweeter than rest, more refreshing than food, dearer than all the treasures upon earth! When you condescend, Lord, to manifest yourself, all pain and want and care, all sense of misery vanishes in a moment, no unkindness or loss of friends, no contempt, reproach of enemies, no evil of any kind does afflict any longer. The noblest wine, the most generous cordial doth not so much exhilarate and cheer the spirit as the least perception of your favour through Jesus Christ doth refresh and glad the soul, when ready to faint under the weight of its corrupt nature and tired with an unsuccessful pursuit of happiness in the enjoyment of what the world calls good. 'Tis in these blessed lucid intervals when the soul by contemplation holds you in view that we say with your apostle, "Master, it is good for us to be here."[110]

Supreme eternal being! Fountain of life and happiness! Vouchsafe to be ever present to the inward sense of my mind. I offer you my heart—take possession by thy Holy Spirit for the sake of Jesus Christ. Amen. Amen.[111]

Notes

1. Fifteen and 18 meditations, respectively, are found in the two notebooks in the Wesley College collection designated Headingley MS B and MS C. Further details on these manuscripts will appear under the two subsections of this chapter.

2. Three characters of what appears to be shorthand seem to complete this sentence. I have been unable to decipher them.

3. The meditation finishes at the bottom of the first notebook page. The next page is entirely blank.

4. See S. W.'s several other quotations from Seneca in her letters—to Samuel Jr. (11 October 1709), to her brother Samuel Annesley Jr. (20 January 1721/22), and to her son John (22

April 1727)—and in her devotional journal (entry 51). As in those places, I cannot find the source of the current quotation, although there are resonances in Seneca's *Epistles* (see *Seneca Ad Lucilium Epistuale Morales*, ed. and trans. Richard M. Gummere [London: Heinemann; New York: Putnam's, 1935] and Roger L'Estrange, ed., *Seneca's Morals by Way of Abstract*, 7th ed. [London: Jacob Tonson, 1699].) My quotation marks.

5. Fairly accurate quotation of John 17:3; my quotation marks.

6. Beginnings, first principles. For a near contemporary example of such usage, the OED cites the Cambridge Platonist Henry More, *Divine Dialogue* (1668) 1:37: "The Primordials of the World Are Not Mechanicall, but Spermaticall or Vital."

7. Followed by the crossed-out "immutability."

8. The phrase, "acting always spontaneously" is crossed out here and inserted below in the same sentence.

9. The entry concludes, leaving nearly half a page blank.

10. Though "humane" was at this time a variant spelling of "human" (as in the original title of Locke's *Essay concerning Humane Understanding*), the OED points out that by the turn of the eighteenth century it was also acquiring the more specialized meaning of refined, compassionate, courteous, and so on that we associate with the word today.

11. Crossed out here and then reworked later in the sentence: "God known to heart, the will and its affections, not barely the Author of our being but."

12. In MS: "humane."

13. Resonances of Song of Solomon 1:7, 3:1–4.

14. S. W. has personified both "heart" and "soul" as female. Interestingly, two young contemporaries of John Wesley sought to "correct" her. John Whitehead, *The Life of the Rev. John Wesley* . . . (New York: R. Worthington, 1881), p. 35, neutered the former ("unless the heart know him to be its supreme good . . .") and turned the latter into a masculine reference: "unless *a man* feel and acknowledge that *he* . . ." (emphasis added). Clarke, transcribing the entry at a slightly later date, followed Whitehead on "heart" but S. W. on "soul" (p. 259).

15. Entry concludes, leaving five or six lines blank at the bottom of the page.

16. Followed by the crossed-out "rather."

17. Replaces the crossed-out "at."

18. Replaces the crossed-out "superior."

19. Followed by the crossed-out "in such."

20. Replaces the crossed-out "bear down."

21. Despite.

22. S. W. seems to be reworking the words of Gilbert Burnet, *Some Passages of the Life and Death of the* . . . *Earl of Rochester*, . . . (London: Richard Chiswel, 1680), facsimile ed. (Menston, Eng.: Scolar, 1972), pp. 45–46: "And that [i.e., "delight in the Dictates of Virtue"] could not be effected, except a mans nature were internally regenerated and changed by a higher Principle: Till that came about, corrupt Nature would be strong, and Philosophy but feeble: especially when it strugled with such Appetites or Passions as were much kindled, or deeply rooted in the Constitution of ones Body. . . . I told him . . . that all his Speculations of Philosophy would not serve him in any stead, to the reforming of his Nature and Life, till he applied himself to God for inward assistances." This popular book is the bishop of Salisbury's account of his conversations with the notorious atheist and loose-living poet (1647–1680) that led to a death-bed conversion. S. W. returns to Burnet in at least two additional meditations in MS B and MS C (entries 199 and 215).

23. Hovering in the background of this meditation is an awareness of Thomas à Kempis's influential work, *The Christians Pattern; Or a Divine Treatise of the Imitation of Christ* (London: John Clark, 1659). See the discussion in S. W.'s correspondence with her son John, 8 June 1725.

24. There follow four characters of indecipherable shorthand and what looks like "c p v-y."

25. Nearly perfect quotation of 1 John 2:15; my quotation marks.

26. See Matthew 6:21ff.

27. Followed by the crossed-out "too."

28. Replaces the crossed-out "carelessness."

29. Losing heart or resolution.

30. Philippians 4:6 with S. W.'s interpretive addition in parentheses, though she omitted the final one; my quotation marks.

31. Matthew 6:25. A space of several lines in the MS indicates that S. W. intended, but did not return to fill in, a longer quotation from Jesus' well-known discourse on anxious care from the Sermon on the Mount, probably through verse 34.

32. The phrases I have placed in quotation marks are from Luke 21:34.

33. Possibly an echo of Galatians 5:13 ("use not liberty for an occasion to the flesh"), which certainly fits the tenor of the entire meditation.

34. Replaces the crossed-out "linked."

35. Replaces the crossed-out "one another."

36. An eclectic list. Cf. the traditional seven virtues: faith, hope, charity, justice, prudence, temperance, and fortitude; and by contrast, the seven deadly sins: pride, covetousness, lust, envy, gluttony, anger, and sloth.

37. Followed by the crossed-out "the effect of which will."

38. The phrase, "sensual objects were wont to make on our minds," is not found in Burnet, *Life of Rochester*, p. 47, but rather seems to be a gloss that indicates her acceptance of Locke's epistemology. See, e.g., John Locke, *An Essay concerning Human Understanding*, ed. Peter H. Nidditch (Oxford: Clarendon Press, 1975), 1.2.15 (p. 55) and 2.19.1 (p. 226).

39. This paragraph is both a loose paraphrase of and a meditation on a section of Burnet's *Life of Rochester*, pp. 43–47. See entry 193 in this chapter.

40. This defense of prayer is a direct quotation, ibid., p. 50. Quotation marks have been added.

41. S. W. gleaned the phrases I have placed in quotation marks, ibid., pp. 51 and 47, respectively. The last phrase of the entry closely echoes two of Burnet's: one on p. 47 ("the strong diversion of thoughts") and another on p. 48 ("if such Methods did only divert the thoughts").

42. Followed by the crossed-out "to a worthy." It appears that the word may have originally been "requisite" but that she altered it to "required" after changing the phrase that followed.

43. This brief meditation is written at the bottom of one side of a single sheet and at the top of its other side. Like the previous one (and, indeed, all the other meditations in MS A and MS B) it is written along the shorter axis of the page. On that same side S. W. turns the notebook and begins to write on the longer axis, a practice she continues for the remainder of the entries.

44. Richard Lucas (1648–1715) was an Oxford-educated Welshman who became a popular preacher and writer in London, finishing his career as a prebendary of Westminster. Upon his blindness he wrote a three-part *Enquiry after Happiness* . . . (London: S. Smith and B. Walford and Edw. Pawlett, 1696–1697), which established his reputation as an authority on the subject of piety. According to the *Dictionary of National Biography*, this work was recommended to John Wesley by his mother, and he esteemed it highly. The source of this supposition is seemingly the recollections of Wesley's friend Alexander Knox, published as counterpoint in Robert Southey's *Life of Wesley*, 2 vols., 3rd ed. (London: Longman, Brown, Green and Longmans, 1846), 2:407–504. Though Knox underscores the importance of Lucas in the formation

of Wesley's doctrine of Christian perfection, he does not give Susanna Wesley any direct credit for recommending the book to her son. The closest he comes is to remark that Wesley was reading Lucas "from his first years of serious reflection" (p. 419) and that both Taylor and Lucas were "guides of his youth" (p. 457). For the extended consideration of Lucas, see p. 457–462.

In the present and in subsequent journal passages, S. W. is reflecting on Lucas's *Religious Perfection. Or, a Third Part of the Enquiry after Happiness*, 2nd ed. (London: Sam. Smith and Benj. Walford, 1697).

45. Ibid., p. 96, my quotation marks. S. W. has omitted the words "and strengthen" after "improve." Her subsequent demur is in response to his assertion further along in the same section: "it is plain, That we ought not to be fond of such a Solitude or Retirement, as cuts off the opportunity of many Virtues, which may be daily practis'd in a more publick and active Life" (p. 97).

46. That is, Satan. See John 12:31, inter alia.

47. See John 14:30: "for the prince of this world cometh, and hath nothing in me."

48. Matthew 6:13; my quotation marks.

49. That is, discusses terms with the enemy.

50. Lucas, *Religious Perfection*, p. 97.

51. Suspect.

52. Titus 3:2; quotation marks added.

53. Apparently S. W.'s underline.

54. Replaces the crossed-out "we."

55. Lucas, *Religious Perfection*, pp. 107–108; my quotation marks. The quotation is nearly word for word, with bracketed words or ellipses representing material from Lucas not incorporated into her meditation.

56. Ibid., p. 109; my quotation marks, with an omitted word from Lucas inserted in brackets.

57. George Herbert, "The Church-Porch," stanza 20, lines 115–117, from *The Temple*, in F. E. Hutchinson, ed., *The Works of George Herbert* (Oxford: Clarendon Press, 1941), p. 11. "Stowre" (stour), that is, sturdy, strong, stalwart. The entire stanza, quoted from *The Temple, Sacred Poems and Private Ejaculations*, 12th ed. (London: Jeffery Wale, 1703), p. 5, runs:

When thou dost purpose ought (within thy power)
Be sure to doe it, though it be but small:
Constancy knits the bones, and makes us [stowre],
When wanton pleasures becken us to thrall.
    Who breaks his own bond, forfeiteth himself:
What nature made a ship, he makes a shelf.

58. In Lucas, *Religious Perfection*: "steadiness." S. W. has miscopied here, reading from the line just above in Lucas's text.

59. Ibid.: "has."

60. Ibid.: "Not very fruitful."

61. Ibid., p. 109, my quotation marks, with Lucas's words inserted in brackets. The meditation concludes, leaving the bottom half of the page blank.

62. *Pascal Thoughts on Religion, and Other Subjects. . . ,* Basil Kennett, trans. (London: A. and J. Churchil, R. Sare, J. Tonson, 1704), chap. 1, par. 1, pp. 11–12; exact transcription with exception of bracketed insert; my quotation marks. The original passage concludes: "an unintelligible Enchantment, a Supernatural blindness and infatuation." S. W. copied a shorter version of the same quotation in entry 131.

63. In Lucas, *Religious Perfection*: "sin."

64. Ibid., pp. 115–116.

65. This sentence is a paraphrase (ibid., p. 116).

66. Ibid.; my quotation marks, with S. W.'s omissions from Lucas in brackets.

67. Nearly exact quotation (with quotation marks added) of Locke, *Essay*, 2.21.29 (p. 249): "The Will being nothing but a power in the Mind to direct the operative Faculties of a Man to motion or rest, as far as they depend on such direction."

68. The sentence (and entry) stop in midstream but are taken up again in the meditation that follows.

69. Locke, *Essay*, 2.21.38, lines 20–29 (p. 255); my quotation marks.

70. S. W. is dealing with material found repetitively in ibid., 2.21.29–40 (pp. 249–258). Part seems to be a close phrase of 2.21.31 (pp. 250–251): "some (and for the most part the most pressing) *uneasiness* . . . successively determines the *Will*, and sets us upon those Actions, we perform. This *Uneasiness* we may call, as it is, *Desire*; which is an *uneasiness* of the Mind for want of some absent good."

71. Close paraphrase of ibid., 2.21.35 (p.253); my quotation marks.

72. Four indecipherable shorthand characters follow, possibly identifying the source of the objection, a publication S. W. has been reading or someone she has been conversing with on the subject, for example, neighboring clergyman Mr. Hoole. See her letter to him, 12 October 1726, discussing Locke.

73. More discussion of material in Locke, *Essay*, 2.21.29ff. (pp. 249–258). See note 70.

74. The meditation breaks off at the bottom of the page.

75. Lucas, *Religious Perfection*, pp. 1–2, somewhat rearranged with some material left out as indicated; my quotation marks. The crucial passage reads: "Religious Perfection therefore, is nothing else but the Moral Accomplishment of Human Nature; such a Maturity of Virtue as Man in this Life is capable of; Conversion begins, Perfection consummates the Habit of Righteousness: In the one, Religion is, as it were, in its Infancy; in the other, in its Strength and Manhood; so that Perfection, in short is nothing else, but a ripe and setled [sic] Habit of true Holiness."

76. Ibid., p. 2, with omissions indicated in brackets; my quotation marks.

77. Lucas spends an entire chapter ("This Notion of Perfection Countenanced by All Sides," ibid., pp. 17–28) dealing with the controversy surrounding the idea of perfection. His definition seeks to take such objections as these into account and thus seems to anticipate S. W.'s, as well. "I never dream of any man's passing the course of Life without Sin: Nor do I contend for such a Perfection as St. Austin calls Absolute, which will admit of no Increase, and is exempt from Defects and Errors" (p. 27).

78. Four indecipherable shorthand characters follow.

79. Lucas, in fact, makes five points (ibid., pp. 33–45), but S. W. gets bogged down in the first only before moving to other material.

80. Ibid.: "unconstant."

81. Added, ibid.: "he that is born of God, overcometh the World, 1 John 5:4."

82. Ibid., p. 33, thus far, with omissions as indicated; my quotation marks. Lucas continues in words dropped by S. W.: "and captivated the Heart, i.e., till we begin to Live by Faith; which is evident from That Corn in the Parable, which though it shot up, yet had it not Depth of Earth, nor Root enough, and therefore was withered up, and brought forth no fruit. Regret and Sorrow for Sin is an Excellent Passion, but till it has subdued our Corruptions, chang'd our Affections, and purified our Hearts, 'tis not that Saving Repentance in the Apostle, 2 Corinthians 7:10 . . ." (pp. 33–34).

83. Note, later on, one of John Wesley's favorite verses.

84. Replaces the crossed-out "denominate."

85. Lucas, *Religious Perfection*, p. 34; my quotation marks. The scriptural resonance at the end is from the second and third chapters of Revelation, particularly 3:11–12.

86. This summary, building on the biblical metaphor of victory, seems to be S. W.'s own.

A one-inch horizontal line is drawn in from the left margin, separating this paragraph from the next.

87. Lucas, *Religious Perfection*, p. 52, with S. W.'s omissions in brackets and my added quotation marks.

88. My quotation marks; paraphrase of Romans 7:24.

89. Lucas, *Religious Perfection*, pp. 52–53; loose paraphrase using many of Lucas's words and phrases, even when not directly quoting. Direct quotations have been so indicated.

90. Ibid.: "reluctances."

91. S. W. has substituted "conquered," for "weaken'd, and reduc'd" (ibid).

92. Ibid.: "brisk and delightful."

93. Ibid., pp. 52–53; paraphrases and, where indicated, direct quotation.

94. Ibid.: "be."

95. Ibid.: "from."

96. S. W. has substituted "freedoms of life," for original word, "liberties" (ibid.).

97. Ibid.: "never be."

98. Ibid.: "indifference."

99. Ibid.: "if these things, I say. . . ."

100. Ibid., pp. 53–54; my quotation marks.

101. John 5:17, slightly altered; my quotation marks.

102. Followed by the crossed-out "[?]of his omnipotent goodness."

103. Nearly exact quotation of Philippians 4:13; my quotation marks. A horizontal line, half the width of the page, separates this paragraph from the next.

104. This paragraph is an unacknowledged quotation (or close paraphrase) from Burnet's, *Life of Rochester*, pp. 48–49; quotation marks added. The original, part of the bishop's conversation with the libertine Rochester, reads: "I added, that Reason and Experience were the things that determined our perswasions: that Experience without Reason may be thought the delusion of our Fancy, so Reason without Experience had not so convincing an Operation: But these two meeting together, must needs give a man all the satisfaction he can desire." The word "satisfaction" in S. W.'s journal is partially underlined, though it is difficult to know if it represents an added emphasis or merely serves to end the entry.

105. George Herbert, "The Crosse," lines 19–22, from *The Temple* in Hutchinson, p. 165. The entire stanza, quoted from the 1703 ed., p. 159, runs:

> Besides, things sort not to my Will,
> Ev'n when my Will doth study thy Renown:
> Though turn'st th' Edge of all things on me still,
>   Taking me up to throw me down:
> So that, ev'n when my Hopes seem to be sped,
> I am to Grief alive, to them as dead.

The final stanza (skipping one in between) gives a heightened sense of the context:

> Ah my dear Father, ease my Smart!
> These Contrarieties crush me: these cross Actions
> Doe wind a Rope about, and cut my Heart:
>   And yet since these thy Contradictions
> Are properly a Cross felt by thy Son,
> With but four words, my words, *Thy will be done?*

106. Worthy of profound respect or reverential awe.

107. S. W. made what appear to be copying errors in this section: she wrote, then crossed out "His goodness" just before the sentence beginning "His justice," and at the end of the

same sentence she has written and crossed out "his truth impartial se," even though it is at the top of the next page between the divided word "immu-table." Probably she was entering material from some other, unacknowledged source.

108. Slightly altered version of Job 11:7; my quotation marks.

109. Hanging over, weighing on the mind, impending, threatening.

110. Peter's comment at the transfiguration in Mark 9:5, Luke 9:33, and Matthew 17:4.

111. This paragraph dramatically concludes the meditations in Headingley MS C. S. W. has filled all her paper: the final phrase of her prayer appears on the same page as the last material already begun from the other end of the notebook (an incomplete draft letter on the Ten Commandments—see part III of this volume).

TWENTY-THREE

"To Feel a Vital Joy Overspread and Cheer the Heart"

*T*his chapter brings together 38 diary entries that survive either as manuscript fragments torn from one of the existing notebooks (or some other one, now lost) or as transcriptions in two nineteenth-century publications. The existing manuscript fragments are located, respectively, in archival collections in Baltimore and Manchester, and the transcriptions are recorded in Adam Clarke's *Memoirs of the Wesley Family* and in the short-lived English periodical, the *Wesley Banner*.

Though somewhat disconnected from one another, these three clusters of entries [1] appropriately conclude this collection from Susanna Wesley's journal. Here we may see once again the array of concerns and issues that typify all of her private writing—from reflections on her spiritual life to quotations from a helpful author to the final revealing entry giving important, if sketchy, biographical details.

Her contemplative writing covers the usual territory. She resolves both to "watch and pray" against sin, in the process setting more rules (230) and more particular "solemn engagements" (250), and yet she tries to achieve spiritual discipline without "ensnaring" herself by "perpetual vows" (249). Her yearning for a closer union with the divine comes across in two entries that talk of enjoying "enough of God" (251, 252) and in her prayer-poem (254) that professes and describes her love for God. She recounts in 253 the spiritual benefits of suffering but also maintains that, even though we are "born to trouble," mercies outweigh afflictions in our lives.

Susanna Wesley's continuing interest in Christian perfection (252) is supported by another long quotation from Richard Lucas, the practical theologian we have already noticed her reading. In 219 she copies a rather long passage arguing that religion should be practiced in every area of life, not just in the "church or closet." Lucas helpfully calls her from the sublimity of the contemplative life to the important struggle of the active life, where one must contend with stubborn children, sour parents, inconstant friends, and all the other "opportunities" the world presents for the exercise of virtue.

The final entry (255) is a fragment that lists what she considers her advantages, among them her parents, "good books and ingenious conversation," and her husband ("a religious orthodox man"). We would certainly like to know more: Is it, in fact, Bishop Bull who helped stop her from becoming a Unitarian? Exactly what were the particulars of her close brush with "violent death"? As usual, she does not provide much in the way of the details of her life; even here the recounting is, typically, not written down for future biographers, but to help her make sense of her own religious pilgrimage.

Journal Fragments: Baltimore Manuscript and Wesley Banner Transcription

Preserved in the United Methodist Historical Society's Lovely Lane Museum, Baltimore, Maryland, are several meditations, written on both sides of a single 6-by-8-inch sheet torn from the binding of one of Susanna Wesley's notebooks, and thus make up four 4-by-6-inch (unnumbered, undated) journal pages. The subject matter is reminiscent of Headingley MS C, but that notebook is slightly smaller and bound along the short rather than the long axis of the page; though the dimensions and binding pattern fit, it is not readily apparent that these pages are from MS A or MS B, either.

Because the writing is on both sides of the sheet, we can easily follow the flow of the meditations from one side to the other. However, because the sheet was removed from a gathering of pages, the left half of the spread and its reverse do not relate to the right half and its reverse.

While they do not connect directly with any known manuscripts, these meditations are part of a larger grouping, now apparently lost, which was transcribed by the Victorian periodical, the *Wesley Banner*. Over the course of seven monthly issues, it published "extracts, now copied from the original . . . never before . . . published." The Baltimore fragments seem to have been faithfully transcribed, and the general trustworthiness of the *Banner* editor is further enhanced by a theological disclaimer suggesting that he is not reponsible for expressions not to his readers' liking and that, at any rate, Susanna Wesley got it right later in life.[2]

🔥

[218. Fragment: "no desire to be known to the world."][3]

[. . .] and you'll never be uneasy [?]though you hear I'll—aspire to be known to God and the Holy Angels, and you'll feel no desire to be known to the world, nor any pain in being contemned of those for whom you've no esteem.

[219. Excerpts from Lucas on the means of attaining perfection.][4]

Morn:[ing]

Lu[cas], Attain[ment of] Per[fection]:[5]

"Religion is not to be confined to the church or closet, nor exercised only in prayer, meditation, etc. [but] everywhere we are in the presence of God, and every word and action is capable of morality. Our defects and infirmities betray themselves in the daily accidents and common conversations of life, therefore they are to be watched over, regulated and governed." [6]

"Let no man that would be perfect or happy abandon himself to his humours, or inclinations towards his children, his acquaintance, or servants [. . . .]" [7]

"To the end he may conform himself to the precepts of the Gospel and train up himself to those rules of wisdom, and virtue, of which he is capable, he must first know himself, and those he has to do with[,] he must discern the proper season, and the just occasion of every virtue, and then apply himself to attain it by exercising it in those things which for want of due reflection do not seem of any great importance. To one thus disposed, the dulness, or carelessness of a servant, the stubbornness of a child, the sourness of a parent, the inconstancy of friends, the coldness of relations, the neglect and ingratitude of the world, will prove useful, and beneficial[;] every thing will instruct him, every thing will afford him an opportunity of exercising some virtue, and he will be daily learning and growing better." [8]

If rich, still remember that it is your principal business to work out your salvation,[9] let the world go which way it will.[10]

[220. "Clear accounts with heaven" before enjoying life's "innocent refreshments."] [11]

Evening

To apprehend God displeased, to feel the vital influences withdrawn, to be sensible neither of the grace nor comfort of the Holy Spirit, and yet to be capable of relishing the childish amusements of the world, is an argument of a vain and irreligious mind. That person that truly loves God above all things, that hath really a higher estimation for him than for any, or all things he hath created, is as incapable of rest, or satisfaction of mind, under a sense of his anger, as his body would be at ease when labouring under an acute distemper. If, therefore, this be your case, be assured you do not love God as you ought to do. First clear accounts with Heaven, and then freely use the innocent refreshments of life.

[221. Consciousness of guilt and inability to atone.]

Morning

To a soul conscious of guilt, sinking under the weight of corrupt nature, there is no solid foundation for hope or comfort, but Jesus Christ. None but the stupidly ignorant can possibly suppose themselves capable of doing anything by way of atonement for sin. The dignity of the Being offended, the condition of the offender, the nature and number of the offences, the deficiencies of our best performances, render this utterly impossible.

[222. Folly, pride, and vainglory.]

Noon

For persons to affect speaking of themselves, shows them either desirous of being taken notice of, and esteemed of men, which proceeds from vain glory; or that they are well opinioned of themselves, which is commonly an effect of pride, or else that their minds are weak and foolish, and that they accustom themselves to talk at all adventures without advertence. In the knowledge of some distempers lies a great part of cure. Folly, pride, and vain glory, are allowed odious by all, and if any sober man can be brought to believe himself guilty of these, he must be uneasy till cured.

[223. Lacking peace of mind: "trust God with the conduct of your soul."]

Evening

Still foolishly disposed to think of————. To what purpose? Either the evil apprehended will come, or not: if it is certainly of Divine appointment, no human prudence, at least not yours, can prevent it; therefore, it is your wisdom, and will be your felicity, too, to fortify your mind with patience, submission, and renewed repentance, that you may be assured of Divine succours when you most need them. If they should never happen, you lose your present quiet, weaken your body, and unfit your soul for present duty for a mere chimera. It is too much, methinks, to be without ease, friend, wealth, reputation, quiet, and peace of mind too! But, perhaps, you will say, "How can this peace of mind be preserved inviolable when we want the others?"[12] I will tell you how patience and submission, where pain is not extreme, are easy to learn, and not difficult to practise, are a sure support, and strengthens [sic] the mind under bodily infirmities. Live so as to deserve a friend, and if you never have one on earth, God will be your friend, and in having him you will have all that is dear and valuable in friendship; and then you will never want a friend though you are without one. Learn by practice to love God above all things, and you will be out of the power of the world, and then to be without wealth will give no uneasiness. Your wealth will be his favour, with the blessed consequences attending it; the virtues of his Holy Spirit, purifying your mind, exalting your nature to the dignity of a divine resemblance, teaching you to undervalue, nay, despise the perishing enjoyments of what a mistaken world calls good, as unnecessary, or rather a hinderance to your spiritual and eternal good, which you will then prize above the others. As for reputation or esteem among men, though a good name is as precious ointment,[13] yet remember, you have long since offered up that to God, and resolved never to make your reputation or the esteem of man the end of any of your actions where the glory of God is not concerned. Now, in this case, trust God with the conduct of your soul, commit yourself to him in ways of well-doing, and he will take care of his own glory, and not suffer you to do anything that may reasonably reflect dishonour on your Christian profession, and when that is safe, despise all popular applause, contemn the reputation of any quality or virtue that terminates in yourself. Be content that all men should despise you. Do well.

[224. Preparation for the Lord's Supper.]

Noon

The design and end of the Lord's Supper is best learned from the words of the institution, "Do this in remembrance of me." Whatever ends in preparation for it we may have in view, this is to be sure is the principal—to commemorate the death of Christ; and though some have supposed the chief end is to renew our baptismal covenant, and I do not deny, that, after a deep lapse into the powers of the flesh or world, it is very convenient, if not necesary, to renew the covenant that we have violated, yet I do not think it essentially requisite to a worthy partaking in case of habitual holiness.[14]

[225. There can be no liberty when a person is beset with "strong conflicts": a likely quarrel with Lucas.]

Morning

This he calls a state of liberty,[15] but I think with the same propriety of speech as a man entered into a good course of physic, excepting a disease may be said to be in a state of health, or two contending nations beginning to treat and debate upon artillery, can be said to be in a state of peace. There is no such thing as liberty under strong conflicts, and when lusts have power to make a vigorous opposition, the man is far from being free. The best that can be said of such a case is, he is in a hopeful way of recovery, and if he persevere, and be not discouraged from doing his duty as well as he can, he may reasonably hope that by the co-operation of the Holy Spirit, through the merits and intercession of his Saviour, he will obtain the victory, and then, and not till then, he will enjoy the "blessed liberty of the children of God."[16]

[226. Lucas on sincere but imperfect Christians—in a "state of grace" but also a "state of childhood."][17]

"That the sinner actually make good his resolutions, break with his lusts, reject their solicitations, and oppose their commands, he must earnestly strive by self denial, meditation, and prayer to extirpate vice, and plant virtue in his mind. [. . .][18] He that has proceeded thus far, though he feel great conflicts, the opposition of lust be strong, and the discharge of his duty difficult, is, nevertheless, in a state of grace, but in a state of childhood too; sincere, but not perfect.[19] Yet this is the state which many Christians continue in all their lives, being abased by false notions, and brought to believe there is no higher or perfecter state, or encumbered by some unhappy circumstances, or the impetus of the soul is abased by prosperity, and the many engagements and diversions of a fortunate life."[20]

[227. Mortify your appetites.]

Noon

It is necessary for you, if you would preserve your liberty, and live free from sin, to mortify your appetites, for if they remain in power, restrain them as you will or can, still some circumstances or seasons will occur, wherein they will betray you and compel you to act contrary to your better judgment.

[228. Lucas on the process of illumination: "repentance in embryo."][21]

Evening

God generally works on man in a manner suitable to his nature. The first operation of the Holy Spirit in conversion is light to discern his state; the medium of which light is usually something extraordinary, either of judgment or mercy.[22] Then "he is presently agitated by various passions, according to his different guilt and temper or the different motives[23] by which he is wrought upon. Fear, shame, indignation, desire, hope, alternately fills his soul.[24] He resents the tyranny of sin, upbraids himself with his folly, observes a meanness in vice which he did not discover before. He is troubled at the mischief his sin and folly have procured him, and apprehends somewhat far more intolerable if he persist in a sinful course.[25] Then he reflects on the goodness and patience of God, the love of Jesus, the 'demonstration of the Spirit and power,'[26] and how distant soever he be from virtue, he discerns a beauty and pleasure in it, and cannot but judge the virtuous[27] happy. These thoughts, if not unhappily stifled by a man's pusillanimity, or diverted by some temptation, do inflame him with thirst of righteousness and liberty, fill him with regret and shame, humble him before God, and inspire him with resolution to shake off the yoke. This may be called a state of illumination, a good preparation, or disposition, for repentance. It is repentance in embryo."[28]

[229. Those who allow appetites and passions to rule are fools and slaves.][29]

Morn[ing]

There is hardly any one that does not resent the being thought or called a fool; yet how few whose words or actions does not every day or hour reproach him with folly. How impatient and angry are we if any man assume a power over us to direct our words or actions, and complain of it as an intolerable violation of our liberty, and yet how often do we suffer our appetites and passions to give law to our superior powers, and without any resentment submit to that worst[30] of slavery. He that without advertence follows his appetites or passions in opposition to his reason is both a slave and a fool.

[230. "Watch," as well as "pray," against sin.]

Even[ing]

"Watch and pray," saith our Lord.[31]

Whatever sin you pray against, if you are not careful to watch against it too, you have little reason to expect your prayers should be answered, and though to a person of your slothful indolent temper this may possibly appear a severe injunction, yet what God your Saviour hath joined together you must in no wise put asunder.[32] In order to perform this duty aright you must observe these rules. [1.] Preserve a sober, equal temper. 2. A habitual advertence. Use frequent recollection. Sincerely pray for divine assistance. Sobriety and equality of mind consists in freedom from all perturbation, for any passion in excess does as certainly inebriate as the strongest liquor immoderately taken.

[231. Lucas's idea of a perfect man is difficult to imagine, yet not impossible.]

Evening

Dr. L[ucas] is of opinon, "that original sin in a perfect man may be so far reduced and mastered as to give him very rare and slight disturbance."[33] This notion of perfection is a confirmed habit of holiness. I confess I have no notion of such perfection; nor has any such person yet come within my observation; yet will I not conclude the thing impossible, for there may be, and doubtless is, sublime degrees of virtue of which such a one as————has no idea.[34]

[232. Reflections on Lucas and defects in those who are "perfect."]

Morning

But if there be any so perfect as to be free from all original sin in the measure he speaks of, how shall we account for the failures we may observe in those we call the best of men? We must not impute them altogether to the depravity of their wills, or suppose that such offend of malicious wickedness; for in this sense they cannot commit sin, being born of God, their seed remaineth in them.[35] Since then, as he acknowledges in another place, when speaking of sins of infirmities, "the best men are not without errors, without defects and failures," even in their regenerate state.[36]

[233. Lucas on venial sin: trifling and indeliberate transgression, "beside the law, but not against it."][37]

Evening

"There are actions properly and truly voluntary. Such are those deliberate transgressions of a Divine law which a man commits in opposition to the remonstrances of conscience. He knows the action is forbidden;[38] he sees the turpitude and obliquity of it; he is not ignorant of the punishment denounced against it; and yet he ventures upon it. This is[39] mortal, damnable sin; and I cannot think that any circumstances or pretences whatever can render it venial. And, therefore,[40] I cannot be of their opinion who suppose that the smallness of the matter, the reluctance[41] of conscience, or length or force of temptation,[42] can so soften or mitigate a voluntary transgression as to diminish it into a sin of infirmity. As to the smallness of the matter, though some think those transgressions venial which are for the matter so small and insignificant[43] that they seem to be attended by no mischievous consequences, nor to offer any dishonour to God nor injustice to man. But I doubt[44] this notion of venial sin hath[45] no solidity in it; for either men perform these actions deliberately, or not knowing them to be sinful, or believing them innocent.[46] Now, if we perform any action deliberately, and knowing it to be sinful, we never ought to look on this as a little sin, much less a venial one. The reason is plain. The first notion we have[47] of sin is, that it is forbidden by, and displeasing to, God; and then to do that deliberately which we know will provoke God, is an argument of a fearless and irreligious heart—a heart destitute of the love of God, of virtue, and of heaven.[48] But if a man transgress in a trifling instance, indeliberately, this alters the case; for the matter not being of importance enough to excite the attention and application of the mind, and there being consequently no malignity of the will in an action where there was no concurrence of the judgment, I think[49] this may very well pass for human infirmity; for all the fault that can here be charged on man is incogitancy or inadvertency, and that, too, as excusable a one as can be. Lastly, where the matter of an action is very trifling and inconsiderable, attended with no ill consequence with respect to God or man;[50] in this case, if a man judge it to be[51] no sin, I cannot think it is any to him, though, by a nice and scrupulous construction, it may fall within the compass of a Divine prohibition. The distinction of the schoolmen is good enough here. It is beside the law, but not against it;[52] it is against the letter, but not against the design and intention of the law of God. I cannot think it consistent with the goodness of God to punish such things as these with eternal misery, or that it can become a man of sense seriously to afflict his soul for them."[53] He supposes by an "idle word" our Saviour means a "wicked one, proceeding from a corrupt,[54] naughty heart, and tending as directly to promote impiety as wholesome discourse does to edification."[55]

[234. Governing the tongue; speaking rarely "in passion of any kind."]

Evening

It is, perhaps, one of the most difficult things in the world to govern the tongue, and he that would excel herein must speak but seldom; rarely, if ever, in passion of any kind, for it is not only in anger we are apt to transgress, but all excess of other passions, whether love, hate, hope, fear, desire, does not often unwittingly cause us to offend in words. Our Blessed Lord hath told us, that "out of the abundance of the heart," the affections, "the mouth speaketh."[56]

[235. Preventing evil speaking.]

Morning

The best way, therefore, to prevent evil speaking of any sort is to purify the heart, for, till that be done, all resolves and caution will be ineffectual. In order to the doing this, it will be requisite to know the state of your soul, to observe what order the passions are in, which is most predominate; whether they are placed on right and proper objects, or if they err in excess or defect, still keeping the main question in view, what you must do that you offend not by your tongue. If your mind be so impotent and weak that anger is wont to get the ascendancy of your reason upon every trivial occasion or inconsiderable provocation, and you are apt to break out into indecent or un-Christian language, give the first check to this most foolish passion, by not speaking one word; resolutely keep silence till the first shock be over; and, to prevent the return of the paroxysms, cleanse your heart by such wholesome considerations as these: first, that you are a Christian, by profession and choice, and that as such you are strictly obliged to observe the example and obey all the commands of the Holy Jesus. His example: he was pure meekness, patience.

[236. Christians should be guided by Jesus' response to reproach.]

Evening

Consider him who endured such contradiction of sinners against himself. In all his reproaches, contumelies, unjust and unworthy censures he met with, he "answered not a word." [57] "When he was reviled, he reviled not." [58] It would be well if those that assure the honour of the Christian name and yet upon every slight provocation indulge themselves in a liberty of using the most reproachful terms and unmanly rudeness their passion can suggest, would use the forementioned text, as Moses commanded the Israelites to do his words, lay them up in their heart and in their soul, and "bind them for a sign upon their hand, that they might be as frontlets between their eyes." [59]

[237. Lucas on the partly voluntary, partly involuntary "sins of infirmity."] [60]

Morning

"The last class of actions are those that are of a mixed nature, partly voluntary, partly involuntary. And here, I think, we must place sins of infirmity. [61] For these surely, if they are to be ranked, as by all they are, among actual sins, must be such actions as have something voluntary, something involuntary, [62] much of human frailty, and something of sinful, much of unavoidable, and something of moral obliquity." [63]

[238. Lucas on venial versus mortal sins.] [64]

"Thus, then, I describe a venial sin. It has in it so much of voluntary as to make it sin, so much of involuntary as to make it frailty. It has so much of the will in it that it is capable of being reduced; and yet too much of necessity as never to be totally extirpated. [65] It hath something in it criminal enough to oblige us to repent and watch against it, [66] and yet so much in it pitiable and excusable, as to entitle us to pardon under the covenant of grace. And thus I distinguish venial from mortal sin. Mortal sin proceeds from a heart either habitually corrupted or deceived and captivated for the time; but venial sin from the infelicities and imperfections of our nature and state. [67] Mortal sin is only [68] voluntary and deliberate in the rise and birth of it, [69] mischievous and injurious in its consequences. [70] Venial sin is very far indeliberate in its beginning and, if not indulged, almost harmless in its effects. Deficiency is, as it were, the essence of the one, malignity of the other. In the one we see more of frailty, in the other of wickedness. In the one something nearly allied to necessity, in the other to presumption. The one is the transgression of the law of perfection, the other of the law of sincerity. The one is repugnant to the letter, the other to the design and end of the law. The one a violation of God's commands taken in the most favourable construction; the other a violation of them in a rigorous one."

Two things to be observed.[71] 1. The matter. 2. The manner. The matter slight, inconsiderable; no room for venial sin in things of a provoking nature, as murder, adultery, drunkenness.[72] But this not to be extended to first motions even of these sins. The manner: ignorance, frailty, surprise.[73] Not only invincible ignorance, but that that has some degree of negligence. Surprise, especially where the temptation is not only sudden but violent, too. This hardly can be extended to gross and carnal sins. Hard to conceive how sins of so high a nature should make their approach so silently, suddenly, or indiscernbily as not to be perceived by him that is alleged to shun all appearance of evil. It is not easy to imagine that one who does, indeed, "strain at a gnat," should "swallow a camel."[74]

[239. Diligence without anxiety.]

Evening

Our blessed Lord reproves Martha's care, because it cumbered and perplexed her mind.[75] She erred not in caring for a decent reception of her Saviour, but in being too anxious and solicitous about it, insomuch that she was not at liberty to attend on his instruction as her sister did. It requires great freedom of mind to follow and attend on Jesus with a pure heart; ever prepared and disposed to observe his example and obey his precepts. To manage the common affairs of life so as not to misemploy or neglect the improvement of our talents; to be industrious without covetousness; diligent without anxiety; to be as exact in each punctilio of action as if success depended upon it, and yet so resigned as to leave all events to God, still attributing the praise of every good work to him. In a word, to be accurate in the common offices of life, yet at the same time to use the world as though we used it not, requires a consummate prudence, great purity, great separation from the world, much liberty, and a firm and steadfast faith in the Lord Jesus.

[240. Lucas on pardonable defects and imperfections.][76]

Evening

"Here comes in the failures and defects in the measures and degrees of duty, if these can properly be called sins;[77] I say, if they can, for I do not see that this is a good argument. We are bound to the highest degree of love by that law, 'Thou shalt love the Lord thy God with all thy heart.'[78] Therefore, whatever falls short of the highest and most absolute degree of love is sin;[79] for at this rate, whatever were short of perfection were[80] sin. We must love nothing better nor equal to God;[81] this will constitute us in a state of sincerity. What is further required is, that we are bound to aim at and pursue the highest degrees of love,[82] but we are not bound under pain of damnation to attain them. But on the other hand, I readily grant that our falling short in the degrees of faith, hope, love,[83] and the like may properly be reckoned sins[84] when they spring from defects of vigilance and industry; and if such defects be such as can consist with sincerity, then, and then only, are the imperfections of our virtues pardonable."[85]

[241. Lucas and Pascal on the tranquility of one's own mind.]

Evening

"Certainly," says Dr. L[ucas], "it were better that all the world should call me fool, knave, or villain than that I should call myself so and know it to be true." He goes on: "My peace and happiness depends on my own opinion of myself, not that of others. It is the inward sentiments I have of myself that raise or deject me; and my mind can no more be pleased with any sensation but its own, than the body can be gratified by the relishes of another palate." [86] He here speaks like a wise and a good man, like one that hath a just dominion over his own passions; and it is what in reason every man ought to be able to say as well as he. But I believe, upon an impartial survey, there will be very few to be found but what are so much in the power of the world that, as Mr. Pascal observes, "they are not satisfied with that life they possess in themselves in their own proper being, but are fond of leading an imaginary life in the idea of others; and it is hence they are so eager and forward of showing themselves to the world. We labour," says he, "indefatigably to retain, improve, and adorn this fictitious being, while we stupidly neglect the true; and if we be masters of any noble endowment of tranquillity, generosity, or fidelity of mind, we press with all our vigour to make them known, that we may transfer and engraft these excellencies on that phantastic existence." [87] Contend not with men's interests, prejudices, or passions, when it can innocently be avoided, for these are things that rarely admit of a calm dispute. Every man ought to be so far a lover of himself as to prefer the peace and tranquillity of his own mind before that of others; and though we should do all we can to make others happy, yet, if any be so obstinately bent to follow those ways that lead to misery that they are not to be reduced, leave them to the mercy of God.

[242. Lucas on inordinate versus natural affections.]

Evening

"I distinguish between inordinate and natural affections. By inordinate I mean the tendencies of the soul towards that which is unlawful. By natural, its propension to the body with which it is invested, the desire of its health and ease, and the conveniences and necessaries of life for this end. Now, when religion enjoins repugnances to the former appetites, the obedience of the perfect man has no reluctancy in it; but when it requires things, as sometimes it occasionally does, which thwart and cross the latter, here the obedience of Christ himself was not exempt from conflict. [. . .] Though good men have preached temperance, chastity, charity, and other virtues of this kind with ease and pleasure, yet nature has shrunk and started at persecution and martyrdom." [88]

[243. Lucas on sin: "Passions for the body and the world" overpower the "desires of virtue."] [89]

Morning

"The nature of sin is founded in subversion of the dignity, and defacing the beauty, of human nature; and that it consists in the darkness of the understanding, the depravity of the affections, and impotence of the will.[90] [. . .] If the strength of sin did not consist in the disorder and impotence of all the powers[91] of the soul, whence is it that the sinner acts as he does? Is it not evident that his understanding is infatuated when he lives as if he were wholly body?[92] As if he had no soul but such as results from and dissolves[93] with its temperament and contexture? One designed to no higher purpose than to contrive, minister to, and partake in, its sensual pleasures?[94] [. . .] All are not equally stupid;[95] but even in those in whom are some sparks of understanding and conscience,[96] how are the weak desires of virtue baffled and overpowered by their much stronger passions for the body and the world."[97]

[244. Hatred of sin, the essence of repentance; a just sense of God, the foundation of penitence.]

Noon

In the hatred and abhorrence of sin as sin, as it is contrary to the purity of the Divine nature and laws, consists the very essence of true repentence. That it weakens the powers and defaces the beauty of human nature, that it is attended with such mischievous consequences in this world and the next, are excellent reasons for that hatred and abhorrence; but they are not the foundation of true penitence—for that derives its origin from a just sense of Almighty God, our dependence on and duty towards him as our creator, redeemer, and sanctifier.[98]

[245. Impossiblity of "a just sense" of God's essence; but we may know God's manifestations in the world and human nature.]

Evening

What is it to have a just sense of Almighty God as he is distinguished into three subsistencies; namely, Father, Son, and Holy Spirit? Indeed I cannot tell. After so many years of inquiry, so long reading, and so much thinking, his boundless essence appears more inexplicable, the perfection of his glory more bright and inaccessible. The farther I search, the less I discover; and I seem now more ignorant than when I first began to know something of him. But if true penitence is founded on a just notion or sense of God, and you cannot tell what it is to have a just sense of him, how can you know when you are truly penitent? It is impossible to speak of God without impropriety, or to think of him without ecstacy. The subject is too vast, the matter too important. His sublimity transcends all thought; words cannot express what is so far above their nature; therefore, the simplest and plainest are the best. There is more significancy in that awful name by which he condescended to manifest himself to the Iraelites, "I am," than can be comprehended or expressed by any or all the words that are comprised in all the languages on earth. When I say I cannot tell what is to have a just sense or notion of God, my meaning therefore is that I cannot do him the justice I would. I cannot attain to an adequate notion of him; but, as when we apply ourselves to the study of any part of physics, though we cannot so far penetrate into the nature of things as to be able to discover or define their proper substances, but must content ourselves with what knowledge we can gain of their accidents and properties—so, when we apply ourselves most diligently and sincerely to know God, though we cannot by the utmost force and energy of all our powers attain to the proper knowledge of his essence, his essential glory, wherein all perfections concentre, or rather are all but one perfection, yet we may discover what he is pleased to call "his back parts," that is, "the emanations of his essential glory or the manifestations it" hath made, or "maketh of itself in the exercise of his divine perfections." In the creation of the world, the redemption and regeneration of the human nature, "the government of the world, particularly in respect to mankind—which last," as Bishop Beveridge observes, "shows forth the glory of God *a posteriori* by its effects and consequences, although *a priori*[99] we can see nothing of it."[100]

[246. God reveals what our reason cannot discover.]

Morning

It is impossible to form right apprehensions of God by the dim light of nature, which that merciful being knowing, as also that the happiness of man could not be secured without his knowing God aright, he hath condescended to reveal that to man which his own reason was too weak to discover. It is to this revelation we owe all the just and true ideas we have of him who dwelleth in inaccessible light, unto which no man can approach.[101] It is this that directeth us to search and find him as he is, by and in Jesus Christ, in whom "dwelleth the fulness of the Godhead bodily."[102] To know him only as a man, as a reasonable creature—to know there is a supreme, just, wise, almighty Being that superintends the thoughts, words, and actions of all men, in order to a future retribution—can administer nothing but horror and amazement to the soul, since, obscure as natural reason is, it is clear enough to show us that we have done, and daily do, many things contrary to the purity of the Divine nature and the dictates of our own reason, which must necessarily lead us to despair. But to behold him in Jesus Christ, "reconciling the world unto himself";[103] to see by faith that infinite, all-glorious Being assuming the character of a Saviour, a repairer of the lapse, and healer of the diseases and miseries of mankind, is—what? It is something that penetrates and melts the soul. It is something the heart feels and labours under, but the tongue cannot express. I adore, O God! I adore!

[247. The difficulties—and the end—of professing Christianity.]

Noon

"What man goeth to war against another, and sitteth not down first to consider whether he be able with ten thousand men to meet him that cometh against him with twenty thousand?"[104] What wise man will take upon himself the profession of a Christian without first considering the end of such a profession, without weighing the difficulties he is to encounter in order to obtain that end? The number and strength of his enemies, what his own powers are, what succours he is to expect and rely upon. The end, the glory of God, his own happiness. Not the happiness of the body, but the mind, which is incapable of true happiness till renewed and sanctified, till restored to its native liberty, till recovered from its lapse, and in all things made conformable to the will and laws of God. Happiness and purity hold just proportion to each other. The difficulties are many and enemies very powerful. "Whoever will come after me," saith our Saviour, "let him deny himself, and take up his cross and follow me." [105] Deny himself! Man is man's worst enemy. There is in every man in his very nature something contrary to the purity and repugnant to the laws of God. An original strong propension to the body and the world—present things. This is what our Lord requires him to deny and conquer. This is what gave occasion for that memorable observation, "Strait is the gate and narrow is the way that leadeth unto life, and few there by that find it." [106] Why few, but because there are not many that will be at the cost and pains to deny themselves the gratifications of their sensual appetites, that will part with present pleasures, however mean or unworthy, for the obtaining future happiness. And so strait is the gate of Paradise as not to admit the least unmortified sin.

🔥

Journal Fragments: Manchester Manuscript

This undated fragment, torn from a notebook much like Headingley MS A (if not the very same), is found in the Methodist Archives, John Rylands University Library, Manchester. A note indicates that in 1825 Charles Atmore gave it to James Everett (whose collection of Methodistica eventually found its way to the Archives).

🔥

[248. Notes on submission, obedience, and the end of religion.]

Entire submission—Impartial obedience—End of religion with respect to self—Healing the lapse of nature, purifying and exalting it to the perfection of its primitive existence; the consequence of which is happiness, pleasure, spiritual, temporal and eternal—with respect to our neighbour—his spiritual and eternal good—present and future happiness.

[249. On discipline, mortification, liberty, and mastery.] [107]

Morn[ing]

Our power is so small [. . .] [108] The end of all discipline, especially voluntary, is to mortify pride and the appetites of the body, and whoever can effect this is at liberty, is master of himself and fortune. This may be obtained without ensnaring ourselves by perpetual vows or obliging ourselves to a multitude of external perform[ances.] [109]

❦

Journal Fragments: Adam Clarke's Transcriptions

Six journal entries, now apparently lost in manuscript, are among those published in Clarke, pp. 263–265. Clarke places these meditations (all but the last) immediately after the material found in MS B, with no indication that they are from any other source. It is possible they were removed from MS B, but they could also be sheets torn from Headingley MS C or just as easily come from a notebook that has itself disappeared. Clarke is a relatively accurate transcriber, though not above an occasional error or editorial change. To check, I have referred also to several excerpts in an earlier (though much briefer) collection of S. W.'s meditations in John Whitehead's The Life of the Rev. John Wesley . . . (New York: R. Worthington, 1881, originally published in two volumes, 1793 and 1796). Whitehead, John Wesley's physician and one of his literary executors, had access to a wide range of manuscripts, including the same set of now missing journal entries that Clarke used.[110]

❦

[250. Experimental knowledge of God; "solemn engagements" against particular sin.]

Evening

The mind of man is naturally so corrupted, and all the powers thereof so weakened, that we cannot possibly aspire vigorously towards God or have any clear perception of spiritual things without his assistance. Nothing less than the same almighty power that raised Jesus Christ from the dead can raise our souls from the death of sin to a life of holiness. To know God experimentally, is altogether supernatural, and what we can never attain to but by the merits and intercession of Jesus Christ. By virtue of what he has done and suffered, and is now doing in heaven for us, we obtain the Holy Spirit, who is the best instructor, the most powerful teacher we can possibly have; without whose agency all other means of grace would be ineffectual. How evidently does the Holy Spirit concur with the means of grace! And how certainly does he assist and strengthen the soul, if it be but sincere and hearty in its endeavours to avoid any evil or perform any good! To have a good desire, a fervent aspiration towards God, shall not pass unregarded.

I have found by long experience that it is of great use to accustom oneself to enter into solemn engagements with God against any particular sin; but then I would have them never made for a longer time than from morning till night, and from night till morning, that so the impression they make on the mind may be always fresh and lively. This was many years tried with good success in the case of ———.[111] Glory be to thee, O Lord!

[251. Thanks for grace already shown but wishes to be "more closely united" to God.]

Evening

Give God the praise for any well spent day. But I am yet unsatisfied, because I do not enjoy enough of God: I apprehend myself at too great a distance from him; I would have my soul more closely united to him by faith and love. I can appeal to his omniscience, that I would love him above all things. He that made me knows my desires, my expectations. My joys all centre in him, and that it is he himself that I desire; it is his favour, it is his acceptance, the communications of his grace, that I earnestly wish for more than anything in the world; and that I have no relish or delight in anything when under apprehensions of his displeasure. I rejoice in his essential glory and blessedness. I rejoice in my relation to him, that he is my Father, my Lord, and my God. I rejoice that he has power over me and desire to live in subjection to him, that he condescends to punish me when I transgress his laws, as a father chasteneth the son whom he loveth.[112] I thank him that he has brought me so far and will beware of despairing of his mercy for the time which is yet to come, but will give God the glory of his free grace.

[252. Two sinful responses to a "new supply of grace": spiritual sloth and fear of loss.]

Morning

It is too common with me upon receiving any light or new supply of grace to think, "Now I have gained my point," and may say, "Soul, [. . .] take thine ease."[113] By which means I think not of going any farther, or else fall into dejection of spirit upon a groundless fear that I shall soon lose what I have gained, and in a little time be never the better for it. Both these are sins. The first proceeds from immoderate love of present ease and spiritual sloth; the other from want of faith in the all-sufficiency of my Saviour.

We must never take up our rest on this side of heaven, nor think we have enough of God, till we are perfectly renewed and sanctified in body, soul, and spirit;[114] till we are admitted into that blessed region of pure and happy spirits, where we shall enjoy the beatific vision according to the measure of our capacities! Nor must we out of a pretended humility, because we are unworthy of the least mercy, dare to dispute or question the sufficiency of the merits of Jesus Christ. It was impossible for God incarnate to undertake more than he was able to perform.

[253. Mercies outweigh afflictions in her life; even sufferings have spiritual benefit.]

Morning

Though "man is born to trouble,"[115] yet I believe there is scarce a man to be found upon earth, but, take the whole course of his life, hath more mercies than afflictions, and much more pleasure than pain. I am sure it has been so in my case. I have many years suffered much pain and great bodily infirmities; but I have likewise enjoyed great intervals of rest and ease. And those very sufferings have, by the blessing of God, been of excellent use and proved the most proper means of reclaiming me from a vain and sinful conversation, insomuch that I cannot say, I had better have been without this affliction, this disease, this loss, want, contempt, or reproach. All my sufferings, by the admirable management of omnipotent Goodness, have concurred to promote my spiritual and eternal good. And if I have not reaped that advantage by them which I might have done, it is merely owing to the perverseness of my own will and frequent lapses into present things and unfaithfulness to the good Spirit of God, who, notwithstanding all my prevarications, all the stupid opposition I have made, has never totally abandoned me. [Eternal][116] glory be to thee, O Lord!

[254. "I do love thee."]

Evening

If to esteem and have the highest reverence for thee! if constantly and sincerely to acknowledge thee the supreme, the only desirable Good be to love thee—I do love thee!

If comparatively to despise and undervalue all the world contains, which is esteemed great, fair, or good, if earnestly and constantly to desire thee, thy favour, thy acceptance, thyself, rather than any or all things thou has created be to love thee—I do love thee!

If to rejoice in thy essential majesty and glory! if to feel a vital joy overspread and cheer the heart at each perception of thy blessedness, at every thought that thou art God and that all things are in thy power, that there is none superior or equal to thee be to love thee—I do love thee!

[255. One Christian's advantages: birth, upbringing, physical and spiritual preservation.][117]

Born in a Christian country; early initiated and instructed in the first principles of the Christian religion; good example in parents and in several of the family; good books and ingenious conversation; preserved from ill accidents, once from violent death; married to a religious orthodox man; by him first drawn off from the Socinian heresy, and afterward confirmed and strengthened by B. B——— . . .[118]

Notes

1. All but a line or two of the Baltimore MS is included in the *Wesley Banner* material.

2. "At the time she wrote her views of many points in Christian theology were defective. When her two distinguished sons obtained the Holy Spirit's witness to their adoption into the Divine family, she attended their ministry, was soon made a partaker of the same blessing, and, a few years after, died in the full triumph of faith" (*Wesley Banner*, June 1852, p. 201).

3. This is the conclusion of an entry begun on another page. In the MS it appears on the right-hand side of the spread, written in normal top-to-bottom fashion, beginning in mid-sentence.

4. With this entry *The Wesley Banner* begins its transcription of S. W.'s journal entries (June 1852, p. 201).

5. Note the extensive quotations of Richard Lucas in journal entries in MS C (202–203, 205, 208, 212–214). Once again she is drawing on his *Religious Perfection. Or, a Third Part of the Enquiry after Happiness*, 2nd ed. (London: Sam. Smith and Benj. Walford, 1697). The *Wesley Banner* transcription has left out S. W.'s abbreviation (in the Baltimore MS) that identifies Lucas as the source of her entry.

6. Ibid., an excerpted quotation; my quotation marks. The original is from sec. 1, chap. 6, p. 99: "Of the Means of attaining Perfection. And the great Ends to be aimed at in Instrumental Duties." It reads (with Lucas's italics): "*Religion* is not to be confin'd to the *Church*, and to the *Closet*; nor to be exercised only in *Prayers* and *Sacraments*, *Meditations* and *Alms*; but everywhere, we are in the Presence of God, and every Word, every Action, is capable of *Morality*. Our Defects and Infirmities betray themselves in the daily Accidents and the common Conversation of Life; and *here* they draw after them very important Consequences; and therefore *here* they are to be watched over, regulated and govern'd as well as in our more *solemn* Actions."

7. S. W. skips an intervening sentence: " 'Tis to the Virtues or the Errors of our *common* Conversation and *ordinary* Deportment, that we owe both our Friends and Enemies, our good or bad Character abroad, our Domestick Peace or Troubles; and in a high degree, the improvement or depravation of our Minds" (ibid., pp. 99–100). She then quotes from the next sentence: "Let no Man then, that will be *Perfect* or *Happy*, abandon himself to his Humours or Inclinations in his Carriage towards his Acquaintance, his Children, his Servants" (p. 100). As the entry continues on the reverse side of the sheet, S. W. is still following Lucas but more loosely than the preceding. See note 8.

8. S. W. continues quoting and paraphrasing, resulting in a précis not unlike the sort that her son John was later to make in his editions of various Christian classics. Again, I have introduced quotation marks, even though the quotation occasionally degenerates into paraphrase. The original passage is this: "Let no Man, that will be *Perfect* or *Happy*, follow *Prejudice* or *Fashion* in the common and customary Actions of Life: But let him assure himself, that by a daily endeavour to conform these more and more to the excellent Rules of the Gospel, he is to train up himself by degrees to the most absolute *Wisdom*, and the most *Perfect Virtue*, he is capable of. And to this end he must first know himself, and those he has to do with; he must discern the proper Season and the just Occasion of every Virtue; and then he must apply himself to the acquiring the Perfection of it by the daily Exercise of it, even in those things, which, for want of due Reflection, do not commonly seem of any great Importance. To one that is thus dispos'd, the dulness or the carelessness of a Servant, the stubbornness of a Child, the Sourness of a Parent, the Inconstancy of Friends, the Coldness of Relations, the Neglect or Ingratitude of the World, will all prove extremely useful and beneficial; every thing will instruct him, every thing will afford an opportunity of exercising some Virtue or another; so that such a one shall be daily learning, daily growing better and wiser" (ibid., pp. 100–101).

9. See Philippians 2:12.

10. This paragraph, which seems to be her own gloss on the Lucas passage, does not appear in the Baltimore fragment but rather at the end of the same entry in the *Wesley Banner*, June 1852, p. 201. The Baltimore fragment ends with the preceding quotation at the bottom of the journal page; the *Banner* editor evidently had access to the succeeding, now missing, page(s).

11. This entry, and all subsequent entries save two in this section (229 and 230), are only to be found in the *Wesley Banner*.

12. My quotation marks.

13. Ecclesiastes 7:1: "A good name is better than precious ointment."

14. S. W. may here be taking off from a passage in Lucas, *Religious Perfection*, in which the

Eucharist is held up as an important "instrumental duty of religion." Lucas touts the benefits of preparation for it, as well as "contemplation of the whole mystery." Also, the "Habit of Holiness" is "improved by that spiritual Pleasure which the sensible Assurances of Grace and Salvation work in us. . . ." Moreover, the sacrament leads to "a most solemn Exercise of Repentance . . ." (p. 123).

15. Ambiguous reference. If "this" refers to the last line of the previous entry, S. W. is a bit off base, defining "liberty" (one part of "Christian Perfection") with something close to Lucas's definition for the whole. This entry is probably a meditation on the passage in Lucas where he describes the "second Stage of the Christian's Advance towards Perfection" in terms of a military metaphor and suggests that one of the impediments to victory in this difficult war is "all false and cowardly Projects of Truces and Accommodations." This second stage, he says, "may be call'd the state of Liberty" (ibid., p. 83). Cf. his definition of perfection: "nothing else, but a ripe and setled Habit of true Holiness" (p. 2). In a further description of the "several parts of perfection" he says, "Illumination is the Perfection of the Understanding, Liberty of the Will, and Zeal of the Affections." The first involves "the Knowledge of our Duty, and our Obligations to it"; the second, "the Subduing our Lusts and Passions, that we may be enabled to perform it"; and the last, "not only a free, but warm and vigorous Prosecution of it" (pp. 150–151). S. W. is probably reading and commenting on Lucas's discussion of liberty—without worrying about some imagined reader missing the reference and the definition. The subject was important to Lucas, who devoted four chapters to the subject (pp. 212–364).

16. Slightly misquoted from Romans 8:21, substituting "blessed" for Paul's "glorious." Quotation marks added.

17. Lucas, *Religious Perfection*, p. 82, paraphrased and cut but close enough to warrant my use of quotation marks.

18. Ibid.: "Secondly, That the Sinner make good his Resolutions, and actually break with his Lusts; he must reject their Sollicitations, and boldly oppose their Commands; he must take part with Reason and Religion, keep a watch and guard over his Soul, and must earnestly labour by Mortification and Discipline, by Meditation and Prayer to root out Vice, and plant Virtue in his Soul." The bracketed ellipses represent the entry's excision of the following: "This in the Language of the Prophet is ceasing to do evil, and learning to do well, Isa. 1.16,17."

19. Ibid.: "He that has proceeded thus far, though he feel a great Conflict within; though the Opposition of Lust be very strong, and consequently the discharge of his Duty very difficult, he is nevertheless in a state of grace, but in a state of childhood too; he is sincere, but far from being perfect."

20. Ibid.: "And yet this is the state which many continue in, to the end of their Lives, being partly abus'd by false Notions, and taught to believe from Rom. 7. that there is no higher or perfecter state; partly intangled and incumbred by some unhappy circumstances of Life: Or it may be, the Force or Impetus of the Soul, towards Perfection, is much abated by the satisfaction of Prosperity, and the many Diversions and Engagements of a Fortunate Life. . . ."

21. Ibid., pp. 80–81; quotation marks added even though S. W. from time to time is quoting loosely and paraphrasing. Cf. Lucas's two chapters on "illumination," one of the "several parts of perfection" (pp. 153–212).

22. Thus far, with the exception of the first sentence, this entry is a paraphrase (ibid., p. 80). The original reads: "First then, As soon as any Judgment or Mercy, or any other sort of Call, awakens and penetrates the Sinner; as soon as a clear Light breaks in upon him, and makes him see and consider his own state. . . ."

23. Ibid.: "different Calls and Motives."

24. Ibid.: "One while Fear, another while Shame; one while Indignation, another while Hope, fills his Soul."

25. A patch of loose quotation and paraphrase. The original, ibid., pp. 80–81, reads: "He resents the Tyranny, and complains of the Persecution of his Lusts; he upbraids himself with his folly, and discovers a meanness and shamefulness in his Vices, which he did not reflect on sufficiently before; he is vex'd and troubled at the plagues and mischiefs his Sin and folly have already procured him, and thinks he has reason to fear, if he persist, others far more intolerable."

26. Ibid.: "Then he calls to mind the Goodness, the Long-suffering of God." Nearly exact quotation of 1 Corinthians 2:4; quotation marks added (indicated by italics in Lucas).

27. In Lucas, *Religious Perfection*: "righteous."

28. Ibid.: "These thoughts, these travels of the Mind, if they be not strangled in the birth by a Man's own wilfulness or pusillanimity, or unhappily diverted upon some Tempatations, do kindle in the Bosom of the Sinner, the desires of Righteousness and Liberty; they fill him with Regret and Shame, cast him down, and humble him before God, and make him finally resolve on shaking off the Yoke. This may be called a state of Illumination; and is a state of Preparation for, or Disposition to Repentance: Or if it be Repentance it self, 'tis yet but an Embrio. . . ."

29. This and the following meditation appear on opposite sides of the Baltimore MS and are written sideways, beginning at the top-right margin of the notebook; they are on the opposite halves of the open sheet from the previous MS entries, 218 and 219. They are also transcribed in the *Wesley Banner*, June 1852, p. 203.

30. Omitted but probably intended here: "form" or "kind."

31. My quotation marks. Matthew 26:41. "Watch and pray, that ye enter not into temptation: the spirit indeed is willing, but the flesh is weak."

32. See BCP, marriage service.

33. Lucas, *Religious Perfection*, p. 282.

34. S. W.'s doubts about Christian perfection may have been one of the views deemed "defective" by the *Wesley Banner* editor. The blank may indicate some conversation on the subject with her husband or with some other person, basically agreeing with her hesitations in the matter, whom she considers authoritative.

35. Slightly rearranged from 1 John 3:9, a key text for the doctrine of Christian perfection.

36. Lucas, *Religious Perfection*, pp. 307–308; quotation marks added. In the last phrase S. W. has paraphrased Lucas's original: "and that not only in their past Life, or unregenerate State, but their best and most Perfect one. . . ." See similar sentiments expressed by S. W. in her journal entry 24, above.

37. S. W. is entering material from Lucas, *Religious Perfection*, pp. 313–317; quotation marks added.

38. Ibid.: "forbid."

39. S. W. omits "plainly" (ibid.).

40. S. W. omits "I must be pardoned if" (ibid.).

41. Ibid.: "reluctancy."

42. Ibid.: "or the Length and Force of a Temptation. . . ."

43. Ibid.: "1. As to the smallness of the Matter. Some cannot but think those Transgressions Venial, which are, for the Matter of them, so slight and insignificant."

44. That is, suspect.

45. In Lucas, *Religious Perfection*: "has."

46. Ibid.: "For either Men perform such Actions Deliberately, or Indeliberately, knowing them to be sinful, or believing them to be innocent."

47. Ibid.: "that every Man has."

48. Ibid.: "the Love of God, the Love of Righteousness, and Heaven."

49. Ibid.: "I cannot but think."

50. Ibid.: "trifling and inconsiderable, and draws after it no ill Consequence, either with respect to God or Man."

51. "To be" not found in Lucas's text (ibid.).

52. S. W. omits the conjunction "or," with which Lucas begins the next phrase: "Or it is against the Letter" (ibid.).

53. S. W. concludes the passage she has been copying, ibid., pp. 313–315, and skips over into pp. 316–317 to round out her entry.

54. S. W. omits "and."

55. "He" at the beginning of the sentence is, of course, Lucas (ibid). Quotation marks have been added. See Matthew 12:36: "every idle word that men shall speak, they shall give account thereof in the day of judgment."

56. Matthew 12:34; quotation marks in the *Wesley Banner* transcription.

57. The quotation she intended is Matthew 27:14, Jesus before Pilate ("And he answered him to never a word"), but it came out closer to Matthew 15:5, Jesus' response to the Canaanite women ("But he answered her not a word"). Quotation marks added.

58. Nearly exact quotation of 1 Peter 2:23; quotation marks added.

59. Paraphrase of Deuteronomy 6:6 and a much closer approximation of verse 8; quotation marks added.

60. Lucas, *Religious Perfection*, pp. 323–324; quotation marks added.

61. S. W. has cut here the phrase "by whatever Names we may call them" (ibid.).

62. Ibid.: "actions as have in them something of voluntary, something of involuntary"

63. That is, deviation, aberration, or perversity.

64. Lucas, *Religious Perfection*, pp. 324–325; quotation marks added.

65. Ibid.: "and yet so much of Necessity in it, it is never utterly to be extirpated."

66. Ibid.: "to oblige us to watch against it, and repent of it."

67. Ibid.: "from the Imperfections and Infelicities of our Nature, and our State."

68. Ibid.: "truly." "Only" may be an error of the *Wesley Banner* editor.

69. S. W. omits the "and" that begins the next phrase in Lucas, *Religious Perfection*.

70. Ibid.: "consequence. But. . . ."

71. S. W. has now stopped writing word for word and started taking notes (ibid., pp. 326–330). Most of the words are Lucas's but have been recast enough to make quotation marks and precise citations excessively cumbersome.

72. The list, ibid., is "adultery, idolatry, murder." S. W. (or the *Wesley Banner* editor?) has added "drunkenness."

73. In Lucas, *Religious Perfection*: "the manner of committing it, it must proceed from Ignorance, Frailty, or Surprise" (p. 327).

74. Matthew 23:24; quotation marks added.

75. See Luke 10:38–42.

76. Lucas, *Religious Perfection*, pp. 331–332.

77. Ibid.: "reckon'd for Sins."

78. Deuteronomy 6:6, Matthew 22:37, Mark 12:30, Luke 10:27; quotation marks are in the *Wesley Banner* transcription, whereas Lucas, *Religious Perfection*, has the passage in italics.

79. In Lucas, *Religious Perfection*: "whatsoever falls short . . . is a sin."

80. Ibid.: "would be."

81. Ibid.: "nothing better than God, nothing equal to Him."

82. Ibid.: "and pursue after the highest and most perfect Degrees of Love."

83. Ibid.: "Faith, Love, Hope."

84. Ibid.: "may be properly reckoned amongst Sins."

85. Ibid.: "And if these Defects be such as can consist with Sincerity, then are the Imperfections or the Abatements of our Virtues, pardonable, and then only."

86. Ibid., p. 240, with only minor changes; quotation marks added.

87. Blaise Pascal, *Thoughts on Religion, and other Curious Subjects,* trans. Basil Kennet, 3rd ed. (London: Pemberton, 1731), chap. 24 ("The Vanity of Man") par. 1, pp. 173–174. Nearly exact transcription; quotation marks added. The original reads: "We are not satisfied with that Life, which we possess in ourselves, and in our own proper Being; we are fond of leading an imaginary Life in the Idea of others. And 'tis hence that we are so eager and forward to shew ourselves to the World. We labour indefatigably to retain, improve, and adorn this fictitious Being, while we stupidly neglect the true. And if we happen to be Masters of any noble Endowment, of Tranquility, Generosity, or Fidelity of Mind, we press with all our Vigour to make them known, that we may transfer and ingraft these Excellencies on that fantastick Existence."

88. Nearly exact quotation of Lucas, *Religious Perfection,* pp. 223–224, quotation marks added. The omitted material (represented by bracketed ellipses) and one significant difference ("practiced," whereas the *Wesley Banner* transcription has "preached") in Lucas's original are as follows: "Here the Obedience even of Christ himself could not be exempt from Conflict; for our Natural Appetites, in this sense of them, will never be put off till our Bodies be. I think this is so clear, it needs not be illustrated by Instances: Or else 'twere easy to shew, that though good men have practised Temperance, Chastity, Charity. . . ."

89. Ibid., pp. 227–228; quotation marks added.

90. Ibid.: "the feebleness and impotence of the Will." The bracketed ellipses represent a half-page discussion on the incapacity of a sinner's understanding and affections.

91. Ibid.: "faculties."

92. Ibid.: "meerly wholly body."

93. Ibid.: "no Soul, or none but one resulting from, and dissolv'd with."

94. Ibid.: "its sensualities?" Several lines of material omitted in the journal entry follow: "Is it not evident, that He has little expectation of another World, who lays up his Treasures only in this; and lives as if he were Born only to make provision for the flesh to fulfil the lusts thereof? 'Tis true all sinners are not equally stupid. . . ."

95. Ibid.: "'Tis true, all Sinners are not equally stupid or obdurate. . . ."

96. Ibid.: "in whome some sparks of Understanding and Conscience remain unextinguished."

97. Ibid.; the sentence concludes with a question mark.

98. A likely source of this descriptive trinitarian language is Bishop William Beveridge's collection, *The Being, Love, and Other Attributes of God, as Our Creator, Redeemer, and Sanctifier, illustrated in Twelve Sermons,* in *The Theological Works of William Beveridge* . . . , 12 vols. (Oxford: John Henry Parker, 1844), 1:232–end. Note the same formula (identifying the persons of the Trinity according to their roles) in the letter to Sammy, 28 December 1710.

99. Italics in the *Wesley Banner* transcription.

100. S. W. is quoting from William Beveridge's sermon CVIII, "All Things to Be Done to the Glory of God," in *Theological Works,* 5:98–99; quotation marks added. Beveridge's original reads: "So by His "back parts" we may understand the emanations of His said Essential Glory, or the manifestations it maketh of itself in the exercise of its Divine perfections, in the government of the world, and particularly in respect to mankind; which last shew forth the glory of God *a posteriori,* by its effects and consequents, although *a priori* we can see nothing of it."

The earlier part of this entry loosely resembles the material on the previous page (p. 97) of the same sermon, but it also resounds with language found in sermon XIII, "The Being and Attributes of God," 1:233–247 (see closer borrowings in S. W.'s journal entry 184).

101. See 1 Timothy 6:16.

102. Nearly exact quotation of Colossians 2:9; quotation marks added.

103. 2 Corinthians 5:19; my quotation marks.

104. Nearly exact quotation of Luke 14:31; quotation marks added.

105. An all but exact quotation of Mark 8:34; quotation marks added. See also Matthew 16:24 and Luke 9:23.

106. Nearly exact quotation of Matthew 7:14; quotation marks added.

107. On the reverse side of the fragment.

108. A half dozen indecipherable shorthand characters follow.

109. Meditation breaks off.

110. John Whitehead transcribes the same six "missing" meditations as does Clarke (250–255), as well as one of the Headingley MS B selections that Clarke also includes (191). It is clear from one significant omission that Clarke, though he was well aware of Whitehead's book (see Clarke, *Wesley Family*, p. 256), was himself working directly with the manuscripts. Whitehead's punctuation strikes me as being closer to S. W.'s original than does Clarke's; the one or two significant differences in content are noted below. His rendition of 191 can be checked against the original from Headingley MS B; see Whitehead, *The Life of the Rev. John Wesley* . . . (New York: R. Worthington, 1881).

111. May reflect either a blank in the missing MS or a series of shorthand symbols, which Clarke, *Wesley Family*, has elsewhere—in a meditation for which the MS exists—represented similarly. In either case S. W. shows her usual reluctance to name names in the diary.

112. A conflation of phrases and ideas from Deuteronomy 8:5 and Hebrews 12:5–7.

113. I have introduced quotation marks; the second phrase is taken from Luke 12:19.

114. The phrase beginning "till we are perfectly renewed" does not appear in Whitehead's transcription, *Life of John Wesley*, p. 36. It is more likely that he, feeling squeamish about the idea of perfection, left it out than that Clarke, *Wesley Family*, concocted it and inserted it in his version. For Whitehead's nervousness about John Wesley's "enthusiasm" and Clarke's advocacy of Wesley's doctrines, see Richard Heitzenrater, *The Elusive Mr. Wesley: Vol. 2. John Wesley as Seen by Contemporaries and Biographers* (Nashville: Abingdon, 1984), pp. 172, 178.

115. Job 5:7; my quotation marks.

116. Whitehead's transcription (*Life of John Wesley*); does not appear in Clarke, *Wesley Family*.

117. Clarke (following Whitehead, *Life of John Wesley*, p. 34) disconnects this fragment from the previous entries in introducing it: "In another of her meditations she mentions the following among the many mercies which God had bestowed upon her" (p. 265). There is no way of telling what MS he is working with here; even the customary morning/noon/evening designation is missing.

118. Clarke, following Whitehead, *Life of John Wesley*, conjectures that the initials stand for Bishop Bull. George Bull (1634–1710) was a high churchman and, from 1705, bishop of St. Davids. Though his most important works were written in Latin, a number of sermons and discourses were published in English during his lifetime. A likely candidate for help in avoiding Unitarianism would have been his "The doctrine of the catholic church for the first three ages of Christianity, concerning the blessed Trinity, considered, in opposition to Sabellianism and Tritheism." See *The Works of John Bull* . . . , ed. Edward Burton (Oxford: At the University Press, 1846), 2:1–16.

PART III

Educational, Catechetical, and Controversial Writings

Introduction to the Writings

*A*s any reader of her letters and journals will affirm, Susanna Wesley was fully capable of sustained theological essays. Her's was a facile pen, her favorite topic was "practical divinity," and more than a few of her letters or longish journal entries might easily pass for publishable essays. Length, subject matter, and even genre alone, therefore, do not necessarily warrant the creation of a third category of her writings. There are, though, a significant group of texts that she intended for a wider audience than herself (in the case of her journals) or than a single correspondent (as for her letters)—texts of considerable length, even by her standards, that cluster topically around her educational and theological concerns. Thus, here is a final section consisting of five essays: Susanna Wesley's long letter, "commissioned" (and later printed) by her son John, outlining her educational method; her exposition on the Apostles' Creed, in the form of a letter to her daughter Susanna (called Suky by the family); a second unfinished letter to Suky beginning an exposition of the Ten Commandments; a theological dialogue or "Religious Conference" constructed as if it were a conversation between herself and her eldest daughter, Emilia; and a final piece, actually published at the end of her life, an anonymous defense of her son John in his public quarrel with his one-time associate George Whitefield over the doctrine of predestination.

Taken together, these writings do not so much express new ideas or address new topics (though there are important exceptions) as reveal a more sustained attention to her favorite issues and a more magisterial persona. Her child rearing finished, she reflected on the method that made it possible, and even successful, under trying circumstances. The family having been scattered after a fire destroyed the Epworth rectory, Susanna Wesley exercised her parental duty as catechist and wrote two treatises interpreting the Creed and the Decalogue for her adolescent daughters—and then crafted an even more sophisticated dialogue that opened up additional areas of current theological debate. Finally, as an older woman, she demonstrated a flare for public controversy, entering the lists against a rising revivalist star and faring quite well. In each instance she drew on her wide stock of reading, as well as her own experience, in constructing these effective and authoritative pieces.

These writings are the work of three decades in the early eighteenth century. Her catechetical writings (the Creed and Decalogue expositions and the "Religious Conference") date from the early 1710s, obviously motivated both by the life stage the Wesley daughters were passing through and the rectory fire that made daily contact with their "tutor" impossible. Her letter outlining how she went about the work of educating (not to mention organizing) her children comes from the early 1730s, by which time her youngest child, daughter Kezia, was about 23, and there was leisure to reflect on past practice. The final piece, her pamphlet arguing against George Whitefield's predestinarian views on behalf of her son John, dates from 1741, at the very end of her life, demonstrating her ability to rise even then to yet another pedagogical occasion. In that each of these occasions was rather different, more detailed introductory material precedes each of the essays.

❦ TWENTY-FOUR ❧

On Educating My Family

*A*rguably the most influential of Susanna Wesley's writings, this essay in the form of a letter was written to her son John at his request in early 1732. Dealing with the household regimen and the early education of her ten children who survived infancy, it has become something of a classic statement of evangelical child-rearing practices. Though not her earliest extended piece on education, we have placed it first in this section as an indication of her methodology and rationale.

Anticipating its composition in a letter to her son John in February 1732, she outlined the project with her own blend of modesty and forthrightness:

> The writing anything about my way of education I am much averse from. It can't (I think) be of service to anyone to know how I, that have lived such a retired life for so many years (ever since I was with child of you), used to employ my time and care in bringing up my children. No one can, without renouncing the world in the most literal sense, observe my method, and there's few (if any) that would entirely devote above twenty years of the prime of life in hope to save the souls of their children (which they think may be saved without so much ado); for that was my principal intention, however unskillfully or unsuccessfully managed.[1]

The letter finally came through in late July, and John Wesley was impressed enough to recommend it to his constituency after his mother's death, both in his published *Journal* and in his house organ, the *Arminian Magazine*, where it appeared as part of a sermon. Leaders in the post-Wesley generation, such as Adam Clarke, followed suit, and soon "her wise and parental intstructions" (accounting for "the rare excellence of the Wesely family") became a staple of Methodist hagiography.[2] Romanticizing aside, however, there are good grounds for tracing something of Methodism's method to the educational discipline of Susanna Wesley's home school.[3] More recently English historian Lawrence Stone has called her educational principles the link between "the caring but authoritarian discipline of the Puritan bourgeois parent of the seventeenth century and the caring but authoritarian discipline of the Evangelical bourgeois parent of the late eighteenth and early nineteenth centuries."[4] Further, according to American historian Philip Greven, the letter may have helped create an evangelical identity in an even wider sphere.[5]

By the time Susanna began raising her family, education of children as a parental duty had long since become a commonplace in both Puritan and Anglican circles. The Geneva Bible, commenting on Deuteronomy 21:18, sounded the note early on: "It is the mothers dutie also to instruct her children."[6] In her own lifetime her father's friend Richard Baxter underscored the point:

> Especially you, mothers, remember this; you are more with your children while they are little ones than their fathers, be you therefore still teaching them as soon as ever they are capable of learning.[7]

But Anglican sources were equally insistent, as a purusal of a section on "Parents Duty to Children" in the influential *The Whole Duty of Man* amply illustrates. After physical nourishment and bringing a child to baptism, parents "must provide for the education of the child."[8]

Though steeped in English Protestant tradition, Susanna's educational methodology was also *au courant*. We have already noticed her fascination with John Locke's *Essay concerning Human Understanding*, portions of which she copied in her journal. As Frank Baker has reminded us, Susanna Wesley appears also to have been one of the early readers of Locke's slightly later work, *Some Thoughts concerning Education*, early echoes of which may be seen in her journal (entries 55 and 103). The yoking of the philosopher with Susanna Wesley has been used to demonstrate both that her methods were not as harsh as may seem (given the intellectual context of the times) and that Locke was not as liberal in his thought as has been supposed.[9] In fact, both may be read as having a severe side: both reserve a place for the rod, and both argue for early and firm parental authority; Locke's goal, "compliance and suppleness of their wills," is a rough equivalent of Susanna Wesley's "conquering the will." Yet both also mitigate such strictness in their disavowal of mean-spirited and senseless beating, as well as in the goals of their practices, which in the long run result in less cruelty than if all early discipline had been abandoned. As the annotations will show, her educational and child-rearing practices are peppered with Lockean resonances, though no direct quotations—she is working from memory, and in any case she has borrowed, not slavishly copied, from him. In one or two instances she contradicts him.

What we seem to have in her letter is a curious yet influential blend of evangelical and Lockean ideas,[10] one that also goes a long way toward explaining the remarkable children of the Epworth rectory and that illustrates the zeal with which Susanna Wesley pursued an educational vocation within the bounds of contemporary social constraints. The letter also sets the stage for the three other (more content-oriented) educational writings that follow.

With no existing holograph I have relied on the text as it appears in John Wesley's *Journals and Diaries*, II (*1738–42*), ed. W. Reginald Ward and Richard P. Heitzenrater, *The Works of John Wesley* (Nashville: Abingdon, 1990), 19:286–291 (1 August 1742), collated with the *Arminian Magazine*, 1784, pp. 462–464, where portions of the letter are incorporated into Wesley's sermon "On Obedience to Parents." John Wesley's editorial hand is probably at work in both. Clarke (pp. 211–212, 215–219) includes most of the letter but probably is following Wesley's *Journal* edition.

❧

July 24, 1732

Dear son

According to your desire, I have collected the principal rules I observed in educating my family;[11] which I now send you as they occurred to my mind, and you may (if you think they can be of use to any) dispose of them in what order you please.

The children were always put into a regular method of living, in such things as they were capable of, from their birth: as in dressing, undressing, changing their linen, etc. The first quarter commonly passes in sleep. After that they were, if possible, laid into their cradles awake and rocked to sleep; and so they were kept rocking till it was time for them to awake. This was done to bring them to a regular course of sleeping;[12] which at first was three hours in the morning and three in the afternoon; afterwards two hours, till they needed none at all.

When turned a year old (and some before), they were taught to fear the rod, and to cry softly;[13] by which means they escaped abundance of correction they might otherwise have had, and that most odious noise of the crying of children was rarely heard in the house, but the family usually lived in much quietness as if there had not been a child among them.

As soon as they were grown pretty strong, they were confined to three meals a day. At dinner their little table and chairs were set by ours, where they could be overlooked; and they were suffered to eat and drink (small[14] beer) as much as they would; but not to call for anything. If they wanted aught they used to whisper to the maid which attended them, who came and spake to me; and as soon as they could handle a knife and fork, they were set to our table. They were never suffered to choose their meat, but always made eat such things as were provided for the family.

Mornings they had always spoon-meat;[15] sometimes on nights. But whatever they had, they were never permitted to eat at those meals of more than one thing, and of that sparingly enough. Drinking or eating between meals was never allowed, unless in case of sickness; which seldom happened. Nor were they suffered to go into the kitchen to ask anything of the servants when they were at meat; if it was known they did, they were certainly beat, and the servants severely reprimanded.[16]

At six, as soon as family prayers were over, they had their supper; at seven the maid washed them; and, beginning at the youngest, she undressed and got them all to bed by eight; at which time she left them in their several rooms awake, for there was no such thing allowed of in our house as sitting by a child till it fell asleep.

They were so constantly used to eat and drink what was given them that when any of them was ill there was no difficulty in making them take the most unpleasant medicine; for they durst not refuse it, though some of them would presently throw it up. This I mention to show that a person may be taught to take anything, though it be never so much against his stomach.

In order to form the minds of children, the first thing to be done is to conquer their will, and bring them to an obedient temper.[17] To inform the understanding is a work of time, and must [with children][18] proceed by slow degrees [as they are able to bear it]; but the subjecting the will is a thing that must be done at once— and the sooner the better. For by neglecting timely correction, they [will] contract a stubbornness [and obstinacy] which is hardly ever [after] conquered;[19] and never, without using such severity as would be as painful to me as to the child.[20] In the esteem of the world they pass for kind and indulgent whom I call cruel parents, who permit their children to get habits which they know must be afterwards broken.[21] [Nay, some are so stupidly fond as in sport to teach their children to do things which in a while after they have severely beaten them for doing.[22]

Whenever a child is corrected, it must be conquered; and this will be no hard matter to do if it be not grown headstrong by too much indulgence. And when the will of a child is totally subdued, and it is brought to revere and stand in awe of the parents, then a great many childish follies and inadvertences may be passed by. Some should be overlooked and taken no notice of, and others mildly reproved; but no wilful transgression ought ever to be forgiven children without chastisement, less or more, as the nature and circumstances of the offence require.][23]

I insist upon conquering the will[24] of children betimes, because this is the only [strong and rational] foundation of[25] a religious education[, without which both precept and example will be ineffectual]. [But] when this is thoroughly done, then a child is capable of being governed by the reason [and piety] of its parent[s], till its own understanding comes to maturity[, and the principles of religion have taken root in the mind].

I cannot yet dismiss this subject. As self-will is the root of all sin and misery, so whatever cherishes this in children ensures[26] their after-wretchedness and irreligion; whatever checks and mortifies it promotes their future happiness and piety. This is still more evident if we [farther] consider that religion is nothing else than the doing the will of God, and not our own; that the one grand impediment to our temporal and eternal happiness being this self-will,[27] no indulgences of it can be trivial, no denial[28] unprofitable. Heaven or hell depends on this alone. So that the parent who studies to subdue it in his child[29] works together with God in the renewing and saving a soul. The parent who indulges it does the devil's work, makes religion impracticable, salvation unattainable; and does all that in him lies to damn his child, soul and body, for ever.[30]

This therefore I cannot but earnestly repeat:[31] break their wills betimes. Begin this great work before they can run alone, before they can speak plain, or perhaps speak at all. Whatever pains it cost, conquer their stubbornness: break the will, if you would not damn the child. I conjure you not to neglect, not to delay this! Therefore, 1. Let a child from a year old, be taught to fear the rod and cry softly.[32] In order to this, 2. Let him have nothing he cries for, absolutely nothing, great or small; else you undo your own work.[33] 3. At all events, from that age, make him do as he is bid, if you whip him ten times running to effect it: let none persuade you it is cruelty to do this; it is cruelty not to do it. Break his will now, and his soul will live, and he will probably bless you to all eternity.[34]

The children of this family[35] were taught, as soon as they could speak, the Lord's Prayer,[36] which they were made to say at rising and bedtime constantly; to which, as they grew bigger, were added a short prayer for their parents, and some collects; a short catechism, and some portions of Scripture, as their memories could bear.

They were very early made to distinguish the Sabbath from other days, before they could well speak, or go. They were as soon taught to be still at family prayers, and to ask a blessing immediately after, which they used to do by signs, before they could[37] kneel or speak.

They were quickly made to understand they might have nothing they cried for, and instructed to speak handsomely for what they wanted. They were not suffered to ask even the lowest servant for aught without saying, "Pray give me such a thing"; and the servant was chid if she ever let them omit that word. Taking God's name in vain, cursing and swearing, profaneness, obscenity, rude, ill-bred names were never heard among them. Nor were they ever permitted to call each other by their proper names without the addition of brother or sister.[38]

None of them were taught to read till five years old,[39] except Kezzy, in whose case I was overruled; and she was more years learning than any of the rest had been months. The way of teaching was this. The day before a child began to learn, the house was set in order, everyone's work appointed them, and a charge given that none should come into the room from nine till twelve, or from two till five; which, you know, were our school hours. One day was allowed the child wherein to learn its letters, and each of them did in that time know all its letters, great and small, except Molly and Nancy, who were a day and a half before they knew them perfectly; for which I then thought them very dull; but since I have observed how long many children are learning the hornbook, I have changed my opinion. But the reason why I thought them so then was because the rest learned so readily; and your Brother Samuel, who was the first child I ever taught, learned the alphabet in a few hours. He was five years old on the 10th of February; the next day he began to learn and, as soon as he knew the letters began at the first chapter of Genesis. He was taught to spell the first verse, then to read it over and over, till he could read it off-hand without any hesitation; so on to the second, etc., till he took ten verses for a lesson, which he quickly did. Easter fell low that year; and by Whitsuntide he could read a chapter very well; for he read continually, and had such a prodigious memory that I cannot remember ever to have told him the same word twice.[40]

What was yet stranger, any word he had learned in his lesson he knew wherever he saw it, either in his Bible or any other book; by which means he learned very soon to read any English author well.

The same method was observed with them all. As soon as they knew the letters, they were put first to spell; and read one line, then a verse, never leaving till perfect in their lesson, were it shorter or longer. So one or other continued reading at school-time without any intermission, and before we left school each child read what he had learned that morning; and ere we parted in the afternoon, what they had learned that day.

There was no such thing as loud talking or playing allowed of; but everyone was kept close to their business for the six hours of school; and it is almost incredible what a child may be taught in a quarter of a year by a vigorous application, if it have but a tolerable capacity and good health. Everyone of these, Kezzy excepted, could read better in that time than the most of women can do as long as they live.

Rising out of their places, or going out of the room, was not permitted unless for good cause, and running into the yard, garden, or street, without leave, was always esteemed a capital offence.

For some years we went on very well. Never were children in better order. Never were children better disposed to piety, or in more subjection to their parents, till that fatal dispersion of them after the fire into several families. In these they were left at full liberty to converse with servants, which before they had always been restrained from;[41] and to run abroad and play with any children, good or bad. They soon learned to neglect a strict observation of the sabbath, and got knowledge of several songs and bad things, which before they had no notion of. That civil behavior which made them admired when at home by all which saw them was in great measure lost, and a clownish accent and many rude ways were learned, which were not reformed without some difficulty.[42]

When the house was rebuilt, and the children all brought home, we entered upon a strict reform; and then was begun the custom of singing psalms at beginning and leaving school, morning and evening. Then also that of a general retirement at five o'clock was entered upon, when the oldest took the youngest that could speak, and the second the next, to whom they read the Psalms for the day and a chapter in the New Testament;[43] as in the morning they were directed to read the Psalms and a chapter in the Old, after which they went to their private prayers, before they got their breakfast or came into the family. And I thank God this custom is still preserved among us.[44]

There were several by-laws observed among us, which slipped my memory, or else they had been inserted in their proper place; but I mention them here, because I think them useful.

1. It had been observed that cowardice and fear of punishment often led children into lying, till they get a custom of it which they cannot leave. To prevent this a law was made, that whoever was charged with a fault, of which they were guilty, if they would ingenuously confess it, and promise to amend, should not be beaten.[45] This rule prevented a great deal of lying and would have done more if one[46] in the family would have observed it. But he could not be prevailed on, and therefore was often imposed on by false colours and equivocations, which none would have used (except one), had they been kindly dealt with. And some, in spite of all, would always speak truth plainly.

2. That no sinful action, as lying, pilfering, playing at church, or on the Lord's day, disobedience, quarrelling, etc., should ever pass unpunished.[47]

3. That no child should ever be chid or beat twice for the same fault; and that, if they amended, they should never be upbraided with it afterwards.[48]

4. That every signal act of obedience, especially when it crossed upon their own inclinations, should be always commended and frequently rewarded, according to the merits of the case.[49]

5. That if ever any child performed an act of obedience, or did anything with an intention to please, though the performance was not well, yet the obedience and intention should be kindly accepted; and the child with sweetness directed how to do better for the future.

6. That propriety[50] be inviolably preserved, and none suffered to invade the property of another in the smallest matter, though it were but of the value of a farthing, or a pin; which they might not take from the owner without, much less against his consent. This rule can never be too much inculcated on the minds of children, and from the want of parents or governors doing it as they ought proceeds that shameful neglect of justice which we may observe in the world.[51]

7. That promises be strictly observed; and a gift once bestowed, and so the right passed away from the donor, be not resumed, but left to the disposal of him to whom it was given; unless it were conditional, and the condition of the obligation not performed.

8. That no girl be taught to work till she can read very well; and then that she be kept to her work with the same application, and for the same time, that she was held to in reading. This rule also is much to be observed; for the putting children to learn sewing before they can read perfectly is the very reason why so few women can read fit to be heard, and never to be well understood.[52]

Notes

1. S. W. discusses her educational projects in several of her other writings: letters to Sammy, 11 October 1709, and to her husband, Samuel, 6 February 1712; journal entries 11, 56, and 57; and in the educational writings themselves, particularly the opening paragraphs of her letter on the Creed and the title page of her "Religious Conference."

2. Clarke, p. 220

3. For a good summary of her educational work (and its Puritan roots) see John Newton, *Susanna Wesley and the Puritan Tradition in Methodism*, (London: Epworth, 1968), chap. 4 ("A Mother in Israel"), especially pp. 105–129.

4. Lawrence Stone, *The Family, Sex and Marriage in England 1500–1800*, abridged ed. (New York: Harper Colophon, 1979), p. 293.

5. Philip Greven, *The Protestant Temperament: Patterns of Child-Rearing, Religious Experience, and the Self in Early America* (New York: Knopf, 1977), pp. 36–38, 44, 48–49, 93–94; reprint ed. (Chicago: University of Chicago Press, 1988). Greven puts S. W. under the category "The Evangelicals: The Self Suppressed," citing her particularly in his chapter "Authoritarian Families: Modes of Evangelical Child-Rearing" in the sections on "Broken Wills: Discipline and Parental Control" and "Regular Methods of Living: External Discipline in Evangelical Households." The other two "modes of piety" Greven explores are "The Moderates: The Self Controlled" and "The Genteel: the Self Asserted." Greven has edited S. W.'s letter on education in his anthology, *Child-Rearing Concepts, 1628–1861: Historical Sources* (Itasca, Ill.: Peacock, 1973), pp. 46–51.

6. Quoted in Richard Greaves, "Foundation Builders: the Role of Women in Early English Nonconformity," in Richard L. Greaves, ed., *Triumph over Silence: Women in Protestant History* (Westport, Conn., and London: Greenwood, 1985), p. 77.

7. Richard Baxter, *The Saints' Everlasting Rest*, 11 ed. (London: Francis Tyton and Robert Boulter, 1677), quoted by Newton, *Susanna Wesley*, p. 105.

8. [Richard Allestree], *The Whole Duty of Man . . .*, in *The Works of the Learned and Pious Author of the Whole Duty of Man* (Oxford: George Pawlet, 1684), pp. 112–117. Underscoring Allestree's

importance, John Spurr borrowed the book's title to label his chapter on the ideal of holy living that permeated the Restoration church: *The Restoration Church of England, 1646–1689* (New Haven and London: Yale University Press, 1991), pp. 279–330.

9. John Locke, *Some Thoughts concerning Education*, ed. John W. Yolton and Jean S. Yolton (Oxford: Clarendon Press, 1989). Frank Baker in his essay, "Susanna Wesley," in Rosemary Skinner Keller, Louise L. Queen, and Hilah F. Thomas, eds. (Nashville: Abingdon, 1982), *Women in New Worlds*, 2:117–19, partially defends S. W.'s emphasis on conquering a child's will by pointing out that it is "one principle which she took from Locke." Cf. Newton, *Susanna Wesley*, pp. 115–117. On the other side, Greven in *Protestant Temperament*, p. 160n, argues, "Although, on balance, John Locke can be put into the category of 'moderate,' his views on early child-rearing . . . were almost as repressive as those of evangelicals such as Susanna Wesley," and he points a finger of blame at Calvinist sources of Locke's thought. In his child-rearing anthology, Greven actually groups Locke with Susanna (and John) Wesley under the rubric "Puritan-Evangelical Concepts," noting that Locke was raised in a Puritan family and "that many of the fundamental assumptions shaping his views on childhood mirrored those of others raised within the Puritan tradition" (p. 18).

10. This combination clouds the distinction that Greven, following Alan Heimart, would like to make: that "evangelicals were not Lockeans." See Greven, *Protestant Temperament*, p. 354n, but cf. his linking of Locke and Puritanism in *Child-rearing*, p. 18.

11. S. W. seems to have heeded Locke's call for as few rules as possible: "Make but few Laws, but see they be well observed, when once made" (*Concerning Education*, sec. 65).

12. Ibid., sec. 21.

13. Though minimizing the necessity of corporal punishment, Locke does occasionally recommend it. In the case of what he calls "obstinate or stomachful crying," he advises "severity to silence it, and where a Look or a positive Command will not do it, Blows must" (ibid., secs. 112 and 114).

14. That is, weak.

15. Soft or liquid food.

16. Cf. Locke, *Concerning Education*, secs. 13–20, 39.

17. Locke recommended physical punishment only for obstinacy or rebellion, not for any other fault. He gives a positive account of a mother who whipped her daughter eight times the same morning to gain compliance on an admittedly "indifferent matter" and "wisely persisting, till she had bent her Mind, and suppled her Will, the only end of Correction and Chastisement, she established her Authority thoroughly in the very first occasion, and had ever after a very ready Compliance and Obedience in all things from her Daughter." He adds that this was not only the first but also the last time she needed to strike her daughter (*Concerning Education*, sec. 78. See also secs. 36, 40, 44, 46). Locke was afraid lest "the Mind be curbed, and humbled too much in Children" or "their Spirits be abased and broken much, by too strict an hand over them" (sec. 46; see also sec. 51). For one of Susanna's earlier meditations on correcting children, see journal entry 55.

18. This paragraph begins a section common to both sources, the previous material having come exclusively from the more extensive edition in John Wesley's *Journal*. Brackets indicate words found in the longer *Journal* version but not in the sermon as published in *AM*; when sections are differently phrased, the *Journal* version is left unbracketed as the preferred text and the *AM* reading is given in footnotes.

19. In *AM*: "to be conquered."

20. In *AM*: "to us as to the children."

21. In *AM*: "Therefore I call those cruel parents, who pass for kind and indulgent: who permit their children to contract habits. . . ." Habits are for Locke central to the discussion. Typical of numerous references is this assertion in a section on diet: "The great Thing to be

minded in Education is, what Habits you settle: And therefore in this, as all other Things, do not begin to make any Thing customary, the Practice whereof you would not have continue, and increase" (*Concerning Education*, sec. 18; cf. sec. 66).

22. Cf. [Allestree], *Whole Duty*, pp. 114–115, who also insists on the wisdom of "seasonable" and moderate correction to forestall bad habits and stubbornness.

23. Achieving a "Compliance, and Suppleness of their Wills" should be "begun early, and inflexibly kept to, till Awe and Respect be grown familiar, and there appears not the least Reluctancy in the Submission and ready Obedience of their Minds." Such reverence—mixed with appropriate indulgence, not more "Beating, Chiding, or other Servile Punishments"—will help govern children as "they grow up to more Understanding" (Locke, *Concerning Education*, sec. 44. Elsewhere, sec. 99, Locke urges that "true Reverence" should be "maintained in both the Parts of it, Love and Fear, as the great Principle, whereby you will always have hold upon him, to turn his Mind to the Ways of Vertue, and Honour." In sec. 41 he states, "Children, when little, should look upon their Parents as their Lords, their Absolute governors; and, as such, stand in awe of them. . . ." When they grow older and wiser "love and reverence" of parents as "their best, as their only sure Friends," will replace the awe.

24. In AM: "wills."

25. In AM: "for."

26. In AM: "insures."

27. In AM: "and that self-will being the grand impediment to our temporal and eternal happiness."

28. AM adds: "of it."

29. In AM: "children."

30. Though without the dire theological consequences, Locke also emphasized the importance of self-denial: "this Habit, as the true foundation of future Ability and Happiness, is to be wrought into the Mind, as early as may be, even from the first dawnings of any Knowledge, or Apprehension in Children." (*Concerning Education*, sec. 45)

31. This paragraph is found only in the AM version.

32. Echoing sentence from third paragraph, above, from the *Journal* version.

33. Somewhat less nuanced, given the short space, than Locke, *Concerning Education*, secs. 111–114.

34. This is the last section of the letter to be found in the AM. The remaining material from John Wesley's *Journal* is therefore transcribed without brackets. On Locke's similar view on the occasional necessity of multiple beatings, see note 17, above.

35. In Clarke: "our children."

36. Though no evangelical, even Locke could recommend that certain religious texts be learnt by heart: the Lord's Prayer, the Creeds, and the Ten Commandments. See *Concerning Education*, sec. 157 and further comments on religious education in sec. 136.

37. Ward and Heitzenrater, *Works of John Wesley*, has "would." "Could" makes more sense and is supported by Clarke and by Curnock's older edition, *The Journal of the Rev. John Wesley, A.M. . . .*, ed. Nehemiah Curnock, 8 vols. (London: Epworth, 1912-16 [reprint 1938]), 3:36.

38. Cf. Locke's *Concerning Education*, on manners, sec. 66, and "good breeding," secs. 141–146.

39. "When he can talk, 'tis time he should begin to learn to read" (ibid., sec. 148). Note, though, that Locke urged that reading be taught as "a Play and Recreation" rather than as a duty (See secs. 149–156).

40. S. W.'s experience stood in direct contraction to Locke on the pedagogical use of the Bible: "the promiscuous reading of it through, by Chapters, as they lie in order, is so far from being of any Advantage to Children, either for the perfecting their Reading, or principling their Religion, that perhaps a worse could not be found" (Locke, *Concerning Education*, sec.

158) His was not a wholesale dismissal of Scripture but an argument that only those parts "suited to a Child's Capacity" should be given (mainly Old Testament stories and "plain moral Rules") until further instruction would make it seem more than just an "odd jumble of Thoughts" (secs. 158–159).

41. Ibid., secs. 68–69.

42. Locke deals with civility and its opposite ("ill-breeding" and various other forms of natural "roughness") in secs. 143–145, ibid.

43. Parallel to Locke's point, "that there cannot be a greater spur to the attaining what you would have the eldest learn, and know himself, than to set him upon teaching it his younger Brothers and Sisters" (ibid., sec. 119).

44. Possibly following the BCP's instructions, "The Order how the Psalter is appointed to be read" and "The Order how the rest of Holy Scripture is appointed to be read." Even Locke could recommend morning and evening devotions for children, as long as they were "suitable to their Age and Capacity" (ibid., sec. 136).

45. Locke made a similar point about a child that admitted a fault: "if he directly confess, you must commend his Ingenuity, and pardon the Fault, be it what it will" (Ibid., sec. 132).

46. Probably her husband, Samuel.

47. This rule has elicited some comment by various editors. Curnock, editor of Wesley's *Journal* (the standard until the completion of the Bicentennial Edition) indicates that the "or" was left out in an erroneous reading, "occasioning severe reflections upon the moralities of the Epworth house regime" 3:38, n. 3. Maldwyn Edwards, *Family Circle: A Study of the Epworth Household in Relation to John and Charles Wesley* (London: Epworth, 1949), p. 61, follows Clarke, p. 219, in reading: "lying, pilfering at church or on the Lord's day. . . ." He maintains that "pilfering" is probably an erroneous reading (especially as the sixth rule covers the same "sinful action") and ought to be "playing." Indeed, singling out ecclesiastical petty larceny as a family concern seems most odd, whereas one with Susanna's sabbatarian concerns might well inveigh against playing on Sunday, as well as in the sanctuary itself.

48. A slightly more pointed version of Locke's "Frequent Beating or Chiding is . . . carefully to be avoided" (*Concerning Education*, sec. 60).

49. "Case" follows Clarke, p. 219, and common usage; the *Journal* version has: "cause." S. W.'s "commendation" bylaw is also present in Locke; see *Concerning Education*, secs. 57 and 62.

50. The right of possession or use.

51. Locke, *Concerning Education*, sec. 110: "great Care is to be taken, that Children transgress not the Rules of Justice: And whenever they do, they should be set right, and if there be occasion for it, severely rebuk'd."

52. This last rule interestingly corresponds to a line of thought from her sister Elizabeth Dunton's funeral sermon: "If good Women would apply themselves to reading and study, as the Men do, or had equal Advantage for Knowledge in their Education, no doubt we should have more of their excellent Composures, many of them have an happy Genius, and a smooth Expression, and might write as well as work, and the Pen might have as good success as the Needle; especially, they may make Observations, or draw up Rules for the good order of their own Families, and when they see fit, communicate them for the Good of others." See Timothy Rogers, *The Character of a Good Woman*. . . (London: John Harris, 1697), pp. 48–49, quoted in Newton, *Susanna Wesley*, p. 107. "Work" in this context has the specific meaning do or make by needlework.

TWENTY-FIVE

The Apostles' Creed Explicated in a Letter to Her Daughter Susanna

*T*he teacher's calling did not dissipate for Susanna Wesley when her children grew. As the correspondence shows, she kept in touch with all three sons when they left home for school, university, and careers in the church. She also felt an obligation to those who remained behind in the rectory, namely, her daughters.

One way to continue her teaching was to write, not just letters but also extended treatises, a project she had already embarked on before the rectory fire struck in early 1709. Corresponding with her son Samuel the following autumn, she recounted her plan: "I had been for several years collecting from my little reading, but chiefly from my own observation and experience, some things which I hoped would ha' been useful to you all." The "little manual" she was assembling dealt with her views on natural and revealed religion, an extended reflection on her decision (at age 12!) to leave the ranks of dissent and join the established church, and a "short discourse" on the sacrament.[1]

The fire not only destroyed this (and all other letters, papers, and books the family possessed) but also necessitated the dispersal of the children to neighbors and relatives while a new rectory was built. That diaspora doubtless prompted Susanna Wesley to take up the project again with new energy: doing some good for their souls was especially crucial now that, temporarily at least, they were not under her day-to-day care and tutelage.[2]

The letter was intended for all her children but addressed particularly to the second eldest daughter, Susanna (Suky), then about 15. Though Adam Clarke reports her residing with her 12-year-old sister Mehetabel (Hetty) in the London home of their uncle Matthew Wesley, in fact she was not so far afield but rather in the neighboring market town of Gainsborough, a dozen miles south of Epworth.[3]

In embarking on her exposition of the Creed and the later, unfinished one on the Decalogue, Susanna Wesley stepped on board the long-standing Reformation tradition of catechesis. Written summaries of Christian teaching for the laity had been known in the Middle Ages, but they gained new stature when the continental reformers developed what quickly became a theological genre in the 1520s and beyond. Given classical statement in Luther's *Small Catechism* of 1529, they generally centered on the Creed, the Ten Commandments, and the Our Father, all explained in a question-and-answer format appropriate either for a parent teaching a child at home or for a pastor instructing all the parish youths in the church. The approach caught on and became an educational staple not only of Lutheranism but also of the Reformed, Anabaptist, and even Roman Catholic traditions.[4]

The English reformation sparked a similar emphasis on educating people in the new (or newly recovered) biblical faith. In its baptismal and confirmation services the Church of England reaffirmed the importance of the Creed, the Lord's Prayer, and the Ten Commandments, and in the church catechism it provided a significant means for such a basic Christian education. As on the continent, catechetical instruction was seen as the duty of parents in the household, as well as of the priest in the church.[5] With the triumph of Puritanism in the mid-seventeenth century, the Larger and Shorter Catechisms of the Westminster Assembly temporarily eclipsed the older Prayer Book catechism, and indeed, even after the Restoration they continued to instill a Calvinistic worldview in the minds of assorted English Dissenters and Scots, particularly in the North American diaspora. However, possibly to counter their popularity and certainly to help consolidate the restored Church of England, Anglican divines turned out a spate of paraphrases and expositions of the reinstated church catechism.[6]

Doubtless some of these (in addition to the Westminster catechism, which she was surely exposed to in her Presbyterian childhood) Susanna Wesley had in mind, if not in hand, when she sat down to write her own explication of the Creed in late 1709 and early 1710.[7] "Though I know there are abundance of good books wherein these subjects are more fully and accurately treated of than I can pretend to write," she wrote her son Samuel, "yet I am willing to think that my children will somewhat regard what I can do for 'em, though the performance is mean, since they know it comes from their mother, who is perhaps more concerned for their eternal happiness than anyone in the world."[8]

Among the "abundance of good books" that Susanna Wesley did draw on, the chief one we have been able to document is Bishop John Pearson's *Exposition of the Creed*, a long and learned work, heavily annotated from Scripture and the church fathers. She refers to it elsewhere in her writings, borrows extensively from it in her own exposition (though without acknowledgement), and apparently generally used it as a key resource for her work. And no wonder: her husband, Samuel, recommended it unequivocally in his *Advice to a Young Clergyman*. He writes, "his tract on the Creed, must last as long as time, and ought to be in every Clergyman's study in England, though he could purchase nothing but the Bible and Common Prayer-Book besides them." My notes will indicate something of her debt to this previously unrecognized source.[9]

Susanna Wesley thus was taking what we might call a catechetical approach, seeking to inculcate the basics of the faith to her growing children by explaining in some detail the Apostles' Creed and the Ten Commandments, two of the three legs on which the church catechism sat.

At the same time, the process was to go deeper than rote learning. There is an experiential note, for instance, in her suddenly switching tenses when she arrives at the article "He was crucified." Whereas in the rest of her exposition she explains and argues and recounts the events of Jesus' life in the past tense, here she attempts to pull the reader into the scene and feel its power as if present: "And now let us by faith attend our Lord to his last scene of misery. . . ." Further, exhibiting a typical eighteenth-century concern for a reasonable and moral Christianity, Susanna writes to Suky in the introductory letter, "you must understand what you say, and you must practice what you know." The Reformation catechetical tradition, now enhanced by various currents of Enlightenment thought, provides the context for this practical primer of the Christian faith.

In preparing this edition I have relied on the two extant holographs, both at Wesley College, Bristol: one is contained in Autograph Letters Illustrated Wesley Papers (folio 44), whose 6-by-8-inch sheets were once in a notebook of some sort; the other is in Headingley MS C, a small notebook, about 3½ by 6 inches, along with a draft letter to Samuel Jr., 11 October 1709; fragments of her devotional journal; and a second letter to Suky, explicating the Ten Commandments. Methodist Archives has a version of the letter in Samuel Wesley Jr.'s hand (SW Jr Letter Book, pp. 107–120), indicating that he also received a copy.

Comparative examination of the two manuscripts indicates that the smaller notebook (MS C) is the prior draft, even though it is dated a day later (14 January 1709/ 10 compared to the Wesley Papers, 13 January). Its insertions and deletions are followed in the cleaner, larger-scale version of the Wesley Papers, though there are additional changes, generally improvements in style, that Susanna Wesley introduces in the latter MS as she copies from the former. I have thus taken the Wesley Papers MS as the primary text, following it almost exclusively. At the same time I have indicated in notes different readings as they appear in MS C. The letter has been published once before; working from the Wesley Papers MS, Adam Clarke edited the exposition (with a rather free hand) for his *Memoirs of the Wesley Family*, crediting it (a bit optimistically, as we now see) with being "entirely original," containing "many fine passages and just definitions." [10] In my transcription, I have introduced an asterisk to indicate Clarke's paragraphing that is not supported in either Wesley College MS.

ʬ

Epworth, January 13, 1709/10

Dear Suky,

Since our misfortunes have separated us from each other, and we can no longer enjoy the opportunities we once had of conversing together, I can no other way discharge the duty of a parent or comply with my inclination of doing you all the good I can, but by writing. You know very well how I love you. I love your body and do earnestly beseech Almighty God to bless it with health and all things necessary for its comfort and support in this world. But my tenderest regard is for your immortal soul and for its eternal happiness; which regard I cannot better express than by endeavouring to instil into your mind those principles of knowledge and virtue that are absolutely necessary in order to your leading a good life here, which is the only thing that can infallibly secure your happiness hereafter.

The main thing which is now to be done is to lay a good foundation, that you may act upon principles and be always able to satisfy yourself and give a reason to others of the faith that is in you.[11] For any one which[12] makes a profession of religion only because 'tis the custom of the country in which they live or because their parents do so or their worldly interest is thereby secured or advanced will never be able to stand in the day of temptation, nor shall they ever enter into the kingdom of heaven. And though perhaps you cannot at present fully comprehend all I shall say, yet keep this Letter by you, and as you grow in years, your reason and judgment will improve, and you will obtain a more clear understanding in all things.

You have already been instructed in some of the first principles of religion—that there is one, and but one, God; that in the unity of the Godhead there are three distinct persons, Father, Son, and Holy Ghost; that this God ought to be worshiped. And you have learnt some prayers, your Creed and Catechism, in which is briefly comprehended your duty to God, yourself, and your neighbour. But, Suky, 'tis not learning these things by rote, nor the saying a few prayers morning and evening, that will bring you to heaven; you must understand what you say, and you must practice what you know. And since knowledge is requisite in order to practice, I shall endeavour, after as plain a manner as I can, to instruct you in some of those fundamental points which are most necessary to be known and most easy to be understood. And I earnestly beseech the great Father of spirits[13] to guide your mind into the way of truth.

Though it hath been generally acknowledged that the being and perfections of God, and a great part of man's duty towards him, as that we should love him and pray to him for what we want and praise him for what we enjoy, etc., as likewise much of our duty towards ourselves and neighbour are discoverable by the light of nature, that is, by that understanding and reason which are natural to all men; yet considering the present state of mankind, it was absolutely necessary that we should have some revelation from God to make known to us those truths upon the knowledge of which our salvation depends and which unassisted reason could never have discovered.[14] For all the duties of natural religion and all the hopes of happiness which result from the performance of them are all concluded within the present life. Nor could we have had any certainty of the future state, of the being of spirits, of the immortality of the soul or of a judgment to come.

And though we may perceive that all men have by nature a strong bent or bias towards evil and a great averseness from God and goodness, that our understandings, wills,[15] and affections, etc. are extremely corrupted and depraved, yet how could we have known by what means we became so or how sin and death entered into the world? Since we are assured that whatever is absolutely perfect, as God is, could never be the author of evil. And we are as sure that whatever is corrupt or impure must necessarily be offensive and displeasing to the most holy God, there being nothing more opposite than good and evil. Nay further, sin is not only displeasing to God, as it is contrary to the purity of his divine nature, but 'tis the highest affront and indignity to his sacred Majesty imaginable.

*By it his most wise and holy laws are contemned and violated and his honour most injuriously treated; and therefore he is in justice obliged to punish such contempt and to vindicate the honour of his own laws, nor can he, without derogating from his infinite perfections, pardon such offenders or remit the punishment they deserve without full satisfaction made to his justice. Now I would fain know which way his justice could be satisfied, since 'tis impossible for a finite being as man is to do it; or how the nature of man should be renewed and he again be admitted into favour with God; or how reason could suggest that our[16] weak endeavours or penitences[17] should be accepted instead of perfect obedience, unless some other were substituted[18] in our stead that would undergo the punishment we have[19] deserved and thereby satisfy divine justice and purchase pardon and favour from God, the merit of whose perfect obedience should atone for the imperfection of ours, and so obtain for us a title to those glorious rewards, to that eternal happiness, which we must acknowledge ourselves utterly unworthy of, and of which we must have despaired without such a Saviour? But what knowledge could we have had of a Saviour? Or how should we have had any certainty of our salvation unless God had revealed these things unto us? The soul is immortal and must survive all time, even to eternity, and consequently it must have been miserable to the utmost extent of its duration, had we not had that sacred treasure of knowledge which is contained in the books of the Old and New Testament. A treasure infinitely more valuable than the whole world, because therein we [find][20] all things necessary for our salvation.[21] There also we learn many truths which though we cannot say 'tis absolutely necessary that we should know them, since 'tis possible to be saved without that knowledge, yet 'tis highly convenient that we should, because they give us great light into those things which are necessary to be known and solve many doubts which could not otherwise be cleared.

*Thus we collect from many passages of scripture that before God created this visible world or ever he made man, he created a higher rank of intellectual beings which we call angels or spirits; and these were those bright morning stars mentioned in Job, which sang together, those sons of God which shouted for joy when the foundations of the earth were laid.[22] And to these he gave a law or rule of action, as he did afterwards to the rest of his creation, and they being free agents, having a principle of liberty, of choosing or refusing, and of acting accordingly,[23] as they must have, or they could not properly be called either good or evil. For upon this principle of freedom or liberty the principle of election or choice is founded; and upon the choosing good or evil depends the being virtuous or vicious, since liberty[24] is the formal essence of moral virtue, that is, 'tis the free choice of a rational being that makes them either good or bad: nor could any one that acts by necessity be ever capable of rewards or punishments.

*The angels, I say, being free agents, must I think necessarily be put upon some trial of their obedience; and so consequently were at first only placed in a state of probation or trial. Those that made a good use of their liberty and chose to obey the law of their creation and acquiesced in the order of the divine Wisdom, which had disposed them into several ranks and orders subservient to each other, were by the almighty fiat confirmed in their state of blessedness, nor are they now capable of any defection. But those accursed spirits that rebelled against their Maker and aspired above the rank in which his providence had placed them, were for their presumption justly excluded the celestial paradise and condemned to perpetual torments, which were the necessary consequences of their apostasy.

After the fall of the angels, and perhaps to supply their defects, it pleased the eternal Goodness to create Adam, who was the first general head of mankind, and in him was virtually included the whole species of human nature. He was somewhat inferior to the angels, being composed of two different natures, body and soul. The former was material, or matter made of the earth; the latter immaterial or a spiritual substance created after the image of God. And as man was also a rational free agent like the angels, so it was agreeable to the eternal Wisdom to place him likewise in a state of probation; and the trial of his obedience was not eating of the tree of knowledge of good and evil, and the penalty of his disobedience was death.[25]

And this trial was suited to the double or mixed nature of man. The beauty, scent, and taste of the fruit was the trial of their[26] senses or appetites, and the virtue of it, it being not only "good for food," but also "to be desired to make one wise," was the trial of their minds.[27] And by this[28] God made proof of our first parents, to see whether they would deny their sensual appetites and keep the body in a due subjection to the mind, or whether they would prefer[29] the pleasures of sense and thereby dethrone their reason, break the covenant of their obedience, and forfeit the favour of God and eternal happiness. And whether they[30] would humbly be content with that measure of knowledge and understanding which God thought best for them,[31] or boldly pry into those things that he had forbidden them to search after.

*Now the devil, envying the happiness of our first parents, being grieved that any less perfect beings should possess the place he had lost, took occasion from the[32] reasonable trial God had proposed to Adam to attack the woman by a subtle question, "Yea, hath God said that ye shall not eat of every tree of the garden?"[33] Hath he created this beauteous world, this great variety of creatures for your use and enjoyment and made these delicious fruits which he himself hath pronounced[34] good and yet forbidden you to taste of them? To which she replied, "We may eat of the fruit of the trees of the garden: but of the fruit of the tree in the midst of the garden, God hath said, ye shall not eat of it, neither shall ye touch of it, lest ye die."[35] Upon which the malicious tempter boldly presumed to give the lie to his Maker. "Ye shall not surely die, for God doth know that in the day ye eat thereof then your eyes shall be opened, and ye shall be as gods knowing good and evil. And when the woman saw that the tree was good for food, and that it was pleasant to the eyes, and a tree to be desired to make one wise, she took of the fruit thereof and did eat, and gave also to her husband with her, and he did eat," etc.[36]

*Thus pride and sensuality[37] ruined our first parents,[38] and brought them and their posterity[39] into a state of mortality. Thus sin entered into the world, and death by sin, and thus was human nature corrupted in its fountain. And as a corrupt tree cannot bring forth good fruit, so of consequence the children of guilty Adam must be corrupted and depraved.[40] And anyone that will but[41] make the least reflection on their own mind may soon be convinced of this great truth, that not only the body is weak and infirm, subject to divers diseases, liable to many ill accidents and even to death itself, but also the superior powers of the soul are weakened and[42] corrupted and, as the apostle expresses it, "at enmity with God."[43]

*The understanding, which was designed chiefly to be exercised in the knowledge and contemplation of the supreme Being, is darkened; nor can it, without the divine assistance, discern the radiant glories of the Deity. And though it should naturally press after[44] truth, as being its proper object, yet it seldom, and not without great difficulty, attains to the knowledge of it, but is subject to ignorance, which is the sin of the understanding (because it generally proceeds from our natural indisposition to search after truth), as error is the sin or defect of the judgment, mistaking one thing for another, not having just and clear and distinct apprehensions of things, for which reason it is so frequently guilty of making wrong determinations. Not choosing or not inclining to good or adhering to and preferring evil before it, is the sin of the will. A readiness in[45] receiving vain, impure, corrupt ideas or images and a backwardness in receiving good and useful ideas, is the sin of the imagination or fancy. And a facility in[46] retaining evil or vain ideas and a neglect of, or a readiness to let slip[47] those which are good, is the sin or defect of the memory.

Loving, hating, desiring, fearing, etc. what we should not love, hate, desire, etc. at all in the least degree, or, when[48] the object of such passions are[49] lawful, to love, hate, desire, etc. more than reason requires, or else not loving, hating, desiring, etc. what we ought to love, hate, etc, in short any error either in defect or excess, either too much or too little, is the vice or sin of the passions or affections of the soul.

Now if we consider the infinite, boundless, incomprehensible perfections of the ever blessed God![50] we may easily conceive that evil, that sin, is the greatest contradiction imaginable to his most holy nature, and that no evil, no disease, pain, or natural uncleanness whatever is so hateful, so loathsome to us as the corruptions and impurities of the soul are to him. He is infinite purity! absolutely separated from all moral imperfection. The divine intellect is all brightness,[51] all perfect! was never, and can never be, capable of the least ignorance! He is truth! Nor can he[52] be weary or indisposed in contemplating that great attribute of his most perfect nature, but has a constant steady view of truth. And as he fully comprehends at once all things past, present, and to come, so all objects appear to him simple, naked, undisguised in their natures, properties, relations, and ends, truly as they are; nor is it possible he should be guilty of error or mistake, of making any false judgment or wrong determination.

*He is goodness![53] And his most holy will cannot swerve[54] or decline from what is so.[55] He always wills what is absolutely best, nor can he possibly be deceived or deceive anyone. The ideas of the divine mind are amiable, clear, holy, just, good, useful, and he is of purer eyes than to behold iniquity![56] His love, desire, etc., though boundless, immense, and infinite![57] are yet regular, immutable, always under the direction of his unerring wisdom, his unlimited goodness, and his impartial justice.

But who can "by searching find out God," who can "find out the Almighty to perfection?"[58] What Angel is worthy to speak his praise, who dwelleth in[59] that inaccessible light, "which no man can approach unto?"[60] And though he is always surrounded with thousands and ten thousands of those pure and happy spirits, yet are they represented to us as veiling their faces, as if conscious of too much imperfection and weakness to behold his glory. And if he chargeth his angels with folly,[61] and those "stars are not pure in his sight," "how much less man that is a worm, and the son of man which is a worm?"[62]

And as we are thus corrupt and impure by nature, so are we likewise "the children of wrath"[63] and in a state of damnation. For it was not only a temporal death with which God threatened our first parents if[64] they were disobedient, but it was also a spiritual death, an eternal separation from him that[65] is our life, the consequence of which separation is our eternal[66] misery.

But the infinite goodness[67] of God, who delighteth that his mercy should triumph over his justice, though he provided no remedy for the fallen angels, yet man being a more simple kind of creature,[68] who perhaps did not sin so maliciously against so much knowledge as those apostate spirits did, he would not suffer the whole race of mankind should be thus ruined and destroyed by the fraud and subtilty of Satan. But he "laid help upon one that is mighty,"[69] that is able and willing to save to the uttermost all such as shall come unto God through him.[70] And this Saviour is that seed of the woman, that was promised should bruise the head of the serpent,[71] break the power of the devil, and bring mankind again into a salvable condition. And upon a view of that "satisfaction" which Christ would make "for the sins of the whole world"[72] was the penalty of Adam's disobedience suspended, and he admitted to a second trial; and God renewed his covenant with man, not on the former condition of perfect obedience,[73] but on condition[74] of faith in Christ Jesus and a sincere though imperfect obedience of the laws of God. I'll speak something of these two branches of our duty distinctly.

By faith in Christ is to be understood an assent to whatever is recorded of him in holy Scripture[75] or is said to be delivered by him, either immediately by himself or mediately by his prophets and apostles or whatsoever may by just inferences or natural consequences be collected from their writings. But because the greater part of mankind either want leisure or capacity to collect the several articles of faith, which lie scattered up and down throughout the sacred writ,[76] the wisdom of the church hath thought fit to sum them up in a short form of words,[77] commonly called the Apostles Creed. Which, because it comprehends the main of what a Christian ought to believe, I shall briefly expound unto you. And though I have not time at present to bring all the arguments I could[78] to prove the being of God, his divine attributes, and the truth of revealed religion, yet this short paraphrase may inform you what you should intend when you make the solemn confession of our most holy faith; and may withal teach you that it is not to be said after a formal customary manner, but seriously as in the presence of the all-seeing God, who observes whether the heart join with the tongue, and whether your mind do truly assent to what you profess when you say,

I believe in God—[79] I do truly and heartily assent to the being of a God, one supreme independent power, who is a spirit infinitely wise, holy, good, just, true, unchangeable.[80] I do believe that this God is a necessary self-existent being; necessary in that he could not but be, because he derives his existence from no other than himself,[81] but he alone is **the Father**—And having all life, all being in himself, all creatures must derive their existence from him, whence he is properly styled the Father of all things, more especially of all spiritual natures, angels and souls of men.[82] And since he is the great Parent of the universe, it naturally follows that he is **Almighty**—And this glorious attribute of his omnipotence[83] is conspicuous in that he hath a right[84] of making anything which he willeth, after that manner which best pleaseth him, according to the absolute freedom of his own will, and a right of possessing all things so made by him, by virtue of direct dominion, as likewise a right of disposing of all things as he pleaseth.[85] Nor can his almighty infinite power admit of any weakness, dependence or limitation, but it extendeth to all things, is boundless, incomprehensible, and eternal. And though we cannot fully comprehend or have any adequate conceptions of what so far surpasseth the reach of human understanding, yet it is plainly demonstrable that he is omnipotent from his being the **Maker of Heaven and Earth**—"of all things visible and invisible."[86] Nor could anything less than almighty power produce the smallest most inconsiderable thing out of nothing. Not the least spire of grass or most despicable insect but bears[87] the divine signature and carries in its existence a clear demonstration of the deity. For could we admit of such a wild supposition as that anything could make itself, it must necessarily follow that a thing had being before it had a being, that it could act before it was, which is a palpable contradiction. From whence among other reasons we conclude that this beauteous world, that celestial arch over our heads, and all those glorious heavenly bodies, sun, moon, and stars, etc. in fine, the whole system of the universe, were in the beginning made or created out of nothing by the eternal power, wisdom, and goodness of the ever blessed God according to "the counsel of his own will"[88] or, as St. Paul better expresses it, Colossians 1:16, "By him were all things created that are in heaven, and that are in earth, visible and invisible, whether they be thrones, or dominions, or principalities, or powers: all things were created by him."[89]

And in Jesus—Jesus signifies a Saviour, and by that name he was called by the angel Gabriel before his birth,[90] to show us that he came into the world to save us from our sins, and the punishment they justly deserve. And to repair the damage human nature had sustained by the fall of Adam. That, as in Adam all died, so in Christ all should be made alive.[91] And so he became the second general head of all mankind. And as he was promised to our parents in paradise, so was his coming signified[92] by various types and sacrifices under the law and foretold by the prophets long before he appeared in the world. And this Saviour, this Jesus, was the promised messiah, who was so long the hope and expectation of the Jews, the **Christ**—which in the original signifies anointed. Now among the Jews it was a custom to anoint three sorts of persons: prophets, priests, and kings.[93] Which anointing did not only show their designation to those offices, but was also usually attended with a special influence or inspiration of the Holy Spirit to prepare and qualify them for the execution of such offices.

Our blessed Lord, who was by his almighty Father sanctified and sent into the world, was also anointed, not with material oil, but by the descent of the Holy Ghost upon him, to signify to us that he was our prophet, priest, and king. And that he should first, as our prophet, fully, clearly reveal the will of God for our salvation, which accordingly he did.[94] And though the Jews had long before received the law by Moses, yet a great part of that law was purely typical and ceremonial, and all of it that was so was necessarily vacated by the coming of our Saviour, and that part which was moral, and consequently of perpetual obligation, they had so corrupted by their misinterpretations and various traditions, that it was not[95] pure and undefiled, as God delivered it on Mount Sinai. Which occasioned the words of our Lord, "Think not that I am come to destroy the Law and the Prophets; I am not come to destroy, but to fulfil."[96] To accomplish the predictions of the prophets concerning himself and to rescue the moral law from those false glosses they had put on it. And though the rest of the world were not altogether without some precepts of morality, yet they lay scattered up and down in the writings of a few wiser and better than the rest, but morality was never collected into a complete system, till the coming of our Saviour, nor was life and immortality ever fully brought to light till the preaching of the gospel.

He was also our priest in that he offered up himself a sacrifice to divine justice in our stead, and by the perfect satisfaction he made, he did atone the displeasure of God, and purchase eternal life for us, which was forfeited by the first man's disobedience.[97]

And as he is our prophet and priest, so likewise he is our king and hath an undoubted right to govern those he hath redeemed by his blood. And as such he will conquer for us all our spiritual enemies: sin and death and all the powers of the kingdom of darkness. And when he hath perfectly subdued them, he will actually confer upon us eternal happiness.[98] This satisfaction and purchase that Christ hath made for us is a clear proof of his divinity, since no mere man is capable of meriting anything good from God; and therefore we are obliged to consider him in a state of equality with the Father, being **his only Son**—Though we are all children of the almighty[99] Father, yet hath he one only Son by an eternal and incomprehensible generation, which only Son is Jesus the Saviour. Being equal to the Father,[100] as touching his Godhead, but inferior to the Father as touching his manhood. "God of God, light of light, very God of very God, begotten, not made."[101] And this only Son of God we acknowledge to be **Our Lord**—In that he is co-equal and co-essential with the Father, and "by him all things were made."[102] Therefore, since we are his creatures, we must with the apostle St. Thomas, confess him to be "our Lord and our God."[103] But besides this right to our allegiance, which he hath by creation, he hath redeemed us from death and hell, he hath purchased us with his own blood, so that upon a double account we justly style him Lord, namely, that of creation and purchase.[104]

And as the infinite condescension of the eternal Son of God in assuming our nature was mysterious and incomprehensible, surpassing the wit of men or angels to conceive how such a thing might be! So it was requisite and agreeable to the majesty of God, that the conception of his sacred person should be after a manner altogether differing from ordinary generations; accordingly it was he **which was conceived by the Holy Ghost**—whose miraculous conception was foretold by the angel when his blessed mother questioned how she which was a virgin could conceive. "The[105] Holy Ghost shall come upon thee, and the power of the Highest shall overshadow thee; therefore also that holy thing which shall be born of thee shall be called the son of God."[106] And as all the sacrifices which represented our Saviour under the law were to be without spot or blemish, so likewise Christ, the great Christian sacrifice, was not only infinitely pure and holy in his divine, but also in his human nature he was perfectly immaculate,[107] having none but God for his

being his onely Son — Tho we are all Children of the Almigh:
Father, yet hath he one onely Son, by an Eternal & incompreh:
sible Generation, wch onely Son, is, Jesus the Saviour. Being
equal to the Father as touching his Godhead, but Inferiour
to the Father, as touching his Manhood. God, of God, Light
of Light, very God of very God begotten n't made. And this
onely Son of God we acknowledg to be Our Lord — In
that he is Co-Equal, and Co-Essential wth the Father, and
by him all things were made. Therfore since we are his
Creatures, we must wth the Apostle St Thomas, confess him
to be, Our Lord, and our God. But besides this Right to our
Allegiance wch he hath by Creation, he hath redeem'd us from
Death, & Hell; he hath Purchas'd us wth his own Blood,
So that upon a double account we justly stile him Lord,
namely, That of Creation, and Purchase.

And as the infinite Condescention, of the Eternal Son
of God, in assuming our nature, was mysterious, and incomprehensible, surpassing the wit of men, or Angels, to conceive
how such a thing might be! So it was requisite, and agruable
to the Majesty of God, that the Conception of his Sacred person
So be after a manner, altogether differing, from ordinary Generations, accordingly it was he, WHICH WAS CONCEIVED
BY THE HOLY GHOST — whose miraculous Conception was
foretold by the Angel, wn his blessed Mother question'd, How
The wch way a Virgin shoud conceive? The Holy Ghost sll
com upon Thee, and the Power of the Highest, shall overshadow Thee, therfore also, that Holy Thing wth shall be
Born of Thee, shall be call'd the Son of God. And as all the
Sacrifices yt represented our Saviour, under the Law, were to
be wthout Spot, or Blemish, so. Likewise Christ, the great Christian
Sacrifice, was n't onely infinitely pure, and holy, in his Divine
but also in his humane nature, he was perfectly Immaculate, having none but God, for his Father, and Being, BORN
OF THE VIRGIN MARY — whose spotless purity, no Age of
the Catholic Church, hath ever presum'd to question.
That the promis'd Messiah shoud be born of a Virgin is plain
from that of Jeremy 31.V.22. The Lord hath created a new
thing on the Earth, A woman, shall compass a man. And from

A portion of Susanna Wesley's commentary on the Apostles' Creed, taken from Headingley Wesley Papers MS at Wesley College, Bristol. This page explicates parts of the
Creed's second article, "[I believe . . . in Jesus Christ] his only Son our Lord, which
was conceived by the Holy Ghost, Born of the Virgin Mary . . ."

Father, being **Born of the Virgin Mary**—whose spotless purity no age of the catholic church hath presumed to question.[108] That the promised messiah should be born of a virgin is plain from that of Jeremiah 31:22: "The Lord hath created a new thing on the earth; a woman shall compass a man." And from Isaiah 7:14: "Behold a Virgin shall conceive and bear a son,[109] and shall call his name Emmanuel."[110] And this seed of the woman[111] must necessarily have assumed our nature, or he could never have been our Jesus, the Saviour of the world. For the divine nature of the Son of God is infinitely happy, utterly incapable of any grief, pain or sense of misery. Nor could its union with humanity any way defile or pollute it or derogate the least from its infinite perfections; so it was only as man that he **Suffered**[112] those infirmities and calamities incident to human nature.

What transactions passed between the Almighty Father and his eternal Son concerning redemption of the world we know not, but we are sure[113] that by a certain and express agreement betwixt them, he was from eternity decreed to suffer for mankind. And in several places of the Old Testament "it was written of the Son of Man that he must suffer many things."[114] And the Spirit of Christ which was in the prophets testified beforehand the sufferings of Christ[115]—particularly in the 53rd chapter of Isaiah[116] we have a "sad, but clear description" of the sufferings of the Messiah.[117] And indeed his whole life was one continued scene of misery.[118] No sooner was he born, but he was persecuted by Herod and forced to fly into Egypt in the arms of a weak virgin under the protection of a poor foster father. And when returned into his own country, he for thirty years lived in a low condition, probably employed in the mean trade of a carpenter, which made him in the eyes of the world despicable, of no reputation. And when after so long an obscurity he appeared unto men, he entered upon his ministry with the severity of forty days abstinence.

Behold the eternal Lord of nature transported[119] into a wild and desolate wilderness, exposed to the inclemency of the air, tempted by the apostate spirits! The Almighty Being that justly claims a right to the whole creation was himself hungry and athirst, often wearied with painful travelling from place to place; and though he "went about doing good,"[120] and never sent any away from him that sought relief without healing their diseases and casting out those evil spirits that afflicted them, yet was he "despised and rejected of men."[121] The possessor of heaven and earth, the sovereign Disposer of all things, from whose bounty all creatures receive[122] what they enjoy of the necessary accommodations of life, was reduced to such a mean[123] estate that though "the foxes had holes, and the birds of the air had nests, yet the Son of man had nowhere to lay his head."[124] And though all his life he was "a man of sorrow and acquainted with grief,"[125] yet his greatest sufferings were **under Pontius Pilate**—who was at that time the Roman governor of Judea under Tiberias then[126] emperor of Rome. His office was that of a procurator, whose business it was not only to take an account of the tribute due to the emperor and to order and dispose of the same for his advantage, but by reason of the seditious and rebellious temper of the Jews, they were further entrusted with some part of the supreme power amongst them, a power of life and death, which was a signal instance of divine providence and a clear proof of the truth[127] of those predictions of the prophets, which had long before foretold that the Messiah should "suffer after a manner that was not prescribed by the law of Moses."[128] And this circumstance of time is mentioned to confirm the truth of our Saviour's history.[129]

And now behold a mysterious scene of wonders indeed![130] The immaculate Lamb of God, that came to save the world from misery, under the greatest most amazing apprehensions of his approaching passion! "He began to be sorrowful," saith St. Matthew;[131] "to be sore amazed and very heavy," says St. Mark.[132] His soul was pressed with fear, horror and dejection of mind! Tormented with anxiety and disquietude of spirit, which he expressed to his disciples in those sad words, "My soul is exceeding sorrowful, even unto death!"[133] See him retire to a solitary garden at a still, melancholy hour of night; behold him prostrate on the ground, conflicting with the wrath of his Almighty Father![134] He perfectly knew what God is, the severe purity of the deity,[135] and was absolutely conformed to his will. He knew the evil of sin in its nature and consequences, the perfect justice, wisdom and goodness of the divine laws; he understood the inexpressible misery[136] man had brought upon himself by the violation of them; and how intolerable it would be for man to sustain the vengeance of an angry God,[137] and perhaps was moved with extreme concern and pity when he foresaw that, notwithstanding all he had already done and was about to suffer for his salvation, there would be so many that would obstinately perish. He had a full prospect of all he had yet to undergo, that the combat was not over, but the dregs of that bitter cup still remained; that he must be forsaken of his father in the midst of his torments, which made him thrice so earnestly repeat his petition that "if it were possible, that cup might pass from him."[138] But the full complement of his sufferings we may suppose to be he did at that time actually sustain the whole weight of that grief and sorrow which is due to the justice of God[139] for the sins of the whole world. And this we may believe occasioned that inconceivable[140] agony when "his sweat was as great drops of blood falling to the ground."[141] And though his torments were so inexpressibly[142] great, yet "the Son of man must suffer many things."[143] He must be betrayed by one disciple, denied by another, and forsaken of all, that, as he had suffered in his soul by the most intense grief and anguish,[144] so he might likewise suffer in his body the greatest bitterness of corporeal[145] pains, which the malice and rage of his enemies could inflict upon it.

And now[146] the sovereign Lord and judge of all men[147] is haled before the tribunal of his sinful creatures. The pure and unspotted Son of God, who could do no wrong, "neither was guile found in his mouth,"[148] accused by his presumptuous slaves of no less a crime than blasphemy. And though the witnesses could by no means agree together, and he was so often declared innocent by Pilate, an infidel judge, yet still the rude and barbarous rabble, being instigated by the envy and malice of the chief priest and elders, persist in demanding that he should be condemned. And when in compliance with their usual custom of having a malefactor released at their feast, Pilate, in order to save him, proposed his release instead of Barabbas, who was a seditious murderer, yet they[149] persisted in their fury and preferred the murderer before the Prince of Life, nor would they be satisfied till he **was crucified**—to which ignominious death the Romans commonly condemned their greatest malefactors, and[150] it was accounted so vile and shameful amongst them that it was esteemed a very high crime to put any freeman to death after such a dishonourable manner. And as the shame was great, so it was usually accompanied with many previous pains. They were first cruelly scourged and then compelled to bear their cross on their bleeding wounds to the place of crucifixion. All which the meek and patient Jesus[151] cheerfully underwent for the love he bore towards mankind. "The plowers plowed on his back and made long their furrows."[152] But there was other painful circumstances attended and increased the sufferings of our Saviour. They had not only accused him of blasphemy, but of treason and sedition. "We found this fellow perverting the nation and forbidding to give tribute to Caesar, saying that he himself was Christ, a king,"[153] which, as it moved Pilate to condemn him, so it caused the rude soldiers to insult him by those mock ensigns of royalty. They arrayed him in a purple robe and put a reed in his right hand, and they bowed the knee before him saying, "Hail, king of the Jews."[154] And that crown of thorns[155] they platted and put on his head[156] not only expressed the scorn of his tormentors, but did by the piercing his sacred temples cause most exquisite pain.[157] That blessed face, which angels rejoice to behold,[158] they buffeted and spit upon, nor was any circumstance of cruelty which their witty malice could suggest might torment him omitted by those inhumane rebels till, wearied with their own barbarity and impatient of his living any longer, they put his own clothes on again and led him away to crucify him.

And now let us by faith attend our Lord to his last scene of misery, let us ascend with him to the top of Calvary and see with what cruel pleasure they nail his hands and feet to the infamous wood,[159] which, having done, they raise[160] him from the earth, the whole weight of his body being sustained only by those four wounds. But though his corporal pains, occasioned by the thorns, the scourging, by the piercing those nervous and most sensible[161] parts of his sacred body, were wrought up to an inexpressible degree of torture,[162] yet they were infinitely surpassed by the anguish of his soul, when there was, but[163] after what manner we cannot conceive, but it is certain that there was, a sensible withdrawing of the comfortable presence of the Deity, which caused that loud and passionate exclamation,[164] "My God, my God, why hast thou forsaken me?"[165]

And now "it is finished"[166]—The measure of his sufferings is completed; and he that could not die but by his own voluntary act of resigning gave up his pure and spotless soul into the hands of his Almighty Father. And though stupid man could insensibly look on this mysterious passion of his blessed Redeemer, yet nature could not so behold her dying Lord, but by strong commotions expressed her sympathy. The sun, as if ashamed and astonished at the barbarous inhumanity and ingratitude of men, withdrew his influence, nor would he display the brightness of his beams when the great Son of God lay under the eclipse of death. The foundations of the solid earth were shaken, the rocks rent, the graves were open—"and the veil of the temple was rent in twain from the top to the bottom,"[167] signifying that all, both Jews and gentiles, have free admission into the holy of holies in the heaven of presence through the blood of Jesus. Which extorted a confession of his divinity even from his enemies, for "when the centurion and they that were with him watching Jesus saw the earthquake and those things that were done, they feared greatly, saying, Truly this was the Son of God."[168]

Now though crucifixion doth not so necessarily involve in it a certain death, but that if a person be taken from the cross he may live, yet since it is evident that the messiah was to die, and for that reason he was born and came into the world,[169] that he by the grace of God should suffer death for every man,[170] so we are bound to believe that he was truly **dead**—that there was an actual, real separation of his soul and body.[171] And for a confirmation of this article it is added **And Buried**— And as his death was foretold, so likewise his burial was typified by the prophet Jonah.[172] For as he was three days and three nights in the belly of the whale, so was the Son of man to be three days and three nights in the heart of the earth. And though by the Roman law those which were crucified were not allowed the favour of a grave, but were to remain on the cross exposed to the fowls of the air and the beasts of the field, yet it was in the power of the magistrate to permit a burial; and the providence of God had so ordered it that those very persons who[173] had caused him to be crucified should petition for his being taken down from the cross.[174] For the law of Moses required that "if a man have committed a sin worthy of death [. . .] and thou hang him on a tree, his body shall not remain all night upon the tree, but thou shalt in any wise bury him that day."[175] And[176] therefore they begged of Pilate that the body[177] should be taken from the cross, and this was the first step towards our Saviour's burial. And "when the even was come, because it was the preparation, that is, the day before the sabbath, Joseph of Arimathea, an honourable counsellor which also waited for the kingdom of God, came and went in boldly unto Pilate and craved the body of Jesus."[178] And "he gave the body unto Joseph, and he bought fine linen [. . .] and wrapped him in the linen and laid him in a sepulchre which was hewn out of a rock, wherein never man before was laid," and "rolled a stone to the door of the sepulchre and departed."[179]

And as our Saviour was really dead and buried, so likewise **He Descended into Hell**—That our Lord did actually descend into hell seems very plain from St. Peter's exposition of that text in the Psalms, "Thou shalt not leave my soul in hell, neither shalt thou suffer thy Holy One to see corruption."[180] When having mentioned this passage he thus explains it—"He (that is David) seeing this before (namely the incarnation of the Son of God) spake of his resurrection, that his soul was not left in hell, neither did his flesh see corruption."[181] Which is clear proof that his soul did really descend into[182] hell after it was separated from his body.[183] But though he underwent the condition of a sinner in this world and suffered and died as a sinner, yet being perfectly holy and having by virtue of the union of the Deity to his human nature fully satisfied the strictest demands of divine justice, we are not to suppose that he either could or did suffer the torment of the damned. Therefore we may reasonably believe that his descent into hell was not to suffer, but to triumph[184] over principalities and powers, over the rulers of the kingdom of darkness in their own sad regions of horror and despair. And for this reason and in this sense we believe he descended into hell.[185]

And[186] as "his soul was not left in hell, neither did his flesh see corruption."[187] But having by his own almighty power loosed the pains of death, because it was impossible that he should be holden of it, **The third day he arose again from the dead**—Friday, on which he suffered,[188] and the first day of the week, on the which he rose, being included in the number of the three days. And this first day of the week the apostles and primitive Christians in their time and all Christians ever since have observed as the sabbath.[189] That[190] as the Jews, who will not believe any greater deliverance than that out of Egypt, still keep the seventh day, and the Turks the Friday, in memory of Mahomet's[191] flight from Mecca, whom they esteem a greater prophet than Christ or Moses, so all Christians are distinguished from the rest of the world by their observation of the first day[192] commemoration of our Saviour's rising from the dead and his finishing the great work of man's redemption on that day.[193] Thus we believe that as Christ died for our sins, was buried and rose again the third day according to the scriptures,[194] so **He ascended into Heaven**—He[195] had for forty days after his resurrection remained upon earth, during which time he appeared frequently to his disciples, ate[196] and drank with them, showed them his hands and his feet, which visibly retained the marks of his crucifixion to convince them that it was the same body which was nailed[197] to the cross, that it was the same Jesus which suffered for our offenses that was raised[198] again for our justification. And that by his so doing we might have a "sure and certain hope" of our own resurrection from death.[199] And when he had spoken to his disciples and blessed them, even while he blessed them he parted from them and ascended into the highest heaven,[200] where he still remains, **And sitteth at the right hand of God the Father Almighty**—God is a spirit, nor hath he any body, so cannot properly be said to have any parts, such as eyes, ears, hands, etc., as we see bodies have; therefore, we may suppose that the right hand of God signifieth his exceeding great and infinite power and glory. And that Christ is said to sit down on the right hand of God in regard of that absolute power and dominion which he hath obtained in heaven, according as he told the Jews, "Hereafter ye shall see the Son of man sitting on the right hand of power."[201] After all the labour and sorrow, the shame, contempt and torments he suffered in this world, he[202] resteth above in a permanent state of endless glory and unspeakable felicity. And **From thence he shall come to judge the quick and the dead**—all that shall be found alive at his coming, as well as all those that have died since Adam,[203] shall appear before the judgment seat of Christ to be by him judged according to what they have done on earth, to be by him determined or sentenced and finally disposed to their eternal condition. Those that have done well, he shall receive into everlasting habitations to remain forever with him in eternal blessedness, and those that have done evil he shall condemn to the kingdom of darkness, there to remain in insupportable misery forever with the devil and his angels.[204]

And as we must thus profess to believe in God the Father and in Jesus Christ his only Son, so we must every one truly and heartily say, **I believe in the Holy Ghost**—that he is a person of a true and real subsistence, neither created nor begotten, but "proceeding from the Father and the Son,"[205] true and eternal God, who is essentially[206] holy himself and the author of all holiness in us by sanctifying our natures,[207] illuminating our minds,[208] rectifying our wills and affections,[209] who cooperateth with the word and sacraments and whatever else is a mean[s] of conveying grace into the soul. He it was that "spake by the prophets"[210] and apostles, and 'tis he that leadeth us into all truth.[211] He helpeth our infirmities,[212] assures us of our adoption[213] and will be with the **Holy Catholic Church** to the end of the world.[214]

The catholic church is composed of all congregations of men whatever who hold the faith of Jesus Christ and are[215] obedient to his laws, wherein the pure Word of God is preached and the sacraments duly administered by such ministers as are regularly consecrated and set apart for such[216] offices according to Christ's institution.[217]

And this church is called holy in respect to[218] its author, Jesus Christ; end, the glory of God and the[219] salvation of souls; institution of the ministry, administration of the sacraments, preaching of the pure word of God;[220] and of the[221] members of this church which are renewed and sanctified by the Holy Spirit and united to Christ, the supreme Head and Governor of the church. 'Tis styled catholic because it is not, like that of the Jews, confined to one place and people, but 'tis disseminated through all nations, extendeth throughout all ages,[222] even to the end of the world. And as there is but one Head, so the members, though many, are but one body, being all firmly cemented and united together by the same Spirit. Principally by the three great Christian virtues, faith, hope and charity.[223] For as we hold the same principles of faith, do all assent to the same truths "once delivered to the saints,"[224] so have we the same hopes and expectation of eternal life which is promised to all. And as our Lord gave the same mark of distinction to all his disciples, "By this shall all men know that ye are my disciples, if you love one another,"[225] so this universal love which is diffused throughout the whole body of Christ is the union of charity; and[226] the same ministry and the same orders in the church makes the unity of discipline. But since Christ hath appointed only one way to heaven, so we are not to expect salvation out of the church,[227] which is also called catholic, in opposition to heretics and schismatics. And[228] if an angel from heaven should preach any other doctrine than Christ and his apostles hath taught or appoint other sacraments than Christ hath already instituted, let him be accursed.[229]

And[230] as the mystical union between Christ and the church[231] and the spiritual conjunction of the members to the head is the foundation of that union and communion which the saints have with each other, as being all under the influence of the same head, so death, which only separates bodies for a time, cannot dissolve the union of minds, and therefore 'tis not only in relation to the saints on earth, but including also those in heaven that[232] we profess to hold **The communion of saints**—And accordingly we believe that all saints, as well those on earth as those in heaven, have communion with God the Father, Son and Holy Ghost, [and] with the blessed angels, who not only join in devotion with the church triumphant above, but are likewise sent forth to minister for those who are the heirs of salvation while they remain in this world.[233] And perhaps we do not consider as we ought how much good we receive by the ministration of the holy angels, nor are we sufficiently grateful to those guardian spirits that so often put by ill accidents, watch over us when we sleep, defending us from the assaults of evil men and evil angels.[234] And if they are so mindful of our preservation in this world, we may suppose them much more concerned for our eternal happiness. There is joy amongst the angels in heaven over one sinner that repenteth.[235] They are present in our public assemblies where we in a more special manner hold communion with them. And 'tis there we join with all the company of the heavenly host in praying and admiring the supreme Being, whom we jointly adore.[236]

What knowledge the saints in heaven have of things or persons in this world we cannot determine, nor after what manner we hold communion with them at present 'tis not easy to conceive. That we are all members of the same mystical body of Christ we are very sure and[237] do all partake of the same vital influence from the same Head and so are united together, and though we are not actually possessed of the happiness they enjoy, yet we have the[238] Holy Spirit given unto us as an earnest of our eternal felicity with them hereafter.[239] And though their faith is consummated by vision and their hope by present possession, yet the bond of Christian charity still remains. And as we have a great joy and complacency in their felicity, so, no doubt, they desire[240] and pray for ours.

With the saints on earth we hold communion by the word and sacraments, by praying with and for each other.[241] And in all acts of public or private worship we act upon the same principles, upon the same motives, having the same promises and hopes of **The forgiveness of Sins** through Jesus Christ, the mediator of the new covenant, who gave his life a sacrifice by way of compensation and satisfaction to divine justice, by which God became reconciled to man and cancelled the[242] obligation that every sinner lay under to suffer eternal punishment. And he hath appointed in his church "baptism for the first remission and repentance for the constant forgiveness of all following trespasses."[243] And now have we confidence towards God, that not only our souls shall be freed from the guilt and punishment of sin by faith in Jesus, but likewise our bodies may rest in hope[244] of **The Resurrection of the Body.**[245] That the same almighty power which raised again our blessed Lord after he had lain three days in the grave shall also "quicken our mortal bodies,"[246] shall reproduce the same individual body that[247] slept in the dust and vitally unite it to the same soul which informed it while on earth.[248] "The hour is coming in the which all that are in the graves shall hear his voice and shall come forth, they that have done good, to the resurrection of life and they that have done evil, to the resurrection of damnation." St. John 5:28–29.[249] "And the sea gave up the dead which were[250] in it, and death and hell (that is, the grave) delivered up the dead that were in them." Revelation 20:13.[251] There shall be a general rendezvous of every particular atom which composed the several bodies of men that ever lived in the world, and each shall be restored to its proper owner so as to make up the same numerical[252] body, the same flesh and blood, etc, which was dissolved at death.[253] And though the bodies of saints shall be glorified heavenly bodies, yet they shall be of the same consistence and figure, but only[254] altered and changed in some properties. And though at first view it may seem hard to conceive how those bodies which have suffered so many various transmutations, have been either buried in the earth, devoured by beasts, consumed by fire or swallowed up in the sea,[255] have been dissolved into the smallest atoms and those atoms perhaps scattered throughout the world,[256] have fructified the earth, fed the fishes and by that means have become the food of animals or other men[257] and a part of their nourishment, till at last the same particles of matter belongs to several bodies, how, I say,[258] the same numerical atoms should at last rally and meet again[259] and be restored to the first[260] owner, make up again the first body, which was so long since consumed,[261] may seem difficult, if not altogether impossible to determine. But since God hath declared that he will raise the dead, we have no manner of reason to question whether[262] he can do it, since omnipotence knows no difficulty. And that almighty power[263] which at first made [264] us of nothing, out of no preexisting matter, can very easily distinguish and preserve unmixed from other bodies our scattered atoms and can recollect and unite them again, how far soever they are dispersed asunder. He can observe the various changes they undergo in their passages through other bodies and can so order it that they shall never become any part of their nourishment, or [265] if they should [266] be adopted into other men, he can cause them to yield them up again before they die, that they may be restored to their right owners. And having collected these scattered [267] particles, he can readily dispose them into the same order, rebuild the same beauteous fabric, consisting of the same flesh and bones, nerves, veins, blood, etc., and all the several parts it had before its dissolution and, by uniting it to the same soul, make the same living man. [268]

But though the body shall be in substance the same after its resurrection it was before its death, yet it shall greatly differ in its qualities. [269] "It was sown in corruption, it shall be raised incorruptible. It is sown in dishonour, it is raised in glory. It is sown in weakness, it is raised in power. It is sown a natural, it is raised a spiritual body." [270] They shall not retain the same principles of corruption [271] and mortality they had before, shall never die, but the bodies of the damned shall eternally remain in most inconceivable torments, [272] while those of the blessed shall [273] "meet the Lord in the air" [274] when he comes to judgment and afterwards ascend with him into heaven, there to enjoy **The Life everlasting.** By everlasting life is not only meant [275] that we shall die no more, for in this sense the damned shall have everlasting life as well as the saints: they shall always have a being, though in intolerable torments, which is infinitely worse than none at all. But we are to understand by it [276] full and perfect enjoyment of solid inexpressible joy and felicity. "Eye hath not seen, nor ear heard, neither hath it entered into the heart of man to conceive what God hath prepared for those that love him." [277] The soul shall be perfectly renewed and sanctified, nor shall it be possible to sin any more. All its faculties shall be purified and exulted: the understanding shall be filled with the beatific vision of the adorable Trinity, shall be illuminated, enlarged and eternally employed and satisfied in the contemplation of the sublimest truths. Here we see as in a glass, have dark and imperfect perceptions of God, [278] but there we shall behold him as he is, shall know as we are known. [279] Not that we shall fully [280] comprehend the divine nature as he doth ours—that is impossible, for he is infinite and incomprehensible and we, though in heaven, shall be finite still—but our apprehensions of his being and perfections shall be clear, just, true; we shall see him as he is, shall never be troubled with misapprehensions or false conceptions of him more. Those dark [281] and mysterious methods of providence which here puzzle and often confound the wisest heads to reconcile them with his justice and goodness shall there be unriddled in a moment, and we shall [282] clearly perceive that all the evils which befall good men in this life were [283] the corrections of a merciful [284] father. That "the furnace of affliction," [285] which now seems so hot and terrible to nature, [286] had nothing more than a lambent flame, [287] which was not designed to consume us, but only to purge away our dross, [288] to purify and prepare the mind for its abode amongst those blessed ones that [289] passed through the same trials before us to the celestial paradise. And we shall forever [290] adore and praise that infinite wisdom, power, and goodness which safely steered and conducted the soul through the rough waves of this tempestuous ocean to the calm haven of peace and everlasting tranquility. Nor shall we have the same sentiments there which we had here, but shall [291] clearly discern [292] that our afflictions here were our choicest mercies. Our wills shall [293] no more be averse from God's, but shall be forever lost in that of our blessed Creator. No conflicts with unruly passions, no pain or misery shall ever find admittance into that heavenly kingdom. "God shall wipe away all tears from our eyes, and there shall be no more death, neither sorrow, nor crying, neither shall there be any more pain, for the former things are passed away." [294] When "we shall hunger no more, neither thirst any more, neither shall the sun light on us, nor any heat. For the lamb which is in the midst of the throne shall feed us and shall lead us unto living fountains of water." [295]

Far be it from us to think that the grace of God can be purchased with anything less precious than the blood of Jesus; but if it could, who that has the lowest degree of faith would not part with all things in this world to obtain that love for our dear [296] Redeemer which we so long for and sigh after. Here we cannot watch one hour with Jesus without drowsiness and weariness, failure of spirits, dejection of mind, worldly regards [297] which damps our devotions and pollutes the purity of our sacrifices. What Christian here does not often feel [298] and bewail the weight of corrupt nature, the many infirmities which [299] molest us in our way to glory? And how difficult is it [300] to practice as we ought that great duty of self-denial, [301] to take up the cross and follow the captain of our salvation [302] without ever repining or murmuring. If shame or confusion could enter those blessed mansions, how would our souls be ashamed and confounded at the review of our imperfect services when we see them crowned with such an unproportionable reward? How shall we blush to behold that exceeding and eternal weight of glory that is conferred upon us for that little (or rather nothing) which we have done or suffered for our God? That God that gave us being, that preserved us, that fed and clothed us [303] in our passage through the world—and what is infinitely more—that [304] gave his only Son to die for us and has by his grace purified and conducted us safe to his Glory! Oh blessed grace! Mysterious love! How shall we then adore and praise what we cannot here apprehend aright! How will love and joy work in the soul! But I cannot express it— I cannot conceive it— [305]

I have purposely omitted many [306] arguments for the being of God, the divine authority of scripture, [307] the truth of revealed religion, a future judgment, and have left the last article very imperfect, because I intend to write on all these subjects for use of my children when I have more leisure. I shall only add a few words to prepare your mind for the second part of my discourse, [308] "Obedience to the Laws of God," [309] which I shall quickly send you.

As the defilement of our nature is the source and original [310] of all our actual impurities and transgressions of the law of God, so the first regular step we can take towards amendment is to be deeply sensible of, grieved and humbled for, our original sin. And though (I believe) the damning guilt of that sin is washed away by baptism in those that die before they are capable of known and actual transgressions, [311] yet experience shows us that the power of it does still survive in such as attain to riper years. [312] And this is what the Apostle complains of in the seventh [chapter] of the [epistle to the] Romans. This is the carnal nature, that "law in our members which wars against the law of the mind, and brings us into captivity to the law of sin."[313] And when the work of conversion or regeneration is begun by the Holy Spirit, yet still corrupt nature[314] maintains a conflict with divine grace, nor shall this enemy be entirely conquered till "death shall be swallowed up in victory," till[315] "this mortal shall put on immortality."[316]

I cannot tell whether you have ever seriously considered the lost and miserable condition you are in by nature; if you have not, 'tis high time to begin to do it, and I shall earnestly beseech Almighty God to enlighten your mind, to renew and sanctify you by his Holy Spirit that you may be his child by adoption here and an heir of his blessed kingdom hereafter.[317]

Epworth, Jan[uary] 13,[318] 1709/10   S.W.

Notes

1. To Samuel Wesley Jr., 11 October 1709.

2. To Samuel Wesley Jr., 7 April 1710.

3. At least she was there when her mother posted the letter in mid-January 1709/10. In the cover letter she sent with the Creed exposition to Samuel Jr., 7 April 1710, S. W. explains, "I have sent you a letter which I writ to your sister Suky at Gainsbro, which I would have you read and copy if you have time." Cf. Clarke, p. 232.

4. See William P. Haugaard, "The Continental Reformation of the Sixteenth Century," in John H. Westerhoff III and O. C. Edwards, Jr., eds., *A Faithful Church: Issues in the History of Catechesis* (Wilton, Conn.: Morehouse-Barlow, 1981), pp. 118–131.

5. In BCP see The Public Baptism of Infants, The Order of Confirmation, and A Catechism. A good overview of catechetical developments in the English Reformation is Frederica Harris Thompsett, "Godly Instruction in Reformation England: The Challenge of Religious Education in the Tudor Commonwealth," in Westerhoff and Edwards, *A Faithful Church*, pp. 174–199.

6. John Spurr, *The Restoration Church of England, 1646–1689* (New Haven, Conn., and London: Yale University Press, 1991), pp. 287–290.

7. For instance, see Bishop Thomas Ken, *An Exposition on the Church-Catechism, or the Practice of Divine Love*, rev. ed. (London: Charles Brome, 1703). Like S. W., Ken was a Nonjuror; his exposition was later edited by John Wesley as volume 13 of his *Christian Library*, 50 vols. (Bristol: Farley, 1749–1755). See also, Archbishop of Canterbury William Wake, *The Principles of the Christian Religion Explained: In a Brief Commentary upon the Church Catechism*, 2nd ed. (London: Richard Sare, 1700). Though Wake held broader ecclesiastical views than the Wesleys, he was, before his move to Canterbury, bishop of Lincoln from 1705 to 1716 and thus would have visited Epworth in the normal course of his diocesan duties; like John and Charles Wesley he was educated at Christ Church, Oxford. Finally, note the brief exposition by William Beveridge, bishop of St. Asaph, *The Church-Catechism Explained: For the Use of the Diocese of St. Asaph*, 2nd ed. (London: Walter Kettilby, 1705). Though she does not seem to have drawn on this work, S. W. did find other of Beveridge's works helpful. Note Samuel Wesley's mention of both Wake's and Beveridge's works in his *Advice to a Young Clergyman* . . . (?1735) in Thomas Jackson, *The Life of the Rev. Charles Wesley* . . . , 2 vols. (London: John Mason, 1841), 2:529–530.

8. To Samuel Wesley Jr., 7 April 1710.

9. Pearson (1613–1686) was a royalist divine who at the Restoration was appointed the head of two Cambridge colleges and Lady Margaret professor of divinity before accepting the bishopric of Chester. His *An Exposition of the Creed*, 6th ed., rev. (London: J. Williams, 1692), originally published in 1659, was in its sixth edition by 1692—a folio of 398 closely reasoned, heavily documented pages. S. W. either possessed it (or had access to it) before the fire, as

she cites it in a letter to Samuel Jr. (27 November 1707). That it continued to impress her years later is evident by another reference in a letter to her son John (18 August 1725). It seems likely that she had acquired another copy by the time she wrote the first letter to Suky on the Creed. For Samuel's assessement, see his *Advice*, p. 521.

Pearson is also available in "A New Edition, carefully revised, and collated with the best copies," ed. James Nichols (London: William Tegg, 1854); and in the 6th ed., revised and corrected by E. Burton (Oxford: At the Clarendon Press, 1870). A recent commentator refers to Pearson's now neglected *Exposition* as "the work which functioned, longer and more widely than any other, as Anglicanism's theological textbook." Richard A. Norris Jr., "Doctor Pearson Construes the Apostles' Creed: A Note on Method and Matter in Christology," in Donald S. Armentrout, ed., *This Sacred History: Anglican Reflections for John Booty* (Cambridge, Mass.: Cowley, 1990), p. 77.

10. Clarke, pp. 232–255; 2nd ed., rev. (London: Thomas Tegg, 1843–1844), 2:38–72, and George Peck, ed. (New York: Lane and Scott, 1851), pp. 347–373.

11. See 1 Peter 3:15.

12. In MS C: "that."

13. See Hebrews 12:9.

14. MS C adds "unassisted."

15. MS C puts both these words in the singular.

16. MS C inserts "partial."

17. Singular in MS C.

18. In MS C: "unless there were some other substituted."

19. In MS C: "had."

20. Clarke's conjecture for a word missing in the Wesley Papers. Crossed out there (and present also in MS C) is the phrase "therein is contained." Note the echo of Article VI, "Of the Sufficiency of the Holy Scriptures for salvation," in the Articles of Religion, BCP. In editing her own sentence in the Wesley Papers, S. W. has crossed out "is contained" and inserted "we" but not provided an active verb.

21. There follows in MS C the crossed-out "and are a most perfect rule of faith and manners and therein likewise."

22. The phrases are culled from Job 38:6–7. See also Revelation 22:16.

23. This complex sentence gave S. W. trouble from the start. Her draft in MS C reads: "and they being free agents or having a principle of [crossed out: *freedom as all rational beings must have or they could not properly be called either good or evil*] liberty or freedom of acting [crossed out: *of chusing or refusing or acting accordingly*] as they must have. . . ."

24. MS C inserts "in created beings."

25. Genesis 2:9 and 3:1–22.

26. In MS C: "his."

27. In MS C: "his mind." Genesis 3:6; quotation marks added.

28. In MS C: "these."

29. In MS C: "give the preference to."

30. In MS C: "he."

31. In MS C: "him."

32. In MS C: "this."

33. Genesis 3:1; my quotation marks.

34. MS C inserts "very."

35. Genesis 3:2–3; quotation marks added.

36. Genesis 3:4–6; quotation marks added.

37. In MS C: "sensuality and pride."

38. See *The Westminster Shorter Catechism, 1648*, in Thomas F. Torrance, ed., *The School of Faith: The Catechisms of the Reformed Church* (London: J. Clarke, 1959), Q. 15: "The sin whereby our first

parents fell from the state in which they were created, was their eating the forbidden fruit." The phrase "our first parents" occurs in Q. 13 and in equivalent places in *The Westminster Larger Catechism, 1648,* ibid. (Q. 21, 26).

39. In MS C: "themselves and all their posterity."

40. See *Shorter Catechism,* Q. 16.

41. Omitted in MS C.

42. Omitted in MS C, which uses a comma instead.

43. An inexact quotation from either Romans 8:7 or James 4:4; quotation marks added.

44. MS C has "press after" above the crossed-out "desire."

45. In In MS C: "of."

46. In MS C: "of."

47. In MS C: "in letting slip."

48. In MS C: "where."

49. In MS C: "is."

50. MS C substitutes a comma for this now quaint use of the exclamation point.

51. MS C has an exclamation point in place of the comma.

52. MS C inserts "ever."

53. No exclamation point in MS C.

54. MS C adds, but crosses out, "from."

55. Crossed out in MS C: "no nor can he."

56. Exclamation point not in MS C.

57. No exclamation point in MS C.

58. Close paraphrase of Job 11:7; quotation marks added.

59. MS C has crossed out "the light that is."

60. Paraphrase of 1 Timothy 6:16; quotation marks added.

61. Paraphrased from Job 4:18.

62. Job 25:5–6; quotation marks added.

63. See Ephesians 2:3: "were by nature the children of wrath"; quotation marks added.

64. Replaces in MS C the crossed out "in case."

65. In MS C: "which."

66. In MS C: "everlasting."

67. In MS C: "& [crossed out: me]." S. W. was probably adding "and mercy," thought better of it, and crossed out "me" but left "&" in her draft.

68. In MS C: "yet men being a more simple kind of beings."

69. Psalm 89:19; quotation marks added.

70. Paraphrased from Hebrews 7:25, a passage later used by John Wesley in buttressing his doctrine of Christian perfection.

71. See Genesis 3:15.

72. BCP, Holy Communion, Prayer of Consecration; quotation marks added.

73. In MS C: "not on the same condition of perfect obedience, as was the first."

74. In MS C: "conditions."

75. In MS C: "is recorded in the holy Scripture of him."

76. In MS C: "the holy Scriptures."

77. MS C adds, but crosses out, "which is."

78. In MS C: "to give you all the arguments I could bring."

79. S. W. writes each phrase of the Creed in slightly larger letters than the rest of her discourse. This emphasis is indicated here by boldface type.

80. MS C lists "holy" as the penultimate divine attribute. Cf. the *Shorter Catechism,* Q. 4: "God is a Spirit, infinite, eternal, and unchangeable, in his being, wisdom, power, holiness, justice, goodness, and truth."

81. In MS C: "he derives not his existence from any other than himself."

82. Pearson, *Exposition* (1870 ed.), p. 73: "this one God is the *Father* of all things, especially of all men and angels."

83. Ibid., p. 74: "After the relation of God's Paternity, immediately followeth the glorious attribute of his Omnipotency."

84. In MS C: "omnipotence gives him a right." S. W. wrote and crossed out "is conspicuous in that he hath" but went back to it in her subsequent version, the Wesley Papers.

85. Pearson, *Exposition* (1870 ed.), pp. 76–77, describes the three branches of God's power: "a right of making and framing any thing which he willeth, in any manner as it pleaseth him, according to the absolute freedom of his own will; . . . a right of having and possessing all things so made and framed by him, as his own, properly belonging to him, as to the Lord and Master of them, by virtue of direct dominion; . . . a right of using and disposing all things so in his possession, according to his own pleasure."

86. BCP Communion, Nicene Creed; quotation marks added.

87. Substituted in MS C for the crossed out "carries."

88. Ephesians 1:11; quotation marks added. Note the similarity with the *Shorter Catechism*, Q. 7 (though in S. W.'s version, without the element of predestination): "The decrees of God are, His eternal purpose, according to the counsel of His will, whereby, for His own glory, He has foreordained whatever comes to pass."

89. My quotation marks.

90. See Pearson, *Exposition* (1854 ed.), pp. 107–108ff.

91. Close paraphrase of 1 Corinthians 15:22.

92. Replaces the crossed-out "foretold" in MS C.

93. See Pearson, *Exposition* (1854 ed.), p. 139, and *Shorter Catechism*, Q. 23.

94. "Now the prophetical function consisteth in the promulgation, confirmation, and perpetuation of the doctrine containing the will of God for the salvation of man"; Pearson *Exposition* (1854 ed.), p. 142. Cf. the *Shorter Catechism*, Q. 24: "revealing to us . . . the will of God for our Salvation."

95. In MS C: "no longer."

96. Nearly exact quotation of Matthew 5:17; my quotation marks.

97. See Pearson, *Exposition* (1854 ed.), pp. 143–144, and *Shorter Catechism*, Q. 25: "in His once offering up of Himself a sacrifice to satisfy divine justice."

98. "The regal office of our Saviour consisteth partly in the ruling, protecting, and rewarding of his people; partly in the coercing, condemning, and destroying of his enemies"; Pearson, *Exposition* (1854 ed.), p. 145. "Christ executes the office of a King, in subduing us to Himself, in ruling and defending us, and in restraining and conquering all His and our enemies"; *Shorter Catechism*, Q. 26.

99. Replaces the crossed-out "eternal" in MS C.

100. In MS C: "being eternally begotten of, and equal to the Father."

101. BCP, Nicene Creed; my quotation marks.

102. Nearly exact quotation from Nicene Creed; quotation marks added.

103. Paraphrased from John 20:28; my quotation marks.

104. Cf. Pearson, *Exposition* (1854 ed.), p. 226: "And in this redemption, though a single word, we shall find a double title to a most just dominion,—one of conquest, another of purchase."

105. MS C initially added, but then crossed out, "power of the."

106. Luke 1:35; my quotation marks.

107. See, for example, Numbers 19:2 and 1 Peter 1:19. In MS C, originally preceded with "spotless and," subsequently crossed out.

108. See Pearson, *Exposition* (1854 ed.), pp. 262–263.

109. MS C substitutes for the crossed-out "bring forth a son."

110. Quotation marks added in both instances.

111. MS C inserts "this promised messiah."

112. The phrase "as a man that he **Suffered**" replaces the original, crossed-out "in his human nature that he **suffered**" in MS C.

113. In MS C, "sure" replaces "certain," which is crossed out.

114. Mark 9:12; my quotation marks.

115. MS C adds "&c."

116. In MS: "Esay."

117. Cf. Pearson, *Exposition* (1854 ed.) p. 266: "The fifty-third chapter of Isaiah is beyond all question a sad, but clear, description of a suffering person"; quotation marks added.

118. In MS C, "misery" replaces "sufferings," which is crossed out.

119. In MS C: "carry'd."

120. Acts 10:38; my quotation marks.

121. Isaiah 53:3; my quotation marks. MS C adds, but crosses out, the next words from the verse: "a man of sorrows and acquainted with grief."

122. MS C inserts "receive" after crossing out "should enjoy."

123. MS C adds "low."

124. Close paraphrase of Matthew 8:20; my quotation marks. MS C more accurately has "not where" in place of "nowhere."

125. Isaiah 53:3; my quotation marks. Both manuscripts put "sorrow" in the singular despite the AV's plural.

126. MS C adds, but crosses out, "present."

127. Wesley Papers has "prophets" here, crossed out. This is a good instance of a scribal error and supports my contention that the MS C copy is the draft. In it the word "prophets" is directly below the word "truth" in the next line; S. W. apparently got lost in her copying, then realized her mistake and corrected it.

128. Cf. Pearson, *Exposition* (1870 ed.), p. 350: "and by the prediction of the Prophets was to suffer in a manner not prescribed by the Law of Moses"; quotation marks added.

129. Pearson, *Exposition* (1870 ed.), p. 288: "a most powerful external testimony to the certainty of our Saviour's death." See also: "It was thus necessary to express the person under whom our Saviour suffered, first, that we might for ever be assured of the time in which he suffered" (p. 352).

130. Note S. W.'s use of the present tense, which she begins here and carries through the passion story, heightening its dramatic effect.

131. Matthew 26:37; my quotation marks.

132. Close paraphrase of 14:33; my quotation marks.

133. Matthew 26:38; my quotation marks; S. W.'s exclamation point.

134. In MS C, "of an Angry God" crossed out here and "Almighty Father" substituted.

135. In MS C: "divinity." S. W. originally copied the same word in the Wesley Papers but crossed it out and substituted "deity."

136. MS C adds "which."

137. In place of "angry God," MS C originally had, but was then crossed out, "incensed Omnipotence."

138. Close paraphrase of Matthew 26:39; my quotation marks. The other two repetitions she refers to are in verses 42 and 44. See also Mark 14:36 and Luke 22:42.

139. MS C substitutes "which the justice of God requires," having originally had (and then crossed out) the wording adopted in the Wesley Papers.

140. In MS C: "prodigious."

141. Nearly exact quotation of Luke 22:44; my quotation marks.

142. In MS C: "inconceivably."

143. Mark 8:31, Luke 9:22; my quotation marks.

144. In MS C: "the most intense grief, the most inexpressible anguish!"

145. In MS C: "corporal."

146. MS C adds "we may behold."

147. See BCP, Communion, General Confession.

148. 1 Peter 2:22; my quotation marks.

149. MS C substitutes "the insolent rabble."

150. MS C in place of "and" reads: "for which reason."

151. MS C has "Son of God" in place of "Jesus."

152. Nearly exact quotation of Psalm 129:3; my quotation marks.

153. Luke 23:2; my quotation marks.

154. Matthew 27:29; my quotation marks.

155. MS C adds "which."

156. See Matthew 27:29, Mark 15:17, John 19:2.

157. MS C originally read, "did not only express the scorn of his Tormenters, but also did" but was corrected as copied into the Wesley Papers.

158. See Matthew 18:10.

159. In MS C: "And now let us by faith ascend with our Lord to the top of Calvary, the place assigned for his last scene of misery and see with what barbarous pleasure."

160. In MS C: "lift,"

161. In MS C: "most nervous and sensible." Nervous: full of nerves; sensible: liable to be quickly or acutely affected by some object of sensation (OED). So used in Pearson, *Exposition* (1854 ed.), p. 300, with my emphasis added: "The exquisite pains and torments in that death are manifest, in that the hands and feet, which of all the parts of the body are *most nervous, and* consequently *most sensible*, were pierced through with nails; which caused, not a sudden dispatch, but a lingering and tormenting death."

162. MS C originally read "torment"; subsequently S. W. crossed out the second syllable and completed the word as "torture."

163. MS C substitutes "though."

164. MS C originally had "that loud and bitter cry," but "cry" was subsequently crossed out and replaced by "exclamation."

165. Matthew 27:46, Mark 15:34; my quotation marks. Cf. Pearson, *Exposition* (1854 ed.), p. 312: "indeed those words infer no more than that he was bereft of such joys and comforts from the Deity, as should assuage and mitigate the acerbity of his present torments."

166. John 19:30; quotation marks added.

167. The passage in quotation marks (which are added here) and the preceding paraphrase are from Matthew 27:51–53. MS C differs: "the graves were opened, &c."

168. Matthew 27:54; my quotation marks.

169. Echoes of John 18:37; see also 1 Timothy 1:15, Hebrews 10:5, and 1 John 4:9.

170. MS C at first read, "that he might suffer death for every man," and was then altered to the longer phrase copied over into the Wesley Papers.

171. That is, as to his humanity. See Pearson, *Exposition* (1854 ed.), p. 311: "it is certain . . . that the union of the parts of his human nature was dissolved on the cross, and a real separation made between his soul and body."

172. Jonah 1:17.

173. In MS C: "that."

174. S. W. begins a new phrase in MS C but crosses it out: "for by commanding."

175. Deuteronomy 21:22–23, with several words omitted, as noted. The final word in the passage is "day," correctly transcribed in MS C but miscopied as "night" in the Wesley Papers.

176. Crossed out in MS C.

177. In MS C: "bodies."

178. Mark 15:42–43; my quotation marks.

179. Mark 15:45–46, with slight additions from Luke 23:53 and Matthew 27:60; quotation marks added.

180. Nearly exact quotation of Acts 2:27 and Psalm 16:10; my quotation marks.

181. Nearly exact quotation of Acts 2:31, into which S. W. has inserted parenthetical explanations of her own; my quotation marks.

182. MS C's reading; Wesley Papers miscopied "in."

183. See Pearson, *Exposition* (1854 ed.), pp. 332–333.

184. MS C repeats "to triumph," apparently for rhetorical effect.

185. MS C reads, "we believe the descent of our Saviour into hell." Pearson, *Exposition* (1854 ed.), pp. 358–363, dismisses this interpretation.

186. In MS C, "But" crossed out and replaced with "And."

187. Again, Acts 3:31; quotation marks added.

188. Here in MS C, inserted but crossed out "and Saturday being the day in which he rested in the grave."

189. Pearson, *Exposition* (1854 ed.), p. 384.

190. In MS C, sentence originally began with "And" but was crossed out and replaced with "That."

191. Transliterated variation of Mohammed or Muhammad.

192. MS C adds "of the week" followed by the crossed-out "which day they celebrate."

193. Note the borrowings from Pearson, *Exposition* (1870 ed.), pp. 475–476: "As therefore the Jews do still retain the celebration of the seventh day of the week, because they will not believe any greater deliverance wrought than that of Egypt; as the Mahometans religiously observe the sixth day of the week in memory of Mahomet's flight from Mecca, whom they esteem a greater Prophet than our Saviour . . . so all which profess the Christian religion are known publicly to belong unto the Church of Christ by observing the first day of the week, upon which Christ did rise from the dead."

194. Echoes of the Nicene Creed; see BCP, Communion.

195. In MS C, the sentence begins "When he had. . . ."

196. Both manuscripts have "eat," an archaic spelling of the past tense.

197. In MS C: "fastened."

198. In MS C, originally read, "which was risen"; "risen" was then crossed off and replaced with "raised."

199. BCP, Burial Service: "in sure and certain hope of the Resurrection to eternal life, through our Lord Jesus Christ"; quotation marks added.

200. Paraphrase of Luke 24:51.

201. Nearly exact quotation of Matthew 26:64; my quotation marks.

202. MS C adds "now."

203. See Pearson, *Exposition* (1854 ed.), pp. 432–433.

204. In MS C: "he shall sentence to depart from him into everlasting fire prepared for the devil and his angels." See Matthew 25:41, from which this is paraphrased.

205. Nearly exact quotation from the Nicene Creed; Communion, BCP; quotation marks added.

206. MS C adds "perfectly."

207. Pearson, *Exposition* (1854 ed.), p. 467: "it is his particular office to sanctify or make us holy . . . he is the cause of this holiness in us."

208. Ibid., p. 468: the Spirit "doth also illuminate the understanding of such as believe, that they may receive the truth."

209. This phrase seems to come from Pearson's summary, *Expositions* (1870 ed.), p. 589, at

the end of this article of the Creed. Among the Holy Spirit's activities are "illuminating the understandings of particular persons, rectifying their wills and affections."

210. Nicene Creed; quotation marks added.

211. See John 16:13.

212. Pearson, *Exposition* (1854 ed.), p. 475.

213. Ibid., p. 471.

214. The original draft in MS C left out "Holy Catholic" in the last clause and failed to employ the larger letters that characterize each phrase from the Creed. However, "Church to the end of the world" is then crossed out and replaced with the wording found in the Wesley Papers.

215. In MS C, followed by the crossed-out "under."

216. In MS C: "their."

217. See BCP, Articles of Religion, XIX. Of the Church:"The visible Church of Christ is a congregation of faithful men, in the which the pure Word of God is preached, and the Sacraments be duly ministered according to Christ's ordinance in all those things that of necessity are requisite to the same."

218. In MS C: "of."

219. In MS C; omitted in Wesley Papers.

220. In MS C: "administration of the pure word of God and the sacraments."

221. MS C is missing "and of the."

222. In MS C: "to all ages in all times." Cf. Pearson, *Exposition* (1870 ed.), p. 620: "not like that of the Jews, limited to one people . . . but . . . disseminated through all nations . . . extended to all places . . . propagated to all ages. . . ."

223. See Romans 12:4–5; I Corinthians 12:11–12, 20, and 13:13.

224. Jude 3; my quotation marks.

225. Nearly exact quotation of John 13:35; my quotation marks.

226. In MS C: "as."

227. Pearson, *Exposition* (1870 ed.), pp. 617–618: "The necessity of believing the Holy Catholick Church appeareth first in this, that Christ hath appointed it as the only way unto eternal life . . . so none shall ever escape the eternal wrath of God, which belong not to the Church." Cf. St. Augustine's dictum "There is no salvation outside the church."

228. In MS C: "So that."

229. Paraphrased from Galatians 1:8–9.

230. MS C begins, "Now."

231. See the Solemnization of Matrimony, BCP, "signifying unto us the mystical union that is betwixt Christ and his Church."

232. Supplied in MS C; missing in Wesley Papers.

233. Pearson, *Exposition* (1854 ed.), pp. 505–507, follows the same pattern.

234. MS C adds "etc."

235. Luke 15:10, paraphrased.

236. See the preface to the Sanctus in Communion, BCP: "Therefore with Angels and Archangels, and with all the company of heaven, we laud and magnify thy glorious Name."

237. MS C follows with the crossed-out "have all the same."

238. MS C follows with the crossed-out "earnest of."

239. Cf. Pearson, *Exposition* (1854 ed.), p. 510: "This communion of the saints in heaven and earth, upon the mystical union of Christ their head, being fundamental and eternal, what acts or external operations it produceth, is not certain. That we communicate with them in hope of that happiness which they actually enjoy, is evident; that we have the Spirit of God given us as an earnest, and so a part, of their felicity, is certain."

240. In MS C: "so, too, do they desire."

241. MS C adds "&c." See Pearson, Exposition (1854 ed.), pp. 508–509.

242. In MS C, originally "every"; subsequently crossed out and replaced by "the."

243. Pearson, Exposition (1870 ed.), p. 653: "God . . . appointed in the Church of Christ the sacrament of baptism for the first remission, and repentance for the constant forgiveness of all following trespasses." Quotation marks added.

244. Resonances of 1 John 3:21, Psalm 16:9, and Acts 2:26.

245. MS C originally read, "**The Resurrection of the dead,**" but S. W. saw her mistake, crossed out the final word, and inserted "**body.**"

246. Paraphrase of Romans 8:11; quotation marks added.

247. In MS C, "body" is inserted as a replacement for the crossed-out "flesh," which is followed by "which."

248. Pearson, Exposition (1870 ed.), p. 671: "as no other substance whatsoever is vitally united to the soul of that man whose body it is while he liveth, so no substance of any other creature, no body of any other man, shall be vitally reunited unto the soul at the resurrection." Pearson also has the Romans 8:11 verse, quoted above by S. W., on the same page.

249. S. W.'s citation; my quotation marks.

250. Replacing the crossed-out "are." S. W. got the quotation right the first time in MS C.

251. S. W.'s citation and parenthetical explanation; my quotation marks.

252. Individual, identical.

253. Unusually, S. W. seems to be indicating this sentence as a quotation. MS C has what seems to be quotation marks in the left margin next to five of the seven lines that the sentence takes up. Though Pearson, Exposition (1870 ed.), uses similar language throughout his long exegesis of Article XI, I have not found there any clear source of S. W.'s sentence.

254. MS C omits "only."

255. Somewhat different order in MS C: "have been either buried in the earth, swallowed up in the sea, devoured by beasts or consumed by fire, etc."

256. In MS C: "have been dissolved into the smallest atoms and perhaps scattered through [replacing crossed-out "over"] the world."

257. MS C reads, "and of other men."

258. MS C follows with crossed-out "these."

259. Followed in MS C by the crossed-out "so as to become the very same."

260. MS C adds, but crosses out, "and pr."

261. In MS C: "dissolved."

262. In MS C: "but."

263. In MS C: "Being."

264. MS C adds, but crosses out, "our."

265. In MS C, but crossed out: "though."

266. MS C adds, but crosses out, "he can."

267. MS C; Wesley Papers substitutes an indecipherable adjective that appears to be "divant," unrecognized by the OED. Several possibilities: a contraction of "divergent"; a hastily scrawled (or misspelled) attempt at the now obscure "divast" (devastated, laid waste), "divers" (various), or "deviant." In his transcription Clarke leaves a blank (p. 252).

268. This account of the problems posed to the resurrection of the body by an inquiry into the food chain is much more graphic than an equivalent passage in Pearson, Exposition (1870 ed.), pp. 657–658. Not surprisingly, they both attest to God's power to overcome such difficulties. A sampling from Pearson: "And as the wisdom is infinite, so the power of this Agent is illimited; for God is as much omnipotent as omniscient. . . . There is not atom of the dust or ashes but must be where it pleaseth God, and be applied and make up what and how it seemeth good to him. The resurrection therefore cannot be impossible."

269. Pearson, stressing the bodily continuity, writes, "the same flesh which is corrupted

shall be restored; whatsoever alteration shall be made shall not be of their nature, but of their condition; not of their substance, but of their qualities" (ibid., p. 676).

270. 1 Corinthians 15:42–44, loosely remembered; my quotation marks. Pearson employs this passage and emphasizes bodily transformation in his discussion of "And the Life Everlasting" (ibid., p. 693).

271. In MS C adds and crosses out "which."

272. In MS C: "misery."

273. MS C adds, but crosses out; "ascend to."

274. 1 Thessalonians 4:17; my quotation marks.

275. MS C adds "a state of immortality."

276. In MS C: "by the life everlasting a" followed by the crossed-out "state."

277. Close quotation of 1 Corinthians 2:9, (cf. Isaiah 64:4); my quotation marks.

278. MS C adds "etc."

279. 1 Corinthians 13:12, paraphrased.

280. MS C omits "fully."

281. MS C adds "involved" and omits the following "and."

282. MS C adds "then."

283. MS C adds, but crosses out, "either."

284. In MS C "a merciful" replaces three crossed-out words: "our heavenly whereby."

285. Isaiah 48:10; quotation marks added.

286. In MS C: "which here seems so hot and terrible to imperfect nature."

287. Playing lightly on or gliding over a surface without burning it.

288. See Isaiah 1:25.

289. In MS C: "which."

290. MS C omits this word.

291. MS C adds "then."

292. In MS C: "perceive."

293. MS C adds "then."

294. Revelation 21:4, slightly altered from the third to the first person plural; my quotation marks.

295. Revelation 7:16–17, altered from third to first person plural; my quotation marks.

296. In MS C: "blessed."

297. In MS C: "worldly regards, dejection of mind."

298. In MS C: "What Christian does not now often feel. . . ."

299. Replaces the crossed-out "and" in MS C.

300. In MS C: "And how difficult do we find it. . . ."

301. MS C adds "and."

302. In MS C: "the great captain of our salvation." See Hebrews 2:10.

303. Followed in MS C by the crossed-out "and."

304. Followed in MS C by the crossed-out "God that."

305. MS C at this point leaves a half page blank before continuing; Wesley Papers continues directly with the same material.

306. Replacing the crossed-out "the" in MS C.

307. MS C adds "for."

308. MS C adds, but crosses out, "namely."

309. My quotation marks.

310. In MS C: "origin."

311. Cf. John Wesley's preface to the *Journal* entry, 24 May 1738, on his famous Aldersgate conversion: "I believe, till I was about ten years old I had not sinned away that 'washing of the Holy Ghost' which was given me in baptism."

312. MS C omits "experience shows us that" and "still" and has as the final clause "in those which attain to riper years." On this last expression, note the title of one of the baptismal services offered in BCP: The Ministration of Baptism to Such as Are of Riper Years.

313. In MS C: "This is that carnal nature, that law in our members that wars against the law in our minds"; paraphrased from Romans 7:23; quotation marks added.

314. In MS C: "is begun in the soul by the Holy Spirit, yet still this corrupt nature. . . ."

315. In MS C: "and."

316. Close quotations, slightly rearranged from 1 Corinthians 15:54; quotation marks added. MS C has "and" connecting the two quoted clauses, whereas Wesley Papers repeats "till." Cf. John Wesley's more optimistic doctrine of Christian perfection, allowing for its realization in some sense in this life.

317. The closing paragraph in MS C reads: "I cannot tell whether you have ever been truly sensible of the lost and undone condition you are in by nature; if you have never thought [?]seriously of these things, 'tis high time to begin to do it, and I shall heartily beseech Almighty God to illuminate your mind, to regenerate you by his grace and to make you his child by adoption here, that you may be an heir of his blessed kingdom hereafter."

318. In MS C: "Jan: 14."

TWENTY-SIX

Obedience to the Laws of God

A Brief (Unfinished) Exposition
on the Ten Commandments

*T*his essay, a sequel to Susanna Wesley's exposition of the Creed, exists only as an incomplete rough draft.[1] Although it had been planned as part of the extended catechetical project that took on new urgency after the rectory fire of 1709, and although she promised her daughter Suky that it would quickly follow the explication of the Creed, it appears to have been no farther along than we see it here by spring 1711. A journal entry in late May of that year, seemingly designed to help strenthen her resolve to get on with her work, implies that the piece was still unfinished. In it she urges herself, "Go through your brief exposition on the Ten Commandments."[2] There is no evidence that it was ever sent to Suky, or indeed that it exists in any other form, and it has never been published.[3]

As it stands, the exposition actually focuses on what seventeenth-century commentators referred to as "the First Table of the law." Although her essay provides a general introduction to the entire Decalogue, its actual commandment-by-commandment exposition stops abruptly after the first four, those that recount humanity's duties to God and that traditionally were thought to have been inscribed on the first of two stone tablets delivered to Moses. However, the advertised sweep of her work turns out to be even more limited: Susanna Wesley's sabbatarianism and, thus, her discussion of the Fourth Commandment dominate. "Remember the Sabbath Day to keep it holy" takes up nearly 15 notebook pages, compared to nine devoted to the first three commandments together.[4]

Interestingly and probably by default (it does not seem to have been her original intention to give extensive treatment only to the First Table—she apparently just ran out of steam), Susanna Wesley's explication draws more on her Puritan heritage than on the Anglican approach she converted to as a young woman. As J. Sears McGee has pointed out with reference to the pre-Restoration period, a stress on the First Table's duties toward God characterized (and implied) a Puritan worldview, and an emphasis on the Second Table's duties toward one's neighbor similarly represented an Anglican one.[5] This development of "moralism" within the Church of England has been decried by C. F. Allison as a way station in the decline of Anglicanism, somewhere between its "classical" (or "orthodox") expression in the early seventeenth century and the Socinianism and Deism of the eighteenth century, which in turn led to the secularism of the nineteenth and twentieth centuries.[6] John Spurr, a more recent student of the Restoration church, attests to the same feature of the era, though with a more nuanced sense of theology and context. While acknowledging the emphasis on "charity, diligence, duties to self and neighbour, social virtues and public piety" he refuses to grant that the Restoration church was "peddling a merely utilitarian system of ethics, and promoting it through an appeal to self-interst and prudence."[7]

Whether an exposition of the First Table or, had she completed the job, First and Second Table commandments, it was this practical, yet pious, view that drew Susanna Wesley to the Decalogue for her second examination of a document central to Christian catechesis. To focus on the Ten Commandments is to acknowledge the continuing claims of "holy living" on the Christian, but it is not to capitulate to an arid moralism. Rather, like many another practical theologian of her age, Susanna Wesley was attempting to instill in the rising generation the importance of both faith and obedience. If she was only partially successful in this instance, her son's maintenance of that tension in the evangelical revival proves that in a broader sense she realized her goal.

A draft of the essay, in Susanna Wesley's hand, is found in the same 3½-by-6-inch Headingley MS C notebook as the rough draft of the Creed exposition.[8] It is undated but probably written after 14 January 1709/10 (the date of her letter on the Creed) and before 24 May 1711 (the date of the journal entry in which she was pushing herself to get her writing and teaching back on track).

Letter 2nd To Suky

Dear Suky,

I suppose by this time you may have read my last letter wherein I mentioned the covenant God made with our First Parents, the condition of which on man's part was perfect obedience to God's laws. And I told you that man, having by temptation of Satan broke this covenant and thereby forfeited God's favour [and] eternal happiness, and brought himself and all his posterity into a state of mortality here and damnation hereafter, how it pleased the eternal Goodness to suspend the penalty of his disobedience and once more admit mankind into a state of probation. And that through Jesus the mediator he hath declared his love and goodwill toward his rebellious creatures, hath renewed his covenant on milder terms than the former, that "as in Adam all died, so in Christ all should be made alive."[9]

What shall become of unbaptized infants, idiots, and such as never heard of a saviour 'tis not my present business to inquire; they are left to God's uncovenanted mercies. 'Tis sufficient that we are assured [that] all which are baptized are certainly admitted into the covenant of grace, baptism being the seal of the new covenant under the gospel[10] as circumcision was the seal of the same covenant under the law, and by it is this general covenant applied and confirmed to particular persons, who are by this mean initiated into the mystical body of Christ, the holy catholic church, and as members of this body have a right to the means of grace [and] the favour and promises of God, provided they are careful to perform the conditions on which they are to be received, namely faith in Christ and [11] a sincere though imperfect obedience to God's laws. I have already discoursed on the first; [12] and before I proceed to the second it may be convenient to premise somewhat concerning laws in general. [13]

A law is a rule of action. [14] And as all beings (the Supreme [Being] as well as natural and rational agents) work for some presupposed end, so 'tis necessary they should have some rule to work by. The eternal fountain of being "who is God over all, blessed for ever," [15] is said to act according to "the counsel of his own will," [16] his infinite perfections giving law to the operations of his almighty power. [17] And though we cannot fathom the depths of infinite wisdom, cannot assign the reasons and causes which move the divine intellect, [18] yet we are assured that his actions are in number, weight, and measure most perfect, which they could never be unless they were designed for some end, were directed by some rule. But though we believe that the divine mind doth in all things act agreeably to the law of its nature, yet this doth not imply any necessity, impulse or dependence on anything but itself, for he always must necessarily enjoy the highest liberty, [19] there being no other cause equal or superior to him that can any way persuade, impel, excite, or animate him to do anything but what seemeth best to himself, but in all his productions he acteth according to the idea and rule which he hath conceived in his own eternal, most perfect mind, and he did in the creation of the world propose an end, answerable to the dignity and perfection of his nature, viz. his own glory, which is the ultimate end of all his actions.

Now since the glory of God was the chief end of all the works of his creation, [20] and since [21] wisdom, power and goodness are perfections inseparable from the Supreme Being, it necessarily follows—that God must give law to his creatures; otherwise they could not answer the end for which they were created. And this law or rule is distinguished by several names according as it relates to various subjects, viz., divine [law], the law of nature, moral law, positive law, etc. [22]

Divine law, or the law of angels, we do not well understand, nor is it necessary that we should at present; [23] only this we know, that their laws are so constantly and exactly obeyed by them that their obedience is proposed as a pattern for ours, and we are directed to pray that the will of God may be done on earth as it is by those blessed spirits in heaven. [24]

The law of nature is that fixed, steady rule which God hath given to all the inanimate and brute creation. And this rule is constantly [25] obeyed by natural agents who, though unwittingly, yet with admirably regularity, pursue the law of their Creator. He made a decree for the rain and gave law to the sea, that the waves thereof should not pass his commandment. And hence arises the beauty and harmony which appears in what we call the works of nature. In the position of the elements, [26] the motions and usefullness of the heavenly bodies, the vicissitudes of night and day, the fertility of the earth, the various seasons of the year, the wonderful production of trees, herbs, flowers, etc., all of which have their proper uses and virtues. The curious fabric and instincts of beasts, birds, fishes and other animals together with their mutual relations, dependencies and subserviency of one thing to another. All which doth clearly demonstrate unto us not only the almighty power, but also the infinite wisdom of the divine Architect, in that he hath so admirably contrived, adapted, and disposed all these things to obey the law of their creation as may most effectually tend to the use of man, for whose service they were created.[27]

Moral law, or the law of reason, is that law which is founded on and results from the unalterable nature of persons and things.[28] And this law is fixed, unalterable, eternal, of equal and perpetual obligation to all persons of what degree soever at all times in all places and circumstances of life. Thus from the absolute perfections of the divine nature and from the rationality and freedom of man's nature arises most of our duties towards God and the greater part of our duties towards ourselves and our neighbour. This law was designed for man and is properly the law of his nature by which he should have always walked, had he not lost his innocence. His conformity to this rule in thought, word, and deed[29] is the perfection of moral virtue, and any deviation from this law in any of these instances is moral evil.[30]

Positive law is a certain temporary alterable rule given upon some particular occasions under some certain emergencies which is determined or vacated when the reason, occasion and circumstances on which it was founded ceases or is taken away.

Of these laws there are various kinds; some are so immediately grafted on the moral law that, though in their own nature they are temporary and alterable, as being only calculated for the meridian[31] of this life, yet are they of longer continuance and more universal obligation than others. Of this kind are all the precepts and rules of Christianity, the whole system of revealed religion, which had never been instituted if man had not fallen. Such as faith in Christ, repentance, and all those duties[32] which naturally tend to cleansing, exalting and restoring the soul to its original purity and perfection. And these laws oblige all that ever did or (if it had not been their own fault) might hear of them.

Other of these laws were enacted for a shorter time as a trial or exercise of some particular virtues of some particular persons under some certain circumstances in some rare and exempt cases.[33] Such were the feasts of charity among the primitive Christians, their kiss of peace, etc., and that command of our Saviour's to the young man mentioned in the gospel,[34] who inquired of him what he might do to inherit eternal life. Our Lord questioned him about several commandments, to which he answered, "All these things have I kept from my youth." Yet one thing was wanting to his perfection, namely a mind disengaged from the love of this world, and therefore our Saviour commands that he should sell all he had and give to the poor and in that poverty follow after Jesus. "But he went away sorrowful." From whence we may observe that if we could live free from all scandalous vices, if we could say as he did, "All the commands of God" as far as they relate to ourselves and neighbours, "we have kept from our youth up," yet if we bear an immoderate love to the things of this world, if riches, honours, friends or any sensual enjoyments be esteemed or valued more than God, or if the possession of them or desires after them prevail so far as to make us unmindful of the "one thing necessary,"[35] it will as infallibly exclude us from the Kingdom of Heaven as the practice of the most black and scandalous vices. But to return.

The Ten Commandments have been generally esteemed a summary of the moral law, yet they are not all strictly speaking moral, but the most of them are positive precepts founded on the moral law. The two first are purely moral, for to acknowledge only one God and "to love him with all the heart, with all the mind," etc.,[36] and to "worship him in spirit"[37] or with the spirit without making any image or representation of him who is a pure spiritual substance, and not to pay any worship or divine honour to any idol is unquestionably a great part of the law of our nature. The third is partly moral and partly positive: the prohibition is positive, that we should not forswear ourselves, which is the thing chiefly intended in the command, but then reverencing the Supreme Being and paying our due homage of adoration, honour, esteem to his person, name, etc. is moral and of perpetual obligation.

The fourth is also a positive rule founded on the moral. That we should devote some part of our time to that God from whom we received our being and all that we have[38] is highly reasonable and seems naturally to spring from the first great branch of the moral law, namely love to God, but what part, how much[39] ought to be and is determined by the God of sabbaths. As the manner how this time should be employed is to be learnt from the general practice of the catholic church ever since the time of our Saviour. The fifth, which teacheth the duty of persons to parents and superiors, is founded on God's most wise and holy providence, that for the sake of order and harmony in the world hath appointed a superiority among[40] the relation men hold to each other, since 'tis plain without such inequality there could be no such thing as discipline in the world, no last appeal in any disputable case, which would soon introduce the wildest anarchy and confusion.

The other five are all positive commands arising from the other branch of moral law, viz. the love of our neighbour.

The sixth is to secure our neighbour's person, the seventh to secure his property in his wife and must necessarily be determined[41] when we arrive to that state wherein we shall never marry nor be given in marriage,[42] as the two following are to secure his goods and his reputation. And the last is guard of all the rest relating to our neighbour. If we are truly humble, if through pride and a too high opinion of our own merit we are not inclined to covet the esteem of men, are not covetous of the honour and reputation of worldly grandeur, we shall not find any reluctance in paying obedience to our natural or civil parents, we shall not affect rule or dominion over others, but with all cheerfulness shall render honour to whom it is due and shall in all things[43] obey the order of divine providence without ever aspiring above that rank in which God hath thought fit to place us.[44]

Again, if we have "the ornament of a meek and quiet spirit,"[45] and are never guilty of immoderate anger nor are urged by too keen a resentment of an injury to covet and desire revenge on our neighbour's person nor do ever covet ought that he possesses, we shall never be tempted to commit any murder, nor shall he that is strictly careful to guard his mind against every impure or wanton thought and shuns all occasions of stirring up in his soul a guilty imagination by avoiding all[46] lewd discourses or looking on any persons or pictures, etc. that might raise a loose desire, in fine, whoever is never guilty of an irregular desire shall never actually defile his neighbour['s] wife, any more than he that, being contented with his own lot and that does not indulge himself in coveting the goods of his neighbour, will be guilty of any fraudulent practices towards him. He will be so far from stealing[47] and oppression and such gross acts of injustice that he will not so much as overreach[48] any in bargaining, nor will he overrate his own goods or undervalue those of his neighbour, nor take advantage of the necessities or weakness of his poor brother to gain the greatest temporal advantage.

And[49] if we do but sincerely and heartily love our neighbour and desire the prosperity of his person, goods, and reputation as truly as we do our own and are not covetous or desirous to raise our own reputation by the ruin of his, we shall be so far from all detraction and evil speaking, lying and slandering, that we shall be sure to discountenance all idle stories, uncharitable censures, or defamatory discourses of our neighbour, much less shall we be wrought upon by either interest, passion, thirst of revenge, etc. to bear any false witness against him in a judiciary way. But I proceed to a brief exposition on the commands themselves, which will more fully show you your duty towards God and your neighbour.

A Brief Exposition on the Ten Commandments

First, **Thou shalt have no other Gods but me.**[50]

Positive duties arising from this command.[51]

1st. A firm rational assent to the being of a God, a pure, simple, uncreated spirit, acknowledging him to be the fountain spring and origin of all being. Necessary, because self-existent, receiving nothing from not having any dependence on anything without himself, but containing in his own most perfect nature all perfection and blessedness.

2nd. An explicit belief of his most glorious perfections. Acknowledging that he is eternal, immutable, omnipotent, omnipresent, omniscient, infinite [?]in wisdom, holiness, goodness,[52] justice, truth. And these perfections we must ascribe to him by way of eminence, so as to admit of no equal or comparison between him and any other being.

3rd.[53] A practical subjection to him of all the powers and faculties of the soul and body, an entire devotedness and resignation to that great God to be by him governed and disposed as shall seem best to his infinite wisdom. And this founded on an acknowledgment of our dependence on him and on his undoubted right to give law unto his creatures and enforcing those laws by rewards and punishments of infinite weight and duration. That he carefully adverts to the actions of each individual with an intention to reward or punish according to their works.

And[54] as we acknowledge his right and fitness to govern the whole system of created beings, so we must with great humility of mind and application and sincerity of heart set ourselves to the study of those laws he hath given us. We must prefer, choose, and delight in his service above all things; in a word, we must "love the Lord our God with all our heart, with all our soul, with all our mind, and with all our strength,"[55] with the full vigour and energy of the soul. And[56] this love[57] is the spring or origin of all the genuine acts of piety toward God, without which no service, no outward expression of [?]desire, no, not the giving the body to be burned[58] shall be accepted, though only giving a cup of cold water to our neighbour out of a principle of love to God shall not only be accepted but rewarded with everlasting happiness.[59]

Love to God naturally inspires us with a desire to please him, and because we know that his most perfect nature is absolutely separated[60] and averse from all moral evil, it therefore makes us also hate sin and puts us upon endeavouring to be conformable to him, makes us rejoice in his glorious perfections, inspires us with a desire of being holy, just, true, good, etc., to be partakers of some small degree of his immutability, that we may constantly and vigourously serve him and do all that is in our power to advance his honour and interest in the world.

Love hath generally been distinguished into two kinds: a love of benevolence and a love of desire.[61] The first is supposed to be a wishing well to or bearing good will towards[62] anyone; the second, a complacency[63] in or desire of union with the person beloved. But this is a mistake arising from want of duly considering the true nature of love. For nothing can be plainer than that love is a simple act of the soul, a pleasing motion towards union with the[64] person beloved.[65] And whether we shall wish well to or have a complacence in and press toward a union with what we love is wholly to be determined by the nature and circumstances of the object. Towards man, which is a weak dependent compound being, that is encompassed on all sides with dangers and temptations, who wants abundance of ingredients to make up the composition of his happiness, we may and ought to express our love by wishing well to him and by contributing all we may to his ease and convenience here and to his eternal welfare in another life.

But the most great and holy God doth in his own divine nature fully comprehend whatever is necessary to his own happiness, and so far is he from receiving or wanting any accession of blessedness from such weak imperfect creatures as we are, that we entirely depend on him for all we are, have, or hope to enjoy. Therefore, since his infinite perfections and essential happiness supersedes all our wishes and desires of that kind, our love to him is determined in a high estimation of him, in adoration, praise, profound reverence, perfect resignation of ourselves to him, complacency in and desire of union and communion with him, zeal for his glory, delight in thinking or speaking of him, love of his name, day, word, sacraments, works, in fine of all his ordinances and all his creatures in which we perceive the smallest faintest ray of his divinity.

Second Commandment
Thou shalt not make unto thyself any graven image, etc.[66]

As we must acknowledge only one God and must not make any image or visible representation of him or form any corporeal idea of him in our mind[67] whom we must acknowledge a pure spirit without body parts, etc., so we must worship him in spirit, or with spirit, and in truth and sincerity,[68] with a spiritual worship internally with our minds. The understanding must contemplate him in the perfections of his nature, in all the operations of his power, wisdom, goodness, etc. visible in the works of creation and providence. The judgment must most highly esteem him and submit to all his determinations. The will must conform to his and acquiesce in the order of his providence. The affections must be fixed upon and terminate[69] in him. Not that we[70] are forbid absolutely to exercise them on anything but God, as has been wildly imagined by some fanciful men of late,[71] but we must principally love, treasure, etc. God above all things, so as not to suffer any creature to come into competition with him. And as the mind must thus be devoted to God, so there must be in our approaches to him a certain reverend, awful prostration of the soul before him, a most profound self-abasement, a kind of self-annihilation, a humble contraction of ourselves into a point, a nothing, before the great, awful and adorable Majesty of earth and heaven. Who is "the high and lofty One that inhabiteth eternity"![72] "Who hath measured the waters in the hollow of his hand, and meted out the heavens with a span, and comprehended the dust of the earth in a measure, and weighed the mountains in scales and the hills in a balance"![73] "Behold the nations are as a drop of a bucket, and are counted as the small dust of the balance; behold he taketh up the isles as a very little thing"![74] For they are all "before him as nothing, and they are counted to him less than nothing and vanity."[75] "It is he that sitteth upon the circle of the earth, and the inhabitants therefore are as grasshoppers, that stretcheth out the heavens as a curtain and spreadeth them out as a tent to dwell in"![76] "To whom then shall we liken God? Or what likeness shall we compare unto him?"[77]

2nd. As we must worship God internally, with or in the spirit, so we must express our inward reverence and devotion by a suitable gesture or posture of body. We must "fall down and kneel before the Lord our Maker."[78] And in all our external actions we must observe a due composure and decency as becomes those that take upon themselves the honour to approach near and speak unto so great a majesty.

Third Commandment
Thou shalt not take the name of the Lord [thy God in vain] etc.[79]

As we must assent to the being, unity, [and] perfections of God and must worship him in a manner agreeable to his nature "in spirit and in truth,"[80] so we must likewise honour his name. And since an oath is a solemn appeal to the God of truth for the confirmation of the truth of what we assert, promise, vow, etc., we must be always very careful (especially if we are called before a lawful judicature to bear testimony in any dubious matter) to speak nothing but the truth out of a high esteem and veneration for that name by which it hath pleased the most high God to make himself known to the children of men. And in all places at all times, whenever we have occasion to make use of that sacred name, we must do it with an awful regard to his presence, with great humility, and the profoundest reverence, especially when we speak to the great and glorious God.

The Fourth Commandment
Remember the Sabbath day to keep it holy etc.[81]

Since it hath pleased Almighty God, whose we are and to whom we are indebted for all the time we enjoy, to appropriate a seventh part thereof to his more immediate service, thereby indulging us rest and leisure after six days labour to attend upon his public ordinances, that we may be somewhat refreshed by the contemplation of himself in the wondrous works of his creation and providence, it is our duty to remember this most happy day before it comes, that we may prevent as much as possibly we can being encumbered or diverted on that day by any unnecessary business, impertinent visits, or whatever else may rob us of any of those sacred moments which ought to be all devoted to God, and therefore 'tis a kind of sacrilege to alienate them from his service.

And as we must remember the day before it comes, so must we be especially careful to sanctify it when present by a conscientious performance of the duties of the day. By remembering the end, the reason of its institution, mentioned in the command, "For in six days the Lord made heaven and earth, the sea and all that in them is, and rested the seventh day. **Wherefore** the Lord blessed the seventh day and hallowed it." [82] **Wherefore** in imitation of our great Creator, we also must rest from all worldly————, [83] that we may adore and praise his infinite power, wisdom, goodness, etc. that is displayed in this beauteous fabric of the world in the noble system of all created beings.

We must praise him for our own "creation, preservation, and all the blessings" [84] which we partake of in common with the rest of his creatures, more particularly for all special or peculiar favours, such as health, friends, a comfortable and convenient habitation, for any extraordinary deliverances from, or supports under, troubles, and for any mercies which upon reflection we can perceive that we enjoy, which perhaps others better than we are may want.

But since our blessed Saviour by his resurrection on the first day of the week, by his sending the Holy Ghost on that day, by his own example, and by his spirit in the apostles and primitive church hath changed the observation of the seventh to the first day of the week, the business of the day is enlarged, and we must now not only bless God for all his works of creation and providence, but we must humbly offer to God the Father, Son, and Holy Ghost our highest praises for the redemption of the world by the Holy Jesus.[85] And this we must do publicly in the assembly of the saints, for the more public our devotions are on that day, provided they are hearty and sincere, the more do we honour God, because we thereby excite others to worship him also, and we show unto the world that we are not ashamed of professing our selves the disciples of a crucified Jesus.

In the morning of the Sabbath 'twill be convenient to rise a little sooner than ordinary (if health permit), that we may have leisure to add to our stated devotions somewhat proper for the day. Let the day be begun with "Glory be to the Father, Son, and Holy Ghost." [86] Then it may not be amiss to repeat the Fourth Command, which I have known some do a great while with very good success, nor is anything more proper to impress a sense of the holiness of the day upon the mind. Proceed to implore the divine assistance to enable you to spend every moment of that most precious time as becomes those that have devoted themselves to God. Let us beg of him to turn our minds from all vain and worldly thoughts, to compose and regulate our affections, and to elevate our souls to such a devout and holy temper, that we may know by experience what it is to be in the spirit on the Lord's Day. That we may know by experience that religion is more than a vain fancy or illusion. 'Tis somewhat above what the carnal trifling world can apprehend. 'Tis a noble vital principle, the perfection and happiness of the soul, which raises it above the trifling pleasures of this life and inspires it with a constant regular tendency towards the divine Origin of being and blessedness, where it rests as on its centre, esteeming itself infinitely more happy in the least degree of his favour than it could be in the possession of all the wealth, honour, or whatever else the whole world contains that foolish mistaken men so much desire and so earnestly seek after. 'Tis that which steers the soul innocently and safely through this tempestuous world and calms and supports it under all the calamities of human life. Peace was the legacy of our dying Lord, and as the world cannot give it, so neither can it take it away.[87] And though the corruption of our natures too often gives advantage to our spiritual enemies to disturb and discompose our minds, yet those persons who are truly devoted to God have habitually such an inward peace and serenity of soul as none else can possible conceive or enjoy, especially on the sabbath, that blessed day of God, which he hath in his abundant infinite goodness given to the sons of men as a type and foretaste of that eternal rest that he hath promised with himself in glory. And indeed I have often admired[88] the stupendous folly and blindness of those bad Christians that account it a task and burden to be one day in seven suspended from the business of this world, when surely, if we have reason to bless the divine Goodness for feeding and clothing us, for so liberally indulging us so many mercies in our passage through this world, much more reason have we to praise, to magnify, to adore his boundless love and goodness to mankind in permitting us to enjoy such an inestimable blessing as a sabbath after six days labour. For surely it would be very sad (I dare not say hard) to command[89] us to spend so much time in making provision for these perishing bodies, which must not withstanding all our care after a little while be resolved into their first principles, must return to their native clay and lie rotting in the dust, if our souls, our nobler and better part had not at least one day in the week to rest and refresh itself, wherein it may have leisure to abstract from all corporeal objects and retire from the world to enjoy those satisfactions that are more proper for its spiritual and celestial nature.

Let us then rejoice when this day approaches and in our morning retirement endeavour to prepare our minds for the solemn happy employment of it.

Then 'tis we may[90] bid adieu to the world for a season, to all our friends and acquaintance[s], to all secular concerns and worldly regards. Farewell the world and all that it contains, I must take my leave of you for a while; tarry ye here at the foot of the mount, I must ascend to converse with God. I have not leisure now to attend or talk with you, nor must you molest or interrupt my soul on this day which my bounteous Lord hath given me for the rest and refreshment of my mind. I do not much affect you at any time and am often weary and apt to say with David, "O that I had wings as a dove that I might fly away from you and be at rest."[91] And though by the order of providence I am determined to spend the greater part of my time here below in business and employments relating to this life, yet now I have not only God's permission but command to abstain from all unnecessary care and labour, 'tis my duty as well as happiness to separate from the world as 'tis man's and retire into it as 'tis God's. And though some persons have taken a great deal of pains to prove that the sabbath is for diversion as well as devotion, and have employed the utmost efforts of their trifling wit to show the difference between the Jewish and Christian sabbath, and to argue themselves out of the benefits their souls might enjoy by a strict observation of the day, yet as I can by no means be of their opinion,[92] so, till they can prove[93] that the deliverance of the Jews out of Egypt under Moses was greater and more worthy of remembrance than[94] our deliverance from sin and misery by Jesus Christ, and that we have no reason to praise God for our being, because none of his creatures and not having[95] any share in the works of creation and providence, and that we are under no obligation of loving God with all the heart, mind, etc.[96], and therefore cannot be obliged by this command which is founded so plainly on that first branch of the moral law, they shall not, I hope, ever prevail against my fixed resolution of devoting this day to the great and holy God. Nay though it were granted that our Saviour did remit somewhat of the strictness required of the Jews on the Sabbath,[97] and if this[98] my purpose should not appear to fall under a positive command, yet if it may but be accepted as a free will offering, I am content. And oh that it would please Almighty God to grant me this one petition, that instead of making my children remarkable[99] for beauty, wit, riches or honour, the love of this day might be engraven on their minds in such indelible characters, that they might by their deportment on the Lord's Day be distinguished from the rest of the world, when I am dust wherever it shall please the divine providence to cast their lot. Amen, Amen.

'Tis needless to inform you how a[100] great part of this day must be employed, since you already know that 'tis our duty to attend upon the public worship of God and that we ought to behave ourselves[101] with great gravity and reverence[102] when we come into his holy temple where we are in the presence and under the more immediate inspection of the great God, where we hold communion with all saints, with all the celestial hierarchy, with angels and archangels, with all the company of the heavenly host[103] we join in worshiping, in praising and adoring our great Creator, our blessed Redeemer and that Holy Spirit by whom we "are sealed unto the day of redemption."[104] I am very sure if we did but actually advert to the awful presence we are then in and did but seriously attend to the business we come about, it would restrain our thoughts and eyes from wandering, nor should we find leisure to observe any about us or desire to be taken notice of ourselves, much less should we stand upon ceremony and compliment, which are at best but trifles in any place, but are scandalous and abominable in the house of God. And if we[105] would but spend more time and care in adorning our[106] minds with such virtues as become those that profess godliness, we should not be so solicitous about these perishing bodies to have them appear well-dressed and amiable to the beholders, which often times proves a snare to ourselves as well as others; not that I disapprove a decency in the habit; on the contrary I like it very well where 'tis an indication of a clean well-ordered mind, but all excessive curiosity and nice observation of every new fashion I think argues too much vanity and delight in sensuality and therefore it ought to be very carefully avoided. I think indeed it would be very commendable if we did forbear putting on anything of apparel that is new, and was never worn before, on the Lord's Day, for 'tis almost incredible how much novelty affects the mind, insomuch that unless we are very careful, we shall be apt to be too much affected with, and take too much notice of, any new thing till custom has made it[107] familiar to us.[108]

There are so many excellent discourses extant of practical divinity, and we are so often[109] and excellently instructed in the particulars of our duty, that 'tis altogether needless for me to enlarge on those subjects; I shall therefore only endeavour to show you how you may fill up the intermediate spaces of time between the public worship, and how you may employ yourself in your morning and evening retirement.

God is a boundless inexhaustible subject for thought! And though we should spend an eternity in contemplation of any one of his divine perfections, we could never attain to an adequate conception thereof. I say not this to discourage, but to inspire your soul with rigor and attention, and to show you that[110] if the mind be but effectually touched with the love of God, it is almost impossible any of that sacred time should lie dead upon our hands, or that such a soul should be idle or not fully employed which hath a strong and clear perception of that most blessed Spirit. But oh what purity! What separation from the world and all material objects, what intenseness of thought and actual advertence to the presence of the great and holy God is necessary when we apply ourselves to the contemplation of his[111] most glorious perfections!

But that we may be able readily and easily to abstract from all corporeal ———[112] on this day, we must endeavour to get a habitual sense of God in the mind, for it is impossible for any creature that is sensual, that is immersed in matter and only (or for the most part)[113] conversant with sensual objects, readily to abstract from them and easily attain such a temper of mind as is requisite for having any clear perception of God. The mind will savour most and be most strongly affected with what it thinks most upon, and if we suffer our thoughts to dwell chiefly on the things of the life, our soul will be earthly, sensual, nay devilish, because by so doing it will contract an enmity against God and a[n] habitual averseness from all spiritual things. Therefore let us with great humility beseech him to purify our minds from the affections of sensuality and to guide us by his Holy Spirit into true and proper notions of himself, that we may love and adore, though we cannot comprehend.[114]

Notes

1. The main title does not appear on the draft MS, which begins with the scrawled "Lre: 2d To Suky," but S. W. used it at the end of her Creed essay, alluding to this next part of her project. She does insert a title at the end of her introductory section before getting into the exposition proper; I have used that, with the parenthetical addition indicating incompleteness, as the subtitle.

2. See my introductory remarks in chapter 25. The last paragraphs of the Creed exposition advertise and prepare the reader for the coming installment on the Ten Commandments. See also journal entry 52, for May 24, 1711—one of the rare dated entries.

3. Adam Clarke would have done so but had no knowledge of the MS that has since come to light (p. 256).

4. Her general introduction takes up an additional 12 pages. In S. W.'s defense it should be noted that much of the discourse on sabbath keeping broadens to more general considerations of worship, contemplation, devotion, and the like—issues pertinent, but not exclusive, to the Lord's Day. She also devoted four of her surviving journal entries, written at about the same period (1709–1710), to similar sabbatarian discussions. See 165–168 in part II of this volume. For background on sabbath observance see James T. Dennison Jr., *The Market Day of the Soul: The Puritan Doctrine of the Sabbath in England, 1532–1700* (Lanham, N.Y., and London: University Press of America, 1983). Though Dennison is primarily occupied with documenting the Sabbath-keeping controversy between Puritans and the "prelatic party" before the middle of the seventeenth century, he does devote a final chapter to practice after the Restoration. Fol-

lowing Christopher Hill, he argues (p. 119) that much of Puritan social doctrine had been brought into the restored church and particularly that "the practice of Sabbath rest had become a national custom." This is certainly borne out in the turn-of-the-century Societies for the Reformation of Manners, which could compete with the strictest congregation of Puritan sabbatarians. See Gordon Rupp, *Religion in England, 1688–1791* (Oxford: Clarendon Press, 1986), pp. 295–298. S. W.'s individual recapitulation of the nation's ecclesiastical change seems to have brought a similar dose of Puritan sabbatarianism into her new Anglican context, but it was enhanced by her husband, Samuel's, early support of the similarly motivated religious societies. For a more restrained Anglican view of the Lord's Day, see Henry Hammond, *A Practical Catechism*, 11th ed. (London: Richard Davis, 1677), pp. 194–197; Bishop Robert Sanderson's 1636 essay (also republished after the Restoration), "The Case of the Sabbath," in *The Works of Robert Sanderson*, 6 vols., ed. William Jacobson (Oxford: At the University Press, 1854), 5:5–16; and Robert Nelson, *A Companion for the Festivals and Fasts of the Church of England . . .* (London: Society for the Promotion of Christian Knowledge; New York: Pott, Young, n.d.), pp. 13–21; original ed. 1703.

5. J. Sears McGee, *The Godly Man in Stuart England: Anglicans, Puritans, and the Two Tables, 1620–1670* (New Haven, Conn. and London: Yale University Press, 1976), p. 70 and passim.

6. C. F. Allison, *The Rise of Moralism: The Proclamation of the Gospel from Hooker to Baxter* (New York: Seabury, 1966), pp. x–xi, 192. The "holy living" tradition that Allison feels distorts the doctrine of justification in the second half of the seventeenth century includes not only Anglicans like Jeremy Taylor but also such Puritans as Richard Baxter.

7. John Spurr, *The Restoration Church of England, 1646–1689* (New Haven, Conn., and London: Yale University Press, 1991), p. 307. For the longer term, cf. Rupp, *Religion in England*, pp. 278–285, 289–322.

8. Headingley MS C, pp. 61–98.

9. Close paraphrase of 1 Corinthians 15:22; quotation marks added. From the reference to "our first parents" to the concluding remarks on a second covenant, this paragraph could be seen as a quick summary of the opening section of the *Westminster Shorter Catechism*. See particularly, questions 12, 13, 15, and 20. See also similar language in several of the more detailed questions of the *Westminster Larger Catechism*, particularly 20, 21, 30–32, and 36. Milton also uses "first parents" in *Paradise Lost*, 3:65 and 4:6.

10. See the *Shorter Catechism*, Q. 94, where baptism "seals our ingrafting into Christ, and partaking of the benefits of the covenant of grace."

11. Followed by the crossed-out "obedience to."

12. A reference to the preceding exposition on the Apostles' Creed.

13. Cf. the *Larger Catechism*, Q. 32, where faith is the condition of salvation and obedience is the "evidence of the truth of . . . faith."

14. This is the gist of the Aristotelian definition as filtered through Aquinas and the Spanish Jesuit Francisco Suarez into mid-seventeenth century England. See Nathaniel Culverwel, *An Elegant and Learned Discourse of the Light of Nature, with Several Other Treatises . . .* , ed. Robert A. Green and Hugh MacCallum (Toronto: University of Toronto Press, 1971), pp. 28–29; original ed. (London: John Rothwell, 1652).

15. Slightly garbled version of Romans 9:5; quotation marks added.

16. Ephesians 1:11; quotation marks added. This verse is also used by the *Shorter Catechism*, Q. 7, the famous issue of God's decrees, by which "He has foreordained whatever comes to pass." S. W. employs the verse but lets the Calvinism lie.

17. Cf. Culverwel, *Light of Nature*, pp. 29–30: "all rectitude has a being, and flows from the fountain of being."

18. Perhaps an Arminian gloss on the *Larger Catechism's* phrase "the unsearchable counsel of His own will." See Q. 13.

19. Followed by the crossed-out "must always."

20. S. W. originally wrote, "the chief end of man's creation," then crossed out "man's" and entered above it "all the works of his." Note the strong echoes of the *Shorter Catechism*, Q. 1: "What is the chief end of man? A. Man's chief end is to glorify God, and to enjoy Him forever."

21. Replaces the crossed-out "seeing."

22. S. W. reworked these examples as she wrote, writing and then crossing out "moral" after "divine" and "&c" after "law of nature."

23. Cf. Culverwel's discussion of the "eternal law" (*Light of Nature*, p. 36): "So then, that there is such a prime and supreme Law is clear, and unquestionable; but who is worthy to unseal and open this Law? and who can sufficiently display the glory of it?"

24. A paragraph on moral law is crossed out here and then reinserted in a slightly rewritten form below; see note 30. S. W. had obviously gotten this out of the previously announced order (divine, natural, and moral and positive) and sought to set it right.

25. Added but crossed out "and regularly."

26. The beginning of this sentence orginally read, "Hence arises the position of the elements," but S. W. crossed out the first two words and inserted "In" to recast the sentence.

27. S. W. ignores (or is unaware of) the debate about whether natural law can ever be applied to nonrational creatures. Culverwel, *Light of Nature*, p. 40, takes the more restrictive view, charging that opposing lawyers "mean to bring beast, birds and fishes into their Courts, and have some fees out of them."

28. Cf. ibid., p. 55: "Natures Law is frequently call'd the Moral Law."

29. Cf. the General Confession in the Holy Communion, BCP: "our manifold sins and wickedness, Which we, from time to time, most grievously have committed, By thought, word, and deed." Also the *Shorter Catechism*, Q. 82 (and *Larger Catechism*, Q. 149), where it is acknowledged that everyone daily breaks God's commandments "in thought, word, and deed."

30. Cf. the first draft of this paragraph, crossed out above, just before the paragraph on natural law: "Moral Law, or the law of reason, is that law which is founded on and results from the unalterable natures of persons and things; thus from the absolute perfections of the divine nature and the rationality and freedom of man's nature arises all our duties towards God and the greater part of our duties towards ourselves and our neighbour. And this law is fixed, unalterable, eternal, of equal and perpetual obligation to all persons of what degree soever at all times in all places and circumstances of life. This law or rule obliges no creature in the world but man, who alone is capable of understanding it, having a principle of reason, and who alone is capable of practicing the precepts thereof, since no creature beside hath a principle of liberty; and therefore his conformity to this law is called moral goodness. And any deviation from this law is moral evil."

31. Context, milieu.

32. Replaces the crossed-out "virtues or graces."

33. Cf. Culverwel, *Light of Nature*, p. 59: "Now, though the formality of humane Lawes do flow immediately from the power of some particular men; yet the strength and sinew of these Lawes is founded in the Law of Nature . . . and whilest they are in their force and vigour, it does oblige and command them not to break or violate them."

34. Matthew 19:16–22, Mark 10:17–22, Luke 18:18–23; quotation marks added.

35. An echo of Luke 10:42; in AV: "needful." Quotation marks added.

36. BCP: "A Catechism," part of the answer (cast there in the first person singular) to the question "What is thy duty towards God?" Quotation marks added. See Matthew 23:37, Mark 12:30, and Luke 10:27.

37. See John 4:24; quotation marks added.

38. Originally followed by "seems," which was subsequently crossed out and replaced by "is."

39. Followed by a line and a half, crossed out: "and in what manner this time is to be employed is to be" (subsequently replaced by "ought to be and is").

40. Replaces the crossed-out "in."

41. Terminated, ended.

42. Close paraphrase of Matthew 22:30. A crossed-out "The" follows.

43. Followed by the crossed-out "with great cheerfulness."

44. Cf. the concluding clause of the church catechism's answer to the question "What is thy duty towards thy Neighbour?": "to do my duty in that state of life, unto which it shall please God to call me."

45. 1 Peter 3:4; quotation marks added.

46. "Avoiding all" replaces the crossed-out "hearing."

47. Followed by the crossed-out "that he will."

48. Outwit; get the better of by cunning or artifice.

49. Replaces the crossed-out "Nor."

50. BCP, catechism: "Thou shalt have none other gods but me"; cf. AV, Exodus 20:3: "Thou shalt have no other gods before me." S. W. writes the commandment, and the subsequent ones she treats, in a somewhat larger hand, indicated here by bold face type.

51. Cf. the patterned explication of the commandments in both Westminster catechisms. After the commandment is repeated the child is asked (in the *Larger Catechism*), "What are the duties required in the [first, etc.] commandment?" and then "What are the sins forbidden in the [first, etc.] commandment?" followed by a third question getting at an important appropriate detail. S. W. seems here to be adopting the first of these approaches.

52. Followed by the crossed-out "patience."

53. This paragraph appears in the MS just above the one numbered "2nd." That S. W. wanted to move it is indicated by her numbering it "3rd" and by the asterisk that links it with the next paragraph, beginning "And as we acknowledge." This order makes better sense, following these initial thoughts on human resignation to God's governing power.

54. Preceded by an asterisk showing the place S. W. wanted the "3rd" paragraph moved. See note 53.

55. Nearly exact quotation of AV, Mark 12:30; cf. BCP catechism; quotation marks added.

56. Originally followed by "from," since crossed out.

57. Followed by "of," crossed out.

58. 1 Corinthians 13:3.

59. See Matthew 10:42.

60. Followed by "from," subsequently crossed out.

61. Note the remarkably similar passage in her letter to Samuel Wesley Jr., 11 March 1704. See also the much later letters to John Wesley, 7 December 1725 and 30 March 1726, indicating her reading of the philosopher John Norris on this subject. Indeed, here S. W. seems to be expanding on the distinction made by Norris in "A Discourse concerning the Excellency of Praise and Thanksgiving," in *[Practical] Discourses upon Several Divine Subjects*, 3rd ed., 4 vols. (London: Samuel Manship, 1697), 2:92–93.

62. Followed by "that," crossed out.

63. In its now more obscure meaning, "pleasure, delight, enjoyment" rather than in its more usual, modern sense of self-satisfaction.

64. Originally followed by "beloved obje," which she deleted in mid-word.

65. Cf. John Norris, *The Theory and Regulation of Love . . .*, 2nd ed. (London: S. Manship, 1694), p. 25, defining "Love in general" as "a Motion of the Soul towards God" and "the Love of Concupiscence or Desire" as "a simple Tendency of the Soul to Good."

66. A seeming conflation of the BCP catechism and AV, Exodus 20:4.

67. This thoroughgoing iconophobia may derive from a youthful exposure to the *Larger Catechism's* Q. 109, which forbids representations of God "either inwardly in our mind or outwardly in any kind of image."

68. Loose paraphrase of John 4:24 with echoes of 1 Corinthians 5:8.

69. Replaces the crossed-out (?)"derar."

70. Followed by the crossed-out "may not."

71. She may be referring to the wildly charismatic sect of Huguenot refugees, known as the French Prophets, which had recently sought refuge in England. See Rupp, *Religion in England,* pp. 216–217.

72. Isaiah 57:15; quotation marks added.

73. Nearly exact quotation of Isaiah 40:12; quotation marks added.

74. Isaiah 40:15; quotation marks added.

75. Isaiah 40:17; quotation marks added.

76. Isaiah 40:22; quotation marks added.

77. Nearly exact quotation of Isaiah 40:18; quotation marks added.

78. From BCP, Morning Prayer, the Venite (Psalm 95), verse 6: "O Come, let us worship and fall down, and kneel before the Lord our Maker." Quotation marks added.

79. BCP, catechism, and AV, Exodus 20:7.

80. John 4:24; quotation marks added.

81. AV, Exodus 20:8, rather than BCP, catechism.

82. BCP and AV, Exodus 20:11, agree. Quotation marks added, but the boldfacing of "wherefore" represents S.W.'s emphasis, in the MS a slightly larger script.

83. Space for the noun is left blank in the MS. The "wherefore" beginning the sentence is also written in a slightly larger hand than the surrounding material; I have represented that emphasis with boldfacing.

84. BCP, Prayers and Thanksgivings, Upon Certain Occasions, a General Thanksgiving. Quotation marks added.

85. Paraphrase from General Thanksgiving.

86. Cf. BCP. The *Gloria Patri* is sung or said after the Psalms and canticles in morning and evening prayer.

87. See BCP, Evening Prayer, the Second Collect; John 14:27.

88. Wondered at.

89. I have corrected the MS's erroneous "commands."

90. Replaces the crossed-out (?)"might."

91. Close paraphrase of Psalm 55:6; quotation marks added.

92. S. W. has crossed out the following words here: "since I am sure we Christians have as much, nay more reason to praise god for the mercies of the Lord's Day as the Jews had. And."

93. Crossed out: "that 'tis a sin to spend the day in the exercises of religion, though it and."

94. Crossed out: "that [?]of the Christian."

95. Syntax has run away with her once again; continuing the list of what she regards as obvious untruths, perhaps S. W. means "because none of his creatures have any share in the works of creation."

96. See Matthew 22:37, Mark 12:30, and Luke 10:27.

97. Followed by the crossed-out "yet."

98. Replacing the crossed-out "it."

99. Followed by the crossed-out "by their."

100. Replaces the crossed-out "the."

101. Originally "you ought to behave yourself." S. W. immediately went back and corrected the pronouns to conform with the previous clause.

102. Followed by the now crossed-out "in the performance of so g."

103. Echoes of the BCP, Holy Communion, preface to the Sanctus.

104. Ephesians 4:30; quotation marks added.

105. Replaces a two- or three-word crossed-out phrase, beginning "our"; the second word (or two words) is intriguingly not just crossed out but also scribbled over so that it is completely illegible. This not being S. W.'s usual editorial custom, it seems likely that she was not just rephrasing for better effect but also nervous about her initial impulse being seen.

106. Originally "their," now crossed out.

107. Replaces the crossed-out "them."

108. S. W.'s negative thoughts about women's fashions are not unusual for religious commentators of her day. For a collection of influential contemporary writings emphasizing the importance of modesty in women see Angeline Goreau, *The Whole Duty of a Woman: Female Writers in Seventeenth Century England* (Garden City, N.Y.: Dial, 1985), pp. 35–64. For another Anglican woman's feelings on the subject, see Elizabeth Burnet, *A Method of Devotion: Or, Rules for Holy & Devout Living . . .* (London: For Joseph Downing, 1709), pp. 99–102. Second wife of the redoubtable Whig bishop Gilbert Burnet, she uses the same language of "Cleanness and Decency" as the appropriate end of dress (p. 101) and inveighs similarly against the "Snares for themselves as well as others" that dressing to attract admiration creates (p. 102).

109. Crossed out: "told what we ought."

110. Crossed out: "'tis impossible for your soul which hath."

111. Originally followed by "divine," now crossed out.

112. Space left blank for noun; S. W. probably intended "objects," easily supplied from the usage later in the same sentence (!) and from the identical phrase she used earlier in this exposition of the Fourth Commandment. See above, p. 417.

113. Followed by two indecipherable words, crossed out.

114. Exposition ends here; the same page contains the final entry in a section of her devotional journal, which she began at the other end of the notebook.

TWENTY-SEVEN

A Religious Conference between
Mother and Emilia

*T*his final piece of catechetical work, dated 1711/12, may be regarded as the last installment on the "little manual" of divinity destroyed in the rectory fire of early 1709 but still very much alive in Susanna Wesley's mind as late as May 1711. Her earlier intention, revealed in a letter to her son Samuel, had been to include details on both natural and revealed religion; her later plan, as sketched in the 1711 journal entry, speaks of explaining "the principles of revealed religion" and discoursing on the "being and attributes of God."[1] Though written as a dialogue between herself ("M" for Mother) and her eldest daughter ("E" for Emilia, at the time a young woman of 19), it is, as the epigraph indicates, intended for the edification of all her children. Nevertheless, it is worth underlining the seriousness with which fairly sophisticated theological teaching is set in the context of a mother-daughter interchange.

The content of the extended dialogue reflects the theological concerns of the age. Dozens of books and hundreds of sermons sought to prove Christianity's reasonableness against the attacks of atheists, both ancient and modern.[2] Some of the issues Susanna raises echo, for instance, those discussed in the Boyle lectures, endowed at the end of the seventeenth century. The well-known scientist Robert Boyle set them up "for proving the Christian Religion against notorious Infidels, viz. Atheists, Deists, Pagans, Jews and Mahometans," and in the process "to answer such New Objections or Difficulties as may be stated, to which good Answers have not yet been made"—that is, to reconcile Christianity with the new science represented by Newton and by Boyle himself.[3] Richard Bentley's 1692 lectures are a significant example of the genre and, as notes to Susanna's dialogue point out, they address some of the same issues she presents to Emilia. Among the common concerns are proving God's existence from the existence of incorporeal substance (the soul), from the harmony and symmetry of the human body, and from the "frame of the world"; and taking particular aim at two notorious atheist positions, the Epicurean notion of creation by chance and the Aristotelian idea of the eternity of the world. While not breaking new theological ground, she has managed (in typical Wesleyan fashion) to break down difficult concepts for easier understanding and application. In the process she has shown herself to be a competent interpreter of apologetic theology, just as in other writings she clearly expounded moral theology and spirituality.

In addition, the essay shows the further influence of French philosopher and mathematician Blaise Pascal. We have already noticed quotations from Basil Kennet's translation of the *Pensées, Thoughts on Religion, and Other Subjects* (London: A. and J. Churchil, R. Sare, J. Tonson, 1704), in her correspondance and spiritual diaries; here there are additional explicit references. However, as Augustin Leger argued early in this century, there are also several other evocations scattered throughout the dialogue.[4]

It is worth noting the interesting stylistic tension in the "Religious Conference" between her typical modest disclaimers (in this case, the phrase that recurs a number of times is "I do humbly conceive") and her sometimes harsh attitude toward the "cultured dispisers," whom she rails against as "stupid" or holders of "senseless opinions." Even Emilia, her "constructed" dialogue partner, comes in for some fairly stern words at the outset ("don't cavil or raise unreasonable questions!"), as if going too far in her inquiry somehow risks being tarred with the atheism under attack—there are limits to reasonableness and toleration! In fact, the cut and thrust of contoversy excite Susanna Wesley and occasionally pull her unawares beyond the self-deprecating modesty women were taught to affect. Emilia and her sisters, if they were paying attention, would have received that message along with the theologically correct line on the "being and attributes of God."

The only extant manuscript appears to be a final copy, not a draft; it is written in Susanna Wesley's fair hand with minimal mistakes or changes, and there is even a title page, indicating that this was intended for circulation, if not actual publication. Indeed it did pass through John Wesley's hands, as an inscription in the flyleaf in his hand indicates: "My Mother's Conference with her Daughter." Owned by Wesley College, Bristol, it consists of a bound notebook with 61 pages of text, each measuring about 6 by 8 inches.

Though now long out of print, the "Religious Conference" was accurately edited (from the same manuscript) and published in the late years of the nineteenth century for the Wesley Historical Society in London.[5] Though that edition has proved helpful as a reference, I have worked from the manuscript for this volume and have managed to correct one or two of the earlier edition's misreadings.

〽

A

Religious Conferrence
Between M. & E.

I write unto you little Children,
of whom I travail in Birth again, until
Christ be formed in you.

may what is sown in Weakness,
be rais'd in Power —

Written for the use of my Children.
$17\frac{11}{12}$

A Religious Conference &c[6]

E.   In obedience to your order, I come to be further instructed in the principals
of religion. And as I do not apprehend that you have any design to deceive or deal
unfaithfully with me, so I humbly beg leave to require, that things may be clearly
and plainly proved before you demand my assent to the truth of them.

M.   Provided that you do not come to cavil or make objections without or
against reason, I am willing to allow what liberty you desire. But then I must tell
you that moral truths must be proved by moral arguments, arguments agreeable to
the nature of the things whence they are drawn, which, being spiritual and remote
from sense, cannot be demonstrated by visible signs like a proposition in mathematics. Nor does their force usually consist in one single evidence, but in the united
strength of several considerations, which, when duly weighed, if the mind perceive[7]
sufficient ground for a rational assent and that there is overweight enough in one
scale to incline the judgement of a wise man, insomuch that he sees 'tis more
reasonable to believe than not to believe, in this case we ought to assent without
further disputation.[8]

E.   I should be very unreasonable if I desired other arguments than the nature
of things will bear. Nor do I design to be troublesome if I can avoid it. My desire
is to be informed of the truth, to have my judgment determined, that I may be

able "to give an answer to every man that asketh me a reason of the faith that is in me." [9]

M.   I am very glad to find you so well disposed. For though the reason of our most holy faith is strong and clear, yet since man's corrupt wit is more fit to pull down than to build up, 'tis very difficult to bring an argument for any point of faith, but what a humoursome [10] captious person may cavil at or find some exception against. And we may humbly conceive 'twas for this reason our Blessed Savior required that his disciples should "become as little children," [11] should divest themselves of all pride, prejudice and passion, should be [12] humble, willing and disposed to learn, capable of being instructed as little children are wont to be. And if our minds were always so prepared, and disposed to entertain the truth, we should not delight in wrangling and disputing as men usually do; but any one conclusive argument for the truth of a proposition would be as good as a hundred.

E.   I am of the same opinion, and therefore desire you'd be pleased to give yourself as little trouble as possible. I shall propose my question in a few words; but since I'm very ignorant, I desire also that you would not be offended, though I sometimes ask the meaning of such things as to you may seem easy to be understood by the meanest capacity. In the first place then be pleased to give me a short explanation of the word religion.

M.   By religion I understand such a firm persuasion of the being and perfection of God as influences our practice. That is, as makes us very serious in studying his nature and will and very careful to perform all the duties he requires of us, to the end we may honour and please him, so as to enjoy his favour. The consequence of which favour is eternal happiness.

E.   By this explanation, I perceive that the belief of a God is the foundation of all religion. Tell me therefore, if you please, how you can prove the being of a God.

M.   By the existence of all things or any one particular thing that hath a being "in heaven above or in the earth beneath or in the waters under the earth." [13] By the clear voice of universal nature that loudly proclaims the power, wisdom, goodness, &c, of the great Creator. [14] Thus, as upon the sight of some noble fabric or curious piece of art we justly infer that some wise builder or cunning artificer has been at work, so when we behold this goodly system of beings, we may [15] reasonably conclude that there must necessarily be some self-existent eternal Being, by whose almighty power all things are created. And this being is God.

There must be something supreme in the order of nature, some First Cause whence all things took their original. For 'tis a self-evident truth that nothing could make itself. To make is to act, and nothing can act before it be; and to say a thing made itself is to affirm that a thing had being before it had a being, which is a palpable contradiction. The cause must necessarily precede the effect; nor is it possible for anything in the same respect to be both cause and effect. Action always presupposes a principle from whence it flows; as nothing hath no existence, so hath it no operation; otherwise, it must be something and nothing at the same time, which is impossible. Therefore, as was said before, there must be something eternally existing that gave being to all things: and every cause must be the effect of some other cause, till we come to the Original Cause of all things, which First Cause is God.

E.   I can easily apprehend that neither the world or anything in it could make itself, nor do I suppose that ever any one was stupid enough to imagine it did so. But what absurdity is there in believing it eternal? This opinion hath been entertained by persons of more sense and learning than I can ever pretend to.

M.   But this opinion was no effect of their sense or learning; but rather shows us that learning and sense are not always sufficient to preserve men from error. And we ought to learn by such men's delusions not to trust to our own weak and fallible understanding, but rely on the assistance of the unerring Spirit of God, if we desire to be led into the way of truth.[16]

Those which have believed the eternity of the world or that the world is eternal should have told us what they meant by the words eternity, eternal, and infinite. I take them to be convertible terms, for we generally use them in the same sense, though with some difference in the application. Thus we apply the word eternity to the duration of existence, as likewise eternal and infinite, and so call it an eternal duration or an infinite duration without succession of parts, such as years, months, weeks, days, hours, also, as there is in time. Infinite and eternal we also apply to the thing or person so existing, signifying that the thing or person so existing is absolutely perfect, immense, or boundless, without beginning or end. Whatever is infinite must of necessity be absolutely perfect, to which perfection nothing can be added nor can anything be taken away. And if absolute perfection be incapable of accession or diminution, it must by consequence be immutable, since all change is wrought either by addition of something wanting or by loss of something it had before; but that can neither lose nor receive must necessarily be always the same, consequently eternal.

Now if you apply what has been said to the matter under debate, you'll easily perceive that neither the world in general nor any particular part of it either is or can be eternal.

For, first, all things on earth are in their nature mutable, as appears by their being in a continual flux, always changing; and whatever is in its nature subject to change may end, and whatsoever may end had a beginning, and therefore cannot be eternal.

Again, all things in the world are of a finite nature. Trees, plants, herbs, flowers, etc., proceed from a small grain or seed, attract each their proper nourishment form the earth, augment and grow to such a point of perfection, and then return back to their original state. And as plants, so animals have their perfection bounded within certain limits. They pass through many sensible alterations from one degree of growth to another; there is not a day but they make some acquisition or suffer some loss, till at last by death they also are resolved into their first principles.

E.   But though each individual had a beginning and be of a finite nature, yet might not the world have been eternally in the same state in which it is now?

M.   No. For if the world were in the same posture as it is now, in a state of generation and corruption, corruption must have been as eternal as generation, and then things that eternally generate and corrupt eternally have been and eternally not have been.

The truth is, 'tis impossible for man's reason to avoid running into inextricable difficulties and endless contradictions, unless we conceive some First of every kind—one first man, one first animal, one first plant, etc., from whence the rest proceeded. And this first must have a cause, not of the same kind, but infinite and independent.

But to make the matter still plainer, pray tell me what you mean by the world. If you mean the whole system of visible beings, it appears plainly that each individual part thereof is mutable and finite, consequently not eternal.[17] For finite added to finite ever so long cannot make an infinite. If you mean first matter, the matter whereof all things were made, is infinite or eternal, you must consider that matter cannot subsist without form nor put on form without the action of some cause, and this cause must necessarily exist before it could endue matter with form, since what has no being cannot act; and if this cause existed before matter, then matter itself could not be eternal, for that cannot be eternal before which another did exist. We must then after all be forced to acknowledge that there is one supreme, infinite, eternal Being, from whom the world and all things therein contained received their being; and this supreme, eternal Being is God!

E.   But though the world could not make itself, and though it be not eternal, yet might it not be made by chance? I have heard of a sect of philosophers that believed all things were reduced into the order we now behold them by a "fortuitous concourse of atoms."[18] That the various innumerable particles of which this world is composed, being in a vigorous motion, did at last by a lucky hit strike on this goodly system of beings. Now, pray, what have you to object against this notion?

M.   Some of the Epicureans did indeed profess to believe this; but I very much question whether they did really believe it for all that. If they did, if there was such a position held among them, it was certainly the most wild and irrational notion that ever entered into the minds of men. And shows the exceeding corruption and depravity of human nature, in that men will believe the most incongruous and impossible thing imaginable, rather than acknowledge the being of that God, from whose mere bounty they received their own.

But suppose for once that matter being in a vigorous motion should at last by a lucky hit, as you call it, give the various and almost innumerable forms to the several parts thereof; yet still the difficulty would recur. For whence was that first matter itself or who inspired it with that motion? It is in its own nature purely passive and therefore can have no principle of motion in or from itself. And if it had existed from eternity, yet still that would not alter the case; for it must have continued to eternity in its pristine state, if there had not been some Superior Power to put it in motion. What can we say then but that there is a God that created matter and inspired it with motion? Since, to suppose motion without a mover or anything to be effected without an active cause, contradicts the general reason of mankind and may justly be pronounced impossible.

Again, if all things were formed by chance at first, how comes it to pass that we see no such wonderful effects of chance now? We now observe a fixed and unalterable rule, a certain admirable method in the production of all things. Did chance appoint the various seasons of the year, and the alternate vicissitudes of day and night? What almighty power and wisdom must we ascribe to this blind cause, if we suppose it able to form the heavenly bodies, those stupendous globes of light, or to contrive their just positions and regular motions? Does chance sustain the earth, which hangs suspended like a ball in the air? Or did that bound the sea within certain limits and make its barriers of weak sand, which prevent it from overflowing the earth, notwithstanding the impetuous violence of its waves? Observe but the vegetable part of the world and tell me whether you think 'twas possible for chance to produce the admirable variety of trees, plants, flowers, and herbs. Can it be chance that causes the earth to bring them forth in their seasons and inspires them with that spark of life that is in them and disposes them to attract nourishment, to grow, increase, and seminate for the preserving themselves and their kind, not to mention their various virtues for food and medicine? 'Tis impossible to conceive this power in so stupid a cause, especially if we consider that the most powerful, the most learned and wisest of men are not able to create one single blade of grass, nay nor so much as to understand and clearly decipher the great varieties in the production, growth, and process of its short yet wonderful continuance.

Observe further the ordinary settled course of generation in animals. You do not see them spring out of the earth like mushrooms; but after such certain stated periods each species generate and produce their like. Nor does man generate man, or a sheep a lamb, as soon as they are brought into the world; but they get strength and vigor by degrees, for till they arrive at a due age, they cannot increase their kind. And as we see nothing but what doth arise from a mutual propagation from another, so all creatures propagate their kind by the same law; not as soon as they are brought forth, but in the interval of some time. Again, what is that which preserves the various species of animals entire and prevents unnatural mixtures, but the law of their great and wise Creator? Chance could never be the cause of such regular productions; nor could it ever endue the several kinds of animals with those curious instincts, by which each creature knows its food and how to avoid such things as would hurt or destroy them. All the brute creation, in working for an end unknown to themselves, do plainly demonstrate that there is a superior Power and Wisdom that directs and guides them in all their operations. For when things act regularly by a rule they know not, to an end they do not understand, and yet work together in the greatest harmony for the attainment of that end, we are compelled to acknowledge an infinite wisdom in the Supreme Cause that ranges all these inferior causes in the order we behold them and imprints on them the laws of their various motions according to their peculiar natures.

Order and harmony can never be the effects of chance. The motions of chance are contingent; but these are constant, uniform, and necessary. Nor will it suffice to evade the acknowledgment of a God, to ascribe all these wonderful effects to nature. For what is nature but the disposition of second causes? And a second proves a first, since the former could never have been but by the efficiency of the latter. Which way soever we turn we must be forced (if we act rationally) to own a First Cause of all things; nor can we possibly give any satisfactory or tolerable account of the world without it. 'Tis therefore the greatest folly imaginable to deny that which all creatures in their existence, constitution, usefulness, and harmony do so strongly assert.

And if there be such stupendous effects of wisdom and power in the lower rank of beings as surpasses the wit of man to discover fully, what shall we say of man himself, or how shall we account for his original without acknowledging the being of a God? If we do but take a view of his grosser part and attentively consider the exact proportions of a human body, we shall be forced to confess with the heathen Galen, that none but a God could make it.[19]

I will not take upon me to read you a lecture of anatomy, but shall only make some general observations, which yet may be sufficient to show that even the body of man bears the impress of infinite power and wisdom in the order, fitness, and usefulness of every part of it.[20] Indeed the whole model is grounded upon reason, every member hath an exact proportion, distinct office, and regular motion; yet all conspiring to make up one entire harmony amidst their diversity. Being all knit together by an admirable symmetry, they orderly perform their functions as acting by a settled law, none swerving from their rule, but in case of some predominant humour. Some parts of it are the organs of sense, some are for motion, some for preparing, others for dispensing, nourishment to the whole. It would be tedious to speak of each individual part; of the wonderful contrivance of the brain, the principal seat of sense, and source of those spirits which animate the whole body by means of the nerves, which take their original from thence. It is guarded outwardly by a skull to hinder ill accidents, and within by a strong membrane to prevent any oppression by the skull. Nor need I detain you long in contemplation of the mouth, though it is curiously framed for the reception of nourishment, wherein are placed two rows of teeth to rough-grind the meat and so prepare it for the stomach, where 'tis more easily digested. And lest the drink should mistake its way in that narrow passage through which it is to pass, the epiglottis is appointed to cover that other passage leading to the lungs by which we respire. Nor shall I speak of the heart, of its admirable position and uses; or of the offices of the liver, diaphragm, spleen, gall, and reins, etc. 'Tis sufficient to say that the wisdom which appears in any one of these (or indeed of any part of the body) is so great, that the dissection thereof would afford discourse to fill a volume. I shall confine my present observation to the organs of sense.

And, first, I would have you observe the noble fabric of the eye, which is placed in the head as in a watch tower, having the finest nerves, most soft for the reception of so many spirits as are necessary for the act of vision. Innumerable ideas enter this way to the soul, all which are represented to her, as it were, in a convex glass, made in an oval form, being most commodious to receive the various species of objects. See how 'tis provided with defence by the variety of coats to secure and accommodate the little humour and part whereby the vision is made. Shaded by the eyebrows and lids that are at once both its ornament and safety, which refresh it when too much dried by heat and prevent the insinuation of too great a light which would offend it, cleanse it from impurities by the quickness of their motion, preserve it from an invasion, and by contraction assist it to discern things more evidently that are at a distance.

Let us next consider the ear and observe how curiously 'tis formed with various turnings to prevent anything from entering that might offend the sense. By this organ the soul makes observation of sounds, which beat upon the drum as they pass through those hollow caverns, wherein is placed the finest echo in the world.

The sense of smelling is likewise of admirable use, and the organ of this sense is not only ornamental, but is also used as a sluice to drain the head of those superfluous humors that would otherwise oppress the brain. Besides 'tis an inlet to such odours as exceedingly comfort and refresh the spirits.

Nor is the sense of feeling of less regard than the former, which is not confined to any single part, but diffused through the whole body. By this power the soul sits like an Arachne in the midst of her loom and is aware of all motions that are made in it, and is awakened by every new impulse to stand upon her guard.

I shall not stay to discourse upon the amicable conjunction of heat and moisture, of the exact temperament of the several juices, or of the multitude of spirits that act in every part. Not the least or most inconsiderable thing in this wonderful machine is made in vain; but the whole symmetry of the body is a worthy object of our contemplation. Each member bears a signature of omnipotent Wisdom, which is visible to every attentive considerer in the formation and beauty of the parts and vigour of the whole. Now who but a fool could think or say that the eye was not made to see, the ear to hear, the tongue to speak, the hands to take hold of things, or the feet to walk, but that each of them being accidentally fitted for such purposes, we use them accordingly? Or who can be so stupid as to imagine that so glorious a fabric, wherein appear the most exquisite art and contrivance, is a work of blind contingency? Could we clearly perceive the successive methods of generation by which the embryo is formed in the womb, and discern how the first designs of the foetus is laid in its warm receptacle, impregnated with the prolific virtue of both sexes, and further observe how many dissimilar parts arise from those small principles, which are joined together in an accurate symmetry without any visible artist attending such excellent operations? What could we imagine but that a God is near, who says, "Grow there a bone, spring here a vein, let this be a heart, etc.?"[21]

But after all, should we grant that this noble fabric was the work of chance, that 'twere possible for a fortuitous concourse of atoms to provide all these wonderful effects, yet how must we account for spiritual substances, such as the souls of men?[22] Whence had they their being? Or how was gross, dull unactive matter disposed and modified to give them existence? What is this reasoning principle we bear within[23] us? Or by what means does it check, control, and govern our outward senses, if it hath not a power superior to matter? Nothing can impart that perfection to another, that it wanteth itself. And since upon the most exact scrutiny we can possibly make into the qualities and properties of matter, we find it utterly void of reason and judgment, we must conclude that it could not possibly be the original of those excellent powers in the mind of man.

E. If there be in man an immaterial substance which we call soul, this last argument for the being of a God must be acknowledged to be unanswerable. But here the learned differ. Some have denied that the soul is a spiritual substance: and others tell us that brutes have as much understanding[24] as we, only they want speech and therefore cannot express their sense in words as men do.

M. To the first part of your objection I shall give this short and plain answer. If the soul of man hath perception, reason, and judgment and can exert these powers in operating about things invisible and remote from sense, if it be capable of knowing many things without the help of sensitive images, then it necessarily follows that it must be a substance different and distinct from body, and what is not body, is spirit. Body, which is mere matter, has not the power of thinking or reasoning;

or if it had that power, it could think only of such things as are made of matter like itself. But it is manifest that the soul is capable of reasoning and judging of things spiritual, that is, of things which have no signatures in matter, and are not ideas of corporal beings derived through our senses or excited in us by the impresses of bodily motion. Such are our ideas of pure intellect, of the ever-blessed God, angels, etc. And I dare challenge the whole world to give a reasonable account how the notion of a God or any other spirit ever entered into the minds of men if there were neither God or other spirit in being. For 'tis an evident truth that such ideas could never take their rise from anything material.[25] I might add innumerable species of reason, the reflex acts of the mind, all our abstracted ideas; notions of moral good and evil, knowledge of truth, simple and complex, of the object and the subject.

E.   I humbly beg pardon for interrupting you. But pray why did you say that 'tis an evident truth that the ideas of God and other spirits could never take rise from anything material?

M.   Because were there no God or spirit, nothing but material beings in the world, then all our ideas or notions could only be an effect of matter moving and reacting,[26] and so our most sublime reasoning could arise no higher than imagination; which imagination can work upon the soul only by corporeal ideas, that is, by those images formed in the brain according to those various impressions which are made upon the organs of sense by the impulses of outward objects. But since 'tis plain that the soul hath a notion of a God and of other spirits, and no such notion or idea could be conveyed to her by any instrument of sense, since 'tis impossible for the imagination to receive an idea of an immaterial substance, for all such ideas are purely spiritual, it is as plain that there are such things as spiritual substances, and such notions are formed in her by the innate power of an immaterial principle reflecting on her own nature and properties.

E.   But has not the soul power to collect several simple ideas together and by compounding them raise an idea of a thing that never was in nature? As suppose I take the idea of a horse, eagle, and fish, and joining these simple ideas together, imagine that I see before me an animal with a head like an eagle, a body like a horse, and[27] a tail like a fish: now will anyone conclude from this wild imagination that there must necessarily be such a creature in the world?

M.   Not to observe (though it may be very material) that all these ideas are objects of sense, I must tell you your objection answers itself; and while you would evade my argument, you do unwittingly prove the soul to be immaterial. For pray tell me how she doth or can collect the representation of sense and from simple raise compound ideas, unless she does it by virtue of her own spiritual powers? The eye may see a horse, and so by that means the idea of a horse may be conveyed to and painted in the imagination; but neither the eye [n]or fancy is capable of judging of this idea. 'Tis the soul perceives the form, judges of its colour and proportion and knows it to be a horse. Nor does she only collect the representations of sense, compare and order the great variety of simple ideas that float in the imagination, but she can likewise form apprehensions of things very contrary to those that are conveyed to her by the organs of sense. Yet she does not say that either the senses or imagination is deceived, for she knows that they only represent their own passions, which are really such as they seem to be. But it knows withal that it would be deceived itself if it always believed things to be as they are represented by the sense or imagination. When the eye beholds a stick half under water, it is pictured in the imagination as crooked; but the soul, knowing that the representations of the sense which are carried to the brain by corporeal motion are without judgment, pronounceth the stick to be straight. So likewise when a man in a boat passes swiftly on water, the eye represents to the imagination the images of earth and trees by the river side moving from the man with equal swiftness. But the soul of the man, which hath a power superior to matter, cannot be so imposed on by the rapidity of corporeal motion and therefore knows that 'tis the boat and man which moves and that the earth and trees stand still.

Thus much is sufficient to prove that the soul is a spiritual substance and that its powers are distinct from and superior to matter. What you would insinuate about beasts does not really deserve a serious answer. And I fancy that any man that is of that senseless opinion would think himself highly affronted to be told that he has no more understanding than an ass or a parrot. Yet I would speak a few words in answer to this also.

It is very true that brutes have admirable properties and instincts given them by the wise God of nature for good and very useful ends. And such of them as are more immediately serviceable to man, as horses, dogs, etc., are more docile and have quicker perception than others. But still all this comes far short of reason, inasmuch as their perceptions and instincts are always confined to the present objects of sense. Nor can we discern that they make reflection on what is past or are solicitous about the future. But man has a great comprehension, a large scope and prospect of the whole universe and takes within his verge[28] as well things past and to come as present. Nor doth he only consider things simply as they lie severally before him, but compares them together, judges of their natures, properties, qualities, mutual respects and influences, etc. And by means of these observations he infers, deduces, concludes, forms general maxims, brings things into order and method, and so raises arts and sciences. All which are the acts of a spiritual being and above any power we could observe in brutes. From whence we must be forced to conclude that man's nature is far superior to theirs and that he was created for higher and more excellent purposes than they.

Furthermore, if we observe the perpetual and universal subjection of the brute creation to man, we may from thence infer that the nature of man must be superior to theirs; otherwise 'twould be hard to conceive how he hath for so long a time preserved his sovereignty. Or why, if brutes have understanding, are they not conscious of their strength, and if conscious of their strength, how comes it to pass that they so long and tamely submit to man without once endeavouring to shake off his yoke? They have the powers[29] of sense in greater perfection than man; and if they had reason to govern those powers and were capable of entering into combinations of forming designs and of using arts and stratagems for compassing such designs, it is impossible to conceive but they might ere now have found some way to communicate their thoughts to each other, though they wanted speech, and that at some time in some age of the world they might have outwitted him and found[30] means to free themselves from the tyrannous usurpations of men.

To sum up all in few words. Since the world could not make itself, because nothing can act before its existence, and since it plainly appears that it is not eternal, by its being made up of finite parts which are in their nature mutable, limited and corruptible; since 'tis as plain that it could not be the work of chance, as appears by the beauty, order and usefulness of the constituent parts and the admirable harmony of the whole, by the law of nature, which is constantly though unwittingly observed by all the vegetable and brute creation, by the exquisite art and contrivance that appears in the formation of the human body, and, what is still of greater regard, by the certainty we have that there are spiritual, immaterial substances, abstracted from and superior to matter, which could never be produced by chance or a fortuitous concourse of atoms; therefore I conclude that there is one Supreme Being who is a pure Spirit and comprehends within himself all perfection of being, which is the Cause of all causes, the Creator, Preserver and Governor of all things, and this Being is God![31]

Have you anything further to object?

E.   No. For though I really did never doubt the being of God, yet if I had questioned it, you have, I think, said enough to prove his existence. As I remember, the perfection of God is next in order to be discoursed of. Be pleased therefore to proceed.

M.   From what hath been already said, 'tis easy to collect that God is a being infinitely and absolutely perfect! For if he be the first, the original Cause of all things, he must necessarily by way of eminence possess whatever powers or virtues he has bestowed on his creatures, since he could not give that to another which he wanted himself.

E.   This I can easily apprehend. But so much depends on our having a just and clear notion[32] of God, that I must humbly entreat you to explain his nature more fully, what he is and wherein the perfection you speak of consists, that I may be better able to form my conceptions aright, since such a general notion cannot be supposed to have much influence on practice.

M.   I must here answer you as once our Lord did two of his disciples in another case: "You know not what you ask."[33] All the angelic and human nature, if united in one mind, would fail in power to define his infinite perfection! **God only knows what God is!**[34] Nor can he be said otherwise to comprehend himself than that nothing in his essence or nature is hid from or unknown to him. I must freely own I am of all others the most unfit and unworthy to speak on this boundless subject! I cannot so much as think of it but I feel my understanding confounded and overwhelmed with the least perception of his majesty and glory! And I am never at so great a loss for words as when I endeavour to express the little and imperfect sense I have of God so clearly as to be well understood by those I speak to. We know but very little of our own nature; how then shall we presume to speak[35] of his that created all things, that infinitely transcends our most sublime apprehensions, who dwells in inaccessible light, unto which no man can approach![36]

Yet since one of the first dictates of natural religion is that we ought to worship and adore the Author of our being, that you may not pay your devotions to an unknown God, I shall endeavour as well as I'm able to assist you in your conceptions of that almighty Being.[37]

God is one pure essence! Fullness, perfection of being! Self-existent, necessary, infinite, eternal! Comprehending in his most blessed nature all the perfection a spirit is capable of! Such as power, wisdom, justice, goodness, truth, holiness, immutability, etc. He is whatever is great or good! Glory! Perfection in the abstract! Absolutely separated from all moral evil, from whatever pollution can possibly defile a spirit! In a word he is being itself! [38]

All these perfections, or to speak more properly, this his glory and perfection, is easily inferred, or rather demonstrated from his being the Creator of the universe. His unity is plain from his infinity! For 'tis impossible there should be more than one infinite being; his self-existence, from his giving being to all things! For if he created all things, he himself must exist before anything else had being. Consequently he must be necessary, self-existent, eternal!

E. I don't well understand what you mean by the infinity of God; therefore desire you would explain that word to me.

M. 'Tis impossible for me so to explain that term as to give you an adequate conception [39] of what is above the brightest created mind to conceive. Finite can never comprehend infinite. There are no words in ours, nor in all the languages on earth whereby to express infinity. I said before that God is pure essence! Being in general! Which includes his infinity, indeed, all that can be said of him! Whatever glory we ascribe to him, as power, wisdom, justice, goodness, truth, and holiness, are not in him distinct powers or virtues acquired and superadded to his essence, but are his very essence itself! Therefore, though we often call him a wise, a powerful, a holy, a just God! Yet if we would speak properly, we should say he is Wisdom! Power! Justice! Goodness! Truth! Etc. For God is one! And those [40] perfections [which] [41] we attribute to him under various appellations are [42] one and the same perfection in God! Distinguished only by several operations on different subjects, all perfection being exerted in every act of the Almighty Mind!

I mean, then, by the infinity of God that his being, his essential perfection is immense! That is, without bounds or limits! His power inexhaustible! His knowledge, wisdom, goodness, etc. absolutely perfect!

Each created being has a certain sphere of activity assigned by its Creator, beyond which it cannot act. But almighty power can effect what it pleaseth by willing it should be done! Therefore we justly style him Omnipotence! So he gave being to all things that are: the heavens and earth, the whole system of spiritual and material beings he called from nothing into actual existence by one pure act of his Almighty Will!

His knowledge is infinite in that he knoweth himself, the boundless perfection of his own essence! He fully understands his power, and whatever is possible to be effected by it, though those possibilities should never spring up into actual being. By knowing his own will he knoweth whatever hath been, is, or shall be executed or brought into being by it. All things that do actually exist he knows by his pure essence, that is, he sees their natures in the ideas of his own mind and the event of things in the decree or permission of his own will. Whatever things he is pleased to appoint, dispose, and execute, he views in their first original causes. He knows them in his power as the physical principle and in his will as the moral principle, as some have expressed it. [43] Thus, he did as in a mirror behold in his pure intellect the various innumerable substances and forms of all things! Their several powers, relations, etc., ere they existed in the universe, or they had never had a being. As God knoweth all things by one simple comprehension of their causes in himself, so he knoweth them distinctly, independently, and eternally by one pure act of intuition! Not by discourse and reasoning,[44] by deducing one thing from another, and from common notions drawing rational conclusions as men do, whose knowledge is successive, being bounded by the measure of their being and capacities, insomuch that it cannot extend itself in an instant to a number of objects so as to make a distinct application of them. But he, by one simple act without any motion doth universally and eternally behold all things which we call past, present, and future! All the various lines drawn from the centre of his will to the circumference of his creatures.[45]

E.   But if God knoweth all things by a simple comprehension of their causes in himself, is he then the cause or author of evil?

M.   If you well considered what is evil, you would not ask that question. We call many things evil that are in their own nature indifferent, but accidentally become evil to us by reason of some circumstances attending them or from the imperfection of our present state or some acquired habit which makes such things necessary to our well-being which, but for that habit, would not be so. And the want of those things men commonly think the greatest evil. Of these I shall here say nothing; 'tis sufficient for the present purpose to speak somewhat of what we call natural and moral evil, which includes whatever is really evil in itself. All evil properly speaking has no positive being. Natural evil is a defect of being, a privation of something necessary to that perfection of being in any creature which God in creation assigned to that species. Of this kind are the diseases, blemishes and defects in the body, such as want of sight, hearing, etc. Moral evil is also a defect; 'tis a privation of the rectitude due to an act. God, when he created man, gave him a just and holy law, which was designed as a rule of action for every individual of human nature. And any voluntary deviation from this rule in thought, word, or action is moral evil. Of either of these evils God cannot possibly be the cause or author. All his works are in number, weight, and measure most perfect! And 'tis impossible they should be otherwise; for the infinite perfection of his power, wisdom, and goodness permits not that anything maimed or imperfect should proceed immediately from God. Nor is it more possible he should be the cause of moral evil, since holiness is his very essence! And were he capable of doing anything morally evil, he could not be infinite purity; consequently he could not be God.

Some have questioned whether God could have so much as any knowledge of evil, because of the absolute perfection of his nature. But this is altogether unreasonable. Indeed I cannot see how evil formally taken can have a distinct conception in the mind, by reason 'tis a privation, and all knowledge is by the apprehension of some being. But then the subject of evil hath a being, and so has a conception. And though what hath no being cannot be known by or in itself, yet it may be known by its contrary. As we know darkness to be a privation of light and folly to be a privation of wisdom. Whoever knows one contrary, knoweth the other.

Others have made it a matter of dispute how God knoweth evil, whether by its opposition to created or uncreated goodness. But this enquiry I think vain and needless. To be sure, he knows it as opposite to created goodness; but he knows it also radically by his own essential goodness. He is the fountain of being and in his being so hath a foundation in himself to know any defect in each degree of being he at first imparted to his creatures. He is the origin of man and endued the reasonable soul with all her powers, knoweth the extent of them and what they are able to effect. He gave man a law to direct and regulate those powers and therefore can't possibly be ignorant of man's deviation from the righteous law he hath given him. In a word God's knowledge is boundless as his essence.

Knowledge is the foundation of wisdom, antecedent to it, and separable from it in man, being seated in the speculative understanding, as wisdom is in the practical. Now because we conceive of God in a manner agreeable to our own nature, we are wont to consider [46] knowledge and wisdom as two distinct perfections in God, though really they are not so. For as the sun melts some things, hardens others, makes some things black, others white, produceth contrary qualities in different subjects, yet is it but one and the same quality in the sun which is the cause of those different productions, [47] so the perfections of God, though they seem to be divers [48] in our conceptions, are one and the same in him! All his operations proceeding from one pure essence!

We may define the knowledge of God to be his most perfect comprehension of, and his understanding, all things! [49] And the wisdom of God, his skillful designing and acting all things! 'Tis that intellectual power in him which directs all his operations to the best and most noble end! [50] Forming, fitting, and disposing all things for attaining that end by the most proper and worthy means that can be! I have already observed that this divine attribute is eminently conspicuous in the works of creation! And 'tis by the same almighty wisdom [51] that God preserves and governs the creatures he has made! As he hath a distinct and certain knowledge of whatever has been effected by his omnipotence, so he hath an infallible wisdom which is the rule that guides and directs the manner of his actions! Nor can the experience of so many ages in the government of the world add anything to the immensity of it! But he eternally hath been and will be original, essential, universal wisdom! [52]

E.   As I remember, the next thing mentioned is the justice of God! And here I desire you'd be pleased to tell me what justice is; for I think I have not a clear notion of it.

M.   Justice is commonly defined by the masters of morality to be a desire to render all their due and is usually distinguished into two kinds, distributive and commutative. [53] Distributive justice is an exact and impartial dispensation of rewards and punishments, a due retribution to every man according to his deserts, good or bad. This is properly the justice of a magistrate and judge or any superior towards their dependents in some measure.

Commutative justice is common to all men and respects all their civil contracts and dealings with each other. 'Tis acting honestly, keeping promises, and using plainness, sincerity and truth in all our words and actions.

All kinds of justice are [54] in God! Or rather he is justice itself! But we may consider it in him, first, as inherent. And then it is the absolute rectitude of his nature [55] wherein all perfection is infinitely exact and regular, so that no one divine attribute does invade the property or restrain the exercise of another!

Secondly, with respect to his creatures. And here also as supreme Lord and Governor of the world his distributive justice is perfectly exact and impartial, utterly incapable of corruption and prejudice! And though it does not always appear in full lustre in this present life, where the methods of providence are sometimes very involved and intricate, far beyond the reach of our apprehensions, and there seems to be an unequal dispensation of what we usually call the good things of this world, yet since 'tis absolutely impossible for the judge of all the earth to act unrighteously,[56] 'tis a strong presumption that a time will come wherein all things shall stand in their proper light; and divine justice will be plainly and fully manifested to angels and men by an impartial distribution of rewards and punishments according as men's lives have been good or bad.

Of the other branch of justice I need say nothing here, because 'twill be necessary to speak of it in another place.[57] I shall therefore proceed to the goodness of God!

E.   Pardon my interrupting you, but before you proceed farther, give me leave to say that I humbly conceive the definition of justice is not full and clear. For both in distributive and commutative justice, 'tis insufficient only to desire to do justly. We should actually render all their due, or we cannot be accounted righteous before God.

M.   The definition is just and good, being grounded on a true observation of the present state of mankind. Man is here considered as an imperfect impotent creature under the direction and government of divine providence. And let his desire or will be never so just, it often happens that he has not power to manifest the justice of his heart and intentions to the world. And where this is the case, his virtue is absolved in the desire and resolution of his soul and is doubtless accepted of God, who knoweth what he would do if he were able. I shall illustrate this by a familiar instance. Suppose two men indebted to a third for a considerable sum of money. Before the assigned time of payment the one, either by loss at sea, fire or some other calamitous accident, is rendered utterly incapable of discharging the debt and is compelled to break his word. The other, having it in his power, keeps his promise and satisfies his creditor. In this case, though the one was more fortunate, none can say but the other might be full as just.

If ever it please God to inspire our souls with a love of justice, and we heartily desire to render all their due, we certainly shall do it if it be in our power. But if any man say that he desires to do justly and in those instances wherein he has it in his power to act justly he does not do so, 'tis plain, let him pretend what he will, his desire is not sincere, his heart is not just.

E.   But how does this[58] affect the magistrate? Can he be supposed to want power? And therefore he is strictly obliged to execute impartial justice in the place wherein he is fixed.

M.   Most certainly the magistrate is obliged to strict and impartial justice. And so is each individual of the community in their respective stations. But it may so happen that he likewise may want power, as in the case of popular tumults and insurrections, wherein it hath fallen out that he has been compelled to suspend the course of justice till such tumults have been quieted. Justice is a moral virtue and as such is seated in the heart or mind. But the power of rendering this virtue conspicuous to the world belongs chiefly to God,[59] who disposes all events. There is one part of justice too much neglected, which yet is rarely out of our power to practice, and that is speaking justly and truly of all men. This, if seriously considered, would teach us to use more advertence in what we speak (nay, and think, too) than we commonly do. For 'tis certain we may really be as unjust in our thoughts and words as in our actions. But 'tis time to return from this digression.

E.   Be pleased then to define the goodness of God.

M.   There are several sorts or kinds of goodness. Simple being is good, and there is a goodness of being which is the natural perception of a thing. And in this sense God's goodness comprehends all his divine attributes. But what we call the goodness of God[60] in distinction from his other glorious perfections I take to be, first, inherent, secondly, communicative and relative.[61]

The first I humbly conceive to be that perfection of God whereby he loveth himself and hath an infinite delight and complacency in his own excellence and blessedness![62] But as it stands in relation to others, 'tis that whereby he delights in the works of his omnipotence,[63] and hath an inclination to deal well and bountifully with them[64] out of a desire that each individual should be happy according to the measure of its capacity and the rank it holds in the order of beings.

E.   But how could there be any relative or communicative goodness in God when there was no creature in being?

M.   Whatever is in God was in him from eternity! His essence, as it is infinite, contains all degrees of being or is endued with all possible perfection! And so he hath in himself the perfection of all other beings, whereby he becomes the representative of them all. And though all creatures began to be, and there was a time when nothing actually existed but God,[65] yet the simple essences of things are eternal and did always exist, not in their natural subsistencies, but in the divine intellect! And as all simple essences had their ideal existence in God before they were in rerum natura,[66] so the same habitudes, respects and relation[s] that attend them and the same beneficent disposition in God towards them did after the same manner eternally exist! The external[67] effluxes of divine goodness began in time, but the principle is eternal! But besides these metaphysical entities there were certain actual communications of the divine goodness from eternity! Hence the eternal generation of the Son of God,[68] to whom the Father communicated the fullness of the Godhead from eternity!

As relative goodness in the notion[69] of it is nothing else but a strong inclination to communicate or do good (which implies diffusiveness), so from this pure fountain of uncreated goodness all creatures derive their being! God did not make the world because he had need of it. His essential glory and blessedness is utterly incapable of access or diminution! Nor is it possible for finite creatures to add anything to infinite perfection! 'Twas therefore to manifest and not increase his glory that he imparted being and happiness to his creatures! Being itself is good, as was said before, and of this common good all things partake, as well the smallest vegetable and most despicable insect as the brightest angel. But then there are as many degrees of good as there are of being. For though God hath liberally conferred on every creature the best being it was capable of in that station and order, and conducing to that end and use in the world he designed it for, yet some beings have greater perfection and far more noble and excellent natures than others. Herbs, plants and flowers are good as they answer the end of their creation in exhibiting the power, wisdom and goodness of God! But being void of sense and having no knowledge of their own virtues and usefulness, they are equally incapable of happiness or misery. Animals hold the next degree of being in the scale of nature. And as they are endowed with the powers of sense, so their bountiful Creator hath provided for each sense its proper object[70] in the enjoyment of which they find a happiness suitable to their natures. But they, not being conscious of those powers nor capable of other pleasure than what animal life can afford, partake not so largely of the divine bounty as man, to whom the almighty Lord hath imparted not only the powers of life and sense but hath after an inexplicable manner to a beautiful body united a spirit[71] of an immortal nature, endued with all spiritual powers, little inferior to the angels![72] For the whole system of matter, however modified and disposed into celestial or terrestrial bodies, is not comparable to the lowest mind or spirit, because spirit is capable of the knowledge of all things, whereas matter is utterly stupid and insensible. But the divine goodness to man extends yet farther. It hath not only vouchsafed to give him an immortal spirit,[73] but hath also created him in his own image of moral goodness,[74] whereby he is rendered capable of divine life and blessedness. For though spirit be superior to body, yet the whole system of intellectual powers is not fit to be opposed in value to the lowest degree of moral goodness or virtue![75]

Can you remember what divine attribute we are to speak of next?

E.   I think it is truth.

M.   You are in the right. 'Tis so. And here I don't think 'tis necessary to trouble you with the various acceptations[76] of the word truth, but shall with much brevity consider this perfection as we may humbly conceive it is in God!

E.   But if 'twas not too great trouble to yourself, I would be gladly informed of the nature of truth in general, because I don't well understand it.

M.   Although these digressions take up more time than I can well spare, yet in as few words as I can I will tell you what I know of it.

Truth hath commonly been distinguished into two parts, truth of the object and truth of the subject. Truth of the object is again divided into simple and complex truth. Simple truth is that whereby everything is what it is, which some call transcendental truth or verity and runs through the whole circle of beings. Truth of the object complex is certain habitudes[77] and relations of things one towards another, whether affirmatively or negatively, which did necessarily and eternally attend them in their ideal subsistences[78] and are inseparable from them in their actual existence.

Truth of the subject is likewise divided into two parts. First, a due conformity between the understanding and the object, when we think of things as they really are, which is logical truth. Secondly, an exact conformity or agreement between the understanding and the words, when we speak as we think, which is moral truth.

E.   Pray give me leave to interrupt you a little. For though I can apprehend truth of the object simple, yet I have not a clear notion of the object complex, of the habitudes and relations of one thing towards another, which you say are inseparable from them and are eternal and immutable.

M.   I think the one as easy to be understood as the other. For can anything be plainer than that there is a certain habitude between some premises and some conclusions?[79] For anything will not follow from anything. That there is certain habitude and relation between some ends and some means, some objects and some faculties, and the like?[80] Nor can it be denied that some habitudes are constant and immutable and, having never been made, they can never be unmade but are independent on any understanding or will whatever. The direct consequence of which is that there are necessary and eternal truths.

E.   I wish you'd be pleased to give me some instances of those truths that are necessary and eternal.

M.   Abundance of instances might be given of truths that are so; but 'tis sufficient to justify the assertion to mention only some few propositions of eternal verity that cannot possibly have an arbitrary dependence on any will or understanding whatever. As in logic, that the cause precedes the effect in order of nature. In physics, that all local motion is by succession. In metaphysics, that nothing can be and not be at once. In mathematics, that parallel lines can never meet or come nearer each other. These truths are necessary and eternal.

E.   But I think some have held that all truths have an arbitrary dependence on the speculative understanding of God! And that he does not understand a thing to be so, because it is so in its own nature, but that a thing is therefore so, because God is pleased so to understand it.[81]

M.   Some have indeed advanced such a position, but 'tis so monstrously absurd, and such a train of mischievous consequences follow it that wise and sober men generally reject it.[82]

E.   Is then Plato's notion of abstract essences true? And may we suppose there ever were any such things as universal natures, subsisting eternally by themselves, separate from a divine Being and all other particular beings? That a man, a beast, a bird, a tree, etc., did eternally exist according to which pattern all things were made?[83]

M.   Though this is not much to the purpose, yet I must tell you that I believe Plato was a wiser man than to entertain any such notion; but he, like other great men, hath been misunderstood and abused. I don't suppose he ever meant more by his ideas than that the exemplars and ideas of all created beings did eternally exist in the divine intellect! Which I think everyone believes as well as he. But the other opinion you mentioned just before, that all truths have a dependence on the speculative understanding of God[84] is well answered and the matter set in a true light by Dr. Rust, Dr. More (if I mistake not) and after them by Mr. Norris, which is as follows.[85]

They consider the divine mind as conceptive and exhibitive. By the mind of God exhibitive they mean the essence of God as thus, or thus imitable or participable[86] by any creature, which is the same with what they call an idea. By the mind of God conceptive they tell us is meant a reflex act of God's understanding upon his own essence as exhibitive or thus imitable! Now 'tis very certain that the divine understanding as conceptive or speculative does not make but suppose[s] bits object, as all speculative understanding does; and the truth of the object is not to be measured by the understanding of God speculative, but the truth of his understanding speculative with its conformity with the object. But if we consider the divine understanding as exhibitive! Then its truth does not depend on its conformity with the nature of things, but on the contrary the nature of things depends upon its conformity with the divine understanding exhibitive! For the divine essence is not imitable because such things are in being, but such things are in being because the divine essence is thus, and thus imitable. For had not the divine essence been thus imitable, it had been impossible for such and such things ever to have had a being. But I shall proceed to speak something of truth, as it is one of the glorious attributes of the great and blessed God! And as such I shall consider it, first, as 'tis an intellectual, secondly, a moral perfection: a perfection of the understanding and a perfection of the will.

The understanding is the highest and most noble power or faculty of the human soul! Truth is the object of it. Knowledge, which is nothing else but an exact agreement between the idea in the understanding and the object (which in other words is truth of the subject), is the proper business or employment of that sublime faculty. Amidst the various degrees of human understanding that is justly accounted the best that hath the largest comprehension and most clear perception of truth of the object simple and complex and that can with the greatest facility apprehend things as they really are. But notwithstanding the action of the mind is so quick that its successive motions are oftentimes imperceptible, yet we know that it can't considerately attend to more than one perception at once. And though proportionable to the goodness of any understanding is its distance from ignorance and error, yet the brightest human understanding cannot comprehend all things and may err and does in fact rarely attain an adequate idea of an object even in view. Angels, who are not determined to such gross material vehicles as ours, may well be conceived to have all spiritual powers in greater perfection than we. But still their understandings are finite, consequently limited; yet is this comprehension and perception of truth vastly superior to ours.

But what are the understandings of all angels and men, could they be united in one mind, in respect of the understanding of God! In whom the original truth of all things does eternally exist! Or rather, who is himself the original Truth of all things! The brightness of such an understanding would not appear so great in his presence as the brightness of one spark when compared with the whole element of fire!

If we consider the divine understanding as exhibitive, his boundless mind comprehends distinctly and eternally the simple essences of all things with their several habitudes, respects or relations! Which is all truth of the object. And if we consider the understanding of God as conceptive, or reflecting on the multifarious ideas of his own exhibitive understanding, which contains within itself all degrees of actual or possible existence,[87] we shall easily perceive that there must necessarily be the most perfect and exact conformity between his speculative understanding and the thing objectively united to it! For truth of the subject is one species of being, as well as truth of the object. Let us therefore contemplate the perfection of the divine understanding under any view we shall find. 'Tis all pure light! Without the least mixture of shade! Absolutely incapable of ignorance or error!

Though there are many practical lessons to be learnt from the contemplation of truth as it is an intellectual perfection in God! Such as the highest estimation,[88] intense and fervent adoration, profound humility, a cheerful resignation of our own understanding to the[89] understanding of God! The effect of which will be a full and ready assent to those truths he hath been pleased to reveal, which are above our comprehension. Yet 'tis of as much, if not more, importance to us to study truth as it is a perfection of the divine will or a moral virtue in God!

The will is that faculty of the mind whereby we make our elections. That is, 'tis the power by which we prefer or choose one thing before or rather than another. And though truth be always an intellectual perfection, yet it must have the concurrence of the will to make it a moral virtue. Good, as good, is the proper object of this faculty, and under the notion of good, truth affects the will. And it is here to be considered as opposite to falsehood, as falsehood is a moral evil. And then we shall find that with these respects the perfection of the will consists in a strong, uniform and constant adherence to truth, preferring and choosing it in all possible instances, which implies an absolute and perfect aversation[90] from falsehood.

E.   Pray give me leave—I don't apprehend truth as a moral virtue in God.

M.   Where lies the difficulty? I'll ask you a few questions. Is there such a thing as the moral virtue of truth in any man? Or thus, is there any man that wills to act sincerely or speak truly, and accordingly does so as far as he is able?

E.   This cannot be denied.

M.   Does the sincerity of such a man's words and actions ever proceed from his love of truth (for love in this case is to considered as an affection of the will) or from what other cause?

E.   Though 'tis possible sometimes for a man to compelled to act and speak sincerely, yet certainly the world is not so bad but someone may be found in it that is sincere in his words and actions because he loves truth and is willing to be so.

M.   Very well. Then such a man's sincerity or truth is a moral virtue in him. Now if a man that hath it in his power to deceive, forbears to do it because he loves and wills to act and speak sincerely, let me ask you,[91] from whence did that man derive that will or power to prefer or choose truth rather than falsehood, since he did not make himself?

E.   To be sure he received it from God, who gave him being.

M.   God could not give man any powers or virtue that he wanted himself. So I need not say more, for you may plainly perceive you've answered yourself.

E.   I have indeed. But yet I'm not entirely satisfied; for methinks moral virtue must be a conformity to some law. Now God being the supreme Lord of all, who can give law to him?

M.   Himself! His own infinite perfection is the rule of his actions! And therefore he is said to act not only according to his will, but "according to the counsel of his own will!"[92] And herein consists the perfection and spotless integrity of the divine will, in that having no superior which might awe, impel, allure or persuade, so that all the motions thereof are absolutely free, yet is it ever under the direction of his infinite wisdom, justice and goodness! And so immutably bent towards or fixed on truth that 'tis impossible for him to err or swerve the least from the most perfect truth and purity in his elections, but he ever wills what is certainly and absolutely best! Nor is he capable of fraud or falsehood, which are diametrically opposite to his nature! And as it is impossible for him to be deceived, so 'tis as impossible for him ever to deceive!

E.   But I thought moral virtue had been a duty.

M.   Justice, goodness, purity, and truth as it respects the will, are moral virtues. The practice of these virtues in obedience to the command and law of God is duty. All moral laws have an antecedent foundation in the nature of God and man, as he was created in his image. For indeed, the moral law which was given to man is a transcript of the pure and blessed nature of God as far as it is imitable by us! And consequently the duties resulting from that law[93] are of perpetual obligation while there is a man in being. But to make the matter still plainer, we must first consider virtue as it is a moral perfection. Secondly, as it is a duty.

As virtue is a moral perfection, it consists in being voluntarily just, good, pure, true, etc.

As virtue is a duty, 'tis a voluntary practice of these or any other virtues in obedience to the law and command of[94] a superior Being.

Now virtue according to the first part of this distinction has its consummate perfection in God! But as 'tis a duty performed in obedience to the command of a superior Being, it neither has nor can have place in him who hath none above him! But if you have nothing more to object, I'll go on.

E.   I am fully satisfied as to this point. But if you please, I would know the reason of your saying that it is of as much if not greater importance to us to study truth as it is a moral virtue in God[95] than as it is an intellectual perfection in him!

M.   This question will be more properly answered when we come to discourse of revealed religion, and therefore I had rather not reply to it here.

E.   Pray follow your own method. And proceed to define the holiness of God[96] which is next in order.

M.   Holiness and purity are the same and signify in God a perfect simplicity of essence! Of all perfection of Being! A thing is said to be pure and simple when it is unmixed or uncompounded of contrary or different qualities. Thus we call gold pure that is refined from all alloy. The purity of God is so transcendent and sublime[97] that he is absolutely separated from all moral evil! From all things, as was said before, that can any way pollute or defile a spirit! Nor is holiness properly a distinct perfection in that most blessed Being! But rather, 'tis the supreme glory of his other attributes!

'Tis the glory of his power that it is perfectly holy! Hath no mixture of weakness! No capacity of being employed in any act of injustice, oppression or cruelty! But is ever under the conduct of his infinite wisdom, justice and goodness! His knowledge and wisdom are pure in that they are absolutely perfect! Unstained by ignorance and error, nor can possibly be applied to any end or use but what is infinitely best! His justice is holy because immutable and strictly impartial! Entire and above all corruption or prejudice! 'Tis the glory of his goodness to be pure! Free from interest and absolutely separated from whatever implies impotence or instability! 'Tis the glory of his truth to be eternal, simple, undisguised,[98] infinitely incapable of being polluted by guile and falsehood! In a word, he is holiness in the abstract! Every perfection in that all glorious Being is altogether simple! So incomprehensibly pure[99] that no words, nay, no thought can reach his immense simplicity! And to crown all, whatever perfection is in God is necessary, essential and by just consequence ever the same! Which leads to the last divine attribute I mentioned, namely, the immutability of God!

I've already observed that what is absolutely perfect can never change, but must be always the same. For all change denotes some imperfection in the subject and is wrought either by addition or subtraction.[100] But what can be added to the infinite fullness of God! What farther access of glory can there be to him that comprehends all degrees of being in his most perfect nature! And for the same reason nothing can be taken from him! For he that is all being and received not that being from himself or any other, but is necessarily and eternally what he is! As he can never change for the better, so neither can he change for the worse! Creatures may be made in some sense immutable by the power and favour of God, but as all things underwent a notable change once, when they passed from nothing into being, so they are still in their own natures capable of increase and diminution and may again be reduced to their original state of nothing by the same power that made them what they are. So 'tis more proper to say of the blessed angels and "the spirits of just men made perfect"[101] that they are unchanged, than immutable, because they are not immutable by nature, but by the sovereign grace of God. For it is the sole incommunicable privilege of the Deity to be immutable in and by his essence! In all perfection he only, by a blessed necessity of nature, is eternally the same! And in him "is no variableness, neither shadow of turning!"[102]

Thus I have, with as much brevity as I could, endeavoured to give you some (though a very imperfect) notion of the infinitely great and all glorious God! And from what has been said the inference is very just that a God of such immense perfection,[103] from whom we received our being and whatever we have that does any way render that being pleasing to ourselves or useful to others, hath a just right to our worship and service. And this is the foundation of all practical religion.

But how to worship and serve God after an acceptable manner is the grand inquiry, in which we ought to use the greatest application and seriousness, because our present and eternal happiness depends on a conformity to the will of our great Creator. Now in order to do the will of God 'tis necessary that we should know it. But we could not know it in our present state had it not pleased Almighty God to reveal his will unto us, what he would have us believe, what do, that we may so please and honour him as to enjoy his favour, the consequence of which I told you is eternal happiness!

E.   You seem to infer a necessity of divine revelation. Whereas some affirm that God in creation impressed a sense of good and evil, of his laws and man's duty, on the heart or mind of man. And from these innate ideas arises that universal consent of mankind in the being of a God, which they make one great argument for his existence.

M.   Far be it from me to endeavour to[104] invalidate any good argument that has been used to prove the being of God. But I've often thought that too much stress hath been laid on this, because I think a universal consent in this point is somewhat dubious and is more easily supposed than proved. Besides, if it could be proved, I see not the consequence that therefore there must be innate ideas or that the being of God is one of those innate ideas, if there be any. For since God hath given understanding to all men, now man that makes the least use of it can withhold his assent to the being of a God, it being, if not a self-evident, yet one of the most obvious truths in the world.[105]

E.   Are there then no principles of virtue or ideas connatural[106] with the soul of man?

M.   I do not think there are and could say somewhat to justify my opinion, but that I don't care to enter into any dispute about it. If people will believe there are such things, let them believe so.[107] Only this I shall observe by the bye, that there is a certain congruity between moral virtue and right reason. And though in the lapse of human nature reason was greatly impaired, yet it never was so totally lost but that sometimes even in bad men it will exert itself; and whenever it does so, this congruity is perceived which compels them often to approve the virtues they do not practice. And I am persuaded that such men's giving their suffrage sometimes[108] on the side of virtue hath induced others to believe that their approbation of virtue proceeds from some innate ideas they have of it, which they have not power to efface.

E.   What then is the meaning of that passage in the 2nd of Romans, 14–15: "For when the gentiles, which have not the law, do by nature the things contained in the law, these, having not the law, are a law unto themselves; which show the work of the law written in their hearts . . ."?[109] What is the law here spoken of, which the apostle says was written in the heart? And who does he mean by those gentiles? I think this text hath been often urged in favour of innate ideas or principles of virtue connatural with the soul of man.

M.   I have known this passage applied to the purpose you speak of, but I think without reason. For when God at first made man, he endued him with understanding, which consists of these three powers: perception, reason and judgment. And this understanding he gave as a law or rule of action to the whole human nature; and it is therefore called the great law or light of nature. There can be no doubt that this is the law which the apostle saith is written in the heart, it being indeed an essential part of man. St. Paul was speaking[110] here to the Jews, who valued themselves exceedingly on account of the Mosaic dispensation and thought it impossible for the uncircumcised gentiles to be saved. This vainglory he reproves and tells them that "God is no respecter of persons,"[111] but "as many as have sinned without law shall perish without law; and as many as have sinned in the law shall be judged by the law. For not the hearers of the law are just before God, but the doers of the law shall be justified."[112] For when the gentiles, which have not the written law, or law of Moses, perceiving by the light of nature the congruity between virtue and reason, do accordingly practice the moral duties required by the written law, these having not the law of Moses are yet a law unto themselves. And therein do greatly reproach you Jews that make your boast of the law and yet notwithstanding lead worse lives than those gentiles whom you despise and condemn for want of it.[113]

Most interpreters agree that those gentiles which the apostle says did "by nature the things contained in the law,"[114] were not the idolatrous gentiles, but such as lived before the law of Moses, as Melchizedek[115] and Job,[116] or were worshipers of the true God, as Cornelius,[117] or repented, as the Ninevites.[118] And I believe he did principally intend them, not excluding any other gentile that obeyd the dictates of reason. But then if any of the gentiles did indeed fear God and work righteousness,[119] I do humbly conceive they did not this by the mere light of nature without any direction or assistance of God's Holy Spirit, which was necessary to preserve them from the powers of "the world, the flesh and the devil."[120] And if God owned any of them as righteous, it was by virtue of their faith in him: that faith by which they believed "he is a rewarder of them that diligently seek him."[121]

E.   This shows, however, that divine revelation is not so absolutely necessary, but that 'tis possible for a man to be saved without it.

M.   'Tis possible for a man oppressed with heavy weight to walk over a narrow bridge in the dark without falling into the water. But what man in such a case would refuse a friendly guide that might secure his passage?[122]

Suppose once in an age there did appear a person of superior sense and learning that by the force of his genius and adverting to the dictates of his reason might endeavour to break through the evil customs of the world. Suppose Almighty God, when he beheld such a one struggling under the weight of his corrupt nature, did afford him some assistance of his Holy Spirit in composing his irregular appetites and passions and vouchsafe him such perceptions of himself[123] as enabled him to acknowledge and worship the true God! Yet what are a few such instances to the bulk of mankind? For one such soul, saved thus by way of prerogative,[124] perhaps many millions perished. Rare and exempt cases, wherein God is pleased to give extraordinary grace to some extraordinary persons, must not be insisted on or brought into computation with his ordinary dealings with the children of men.

I do not deny but that God, to whom all things are possible, may save a man without his having an explicit knowledge of Jesus Christ; but I think 'tis impossible for us to be certain whether he will do so or no. This we are sure of, that such a man must be saved (as before) by way of prerogative and not according to the stated method of salvation which God has established in his church. Faith and repentance are the conditions of salvation by Jesus Christ! But how 'tis possible for us to know what to believe or that (if we could repent) our repentance will be accepted in lieu of perfect obedience, unless God had revealed these things unto us, I cannot conceive. Christian religion, as distinguished from natural religion, is a complete system of rules for faith and practice, calculated for the present state of mankind. And 'twas necessary this religion should be revealed, because man had forgotten his God and was perfectly ignorant of himself. Nor was it in the power of human reason to discover it unto him;[125] and none but the Christian religion ever taught man the true knowledge of God and of himself. Ever represented the divine Being so awful, yet so amiable! So full of majesty and purity, yet so full of love and tenderness towards his creatures![126] 'Tis revelation has instructed us in the knowledge of our own condition, how human nature became corrupted and by what means 'tis capable of being restored to its primitive purity, and hath assured us of the certainty of future happiness, if we perform the conditions on which 'tis promised. We might in these matters study, project and propose, but 'tis hard trusting to nice and curious speculations when eternal misery is the consequence of a mistake.

E.   But pray then what is that natural religion which deists and free thinkers affirm to be sufficient to save us without any revelation?

M.   Those that in opposition to Christianity affect to call themselves by such names seem to me to have the least knowledge of natural religion of any men in the world; neither do they well understand what they say or whereof they affirm. I do very much question whether we should have known anything at all of natural religion, if it had not pleased God to afford us the light of the gospel. For in our corrupt state "such knowledge is too wonderful and excellent for us; neither can we attain unto it."[127]

I suppose their notion of natural religion is some kind of religion that they fancy we are capable of finding out and practicing by the mere light of nature without any divine revelation or assistance. But in truth had we no other than what that very dim and imperfect light could discover, and were we left to our own conduct without any direction and[128] assistance from above, the far greatest part of mankind would have no religion at all.

Natural religion is the religion of the genuine uncorrupted nature of man. The religion of Adam in paradise, while he remained under the conduct of right reason and exactly conformable to all the dictates thereof in "thought, word, and deed."[129]

I do humbly conceive that it consists in a sincere fervent[130] love of God, which presupposes all necessary knowledge of him. In an imitation of his divine perfections, as far as they are imitable and our limited powers will permit. And in a uniform impartial obedience to the whole will or law of God, which includes not only our duty towards him, but also our duty to ourselves and neighbour. But this pure religion Adam lost with his innocence; and as he was excluded paradise for his offence, so all his unhappy offspring are born out of it. Nor have we power to approach the tree of knowledge or any right to the tree of life[131] by virtue of the covenant God made with our first parents.[132] But all the power or capacity we have of attaining to the knowledge of God and ourselves, all the right we have to the tree of life (or eternal life) is only on account of the second covenant made in and by the Lord Jesus![133] Who united his divine person not to this or that particular man, but to the whole human nature. For which reason he is called the second Adam, or man in general, as the name Adam signifies. That "as in Adam all died, so in Christ all might be made alive."[134] I.e., as in or by the sin of the first Adam all men were brought into a state of mortality in danger of an endless separation from God with all the dreadful consequences thereof, so by the second Adam all men are brought into a salvable condition, may have the lapse of their nature cured and thereby become capable of enjoying God's favour and presence, the effects of which is life eternal!

E.   I wish you would be pleased to inform me of the difference between natural and revealed religion. And for what reason those people do so earnestly contend for the one while they reject the other?

M.   Do you think our Saviour taught any other than natural Religion? If you do, you are mistaken. For true religion, like Almighty God, the supreme object and author of it, is but one! Nor is there any essential difference between the religion of Jesus Christ and that of Adam in paradise. And one reason why deists and free thinkers contend for natural in opposition to revealed religion is because they don't understand it. All the ordinances and positive precepts of the gospel which have been thought sufficient to justify a distinction between natural religion and that revealed are in truth necessary[135] ways and means of religion, or a course of duties adapted to our present state for the purifying our natures and restoring us to that divine resemblance we lost in the lapse of our first parents. Again, they reject our blessed Lord, because he obliges them to observe greater strictness and purity of life than is consistent with those sensual pleasures they are unwilling to part with and to mortify that pride of nature which is wont to suggest that man is a law to himself and therefore need not be brought under subjection to the law of Christ, never considering that the rules of right reason are as severe as the precepts of the gospel, being in truth all one. Nor that 'twould be impossible for man in his present condition to live according to those rules, had it not pleased God by revelation to put him in the way and promised him the assistance of his Holy Spirit that he may be able to do it. For there's a mighty difference between man innocent and pure, endued with perfect knowledge of his duty and sufficient strength to perform it, and man fallen from a state of innocence, light and strength into a state of sin and misery, his understanding dark and perpetually subject to ignorance and error, his will impotent to the last degree, naturally averse from God and moral goodness, by consequence under the divine displeasure, and liable to suffer the sad effects thereof forever. But these things they do not apprehend, nor have they any sense of the depravity of human nature. For if they had, they would easily perceive that this inversion of nature necessarily requires a course of duties that were altogether needless in a state of innocence. That it was requisite there should be some way appointed to vindicate the honour and authority of God, to satisfy his justice for the violation of his laws, and means used to heal the lapse of human nature, in order to reconcile God to man and man to God. Since 'tis impossible for a creature guilty and impure to be capable of divine favour or to have any title to eternal life and blessedness. This therefore was the very end for which Jesus Christ was promised in paradise and in the fullness of time appeared in the world, namely, to vindicate the honour and satisfy the justice of God! To instruct us in the ways and means of healing the diseases of our nature; and to conquer in and for us those spiritual enemies which without him we could never overcome; and to give us a new and better title to eternal happiness. In a word, our Saviour came not to teach us a new, but to retrieve the old natural religion and to put us again under the conduct of right reason by the direction and assistance of his Holy Spirit. And if we do but bear in mind a constant sense of the present state of mankind, we shall plainly discern that the system of the gospel is a most noble and reasonable institution. All its precepts are pure and holy as the incarnate God that gave them! All the positive laws thereof are such as[136] directly tend to the healing and perfecting our nature! All the sanctions used to enforce them are weighty and proper to excite and work on reasonable free agents! The whole design is worthy of God! Agreeable to primitive human nature and finally conducive to God's glory! And the happiness of mankind!

E.   It seems by what has been said that the whole system of the gospel stands upon the supposition of the fall of man. But I think these gentlemen do not grant the authority of scripture, nor will allow human nature to be corrupted and depraved.

M.   What they will allow or grant I neither know nor care, since the truth of the fact is too obvious to be denied by any man of common sense. And let anyone otherways account for the prodigious contrarieties in human nature[137] and for our moral impotence and utter insufficiency for attainment of solid piety and virtue by our own strength, notwithstanding the congruity between virtue and right reason. We may plainly perceive[138] in our minds some faint ideas of a divine resemblance, a native principle of grandeur within us, directing us to despise a sensual life and aspire to a happiness beyond what the world can give. Yet at the same time we feel an innate concupiscence which subjects us to present things and renders us incapable and unworthy of that happiness. Insomuch that men, though by far the most noble and excellent, are yet the most despicable and wretched creatures of the visible creation. Excellent in their powers and capacities, despicable and wretched by the abuse of those powers and voluntary subjection of them to serve the propensions[139] and pleasures of the animal life. And indeed I can't conceive how a man that has made the least observation of mankind or reflection on his own mind and has withal a just sense of the absolute perfection of God[140] but he must acknowledge it was utterly impossible for that all glorious Being[141] to make man so corrupt and imperfect as he is. And this the wiser sort even of heathens were well apprised of, though how human nature became so depraved was beyond the power of their natural light to discover. Much less could we have known how that deadly wound might be healed, had not God of his boundless mercy revealed it unto us in the gospel of his Son!

E.   But did not they tell us that all the distempers of our minds might be cured by making a right use of our reason? And that reason, if not diverted by interest or passion, always tends directly to what is honourable and just?[142]

M.   Plutarch does indeed tell us so.[143] But what is this more than begging the question? For any man that will use his reason may know that reason itself is depraved and has as little liberty as any other power of the soul. This will evidently appear upon a sober advertence to the general conduct of the world. There we shall find that many have little or no understanding scarce enough to distinguish them from "the beasts that perish."[144] And oftentimes what we call reason in men of brighter parts is little better than fancy and conjecture. In truth very few make a right use of the small share of reason they enjoy, but men commonly act as much without, and oftentimes as contrary to, reason, as if they had none at all, even in the ordinary affairs of life, where one would think it should not fail them. And if we turn our eye inward and strictly observe the powers and motions of our own minds, we shall not much mend the prospect; for we shall quickly perceive that our own understanding is like that of our neighbours, weak and fallible. Unable to regulate and compose our roving desultory thoughts and fix them at pleasure or to apprehend and clearly discern between truth and falsehood, right and wrong, good and evil. Nor has our reason such power to direct and govern our passions as to reduce them to a true mediocrity,[145] insomuch that they shall never err either by excess or defect. And human reason is still at a greater loss to direct in matters of the highest importance and such whereon man's eternal happiness depends, even answering the end of our creation, worshipping and serving God after a manner acceptable to him.[146] This is plain by the practice of all those that have nothing to guide or govern them but what we call reason. By the old heathens, who notwithstanding they had a confuse[d] idea of some supreme being and that some honour ought to be given him, yet when they came to apply it to particulars, they ran into such idle and[147] ridiculous extravagancies as evidently showed they knew not what to do.

E. Ought we then to discard our reason from having anything to do in matters of religion?

M. By no means. For though it is of itself too weak and insufficient to direct us the way that leads to eternal life,[148] yet when enlightened and directed by God's Holy Spirit, 'tis of admirable use to strengthen our faith, and those are alike to blame that either idolize[149] or despise it. A little learning and study will serve to convince us that there are innumerable things which surpass the force of human understanding. Nor is it hard for an honest mind that is willing to know the truth to discern when reason ought to submit and when 'tis able to comprehend, where it should doubt and when it should rest assured. And if we would act reasonably, we shall neither stifle the principles of reason nor build too much upon them. For by doing the first, we make our religion childish and ridiculous; and by the other, we exclude all supernatural assistance and mysterious truths from it and thereby cut off all hope of salvation by Jesus Christ. As M. Pascal has well observed.[150]

E. But pray what do you mean by saying that 'tis not hard for an honest mind that is willing to know the truth, etc.? I don't understand what the will has to do in this case.

M. I say so because I'm of opinion that most errors in point of religion take their rise rather from the depravity of our wills than from defect of[151] understanding. We commonly choose one side of the question and then employ all our wit to find out a reason for doing so; and 'tis odds but we choose that side which seems most to favour our corrupt animality. Whereas we ought by all means, if we would know of any doctrine whether it be of God,[152] to endeavour first to correct the moral impotence and disinclination of the will to divine truth and throw that bias (of the will) on the side of virtue, which having done, we shall find a sensible alteration in the understanding. For then all things will appear in a different light, and we shall have other views than we had before. We shall have a better sense of spiritual objects and be able more clearly to perceive, reason and judge of moral truths than we were wont to do.

E. I believe it may sometimes be as you say. Yet certainly there are some people which are willing to embrace truth, if they knew where to find it and, for want of some distinguishing characters whereby to know it from falsehood, are unwittingly led into error.

M. Those characters will be easily found and discerned by a sincere lover of truth. We may lay this down for a general rule that I think will admit of no exception: whatever doctrine or point of truth is worthy of God, perfective of man's nature, and conducive to his spiritual and eternal happiness is certainly true. And I hold to my first assertion, that if we are but heartily willing to know the truth in this case, we shall certainly know it. But men are apt to impose upon themselves and to conclude without good ground that they are willing to know and embrace truth, when in reality they are not so. I do not take every simple act of volition for willing here; but I mean by willing[153] when the will is so strongly bent towards and fixed on truth as to carry the affections of love and desire along with it, insomuch that it peremptorily resolves to embrace and adhere to it without regarding the consequences of doing so. A man thus disposed will use his utmost efforts to bring under subjection the powers of his animal[154] nature, will endeavor to preserve great purity of life, and improve all advantages of time, study or[155] converse. Will divest himself of all pride and prejudice as much as possibly he can, that he may more easily and clearly discern truth; and to his own endeavours he will be sure to add fervent and constant prayer to Almighty God[156] for his direction and assistance. Now 'tis inconsistent with all the notions we have of divine goodness to suppose that God, to whom all power belongs,[157] should suffer such a man to fall into any damnable error or withhold from him the guidance of his Holy Spirit in his search of truth. Especially if we consider the blessed promise of him that cannot deceive, Proverbs, second: "My son, if thou wilt receive my words [. . .], so that thou incline thine ears unto wisdom and apply thine heart to understanding: yea if thou criest after knowledge and liftest up thy voice for understanding: If thou seekest her as silver, and searchest for her, as for hid treasures: Then shalt thou understand the fear of the Lord; and find the knowledge of God."[158] If all men were thus prepared and disposed to receive the truth in the love of it, there would be no such thing as an Arian, Socinian or heretic of any denomination whatever in the Christian world. For the great truths of the gospel are so legible that he which runs may read;[159] and those on which our happiness does more immediately depend carry in them such a congruity with all the unprejudiced sense and reason of mankind as upon proper application to the study of them will effectually serve to convince our judgments and direct and regulate our practice.

E.   But since the desire of happiness is equally natural to all men, why do not all men alike apply themselves to find out the true way that leads to it?

M.   Men differ more in their notions of the thing than about the true way of finding it. For almost every man believes that he already knows what would make him happy. And this is one reason why 'tis one of the most difficult things in the world, to make men apprehend wherein their true happiness consists, so as to have such a deep and solid sense of it as will excite them to use their utmost endeavours to attain it. For since the heart is wont to apply the name of good to the object of its love, men naturally believe that their happiness lies in the possession and enjoyment of that good, be it what it will. And this is the reason that, though all men equally desire happiness, yet they pursue it in such various ways and take such different methods to obtain it. Man is a compound being, a strange mixture of spirit and matter. Or rather a creature wherein those different principles are united without mixture, yet each principle subject to the influences of the other. The happiness of man thus considered consists in a due subordination of the inferior to the superior powers, of the animal to the rational nature, and of both to God. And the inversion of this order is the true source of human misery here and hereafter. Now, though this truth will appear very evident to a sober unprejudiced mind, yet 'twould be exceeding hard, if not impossible, to make anyone assent to it, whose animal part has got the ascendant of his reason.[160]

Notes

1. To Samuel Wesley Jr. 11 October 1709; Journal, entry 52 (24 May 1711).

2. An early and encyclopedic essay in this genre was by the Cambridge Platonist Ralph Cudworth, *The True Intellectual System of the Universe* . . . *Wherein, All the Reason and Philosophy of Atheism Is Confuted* . . . (London: Richard Royston, 1678). A more accessible work is John Ray, *The Wisdom of God Manifested in the Works of Creation* (London: Samuel Smith, 1691), which covers much of the same territory (e.g., an extended description of the human eye) as S. W. but does not seem to have directly influenced her. Another example, much briefer and in the same dialogue format as S. W.'s "Conference," was the 56-page pamphlet of Samuel Wesley Sr.'s collaborator on the *Athenian Mercury*, Richard Sault, *A Conference betwixt a Modern Atheist, and His Friend* . . . (London: John Dunton, 1693). Though there seems to be no direct influence, Sault's work demonstrates that people in the Wesleys' intellectual and ecclesiastical circle were dealing with similar issues in a nearly identical format.

3. See Richard Bentley, *The Folly of Atheism, and (What Is Now Called) Deism* . . . in *Eight Boyle Lectures on Atheism, 1692* (New York and London: Garland, 1976); reprint of eight sermons (London: Tho. Parkhurst and H. Mortlock, 1692–1693, sig. A2f. Another important voice in the effort to harmonize theology and the new science was John Wilkins, *Of the Principles and Duties of Natural Religion* . . . (New York and London: Johnson Reprint Corporation, 1969); reprint of London: T. Basset et al., 1693.

4. Augustin Leger, *La Jeunesse de Wesley* . . . (Paris: Librairie Hachette, 1910), pp. 48–49.

5. G. Stringer Rowe, ed., *Mrs. Wesley's Conference with Her Daughter: An Original Essay by Mrs. Susannah Wesley, Hitherto Unpublished*, Publications of the Wesley Historical Society, no. 3 (London: Charles H. Kelley, 1898).

6. See 1 Corinthians 15:43 for the source of the second epigraph.

7. Rowe, *Conference*, misreads "receive."

8. Leger finds this paragraph reminiscent of Pascal. See *Jeunesse de Wesley*, p. 49, n. 1.

9. Paraphrased from 1 Peter 3:15, changed to first person singular and substituting "faith" for the AV "hope." Quotation marks added.

10. Capricious, peevish.

11. Matthew 18:3; quotation marks added.

12. "Should be" is inserted in place of the crossed-out "which would render them."

13. Close paraphrase of Exodus 20:4, the commandment against graven images; quotation marks added.

14. Cf. Addison's ode, still sung as a hymn. Composed the same year as S. W.'s *Religious Conference*, it expresses the same natural theology:

The spacious firmament on high,
With all the blue ethereal sky,
And spangled heavens, a shining frame,
Their great Original proclaim. . . .

15. Written heavily over the original "must."

16. See Richard Bentley's approach in his Boyle lectures, *A Confutation of Atheism from the Origin and Frame of the World* . . . , 3 parts (London: Henry Mortlock, 1692–1693), especially part 1, pp. 20ff.

17. Followed by the beginnings of a crossed-out sentence: "If you mean first matter, the matter whereof all things were made. . . ." Evidently copying from an earlier draft, S. W. mistakenly inserted the sentence too soon. Note its inclusion after the next sentence.

18. Quotation marks added. The OED attributes the phrase to the English translation of Cicero explaining Leucippus and Democritus on the origin of the world (s.v. concourse, 3).

By the time S. W. wrote, however, it was a staple of theological debate. See Edward Still-ingfleet, *Origines Sacrae or a Rational Account of the Grounds of Christian Faith* . . . (London: Henry Mortlock, 1666), p. 375: "it must necessarily follow according to the different principles of the Aristotelian and Epicurean Atheists, that either the world was as it is from all eternity, or else that it was at first made by the fortuitous concourse of Atoms." Cudworth, *True Intellectual System*, p. 674, remarks on the absurdity of supposing the world "to have Resulted from the Fortuitous Motion of Sensless Atoms. . . ." Cf., closer to the end of the century, Richard Bentley on the odds against "fortuitous hits" explaining the wonders of the human body if "divine Wisdom and Skill" were not involved: *A Confutation of Atheism from the Structure and Origin of Humane Bodies. The Third and Last Part* (London: Henry Mortlock, 1692), p. 32. In his next to last Boyle lecture, Bentley uses the same phrase: "as to that ordinary Cant of illiterate and puny Atheists, the fortuitous or casual concourse of Atoms. . . ." *A Confutation of Atheism from the Origin and Frame of the World* . . . Part II (London: H. Morlock, 1693), p. 4. Cf. also Sault, *A Conference*, p. 18: "the first Trees cou'd not be made by the fortuitous justlings of Atoms and fine Particles of Matter, but [. . .] there is an Intelligent, Wise Author. . . ."

19. Galen of Pergamon (130–c. 200), along with Hippocrates, was a primary influence on Western medicine. His works, like Aristotle's, were preserved in the Arab world and by the eleventh century began to be introduced into Europe. The Greek originals became available at the time of the fall of Constantinople in the mid-fifteenth century. English translations were published beginning in the sixteenth century, and, despite the anatomical advances of William Harvey (1578–1657), Galen continued to have considerable influence. Here, of course, S. W. is following other theological apologists in employing this "pagan" support for the teleological argument for God's existence. See, for example, Wilkins, *Principles and Duties*, pp. 80–82, writing of human bodies, "upon consideration of which, Galen himself, no great Friend of Religion, could but acknowledge a Deity." Wilkins cites Galen's *de formatione Foetus* as his source. Cudworth, *True Intellectual System*, pp. 671–672, also drew on Galen to make similar points, citing *Of the Use of Parts.*

20. Cf. Richard Bentley's Boyle lecture, *A Confutation of Atheism from the Sturcture and Origin of Humane Bodies* . . . , parts I–III (London: Thomas Parkhurst and H. Mortlock, 1692), particularly part I, pp. 8–9; part II, p. 14.

21. Quotation marks added.

22. See Richard Bentley's Boyle lecture, *Matter and Motion Cannot Think: Or, A Confutation of Atheism from the Faculties of the Soul* . . . (London: Thomas Parkhurst and Henry Mortlock, 1692), particularly pp. 32–33.

23. Replaces the crossed-out "about."

24. Followed by the crossed-out "as well."

25. This entire sentence was at first left out, then inserted above the line.

26. Rowe, *Conference*, misreads it as "reaching."

27. Replaces the crossed-out "with."

28. That is, within his area of power, control, or jurisdiction.

29. Rowe, *Conference*, misreads "power."

30. Followed by "some," now crossed out.

31. Trying to preserve its flow, I have punctuated this summary as one long sentence, even though S. W. broke it up into numerous fragments.

32. Replaces the crossed-out "idea."

33. Nearly exact quotation of Mark 10:38; my quotation marks.

34. This sentence is written in large script; I have emphasized it in boldface.

35. Rowe, *Conference*, misreads "think."

36. Paraphrase of 1 Timothy 6:16.

37. Note the similar tack on the "Excellencies and Perfections of the Divine Nature" taken by Wilkins, *Principles and Duties*, chaps. 8–11, pp. 100–175.

38. Note the similarity of expression in her letter to her son John, 27 November 1735, with its echoes of Malebranche and/or Norris.

39. Replaces "idea," now crossed out.

40. Rowe, *Conference*, misreads "these."

41. Inserted above the line, not in S. W.'s hand.

42. Inserted above the line in S. W.'s hand, replacing the crossed-out "is."

43. S. W. is playing with the same assumptions Wilkins outlines in *Principles and Duties*, p. 102, when he divides the "communicable" attributes of God into three categories: the divine understanding, the divine will, and the divine "faculties of acting." The first encompasses knowledge, wisdom, and particular providence; the second, goodness, justice, and faithfulness; the third, power, "dominion over us in this life," and "distributing of future rewards and punishments."

44. An "and" appears here in the MS, crossed out; Rowe, *Conference*, mistakenly inserts it in his edition.

45. On God's "perfect comprehension of all things" see Wilkins, *Principles and Duties*, pp. 126–127.

46. Followed by the crossed-out "his."

47. S. W. originally wrote, then crossed out, "contrary operations," replacing it with "different productions."

48. Rowe, *Conference*, has "diverse," but S. W.'s original makes more, or at least adequate, sense: several, sundry, more than one (rather than unlike in nature or qualities, varied, changeful).

49. Cf. Wilkins, *Principles and Duties*, p. 126, on God's universal knowledge: "He hath a perfect comprehension of all things, that have been, that are, or shall be. . . ."

50. Ibid., p. 128: "As Knowledge doth respect things absolutely; so Wisdom doth consider the relations of things one to another, under the notion of Means and End, and so their fitness or unfitness for the various purposes to which they are designed."

51. S. W. puts an exclamation point after "wisdom," not for punctuation but for emphasis.

52. Again the MS has exclamation points inside the sentence, this time after "original" and "essential."

53. Aristotelian terms; see OED, s.v. "commutative" and "distributive." I have been unable to trace the actual source of her definitions. Wilkins, *Principles and Duties*, p. 139, does not go into such detail, defining justice merely as God's "dealing with his creatures according to the desert of their deeds."

54. Replaces the crossed-out "is."

55. S. W. adds an exclamation point here.

56. S. W. puts an exclamation point here.

57. Discussions of moral issues (which might fit under the label of "commutative justice") are sprinkled throughout the rest of the MS.

58. "This" is inserted in place of an awkward-sounding phrase, which S. W. crossed out: "what you speak of want of power."

59. S. W. adds an exclamation point here.

60. S. W. adds an exclamation point here.

61. I have eliminated S. W.'s mid-sentence exclamation points: "goodness of God!" and "glorious perfections!"

62. The MS also has an exclamation point after "excellence."

63. S. W. has an exclamation point here.

64. The following phrase is crossed out (and recast later in the sentence): "according to the measure of their capacities, and."

65. S. W. adds an exclamation point here.

66. Latin: "in nature"; emphasis added.

67. Rowe, *Conference,* misreads "eternal."

68. S. W. adds an exclamation point here.

69. S. W. originally wrote "nothing" but realized her mistake and crossed it out—a further indication that she is copying from another source or draft.

70. S. W. has added an exclamation point here.

71. Replaces the crossed-out "soul."

72. Paraphrase of Psalm 8:5.

73. She has crossed out her original word, "soul." Before that change she also altered the sentence from its original form, "vouchsafed to make him a reasonable creature."

74. S. W. adds an exclamation point here.

75. John Barker, *Strange Contrarieties: Pascal in England during the Age of Reason* (Montreal and London: McGill-Queen's University Press, 1975), p. 182, follows Leger, *Jeunesse de Wesley,* pp. 48–52, in indicating that this passage is S. W.'s gloss and paraphrase of Pascal's observation, *Thoughts,* chap. 14 ("Jesus Christ"), par. 1, p. 120: "The whole System of Bodies, the Firmament, the Stars, the Earth and the Kingdoms of it, are not fit to be opposed in Value to the lowest Mind or Spirit: because Spirit is endued with the knowledge and apprehension of all this, whereas Body is utterly stupid and insensible. Again, the whole united Systems of Bodies and Spirits are not comparable to the least Motion of Charity; because this is still of an Order infinitely more exalted and Divine.

"From all Body together we are not able to extract one Thought. This is impossible, and quite of another Order. Again, all Body and Spirit together are unable to produce one Spark of Charity. This is likewise impossible, and of an Order above Nature."

76. Received meanings.

77. Manner of being with relation to something else; relation, respect.

78. Existence as a substance or entity; substantial, real, or independent existence.

79. My question mark; S. W. uses a colon here.

80. My question mark; S. W. uses a period.

81. Probable reference to Malebranche's theory that "we see all things in God." *De la recherche de la vérité,* 3,2,6; quoted in Frederick Coppleston, *A History of Philosophy,* 6 vols. (Garden City, N.Y.: Doubleday Image Books, 1963), 4:200.

82. See Locke, *An Examination of Malebranche's Opinion of Seeing All Things in God,* in *Posthumous Works of Mr. John Locke* (London: A. and J. Churchill, 1706), written in 1695 but not published until two years after the author's death.

83. My question mark; S. W. ends with a dash.

84. S. W. adds an exclamation point here.

85. For an example of such language among the "Cambridge Platonists," see George Rust, *Two Choice and Useful Treatises: The One Lux Orientalis . . . the Other a Discourse of Truth . . . with Annotations on Them Both* (London: James Collins and Sam. Lowndes, 1682). pp. 264–265: "Pg. 194. *Now all that Truth that is in any created Being, is by participation and derivation from this first Understanding* (that is, from the Divine Understanding *quatenus Exhibitive*) *and Fountain of Intellectual Light.* That is, according to the *Platonick* Dialect, of those steady unalterable and eternal Idea's [Greek: *to gar eidos phos*] of the natures and respects of things represented there in the Divine Understanding *Exhibitive* in their *Objective Existence;* In conformity to which the Truth in all created things and Understandings doth necessarily consist.

"Pg. 195 *Antecedently to any Understanding or Will,* &c. That is, Antecedently to any Understanding *Conceptive, Observative or Speculative* whatsoever, or to any *Will;* but not antecedently to the

Divine Understanding *Exhibitive*. For that is antecedent to all created things, and contains the steady, fixt, eternal and unalterable natures and respects or habitudes, before they had or could have any Being. I say it contains the Truth and measure of them; nor can they be said to be truly what they are, any further than they are found conformable to these eternal, immutable Idea's, Patterns and Paradigms, which necessarily and eternally are exerted, and immutably in the Divine Understanding *Exhibitive*. And of these Paradigmatical things there, what follows is most truly affirmed."

Also, cf. this passage from John Norris, "A Metaphysical Essay toward the Demonstration of a God, from the Steddy [*sic*] and Immutable Nature of Truth," in *A Collection of Miscellanies* . . . (Oxford: John Crosley, 1687), p. 207: "that celebrated Distinction of the Platonic School, of the Divine Mind into [Greek: *nous noeros?*] and [Greek: *nous noetos*], *Conceptive* and *Exhibitive*. Truth does by no means *depend* upon any mind as *Conceptive*, whether Human or Divine, but is *supposed* by it. . . . But upon mind as *Exhibitive* it may and does *ultimately* depend; so that if there were no *God* or Eternal Mind, there could be no *Truth*. . . ."

Leger also detects an evocation of Pascal in the ensuing discussion. See *Jeunesse de Wesley*, p. 49, n. 1.

86. Liable or entitled to participate or share.

87. My comma replacing S. W.'s exclamation point.

88. Exclamation point omitted.

89. Originally "that," now crossed out.

90. Aversion, turning away.

91. S. W. originally followed with "again," then crossed it out.

92. Close paraphrase of Ephesians 1:11; quotation marks added. The exclamation point is S. W.'s.

93. Crossed out: "those laws."

94. S. W. follows with "some," then crosses it out.

95. Exclamation point omitted.

96. Exclamation point omitted.

97. Exclamation point omitted.

98. Exclamation point omitted.

99. Exclamation point omitted.

100. S. W. uses the archaic alternative, "substraction."

101. Hebrews 12:23; my quotation marks.

102. James 1:17; my quotation marks; S. W.'s exclamation point.

103. Exclamation point omitted.

104. "Endeavour to" omitted by Rowe, *Conference*.

105. S. W. here alludes to the debate over innate ideas. Against prevailing opinion, Locke argued there were none; rather, the mind gets its ideas from two sources, sensation and reflection. Though Locke's opponents felt that this argument destroyed the credibility of Christianity, he believed he was setting the truth of religion on a stronger, experiential basis. See S. W.'s references to Locke's *An Essay concerning Humane Understanding* . . . 5th ed. (London: Awnsham and John Churchill and Samuel Manship, 1706), in her journal, particularly her entries 19, 169, and 182.

106. Belonging to as a natural accompaniment or as a property inherent by nature or from birth; congenital, innate, natural.

107. Ever the practical theologian, S. W. does not insist on Locke's epistemology, though she prefers it. Rather, she opts for something akin to her son John's "catholic spirit," permitting people to "think and let think" about issues she believes are not central to the faith.

108. "Sometimes" inserted above the line as an afterthought.

109. My quotation marks and question mark.

110. S. W. originally wrote "writing" but then crossed it out.

111. See Romans 2:11, though the more familiar quote she is using is from Peter's speech in Acts 10:34; my quotation marks.

112. Romans 2:12–13; my quotation marks.

113. S. W. here paraphrases, glosses, and summarizes Paul's argument from verse 14 to the end of the chapter.

114. My quotation marks.

115. See Genesis 14:17–20; Psalm 110:4; and Hebrews 5:6, 10, 6:20–7:22.

116. See the book of Job, especially chaps. 1 and 42.

117. A primary Gentile convert to Christianity, whose story is told in Acts 10–11.

118. For their conversion, see Jonah 3:5–10.

119. See Acts 10:35.

120. BCP, Litany; my quotation marks.

121. Hebrews 11:6; my quotation marks.

122. The illustration is as least as old as St. Anselm of Canterbury (1033–1109); see his meditation quoted in Paul Hindley et al., eds., *The English Spirit: The Little Gidding Anthology of English Spirituality* (Nashville: Abingdon, 1987), pp. 17–18. Leger again sees reflections of Pascal in the ensuing two paragraphs. See *Jeunesse de Wesley*, p. 49, n. 1.

123. S. W. capitalizes "Himself"; the reference is to God.

124. The power, usually associated with royalty, "to act according to discretion . . . without the prescription of the law and sometimes even against it." OED, s.v. prerogative, quoting Locke, *Two Treatises of Government* (1690), II, xiv, 160.

125. The clause originally concluded "discover this religion to him," but S. W. crossed out the final four words and completed it as in the text.

126. A classic example of Rudolph Otto's description of the Holy as *mysterium tremendum et fascinans*. See *The Idea of the Holy* (London and New York: Oxford University Press, 1932). I have omitted the exclamation point S. W. used mid-sentence after "purity."

127. Close paraphrase of Psalm 139:5, BCP; my quotation marks.

128. Rowe, *Conference*, mistranscribes "or."

129. BCP, Communion, General Confession; my quotation marks.

130. "Fervent" originally preceded "sincere," but S. W. crossed it out there and wrote it in to follow.

131. Genesis 2:9ff.

132. *Shorter Catechism*, Q. 13. *Larger Catechism*, Q. 21. Cf. John Milton, *Paradise Lost*, 3:65 and 4:6.

133. See the *Larger Catechism*, questions 30–31.

134. Close paraphrase of 1 Corinthians 15:22; my quotation marks.

135. Replaces crossed-out, indecipherable word(s) (possibly "more necessary"), followed by "than," also crossed out.

136. Crossed out at this point: "are necessary and."

137. Cf. Pascal, *Thoughts*, heading of chap. 21: "The strange contrarieties discoverable in Human Nature, with regard to Truth, and Happiness, and many other things." Barker has taken part of that as the title of his helpful book, *Strange Contrarieties*, p. xii.

138. Followed by the crossed-out "so." Apparently, S. W. began to write "some" before deciding it fit better a few words later.

139. Inclinations, leanings, propensities.

140. Exclamation point omitted.

141. Exclamation point omitted.

142. My question mark.

143. Plutarch was a favorite author of both Renaissance and Enlightenment England. His

works were available in a number of contemporary translations. The allusion here is probably to either *Plutarch's Lives* . . . , 5 vols. (London: Jacob Tonson, 1693), translated by Samuel Wesley's friend John Dryden and others and first published in 1683 (with more than a dozen editions or reprintings by 1770), or *Plutarch's Morals* . . . , 5 vols., 4th ed. (London: Tho. Braddyll, 1704), first published in 1684. Each of these major works was also abridged or abstracted early in the eighteenth century. Or S. W. may have taken the quotation from a collection, such as the now rare *Miscellany Poems and Translations by Oxford Hands* (London: Anthony Stephens, 1685).

144. See Psalm 49:20; quotation marks added.

145. Moderation, temperance.

146. Cf. *Shorter Catechism*, Q. 1: "Man's chief end is to glorify God, and to enjoy him forever."

147. Followed by the crossed-out "such."

148. See Matthew 7:14.

149. Rowe, *Conference*, misreads "indulge."

150. Loose paraphrase of chap. 5 ("The Submission and Use of Reason") par. 3, Pascal's *Thoughts*, p. 52: "If we bring down all things to Reason, our Religion will have nothing in it Mysterious or Supernatural. If we stifle the Principles of Reason, our Religion will be absurd and ridiculous."

151. Followed by the crossed-out "our."

152. See 1 John 4:1.

153. Followed by the crossed-out "I speak of."

154. Followed by an indecipherable, crossed-out word.

155. Rowe, *Conference*, substitutes "and."

156. Exclamation point omitted.

157. Exclamation point omitted.

158. Proverbs 2:1–5; nearly exact quotation but missing the second half of verse 1: "and hid my commandments with thee. . . ." S. W. has set the passage off in her MS by writing it in a slightly larger hand; I have done so with quotation marks.

159. See Habakkuk 2:2.

160. The essay ends rather abruptly here at the top of MS p. 61.

TWENTY-EIGHT

Some Remarks on a Letter
from Whitefield

Near the end of her life Susanna Wesley found herself in a position to defend one of her former pupils, her son John, then in the middle of a public theological controversy with his old friend George Whitefield. Whitefield (1714–1770) came under John Wesley's influence while a student at Pembroke College, Oxford, becoming not only an ardent member of the undergraduate religious organization nicknamed the Holy Club but subsequently a major leader of the evangelical revival in both Britain and North America. In fact, it was the more innovative, less churchly Whitefield who introduced Wesley to field preaching in 1739. Though they were able to maintain their personal friendship, a fact that partially accounted for Whitefield's visit to the widowed Susanna Wesley while she was staying with the Halls in Wooton,[1] a professional rivalry developed. The two men soon broke theological ranks over predestination, the Calvinist doctrine asserting that God "before the foundation of the world" irrevocably chose some for salvation ("election"), others for damnation ("reprobation"). Whitefield, whose predisposition in this direction was abetted by his evangelistic work in Wales, Scotland, and America, became its champion, while his former mentor steadfastly held to his birthright Arminian position, which supported divine love (though perhaps at the expense of divine power) and gave humanity a greater role in the process of salvation.

The disagreement became more than a private dispute when Wesley preached and published a sermon critical of predestination entitled "Free Grace." Making matters worse, Whitefield was out of the country at the time and expressed his shock in the form of a letter from Georgia, published as *A Letter to the Reverend Mr. John Wesley: In Answer to His Sermon, Entitled, Free-Grace* (London: T. Cooper and R. Hett, 1741).[2] Though Wesley provided his own more general rejoinder in *A Dialogue between a Predestinarian and His Friend*, 2nd ed. (London: Strahan, 1741), his mother, within a year of her death, also took up her pen in this point-by-point rebuttal of Whitefield.

After all her letters, journals, and extended essays, this last piece of theological writing was the only one to see publication during her lifetime. Even at that, it was published anonymously, and though her authorship was suspected, it was never conclusively proven until the 1960s. Frank Baker has convincingly marshaled the evidence, which includes the work's similarity with some of her catechetical writings; a diary entry from one of John Wesley's assistants, describing the pamphlet and noting, "Mr. W. told me his Mother wrote it"; and the suggestive note in the ledger of Wesley's printer, "For the printing and Paper of Mrs. W.'s pamphlet £3.5.——."[3]

Just another skirmish in one more pamphlet war before the identification of its author, *Some Remarks* now begs for scrutiny. In general, it reveals Susanna Wesley capably defending one of her own by holding her own against a formidable and increasingly popular public figure. A decade and a half earlier she had expressed her aversion to "rigid Calvinists" in a letter to John,[4] demonstrating that these were issues she had carefully thought about and doubtless confirming him in his position.

As in her "Religious Conference," she tempers an appropriately modest female persona (in that case "Mother," in this one a "gentlewoman") with a fairly bold one. In *Some Remarks* she is, if not licensed to kill, at least authorized as a controversialist, expected to make trenchant points against an opponent; and this she clearly enjoys.

Her forthright, not to say harsh, strategy is immediately apparent on the title page with the choice of epigraphs. The two scriptural references and the quotation from Athanasius imply at best Whitefield's instability; at worst, his blasphemy and his status as a fallen angel. Indeed, following a few opening niceties, the attack begins in a similar vein: Whitefield is "not the first . . . that have done the Devil's work in the great and sacred name of God" in acts of treachery and betrayals of trust. Not shrinking from ad hominem argument, she accuses Whitefield of jealousy and a susceptibility to bribes and expresses pity for his "youth and inexperience," which have not well equipped him for the temptations that come with popularity. Finally, before turning her attention to content, she scores Whitefield for raising controversy and causing divisions among Christians—while in the process she abets both.

In responding to Whitefield's attack on her son and advancing her own argument, Susanna Wesley covers the well-worn territory of Calvinist-Arminian debate, though there are several unexpected moments. Among the traditional anti-Calvinist points, she cites the cruelty of preaching to the reprobates, if in fact they cannot be saved; she argues that the nature of God, particularly God's infinite love, is blasphemed in the doctrine of election; she wonders how predestination leaves any room for moral choice and, therefore, the promised reward and punishment of the last judgment. But there are also some interesting new twists: her suspicion that "gospel perfection," as preached by the Wesleys, was part of what had got stuck in Whitefield's craw; her analysis (from having herself known "many predestinarians") of the problems Calvinists necessarily suffer, either despairing of their election or being so sure of it as to fall into a self-indulgent Antinomianism; her charge that a Calvinist God is a kind of projection of an earthly absolute monarch (a statement indicating she had by then probably outlived the divine right philosophy she espoused some four decades before);[5] and in contending that Calvinists often hide behind the inevitability of original sin, her asertion that Eve was really less culpable than Adam in the fall.

High-minded, sophisticated theology it is not, but it is practical, if not particularly irenic, and displays a rhetorical flare that effectively clarifies some of the factors, theological and psychological, contributing to the growing rift between the two great leaders of the evangelical revival. It deserves our special attention as her last and most public attempt at giving voice to her convictions.

〰

SOME
REMARKS
ON A
LETTER

From the REVEREND

Mr. *WHITEFIELD*

To the REVEREND

Mr. *WESLEY*,

In a LETTER from a *Gentlewoman*
to her FRIEND.

---

*How art thou fallen from Heaven, Oh! Lucifer, Son of
the Morning!* Isaiah xiv. 12.

Unstable as Water, thou shalt not excel. Genesis xlix. 4.

*Between Sin in general and Blasphemy this is the Difference,
He that sinneth transgresseth the Law: He that blasphe-
meth, committeth Impiety against the Godhead itself.*
St. Athanasius.

LONDON:
Printed, and sold at the Pamphlet-Shops of *London*
and *Westminster*. MDCCXLI.

[Price Sixpence.]

SOME
REMARKS
ON THE REVEREND
MR. WHITEFIELD's
LETTER

Dear FRIEND,

In compliance with your request, I send you my thoughts at last concerning this strange letter, which you observe has made such a noise in town; but before I make any remarks on the letter itself, I must take notice of its publication to the world, which, not to insist upon the wonderful absence of good sense, good manners, friendship, and above all Christian charity in the writer, is so exceeding shocking, that every well-tempered, honest, generous mind, must look upon it with a just abhorrence.

Supposing (but in no wise granting) that Mr. Wesley had fallen into any error, did he take a proper way to apprize him of it? If he had been the Christian or friend he pretended to be, he would never have appeared against Mr. Wesley in print, but would have much rather gone to him in private and in a calm and friendly manner have endeavoured to show him his errors, and if he could have convinced Mr. Wesley of any mistake, well; if not, the matter was not of such importance to the world as to lay him under any obligation of exposing his friend. Oh! but says Mr. Whitefield, "I should never have published this private Transaction to the World, had not the Glory of God called upon me to do it."[6] He is not the first, by many thousands, that have done the Devil's work in the great and sacred name of God. But be it known to him and all the world, that it is an impious profanation of that most holy name to use it in vindication of any act of treachery, in abusing the confidence of any man, betraying a trust, revealing of secrets, declaring what is spoken by a friend to the ear in private on the house-top. This is a practice which no pretence can justify: for it is not religion, but the want of it that make a man capable of doing a base unworthy action.

"Oh! my soul, come not thou into the secret of such treacherous men; unto their assembly, mine honour, be not thou united."[7]

But I take the true state of the case to be this; when Mr. Whitefield returned from Georgia, he found the Wesleys were men of an established reputation among the better sort of people for the purity of their doctrine and integrity of their lives ("the Spirit that is in us lusteth to envy"),[8] and as he too much affected popularity himself, as appears in some of his writings, he might probably think his own glory suffered some diminution by the increase of their reputation. Besides, he had held a close correspondence with the Dissenters while he was abroad and could not be ignorant of what they were not careful to conceal in England, that if Mr. Whitefield would return and preach up predestination in opposition to the Wesleys, they would pave his way with gold. Interest hath an agreeable way of putting out a man's eyes and making him mistake that for good which indeed is evil. Had it not been so, perhaps Mr. Whitefield would not so readily have forsaken his old faithful friends to make his court to the Dissenters.

But after all, his youth and inexperience renders him somewhat pitiable.[9] He appeared young in the world and was not apprized that popular applause had such an intoxicating quality, that few men have heads strong enough to bear it. Nor did he consider that praise is the most contagious breath, nor knew that the sails of native pride are ever ready to receive such winds, which frequently increase a man's sins, but never add one cubit to the stature of his worth.[10]

As to his compellations to Mr. Wesley of "Honoured" and "Dear," etc.[11] I look upon them only as so many cant words which are of no signification, tho' possibly he might intend by the frequent use of them to cut his friend's throat with a feather.

Mr. Whitefield might well be aware that the publishing of his letter would have different (tho' no good) effects in the minds of the readers. "Many of my Friends," says he, "that are Advocates for universal Redemption, will be offended; many, that are zealous on the other Side, will be much rejoiced." Thus far he is right, but in what follows he mistakes the truth totally. "They that are lukewarm on both Sides, and are carried away with carnal Reasoning, will wish this Matter had never been brought under Debate."[12] Did ever man think like this! Alas! my friend, it is not the lukewarm and carnal reasoner on either side (for God is seldom in their thoughts, neither are such zealous for his glory.) But it is the truly spiritual man, it is he that "loves the Lord Jesus Christ in sincerity," who is grieved to see him again "wounded in the house of his friends,"[13] that deeply mourns at observing the miserable divisions this unwary man hath made in the church by reviving a controversy which had been very wisely laid asleep. God forgive him. He had been much better employed in exhorting his followers to let controversy alone and to mind the "working out their own salvation with fear and trembling," as St. Paul directs.[14]

He begins his letter with a protestation against fact, of which I shall say nothing. Then he accuses Mr. Wesley of having by preaching and printing propagated the doctrine of universal redemption, which doctrine more than once or twice I have heard Mr. Whitefield preach himself. But that was before he was so loudly called upon to oppose Mr. Wesley, and then he probably thought his own interest would be better supported by an union with the Wesleys and therefore preached the true Gospel as they did then, and, blessed be God, continue to do still. But now he finds his interest lies another way. Then who shall blame him if his mind alter with the occasion? 'Tis a common case, so let that pass also.

Mr. Whitefield falls severely enough on Mr. Wesley about casting a lot.[15] I cannot say that I approve of lots in any trifling matter, but to use them in a case of importance, as this certainly was, is not to be condemned, since we find them so used both in the Old and New Testament. He tells Mr. Wesley, "a due Exercise of religious Prudence, without a Lot, would have directed you in that Matter."[16] And I must tell him, that a due exercise of religious prudence or common honesty would have restrained Mr. Whitefield from publishing what passed[17] in private between him and Mr. Wesley. But Mr. Whitefield goes on, "Besides I never heard that you enquired of God, whether or not Election was a Gospel Doctrine?"[18] I suppose he means that doctrine of election which he says must stand or fall with that of reprobation; and if so, what high presumption must Mr. Wesley have been guilty of had he brought such a lot as that before the Lord, since it would, in effect, have given the lie to all the merciful declarations God hath vouchsafed to make of his free grace and universal love to lost mankind!

He then cavils at Mr. Wesley's text and wonders that he should choose a text out of the eighth of the Romans to disprove the doctrine of election.[19] Now I cannot see where Mr. Wesley could have chose a better. It is plain indeed that St. Paul throughout the whole Chapter is speaking of the privileges of those who are in Christ true believers. Yet if we compare spiritual things with spiritual and observe how often the word "all," when used to declare God's grace and love to mankind, must be taken in the largest and most comprehensive sense, unless we strangely pervert the text, we shall not see reason (notwithstanding the Apostle did speak chiefly to believers here) to confine the word "all" within such narrow limits as Mr. Whitefield has done. And I rather approve of Mr. Wesley's choice of this text because the true doctrine of election is more clearly and explicitly taught in the twenty-ninth and thirtieth verses of this chapter than any where else in scripture. And these two verses always preserved me from the errors of these predestinarians, with whom I frequently conversed. Verse 29: "For whom he did foreknow, whom in his eternal prescience he saw would accept of offered mercy, and believe in Jesus Christ, as their Redeemer, their Saviour," etc.[20] He approves, chooses them for heirs of his kingdom, and appoints or wills their conformity to the image of his Son in righteousness and true holiness. And to this they are called, either by the inward voice of their Redeemer or the outward voice of his ministers, and Providence, commonly by all these means. And wherever the elect, the children or sons of God, etc. are spoken of in scripture, it is always to be understood of true believers. (Here is not a word of reprobation.) Now since prescience doth not infer causality, the predestinarians, if they would ever so fain have all men damned but themselves, cannot conclude that one single man is damned from this place. But to go on, "Your Discourse," says Mr. Whitefield, "is as little to the Purpose as your Text.[. . .] I shall not mention how illogically you have proceeded.—Had you wrote clearly, you should first [. . .] have proved your Proposition, that God's Grace is free to all."[21]

How inconsistent is this man with himself! A few pages farther he advises Mr. Wesley to "down with his carnal Reasonings,"[22] and here he blames him for not using carnal reason, for "illogical Proceeding, in not proving the Truth of this Proposition, that God's Grace is free to all."[23] Is there then need of logic to prove the truth of any thing that God hath so often and clearly revealed throughout the whole bible? For my part I always thought that God was infinite, original Truth! And if we were once secure that he had revealed any thing to us, we might safely depend on his authority for the truth of it, whether we do or do not understand it.

But Mr. Whitefield further adds, "Passing by this, as also your equivocal Definition of the Word Grace, and your false Definition of the Word Free . . ."[24] Mr. Wesley's definition of the word "grace" is good, and Mr. Whitefield must own it to be so, or else deny that the favour or grace (for the words are of the same signification) God hath showed to men in sending his only Son into the world to save them proceeded from his infinite love to mankind! If he be hardy enough to deny this, our Lord will answer him by himself.

As for the word "free" as used in this place, I challenge Mr. Whitefield and all his adherents to define it better than Mr. Wesley hath done; but this is mere trifling, as indeed is what follows.

Mr. Wesley had justly inferred from the Calvinists doctrine, Sermon p. 7th, that "by virtue of an Eternal, Unchangeable, Irresistible Decree of God, one Part of Mankind are infallibly saved, and the rest are infallibly damned." That if it "be so, then is all Preaching vain." [25] Mr. Wesley speaks too modestly here in only saying preaching is vain (for certainly infinite Wisdom might have appointed some other way to have called the elect). He might have safely affirmed preaching the gospel to be a cruel ordinance: for if, as Calvin says, "God speaketh by his Ministers to Reprobates that they may be deafer; he gives Light to them that they may be the blinder; he offers Instruction to them that they may be the more ignorant; and uses the Remedy that they may not be healed," [26] what good man would not rather choose to be a hangman than a minister of the gospel? For the former, as the executioner of public justice, is only employed to put an end to a man's temporal life, which may prove the salvation of his soul. But the latter must be employed to confirm and harden men in sin and thereby insure their damnation and increase their eternal torments. Therefore it might well be said (as before) that Mr. Wesley spake too modestly in only saying that upon their principles preaching and hearing are vain. [27]

Mr. Whitefield seems to me to be beating the air, sometimes arguing against self-evident truth, at other times he argues against the truth of God himself. Mr. Wesley says, "that the Doctrine of Election and Reprobation directly tends to destroy that Holiness, which is the End of all the Ordinances of God: For it takes away these first Motives to follow after it, so frequently proposed in Scripture, the Hope of future Reward, and Fear of Punishment, the Hope of Heaven, and the Fear of Hell, &c." [28]

One would think this is too clear to be denied. For since this doctrine hath a natural tendency to lead men either into presumption or despair, it must take away those first motives to Christian holiness so often proposed in scripture, viz. "the Hope of Heaven, and Fear of Hell," etc. What Mr. Wesley says further under this head (if duly considered) will appear to be very good arguing against predestination. But Mr. Whitefield says, "I thought one that carries Perfection to such an exalted Pitch as Mr. Wesley does" (doth Mr. Wesley then set the mark of Christian perfection one jot higher than Christ and his apostles did? I wish Mr. Whitefield would attempt to prove that.) "would know that a true Lover of the Lord Jesus Christ would strive to be holy, for the sake of being holy." [29] I think also that Mr. Whitefield might know that a person must have made a good progress in Christianity before he can "strive to be holy, for the sake of being holy"; [30] and must have attained to a great degree of faith and love, before he can act for Christ upon the pure principles of gratitude and love, without any regard to the rewards of heaven or fear of hell. Hope and fear are the two great principles of human action; no man of sense ever undertaking anything of moment, but either out of hope to get something he thinks may do him good or else out of fear of some evil which otherwise may fall upon him; therefore he that made us, and indued us with these principles, the better to keep us within the compass of our duty, hath been graciously pleased to promise the best things we can ever hope for to those who keep his commandments, and to threaten the worst we can ever fear to those who keep them not.

Here we may observe that God works on man as man, a rational free agent, in that he proposes rewards and punishments as motives to obedience. And indeed we must own man has some liberty or deny him to be a subject capable of reward or punishment. And if he be a necessary agent, what becomes of the resurrection from the dead, a general judgment, and a future state of happiness or misery? But of man's free-will more hereafter.

Mr. Wesley says, "this Doctrine (of Election) tends to destroy the comforts of Religion, the Happiness of Christianity, etc." [31] Now to him who hath a zeal for the glory of God according to knowledge, and whose heart is full of universal benevolence to mankind, this appears a self-evident truth. And those that hold the doctrine of election and reprobation, even against their wills confirm this truth, that they who hold the blessed doctrine of universal redemption are much happier than themselves. For they cannot shake off their doubts and fears, but they will frequently return upon them, do what they can, which plainly shows that they are far from solid happiness. I have been well acquainted with many predestinarians and have observed two sorts of people amongst them. The one were serious and, I believe, sincerely desirous of salvation, and striving to enter by the strait gate [32] into the kingdom of heaven. These were generally much dejected and (excepting a few) always seeking after marks of grace, being doubtful of their own election often upon the point of despair, being ignorant of that true gospel liberty which is attainable in this life and which many, who hold universal redemption do actually enjoy.

Others, and they far the greater number, were very confident of their own election, thought it a great sin to make any doubt of it, and could not patiently hear it questioned. These were commonly sunk in carnal security and without scruple gave in to all manner of self-indulgence, fancying that what would be sin in a reprobate would be none in them. Of these I know several at this time, and so does Mr. Whitefield, too.

Mr. Whitefield says, "I admire the Doctrine of Election, and am convinced that it should have a Place in Gospel Ministry, and should be insisted on with Faithfulness and Care." [33]

Now if Mr. Whitefield can prove that without believing this doctrine a man cannot possibly be saved, he is in the right; but if he cannot prove this, he is palpably in the wrong. And considering what fierce contentions and sad divisions the doctrine of election and reprobation hath occasioned in the church of Christ, wise and good men can never come into his way of thinking in this particular.

Young men and novices in divinity commonly delight in controversy; but sober experienced Christians much abhor it, well knowing that it usually destroys the vitals of true saving religion and that while men are disputing the way, the power of godliness is lost. And I very much fear that Mr. Whitefield's reviving this pernicious controversy is one reason why our Lord hath permitted him to fall into that dangerous most shocking practice of making public opposition against gospel holiness, which is the only Christian perfection the Wesleys ever taught; for absolute perfection they never preached.

If men would have been content with the plain account given in scripture of the creation of the world and redemption of mankind by our Lord Jesus Christ and had not affected to be wise above what is written, there had never arose any controversy in the church about election and reprobation. Nor would the predestinarians so vilely have blasphemed the great and holy God as they have done, if they had believed and rested in the manifestations he hath vouchsafed to make of himself to us in sacred writ. 'Tis past all dispute "that none but God know what God is!" [34] nor can a finite being possibly have any true conceptions of him unless they be taught of God.

If we look into holy scripture, we shall find, when Moses enquired of God what he should say to the children of Israel when they asked him what was the name of God, God said unto Moses, "I am that am; and he said, thus shalt thou say unto the children of Israel, I am hath sent me unto you." [35] We see God defines himself by himself, "I am that I am," or as the words also signify, "I will be that I will be." [36] There is no doubt but Moses, designing to know God's name, intended by that to understand his nature, who and what he is. But that could not be; for there are no words in any or all the languages on earth whereby to express the glory of an infinite Being so as finite creatures should be fully able to conceive it. Therefore God is pleased to return him this answer, "I am that I am." [37] And if we could rightly apprehend what is couched under these words, we should certainly have as high and true conceptions of God as is possible for creatures to attain. However, we may learn from this awful name what he would have us think of his nature, so as to distinguish him from all things beside. We are wont to conceive and speak of the great God after the manner of men and to call him a powerful, a wise, a just, a true, a loving and holy God, etc., whereas we ought rather to say, he is Power, Wisdom, Goodness, Justice, Truth, Love, Holiness, etc. For as all these perfections are in him, they are neither distinguished from one another, nor from his nature or essence, in whom they are said to be. For, to speak properly, they are not in him, but are his very essence or nature itself, which, acting severally upon several objects, seems to us to act from several properties or perfections; whereas all the difference is in our different apprehensions of the same thing. God in himself is one most pure and simple act and therefore cannot have any thing in him but what is that most pure and simple act. We may observe, he admits nothing into the manifestation of himself but pure essence, without any mixture or composition. "I am that I am! I am Jehovah! Being itself!" [38] To which name nothing can be added, from which nothing can be taken away. To add anything to it would be a mere tautology, or rather a diminution from it, as limiting or confining it to one perfection, whereas all are signified by it.

Now it is inconceivable to me how anyone who believes God to be this all-great all-glorious, infinite Being that he hath declared himself to be, can possibly sink into such low, vile, unworthy conceptions of him as these Calvinists do! How is it possible for them to think that evil, which, properly speaking, hath no Being (tho' the subject of evil hath a being) can proceed from him who is Being itself! How sin, the greatest of evils, could ever proceed from God, from him that is the only infinite, supreme, original Good! [39]

Now, if Mr. Whitefield would have answered Mr. Wesley to any purpose, the first thing he had to do was to vindicate the honour and glory of God by clearing the predestinarian scheme from those monstrous absurdities and horrible blasphemies which necessarily attend it. He should have tried to reconcile God's being the author of sin, with his infinite holiness, and his deceiving his creatures by so many and often repeated declarations of his universal love and free grace for all that will accept of it, to his infinite Truth, and creating so many millions of souls on purpose to damn them, with his infinite justice, mercy and love.

But the Calvinists very well know that their doctrine is irreconcilable with the perfections of the divine nature; and therefore when they are hard pressed with any argument taken from thence, they strive to evade the force of it, not by clearing their doctrine from the blasphemy attending it, but by having recourse to the sovereignty of the Almighty, which, they say, may do whatever he pleaseth; which in some sense is true, but in theirs absolutely false. And they grossly betray their ignorance, when they attempt to speak of sovereign power as it is in God. For it is plain the authors Mr. Whitefield mentions and recommends to Mr. Wesley were very weak injudicious writers and had no true conceptions of the sovereign power of God,[40] but took their notion from the arbitrary sway which those whom we call sovereign princes exercise with in their dominions; these absolute monarchs usually act arbitrariously, and their will is commonly their rule of government. The sad effects of such government are too well known, especially to their unhappy subjects.[41] But true infinite sovereign power never was nor can be employed in any acts of oppression, injustice, or cruelty. Never acts arbitrariously, after the manner of men, but all his works and ways are in number, weight and measure most perfect! In that blessed Being wisdom and power, truth, holiness, justice and mercy, etc. are one act. And tho' he be the true and only potentate, "king of kings and lord of lords," "and none can stay his hand (his power) or say unto him, What dost thou?"[42] Yet notwithstanding his infinite, absolute sovereignty, which none can dispute and to which all must submit, we may with humble reverence affirm that there are things which this almighty, all-glorious Being cannot do. But some may say, how can this be? God knoweth no superior, no equal; "he doth whatever pleaseth him" in heaven and earth.[43] Who then can give law to him?

Himself, the infinite perfection of his divine nature, is the constant unerring rule of all his actions; therefore he is said in scripture "to work according to the counsel of his own will."[44] The will of God is the pure origin or fountain of all moral goodness! And therefore it is absolutely impossible that he should will anything which is evil. 'Tis true he permits many things that are evil, but 'tis impiety to think or say he is pleased with anything that is so. He is "of purer eyes than to behold iniquity"[45] with the least degree of approbation; nor can he possibly decree or act anything that is inconsistent with the infinite perfection of his most blessed nature, which is his essential glory!

We have seen that this horrible decree of reprobation is utterly inconsistent with the manifestations the great Jehovah hath condescended to make of himself to his unworthy creatures. Let us now consider whether this doctrine be more agreeable to the gracious declarations he hath been pleased to make of his universal love and free grace to fallen man.

And here I shall follow the plain account which holy scripture gives of those two great events, namely, the creation of man and his redemption by our Lord Jesus Christ.[46] But first I shall observe that before God made man, he created the angels, an order of spirits superior to those of humankind. These were the "morning stars which sang together, those sons of God that shouted for joy" when he "laid the foundations of the earth."[47] These were all free agents and consequently were at first entered into a state of probation, otherwise they must have been incapable of rewards of punishments. "Some of these," St. Jude tells us, "kept not their first estate, but left their own habitation (heaven) having fallen, self-tempted."[48]

After the apostasy of the angels God created man, a compound being, having an immortal spirit united to a material body, formed of the dust of the ground, and placed him in Paradise before prepared for them; and gave them "dominion over the fish of the sea, and over the fowls of the air, and over the cattle, and over all the earth, and over every creeping thing that creepeth upon the earth."[49]

Man, also being a rational free agent, was put upon a trial of his obedience, as we read in the third of Genesis. And as God had created him in his own image, while he retained his integrity, there was a perfect union between the will of his Maker and his own. He had perfect knowledge of his duty and sufficient strength to do it, and therefore perfect obedience was justly required. How long our first parents continued in their state of happy innocence we know not, scripture being silent about it. But this we know and feel, that they also fell and thereby broke the union between the divine and human nature, forfeited their interest in God, became servants to Satan, and subject to death temporal, spiritual and eternal.

Adam (or man in general, as the word Adam signifie[s]) being the first head of mankind, in whom the whole human species was virtually included, the whole human nature was corrupted in him and involved in the consequences of their first parents['] fall.[50]

But here let us admire, praise and adore the incomprehensible glory of God in his universal love and goodness to all mankind! In providing (all men) a second parent or common head, who after the fall of the first, and the fallen state he had brought upon his posterity, should be a common Restorer, and put it in the choice of every individual man to have life or death as the first man had; that so they, who were lost before they were born and made inheritors of a corrupt and miserable nature without their choice, might have a divine life restored to them in a second parent, which should not be in the power of anyone to lose for them. But I choose to speak of this matter in the words of an excellent man, Mr. Law, in a book of his entitled *A Demonstration of the gross and fundamental Errors of a late Book, called, A plain Account of the Nature and End of the Lord's Supper* etc., a book much better worth reading than any Mr. Whitefield hath recommended to Mr. Wesley. His words are these:

> The Declaration which God made to Adam immediately after his Fall, of a Seed of the Woman to bruise the Serpent's Head, was a Declaration of Pardon and Redemption to Adam, and in him to all Mankind: For what he said to Adam, that he said to all that were in the Loins of Adam, who, as they fell in his Fall before they were born, without the Possibility of any one Man's being exempted from it; so were they all put into his State of Pardon and Redemption before they were born, without the Possibility of any one Man's being excluded, or left out of it.
>
> Thus revealed Religion begins with an Offer of a second Adam, and upon the Foot of an universal Pardon and Redemption to all Mankind.[51]

In that instant that God declared the seed of the woman should bruise the serpent's head[52] (break the power of the devil) our blessed Redeemer united his divine power to the whole human nature and thereby brought all mankind into a salvable condition. And had he not thus healed the breach between the divine and human nature, which Adam had made by his voluntary disobedience, neither Adam himself or anyone of his posterity could possibly have been saved. The very reason why the apostate angels remain devils is because our dear Lord passed them by. "For he took not on him the nature of angels, but he took on him the seed of Abraham." [53] For it is very probable, had our Savior assumed their nature as he did ours, very few, if any, of these unhappy spirits had been lost. But every child of Adam is in the same covenant, hath the same Saviour, and an equal share in the first general pardon that Adam himself had. To this purpose the Apostle: "As by the offence of one, judgment came upon all to condemnation; even so by the righteousness of one, the free gift came upon all men unto justification of life." [54] What becomes then of their decree of reprobation? There is no partiality in God; he bears equal respect to all his creatures, and if any one soul be lost, the destruction of that soul is from itself. The soul of Judas was as much interested in the original pardon and redemption as the soul of St. Paul, and the reason why the one was saved and the other lost was not because one was ordained to eternal life, the other to eternal death, but St. Paul accepted an offered Saviour and was faithful to given grace, whereas Judas rejected his offered Saviour and despised his offered mercy; he would not believe, therefore he could not be saved. Otherwise he was one of the human nature a well as St. Paul and had as much right to the first covenant as he, but wanted faith to lay hold of it.

In God as Parent to the universe we have our natural life; "for in him we live, and move, and have our being." [55] So in God the Son as Redeemer of mankind we live, and move, and have our spiritual being. He is our second Adam, from whom we derive as real a birth, life, and nature as we do from the first Adam; he is the Life of our life, Spirit of our spirit. "He is the true light, that lighteth every man which cometh into the world" [56] and doth impart to every man so much liberty, so much strength and power against the Serpent as, if carefully improved by the continual succours of divine grace, will enable him to "work out his own salvation." [57] And the assistance of the Spirit of Jesus shall never be wanting; for Christ hath said, "To him that hath shall be given." [58] But if a man will not accept this liberty, if he will not attend to what his Saviour inwardly speaks to his soul, if he will shut his eyes against the light and quench that spark of life communicated to every man by the seed of the woman, when the body falls off by death, he must find himself in his own hell and feel the torments of a diabolical, self-tormented nature for ever, that would not suffer itself to be redeemed.

What hath been already said is sufficient to convince any man (who will be convinced) that the doctrine of eternal reprobation is contrary to the infinite perfection of the nature of God and as contrary to all the declarations he hath made of his universal love and free grace to all mankind. Indeed, as Mr. Wesley hath observed, this doctrine "flatly contradicts [. . .] the whole scope and tenor of scripture," [59] and therefore ought to be exploded and rejected by all men. But to go on; Mr. Whitefield says, "The Principles of those that hold universal Redemption, has a natural Tendency to keep the soul in Darkness for ever; because the Creature is thereby taught, that his being kept in a State of Salvation is owing to his own free Will." [60] How well Mr. Whitefield knows his own principles or their tendencies, I don't know; but it is plain he knows very little of their principles against whom he disputes. Those who believe Christ an almighty universal Saviour arrogate nothing to themselves, but give him the glory of all and acknowledge that they can neither will or do according to his good pleasure [61] but by his grace preventing and assisting them; they plead no exemption from original sin, nor lay claim to any merits or righteousness of their own. "They have not so learned Christ." [62] I think Mr. Whitefield might well have spared his invidious reflections on Mr. Wesley and his followers; for suppose he doth not in such triumphant language boast of his privileges or speak of himself as if, like St. Paul, he had been "caught up into the third heaven," [63] and suppose his followers should be infected with the same humility and are not so profuse in their professions or so positive they can never fall from grace. Can it be fairly inferred from thence, that he and his people are all dead and cold and that, having begun in the spirit, they have all ended in the flesh? I wish Mr. Whitefield and those who follow him would return to a better mind, that they also might be in that state of gospel liberty which they enjoy whom he now despises.

I shall take no farther notice of what Mr. Whitefield says concerning the final perseverance of his saints than to quote a passage I lately met with in a *Dissenter's Letter to his Friend*:

> This is certain, that there is such a State of Perfection to be attained in this Life, from which a Man shall never fall: But yet it is high Presumption for a Man to affirm of himself, or any other, that it is impossible for him to fall. 'Tis best for all People to follow the Apostle's Advice, "Let him that thinketh he standeth, take heed lest he fall." [64]

Mr. Wesley had very justly observed, "how uncomfortable a thought it is, that thousands and millions of men, without any preceding offence or fault of theirs, were unchangeably doomed to everlasting burnings!" [65]

To which Mr. Whitefield replies, "Do not they who believe God's dooming Men to everlasting Burnings, also believe that God looked upon them as Men fallen in Adam, and that Decree which ordained the Punishment, first regarded the Crime by which it was deserved? How then are they doomed without any preceding Fault? Surely Mr. Wesley will own God's Justice in imputing Adam's Sin to his Posterity, and also, that after Adam fell, and his Posterity in him, God might justly have passed them all by, without sending his own son to be a Saviour for any one." [66]

Now, all this reply is just so much of nothing to the purpose. 'Tis presumption for anyone to dispute whether God might justly have passed Adam and all his posterity by, since 'tis plain he did not pass any one of them by, but provided a second head for mankind and called his name Adam as the first; signifying thereby, that he should not unite his divine Person to the nature of this of that particular man, but to the whole human nature in general, that the redemption might be equal to the fall. But enough hath been said of this already, and I only mention it here to show, that tho' God doth look upon all men as an order of fallen spirits, yet in the same view he beholds them as an order of redeemed spirits too. Therefore it is highly unreasonable (to say no more of it) for us to believe that any single soul of Adam's posterity ever was or ever will be damned merely for their original sin; therefore we may conclude that infants and idiots are certainly saved.

I cannot forbear observing here how incident it is to mankind to follow the example of their first parents. When God questioned Adam whether he had eaten of the forbidden fruit, he replied, "The woman whom thou gavest to be with me, she gave me of the tree, and I did eat." And when the Lord God said unto the woman, "What is this that thou hast done?" she said, "The serpent beguiled me, and I did eat." [67] How ready they were to excuse themselves and lay the blame upon another. The woman indeed seemed more modest of the two; for she only accuses the serpent, but Adam would have transferred his guilt upon God himself.

After this manner do we charge all of our voluntary transgressions upon original sin; and 'tis a sad truth, that we were all conceived and born in sin, and if in this case "we say that we have no sin, we deceive ourselves, and the truth is not in us." [68] And of this important truth all are, or ought to be, deeply sensible, in order to bring them to Christ. For he who sees no sin in himself, will seek no Saviour. But then we must not lay the blame of all our personal sins upon Adam, rather let us forbear sewing fig-leaves together to hide our nakedness and take shame to ourselves by confessing our faults are all our own. We brought indeed a corrupted nature into the world, but we had the seed of the woman too; and what everyone that calls himself a Christian ought principally to be grieved and humbled for is that, knowing the disease, we shunned the cure and suffered either the "lust of the flesh, or the lust of the eye, or the pride of life" [69] to extinguish that spark of divine life we received from our blessed Redeemer. If we still feel the weight of our corrupt nature and that our original sin hath dominion over us, whose fault is it? Is it not our own? Had we carefully listened to the still small voice of Jesus within us, had we diligently improved each degree of light and liberty he imparted to us and obediently followed every motion of his Holy Spirit, the old Adam had been crucified long ago, and we had been fully born of God. Then there would be no dispute amongst Christians whether a man can live without sin; for every Christian's experience would answer that question in the affirmative.

Sufficient hath been said to obviate Mr. Whitefield's objection, "That the Doctrine of universal Redemption makes Salvation depend, not on God's free Grace, but on Man's free Will." [70] But this is a gross mistake; for none who believes universal redemption but acknowledges also "that we are not sufficient of ourselves to think or do any thing as of ourselves, but our sufficiency is of God." [71] But then we most humbly believe and dare boldly assert that every man receives so much light and liberty from the universal Redeemer as will render him altogether inexcusable at the last great day, if he has been unfaithful to the grace he had or might have received. Of which truth this is a proof, that God hath fixed a conscience in every man's heart as his [72] vicegerent, to which men are accountable. Thus St. Paul: "When the Gentiles (heathens) which have not the (written) law, do by nature (redeemed nature) the things contained in the (written) law, these having not the (written) law, are a law unto themselves; which show the work of the law written in their hearts (by the inward Redeemer) their consciences also bearing witness, and their thoughts the mean while (before the general judgment) accusing, or else excusing one another." [73] I am very sure our blessed Lord will sit as judge on no man for whom he hath done nothing as a Saviour. And tho' our original sin is that root of bitterness from whence all our evil thoughts, words and actions took their rise, yet not one of those wretched creatures, which must stand at the left-hand in the last judgment, will dare before that awful tribunal to plead his original sin in excuse of his unbelief or any other sin he ever committed, any more than he will dare to mention a decree of reprobation. No, no, all those idle presumptuous thoughts will then be over, and conscience, which is more than a thousand witnesses beside, will compel them to acquit their judge for condemning them and force them to own before God, angels and men that their destruction is from themselves; Christ would have saved them, but they would not be saved.

Mr. Whitefield seems much displeased with Mr. Wesley for saying, "That their Doctrine hath a direct and manifest Tendency to overthrow the whole Christian Revelation."[74] This Mr. Wesley hath well proved; read the twelfth, thirteenth, and part of the fourteenth pages of his sermon on free grace.[75]

In answer to this assertion Mr. Whitefield says some things true, but is wrong in the application. For none has more clearly and strongly proved the necessity of using the divine ordinances than the Wesleys have done, showing at the same time the danger of resting in outward performances, and how they ought to be used in obedience to God as means of bringing us to Christ. Their judgment in these cases is best known by their practice. "Do they not labor more abundantly than they all?"[76]

I know no one that questions our Lord's having appointed preaching the gospel as means of converting men to himself; but this divine institution stands upon the foot of universal redemption, as appears by the commission he gave his disciples a little before his ascension, which runs in these general terms, "Go ye," saith our blessed Saviour, "into all the world, and preach the gospel to every creature. He that believeth and is baptized shall be saved; but he that believeth not shall be damned."[77] This is the irrevocable decree which concerns us, as Mr. Wesley lately proved in an excellent sermon on this text.[78]

After what Mr. Wesley hath said upon this head, Mr. Whitefield had no reason to ask how their doctrine of election "has a direct tendency to overthrow the Christian revelation."[79] Does he need to be told again that their doctrine has a direct tendency to overthrow the Christian revelation by undermining the foundation on which it stands, *viz. the eternal love and truth of God?*[80] For if they can prove that God is not infinite love and that he can lie, that he can deceive his creatures by declaring one thing and meaning another, there is an end of all revelation, of all revealed religion at once. And they plainly join with, and encourage all unbelievers, even those who deny there is a God, by representing the All-glorious Majesty of heaven, the supreme and only Good, after such a manner as befits a devil rather than a God. For who could believe in such a God as they have made; for found such a one they have not, "either in heaven above, or in the earth beneath, or in the waters under the earth."[81] Or who would not choose, rather than acknowledge and pay homage to such a God, to acknowledge none at all? But, blessed be God, their doctrine is as false as the grand artificer of fraud who invented it.

Mr. Whitefield's ranking Mr. Wesley with Infidels, Deists, Arians, etc.[82] puts me in mind of what Hugh Peters advised his brethren to do. "Let us," said he, "cast dirt enough upon him (King Charles I). If some should fall off, more will stick."[83] Thus Mr. Whitefield harangues the populace with Mr. Wesley's joining with Infidels, Arians, Socinians, Deists, etc. while perhaps not one in a hundred of his hearers understands what he means, any more than if he spake to them in Greek or Arabic.

Yet they think those Mr. Wesley joins with are very bad creatures, but whether they walk on four feet or two they don't know; yet this is casting dirt, and some may stick. But all personal reflections are nothing to the merits of the cause; and what follows in the 23d, 24th, and 25th pages is as little to the purpose, tho' most of it hath been already answered. I should here conclude, but that in justice to Mr. Wesley I think myself obliged to take notice of two or three things in page 26. Mr. Whitefield, after he had accused Mr. Wesley of using so much sophistry in his sermon, hath these words: "You beg the Question, in saying, that God has declared that He will save all; i.e. every individual Person."[84] Now this is a great mistake (I would hope it is not willful) in Mr. Whitefield; for certainly Mr. Wesley, either in preaching or print, did never say that God had declared he will save all men. Mr. Wesley had said, (which is true) "that all might be saved"; but I am sure he never said, "that all will be saved"; and I think there is a great difference between those two words, "might" and "will."[85]

I pass by his needless advice to Mr. Wesley, such as, "To give himself to Reading, to study the covenant of Grace; down with your carnal Reasoning; be a little Child, and then, instead of pawning (an ugly Word) your Salvation, as you have done in a late Hymn Book, if the Doctrine of Universal Redemption be not true."[86] I don't like the word Mr. Whitefield uses here, but if I had a thousand souls, I durst venture them all upon the unchangeable word of God, as well as Mr. Wesley hath his, and I am sure they would be very safe too. Mr. Whitefield goes on, "Instead of talking of sinless Perfection, as you have done in the Preface to that Hymn Book."[87] Now Mr. Whitefield speaks out, Plain dealing is best.

I am verily persuaded that many of the predestinarians are more angry with the Wesleys for preaching up gospel holiness than for their pleading so strongly for universal redemption, and if they would let the former alone, they would forgive them the latter. "If instead of preaching right, they would preach to them smooth things; if they would cause the holy One of Israel (or Holiness of God) to cease from before them,"[88] they would be content to hear them. But to press people so earnestly to endeavour to live without committing sin, to talk of plucking out right eyes and cutting off right hands, to tell them they must spare no evil inclination, indulge no worldly temper, not to leave them one Herodias, but to insist upon the necessity of having clean hearts, is strangely provoking. "These are hard sayings; who can hear them?"[89]

Mr. Wesley, in the beginning of his sermon on free grace hath these words: "Whatsoever good is in man, or is done by man, God is the author and doer of it."[90] Now with what reason does Mr. Whitefield say, as he does a little further, that Mr. Wesley "makes Man's Salvation depend on his own free Will in this Sermon,"[91] unless it be to insinuate to his followers that Mr. Wesley is an Arminian, which Mr. Whitefield knows he is not.[92] But I would hope that in a while Mr. Whitefield will know himself better than he does now and that Mr. Wesley also will have the satisfaction of seeing him retract his errors and return to preach the same gospel he did formerly.

In the mean time I cannot but observe how signally God hath honoured those two brethren (the Wesleys) by calling them forth and enabling them with great power to preach the truth of the gospel as it is in Jesus[93] and by setting his seal to their ministry. And I am persuaded you will join with me in prayer to our Lord, that he would strengthen and bless them more and more and protect them from evil men and evil angels, and that they may "be stedfast, immoveable, always abounding in the work of the Lord, for as much as they know that their labour is not in vain in the Lord."[94]

My dear Friend, Yours.

Notes

1. See her letter to Samuel Jr., 8 March 1738/39.

2. The original is rare, but it is also available in the Microbook Library of American Civilization reproduction (LAC 21966–69) of *The Works of the Reverend George Whitefield* . . . , 4 vols. (London: Edward and Charles Dilly, 1771–1772), 4:53–73.

3. "Susanna Wesley, Apologist for Methodism," in PWHS 35 (1965–1966): 68–71.

4. To John Wesley, 18 August 1725. In it she gave her reading of Romans 8, a key passage in the ongoing debate.

5. And yet, apropos Whitefield's lumping John Wesley together with various heretics, she could still employ a saying of one of the more notorious of the executed regicides of the previous century, that mudslinging can pay off—another instance of fighting guilt-by-association fire with fire!

6. Whitefield, *Letter*, p. 8. *Some Remarks* puts this and the subsequent Whitefield quotations in italics; I have set them apart with quotation marks. I have not modernized Whitefield's punctuation, capitalization, and spelling in these quotations.

7. A slightly altered quotation from Genesis 49:6. The original says, "come not into their secret"; S. W. has made it "the secret of such treachreous men." Note that this passage follows two verses after one that appears as an epigraph on the title page. Both are part of Jacob's prophecy concerning his sons, the earlier one directed toward Reuben ("unstable as water") and this one toward the murderous cruelty and self-will of Simeon and Levi.

8. Nearly exact quotation of James 4:5.

9. Whitefield was 27 at the time and had been ordained a deacon some five years and a priest for only two.

10. See Matthew 6:27, Luke 12:25.

11. Whitefield, *Letter*, pp. iii–iv and passim. "Compellation" is archaic usage for the "name, title, or form of words by which a person is addressed" (OED).

12. Ibid., p. iii.

13. Close paraphrases of Ephesians 6:24 and Zechariah 13:6, respectively; quotation marks added.

14. Close paraphrase of Philippians 2:12; quotation marks added.

15. Whitefield, *Letter*, pp. 7–8.

16. Ibid., p. 7.

17. In MS: "past."

18. Whitefield, *Letter*, p. 7.

19. Ibid., p. 9. Wesley's text was Romans 8:32: "He that spared not his own Son, but delivered him up for us all, how shall he not with him also freely give us all things?" John Wesley, *Sermons*, III (71–114), in Albert Outler, ed., *The Works of John Wesley* (Nashville: Abingdon, 1986), p. 544. Certainly it was not only audacious but also shrewd to draw on the chapter that provides the classic proof text for predestination. S. W. recognizes as much below in the same paragraph.

20. Romans 8:29's first phrase, "For whom he did foreknow," is the only part actually

quoted. The rest, though also italicized in the text, is her own Arminian gloss on it. The "etc." represents the omitted fighting words, "he did predestinate to be conformed to the image of his Son. . . ."

21. Pages 9–10 of Whitefield, *Letter*, with several words omitted: at the first ellipses, S. W. skipped over "and instead of warping, does but more and more confirm me in the Belief of the Doctrine of God's eternal Election"; at the second, "Honoured Sir."

22. Ibid., p. 26.

23. Ibid., p. 10, paraphrased to fit her syntax.

24. Ibid.

25. S. W. is quoting from her son's sermon, "Free Grace," par. 9–10. See *Sermons*, p. 547. In S. W.'s pamphlet the first quotation is both in italics and parentheses; the second is in quotation marks. I have used quotation marks for both.

26. See John Calvin, *Institutes* III.24.12. The translation available in early-eighteenth-century England was by Thomas Norton (1532–1584), *Institutio Christianiae Religionis. English. The Institvtion of Christian Religion* . . . (London: For Ioyce Norton and R. Whitaker, 1634).

27. A loose paraphrase of John Wesley's statement quoted above. Nevertheless, the MS puts the phrase (from "upon" through "vain") in italics.

28. "Free Grace," par. 11 (*Sermons*, p. 548). The sentence's subject in the original is "it," despite the appearance given by S. W.'s quotation marks that the longer phrase fills that function ("that the doctrine of election and reprobation . . .").

29. Whitefield, *Letter*, p. 11.

30. Quotation marks added.

31. "Free Grace," par. 13 (*Sermons*, p. 549). The prepositional phrase within parentheses is S. W.'s insertion.

32. See Matthew 7:13–14 and Luke 13:24.

33. Whitefield, *Letter*, p. 15. Whitefield, *Works*, 4:63, reads, "gospel ministrations."

34. Quotation marks represent italics in the MS; perhaps a broad paraphrase of 1 Corinthians 2:11.

35. Exodus 3:14; quotation marks replace the mixture of italics and regular type in the pamphlet.

36. Quotation marks replace the italics in the text. Note S. W.'s attraction to the same "I am" text in her letter to her son John, 27 November 1735, and in her journal entry 245, where she follows Bishop Beveridge in also attesting to our inability ultimately to know God. In each case she understands the revelation of the divine name implying in some sense the divine nature and perfections.

37. Quotation marks replace the italics of the text.

38. Quotation marks replace the text's italics.

39. The concluding clause, beginning "the only" appears in italics in the text. It is unclear whether she intends emphasis or quotation.

40. In lieu of arguing against Wesley's text (Romans 8:32) himself, Whitefield had recommended three authors to him: "Ridgley, Edwards, Henry" (Whitefield, *Letter*, p. 25). Though he did not specify further on the first and the last, he probably had in mind Thomas Ridgley (1667?–1734), *A Body of Divinity . . . Being the Substance of Several Lectures on the Assembly's Larger Catechism*," 2 vols. (London: Daniel Midwinter and Aaron Ward, 1731); and Matthew Henry (1662–1714), *An Exposition of the Old and New Testament*, 6 vols. in 3 (Edinburgh: C. Macfarquhar and Co., 1767–1770 ([original ed., London: 1704–1710])). The middle author is clearly John Edwards (1637–1716), whose *Veritas Redux: Evangelical Truths Restored: Namely, Those Concerning God's Eternal Decrees* . . ., 3 vols. (London: Jonathan Robinson et al., 1707–1708, 1725–1726), Whitefield mentions by name (*Letter*, pp. 6, 24).

Whitefield dropped several other names (and categories of people) he believed supported his side of the issue, men of such stature as could not easily be dismissed by Wesley: "Bunyan, Henry, Flavel [John Flavel, 1630?–1691, author of *Divine Conduct, or, The Mysterie of Providence* . . . (London: Francis Tyton, 1678)], Halyburton [Thomas Halyburton, 1674–1712, author of *The Great Concern of Salvation* . . . , 2d. ed. (Glasgow: J. Meuros, 1751 [original ed., Edinburgh, 1722])], . . . the New-England and Scots divines" (p. 20); the Anglican Bishop Gilbert Burnet, who wrote in support of Article XVII, "Of Predestination and Election" in an *Exposition of the XXXIX Articles* (London: Ri. Chiswell, 1699), (p. 10); the Scottish Episcopalian devotional writer Henry Scougal (one of S. W.'s own favorites) (p. 12); the pietist Johan Arndt; and Martin Luther (p. 20). He also mentioned (p. 24) Elisha Cole on God's Sovereignty (a book and author I have not been able to trace) and the sermons of "Mr. Cooper of Boston," no doubt William Cooper, 1694–1743, author of *The Doctrine of Predestination unto Life: Explained and Vindicated, in Four Sermons* . . . (Boston: For J. Edwards and H. Foster, 1740).

41. Has the old Nonjuror finally forsaken divine-right monarchy and come round to the point of parliamentary supremecy?

42. Revelation 19:16 and Daniel 4:35; quotation marks added. Interestingly, Handel's *Messiah*, whose "Hallelujah Chorus" further ingrained the first verse into English consciousness, was not performed until the following year.

43. Ecclesiastes 8:3, slightly altered; quotation marks added.

44. Ephesians 1:11, closely paraphrased; quotation marks substituted for the text's italics.

45. Habakkuk 1:13, paraphrased; quotation marks added.

46. The text has the phrase "namely . . . Christ" in italics.

47. Job 38:7 and 4, slightly paraphrased; quotation marks added.

48. Jude 6, considerably embellished. The direct quotation is from "kept" through "habitation," but the text puts the entire section (represented here by quotation marks) in italics.

49. Nearly exact quotation of Genesis 1:26; quotation marks added.

50. The language of this and the surrounding paragraphs is reminiscent of similar material in the introductory section of S. W.'s explication of the Apostles Creed.

51. William Law, *A Demonstration of the Gross and Fundamental Errors of a Late Book* . . . , in *Works*, 3rd ed. (London: W. Innys and J. Richardson, R. Manby and J. S. Cox, 1752), 3:165. I have indented the quoted paragraphs where the text has italics. Originally published in 1737, the tract is mainly pointed against the rationalistic interpretation of the Eucharist offered by Bishop Benjamin Hoadley (1676–1761) of Winchester. Secondarily, however, it also takes on those who pushed the doctrines of "particular absolute election and reprobation" (p. 258). Among other passages that Whitefield would not have appreciated, had he followed Susanna Wesley's recommendation to read it, is the following: "If my zealous Christian should find it a disagreeable thought to him, to think that *all Mankind* have had some *Benefit* from Christ . . . I must tell him, he need have no greater proof than this, that his own Heart is not yet truly Christian, that he is not a true Disciple of that Lord who *would have all men to be saved*." (pp. 255–256). There are other hints of S. W.'s reading of Law in the remainder of her pamphlet (see below).

52. Genesis 3:15, paraphrased.

53. Nearly exact quotation of Hebrews 2:16; quotation marks substituted for italics.

54. Nearly exact quotation of Romans 5:18; quotation marks substituted for the text's italics. S. W. cleverly builds her argument by continuing to appeal to Paul and Romans, usually considered the predestinarians' best ammunition.

55. Acts 17:28; quotation marks added.

56. Nearly exact quotation of John 1:9; quotation marks substituted for the text's italics.

57. Close paraphrase of Philippians 2:12; quotation marks added.

58. Close paraphrase of Matthew 25:29; cf. Matthew 13:12, Mark 4:25, and Luke 8:18; quotation marks added.

59. "Free Grace," par. 20 (*Sermons*, p. 552); quotation marks added.

60. Whitefield, *Letter*, p. 18; quotation marks substituted for the texts's italics. The actual quotation begins with "has a natural Tendency." S. W. italicized her whole previous phrase as if it were also Whitefield's; however, it is merely her attempt to supply the antecedent for Whitefield's pronoun in his real sentence "For that . . . has a natural Tendency. . . ."

61. Loose paraphrase of Philippians 2:13: "For it is God which worketh in you both to will and to do of his good pleasure."

62. Ephesians 4:20, with changed pronoun; quotation marks substituted for the text's italics.

63. Nearly exact quotation of 2 Corinthians 12:2; quotation marks added.

64. I have been unable to trace this pamphlet. I have indented the entire block where S. W. had it printed in italics; I have also introduced quotation marks to indicate the author's use of 1 Corinthians 10:12.

65. "Free Grace," par. 17 (*Sermons*, p. 550); quotation marks already in the text.

66. Whitefield, *Letter*, pp. 20–21; quotation marks already in text. Interestingly, Whitefield, as if to twit Wesley's Arminianism, has had the word "all" set entirely in capitals, whereas S. W. has elected not to record the emphasis in her quotation.

67. Genesis 3:12–13, somewhat adapted; quotation marks substituted for the text's italics.

68. 1 John 1:8; quotation marks substituted for the text's italics.

69. 1 John 2:16, changing the "and"s to "or"s; quotation marks added.

70. Whitefield, *Letter*, pp. 25–26; quotation marks substituted for the text's italics. S. W. has again altered the quotation slightly; Whitefield's original begins, "You plainly make Salvation depend. . . ."

71. Nearly exact quotation of 2 Corinthians 3:5; quotation marks substituted for the text's italics.

72. The capital "H" in the text leaves no doubt that the reference is to God.

73. Romans 2:14–15; quotation marks and S. W.'s parenthetical glosses already in the text.

74. "Free Grace," par. 19 (*Sermons*, p. 551), slightly altered; quotation marks replace the italics in the text.

75. I have not been able to attain a copy of the edition of her son's sermon that S. W. was working from and consequently cannot connect her page references with Outler's edition of *Sermons*, though they are probably paragraphs 19–23. She was probably using one or the other of Strahan's 24-page editions, *Free Grace: A Sermon Preach'd at Bristol* (London: Strahan, 1740 and 1741).

76. 1 Corinthians 15:10, slightly altered; quotation marks replace the text's italics.

77. Mark 16:15–16; quotation marks replace the text's italics.

78. Such a sermon does not seem to exist, but S. W. might still be right. Though Outler records no published sermons on this text (*Sermons*, 4:548–554), Wesley's sermon registers are far from complete (nonexistent, in fact, for his early career), so it is quite possible he did deliver a sermon, orally, from Mark 16:15–16 and there is no further record. Wesley does refer to the passage elsewhere in his published sermons, and there is an outside possibility S. W. is thinking of his landmark "Justification by Faith" (5 in *Sermons*, 1:181–199), in which par. 7 (p. 197) uses the Mark text to prove that faith is the only condition of justification. The sermon as it stands now was preached in 1746, but Outler has traced references to possible predecessors as early as 1738 (1:181), and the sermon S. W. alludes to might be such a one.

79. Whitefield, *Letter*, pp. 21–22, quoting and responding to John Wesley's accusation already mentioned in S. W.'s pamphlet, three paragraphs above. Quotation marks substitute for the text's italics, which begin there with "how their doctrine of election," that is, material not actually quoted.

80. I have let the italics in the text stand to maintain S. W. emphasis; this does not seem to be a quotation, though it captures the tenor of her son's argument in, for example, "Free Grace," par. 26 *Sermons*, p. 556).

81. Close paraphrase of Exodus 20:4; quotation marks substituted for the text's italics.

82. Whitefield, *Letter*, p. 22. All such, writes Whitefield to Wesley, "are on your side of the question."

83. Hugh Peters (1598–1660), Cambridge graduate and Independent divine, preached in Holland and Massachusetts (as one of the chief accusers of Anne Hutchinson) before returning to London and supporting the parliamentary cause. At the Restoration he was arrested and executed for having preached what the DNB calls "incendiary sermons" during the trial of Charles I and was the butt of royalist hatred even after his death. See *The Tales and Jests of Mr Hugh Peters* . . . (London: S. D., 1660); the anonymous editor makes Peters occasionally sound witty but usually buffoonish and often cruel. The final account of his execution leaves no doubt about the author's opinion: "Thus did he that called his sacred Majesty a Barrabas, a murderer, and seditious, die for murther and sedition himselfe . . ." (p. 32). I cannot find in this collection the source of the remark S. W. quotes, though it could easily have been circulated in such an anti-Peters tract as William Yonge's *England's Shame, or the Unmasking of a Political Atheist, Being a Full and Faithful Relation of the Life and Death of That Grand Imposter Hugh Peters* (London: Theodore Sadler, 1663).

84. Whitefield, *Letter*, p. 26; quotation marks replace the italics in the text.

85. John Wesley deals with this issue (though not so succinctly) in "Free Grace," par. 22 (*Sermons*, pp. 553–554). Quotation marks substituted for italics.

86. Whitefield, *Letter*, p. 26; quotation marks substituted for italics. An excerpt will give a sense of how S. W. has altered the quotation and also provide a sense of Whitefield's own rhetorical approach: "Dear, dear Sir, O be not offended! For CHRIST's sake be not rash! Give yourself to reading. Study the covenant of grace. Down with your carnal reasoning. Be a little child; and then, instead of pawning your salvation, as you have done in a late hymn book, if the doctrine of *universal redemption* be not true; instead of talking of *sinless perfection*, as you have done in the preface to that hymn book, and making man's salvation to depend on his own *free-will*, as you have in this sermon; you will compose an hymn in praise of sovereign distinguishing love. You will caution believers against striving to work a perfection out of their own hearts, and print another sermon the reverse of this, and entitle it free-grace *indeed*. Free, because not free to all; but free, because GOD may withhold or give it to whom and when he pleases."

87. Ibid.; quotation marks substituted for italics. See note 86. The reference is probably to the first edition of Wesley's *A Collection of Psalms and Hymns* (London: Strahan, 1741).

88. A composite quotation, made up of a rough paraphrase of Isaiah 30:10 and a slightly more accurate paraphrase of the second half of verse 11. Quotation marks replace the text's italics; the parenthetical insertion is S. W.'s.

89. John 6:60, altered to the plural; quotation marks replace the italics of the text. Other references in S. W.'s counsels of perfection are Matthew 5:29–30, 18:8–9; Mark 9:43, 47. Herodias was the sister-in-law and paramour of Herod, who tricked him into executing John the Baptist through her daughter's dancing (see Matthew 14:3–12 and Mark 6:17–29). The metaphorical usage here implies fleshly temptation.

90. "Free Grace," par. 3 (*Sermons*, p. 545); quotation marks substituted for text's italics.

91. Whitefield, *Letter*, p. 26, slightly adapted; quotation marks substituted for the text's italics.

92. Of course, John Wesley *was* an Arminian, and later on proudly wore the label when in 1778 he designated his new monthly publication the *Arminian Magazine*. However, in the early days of the revival, Dissenters particularly lumped it together with heresy. Writing in

1745, Isaac Watts decried how "the popish and pelagian doctrines of justification by works, and salvation by the power of our own free-will, are publically maintained. . . . The socinian and the arminian errors are revived and spread exceedingly. . . ." Quoted in Isabel Rivers, *Reason, Grace, and Sentiment: A Study of the Language of Religion and Ethics in England, 1660–1780*, vol. 1, *Whichcote to Wesley* (Cambridge: Cambridge University Press, 1991), p. 177.

93. See Ephesians 4:21.

94. 1 Corinthians 15:58, altered from the second to the third person; quotation marks replace italics in the text.

Bibliography

Susanna Wesley's Writings

Manuscript Sources

Peter Conlan, Bromley, Kent
Methodist Archives, Manchester
State Library of Victoria, Melbourne
United Methodist Historical Society, Baltimore
Wesley College, Bristol
Wesley's Chapel, London

Printed Sources

Arminian Magazine. London: J. Fry, 1778–1797.

Clarke, Adam. *Memoirs of the Wesley Family; Collected Principally from Original Documents*, pp. 263–265. New York: N. Bangs and T. Mason for the Methodist Episcopal Church, 1824.

———. *Memoirs of the Wesley Family*. 2nd ed., rev. 2 vols. London: Thomas Tegg, 1843–1844.

———. *Memoirs of the Wesley Family*. 2nd ed., rev. edited by George Peck. New York: Lane and Scott, 1851.

Coke, Thomas, and Henry Moore. *The Life of the Rev. John Wesley, A. M.* . . . . London: Paramore, 1792.

Priestly, Joseph, ed. *Original Letters, by the Rev. John Wesley, and His Friends, Illustrative of His Early History.* . . . Birmingham: Thomas Pearson, 1791.

Rowe, G. Stringer. *Mrs. Wesley's Conference with Her Daughter: An Original Essay by Mrs. Susanna Wesley, Hitherto unpublished*. Publications of the Wesley Historical Society, no. 3. London: Charles H. Kelly, 1898.

Stevenson, George J. *Memorials of the Wesley Family*. London: S. W. Partridge; New York: Nelson and Phillips, 1876.

Wallace, Charles, and Elizabeth Hart, eds. "Discovery: A 'New' Letter of Susanna Wesley." *Methodist History* 28.3 (1991): 202–209.

Walmsley, Robert. "John Wesley's Parents: Quarrel and Reconciliation." *PWHS* 29 (1953–1954): 50–57.

Wesley, John. *Journal and Diaries, II (1738–43).* In *The Works of John Wesley,* vol. 19. Edited by W. Reginald Ward and Richard P. Heitzenrater. Nashville: Abingdon, 1990.

———. *The Journal of the Rev. John Wesley, A. M. . . .* 8 vols. Edited by Nehemiah Curnock. London: Epworth, 1912–1916 (reprint, 1938).

The Wesley Banner (London: Partridge and Oakley, 1852), pp. 201–205, 245–248, 281–287, 323–326, 365–366, 404–406, 443–445.

Whitehead, John. *The Life of the Rev. John Wesley, M.A., with Some Account of His Ancestors and Relations. . . .* 2 vols. Dublin: John Jones, 1805; New York: R. Worthington, 1881.

Susanna Wesley: Biographies and Studies

Baker, Frank. "Investigating Wesley Family Traditions." *Methodist History* 26.3 (April 1988): 154–162.

———. "Salute to Susanna." *Methodist History* 7.3 (1969): 3–12.

———. "Susanna Wesley, Apologist for Methodism." *PWHS* 35 (1965–1966): 68–71.

———. "Susanna Wesley: Puritan, Parent, Pastor, Protagonist, Pattern." In *Women in New Worlds: Historical Perspectives on the Wesleyan Tradition,* 2:112–131. Edited by Rosemary Skinner Keller, Louise L. Queen, and Hilah F. Thomas. Nashville: Abingdon, 1982.

Brailsford, Mabel R. *Susanna Wesley: The Mother of Methodism.* London: Epworth (Edgar C. Barton), 1938.

Clarke, Eliza. *Susanna Wesley.* Eminent Women Series. London: W. H. Allen, 1886.

Dallimore, A. A. *Susanna: The Mother of John and Charles Wesley.* Darlington: Evangelical Press, 1992.

Doughty, W. L. *The Prayers of Susanna Wesley.* London: Epworth, 1956.

Edwards, Maldwyn. *Family Circle: A Study of the Epworth Household in Relation to John and Charles Wesley.* London: Epworth, 1949.

Greetham, Mary. *Susanna Wesley: Mother of Methodism.* Peterborough: Foundery Press, 1988.

Harmon, Rebecca Lamar. *Susanna: Mother of the Wesleys.* Nashville and New York: Abingdon, 1968.

Harrison, G. Elsie. *Son to Susanna: The Private Life of John Wesley.* London: Ivor Nicholson and Watson, 1937.

Hart, Elizabeth [Hannon]. "Susanna Annesley Wesley—An Able Divine." *Touchstone,* May 1988, pp. 4–12.

———. "Susanna Wesley and her Editors." *PWHS* 48.6 (October 1992): 202–209; 49.1 (February 1993): 1–10.

———. "A Tinge of the Ideal: Trans-Atlantic Interpretation in Portraits of Susanna Wesley." *Canadian Methodist Historical Society Papers,* Vol. 8, 1991 (for 1988 and 1990), ed. Neil Semple, pp. 137–157.

Kirk, John. *The Mother of the Wesleys: A Biography.* 6th ed. London: Jarrold, 1876.

Kline, Donald L. *Susanna Wesley: God's Catalyst for Revival.* Lima, Ohio: C.S.S., 1980.

Ludwig, Charles. *Susanna Wesley: Mother of John and Charles.* Milford, Mich.: Mott Media, 1984.

Maser, Frederick E. *Susanna Wesley.* Lake Junaluska, N.C.: Association of Methodist Historical Societies, 1967.

Moore, Robert L. *John Wesley and Authority: A Psychological Perspective.* AAR Dissertation Series 29. Missoula, Mon.: Scholars Press, 1979.

Newton, John. *Susanna Wesley and the Puritan Tradition in Methodism.* London: Epworth, 1968.

———. "Susanna Wesley (1669–1742): A Bibliographical Survey." *PWHS* 37 (June 1969): 37–40.

Stevens, Abel. *The Women of Methodism: Its Three Foundresses, Susanna Wesley, the Countess of Huntingdon, and Barbara Heck.* . . . New York: Carlton and Porter, 1866.

Wallace, Charles I., Jr. "'Some Stated Employment of Your Mind': Reading, Writing, and Religion in the Life of Susanna Wesley." *Church History* 58 (1989): 354–366.

———. "Susanna Wesley's Spirituality: The Freedom of a Christian Woman." *Methodist History* 22.3 (April 1984): 158–173.

Whitehead, John. *The Life of the Rev. John Wesley.* . . . New York: Worthington, 1881.

Young, Betty. "Sources for the Annesley Family." PWHS 45 (1985): 47–57.

Books Read by Susanna Wesley, and Other Related Seventeenth-
and Eighteenth-Century Works

[Allestree, Richard]. *The Whole Duty of Man.* . . . In *The Works of the Learned and Pious Author of The Whole Duty of Man,* pp. 1–149. Oxford: George Pawlet, 1684.

Barrow, Isaac. *Theological Works.* Vol. 7. *An Exposition of the Creed; the Lord's Prayer; the Decalogue; the Doctrine of the Sacraments.* Edited by Alexander Napier. Cambridge: At the University Press, 1859.

Baxter, Richard. *A Christian Directory: Or, a Summ of Practical Theologie, and Cases of Conscience.* . . . 2nd ed. London: Nevil Simmons, 1678.

———. *The Life of Faith. In Three Parts.* . . . London: Nevil Simmons, 1670.

———. *The Practical Works of the Rev. Richard Baxter.* . . . 23 vols. Edited by William Orme. London: J. Duncan, 1830.

———. *The Saints' Everlasting Rest: Or a Treatise of the Blessed State of the Saints in Their Enjoyment of God in Glory.* . . . 11th ed. London: Francis Tyton and Robert Boulter, 1677.

Bentley, Richard. *A Confutation of Atheism form the Origin and Frame of the World.* . . . 3 parts. London: Henry Mortlock, 1692–1693.

———. *Eight Boyle Lectures on Atheism, 1692.* New York and London: Garland, 1976. Reprint of originals, London: Tho. Parkhurst and H. Mortlock, 1692–1993.

———. *The Folly of Atheism, And (what is now called) Deism.* . .*Being the First of the Lecture Founded by* . . . *Robert Boyle.* . . . London: Tho. Parkhurst and H. Mortlock, 1692.

———. *Matter and Motion Cannot Think: Or, A Confutation of Atheism From the Faculties of the Soul.* . . . London: Thomas Parkhurst and Henry Mortlock, 1692.

Berkeley, George. *Three Dialogues between Hylas and Philonous.* . . . London: Henry Clements, 1713.

Beveridge, William. *The Church-Catechism Explained: For the Use of the Diocese of St. Asaph.* 2nd ed. London: Walter Kettilby, 1705.

———. *Private Thoughts upon Religion, Digested into Twelve Articles, with Practical Resolutions Form'd Thereupon.* 2nd ed. London: E. Smith, 1709.

———. *The Theological Works of William Beveridge, D.D., Sometime Lord Bishop of St. Asaph.* 12 vols. The Library of Anglo-Catholic Theology. Oxford: John Henry Parker, 1844.

The Book of Common Prayer. Oxford: At the University Press, ca. 1970.

Bull, George. *A Companion for the Candidates of Holy Orders. Or, the Great Importance and Principal Duties of the Priestly Office.* London: Richard Smith, 1714.

———. *The Works of George Bull, D.D., Lord Bishop of St. David's.* . . . 8 vols. Edited by Edward Burton. Oxford: At the University Press, 1846.

Burnet, Elizabeth. *A Method of Devotion: or, Rules for Holy & Devout Living.* . . . London: Joseph Downing, 1709.

[Burnet], Gilbert, Bishop of Salisbury. *An Exposition of the Church Catechism, for the Use of the Diocese of Sarum.* London: Joseph Downing, 1710.

———. *An Exposition of the XXXIX Articles.* . . . London: Ri. Chiswell, 1699.

[Burnet], Gilbert, Bishop of Salisbury. *Some Passages of the Life and Death of the Right Honourable John, Earl of Rochester.* . . . London: Richard Chiswel, 1680. Reprint ed. Menston, Eng.: Scolar, 1972.

Calvin, John. *Institutio Christianiae Religionis. English. The Institution of Christian Religion.* . . . Translated by Thomas Norton. London: For Ioyce Norton and R. Whitaker, 1634.

de Castaniza, John [supposed author; now attributed to Lorenzo Scupoli]. *The Spiritual Combat: Or the Christian Pilgrim in His Spiritual Conflict and Conquest.* Translated by Richard Lucas. London: Samuel Keble, 1698.

Clarendon, Edward [Hyde], Earl of. *The History of the Rebellion and Civil Wars in England.* . . . 3 vols. Oxford: Printed at the Theatre, 1712.

Clarke, Samuel. *A Demonstration of the Being and Attributes of God: More Particularly in Answer to Mr. Hobbs, Spinoza, and Their Followers.* . . . Boyle Lectures, 1704; published together with *A Discourse Concerning the Unchangeable Obligations of Natural Religion, and the Truth and Certainty of the Christian Religion.* . . . Boyle Lectures, 1705. London: James Knapton, 1705 and 1706.

———. *An Exposition of the Church-Catechism.* London: James and John Knapton, 1729.

The Compleat Library: Or, News for the Ingenious . . . *by a London Divine, etc.* 3 vols. London: John Dunton, 1692–1694.

Cooper, William. *The Doctrine of Predestination unto Life: Explained and Vindicated, in Four Sermons.* . . . Boston: J. Edwards and H. Foster, 1740.

Cudworth, Ralph. *The True Intellectual System of the Universe* . . . *Wherein, All the Reason and Philosophy of Atheism Is Confuted.* . . . London: Richard Royston, 1678.

Culverwel, Nathaniel. *An Elegant and Learned Discourse of the Light of Nature, with Several Other Treatises* . . . . Edited by Robert A. Green and Hugh MacCallum. Toronto: University of Toronto Press, 1971. Original publication, London: John Rothwell, 1652.

D., S. *The Tales and Jests of Mr. Hugh Peters.* . . . London: S. D., 1660.

[Defoe, Daniel]. *The Character of the Late Dr. Samuel Annesley, by Way of Elegy: With a Preface. Written by One of His Hearers.* London: E. Whitlock, 1697.

———. An Essay upon Literature: Or, An Enquiry into the Antiquity and Original of Letters. . . . London: Thomas Bowles, 1726.

Dunton, John. *The Life and Errors of John Dunton.* . . . 2 vols. London: J. Nichols, Son, and Bentley, 1818. Original ed. London: S. Malthus, 1705.

Ferguson, Moira, ed. *First Feminists: British Women Writers, 1578–1799.* Bloomington: Indiana University Press; Old Westbury, N.Y.: Feminist Press, 1985.

Fiddes, Richard. *Fifty Two Practical Discourses on Several Subjects. Six of Which Were Never before Published.* London: John Wyat, Benjamin Tooke, John Barber, H. Clements, 1720.

———. *A General Treatise of Morality, Form'd upon the Principles of Natural Reason Only.* . . . London: S. Billingsley, 1724.

Flavel, John. *Divine Conduct, or, The Mysterie of Providence* . . . . London: Francis Tyton, 1678.

Galen. *Galen on the Natural Faculties.* Edited and translated by Arthur John Brock. London: Heinemann; New York: Putnam's, 1916.

Hales, John. *A Discourse of the Several Dignities, and Corruptions, of Man's Nature, since the Fall.* London: E. Curll, 1720.

———. *Golden Remains, of the Ever Memorable Mr. John Hales, Eaton-Colledge, &c.* 3rd impression. Letter to the Reader by John Pearson. London: George Pawlet, 1688.

Halyburton, Thomas. *The Great Concern of Salvation.* . . . 2d ed. Glasgow: J. Meuros, 1751. Original ed., Edinburgh, 1721 and 1722.

Hammond, Henry. *A Practical Catechism.* 11th ed. London: Richard Davis, 1677.

Henry, Matthew. *An Exposition of the Old and New Testaments.* . . . 6 vols. in 3. Edinburgh: C. Macfarquhar and Co, 1767–1770. Original ed., London, 1710.

Herbert, George. *The Temple. Sacred Poems, and Private Ejaculations. Together with His Life.* 12th ed. London: Jeffery Wale, 1703.

———. *The Works of George Herbert.* Edited by F. E. Hutchinson. Oxford: Clarendon Press, 1941.

Jefferson, Thomas. *The Life and Morals of Jesus of Nazareth. . . .* Washington: Government Printing Office, 1904.

Ken, Thomas. *An Exposition on the Church-Catechism, or the Practice of Divine Love.* Revised ed. London: Charles Brome, 1703.

King, William. *Divine Predestination and Fore-knowledge, Consistent with the Freedom of Man's Will: A Sermon Preach'd at Christ-Church, Dublin, May 15, 1709. . . .* Dublin and London: for A. Bell . . . and J. Baker, 1710.

Law, William. *A Demonstration of the Gross and Fundamental Errors of a Late Book, Called "A Plain Account of the Nature and End of the Sacrament of the Lord's Supper, etc. . . ."* 3rd ed. In *Works, 1717–1774,* vol. 3. London: W. Innys and J. Richardson, R. Manby and J. S. Cox, 1752. 1st ed. 1737.

———. *A Practical Treatise upon Christian Perfection.* London: William and John Innys, 1726.

———. *A Serious Call to a Devout and Holy Life. Adapted to the State and Condition of All Orders of Christians.* London: William Innys, 1729.

Locke, John. *An Abridgement of Mr. Locke's Essay concerning Humane Understanding.* 2nd ed. Edited by John Wynne. London: A. and J. Churchil, 1700.

———. *An Essay concerning Humane Understanding. In Four Books.* 5th ed. London: Awnsham and John Churchill and Samuel Manship, 1706.

———. *An Essay concerning Human Understanding.* The Clarendon Edition of the Works of John Locke. Edited by Peter H. Nidditch. Oxford: Clarendon Press, 1975.

———. *An Examination of Malebranche's Opinion of Seeing All Things in God.* In *Posthumous Works of Mr. John Locke. . . .* London: for A. and J. Churchill, 1706.

———. *A Letter to the Right Revered Edward Ld Bishop of Worcester, concerning Some Passages Relating to Mr. Locke's Essay of Humane Understanding. . . .* London: A. and J. Churchill and Edward Castle, 1697.

———. *Mr. Locke's Reply to the Right Reverend the Lord Bishop of Worcester's Answer to His Letter, concerning Some Passages Relating to Mr. Locke's Essay of Humane Understanding. . . .* London: A. and J. Churchill and E. Castle, 1697.

———. *Mr. Locke's Reply to the Right Reverend Lord Bishop of Worcester's Answer to His Second Letter. . . .* London: A. and J. Churchill and E. Castle, 1699.

———. *Some Thoughts concerning Education.* Edited by John W. and Jean S. Yolton. Oxford: Clarendon Press, 1989. 1st ed. London: 1693.

———. *The Works of John Locke.* 12th ed., 9 vols. London: C. and J. Rivington, 1824.

Lucas, Richard. *An Enquiry after Happiness, in several Parts: Vol. 1. Of the Possibility of Obtaining Happiness.* 3rd ed. London: S. Smith and B. Walford and Edw. Pawlett, 1697.

———. *Humane Life: Or, a Second Part of the Enquiry after Happiness.* 3rd ed. London: Sam. Smith and Ben. Walford and Edw. Pawlet, 1696.

———. *Religious Perfection. Or, a Third Part of the Enquiry after Happiness.* 2nd ed. London: Sam. Smith and Benj. Walford, 1697.

Maimbourg, Lewis. *The History of the Crusade; or, the Expeditions of the Christian Princes for the Conquest of the Holy Land.* Translated by John Nalson. London: Thomas Drink, 1685.

Malebranche, Nicolas. *Malebranch's Search after Truth. Or a Treatise of the Nature of the Humane Mind. And of Its Management for Avoiding Error in the Sciences.* 2 vols. Translated by Richard Sault. London: J. Dunton, 1694.

———. *The Search after Truth.* Translated by Thomas M. Lennon and Paul J. Olscamp. Columbus: Ohio State University Press, 1980.

Millington, Edward. *Bibliotheca Annesleiana: Or a Catalogue of . . . Books . . . Being the Library of the Reverend Samuel Annesley. . . .* London, 1696.

Miscellany Poems and Translations by Oxford Hands. London: Anthony Stephans, 1685.

More, Henry. *The Immortality of the Soul.* In *A Collection of Several Philosophical Writings of Dr. Henry More. . . .* 2nd ed., "more correct and much enlarged." London: William Morden in Cambridge, 1662.

Murray, Iain, ed. *George Whitefield's Journal.* London: Banner of Truth Trust, 1960.

Du Moulin, Peter [Pierre (1601–1684)]. *A Treatise of Peace & Contentment of Mind.* 3rd ed., rev. and much amended by the Author. London: John Sims, 1678.

Nelson, Robert. *A Companion for the Festivals and Fasts of the Church of England. . . .* London: Society for the Promotion of Christian Knowledge; New York: Pott, Young, n.d. Original ed. 1703.

Norris, John. *A Collection of Miscellanies: Consisting of Poems, Essays, Discourses, and Letters. . . .* Oxford: John Crosley, 1687.

———. *Cursory Reflections upon a Book Call'd, an Essay concerning Human Understanding.* London: S. Manship, 1690. The Augustan Reprint Society Publication Number 93. Edited by Gilbert D. McEwen. Los Angeles: William Andrews Clark Memorial Library, 1961.

———. *An Essay towards the Theory of the Ideal or Intelligible World.* 2 vols. London: Manship and Hawes, 1701–1704.

———. *Letters concerning the Love of God, between the Author of the Proposal to the Ladies and Mr. John Norris. . . .* London: Manship and Wilkin, 1695.

———. *A Philosophical Discourse concerning the Natural Immortality of the Soul. . . .* London: S. Manship, 1708.

———. *[Practical] Discourses upon Several Divine Subjects.* 2nd ed., 4 vols. London: Samuel Manship, 1697–1701.

———. *Reason and Religion: Or, the Grounds and Measures of Devotion, Consider'd from the Nature of God, and the Nature of Man.* London: Samuel Manship, 1689.

———. *The Theory and Regulation of Love. A Moral Essay, in Two Parts. To Which Are Added Some Letters Philosophical and Moral, between the Author and Dr. Henry More.* 2nd ed. London: S. Manship, 1694.

Osborne, Francis. *Advice to a Son. . . .* Oxford: Thomas Robinson, 1656.

Pascal, Blaise. *Pascal's Pensées.* Introduction by T. S. Eliot. New York: Dutton, 1958.

———. *Thoughts on Religion, and Other Curious Subjects. . . .* Translated by Basil Kennet. 3rd ed. London: John Pemberton, 1731.

———. *Thoughts on Religion, and Other Subjects. By Monsieur Pascal.* Translated from the French [by Basil Kennett]. London: A. and J. Churchil, R. Sare, J. Tonson, 1704.

Pearson, John. *An Exposition of the Creed.* 6th ed., rev. London: J. Williams, 1692.

———. *An Exposition of the Creed.* Edited by James Nichols. London: William Tegg, 1854.

———. *An Exposition of the Creed.* Edited by E. Burton. Oxford: At the Clarendon Press, 1870.

Peters, Hugh. *The Tales and Jests of Mr. Hugh Peters. . . .* London: S. D., 1660.

Plume, Thomas. *An Account of the Life and Death of the Right Reverend Father in God, John Hacket, Late Lord Bishop of Lichfield and Coventry.* Edited by Mackenzie E. C. Walcott. London: J. Masters, 1865. Original ed. London: Robert Scott, 1675.

Plutarch. *Plutarch's Lives. Translated from the Greek by Several Hands. . . . To which Is Prefixt the Life of Plutarch* [by John Dryden]. 5 vols. London: Jacob Tonson, 1693.

———. *Plutarch's Morals: Translated from the Greek by Several Hands.* 5 vols., 4th ed. London: Tho. Braddyll, 1704.

Ray, John. *The Wisdom of God Manifested in the Works of Creation.* London: Samuel Smith, 1691.

Ridgley, Thomas. *A Body of Divinity . . . Being the Substance of Several Lectures on the Assembly's Larger Catechism.* London: Daniel Midwinter and Aaron Ward, 1731–1733.

Rogers, Timothy. *The Character of a Good Woman . . . in a Funeral Discourse. . . . Occasioned by the Decease of Mrs. Elizabeth Dunton . . . with an Account of Her Life and Death. . . .* London: John Harris, 1697.

Rust, Goerge, *A Discourse of the Use of Reason in Matter of Religion, Showing That Christianity Contains Nothing Repugnant to Right Reason, against Enthusiasts and Deists.* London: for Walter Kettilby, 1683.

———. *Two Choice and Useful Treatises: The One Lux Orientalis . . . the Other a Discourse of Truth . . . with Annotations on Them Both.* London: James Collins and Sam. Lowndes, 1682.

Sanderson, Robert. "The Case of the Sabbath." London, 1636. In *The Works of Robert Sanderson, D.D., Sometime Bishop of Lincoln.* 6 vols. 5:5–16. Edited by William Jacobson. Oxford: At the University Press, 1854.

[Sault, Richard]. *A Conference betwixt a Modern Atheist, and His Friend. . . .* London: John Dunton, 1693.

[Scougal, Henry.] *The Life of God in the Soul of Man: Or, the Nature and Excellency of the Christian Religion. . . .*2nd ed. Preface by Gilbert [Burnett], Lord Bishop of Sarum. London: T. Dring and J. Weld, 1691.

Seneca, Lucius Annaeus. *Seneca Ad Lucilium EpistULAE Morales.* 3 vols. Edited and translated by Richard M. Gummere. London: Heinemann; New York: Putnam's, 1935.

———. *Seneca's Morals by Way of Abstract.* 7th ed. Edited by R. L'Estrange. London: Jacob Tonson, 1699.

———. *The Workes of Lucius Annaeus Seneca, Newly Inlarged and Corrected. . . .* Edited by Thomas Lodge. London: Willi: Stansby, [1620].

Shelton, Thomas. *A Tutor to Tachygraphy, or, Short-Writing (1642) and Tachygraphy (1647).* Introduction by William Matthews. The Augustan Reprint Society, nos. 145–146. Los Angeles: Clark Memorial Library, UCLA, 1970.

Sherlock, Thomas. *The Use and Intent of Prophecy, in the Several Ages of the World. In Six Discourses, Delivered at the Temple Church In April and May, 1724. . . .* 6th ed. London: J. Whiston and B. White, 1755.

———. *The Works of Bishop Sherlock. With Some Account of His Life. . . .* 5 vols. Edited by the Rev. T. S. Hughes. London: A. J. Valby, 1830.

Sherlock, William. *A Discourse Concerning the Divine Providence.* London: William Rogers, 1694.

Sprat, Thomas. *Sermons Preached on Several Occasions.* London: R. Bonwicke, J. Walthoe, R. Wilkin, B. Tooke, J. Ward, and E. Nutt, 1722.

Stillingfleet, Edward. *The Bishop of Worcester's Answer to Mr. Locke's Letter, concerning Some Passages Relating to His Essay of Humane Understanding, Mention'd in the Late Discourse in Vindication of the Trinity. . . .* London: Henry Mortlock, 1697.

———. *The Bishop of Worcester's Answer to Mr. Locke's Second Letter; Wherein His Notion of Ideas Is Prov'd to Be Inconsistent with It Self, And with the Articles of the Christian Faith.* London: Henry Mortlock, 1698.

———. *A Discourse in Vindication of the Doctrine of the Trinity: With an Answer to the Late Socinian Objections Against It from Scripture, Antiquity and Reason. . . .* London: Henry Mortlock, 1697.

———. *Origines Sacrae or a Rational Account of the Grounds of Christian Faith. . . .* London: Henry Mortlock, 1666.

Taylor, Jeremy. *The Rule and Exercises of Holy Dying. . . .* 15th ed. London: Luke Meredith, 1690. (Bound together with the following.)

———. *The Rule and Exercises of Holy Living. . . .* 15th ed. London: Luke Meredith, 1690. (Bound together with the preceding.)

Thomas à Kempis. *The Christian's Pattern; or a Divine Treatise of the Imitation of Christ.* London: John Clark, 1659; London: John Williams, 1677.

———. *The Christian's Pattern: Or, a Treatise of the Imitation of Jesus Christ. . . . To Which Are Added,*

Meditations and Prayers, for Sick Persons. Translated by George Stanhope. London: Gillyflower et al., 1698.

Thomas à Kempis. *The Christian's Pattern; or, a Treatise of the Imitation of Christ. . . .* Edited by John Wesley. London: C. Rivington, 1735.

Two Choice and Useful Treatises: The One Lux Orientalis . . . [by Joseph Galnvill]. The Other a Discourse of Truth by . . . Dr. Rust. . . . With annotations on Them Both [by Henry More]. London: James Collins and Sam. Lowndes, 1682.

Wake, William. *The Principles of the Christian Religion Explained: In a Brief Commentary upon the Church-Catechism.* 2nd ed. London: Richard Sare, 1700.

Wesley, John. *A Christian Library: Consisting of Extracts from, and Abridgements of, the Choicest Pieces of Practical Divinity Which Have Been Publish'd in the English Tongue.* 50 vols. Bristol: Farley, 1749–1755.

———. *A Dialogue between a Predestinarian and His Friend.* 2nd ed. London: Strahan, 1741.

———. *A Collection of Psalms and Hymns.* London: Strahan, 1741.

———. *Free Grace: A Sermon Preach'd at Bristol.* London: Strahan, 1740 and 1741.

———. *Journal and Diaries, II (1738–43).* In *The Works of John Wesley,* vol. 19. Edited by W. Reginald Ward and Richard P. Heitzenrater. Nashville: Abingdon, 1990.

———. *Letters, I: 1721–1739.* In *The Works of John Wesley,* vol. 25. Edited by Frank Baker. Oxford: Clarendon Press, 1980.

———. *Letters, II: 1740–1755.* In *The Works of John Wesley,* vol. 26. Edited by Frank Baker. Oxford: Clarendon Press, 1982.

———. *Primitive Physick: Or an Easy and Natural Method of Curing Most Diseases.* London: Strahan, 1747.

———. *Sermons, III (71–114).* In *The Works of John Wesley,* vol. 3. Edited by Albert Outler. Nashville: Abingdon, 1986.

Wesley, Samuel. *Advice to a Young Clergyman, in a Letter to Him . . .* [?1735]. In Thomas Jackson. *The Life of the Rev. Charles Wesley, M.A. . . .* 2 vols. 2:499–534. London: John Mason, 1841.

———. *The Young Student's Library: Containing Extracts and Abridgements of the Most Valuable Books. . . .* London: John Dunton, 1692.

The Westminster Larger Catechism, 1648. In *The School of Faith: The Catechisms of the Reformed Church,* pp. 183–235. Edited by Thomas F. Torrance. London: J. Clarke, 1959.

The Westminster Shorter Catechism, 1648. In *The School of Faith: The Catechisms of the Reformed Church,* pp. 261–278. Edited by Thomas F. Torrance. London: J. Clarke, 1959.

Whaling, Frank, ed. *John and Charles Wesley: Selected Prayers, Hymns, Journal Notes, Sermons, Letters and Treatises.* Classics of Western Spirituality Series. New York, Ramsey, and Toronto: Paulist Press, 1981.

Whitefield, George. *A Letter to the Reverend Mr. John Wesley: In Answer to His Sermon, Entitled, Free-Grace.* London: T. Cooper and R. Hett, 1741.

———. *The Works of the Rev. George Whitefield. . . .* 4 vols. London: Edward and Charles Dilly, 1771–1772.

Wilkins, John. *Of the Principles and Duties of Natural Religion. . . .* New York and London: Johnson Reprint Corporation, 1969. Reprint of London: T. Basset et al., 1693.

Yonge, William. *England's Shame, or the Unmasking of a Political Atheist, Being a Full and Faithful Relation of the Life and Death of That Grand Imposter Hugh Peters. . . .* London: Theodore Sadler, 1663.

[Ziegenbalg, Bartholomaeus (1683–1719)]. *An Account of the Religion and Government, Learning and Oeconomy, etc., of the Malabarians, Sent by the Danish Missionaries to Their Correspondents in Europe.* Translated from the High-Dutch. London: J. Downing, 1717. (Bound with his *Propagation of the Gospel in the East.* London, 1714–1718.)

Background Material: Secondary Studies and Reference Works

Abelove, Henry. *The Evangelist of Desire: John Wesley and the Methodists.* Stanford, Calif.: Stanford University Press, 1990.

Acworth, Richard. *The Philosophy of John Norris of Bemerton (1657–1712).* Hildesheim, Ger., and New York: Georg Olms, 1979.

Allison, C. F. *The Rise of Moralism: The Proclamation of the Gospel from Hooker to Baxter.* New York: Seabury, 1966.

Anderson, Thomas. *History of Shorthand with a Review of its Present Condition and Prospects in Europe and America.* London: Allen, 1882.

Ashcraft, Richard. "Faith and Knowledge in Locke's Philosophy." In *John Locke: Problems and Perspectives: A Collection of New Essays,* pp. 194–223. Edited by John W. Yolton. Cambridge: Cambridge University Press, 1969.

Barker, John. *Strange Contrarieties: Pascal in England during the Age of Reason.* Montreal and London: McGill-Queen's University Press, 1975.

Beecham, H. A. "Samuel Wesley Senior: New Biographical Evidence." *Renaissance and Modern Studies* 7 (1963): 78–109.

Bell, Maureen, George Parfitt, and Simon Shepherd, eds. *A Biographical Dictionary of English Women Writers, 1580–1720.* Boston: G. K. Hall, 1990.

Blain, Virginia, Patricia Clements, and Isobel Grundy, eds. *The Feminist Companion to Literature in English: Women Writers from the Middle Ages to the Present.* New Haven, Conn., and London: Yale University Press, 1990.

Blodgett, Harriet. *Centuries of Female Days: Englishwomen's Private Diaries.* New Brunswick, N.J.: Rutgers University Press, 1988.

Brantley, Richard E. *Locke, Wesley, and the Method of English Romanticism.* Gainesville: University of Florida Press, 1983.

Brown, Earl Kent. *The Women of Mr. Wesley's Methodism.* New York and Toronto: Edwin Mellen, 1983.

Brueggemann, Lewis William. *A View of the English Editions, Translations and Illustrations of the Ancient Greek and Latin Authors, with Remarks.* Stettin, Eng.: John Samuel Leich, 1797.

Butler, E. H. *The Story of British Shorthand.* London: Pitman, 1951.

Cahn, Susan. *Industry of Devotion: The Transformation of Women's Work in England, 1500–1660.* New York: Columbia University Press, 1987.

Chilcote, Paul W. *John Wesley and the Women Preachers of Early Methodism.* Metuchen, N.J.: Scarecrow, 1991.

Clark, Elizabeth, and Herbert Richardson, eds. *Women and Religion: A Feminist Sourcebook of Christian Thought.* New York: Harper and Row, 1977.

The Compact Edition of the Oxford English Dictionary. New York: Oxford University Press, 1971.

Coon, Lynda L., Katherine J. Haldane, and Elisabeth W. Sommer, eds. *That Gentle Strength: Historical Perspectives on Women in Christianity.* Charlottesville and London: University of Virginia Press, 1990.

Copleston, Frederick. *A History of Philosophy.* 6 vols. Garden City, N.Y.: Doubleday, Image Books, 1963.

Crawford, Patricia. "Public Duty, Conscience, and Women in Early Modern England." In *Public Duty and Private Conscience in Seventeenth-Century England: Essays Presented to G. E. Aylmer,* pp. 57–76. Edited by John Morrill, Paul Slack, and Daniel Woolf. Oxford: Clarendon Press, 1993.

———. *Women and Religion in England 1500–1720.* London and New York: Routledge, 1993.

———. "Women's Published Writings 1600–1700." In *Women in English Society 1500–1800,* pp. 211–282. Edited by Mary Prior. London and New York: Methuen, 1985.

Dennison, James T., Jr. *The Market Day of the Soul: The Puritan Doctrine of the Sabbath in England, 1532–1700.* Lanham, N.Y., and London: University Press of America, 1983.

Di Cesare, Mario A., and Rigo Mignani, eds. *A Concordance to the Complete Writings of George Herbert.* Ithaca, N.Y., and London: Cornell University Press, 1977.

Dictionary of National Biography. 21 vols. and supplements. Edited by Leslie Stephen and Sidney Lee. Oxford: Oxford University Press; London: Humphrey Milford, 1917.

Dupre, Louis, and Don E. Saliers, eds. *Christian Spirituality: Post-Reformation and Modern: Vol. 18. World Spirituality: An Encyclopedic History of the Religious Quest.* New York: Crossroad, 1989.

Ezell, Margaret J. M. "John Locke's Images of Childhood: Early Eighteenth Century Response to *Some Thoughts concerning Education.*" *Eighteenth-Century Studies* 17.2 (Winter 1983/1984): 139–155.

———. *The Patriarch's Wife: Literary Evidence and the History of the Family.* Chapel Hill and London: University of North Carolina Press, 1987

———. *Writing Women's Literary History.* Baltimore and London: Johns Hopkins University Press, 1993.

Ferguson, J. P. *An Eighteenth Century Heretic: Dr. Samuel Clarke.* Kineton, Eng.: Roundwood, 1976.

Fletcher, Anthony. *Gender, Sex and Subordination in England 1500–1800.* New Haven and London: Yale University Press, 1995.

George, Edward A. *Seventeenth Century Men of Latitude.* New York: Scribner, 1908.

Gill, Sean. *Women and the Churcch of England: From the Eighteenth Century to the Present.* London: S.P.C.K., 1994.

Goreau, Angeline. *The Whole Duty of a Woman: Female Writers in Seventeenth Century England.* Garden City, N.Y.: Dial, 1985.

Greaves, Richard L. "Foundation Builders: The Role of Women in Early English Nonconformity." In *Triumph over Silence: Women in Protestant History,* pp. 75–92. Edited by Richard L. Greaves. Westport, Conn., and London: Greenwood, 1985.

———. ed. *Triumph over Silence: Women in Protestant History.* Westport, Conn., and London: Greenwood, 1985.

Greven, Philip. *The Protestant Temperament: Patterns of Child-Rearing, Religious Experience, and the Self in Early America.* New York: Knopf, 1977.

———, ed. *Child-rearing Concepts, 1628–1861: Historical Sources.* Itasca, Ill.: Peacock, 1973.

Haller, William. *The Rise of Puritanism.* New York: Columbia University Press, 1938. Reprint, Philadelphia: University of Pennsylvania Press, 1984.

Handley, Paul, et al., compilers. *The English Spirit: The Little Gidding Anthology of English Spirituality.* Nashville: Abingdon, 1987.

Hastings, James, ed. *Encyclopedia of Religion and Ethics.* New York: C. Scribner's Sons; Edinburgh: T. and T. Clark, 1908–1926.

Hefelbower, S. G. *The Relation of John Locke to English Deism.* Chicago: University of Chicago Press, 1918.

Heitzenrater, Richard P. *The Elusive Mr. Wesley: Vol. 1. John Wesley His Own Biographer; Vol. 2. John Wesley as Seen by Contemporaries and Biographers.* Nashville: Abingdon, 1984.

Hobby, Elaine. *Virtue of Necessity: English Women's Writing, 1649–88.* Ann Arbor: University of Michigan Press, 1989.

Johnson, Dale, ed. *Women in English Religion, 1700–1925.* New York and Toronto: Edwin Mellen, 1983.

Jones, Cheslyn, Geoffrey Wainwright, and Edward Yarnold, S.J., eds. *The Study of Spirituality.* New York and Oxford: Oxford University Press, 1986.

Keeble, N. H. *Richard Baxter: Puritan Man of Letters.* Oxford: Clarendon Press, 1982.

———, ed. *the Cultural Identity of Seventeenth-Century Woman: A Reader.* London and New York: Routledge, 1994.

Knox, Alexander. *Remains of Alexander Knox, esq.* 2nd ed., 4 vols. London: James Duncan, 1836.

————. *Remarks on the Life and Character of John Wesley*, 2:407–504. In Robert Southey, *The Life of Wesley.* . . . 3rd ed., 2 vols. Edited by Charles Cuthbert Southey. London: Longman, Brown, Green, and Longmans, 1846.

Leger, Augustin. *La Jeunesse de Wesley: L'Angleterre religieuse et les origines du Méthodisme au XVIII siècle.* Paris: Librairie Hachette, 1910.

Leland, John. *A View of the Principal Deistical Writers.* . . . 2 vols. London: W. Baynes, 1807.

Ludlow, Dorothy P. "Shaking Patriarchy's Foundations: Sectarian Women in England, 1641–1700." In *Triumph over Silence: Women in Protestant History*, pp. 93–123. Edited by Richard L. Greaves. Westport, Conn., and London: Greenwood, 1985.

McCracken, Charles J. *Malebranche and British Philosophy.* Oxford: Clarendon Press, 1983.

McEwen, Gilbert D. *The Oracle of the Coffee House: John Dunton's Athenian Mercury.* San Marino, Calif.: Huntington Library, 1972.

McGee, J. Sears. *The Godly Man in Stuart England: Anglicans, Puritans, and the Two Tables, 1620–1670.* New Haven, Conn., and London: Yale University Press, 1976.

MacHaffie, Barbara J. *Her Story: Women in Christian Tradition.* Philadelphia: Fortress, 1986.

Mack, Phyllis. *Visionary Women: Ecstatic Prophecy in Seventeenth-Century England.* Berkeley, Los Angeles, and London: University of California Press, 1992.

MacKinnon, Flora Isabel. *Philosophical Writings of Henry More.* New York: Oxford University Press, 1925.

Marshall, Sherrin, ed. *Women in Reformation and Counter-Reformation Europe: Public and Private Worlds.* Bloomington and Indianapolis: Indiana University Press, 1989.

Maser, Frederick E. *Seven Sisters in Search of Love.* Rutland, Vt.: Academy Books, 1988.

Matthews, William. *English Pronunciation and Shorthand in the Early Modern Period.* University of California Publications in English, vol. 9, no. 3, pp. 135–214. Berkeley and Los Angeles: University of California Press, 1943.

Mendelson, Sara Heller. *The Mental World of Stuart Women: Three Studies.* Amherst: University of Massachusetts Press, 1987.

————. "Stuart Women's Diaries and Occasional Memoirs." In *Women in English Society 1500–1800*, pp. 181–210. Edited by Mary Prior. London and New York: Methuen, 1985.

Norris, Richard A., Jr. "Doctor Pearson Construes the Apostles' Creed: A Note on Method and Matter in Christology." In *This Sacred History: Anglican Reflections for John Booty*, pp. 77–88. Edited by Donald S. Armentrout. Cambridge, Mass.: Cowley, 1990.

Nussbaum, Felicity A. *The Autobiographical Subject: Gender and Ideology in Eighteenth-Century England.* Baltimore and London: Johns Hopkins University Press, 1989.

————. "Eighteenth-Century Women's Autobiographical Commonplaces." In *The Private Self: Theory and Practice of Women's Autobiographical Writings*, pp. 147–171. Edited by Shari Bentock. Chapel Hill and London: University of North Carolina Press, 1988.

Nuttall, Geoffrey F. *Richard Baxter.* London: Nelson, 1965.

Obelkevich, James. *Religion and Rural Society: South Lindsey, 1825–1875.* Oxford: Clarendon Press, 1976.

Orcibal, Jean. "Les spirituels français et espagnols chez John Wesley et ses contemporains." *Revue de l'histoire des religions* 139 (1951): 50–109.

Otto, Rudolph. *The Idea of the Holy.* London and New York: Oxford University Press, 1932.

The Oxford Dictionary of the Christian Church. Edited by F. L. Cross. London, New York, Toronto: Oxford University Press, 1958.

Pascoe, C. F. *Two Hundred Years of the S. P. G.: An Historical Account of the Society for the Propagation of the Gospel in Foreign Parts, 1701–1900.* 2 vols. London: SPG, 1901.

Perry, Ruth. *The Celebrated Mary Astell: An Early English Feminist.* Chicago and London: University of Chicago Press, 1986.

Primus, John H. "Sunday: the Lord's Day as a Sabbath—Protestant Perspectives on the Sabbath." In The Sabbath in Jewish and Christian Traditions. Edited by Tamara C. Eskenazi, Daniel J. Harrington, S.J., and William H. Shea. New York: Crossroad, 1991.

Quiller-Couch, Arthur Thomas. Hetty Wesley. London and New York: Macmillan, 1903.

Rack, Henry D. Reasonable Enthusiast: John Wesley and the Rise of Methodism. Philadelphia: Trinity Press International, 1989.

Raitt, Jill, ed. Christian Spirituality: High Middle Ages and Reformation: Vol. 17. World Spirituality: An Encyclopedic History of the Religious Quest. New York: Crossroad, 1988.

Redwood, John. Reason, Ridicule and Religion: The Age of Enlightenment in England, 1660–1750. London: Thames and Hudson, 1976.

Reuther, Rosemary, and Eleanor McLaughlin, eds. Women of Spirit: Female Leadership in the Jewish and Christian Traditions. New York: Simon and Schuster, 1972.

Rivers, Isabel. Reason, Grace, and Sentiment: A Study of the Language of Religion and Ethics in England, 1660–1789: Vol. 1. Whichcote to Wesley. Cambridge: Cambridge University Press, 1991.

Rogers, Katharine M. Feminism in Eighteenth-Century England. Urbana, Chicago, and London: University of Illinois Press, 1982.

Rupp, Gordon. "A Devotion of Rapture in English Puritanism." In Reformation, Conformity and Dissent: Essays in Honour of Geoffrey Nuttall. Edited by R. Buick Knox. London: Epworth, 1977.

———. Religion in England, 1688–1791. Oxford: Clarendon Press, 1986.

Salvaggio, Ruth. Enlightened Absence: Neoclassical Configurations of the Feminine. Urbana and Chicago: University of Illinois Press, 1988.

Sarton, George. Galen of Pergamon. Lawrence: University of Kansas, 1954.

Sheils, W. J., and Diana Wood, eds. Women in the Church: Papers Read at the 1989 Summer Meeting and the 1990 Winter Meeting of the Ecclesiastical History Society. Oxford: Basil Blackwell, 1990.

Sommerville, C. John. Popular Religion in Restoration England. Gainesville: University of Florida, 1977.

Southey, Robert. The Life of Wesley . . . with . . . Remarks on the Life and Character of John Wesley, by the late Alexander Knox. . . . 3rd ed., 2 vols. London: Longman, Brown, Green and Longmans, 1846.

Spacks, Patricia Meyer. "Female Rhetorics." In The Private Self: Theory and Practice of Women's Autobiographical Writings. Edited by Shari Bentock. Chapel Hill and London: University of North Carolina Press, 1988.

Spurr, John. The Restoration Church of England, 1646–1689. New Haven, Conn., and London: Yale University Press, 1991.

Stenton, Doris Mary. The English Woman in History. London and New York: George Allen and Unwin and Macmillan, 1957.

Stephen, Sir Leslie. History of English Thought in the Eighteenth Century. 2 vols. New York and Burlingame, Cal.: Harcourt, Brace and World, 1966.

Stone, Lawrence. The Family, Sex and Marriage in England 1500–1800. Abridged ed. New York: Harper Colophon, 1979.

Thomas, Keith. "Cases of Conscience in Seventeenth-Century England." In Public Duty and Private Conscience in Seventeenth-Century England: Essays Presented to G. E. Aylmer, pp. 29–56. Edited by John Morrill, Paul Slack, and Daniel Woolf. Oxford: Clarendon Press, 1993.

Thornton, Martin. "The Caroline Divines and the Cambridge Platonists." In Cheslyn Jones et al., eds., The Study of Spirituality. New York and Oxford: Oxford University Press, 1986. PP. 431–437.

Todd, Janet, ed. A Dictionary of British and American Women Writers, 1660–1800. London: Methuen, 1987.

Tuveson, Ernest Lee. The Imagination as a Means of Grace: Locke and the Aesthetics of Romanticism. Berkeley and Los Angeles: University of California, 1960.

Tyerman, Luke. *The Life and Times of the Rev. Samuel Wesley, M.A., Rector of Epworth*. . . . London: Simpkin, Marshall, 1866.

Watkins, Owen C. *The Puritan Experience: Studies in Spiritual Autobiography*. New York: Schocken, 1972.

Weber, Alison. *Teresa of Avila and the Rhetoric of Femininity*. Princeton, N.J.: Princeton University Press, 1990.

Westerhoff, John H., III, and O. C. Edwards Jr., eds. *A Faithful Church: Issues in the History of Catechesis*. Wilton, Conn.: Morehouse-Barlow, 1981.

Wiesner, Merry E. *Women and Gender in Early Modern Europe*. Cambridge: Cambridge University Press, 1993.

Willen, Diane. "Godly Women in Early Modern England: Puritanism and Gender." *Journal of Ecclesiastical History* 43.4 (October 1992): 561–580.

Willey, Basil. *The Eighteenth Century Background: Studies on the Idea of Nature in the Thought of the Period*. Boston: Beacon, 1961.

———. *The Seventeenth Century Background: Studies in the Thought of the Age in Relation to Religion and Poetry*. New York: Doubleday, 1953.

Williamson, Marilyn L. *Raising Their Voices: British Women Writers, 1650–1750*. Detroit: Wayne State University Press, 1990.

Woolf, Virginia. *A Room of One's Own*. London: Triad Grafton, 1977. Original ed. London: Hogarth Press, 1929.

Yolton, John W. *John Locke and the Way of Ideas*. London: Oxford University Press, 1956.

———. *Locke: An Introduction*. Oxford and New York: Basil Blackwell, 1985.

Index